COUNSEL TO THE PRESIDENT

COUNSEL TO THE PRESIDENT

A MEMOIR

CLARK CLIFFORD

with

Richard Holbrooke

ANCHOR BOOKS

DOUBLEDAY

New York London Toronto Sydney Auckland

An Anchor Book
PUBLISHED BY DOUBLEDAY
a division of Bantam Doubleday Dell Publishing Group, Inc.
666 Fifth Avenue, New York, New York 10103

Anchor Books, Doubleday, and the portrayal of an anchor
are trademarks of Doubleday, a division of Bantam Doubleday
Dell Publishing Group, Inc.

Counsel to the President was originally published in hardcover by Random House in 1991. The Anchor Books edition is published by arrangement with Random House.

Library of Congress Cataloging-in-Publication Data
Clifford, Clark M., 1906–
Counsel to the president : a memoir / Clark Clifford with Richard
Holbrooke. — 1st Anchor Books ed.
p. cm.
"Originally published in hardcover
by Random House in 1991"—T.p. verso.
Includes bibliographical references (p.) and index.
1. Clifford, Clark M., 1906– . 2. Statesmen—United States—
Biography. 3. Lawyers—United States—Biography. 4. United
States—Politics and government—1945–1989. I. Holbrooke, Richard
C. II. Title.
[E840.8.C55A3 1992]
973.9'092—dc20
[B] 92-3569
CIP

ISBN 0-385-42398-5

Printed in the United States of America
First Anchor Books Edition: June 1992
10 9 8 7 6 5 4 3 2 1

To the loving memory
of my
mother and father

Contents

Preface to The Anchor Edition

When I began writing these memoirs in 1987, I envisioned them, as I wrote in the Author's Note to the hardcover edition (published by Random House), as an exercise in recall. The events that have taken place in the world since I began this project—particularly the collapse of communism in Europe—have strongly reinforced my original view that it was important for those people fortunate enough to have played a role in the formative years of the Cold War to preserve their memories for future generations. With the end of that extraordinary forty-five-year era, a new generation of Americans has begun a great national debate over the nation's priorities, and, although so far this debate has been disappointing and desultory in nature, I believe that over time a new consensus will emerge on America's goals and role in the world. But this cannot be accomplished without a clear understanding of what our nation did, and how, and why, in the almost half-century that followed the end of World War II.

It is now a commonplace that the policies put into place by President Truman and his extraordinary foreign policy team, and followed by all eight of his successors, succeeded. But a new generation of Americans is too young to remember that the policies we now look back on with such pride were the subject of ferocious and continual warfare within each Administration, between the Congress and the Executive branch, within the intellectual and journalistic communities, between conservatives and liberals. Some of today's most assertive proponents of the policies that succeeded were, at the time, their most violent critics. The right wing (which at one time would have included Richard Nixon among its leading spokesmen) regularly castigated the Dean Achesons and George Marshalls for their alleged "softness" toward communism, while the left wing (for example former vice-president Henry Wallace) often accused the same men of "warmongering." To the reader old enough to remember these battles, I hope this book will help place the blizzard of events into a more coherent whole—for there was a pattern in what we lived through, even if it was not evident at the time.

As for the generation for whom I really wrote this book—those too young to remember the Berlin Blockade or the Berlin Wall, the Bay of Pigs or even the Tet Offensive—I fear that, to the extent they learn history at all, it will be through television soundbites—the headline news service version of history. Such oversimplifications may be inevitable in a television age, but they are dangerous and risk the replacement of facts with myths. There is only one antidote for these distortions—and that is the study of the events themselves. This will, of course, often produce additional controversy and disagreement; the truth can be as elusive to historians as it is to politicians and journalists. The continuing debate over the 1968 Tet Offensive is a perfect illustration of this. Nonetheless, to paraphrase the architect Mies van der Rohe: truth, or something approaching it, can be found in the details.

This exercise in recall was designed as a contribution to that process. The broad outlines of the events I have witnessed and in which I have sometimes participated are well known. But details, mostly long forgotten, matter, at least to anyone who wants to understand how events happen. I think, for example, of Winston Churchill's now legendary "Iron Curtain" speech at Fulton, Missouri, excerpts of which can be found in every headline history or television documentary of our time. Looked at in closer detail—how Churchill was invited and decided to give the speech, President Truman's initial hesitation in endorsing the message despite his reverence for the messenger, the oddly ambivalent reception the speech received—the speech becomes a more complicated event, not the universally admired and quoted speech that it would become in history books, but a part of the controversy of those times that shaped our own. Such detail is not just a footnote to history—it is *history itself*. Similarly, the fierce battle over how to present to Congress what history now calls the Truman Doctrine (a phrase, of course, that none of us even imagined at the time the speech was given, in March 1947); or the murky and disputed origins of the much acclaimed Point Four program; or the step-by-step descent into the the quagmire of Vietnam—

without these details, our history is reduced to one-line headlines about the containment policy. Such a simple story line, so satisfying to politicians and commentators, contains, of course, a kernel of truth; one of the most astonishing facts of the Cold War is that the American people were willing to see it through for close to half a century immediately after having fought and won a world war. But it also obscures an even more essential lesson of that period: that without strong leadership we might not have stayed the course or even embarked on the right one.

There were times when the outcome of that struggle seemed uncertain or hopeless. In 1948, for example, on the same day that the Republicans nominated Thomas E. Dewey as their candidate for a Presidency they assumed would be theirs within months, the Soviet Union imposed a complete blockade of all highway, rail, and water traffic in and out of Berlin. That day, less than three years after the end of World War II, President Truman and his senior advisors confronted the possibility of another war in Europe, and prepared to take that risk in defense of freedom. In the forty-plus years that followed, McCarthyism, Korea, the fall of China, Cuba and the Bay of Pigs, Watergate, and above all, Vietnam, would challenge the consensus that President Truman had set into place. Soviet military power would be strong for more than three decades before it suddenly crumbled under its own internal contradictions.

I recognize, of course, that despite our success in the Cold War we live in an era of widespread self-doubt about America's purpose and will. Yet, while I am aware as any citizen of the problems we face, especially at home, I do not share the pessimism of some, nor do I see America as being in decline. Our global dominance immediately following World War II, when we produced fully half the world's goods, was a temporary phenomenon. In a noble act that was also in our own self-interest, we did not seek to perpetuate American dominance, but rather to export our capital, our know-how, and our ideals to other parts of the globe. The economic and political revival of nations from Japan and South Korea to Western Europe and now, finally, to Eastern Europe owes a great deal to that enlightened policy, and we should take great pride in its success rather than lament the economic challenge from the very nations whose revival we encouraged and guided. Rather than criticize them, I would prefer to focus American attention on restoring to our own nation the sense of pride and purpose that animated us when I was growing up early this century in St. Louis, and later, when we faced down the dictatorships that threatened the world for half a century.

National security, as the readers of this book will see, was a new concept, developed specifically for the challenge posed by a struggle that would involve everything except, we hoped, a shooting war. It was no accident that the phrases "national security" and "Cold War" came into general usage at about the same time, in the late 1940s.

Today we face an entirely new challenge, as unprecedented in its own way as the Cold War was in 1947. Accordingly, I believe that it is time to restructure the United States government once again, so that the energy, resources, and talents of the nation can be focused on the new challenges that face us. Some will wish to redefine "national security" to include such matters as the environment, world health problems, overpopulation, and drugs. This suggestion deserves careful consideration, especially since the national security and foreign policy structure of the United States government has worked more efficiently than its domestic counterpart over the last fifty years. But that greater efficiency may have been due more to the relatively singular—that is, easily defined—nature of the threat rather than to any inherent advantage in the National Security Council structure. After all, when it confronted its greatest challenge, in Vietnam, the system did not perform well.

Whatever the next generation of Americans faces, I am certain that our challenges will continue to include foreign policy. In the new and increasingly interconnected world in which we live, old-fashioned isolationism is not an option, no matter how tempting it sounds to some. The demise of the Soviet Union may make the world a safer place for Americans, but paradoxically, it also makes it a less stable place, as events in Yugoslavia have so starkly illustrated. While some other nations will grow, the United States will remain the world's preeminent power. As long as we continue to believe in ourselves and invest in the future, I am confident of the nation's ultimate success.

I must close on a bittersweet personal note. When I began these memoirs, I thought solely in terms of looking backward. I could not have imagined that they would be published in the midst of the most serious personal problem of my career. I refer, of course, to the question of the relationship between First American Bankshares of Washington, D.C., and the Bank of Commerce and Credit International (BCCI), which has been under intense investigation for the past two years. Given the fact that I served as chairman of First American from 1982 to 1991, and as a lawyer to BCCI for much of that same period, it is not surprising that, once the massive investigations of BCCI began, questions would arise concerning my relationship to each of these two institutions. I have stated repeatedly that, to my knowledge, the two institutions were entirely separate, and that no one from BCCI, at any time, gave me instructions on how to run First American. Each time that I have been requested or invited to appear before a governmental body, including Congressional committees, I have appeared and answered every question put to me. But because at this writing these matters are under continuing investigation by federal and other authorities, I am still constrained as to what I can appropriately add in this forum.

It is difficult for anyone to face up to the fact that his actions have been interpreted in a manner that invites suspicion. Many people have asked me how I have managed to "get through" the last year, in which the press has been filled with a seemingly endless series of critical articles to which I have been unable to respond. The answer is simple. I have been able to get through this difficult period for one reason: I am secure in the knowledge that I did not participate, in any way, in any wrongdoing.

It is ironic to begin this voyage into the past with such a current problem. But even though this book is not about these current events, I feel that I owe it to my readers to mention them at the outset.

I trust that whatever the readers' views on this matter, they should not affect the rest of the story, which concerns the fate of our great nation, as seen through the eyes of someone who was fortunate enough to arrive in Washington at exactly the right moment—in Arthur Schlesinger, Jr.'s words, at the "high noon of American power." For the opportunities that fate offered me, I shall always be grateful.

C. C.
February 3, 1992

Author's Note

Life is lived forward, but understood backward.
—SOREN KIERKEGAARD

I began this work as an exercise in recall, persuaded that there was value in a review of some of the events that have shaped the world we live in, as seen through the eyes of a participant. My original purpose has not changed, but the nature of the work has broadened.

I have never kept a diary, although, as a lawyer, I did keep careful records of many of my activities. Yet gaps existed—events that had, so to speak, dropped off my radar screen. Without them, my life had assumed a certain shape with which I was comfortable; but that shape, I realized, was not complete. Thus I embarked on a voyage to reduce the gap between memory and forgetting, hoping to share with my readers a better understanding of my role, large or small, in certain events of the last half century. In the process, I depleted my own memory several times over, tapped the generosity and time of over seventy friends and colleagues, and mined the splendid archives of five Presidential libraries and numerous other institutions. Their assistance is gratefully acknowledged at the end of this work.

One should distrust memoirs that portray their author in an excessively favorable light. At the savage intersection of policy, ambition, and history, it is impossible to be right all the time. There is, however, an amazingly strong subconscious drive to remember clearly those instances in which one exercised good judgment and to forget or blur those times when one was guilty of poor judgment or just plain error. I have fought the natural temptation to accentuate one's successes and minimize one's failures. The reader will judge to what degree my effort has been successful.

Understood backward, my career may seem to build inexorably to the crisis over Vietnam in 1968. But no one could have foreseen the convergence of events in that dreadful year, and nothing foreshadowed my role in them. The record of that decisive year in our nation's history is complex and, in some ways, inconclusive. Other participants may wish to remember events differently, but I have described that last year of the Johnson Administration as honestly as possible. It is neither productive nor fair to the reader to continue at this late date to withhold parts of the truth about these events, especially if the next generation is to learn from the mistakes we made.

Where direct quotations have been used in this work, I have taken great care to ensure accuracy. They come from contemporaneous sources, usually White House or Pentagon notes taken at the time, or from my own records and memory. Where my memory and historical records are in conflict, I have deferred to the higher accuracy of contemporary accounts.

Even before I first set foot in the White House in July of 1945, I had held the office of President of the United States in special reverence. I have known, in varying degrees, its last nine occupants, almost one fourth of all the Chief Executives in our nation's history, and I have been an adviser to every Democratic President since the end of World War II. To me, the creation, by our Founding Fathers, of this unique and noble institution was an almost divine inspiration. Yet Presidents are human, and I could not always agree with them. If I had, I doubt they would have bothered consulting me very often. I felt that my advice, when solicited, had to be honest, direct, and objective. I could not let myself be awed by the man, even though I revered the institution.

I am indebted to my collaborator, Richard Holbrooke, for his invaluable role in this work. Like me, he had not written a book before, but I asked him to assist me because of his substantial experience in government. We had known each other for almost twenty years when we began this project, and I felt confident that he would be both ruthless and understanding in the quest for the elusive truth. We were both ably assisted by an outstanding young research associate, Brian VanDeMark, who worked with us while completing his own splendid work on the Vietnam War.[1] Needless to say, responsibility for the final product is solely my own.

This project began as a form of reminiscence. It ended as something much more, as an exciting voyage of rediscovery. As I wrote, the Cold War was coming to an end in Eastern Europe, and the policies President Truman and his advisers created in the late forties seemed to be achieving their original objective. By ironic coincidence, we were editing the concluding passages of the Vietnam section when we heard the initial reports from Baghdad that the nation was once again at war, one whose central motif was, in the oft-repeated words of the Bush Administration, "No more Vietnams." Thus, even in the midst of another war, our nation continued to try to come to terms with the uncertain legacy of the war in Vietnam. I hope that this volume will help a new generation of Americans to greater understanding of their nation's recent past, so that, in the words of T. S. Eliot,

. . . the end of all our exploring
Will be to arrive where we started
And know the place for the first time.

At the end of my exploring I have arrived, in a sense, where I started. I see a young man whose career and life would be transformed by events on faraway continents, yet who would never change certain values and attitudes he had first acquired in St. Louis just after the turn of the century. On that note, let me begin.

C.C.

Part I

BEGINNINGS

1

Showdown in the Oval Office

A people without history
Is not redeemed from time, for history is a pattern
Of timeless moments.
—T. S. ELIOT, *Little Gidding*

My mind's eye roams over forty-five years of a life in Washington. Still-vivid images of people and incidents flash by: Harry Truman and Winston Churchill on the train to Fulton, Missouri, for the "Iron Curtain" speech; Jack Kennedy adrift after the Bay of Pigs and triumphant after the Cuban Missile Crisis; Lyndon Johnson searching in vain for escape from Vietnam; Jimmy Carter baffled by a darkening political scene he cannot control. But my memory comes to rest first on a meeting in the President's office on a Wednesday afternoon in the spring of 1948, when the Truman Administration faced a decision whose consequences are still with us today. This is where I shall start. The rest will follow.

MAY 12, 1948

Of all the meetings I ever had with Presidents, this one remains the most vivid. Not only did it pit me against a legendary war hero whom President Truman revered, but it did so over an issue of fundamental and enduring national security importance—Israel and the Mideast, an issue as relevant and contentious in the nineties, in the wake of the war with Iraq, as it was then.

The President regarded his Secretary of State, General of the Army George C. Marshall, as "the greatest living American." Yet the two men were on a collision course over Mideast policy, which, if not resolved, threatened to split and wreck the Administration. British control of Palestine would run out in two days, and when it did, the Jewish Agency intended to announce the creation of a new state, still unnamed, in part of Palestine.

Marshall firmly opposed American recognition of the new Jewish state; I did not. Marshall's opposition was shared by almost every member of the brilliant and now-legendary group of men, later referred to as "the Wise Men,"[1] who were then in the process of creating a postwar foreign policy that would endure for more than forty years. The opposition included the respected Undersecretary of State, Robert Lovett; his predecessor, Dean Acheson; the number-three man in the State Department, Charles Bohlen; the brilliant chief of the Policy Planning Staff, George F. Kennan; the dynamic and driven Secretary of Defense, James V. Forrestal; and a man with whom I would disagree again twenty years later when we served together in the Cabinet, Dean Rusk, then the Director of the Office of United Nations Affairs.

Some months earlier, during one of our weekly breakfasts at his elegant Georgetown home, Forrestal had spoken emotionally and frankly to me concerning his opposition to helping the Zionists, as advocates of the creation of a Jewish state were called. "You fellows over at the White House are just not facing up to the realities in the Middle East. There are thirty million Arabs on one side and about six hundred thousand Jews on the other. It is clear that in any contest, the Arabs are going to overwhelm the Jews. Why don't you face up to the realities? Just look at the numbers!"

"Jim, the President knows just as well as you do what the numbers are," I replied, "but he doesn't consider this to be a question of numbers. He has always supported the right of the Jews to have their own homeland, from the moment he became President. He considers this to be a question about the moral and ethical considerations that are present in that part of the world. For that reason, he supports the foundation of a Jewish state. He is sympathetic to their needs and their desires, and I assure you he is going to continue to lend our country's support to the creation of a Jewish state."

Forrestal answered bluntly: "Well, if he does that, then he's absolutely dead wrong." His attitude was typical of the foreign policy establishment, especially the pro-Arab professionals at the State Department, who, deeply influenced by the huge oil reserves in the Mideast, supported the side they thought would be the likely winner in the struggle between the Arabs and the Jews. Officials in the State Department had done everything in their power to prevent, thwart, or delay the President's Palestine policy in 1947 and 1948, while I fought for assistance to the Jewish Agency. Watching them find various ways to avoid carrying out White House instructions, I sometimes felt, almost bitterly, that they preferred to follow the views of the British Foreign Office rather than those of their President.

At midnight on May 14, 1948—6 P.M. in Washington—the British would relinquish control of Palestine, which they had been administering since World War I under mandate from the League of Nations. One minute later, the Jewish Agency, under the leadership of David Ben-Gurion, would proclaim the new state. (The name "Israel" was as yet unknown, and most of us assumed the new nation would be called "Judaea.") The neighboring Arabs made it clear that the fighting, which had already begun, would erupt into a full-scale war against the new state the moment the British left. In order to avoid this, the British and the State Department wanted to turn Palestine over to the trusteeship of the United Nations—a position I strongly opposed as dangerous to the survival of the beleaguered Jews in Palestine. I already had had several serious disagreements over State's position with General Marshall's protégé, Dean Rusk, and with Loy Henderson, the Director of Near Eastern and African Affairs. Henderson, a mustachioed, balding, tightly controlled and somewhat pompous career diplomat, was strongly pro-Arab and heavily influenced by the British. I had no firsthand evidence of it, but I knew Henderson was among a group of Mideast experts in the State Department who were widely regarded as anti-Semitic. He had no use for White House interference in what he regarded as his personal domain—American policy in the Mideast.

On May 7, a week before the end of the British Mandate, I met with President Truman for our customary private day-end chat in the Oval Office. In these informal sessions, which were never listed on his official schedule, he was often very blunt. No one else knew what passed between us in those sessions unless he wanted them to. In this case he didn't.

I handed him a draft of a public statement I had prepared, and proposed that at his next press conference—scheduled for May 13, the day before the British Mandate would end—he announce his intention to recognize the Jewish state. The President was sympathetic to the proposal; keenly aware of Secretary Marshall's strong feelings, though; he picked up the telephone to get his views. As I sat listening to the President's end of the conversation, I could tell that Marshall objected strongly to the proposed statement. The President listened politely, then told Marshall he wanted to have a meeting on the subject.

I was sitting, as usual, in a straight-backed chair to the left of the President's desk. As he ended the conversation with Marshall, he swiveled his chair back toward me. "Clark, I am impressed with General Marshall's argument that we should not recognize the new state so fast," he said. "He does not want to recognize it at all, at least not now. I've asked him and Lovett to come in next week to discuss this business. I think Marshall is going to continue to take a very strong position. When he does, I would like you to make the case in favor of recognition of the new state." He paused, then looked at me intently for a moment. "You know how I feel. I want you to present it just as though you were making an argument before the Supreme Court of the United States. Consider it carefully, Clark, organize it logically. I want you to be as persuasive as you possibly can be."

PREPARING FOR THE SHOWDOWN

The long and bitter battle with Marshall, Forrestal, Lovett, Rusk, and Henderson over Palestine was about to come to a climax. Confusion, bitter disagreements, and procrastination had marked the preceding year, but we could no longer avoid a decision. President Truman had asked me to debate the man he most admired, whose participation in the Administration was essential to its success. I was forty-one years old, in my third year at the White House as a Presidential aide. Virtually every American regarded General Marshall, then sixty-seven, with respect bordering on awe. He had capped his central contribution to victory in World War II with his speech at Harvard a year earlier, proposing what became known as the Marshall Plan. Alone among soldiers, his name was now associated with a peaceful purpose—the reconstruction of Europe—and alone among statesmen, he carried the credentials of a great soldier. Without his towering presence, the Administration would be much diminished, perhaps even mortally wounded, at home and abroad, at a time of great challenge. The Berlin crisis was challenging American leadership as nothing had since the end of the war. The Soviet-inspired coup in Czechoslovakia had taken place only ten weeks earlier. And the Republicans controlled both Houses of Congress.

How firmly would Marshall continue to oppose something the President wanted badly? Could we find a way out of the bind we were in? Out of respect for Marshall and a keen sense of his own political interests, the President knew he should not overrule Marshall; rather, he would see if I could convince the great man.

Marshall did not like me. As far as he was concerned, I was a domestic Presidential adviser who had no business meddling in foreign policy. There was as yet no National Security Adviser, and I often functioned in a manner which presaged the present system. In a sense, Marshall's attitude toward me foreshadowed the conflicts between the State Department and the National Security Council, which would later become a standard part of the Washington landscape.

In preparing for the meeting, I told only three people what I was doing. One was my sole assistant, George Elsey, a brilliant history graduate student from Harvard who had begun working in the Roosevelt White House and stayed on under President Truman. The others were David Niles and Max Lowenthal.

Niles, one of the few holdovers from the Roosevelt White House, was virtually unknown to the public. With outsiders, he cultivated an air of mystery, and insiders said that his enigmatic style either masked real power or created a useful illusion of power. Round-faced, elusive but serious, he was born in Russia and grew up in Boston. Unmarried, he returned to Boston almost every weekend to stay with his sister, even while working at the White House. I respected him for his role in formulating the policies of the late Roosevelt and early Truman period on the plight of the displaced and homeless Jews of Europe; he was the key drafter of many of the directives concerning American policy in this area, which the State Department had long neglected.

If Niles seemed a little strange, that was nothing compared to Max Lowenthal, who was never an official member of the White House staff at all, although he came and went as he pleased. Lowenthal had been a consultant and counsel to Senator Truman in the early forties. Convinced he was under surveillance by J. Edgar Hoover, when Lowenthal wanted to discuss matters he considered sensitive, he insisted that we conduct some of our discussions on a bench in Lafayette Park.*

As I prepared, with assistance from Niles and Lowenthal, for the showdown with Marshall, I felt that I knew what the President wanted, and, more important, how he felt. From our many talks over the past year, I knew that five factors dominated his thinking. From his youth, he had detested intolerance and discrimination. He had been deeply moved by the plight of the millions of homeless of World War II, and felt that alone among the homeless, the Jews had no homeland of their own to which they could return. He was, of course, horrified by the Holocaust and he denounced it vehemently, as, in the aftermath of the war, its full dimensions became clear. Also, he believed that the Balfour Declaration, issued by British Foreign Secretary Arthur Balfour in 1917, committed Great Britain, and by implication, the United States, which now shared a certain global responsibility with the British, to the creation of the Jewish state in Palestine.** And finally, he was a student and believer in the Bible

*As it turned out, he was justified: Hoover, suspecting him a communist, had had Lowenthal under observation for years. A few years later, Lowenthal created a stir by writing the first openly critical book about Hoover.[2] For this act of conscience and courage—decades ahead of its time in discussing Hoover's abuses of power—Lowenthal came under severe public attack. One Congressman called him "a menace to the best interests of America," and he was summoned before the House Committee on Un-American Activities, where he denied absurd charges, stimulated by Hoover, that he had "aided and abetted" communists in the government.

**I recognize that historians have long disagreed as to whether or not British Foreign Minister Balfour committed anyone to anything, but President Truman's view was clear on this point.

since his youth. From his reading of the Old Testament he felt the Jews derived a legitimate historical right to Palestine, and he sometimes cited such biblical lines as Deuteronomy 1:8: "Behold, I have given up the land before you; go in and take possession of the land which the Lord hath sworn unto your fathers, to Abraham, to Isaac, and to Jacob."

From the beginning, I had also supported the creation of the Jewish state, even though this put me in opposition to an entire generation of senior foreign policy makers whom I admired and numbered among my friends, because I considered such action a historical and strategic necessity. I recognized then, of course, that oil, historic antagonisms, and numerical imbalances might create many of the problems Israel's opponents in Washington predicted. Many of their fears, in fact, came true; the Mideast remains today the single most volatile place on earth, a legacy, in part, of the events of 1948. And Israel, having survived four wars and awed the world with its courage and energy, has also veered toward policies that sometimes fall short of the dreams of its founders and their American supporters.

The Zionist position in 1948 was simple: Partition Palestine into two parts, one Jewish, one Arab. On its surface, the joint British–State Department position favoring trusteeship might have seemed a reasonable way to avoid conflict, but the President feared that if Palestine was turned over to the U.N., the Arabs would combine military action and diplomatic footdragging in an effort to throttle the Jewish state at its birth. I fully agreed. I knew Marshall and Lovett would argue that we should continue to support trusteeship, and delay in recognizing the new state—but by "delay" I was convinced that State in fact meant "deny."

My fears about the State Department had crystallized after a bitter incident in March, when, without informing the President, it had permitted the American delegation to the U.N. to reverse its support for partition and switch to trusteeship for Palestine—a contradiction of a personal commitment the President had given the previous day to Chaim Weizmann, the Zionist leader who would later become the first President of Israel. Furious and depressed when he learned what had happened, President Truman wrote on his calendar for March 19, 1948:

> The State Dept. pulled the rug from under me today. . . . The first I know about it is what I see in the papers! Isn't that hell? I am now in the position of a liar and a double-crosser. I've never felt so low in my life. There are people on the third and fourth level of the State Dept. who have always wanted to cut my throat. They've succeeded in doing it.

That afternoon, the President had angrily instructed me to "read the riot act" to those "third- and fourth-level" people at State. A few hours later, I held a contentious meeting with Rusk, Henderson, and State Department Counselor Charles Bohlen, which left us barely on speaking terms. Despite his annoyance, though, the President did not order the State Department to reendorse partition, lest he create a crisis with Marshall. Thus, with the May 14 deadline fast approaching, the U.S. was in the awkward position of having its U.N. delegation still rounding up votes for trusteeship while the President favored partition and prompt recognition of the soon to be proclaimed Jewish state.

Sixteen years as a trial lawyer in St. Louis before my World War II naval service shaped my approach to the May 12 showdown with Marshall. For me the key to successful advocacy was and remains preparation—careful preparation. Even today, when going into court, I rise very early the day of my court appearance, and rehearse my presentation as I shave, sometimes going over it again for several hours alone in my bedroom or office. I have seen many good cases lost simply because they were badly presented. But this was the only time I would ever argue a case against General Marshall. Knowing the President was privately on my side did not reduce the difficulty of the task—after all, he was counting on me to turn Marshall around.

George Catlett Marshall was a man of the strictest rectitude, with little noticeable sense of humor. Not even Presidents Roosevelt and Truman called him by his first name, a privilege reserved for his wife and a handful of early military contemporaries; he called even his closest associates only by their last names. He had planned to spend his time in quiet retirement with his wife at their home in Virginia, but when President Truman asked him to return from his thankless mission in China at the beginning of 1947 to become Secretary of State, just as the Cold War was beginning its most dangerous phase, he agreed without complaint. It was this devotion to the President—or more accurately, the Presidency—that so impressed President Truman and everyone else, including me.

Marshall and Lovett had prepared a position paper for the President's consideration. Reading it before the meeting, I saw it amounted to a clever way to avoid recognizing the new nation. And I feared that the President's respect for Marshall might prevail.

At 4 P.M. on Wednesday, May 12, a cloudless, sweltering day, we assembled in the Oval Office.[3] President Truman sat at his desk, his back to the bay window overlooking the lawn, his famous THE BUCK STOPS HERE plaque in front of him on his desk. In the seat to the President's left sat Marshall, austere and grim, and next to Marshall sat his deputy, Robert Lovett. Behind Lovett were two State Department officials, Robert

McClintock and Fraser Wilkins. I wondered why Rusk and Henderson, who had been centrally involved in every phase of the policy debate for months, were not present. Only forty years later did I learn from Wilkins that just before the meeting Lovett had decided the presence of Rusk and Henderson in the same room with me would be too inflammatory, and he had substituted their deputies.*

David Niles, White House Appointments Secretary Matthew Connelly, and I sat together in chairs to the right of the President. As the meeting began, exactly fifty hours remained before the new nation, still without a name, would be born.

The meeting began in a deceptively calm manner. President Truman did not raise the issue of recognition; he wanted me to raise it, but only after Marshall and Lovett had spoken, so he would be able to ascertain the degree of Marshall's opposition before showing his own hand. Lovett began by criticizing what he termed signs of growing "assertiveness" by the Jewish Agency. "On the basis of some recent military successes and the prospect of a 'behind the barn' deal with King Abdullah," Lovett said, "the Jews seem confident that they can establish their sovereign state without any necessity for a truce with the Arabs of Palestine."**

Marshall interrupted Lovett: he was strongly opposed, he said, to the behavior of the Jewish Agency. He had met on May 8 with Moshe Shertok, its political representative, and had told him that it was "dangerous to base long-range policy on temporary military success." Moreover, if the Jews got into trouble and "came running to us for help," Marshall said he had told them, "they were clearly on notice that there was no warrant to expect help from the United States, which had warned them of the grave risk they were running." I was surprised to hear, from Marshall himself, how bluntly he had dealt with Shertok. He had laid down a tough opening position.

As Marshall spoke, he was interrupted by an urgent message from his special assistant. The United Press had reported that Shertok had returned to Tel Aviv carrying Marshall's personal warning to David Ben-Gurion. Clearly displeased, Marshall told us that not only had he not sent Ben-Gurion a message, but he had never even *heard* of Ben-Gurion—a surprising statement about the leader of the Jewish Agency, who was about to become the new nation's Prime Minister.

Marshall directed the State Department to refuse to comment on the

*Both men subsequently had distinguished Foreign Service careers. McClintock served as Ambassador to Lebanon during the 1958 crisis, Wilkins as Ambassador to Cyprus.

**King Abdullah of Transjordan, who was assassinated in 1951, was the grandfather of King Hussein of Jordan. Lovett was referring to the highly secret talks between the Jews and the Jordanians. Some of these contacts involved Golda Meir and King Abdullah himself, but this was not known at the time.

UP news story, and then concluded his presentation. The United States, he said, should continue supporting U.N. trusteeship resolutions and defer any decision on recognition.

It was now my turn. Even though I disagreed with many of Marshall's and Lovett's statements, I had waited without saying a word until the President called on me—in order to establish that I was speaking at his request, not on my own initiative.

I began by objecting strongly to the State Department's position paper reaffirming American support of Security Council efforts to secure a truce in Palestine. "There has been no truce in Palestine and there almost certainly will not be one," I said. I reminded everyone that in a meeting chaired by the President on March 24, "Dean Rusk stated that a truce could be negotiated within two weeks. But this goal is still not in sight."

"Second," I went on, "trusteeship, which State supports, presupposes a single Palestine. That is also unrealistic. Partition into Jewish and Arab sectors has already happened. Jews and Arabs are already fighting each other from territory each side presently controls."

The time had now come to join the issue. "Third, Mr. President," I said, "I strongly urge you to give prompt recognition to the Jewish state immediately after the termination of the British Mandate on May 14. This would have the distinct value of restoring the President's firm position in support of the partition of Palestine. Such a move should be taken quickly, before the Soviet Union or any other nation recognizes the Jewish state."

I knew my comment would displease Marshall and Lovett, since I was implying that State had embarrassed the President by reversing the American position in the U.N. two months earlier. But I strongly believed this, and I saw no reason not to bring it up.

"My fourth point," I continued, "is that the President should make a statement at his press conference tomorrow which announces his intention to recognize the Jewish state, once it has complied with the provision for democratic government outlined in the U.N. resolution of November 29. I understand this is in fact the case, and therefore presents no problem." I handed around the room a proposed press statement, and read aloud its conclusion: "I have asked the Secretary of State to have the Representatives of the United States in the United Nations take up this subject with a view toward obtaining early recognition of the Jewish state by the other members of the United Nations." When everyone had examined it, I went on, "My fifth point relates to the Balfour Declaration. Jewish people the world over have been waiting for thirty years for the promise of a homeland to be fulfilled. There is no reason to wait one day longer. Trusteeship will postpone that promise indefinitely. Sixth, the United States has a great moral obligation to oppose discrimination such as that inflicted on the Jewish people. Alarmingly, it is reappearing in communist-controlled Eastern Europe. There must be a safe haven for these people. Here is an opportunity to try to bring these ancient injustices to an end. The Jews could have their own homeland. They could be lifted to the status of other peoples who have their own country. And perhaps these steps would help atone, in some small way, for the atrocities, so vast as to stupefy the human mind, that occurred during the Holocaust.

"Finally," I concluded, "I fully understand and agree that vital national interests are involved. In an area as unstable as the Middle East, where there is not now and never has been any tradition of democratic government, it is important for the long-range security of our country, and indeed the world, that a nation committed to the democratic system be established there, one on which we can rely. The new Jewish state can be such a place. We should strengthen it in its infancy by prompt recognition."

I had noticed Marshall's face reddening with suppressed anger as I talked. When I finished, he exploded: "Mr. President, I thought this meeting was called to consider an important and complicated problem in foreign policy. I don't even know why Clifford is here. He is a domestic adviser, and this is a foreign policy matter."

I would never forget President Truman's characteristically simple reply: "Well, General, he's here because I asked him to be here."

Marshall, scarcely concealing his ire, shot back, "These considerations have nothing to do with the issue. I fear that the only reason Clifford is here is that he is pressing a political consideration with regard to this issue. I don't think politics should play any part in this."

Lovett joined the attack: "It would be highly injurious to the United Nations to announce the recognition of the Jewish state even before it had come into existence and while the General Assembly is still considering the question. Furthermore, such a move would be injurious to the prestige of the President. It is obviously designed to win the Jewish vote, but in my opinion, it would lose more votes than it would gain." Lovett had finally brought to the surface the root cause of Marshall's fury—his view that the position I presented was dictated by domestic political considerations, specifically a quest for Jewish votes.

"Mr. President, to recognize the Jewish state prematurely would be buying a pig in a poke," Lovett continued. "How do we know what kind of Jewish state will be set up? We have many reports from British and American intelligence agents that Soviets are sending Jews and communist agents into Palestine from the Black Sea area." Lovett read some of these intelligence reports to the group. I found them ridiculous, and no evidence ever turned up to support them; in fact, Jews were fleeing communism throughout Eastern Europe at that very moment.

When Lovett concluded, Marshall spoke again. He was still furious. Speaking with barely contained rage and more than a hint of self-righteousness, he made the most remarkable threat I ever heard anyone make directly to a President: *"If you follow Clifford's advice and if I were to vote in the election, I would vote against you."* (Emphasis added.)

Everyone in the room was stunned. Here was the indispensable symbol of continuity whom President Truman revered and needed, making a threat that, if it became public, could virtually seal the dissolution of the Truman Administration and send the Western Alliance, then in the process of creation, into disarray before it had been fully structured. Marshall's statement fell short of an explicit threat to resign, but it came very close.

Lovett and I tried to step into the ensuing silence with words of conciliation. We both knew how important it was to get this dreadful meeting over with quickly, before Marshall said something even more irretrievable. My suggested Presidential press statement was clearly out of the question, and I withdrew it. Lovett said that State's Legal Adviser, Ernest Gross, had prepared a paper on the legal aspects of recognition, and he would send it to us immediately.

President Truman also knew he had to end the meeting. He said he was fully aware of the dangers in the situation, to say nothing of the political factors involved on *both sides* of the problem; these were his responsibility, and he would deal with them himself. Seeing Marshall was still very agitated, he rose and turned to him and said, "I understand your position, General, and I'm inclined to side with you in this matter."

We rose with the President and gathered our papers. Marshall did not even glance at me as he and Lovett left. In fact, not only did he never speak to me again after that meeting, but, according to his official biographer, he never again mentioned my name.[4] Then, at the end of that day, still steaming, he did something quite unusual, although the President and I were unaware of it at the time. Certain that history would prove him right, he wanted his personal comments included in the official State Department record of the meeting. It is normal for the records of such meetings kept by the State Department to water down or leave out personal comments; Marshall did exactly the opposite. His record, exactly as he wanted historians to find it when it was declassified almost three decades later, reads as follows:

> I remarked to the President that, speaking objectively, I could not help but think that suggestions made by Mr. Clifford were wrong. I thought that to adopt these suggestions would have precisely the opposite effect from that intended by Mr. Clifford. The transparent dodge to win a few votes would not in fact achieve this purpose. The

> great dignity of the office of the President would be seriously diminished. The counsel offered by Mr. Clifford was based on domestic political considerations, while the problem which confronted us was international. I said bluntly that if the President were to follow Mr. Clifford's advice and if in the elections I were to vote, I would vote against the President.[5]

General Marshall's position was grossly unfair: he had no proof to sustain the charge, nor did he offer any—nor had I given him any, for I had not mentioned politics in my presentation. My growing involvement in foreign policy was at the President's direction. I believed then, as I do now, that the President's position was based on the national interest.

Marshall and Lovett's view was based on the assumption that the Palestine issue would decide how Jewish Americans voted. In my opinion, their assumption was incorrect. In fact, a significant number of Jewish Americans opposed Zionism: some feared that the effort to create a Jewish state was so controversial that the plan would fail. In 1942 a number of prominent dissident Reform rabbis had founded the American Council for Judaism to oppose the establishment of a Jewish state in Palestine. It grew into an organization of over fourteen thousand members, which collaborated closely with State Department officials, including Dean Acheson and Loy Henderson. Its leaders believed that the establishment of an exclusively Jewish state was "undemocratic and a retreat from the universal vision of Judaism," and would lead to "ghettoizing Jews by segregating them from their compatriots and turning them into aliens."[6] Other individuals, including Arthur H. Sulzberger, the publisher of *The New York Times* (who supported the American Council for Judaism), and Eugene Meyer, the publisher of *The Washington Post,* opposed Zionism. Sulzberger's wife, the redoubtable Iphigene Ochs Sulzberger, who disagreed strongly with her husband, later recalled that "Zionism was a heavily debated issue among American Jews." Many Jews opposed American backing for any Jewish state in Palestine.[7]

As for domestic politics, neither the President nor I believed that Palestine was the key to the Jewish vote. As I had written the President in 1947, in a lengthy memorandum proposing a strategy for the 1948 election campaign, the key to the Jewish vote in 1948 would not be the Palestine issue, but a continued commitment to liberal political and economic policies. Noting the sharp divisions over Zionism within the Jewish community, I concluded, "In the long run, there is likely to be greater gain if the Palestine problem is approached on the basis of reaching a decision founded upon intrinsic merit." (For further discussion of this memorandum, see Chapter 13.)

"LET THE DUST SETTLE A LITTLE"

Marshall had deeply disappointed me. I thought his implied threat had crossed the bounds of what was permissible and proper in a meeting with the President. I thought I had lost. In the course of the meeting in the Oval Office, I had left the proposed press statement and some other papers on the front of the President's desk. I lingered a moment to pick them up.

Seeing my face, President Truman thought I needed to be cheered up. "Well, that was rough as a cob," he said, using one of his favorite Missouri farm phrases. "That was about as tough as it gets. But you did your best."

"Boss," I replied, "this isn't the first case I've lost. I never expected to win them all." Then, to see if he wanted to try again, I said, "Maybe it's not over yet. I'd like approval to test the waters one more time."

The President's reply was ambiguous: "You may be right, I don't know. I never saw the General so furious. Suppose we let the dust settle a little—then you can get into it again and see if we can get this thing turned around. I still want to do it. But be careful. I can't afford to lose General Marshall."

It might be argued that a Presidential telephone call to Marshall or Lovett would have resolved the issue. While this would normally be correct in relationships between the President and anyone in his Cabinet, it did not fit this unique situation. Harry Truman, as yet an unelected President, was viewed by most people as a temporary custodian of the giant legacy of Franklin Roosevelt. Facing the central political fact of 1948—Republican control of both Houses of Congress—he could not afford an open break with Marshall. Besides, he genuinely liked and respected Marshall, and on every other important issue they were in agreement.

Thus, as I left the Oval Office, I understood that the chances for salvaging the situation were very small—but not quite zero. As I was in my office going over the day's events with Elsey, the telephone rang—it was Bob Lovett. "I have been deeply disturbed ever since the meeting in the President's office this afternoon," he said, and then he paused. I felt like saying, "You didn't help much," but, barely resisting the temptation, waited to see what was coming next. "It would be a great tragedy if these two men were to break over this issue."

I certainly agreed: "It would be about the worst thing that could happen to the President and to the country." I was thinking of how difficult it would be to conduct our foreign policy if we lost Marshall, or even if his opposition and threat to President Truman on this issue were to become known publicly.

"Could you drop by my house for a drink on your way home tonight?"

Lovett asked. "I would like to talk to you more about this." I was delighted. I knew him to be a sensible and thoughtful man. He had not suggested any change in his attitude, but apparently he was willing to try to find a solution to this dreadful turn of affairs.

* * *

Robert Lovett's life and career had been closely linked with that of his close friend from childhood, Averell Harriman. Lovett's father had been president of the Union Pacific Railroad under the legendary E. H. Harriman, Averell's father, and upon the elder Harriman's death, the senior Lovett had become chairman of the railroad. Lovett and Harriman had been at Yale together, and later became colleagues when they merged their two firms to form Brown Brothers Harriman—to this day a respected New York investment bank. Lovett's wife Adele was the great-granddaughter of one of the Browns who had founded Brown Brothers in 1835. In World War II, Lovett had served with great distinction as Assistant Secretary of War, working closely with General Marshall. Now he was back as Marshall's deputy at State, a position whose normal power was heightened by the fact that Marshall believed deeply in delegating authority through a formal chain of command. Lovett, a Republican who served Democrats with loyalty and skill, would later become President Truman's Secretary of Defense. A dozen years later, I would find myself calling on him, at President-elect Kennedy's request, to offer him the post of Secretary of the Treasury, a job which he turned down for health reasons (see Chapter 21).

I was pleased President Truman had asked Lovett to become Undersecretary of State, replacing Dean Acheson, who had returned to his law firm in 1947. Because Lovett did not leave behind policies or theories in the manner of Acheson and Kennan, later historians would find it hard to understand his great value to any Administration fortunate enough to have him. I respected Acheson greatly for his achievements, his intellect, and his conceptual abilities; but despite his great stature, he did not possess Lovett's ability—unsurpassed in my entire Washington experience—to get people to work together with a minimum of friction. Where Acheson was decisive and impatient, Lovett was thoughtful and conciliatory. In informal settings, he was witty and charming, with a fine sense of detachment and irony—he was one of the best raconteurs I have ever met. But these charming qualities would have been of interest only to hostesses if they had not skillfully covered an immensely tough interior. All in all, he was close to the model of a perfect public servant. If anyone could turn Marshall around, it might be the man whose appointment as Undersecretary of State General Marshall had made a condition of his becoming Secretary, calling him, with a rare display of personal affection, "my old copilot." But was Lovett willing to try?

The Lovetts had rented a house in the Kalorama area off Connecticut Avenue, a quiet, tree-lined section of Washington, about ten minutes from the White House. When I arrived, we went into his library. In those days bourbon and branch water was virtually the official drink of the Administration; I had one, while Lovett, always concerned about his health, drank a sherry. His wife left us alone to talk.

Lovett opened on a positive note: a break between the President and General Marshall, he said, would have unacceptable consequences. We were in the midst of the most difficult months of the Cold War and we had to avert a split in our ranks—any leak of the astonishing events of that afternoon would be catastrophic.

Lovett stressed the reasonableness of his own views. "Let's get through this crisis, then sit down and review the issue again in a more thorough manner," he suggested. Gentle and conciliatory though Lovett's style was, this seemed to be more of the same from State—delay and circumvention of the President's policy objectives. In order not to return to the contentious tone of the Oval Office meeting, I observed that the "very persuasive critique" by Lovett and Marshall had caused the President to set aside any thought of announcing recognition the following day. Lovett probed to see to what extent my comments in the meeting represented the President's position.

"Do you think," Lovett asked, "that if you were to present some modification of State's views to the President as something he could live with, he might be persuaded to moderate his position and work something out with General Marshall that would get us past this crisis—at least past the next two days?" His question forced me to make an immediate choice. I could have said I needed to check with the President and reply the next day, but time was running out. "Bob, there is no chance whatsoever that the President will change his mind on the basic issue. My presentation today was made at his instruction and represented his views. He wants to recognize the new state. So all I can say is that if anyone is going to give, it is going to have to be General Marshall, because—I can tell you now—the President is not going to give an inch." Because I saw no value in even hinting that compromise was possible, I had stated President Truman's views more strongly than he himself would have. It was essential to turn the pressure back on Marshall, and Lovett was the only channel through which to do it.

"Well, then," said Lovett thoughtfully, "let's see what can be done at State." I left on that slightly encouraging note, hopeful that Lovett could somehow bring *his* copilot around.

The next morning, Thursday, May 13, I began by reporting to the President on my meeting with Lovett the previous evening. "Okay, this is part of the process of letting the dust settle," he said. "Keep encouraging Lovett to work on the General."

In the middle of a day of tense waiting, Lovett called with a new suggestion—to make a formal decision to recognize the new state, but delay announcing or implementing it for an unspecified period. I saw no value in this suggestion, and without checking with the President told Lovett so: "That's a nothing approach, Bob. I've talked to the President, and I want to tell you that he is not going to budge an inch in his basic view. He is rock solid."

Lovett suggested recognizing the new state de facto instead of de jure. Here at last was an issue on which I felt we could yield to State, and said so—again without checking with the President. The difference, while extremely important to governments in defining and justifying international boundaries, was not something I felt was critical at this moment, since we could upgrade the nature of our recognition to de jure later.*

May 13 ended with no resolution of the crisis. Amazingly, there had been no leaks. At his press conference, asked what he planned to do when the Jewish state was proclaimed, the President replied curtly, "I will cross that bridge when I get to it." As I listened, I thought, *We reach that bridge tomorrow.*

THE DAY OF DECISION

This was the beginning of a historic day in Palestine, but the American government still had not decided what it would do when 6 P.M. came. The unseasonably hot and muggy weather in Washington finally showed signs of breaking; when I reached the office, earlier than usual, I called Lovett. He was looking for ways to calm things down, but he and Marshall were still opposed to recognition of the Jewish state.

I was also in close contact, directly and through David Niles, with Eliahu Epstein, the Jewish Agency representative in Washington. Through Epstein, I had been able to learn much about the situation in the Mideast, in particular the position of the Jewish Agency—information that went beyond what the State Department, with its pro-Arab bias, allowed to filter across the street to the White House through official channels.

In our conversations, Lovett searched for the minimum that would satisfy the President. Finally, I had an idea: "Look, Bob, the President

*I had another battle with State in the fall of 1948 over this issue, finally overcoming their objections to de jure recognition, conditional on Israel holding parliamentary elections. These elections were held and the U.S. granted de jure recognition early in 1949.

understands General Marshall is not going to support him on this. Let's forget Wednesday. We're not seeking a formal retraction of what the General said. The President doesn't care whether he supports this now or never. If you can get him simply to say that he will not oppose this, that's all the President would need." There was a brief pause at the other end of the line. "Let me see what I can do," was all Lovett said in reply.

Even without a clear signal from Lovett and Marshall, I felt we had to set in motion the machinery for recognition, in the event a favorable decision was made. At 10 A.M., I made a different call, one that I would look back on later with great pleasure. "Mr. Epstein," I told the Jewish Agency representative, "we would like you to send an official letter to President Truman before twelve o'clock today formally requesting the United States to recognize the new Jewish state. I would also request that you send a copy of the letter directly to Secretary Marshall."

Epstein was ecstatic. He did not realize that the President had still not decided how to respond to the request I had just solicited. It was particularly important, I said, that the new state claim nothing beyond the boundaries outlined in the U.N. resolution of November 29, 1947, because those boundaries were the only ones which had been agreed to by everyone, including the Arabs, in any international forum.

A few minutes later, Epstein called back: "We've never done this before, and we're not quite sure how to go about it. Could you give us some advice?" I told him that I would check with the experts and get back to him. With my knowledge and encouragement, he then turned for additional advice to two of the wisest lawyers in Washington, David Ginsburg and Benjamin Cohen, both great New Dealers and strong supporters of the Zionist cause. Working together with me during the rest of the morning, Epstein and his team drafted the recognition request.

It was short: "My dear Mr. President," it began, "I have the honor to notify you that the state of. . . ." Here Epstein and I had a problem—we did not know the name of the new state. After some discussion, Epstein simply typed in "the Jewish State" and finished the letter. I asked Epstein to be sure the letter explicitly referred to the November 29 U.N. resolution. The document ended with a minor rhetorical flourish that we worked out over the telephone together:

> With full knowledge of the deep bond of sympathy which has existed and has been strengthened over the past thirty years between the Government of the United States and the Jewish people of Palestine, I have been authorized by the provisional government of the new state to tender this message and to express the hope that your government will recognize and will welcome [the new state] into the community of nations.

Epstein handed the letter to his press aide, Harry Zinder, and told him to take it to my office immediately. As I waited anxiously for it, Epstein got word on his shortwave radio that the new state would be called "Israel." He immediately sent a second aide after Zinder to change the letter. Two blocks from the White House, Zinder, sitting in the car Epstein had provided, crossed out with a pen the words "Jewish State" and inserted the word "Israel." Zinder then proceeded to my office. It was the first time I had heard the name of the new state.

When we received Epstein's letter, Niles and I began drafting the reply, checking with State on technical details. Niles also checked with, of all people, Ben Cohen, who thus found himself on both sides of the first official exchange between the U.S. and Israel. However, there was still no word from Lovett or Marshall. In the late morning, unable to contain my concern and tension, I called Lovett again and said we should move to resolve the matter; in response, he suggested we meet for lunch at a small, private club to which he belonged, the F Street Club, not far from the White House.

The luncheon with Lovett was a remarkable example of the way we were operating. With time literally slipping away, Lovett and I functioned in a sort of never-never land; while we calmly and professionally discussed technical aspects of the decision, we continued to disagree profoundly as to whether or not the decision should be made at all. Lovett's ability to function effectively on such murky terrain was one reason I respected him so much.

I brought Epstein's request for recognition, our proposed reply, and a draft of a Presidential statement with me. I wanted to increase the pressure on State. In a friendly but firm manner, Lovett continued to argue against recognition: delay, he said, was essential. Delay, I said, was the equivalent of nonrecognition in the explosive conditions that existed at that moment in the Mideast.

There were less than four hours remaining until the new nation would be proclaimed. I picked my way carefully through the conversation. "The President was impressed, as I was by your argument, but at 6 P.M. tonight, without action by us, there will be no internationally recognized government or authority in Palestine," I said. "A number of people have advised the President that this should not be permitted. The President wishes to take action on recognition."

Lovett still had not given up: "Indecent haste in recognizing the new state would be unfortunate for the very reasons that I mentioned on Wednesday. Please get the President to delay for a day or so. It is hard for me to believe that one day could make so much difference. There will be a tremendous reaction in the Arab world. We might lose the effects of many years of hard work with the Arabs. We will lose our position with Arab leaders. It will put our diplomatic missions and consular representatives into personal jeopardy."

"Speed is essential to preempt the Russians," I replied, and reminded him that he and Marshall had been expressing great concern that the Soviet Union might take advantage of indecision on our part to gain a toehold in the area. "And a one-day delay will become two days, three days, and so on. . . ."

Lovett could see that our position was absolutely firm. If the State Department did not change its attitude the feared explosion between the President and the General could not be averted. He simply had to back down.

"It is impossible to time our messages to arrive in so many distant capitals when we still don't know when the final decision will be made," he said, somewhat weakly. He again suggested a one-day delay.

"We have the formal request from the Jewish Agency, and the President will make the final decision this afternoon," I replied. On this ambiguous note our luncheon—friendly in tone, contentious in content—ended, and I returned to the White House, still uncertain if Lovett could "deliver" Marshall.

The President viewed my luncheon as a sign Lovett was trying to lead Marshall and his colleagues out of their bunker a step at a time. If Lovett wanted me to play the heavy in this minuet, by allowing me to reject their arguments one by one, partly in the name of the President, I was more than willing. And if he was trying to get himself and State off the hook by saying the decision was dictated by domestic politics, I thought that was an acceptable price for us at the White House to pay to get the job done. The only important thing, with time running out, was to get it done quickly.

Around 4 P.M., Lovett made the telephone call I had waited so long to receive: "Clark, I think we have something we can work with. I have talked to the General. He cannot support the President's position, but he has agreed that he will not oppose it."

"God, that's good news." I was truly thrilled. I thanked Lovett for his efforts, and asked if he could get Marshall to call the President directly with the news. Lovett said he would try. Marshall never did make the call himself—I assume it was too painful for him to do so—but Lovett confirmed Marshall's position directly with the President a few minutes later. As Lovett called the President, I called Epstein and told him, in strict confidence, the good news.

Only thirty minutes remained before the announcement would be made in Tel Aviv. The American segment of the drama was now coming to its climax in three places simultaneously—the mini–command center in my office; the State Department; and the floor of the U.N. General Assembly, then located at Flushing Meadow, New York.

I had thought the issue was finally behind us, but to my astonishment, Lovett called to suggest another delay. Would the President agree to defer any action until after the General Assembly adjourned around ten that night?

Saying I would check with the President, I waited about three minutes and called Lovett back to say that delay was out of the question. It was about 5:40, and the State Department had run out of time and ideas.

But one last, suitably bizarre scene was still to be played out. At 5:45 I called Dean Rusk to ask him to inform Ambassador Warren Austin, the head of our U.N. delegation, that the White House would announce recognition of Israel right after 6 P.M. I realized as I talked to Rusk that Lovett had not yet told him that the decision had been made. He reacted as if he had been stung: "This cuts directly across what our delegation had been trying to accomplish in the General Assembly—and we have a large majority for it," he responded testily.

"Nevertheless, Dean, this is what the President wishes you to do."

Reluctantly, Rusk called Austin off the floor of the General Assembly and told him what was about to happen. Stunned at the news, Austin decided not to return to the floor in order to signal that he had not known in advance of the President's decision. Instead, he got into his car and went home. Thinking that Austin had simply gone to the washroom, his colleagues in the American delegation continued to round up votes for trusteeship.

Just after 6 P.M., I walked hurriedly past the White House press corps, who were lounging, as usual, on the worn sofas in the lobby of the West Wing, to the office of Charlie Ross, the President's press secretary. Impatient to be told there would be no more news that day, the reporters wondered what story they were waiting for so late in the day. Handing Ross a piece of paper, I asked him to gather the press as quickly as possible. At 6:11 P.M. Ross read aloud to them:

> Statement by the President. This government has been informed that a Jewish state has been proclaimed in Palestine. . . . The United States recognizes the provisional government as the de facto authority of the new State of Israel.

Back at the U.N., the situation unraveled. Unaware of the White House announcement, the delegates continued to debate trusteeship status for Palestine. Suddenly a rumor swept the floor: the U.S. had recognized the Jewish state! As *The New York Times* reported the next morning, "the first reaction was that someone was making a terrible joke, and some diplomats broke into skeptical laughs." In the ensuing chaos, American delegates had to restrain physically the Cuban delegate, who tried to march to the podium to withdraw his nation from the world assembly!

* * *

It had been a near-run thing, but the deed had been done. The U.S. had been the first to recognize Israel, as the President had hoped and wanted. (The Soviet Union followed suit three days later.) The struggle with Marshall, Lovett, Forrestal, and the entire foreign policy establishment had been contained—but only barely.

Lovett never told me exactly what had passed between him and Marshall in those last two days. From his general comments I concluded that Lovett had finally sat down alone with Marshall on Friday and said, in effect, that, having argued their position, they had an obligation to accept the President's policy or resign.

Although Marshall never forgave me, these events did nothing to impair my relations with Lovett. In fact, the curious combination of disagreement over substance and collaboration to solve the crisis had forged stronger and closer bonds between us. At the beginning of 1949, just before he left the government and returned to New York, we exchanged personal letters. In his, he wrote, "One of the happiest recollections of my tour of duty down here is the basis on which we worked on our common problems, and I am grateful to you beyond words for the understanding and help you always gave me." I certainly felt the same way.

Lovett remained adamant for the rest of his life, however, that the President and I had been wrong—as did most of his colleagues. Nothing could ever convince him, Marshall, Forrestal, Acheson or Rusk otherwise. Like Marshall, Lovett made sure that historians would find a personal record of his views—something that he rarely did in his long and distinguished career. In a vivid closing paragraph of his memorandum, written three days after these events but classified top secret for almost thirty years, Lovett revealed his true feelings:

> In this memorandum I have omitted, for the sake of brevity, the long arguments back and forth through the afternoon [of May 14]. My protests against the precipitate action and warnings as to consequences with the Arab world appear to have been outweighed by considerations unknown to me, but I can only conclude that the President's political advisors, having failed last Wednesday afternoon

> to make the President a father of the new state, have determined at least to make him the midwife.

When I read this memorandum, I knew exactly whom Lovett meant when he referred to "the President's political advisors." In the same memorandum, he quoted me as saying, "The timing of this action is of the greatest possible importance to the President from a domestic point of view." It is regrettable that Lovett must have misunderstood some comment I had made. At no time did I suggest, or intend to suggest, that President Truman's major concern was domestic politics. During the luncheon we did discuss the election that would take place later that year, and three days later, when he dictated his record, it is possible that Lovett merged the two subjects. But his view that my desire to recognize Israel was motivated by political considerations was incorrect. Although domestic considerations are in fact a legitimate part of any important foreign policy decision, I never rested the case for recognition upon politics.

* * *

It is now more than forty years since those "timeless moments" in May. I can still see General Marshall exploding in anger; Bob Lovett fixing a drink while testing our determination; Loy Henderson looking for every possible way to stop the President; Eliahu Epstein joyfully asking how to request recognition for his new, still-unnamed nation; and Dean Rusk telling me that the President's decision contradicted American policy.

But never once, in these forty-plus years, have I wavered in the conviction that what Harry Truman did was correct. Lovett had been right on one point—the U.S. *was* "midwife" to Israel's creation. But he was wrong to ascribe this to the President's "political advisors." I believed in the advice we gave the President, but it was he who made the decision.

Under our system, political considerations are present in every important decision a President makes, but in this case it was in no way the central factor. The charge that domestic politics determined our policy on Palestine angered President Truman for the rest of his life. I shared his anger at the implication that the President and those Americans who supported the Zionists were somehow acting in opposition to our nation's interests. In fact, though, the President's policy rested on the realities of the situation in the region, on America's moral, ethical, and humanitarian values, on the costs and risks inherent in any other course, and—of course—on America's national interests.

What would have happened if President Truman had not acted as he did? History does not allow us to test alternatives, but in my view American recognition and the support that followed was vital in helping Israel survive. Had the U.S. continued to support trusteeship status for Palestine, Israel's condition at birth would have been infinitely more precarious, and in the war that followed, the Israelis would have been at an additional disadvantage. Emboldened by less American support for Israel, the Arabs might have been more successful in their war against the Jews. If that had happened, the U.S. might have faced a far more difficult decision within a year: either offer the Israelis massive American military support, or risk watching the Arabs drive the Israelis into the sea.

Because President Truman was often annoyed by the tone and fierceness of the pressure exerted on him by American Zionists, he left some people with the impression he was ambivalent about the events of May 1948. This was not true: he never wavered in his belief that he had taken the right action. He felt particularly warmly toward Chaim Weizmann, Israel's first President, and David Ben-Gurion, its first Prime Minister. In 1961, years after he left the White House, former President Truman met with Ben-Gurion in New York. Ben-Gurion's memory of that meeting is revealing:

> At our last meeting, after a very interesting talk, just before [the President] left me—it was in a New York hotel suite—I told him that as a foreigner I could not judge what would be his place in American history; but his helpfulness to us, his constant sympathy with our aims in Israel, his courageous decision to recognize our new State so quickly and his steadfast support since then had given him an immortal place in Jewish history. As I said that, tears suddenly sprang to his eyes. And his eyes were still wet when he bade me goodbye. I had rarely seen anyone so moved. I tried to hold him for a few minutes until he had become more composed, for I recalled that the hotel corridors were full of waiting journalists and photographers. He left. A little while later, I too had to go out, and a correspondent came to me to ask, "Why was President Truman in tears when he left you?"[8]

I believe that I know. These were the tears of a man who had been subjected to calumny and vilification, who had persisted against powerful forces within his own Administration determined to defeat him. These were the tears of a man who had fought ably and honorably for a humanitarian goal to which he was deeply committed. These were tears of thanksgiving that his God had seen fit to bless his labors with success.

I admired President Truman enormously for the courage he showed in this crisis. But then, I admired Harry Truman more than any other man I have ever known. He was not only my boss, he became my friend. Because of him, I came to Washington almost half a century ago, and never left.

2

St. Louis

That great Cathedral space which was childhood.

—VIRGINIA WOOLF

My first political memory is of Election Day, 1916. My father was a loyal Democrat, and our family supported President Wilson against his opponent, Charles Evans Hughes. In order to inform the people of St. Louis of the results as quickly as possible, the *St. Louis Post-Dispatch* had made an ingenious arrangement with the local utility company. In the evening, the newspaper proudly announced, "the electric lights in homes and street cars will flicker out once and be turned on again if President Wilson has been re-elected. If Hughes is elected, the lights will flicker out three times."[1] I was nine, it was the first election I was aware of, and this novel way to learn the outcome especially excited me because it might allow me to stay up late. I begged my parents to allow me to await the signal, and they agreed.

We waited in our living room as the evening wore on. Finally, near midnight, our lights blinked once. As we began cheering for Wilson, our lights suddenly blinked twice more. Plunged into despair, we went to bed thinking Hughes had been elected. It was not until a day later that we, and the nation, learned that California's vote, which was counted late, had gone to Wilson, and with it, the 1916 election. I have lived through many other election nights since then, but only one was as memorable—1948.

St. Louis was then the fourth-largest city in the nation, and the jumping-off point for the West. From St. Louis west, the land was more lightly settled, mostly by the last generation of frontiersmen. For the Mississippi River traveler, also, St. Louis was a great destination. Two years before my birth, St. Louis had played host to two great events, the 1904 Olympics, and the World's Fair, which was given immortality in the famous song and movie *Meet Me in St. Louis.* We felt we lived in a special place with a great destiny, not simply another middle-sized American city.

Life was, to a far greater degree than is true in most families today, centered around my parents and our family. Both of my parents came from families of eight children, all of whom lived. But the two families were very different. My father, Frank Andrew Clifford, was a quiet man, well balanced, with an even disposition—but he was not creative, and I sensed after a while that to him life was a rather uneventful experience. He had been trained to have limited expectations as to what life had in store for him. When I was born, on December 25, 1906, in Fort Scott, Kansas, he was an auditor with the Missouri Pacific Railroad, on temporary assignment in Fort Scott. When my father's assignment ended, we moved back to St. Louis, where my memories begin. My father was making the long slow climb up the corporate ladder during an era when the railroads were enormously important and had great prestige.

My mother, Georgia McAdams Clifford, was quite beautiful, had a strong dramatic bent, and loved to appear before audiences as a speaker or storyteller. An innate charm, an attractive speaking voice, and an active and wide-ranging mind were the hallmarks of her unique personality. She achieved some national recognition in the thirties with her own weekly program on the CBS radio network, which ran for three years. For years, she served as the President of the National Story Teller's League. Each summer she lectured, told stories, and taught children at Chautauqua, New York.

There was very little family feeling among my father's family. Grandfather Clifford, who was English, had a wholesale grocery business, and did quite well with it. Of Grandmother Clifford, a German born in Alsace-Lorraine, my father told me she had been so strict with her children that she squeezed practically all the enjoyment out of their lives. It might be accurately described as a not very attractive family.

The McAdams side of my family was much more interesting, at least to me. My maternal grandfather, William Douglas McAdams, was a well-known geologist, archeologist, and scholar, whose collection of Indian artifacts reposes today in the Smithsonian Institution as the William Douglas McAdams Collection. Grandmother McAdams, born Annie Curtis, came from English stock that had settled and operated a farm for some generations in Jerseyville, Illinois.

There was a strong literary and artistic strain in the McAdams family. My mother's eldest brother, Clark McAdams, after whom I was named, was a journalist who rose to become a well-known crusading editor of the *St. Louis Post-Dispatch,* the flagship newspaper of the great publisher,

Joseph Pulitzer. My uncle believed deeply in the responsibility of both the individual and the government to try to improve the general condition of all Americans; much of my basic liberal orientation came from him. John, another brother, also went to work for a newspaper, the *Alton Evening Telegraph,* and ended up as its editor and owner. Bessie became a pianist, Maggie wrote poetry, and the youngest daughter, Anne, became an accomplished pianist and organist. My mother's youngest brother, William Douglas McAdams, went into the advertising business, moved to New York, and founded the William Douglas McAdams Agency, which still exists today.

The startling difference between the families of my parents intrigued me. While the Cliffords expected little from life, the McAdamses thought that anything was possible if one strived. I concluded, not surprisingly, that one's expectations were a powerful, guiding factor in how one's life developed. If one did not expect much, one did not get much; if one expected a lot, there was at least the chance of achieving a substantial part of it.

It would be difficult today for a young person to understand how different life was at that time. There was no radio, no television, few electric lights (at first), no commercial airplanes, only a few telephones, and almost no automobiles. If one needed to go from one place to another, one went by foot or horse or train. But the absence of today's marvels of modern technology did not mean we led dull lives. Almost every day, stimulating events took place. One of the most exciting was the appearance of the lamplighter, who came to our neighborhood each evening to turn on the street lights. Everyone in the neighborhood knew him, and we enjoyed walking along with him for part of his journey. In the summer, the excitement revolved around the visit of the iceman, who, with horse and wagon, brought ice to our kitchen. Our greatest thrill came on Saturday nights, when we were permitted to go to the movies (silent, of course)—admission was a nickel.

We also had sports, of course: neighborhood baseball, track, and football, and later tennis. I became a member of the Knothole Gang, an organization that allowed youths to go to the games of either of our two major league baseball teams, the Cardinals and the Browns, for twenty-five cents—a bargain even in those days. In addition to sports, we read much more than most children do today. I probably read every Horatio Alger book during my childhood. The theme was always the same: a poor boy with no assets would ultimately rise to the top because of his honesty, industry, and decency. The books offered various slogans and precepts that would be scoffed at and referred to as being "square" today, but were the wisdom of the day. They were immensely valuable in shaping enduring values: "Honesty is the best policy," "Haste makes waste," "Time waits for no man," "Look before you leap," "Penny wise and pound foolish," "God helps those who help themselves," and so on. I regret that young people today, bombarded by an overdose of conflicting information, advice, and contradictory role models, no longer share such a simple but valuable set of universal and socially beneficial precepts.

Good manners were drummed into me from an early age. A child stood immediately when an adult entered the room, and listened politely to adult conversation. A man always rose upon a lady's arrival. It was the man's task to help women get seated at the table. In those days men wore hats, and I was taught to tip my hat when passing a lady on the street, and to remove it in an elevator when a lady entered.

The general attitude on the part of men toward women remains remarkably clear in my mind: women were nicer than men. They were to be protected, they were to be cherished, and they were to be helped because they were the weaker sex. Men were familiar with the harsh and ugly side of life, but one of their basic responsibilities was to shield women from knowledge of this unfortunate aspect.

In my immediate family, I had one sister, Alice, who was four years older than I. Because she was a girl, we had different interests and did not compete. Her goal was to get me through the "brat" stage and help me to amount to something. I thought she was almost as beautiful as my mother, and I adored her.

In his quiet and unobtrusive manner, my father guided and taught me as I grew up. From the time I was four or five he began to impress me with the fact that to live was to work. As a child, I had certain chores to perform and as time went on they became more important and oftentimes more onerous. The responsibility I hated most was to take the ashes out of the coal furnace, and carry them to the ash pit in our back yard.

In later years, when he and I talked, my father explained that he felt most boys were raised in an atmosphere of indolence, while a lesser number were taught that industrious habits must be a way of life. He believed that early work habits would last a lifetime, but he warned me that this was also true for habits of indolence. His philosophy was that the really important accomplishments in life had to flow from one's own efforts. I have always been deeply grateful to him for instilling this in me, although through the years my wife has on occasion teasingly complained that she felt my father had overdone it.

He also stressed the importance of independence, and advised me to structure my life so I could achieve this goal. Unfortunately, a turning point in his own career provided me with the most lasting illustration of his lesson. He had been befriended and promoted at the railroad by the executive vice president, a man named Egan, who planned a series of moves for my father that would have led to high positions in the railroad.

The future looked exciting and challenging. Then, one day, Egan's secretary came into his office and found him slumped across his desk, dead from a heart attack. With Egan's death, the curtain abruptly rang down on my father's career.

The board of directors selected as Egan's successor an experienced man from another railroad, who brought with him men he had worked with for many years. The spirit went out of my father like the air out of a balloon: his hopes and dreams were crushed, and the spring in his step departed, never to return. From then until his retirement, he remained in the same position with no further progress.

It was an enduring lesson to me in the importance of planning one's life and career as free as possible from dependence upon the decisions of others, and contributed greatly to my choice of a career in law, where one is essentially dependent only on oneself.

Other times my father delivered his lessons more directly. One day, when I was about halfway through high school, my Latin teacher, Miss Wayney, whom I remember as a stern and forbidding elderly lady, called on me in class. I fumbled my answer badly, and finally she said, "Sit down. You obviously do not know what you are talking about." Turning to the rest of the class, she added, "This is a perfect illustration of someone who could accomplish something if he wanted to, but he just won't do it."

I was angry throughout the rest of the day. But that afternoon, a thought occurred to me: I didn't *have* to take that course—I didn't need the credit. I would just drop the course. What a lovely way, I thought, to show her that I thought she had been unfair to me.

At the dinner table that evening, I described the day's events, including my intention to drop Latin. My father listened carefully. After dinner, he suggested that we go into the living room to talk. I would never forget his words: "I listened with great interest, son, to the incident that occurred in your Latin class. I have a certain regard for your judgment, but you are so wrong on this matter that it really shakes my confidence in you. You are intelligent—but when you run into a difficult situation, what do you do? You stick your tail between your legs and quit. That is not the way we conduct ourselves in this family. You are not going to drop out of Latin. If you do not like Miss Wayney, that is your misfortune, not hers. You are going to pass that course. If by chance you do not pass it, then you will take it each term until you do pass it. There is a lot more at stake here than your dislike of Miss Wayney.

"Let me tell you what is involved here. You can take one of two paths. You can either meet your responsibilities, and when you do, each time it gets easier to meet the next one. Or you can say, I do not like the way she treats me, so I will drop the course. I cannot imagine a more serious mistake. You would begin to develop a pattern in your life that will guarantee failure."

I thought my father terribly wrong; it was I who had suffered this slanderous attack, not he. But I did what he said, returning to Latin class. Although I never did very well, I passed and got it behind me—and came to see the wisdom of his words. I was only about fifteen at the time, but the memory of our conversation was deep and permanent, and I was eternally grateful to him.

While my father was influential in shaping my character, my mother was unquestionably the star of the family, and at an early age she began to impart to my sister and me the values she held. One of her convictions was that the English language was one of the greatest blessings given to us as a people. She often told me that it was the finest instrument ever developed by human ingenuity, comparable to the delicate, sensitive music produced by a string quartet, or the massive and sonorous and thrilling sounds produced by a full symphony orchestra.

We were taught by my mother, even more than in school, the importance of grammar, not as an end in itself, but as a way of utilizing the best in the language. If at the table either my sister or I would slip and say, for example, "Charles spoke to she and I," a forbidding silence would take control of the room that would compare favorably with Greenland's icy mountains, until a correction was made. A sentence like "He came up and spoke to Helen and myself" brought expressions of great distress from her for the misuse of the word "myself." I believe that by the age of five I knew that it was a capital offense not to use an adverb after a verb of motion. My mother regretted ostentatious speech more than ignorant speech because, she said, the speaker should have known better.

Perhaps thanks to the influence of my parents, I finished high school at the age of fifteen. My father thought it would be wise if I worked before going to college, so he obtained a clerical job for me at the Missouri Pacific Railroad, at which I worked for almost a year. Then, he felt, I was ready for college. I entered Washington University in September 1923.

WASHINGTON UNIVERSITY

Washington University was perched on a gentle plateau at the western edge of St. Louis's beautiful Forest Park, with ivied gothic halls, quadrangles, and tree-lined walkways. In addition to the academic work, I found time for both tennis and, at my mother's urging, dramatics. The latter was invaluable to me in later life when I had to appear before juries and make public speeches.

At the time I entered college, inspired by a dynamic family friend named Franklin Walton who was the chief of surgery at St. Louis's City Hospital, I thought I would become a doctor. Over time, however, my father gently steered me in another direction. He had nothing against medicine, he told me, but he stressed what he felt were some special advantages possessed by those with legal training—logically ordered minds, ease at handling complex questions, forensic skills. "Besides," he would add when we talked about careers, "if you get into the law and find that it is not particularly appealing to you, you wouldn't have wasted your time, because if you then decide to go into business, the law will have been an invaluable asset."

Eventually, the arguments for the law won out over medicine, and in the fall of 1925, after two years as an undergraduate, as was done in those days, I transferred into Washington University's law school. After graduating in June 1928, I took and passed the bar examination, and became a member of the bar on July 1, 1928, at the age of twenty-one. I set out to find a job.

I already had a role model. During my senior year in law school, I had taken a course with Jacob M. Lashly, widely considered one of the Midwest's leading trial lawyers. Deeply impressed with him, I applied to work for his firm, Holland, Lashly, and Donnell, but found, to my dismay, they had no openings. I was to hear the same story from other firms in St. Louis as well. Some invited me to try again in the fall, but, anxious to start work immediately, I returned to Lashly and offered to work for free, filing papers in court and running errands, until I could resume my search for permanent employment in the fall. What I wanted most, I told him, was the experience that would come from an association with the firm. Lashly was surprised at my suggestion, but he had nothing to lose, and accepted. Lacking office space, he told me to work out of the library.

Over the summer I learned the rhythms of the firm, carrying papers to the courthouse, dusting and straightening up the library, getting to know the clerks and associates. In early September I went to thank Lashly for the splendid opportunity he had given me. He responded with some surprise. "What is the matter? Don't you like it here?"

My heart leaped. "I like it very much," I replied, "but our agreement was that I would leave in the fall to seek permanent employment."

"That doesn't make much sense," Lashly replied. "The men here have gotten to know you, and we would be delighted if you stayed." I thought these the sweetest words I had ever heard. "However, as you know, we have filled all the spots in the firm, so we cannot offer you a salary. What we can offer is to pay you for services on individual cases, on an hourly basis."

Although it offered no security, I accepted his offer on the spot. At first, this arrangement was hardly different from working without pay. My total income for the first six months was thirty dollars—including the fee I received from the friend of a secretary in the office for getting her a divorce. But living with my parents, who encouraged my arrangements with Lashly, made it possible. Later I added an important fifteen dollars per week to my income by teaching a course on contracts at a night law school downtown.

In this class, I stressed the importance of reaching a complete and full understanding, a "meeting of the minds," between two persons entering into a contract. Often, I said, people thought they had such understanding until they were ready to execute the agreement, at which time they found out that each had a different notion of what the contract meant. I illustrated my point with a story that has always remained one of my favorites; I think that I eventually told it to every President I ever knew, as well as to most of my friends. It goes as follows: A man walking down the street noticed a sign in the window of a restaurant that said, SPECIAL TODAY—RABBIT STEW. He said to himself, "That's a favorite of mine," and went in to order the stew. After he had taken three or four bites, which did not taste quite right, he asked the waiter to call over the proprietor. "By any chance is there any horsemeat in this rabbit stew?" the customer asked. "Well, now that you ask, there is some," responded the owner. "What is the proportion?" asked the man. "Fifty-fifty," came the reply. Now, most people would have felt that no further questions were needed, that there was a clear understanding. But this man pursued the issue. "What do you mean by fifty-fifty?" he asked, and the proprietor replied, "One horse to one rabbit."

* * *

My career at the firm progressed gradually. By September 1929, I was earning the princely sum of thirty dollars per week—not much perhaps, but a steady income. With the Wall Street crash the following month, followed by the beginning of the long slide into the Great Depression, a regular income, no matter how small, would prove to be something for which I would be most grateful. As the economic situation steadily deteriorated in 1930, I concentrated on a very personal goal—to gain some courtroom experience. In those days, before the advent of public defenders, young attorneys often volunteered to represent persons who could not afford a lawyer. So, with the firm's encouragement, I went to the judges of the criminal court and asked for some trial experience. About two weeks later, the court's clerk called—I had my first client.

JOHN PIPER

He was a young man, about my age, named John Piper, charged with stealing a car. The case presented several difficulties, not the least being the fact that the arresting officer had discovered a set of burglar tools on the back seat of the car.

No matter. With eagerness for battle and unwarranted optimism about my client's case, I plunged into battle for John Piper. I spent hours talking to him in the city jail. I interviewed every witness I could find. I studied many previous car-theft cases. I read Wellman's *Art of Cross-Examination.* Finally, the case came to trial in early March 1930. I sought to poke holes in the prosecuting attorney's case. I impatiently awaited the closing argument, looking forward to delivering an historic address, but the jury needed less than a half hour of deliberation before returning a verdict: guilty. Because Piper had two prior felony convictions, the judge gave him a heavy sentence: twenty-five years in the state penitentiary.

The decision of the jury left me reeling in disbelief and embarrassment, and with a feeling of total disaster. The judge, John W. Calhoun, saw that I was upset, and motioned me to approach the bench. "I am going to assign you another case as soon as I can find one," he said. "Losing your first case this way is like getting thrown off a horse. You have to get right back on again."

For years afterward, I had reason to remember my first client. Each December, a Christmas card would arrive from the state prison signed "John Piper."

Three days later, Judge Calhoun's clerk called to assign me another case. I went through the same process, and did better: my client got only fifteen years. As I was picking myself up from this second dismal experience, calls came from the clerks of the other two judges, assigning me two more cases. I lost them both.

I felt a certain stubbornness growing within me, and a determination to stay with this until I finally won one. But I continued to lose cases steadily over the next year, sending ten clients in a row to the state penitentiary. Other lawyers around the courtroom joked that authorities had opened a "Clifford Wing" at the Missouri State Penitentiary in Jefferson City. I laughed, but it hurt. I continued to struggle on behalf of my court-appointed clients. Finally, after well over a dozen cases, a jury returned a verdict of not guilty in a case. I was elated.

A week after this stirring success, the presiding judge, Moses Hartman, heard a motion filed in civil court by the senior member of our firm, Robert Holland. A classic nineteenth-century lawyer, Holland was a crusty but dignified man who wore stiff, high-necked collars of the sort popularized by President Hoover. He was referred to only as "Mr. Holland" around the offices, and was respected by his partners and feared by the younger associates. After the court had adjourned, Judge Hartman mentioned that the previous week a young member of Holland's firm had argued and won a splendid verdict in criminal court. "What's his name," Holland asked. "Clifford," the judge replied. "Clifford?" Holland said, "Clifford? No, we don't have anybody by that name. What does he look like?" When Hartman described me—a tall slender fellow with wavy blond hair, as I was told later—Holland nodded, and said, "Oh, you mean that young man who sits in the library!" I obviously had not made much of an impression on him.

Although this was a laborious and discouraging way to spend my time, I was learning a great deal—especially the unique importance of preparation. Cases are rarely won by oratory, rather, they are won by careful, meticulous mastery of the facts and of the law. I learned a great deal about the rules of evidence. I began to understand the reactions of a jury. After each case I would consult with one or two members of the jury in order to learn what had impressed them and what had not.

Over sixteen years in St. Louis, I handled many cases, though only a few were memorable—like the important client whose will I reluctantly but dutifully drew up on a beautiful weekend when I would rather have been playing tennis, only to learn on Monday morning that he had suffered a severe stroke just hours after I had gotten his signature on the document; or the occasion when I accompanied the police and our client, the head of a furniture company, to a house of ill repute to repossess a piano, only to watch the proprietress triumphantly hand over the money just in time to save what I assumed was an indispensable piece of equipment in any such establishment.

My work load was immense: in one year alone in the midthirties, I tried nearly thirty cases. At the time it just seemed like a lot of work; but I realized later, especially after I started working in Washington, that it was the most valuable period of training and preparation of my life. Today lawyers specialize early in their careers, perhaps an unavoidable necessity in the more complex modern world. But most of them sacrifice the invaluable experience of courtroom combat. A trial lawyer must confront an enormous amount of facts, sift through them, and identify the most salient. Then he must organize them logically and present them articulately and persuasively in order to convince the jury. Such courtroom experience was priceless to me when I arrived in Washington in 1945. Substitute the President or Cabinet members for the jury; in both cases, the key art to be mastered was the art of persuasion.

MARNY

In the summer of 1929 a friend of mine at the law firm, Louis McKeown, and I made a trip to Europe. I was practically engaged to a girl in St. Louis named Dorothy Ladd, and I thought of the trip, in part, as a last youthful fling before embarking on the domesticity of settled adult life. Naturally, we referred to our trip as "the Louis and Clark expedition." At one point, after a few days in Heidelberg, we found ourselves in the great cathedral city of Cologne, where in the evenings we went to an open-air beer garden to mix with other young people. After a few days, we decided to take the 8 A.M. steamer down the Rhine. But the night before, my friend Lou had done more than simply mix with the young people, and I couldn't get him up in time for the 8 o'clock boat. We took the 9 o'clock boat instead.

Onboard was a group of six young American girls on a college tour. I noticed immediately a tall, slender blonde, and Lou picked a gorgeous redhead. After Lou and I had eyed them for a while from a distance, we approached them, and rather boldly asked if we might join them for the day so that we might speak English instead of our fractured French and German. Our offer was courteously accepted.

The blonde whom I had noticed turned out to be Margery Pepperell Kimball, from Boston, and Lou's redhead was Angela Higgins, from Pittsburgh. Gradually we managed to separate the two girls from their friends and talk to them privately, obtaining from them the rest of their itinerary. We then adjusted our itinerary in order to meet them again in Rome, Florence, and Venice. Our trip continued on to Paris, where we concluded a marvelous all-night party with the famous onion soup in Les Halles in the morning's early light.

Early in our peripatetic voyage across Europe, Marny—for that was what her friends always called her—and I each confided to the other that we had a "situation" at home. Marny told me that upon her return there would be a formal announcement of her engagement to a former Harvard hockey player to whom I took an instant, and no doubt unfair, dislike. And, of course, I had Dorothy Ladd back in St. Louis. So, when we bade farewell as she and her companions boarded the train for Le Havre and home, I wrote the summer off as a wonderful memory.

Because she was about to be married, I made no effort to contact her again. But I found that the events of the summer had had a profound impact upon me, and within a few months, my relationship with Dorothy Ladd had faded.

A year later, I ran into a friend of mine, Ben Lang, on the street. He had just returned from Boston, where, he said, he had met a friend of mine named Marny Kimball.

"What is her married name?" I asked.

"Her name is Marny Kimball, and she is not married."

Much excited, I said, "Ben, you are a great fellow and I am delighted that we ran into each other." Then, almost running to my office, I got Marny's telephone number and called her. She was not home, but the next morning I finally reached her. She told me that when she returned from the trip the situation with the hockey player had lost its attraction. When I told her that the same had happened to me, I thought she sounded quite pleased. I said that if it was agreeable, I would like to pay her a visit between Christmas and New Year's.

I visited with her and her family for three days, and we immediately picked up the wonderful relationship of the previous summer. Proceedings were more formal in those days, and after I had made several more visits to Boston, we approached Marny's parents with a statement, rather stiffly delivered, that we wished to become engaged. This discussion led to arrangements for my parents to meet with Marny's parents, an event that took place in New York a month or so later. Fortunately, they got on very well; we announced our engagement in the late spring of 1931, and were married in Boston on October 3, 1931.

STUART SYMINGTON

Life in St. Louis was active and busy for me in the years after our marriage. The cases assigned to me steadily became more important. Marny made friends easily, and she was soon active in organizing the Grand Opera Guild, later becoming its president. We had three daughters, Margery, Joyce, and Randall, and bought a house on Westminster Place.

For the first time, I became involved in some public activities. During the thirties, I was appointed to the State Social Security Commission, and I became a member, and later chairman, of the Trial Practice Committee of the St. Louis Bar Association.

Sometime around 1936, after a late-afternoon game of squash at the St. Louis Racquet Club, I entered the bar with my opponent for a drink, and was introduced to a new member of the club. I have long forgotten the name of my opponent, but I will always remember the tall, slender, very handsome man to whom I was introduced. His name was Stuart Symington. He had come from New York to become the President of Emerson Electric Company, at that time the largest employer in Missouri. He was in his mid-thirties, five years older than I.

Our chance meeting at the racquet club was the beginning of a fifty-year friendship, which eventually would also include close professional collaboration during the unification of the armed services, the creation of the Defense Department and the CIA, the fight against Joseph McCarthy, an unsuccessful Presidential campaign, and the Vietnam War. Until his death in 1989, he was my closest friend.

Everything seemed clearly set for an enjoyable life in St. Louis. My father had always wanted me to set goals for myself, and I had one in mind: to be the most successful trial lawyer in the St. Louis area. After ten years with the law firm, I was invited to become a partner, and the name of the firm was changed to Lashly, Lashly, Miller, and Clifford. I felt that I was on my way. But, like our nation itself, my plans did not include Adolf Hitler and the Third Reich, or the rise of Japanese militarism.

PEARL HARBOR

If it had not been for the war, I would probably have remained a St. Louis lawyer for the rest of my life, with limited interest in international affairs. But on December 7, 1941, my life, like that of almost every American of my generation, changed forever.

Marny and I were at the home of close friends, Joseph and Jamie Folk, for a Sunday luncheon party, when the telephone rang. Folk answered it, listened for a moment, and turned, very agitated, to his guests. "*The Japanese have attacked us!*" he exclaimed. We rushed to the radio to listen to news bulletins on the unfolding disaster at Pearl Harbor.

The next day, along with the rest of the nation, I listened to President Roosevelt ask Congress for a formal declaration of war against Japan. Catastrophic as the news was, I thought the war would probably end within a year, and I could not yet imagine that it would affect me so personally—at thirty-four, married, with three children, I was not subject to the draft.

Until then, the outside world had been of only passing interest to me. Life in the center of the great American continent seemed remote from, and unaffected by, the dramatic events unfolding in such faraway places as China and Czechoslovakia. New York was as far as one's thoughts and imagination normally reached.

Gradually, though, the international drama began to interest me. Long before Pearl Harbor, Stuart Symington, who had been in London during part of the Battle of Britain, had described to me with great passion how important it was to us for the British to win. Symington's father-in-law, James Wadsworth, was a distinguished Republican Congressman from New York, and Stuart often described, with understandable pride, how Wadsworth's impassioned plea had helped save the draft in 1941 by the margin of one vote.

THE MISSOURI STATE GUARD

Shortly after Pearl Harbor, Congress federalized all Reserves and National Guardsmen in order to relieve the Army's severe manpower shortage. This meant that many duties previously performed by the Reserves and the National Guard were left unattended; so many states, including Missouri, created a State Guard, staffed largely by older men, to fill the gap. In June 1942, I volunteered, as an infantry reservist.

Three months later, I received a telephone call from a prominent St. Louis businessman, C. W. Gaylord, who had been appointed Commanding General of the State Guard, asking me to serve as its Judge Advocate General.

For the next fifteen months, I handled various legal chores for the State Guard: conducting courts-martial, submitting requests for state appropriations, reviewing legal opinions at the regimental level, and so on. My most interesting assignment—and one that served me well four years later during my work at the Truman White House on military unification—involved drafting a bill for submission to the Missouri General Assembly, which reorganized and expanded the powers of the State Guard. The work was tedious and frustrating, but it gave me an appreciation for the give-and-take of the political process.

THE NAVY

By 1943, it was clear that the war was not going to be as short as I had originally expected. I began to feel increasingly uncomfortable sitting out the fighting in the State Guard while friends were in the military. I discussed my concerns with several of my friends, including Richmond Coburn, who had come to the St. Louis bar two years ahead of me. He had joined the Navy, and he wrote me letters encouraging me to join him. Most of my other friends took the opposite position. Symington tried to persuade me that I was more valuable to the war effort as a civilian than I would be in uniform. (There was no question of Symington himself joining the armed forces; not only was he five years older than I, but as president of Emerson Electric he was overseeing the production of equipment vital for our airplanes.)

In 1942, my father died. While he was alive and in poor health, as he had been for several years, I would not have considered leaving St. Louis; but after his death, my mother, who was completely self-sufficient, with her own career, said she would back me in whatever I decided to do. My father-in-law in Boston said that if I entered the military, he would be delighted to have Marny and our daughters stay with him.

Symington still thought it was a mistake. But as the war entered its third year of American involvement, I felt I had to leave my comfortable perch at the law firm. In the fall of 1943, I told Symington I was going to sign up. I chose the Navy because it was smaller than the Army, and I thought it would prove more interesting. A month later, in order to speed up the paperwork, I went to the Missouri Pacific Building, where the Navy had established its personnel offices. I had been in the building on many visits to my father's office, but this time I had the distinct feeling that I was entering a different building, and a different life.

After various bureaucratic delays, I executed the oath of office as Lieutenant, Junior Grade, in the United States Naval Reserve, on April 28, 1944, at the age of thirty-seven. Armed with my new commission, I went downtown to purchase a uniform as well as a "how-to" book on Navy customs and regulations. I knew absolutely nothing about military procedures, not even such basics as how to give and receive a salute.

A few days later, I received orders to report to the Office of the Chief of Naval Operations in Washington, D.C. I arrived by train in a city, like the nation it governed, transformed by the war. Washington in 1944 buzzed with energy, excitement, and purpose. Men and women in uniform rushed through the once-sleepy streets. I found the commotion a bit overwhelming at first. I had visited Washington a few times on legal business, but I had never gotten to know the city, its people, or its culture.

I found a bunk at the Navy League Club on 21st Street in northwest Washington, which gave reserve officers a place to sleep and eat at modest prices—a welcome benefit, given the housing squeeze then gripping the capital.

At the club I met an enchanting and witty New Hampshire lawyer named Dudley Orr, who became a lifelong friend, and who, after the war, founded what became one of his state's great law firms, Orr and Reno.* After a month or so at the Navy League Club, the two of us decided to strike out on our own, and found a small apartment a few blocks away.

I was assigned routine staff work at the Navy Department. The massive Pentagon building across the Potomac River had been completed just the year before, but Navy personnel still worked in the "temporary" buildings on the Mall. These infamous "temporaries" had been built during World War I; amazingly, some of them were to remain in use into the early sixties. They were low-slung and ugly, hot as a sauna in summer and cold as a freezer in winter.

I remained there through May and June of 1944, handling very ordinary administrative duties at a most extraordinary moment: D-Day, the invasion of Western Europe. When the long-awaited assault finally began

*One of the junior lawyers who worked for Orr's firm was David Souter, President Bush's first appointment to the Supreme Court.

on June 6, we in the Navy Department anxiously followed the reports of the landings. As the Allied armies broke out from their beachheads and began their dash toward Paris and the Rhine, the end of the war in Europe seemed in sight. Our attention shifted to the war in the Pacific, a shift that would soon take me west.

Shortly after D-Day, I was selected as one of two officers to make a survey of Navy logistical activities on the West Coast, in preparation for the push against Japan. My partner on this mission was a reserve Lieutenant Commander from Pittsburgh named Nathan Pearson, who had worked in market research for U.S. Steel before the war.

On July 29, we left Washington by military aircraft for San Francisco. After further briefings, we flew to San Diego on August 15, then slowly worked our way back up the southern California coast, visiting Terminal Island, Port Hueneme, and Los Angeles. After a visit to Seattle and a stop in San Francisco for a final review, we returned to Washington, D.C. on September 9 to make our report.

Our inspection tours followed a familiar pattern. At each stop, Pearson and I would hand the base commander a letter from the top Navy brass in Washington requesting his full cooperation. Invariably, we received an effusive welcome—and almost no information of substance. After several hours of this empty ritual, we searched out lower-ranking reserve officers stationed at the installation; from them we would invariably get a different story, including the needed information about each base's strengths and weaknesses.

I learned an important lesson from this assignment that would serve me well in the distant future: in order to find out what is really going on in the military, it is necessary to look beyond the official chain of command. Top commanders, whether in World War II or Vietnam, were predictably defensive about any sign of weakness. One had to look behind the official briefings in order to assemble an accurate picture. In dealing with the military, my legal experience was useful, but a different and less confrontational procedure was necessary. I believe that my real preparation for service as Secretary of Defense twenty-four years later began on that inspection tour in 1944.

Once we were back in Washington, Pearson and I assembled our conclusions and submitted a lengthy report. We also observed, but could not solve, a more serious problem: the costs of interservice rivalry. Almost every Navy installation we visited lay near an Army base or airfield, and the two (or three, in some cases) invariably competed for the same equipment, bidding up prices to exorbitant levels. This picture of wasteful rivalries would also prove to be an invaluable lesson for me a few years later when I worked on military unification.

ADMIRAL INGERSOLL AND THE WESTERN SEA FRONTIER

In our report, Pearson and I emphasized the need to unify Navy logistical operations on the West Coast. Acting on these recommendations, the Navy reorganized and strengthened the Western Sea Frontier—the command responsible for coordinating supply activities on the West Coast. To direct this new effort Washington chose the Commander in Chief of the Atlantic Fleet, Admiral Royal E. Ingersoll. An Annapolis classmate of Pacific Fleet Commander Chester Nimitz, Ingersoll was greatly respected in the Navy for his defense of the East Coast against German submarine attacks in 1942 and 1943. More important, he had the experience and the four-star rank essential to exercise effective control over the flow of matériel from the West Coast's ports into the Pacific theater.

Admiral Ingersoll was so impressed with our report that he asked we be assigned to his staff in San Francisco. Soon, Pearson and I were headed back to San Francisco, this time as Ingersoll's special assistants. Upon arrival at the Western Sea Frontier headquarters, we began organizing Navy supply lines from the West Coast to the forward areas in the Pacific. It was a massive and exhausting effort: the eastern Pacific had become a huge highway for the passage of troops, ammunition, aircraft, and other war matériel to forward bases in the Marianas and the Philippines, requiring a staggering shipping capacity of more than 500,000 tons a month.

Admiral Ingersoll looked to Pearson and me as personal troubleshooters who could operate from slightly outside the official system while remaining part of it. One day in early 1945, he called me in to his office overlooking the beautiful San Francisco Bay and said, "There are some things that I am going to ask you to do for me that I could not ask a regular officer to do because you have no ambitions for a naval career and can afford to take chances in order to get things done." It turned out that what he had in mind was assuring that the Navy got what it needed for its Pacific operations. This sometimes involved "liberating" materials under Army control. Accomplishing this involved some fast paper shuffling, and the quick deployment of Navy trucks to "capture" equipment that might otherwise have reached the Army.

I was thus busily engaged preparing for the invasion of Japan, when another event occurred that would change my life completely. Franklin Roosevelt died.

Part II

THE TRUMAN WHITE HOUSE

3

To the White House

TRUMAN TAKES OVER

The news from Washington reached the headquarters of the Western Sea Frontier in the middle of a cool, clear, and breezy San Francisco afternoon, April 12, 1945: President Roosevelt was dead. Like everyone else, I was stunned, and wholly unprepared for his death, but I could not have imagined that the President's death would lead me to the White House in less than three months, and launch a career that would last for the rest of my life.

Even at the moment of initial shock, however, I felt a small, personal flutter when I realized that I had once met the man who was now President of the United States. It was in 1939 at a cocktail party at the home of a friend and client, James K. Vardaman, Jr., one of the few St. Louis businessmen who had supported Harry Truman's successful bid for the Senate in 1934. My meeting with Senator Truman had been brief and inconsequential. But my acquaintanceship with Vardaman turned out to be the key to my career in Washington.

J. K. VARDAMAN

Marny and I had become friends of the Vardamans in the thirties through our shared love of music. Marny and Vardaman had been founding members of the Grand Opera Guild of St. Louis. Almost every Saturday afternoon before the war, the Vardamans would give a luncheon party at their farm for members of the Opera Guild, and we would gather around their radio, a large and bulky Capehart, to listen to the famous live broadcasts from the Metropolitan Opera in New York, which Texaco sponsored. Elegant and good-looking, but unfortunately possessed of a strong temper, Vardaman could alternately charm and infuriate people. He was originally from Mississippi, and his father, James Kimble Vardaman, had served the state as both Governor and Senator. J.K.—as we always called him—lived, I felt, in the shadow of his father. He spoke often of his father's Senate career, which had lasted only one term (1913–1919). He said his father had a tendency to make enduring enemies out of people with whom he had some minor disagreement. Sadly, J.K. suffered from the same problem.

In 1942 Vardaman became a Naval Reserve officer, and the following year he was slightly wounded during the invasion of Sicily. While he was overseas, he asked me to act as his personal lawyer, and to keep in touch with his wife Bea.

Shortly after Roosevelt's death, I got an unexpected telephone call from Vardaman: he was in San Francisco and wanted to see me right away. We met a few hours later at a downtown hotel. Almost vibrating with excitement, he told me that he was going to be Naval Aide to the new President. We both knew it would be unprecedented for the Naval Aide to come from the Naval Reserve rather than the regular Navy. This may have seemed like a distinction without a difference to the rest of the world, but it meant everything in the tradition-laden Navy, which believed that the prestigious post should always be reserved for a career officer. Vardaman, angry at the way the regulars scorned the Reserves, saw his new post as a way of settling some scores.

During our discussion, Vardaman raised an intriguing possibility: that I might eventually join him in Washington, either at the White House or in the Office of the Chief of Naval Operations. I asked Vardaman to let me think about it while he learned what possibilities might exist in Washington. We said good-bye warmly, and he left with me one of his heavy duffel bags to ship to Washington as he raced to catch a plane east.

With people I knew from St. Louis moving into positions in the new Administration, I could see the attraction of serving in Washington. I responded to Vardaman's suggestion positively at the end of a letter to him on May 10, 1945, which was otherwise concerned with his duffel bag, lost somewhere between San Francisco and Washington. Upon reflection, I said, I "would like nothing better" than to be of assistance in Washington. Vardaman replied almost immediately:

> This is the first time that I have had a minute to write any letters since getting here. . . . The rapidity with which I was thrown into the hopper here has just about swamped me. . . . I hope to develop over the next several months something of interest and value to you. I am taking this slowly and deliberately because I want to be sure of my ground, and I want to be sure that whatever is offered is attractive and worthwhile. . . . This is, of course, between you and me. I have no idea when something will develop, but hope it will not be long as I will be much more comfortable with you around here.

My interest in Washington whetted, I replied that I would await further guidance. Vardaman responded on June 1:

> For your confidential information, I have been discussing your possible return to Washington for duty in the Office of the Secretary of the Navy. Right now it has been held up because of the importance attached to your duties with Admiral Ingersoll. However, I shall continue my efforts to get you back here. . . .

June 8, 1945, Clifford to Vardaman:

> I note your emphasis on the word "confidential" in your letters. I have mentioned to no one (not even Marny) that there was anything discussed by you and me regarding the possibility of my returning to Washington. I shall continue to maintain complete silence. . . .

June 22, 1945, telegram to Lieutenant Clark M. Clifford, U.S.N.R., Staff Headquarters, Western Sea Frontier, San Francisco 2, California:

> EXPECT ARRIVE FAIRMONT HOTEL SATURDAY JUNE 23 EIGHT P.M. WOULD LIKE TO SEE YOU THEN OR SUNDAY MORNING. JAMES K. VARDAMAN, JR.

Vardaman had come to San Francisco along with the Presidential advance team for a momentous event: the signing of the charter of the United Nations. America seemed to stand at the absolute height of its power and self-confidence, and its hopes for its new President, the new world organization, and a peaceful postwar world all seemed to converge on that lovely city in June of 1945. Only the war in the Pacific cast a shadow on the mood. Some of the men dealing with Stalin—future colleagues like Averell Harriman, Robert Lovett, James Forrestal, George Kennan, and Dean Acheson—may already have seen the clouds of Cold War, but they were not visible to a slightly overage Naval Lieutenant thinking about his meeting with the President's new Naval Aide.

When we met, Vardaman told me in confidence that the President would shortly be going to a place called Potsdam for a meeting with Churchill and Stalin to settle the future of postwar Europe and plan the final phase of the Pacific war. But Vardaman's immediate concern was not Russia or Japan; instead, he gave me my first glimpse of Washington power struggles. His problem was with the Navy, and its strong-willed Secretary, James V. Forrestal. As we had both anticipated, the Navy was upset that a Naval Reserve officer held the job of Naval Aide to the President. Forrestal had offered to send someone over to "take care" of Vardaman's office while he was at Potsdam. Vardaman interpreted this offer as a Navy effort to protect its parochial interests and spy on him, and he had a solution to this problem which would also bring me to Washington, if only temporarily: assign me to the White House as his assistant while he and the President were at Potsdam. My main function would be to keep any regular Navy officers—Navy "spies"—from entering his offices while he was away. Vardaman even thought that he could get me a temporary promotion on the grounds that the position required someone of a higher rank. Needless to say, the idea was irresistible—I might get a chance to observe, and even participate in, some history, and I would be nearer my family, who were still in Boston.

After our conversation, Vardaman gave me a ticket for the climactic event, the signing of the U.N. Charter at the War Memorial Opera House on June 26.

I had high hopes for the U.N. Some of my earliest political memories were of Woodrow Wilson's desperate and unsuccessful fight to get the Senate to ratify American membership in the League of Nations, and I believed this had been a root cause of World War II. Losing the peace after winning the war had to be avoided this time around, and I believed completely in the new organization.

From a red plush seat in the balcony of the Opera House, I looked down at a wondrous sight: the brilliant colors of the flags of the fifty nations present, each draped from a gilded flagpole, arrayed behind a large circular table covered with green baize, on which lay two large books, bound in gleaming hand-tooled blue leather, waiting to be signed. Below me, I could see the delegates of many countries, bathed in floodlights.

At exactly noon the Chinese delegate, Wellington Koo, chosen because his country had been the first victim of Axis aggression, strode onto the stage, seated himself in the blue chair behind the table, and signed the charter. Then, one by one, the representatives of the other nations signed. Andrei Gromyko, then the Ambassador to the United States, signed for the Soviet Union.

When the time came for the U.S. to sign, I felt a sense of euphoria and pride as I watched our President walk onstage, accompanied by the

Secretary of State, Edward R. Stettinius, and next to him, the President's military aide* and Vardaman. Escorting the delegation onstage was a man I did not recognize, but who was later to play an important role in the history of the era—the Secretary-General of the conference, Alger Hiss. In honor of the official color of the U.N. the President had dressed himself in a navy blue suit, a blue necktie, and a blue handkerchief. I watched with growing enthusiasm, thrilled to think that I might soon be working for one of his aides.

* * *

When he returned to Washington, Vardaman moved fast. For the first time, I saw the immense reach of the White House. At the beginning of July, the Western Sea Command received a high-priority order, with no explanation, that I report immediately to the Office of the Chief of Naval Operations in Washington. Worried, Admiral Ingersoll called me in to express concern that perhaps I was going to be questioned about our "liberation" of equipment earmarked for the Army.

Suspecting Vardaman's hand, I called him in Washington: "J.K., I may be in a lot of trouble out here. Do you know what's going on?" He laughed and explained that he was behind the mysterious orders. The Admiral was visibly relieved when I passed this information on. The next day I flew to Washington to meet with Vardaman.

"BIG FELLA, AIN'T HE?"

I had never set foot in the White House before. I was awed by the hallowed premises, and I was deeply conscious that it was from this building that Lincoln and Wilson and Roosevelt had led the nation through crises that had threatened its very survival. It was still in transition from its previous occupant, but no physical traces of Franklin Roosevelt remained—only his aura and a few remaining senior aides. Today, all the offices of key White House aides are located either in the West Wing or the Old Executive Office Building next door, and the East Wing is reserved for the First Lady's staff; in the forties, though, the East Wing, which had been built during the war, still housed some of the President's staff. Among these were Roosevelt's closest aide, Harry Hopkins—who, despite his declining health, had stayed on at President Truman's request—and Fleet Admiral William D. Leahy, who had served throughout most of the war in a job that evolved into that of the Chairman of the Joint Chiefs of Staff. Vardaman's office was also in the East Wing.

He greeted me warmly, and turned, a bit conspiratorially, to the reason

*This was Colonel Harry Vaughan, later my Army counterpart at the White House.

for my sudden trip: he had indeed succeeded in getting me assigned to watch over his office while he was at Potsdam. He still wanted me assigned permanently as his assistant, he said, but had as yet been unable to overcome Navy opposition to my leaving Western Sea Frontier on more than a temporary basis. A regular Navy officer, Commander John A. Tyree, was already assigned to Vardaman as the Assistant Naval Aide. I later learned that Tyree was a highly capable officer, but Vardaman was not about to leave a regular Navy officer in the White House while he was away. Vardaman took Tyree with him to Potsdam to keep an eye on him, and had him reassigned shortly thereafter.*

Before leaving for Potsdam, Vardaman took care of two important details. First, he wanted me to meet the President: so, for the first time in my life, I walked through the ground floor of the mansion, along the colonnade to the West Wing, and into the Oval Office. As we walked in, President Truman was seated behind his desk, signing a few papers. He did not look up until we had reached his desk. Finally, he glanced up, and Vardaman said, "Mr. President, this is Lieutenant Clark Clifford, the young naval officer I told you about. He is going to look after my office while we are gone."

The President did not rise. Looking up at me from his desk through his thick glasses without any change of expression, he said, "Big fella, ain't he?" Then he put out his hand and I shook it. It was clear he had nothing more to say, so after thanking him, we left immediately. I did not mention that we had met before; he clearly did not recognize or remember me.

After that brief introduction to the President, Vardaman took me to the most secret area of the wartime White House, the Map Room, located on the ground floor of the mansion. Throughout the war, a group of young officers had been responsible for maintaining in it up-to-date reports on military activity around the world. Access was strictly limited to the President, Leahy, Hopkins, and the military aides, and the door was locked and guarded at all times. In this room Roosevelt and Churchill had discussed the invasion of Europe, and Marshall, King, and Leahy had met with their Commander in Chief. The most closely guarded secrets of the war were in this room: reports on the Manhattan Project, the twice-daily summaries from the Navy of the positions of the Japanese Fleet (based on the broken Japanese naval codes), the President's personal copies of war plans, and records of the summit conferences and personal messages with Churchill, Stalin, and Chiang Kai-shek. Nothing like the Map Room had existed in the White House before Pearl Harbor, but the need for such a room continued after the war, and led directly to the establishment

*I finally encountered Tyree in Bonn over twenty years later, when, as a three-star Admiral assigned to NATO, he met me during one of my trips as Secretary of Defense. We shared a laugh at the strange route our paths had taken before they eventually intersected.

of today's Situation Room, the windowless and far less colorful area in the White House basement which serves the same functions.

Maintaining the Map Room was a responsibility of the Naval Aide. Tyree had been the man directly supervising the Map Room, and Vardaman told me I should take over this duty while he was away. He introduced me to a number of officers who were moving briskly around, changing the position of units on maps. With the European war over, the movement was in the Pacific, but the maps of Europe were still up, showing the zones of occupation in Germany and Soviet troop positions. One of the maps I glimpsed that day particularly impressed me—the plan for the invasion of Japan. Some officers were busy rolling up maps and putting documents into folders, preparing to transport part of the Map Room to Potsdam for the conference. I was impressed by the sight of these efficient young men, and noted that I was older than any of them.

One of the men I met in the Map Room that day was a twenty-seven-year-old Naval Reserve Lieutenant named George M. Elsey, who was to become my closest associate and collaborator over the next twenty-five years. Elsey told me later of the intense curiosity with which he and his colleagues greeted me. They were already extremely uncomfortable with what they viewed as Vardaman's abrupt and crude style, and were wary of the man he had brought in to replace the popular and respected Tyree.

FIRST DAYS AT THE WHITE HOUSE

I returned briefly to San Francisco to report to Admiral Ingersoll and receive official orders for my assignment. To the astonishment of the command at Western Sea Frontier, a "spot," or temporary, promotion to Lieutenant Commander suddenly arrived on July 3, while I was en route back from Washington. On July 9, I received the orders that were to change my life, written in the deadly prose of the Navy bureaucracy:

> On or about 10 July 1945, you will proceed to the Office of Naval Aide to the President, Washington, D.C., for temporary duty in connection with naval matters. This is in addition to your present assignment duties and upon completion thereof, you will return to this station and resume your regular duties. . . . A per diem of $7.00 in lieu of subsistence will be allowed while absent from this station.

While I was excited by the opportunity that Vardaman had offered me, I looked at Washington simply as another assignment. As soon as the war was over, I planned to return to St. Louis and rejoin Lashly, Lashly, Miller, and Clifford. My ambition remained at that time exactly what it had been since 1929: to be the best trial lawyer in St. Louis, to live there for the rest of my life and bring up my family there. Washington—even the White House—was simply another, albeit better, assignment in my World War II service. I had been explicit on this point in my June 8 letter to Vardaman, when I said I looked forward to the moment "when the time comes to return to my practice" in St. Louis.

I could never have imagined that the discussion with Vardaman at the Fairmont Hotel in June of 1945 would lead to a one-way trip to Washington that would last over forty-five years. I had been educated in St. Louis, lived for only the briefest time in the East, and did not feel myself in any way to be part of the so-called Eastern Establishment, which dominated the corridor of financial, legal, and political power between New York and Washington. But I welcomed a chance to see how it worked.

On the evening of July 9, I left San Francisco on a commercial night-flight (with a refueling stop), arriving in Washington the following afternoon. There had been no farewells at the Western Sea Frontier; after all, I was scheduled to return within a month or so.

I reported to the White House on July 11, four days after the Presidential party had left for the long sea trip to Europe. The White House was quiet, compared to the bustle I had seen only a few days earlier. When I arrived, however, a pleasant surprise awaited me: a temporary office on the second floor on the northwest corner of the East Wing, facing Pennsylvania Avenue. It was not a large office, but that was of no importance—I had an office in the White House!

By good fortune, Dudley Orr, my friend from my brief tour in 1944 in the Office of the Chief of Naval Operations, was still working in the Office of the Navy's General Counsel. I called him as soon as I was alone in my new office. He was not in, and with a feeling of sudden pleasure, I left word with his secretary that he should call me at the White House when he returned. Dudley returned to his office a few hours later and looked over his messages. As he told me later, he then turned to his secretary and said, "Is this a message from Lieutenant Clifford in San Francisco?" "No," she replied, "this call is from a Lieutenant *Commander* Clifford at the White House." Dudley called the White House and, to his astonishment, found me there.

He again invited me to share his apartment on 21st Street. Marny and I had already agreed that, since the White House assignment was temporary, she should stay in Boston with the children for the time being, and visit Washington often. After my temporary assignment was extended, Dudley and I decided that 21st Street had become far too cramped for us, and we drafted a somewhat misleading advertisement for the newspapers: WANTED: APARTMENT. TWO ELDERLY NAVAL OFFICERS REQUIRE APARTMENT IN QUIET NEIGHBORHOOD NEAR CHURCHES. Through this shameless device, we found a splendid apartment on Connecticut Avenue, near the bridge over Rock Creek Park. It had two bedrooms, and was available on a short-term lease which, by pooling our resources, we could afford. We were to share that apartment until the spring of 1946, when Marny and the children moved to Washington.

As I settled into the White House, I made an immediate discovery: there was very little for an assistant to the Naval Aide to the President to do when the President and his Naval Aide were both away. The only specific assignment Vardaman had given me was to oversee the redesign of the Presidential seal and flag, a project which George Elsey, who had gone to Potsdam, had already begun. Guarding Vardaman's office, taking care of his mail, and keeping an eye on the Map Room took, at the most, only a few hours a day. It was quite a change from the hectic pace of the Western Sea Frontier.

Nevertheless, I was thoroughly enjoying myself. Thrilled to be a member of the White House staff, even temporarily, I wanted to make the most of the assignment. I decided to get to know the White House better. In those days, before the Secret Service had subdivided even the inside of the White House into internal security zones, one could pretty much go anywhere except the family quarters. As I explored, the feeling of being at the center of history affected me deeply. The Cabinet Room, the Fish Room (now called the Roosevelt Room), and the rest of the West Wing seemed accessible and inviting on one hand, and highly formal and intimidating on the other. Although filled with the offices of powerful Presidential aides, the White House did not have the feeling of an office building. Partly because it is also the family home of the President and his family, the White House has always reflected the style and personality of its current residents. Compared to later Presidents, who benefited from the complete reconstruction that took place during the Truman Administration, the Truman White House would have seemed rundown and dowdy. But that judgment comes with the benefit of hindsight, and our knowledge of the magnificent redecorating that took place under the Kennedys—a project in which I was to play a supporting role. At the time, the White House just seemed simple and informal, like the Trumans themselves.

JUDGE ROSENMAN

With free time on my hands, I began to look around to see if there was anything I could do to make myself more useful. As was the custom in those more civilized times, I made courtesy calls on people with whom the Office of the Naval Aide worked. The most important of these early calls was on the Special Counsel to the President, Judge Samuel I. Rosenman.

If I owed my arrival in the White House to an old friendship with J. K. Vardaman, then I owe my job as Special Counsel to the President to Sam Rosenman. But that is only part of my debt to Rosenman: through hours of listening to him and watching him, I learned more than from anyone else with whom I ever worked in Washington. From our association, I developed many of the ideas and values that shaped my attitude toward the Presidency.

History may not accord him as prominent a place in the list of senior advisers to Franklin Roosevelt as some of his contemporaries, such as Harry Hopkins, but Judge Rosenman was one of FDR's most valued associates, and the most important Roosevelt holdover in the Truman White House. Roosevelt so valued Rosenman's advice that he had wanted to create for Rosenman the simple and elegant title of "Counsel to the President," but had been dissuaded at the last minute by Attorney General Francis Biddle, on the grounds that such a title would undercut the role of the Attorney General as the President's chief legal adviser. So FDR simply added the word "special" to the title he had in mind, and Rosenman became the Special Counsel to the President.*

Rosenman's relationship with FDR had been long and close, dating back to the twenties. Roosevelt valued his judgment and ability as a speech writer immensely, and trusted him totally. Born in Texas but educated in New York, Rosenman greatly preferred a seat on the New York State Supreme Court to the glories of Washington, and as Governor, Roosevelt obliged in 1932, appointing him to the Court, where he won a reputation for his learning and fairness. But Roosevelt continued to call on Rosenman for special assignments and advice, and finally in 1943 persuaded Rosenman to come to Washington on a full-time basis. He functioned as a sounding board for ideas and as the senior Presidential speech writer.

Rosenman had the second-largest and best office in the White House, located approximately where the Vice President's office is today, facing the magnificent Old Executive Office Building. (It is surprising but true that no Vice President had an office in the White House until 1977, when Walter F. Mondale moved into the old offices of the Special Counsel, setting a precedent that has continued.) I noticed immediately that while much of the rest of the White House seemed to slumber in the President's absence, Rosenman's office was a beehive of activity. Three typists were constantly busy, and Rosenman himself was buried in papers. He told me he had just been ordered to meet President Truman in Europe, in order to take charge of drafting a sort of interim State of the Union message

*In the seventies, as the power of the White House staff grew, one of my successors removed the word "Special" from the title, finally establishing Roosevelt's original title for the position.

which the President wished to give upon his return. That the President, surrounded by the rest of his staff in Potsdam, still needed Rosenman, truly impressed me: it was evident no one on the new team possessed anything approaching Rosenman's vast experience as a Presidential assistant.

From the moment I met Rosenman we hit it off. We shared a reverence for the law and an enjoyment of the nuances of the legal profession, which we discussed often as we got to know each other. His bright, intelligent eyes contrasted with his heavy, ponderous bearing. He had a wise and thoughtful manner, and his advice was always carefully thought out and carefully presented—and tinged, as all he said was, with a subtle wit and a fine sense of irony. His advocacy on a matter was powerful and usually decisive with President Truman; later I was to see him confront, without the slightest concern for his own bureaucratic position, men who were much closer personally to the President. He was a confirmed liberal, who believed deeply in resuming the New Deal as soon as the war was over.

In many conversations, Rosenman gave me his view of the proper role of a Presidential aide; it has guided me ever since. He stressed one basic point: the White House staff exists for a single purpose—to serve the President. Presidential assistants who become controversial violate the first rule of their service to the man whom the American people have elected: they should never advance a personal agenda if it conflicts in any way with the President's policies or interests. If a member of the President's staff becomes controversial, he weakens the man who has chosen him, and should, if he is honorable, offer the President his resignation.

Rosenman's comments may seem unsurprising or self-evident, but it is remarkable how many Presidential assistants, in almost every Administration from Truman to Bush, have not understood this basic obligation. I believe Roosevelt was entirely correct in his feeling—shared fully by Rosenman—that Presidential staff members should not become public personalities, although in recent years the rise of a larger and ever-more voracious press corps in Washington, plus the temptations of publicity and fame, have made his dictum increasingly difficult for many senior aides to live up to. However, in those long-ago days when White House aides did not make regular public and press appearances, Rosenman epitomized this philosophy.

Unlike today's senior White House officials, who often build their personal staff in order to enhance their own position, Rosenman worked without any aides, simply reaching out to anyone he thought could be of help. One of the many issues on his agenda was a message to Congress on Universal Military Training. Because I was available, he asked me to assist him on it.

Rosenman left for Europe to meet the President on July 27, only about two weeks after I had arrived. But so informal and small was the White House in those days that neither of us saw anything odd in the fact that upon leaving, the President's Special Counsel left a temporary Assistant Naval Aide with responsibility for continuing research and drafting of a message on Universal Military Training—a project I plunged into with great energy and enthusiasm.

UNIVERSAL MILITARY TRAINING

President Truman fought hard and long for Universal Military Training, repeatedly submitting it to Congress for approval, and proposing it in several State of the Union addresses as well as special messages. It would be, he hoped, a way of creating a "citizen army" in peacetime, which could be mobilized quickly in time of war or emergency. President Truman told me once that he had favored something like it since 1905, the year he joined the National Guard. He conceived of it as an alternative to a large standing army, which he assumed would not be supported by the nation after the end of World War II. Although it was a program close to the President's heart and was also supported by Generals Marshall and Eisenhower, it never won public or Congressional support.

From the beginning, despite this high-level support, most of the military bureaucracy viewed UMT as a threat to their private postwar preserve. After Pearl Harbor, the services felt that the ability to mobilize quickly was less important than having a capability in place that could absorb an enemy attack and respond immediately. Furthermore, they were determined to protect their own status and privileges. Aware of this, I sent Rosenman a memorandum on September 28, 1945, stressing the importance of getting approval from the staffs of both the Army and the Navy if UMT was "to have any real opportunity of passage"; I also recommended that the White House "make an effort to agree upon a plan acceptable to both Services and the President." In the rush of events, however, this was not done, and on October 23, the President sent to Congress a Message on Universal Military Training, much of which I had drafted under Sam Rosenman's guidance. This proposal floundered in Congress for a year, after which the President appointed a blue-ribbon advisory commission on UMT, headed by Karl Compton, a distinguished scientist. In May 1947 the Compton Commission recommended that every able-bodied seventeen- or eighteen-year-old male take basic military training for six months, followed by a post-training military obligation. The President's opponents jumped on this proposal once more, calling it a disguised form of conscription, undemocratic, excessively expensive, and alien to American traditions. Although the President submitted a new call for UMT in 1948, and never gave up trying, it was effectively dead. Later, when I was working directly with President Truman, he told me that his main objective had been to democratize the armed services and break up the power of the West Point and Annapolis cliques—a noble but impossible goal.

THE ATOMIC BOMB

As I toiled in obscurity in the East Wing in July, momentous events were unfolding at the conference of the Big Three in Potsdam, and at a place code-named "Trinity" in the desert near Alamogordo, New Mexico. Since the Manhattan Project was run by the Army, operating directly under the President through Major General Leslie Groves and Secretary of War Henry L. Stimson, and, since information about the bomb was carefully compartmentalized, I knew nothing of the July 16 test of the atomic bomb at Trinity or of the plans to drop the bomb on Japan.

I was in my office in the White House on August 6 when I heard about Hiroshima. My initial thought upon hearing the news was as simple as that of most other Americans: the war would be over sooner than we had expected, with less loss of American life. Mercifully, this proved to be the case, but I knew too little at first to suspect the larger truth: that we had entered an age in which warfare would never be the same—that, in fact, the development of nuclear weapons would turn out to be the most significant event of the century, even more than the rise and fall of communism and fascism. Had I known that over twenty years later, as Secretary of Defense, I would be the direct link between the President and the Joint Chiefs of Staff in the nuclear chain of command, my excitement undoubtedly would have been tempered by more somber reflections.

Later, when President Truman and I became closer, he talked often about the decision. Although he never evinced any doubt about his actions, he wanted them to be understood. He always emphasized that no one had told him anything about the Manhattan Project before he became President. This was not an oversight, but a deliberate—and, I believe, irresponsible—decision by President Roosevelt and his senior advisers to withhold from the man next in the chain of command the most vital secret of the war.*

He told me he first heard of the existence of "the most terrible weapon" on the evening he became President, less than four hours after Roosevelt had died and only twenty minutes after being sworn in as President, when

*I am aware of the assertion that President Roosevelt told Senator Truman of the existence of the Manhattan Project shortly after selecting him as his running mate in 1944, but I can only report what President Truman told me on many occasions.

Secretary of War Stimson took him aside and told him that Roosevelt had set up a special organization to develop a super-bomb that was almost ready for its first test. President Truman said he was so overwhelmed by the events of the day that the information about the bomb did not sink in—a clear demonstration, if any were needed, of the necessity to keep the Vice President *fully* informed of important events so that he (or she) can make decisions quickly if the President is unable, for whatever reason, to perform the duties of office.

Stimson was then seventy-eight and, when I met him only a few months later, enormously weary and physically weakened by the burdens he had carried through the war. He was, however, the very model of the Eastern Establishment Republican gentleman—a breed now all but extinct—and was prepared to carry on as long as his country and its President needed him. When he heard nothing more from the new President for two weeks, he asked to see him "on a highly secret matter," and brought with him Major General Leslie Groves, head of the Manhattan Project. They handed President Truman a detailed memorandum that contained a heart-stopping sentence: "Within four months we shall in all probability have completed the most terrible weapon ever known in human history, one bomb which could destroy a whole city."

Given the number of other matters pressing upon him, there was no time for him to educate himself adequately; but from that moment he understood that the final decision would have to be his and his alone. "I am going to have to make a decision which no man in history has ever had to make," he said to Leonard Reinsch,* the very next person he saw after Stimson and Groves had left his office. "I'll make the decision, but it is terrifying to think about what I will have to decide."

When President Truman discussed these events later, he always emphasized that he had only one goal: ending the war as soon as possible. I stress this because of the controversy that continues to this day concerning three aspects of these events.

First, there has been speculation over the years that the use of the bomb against Japan instead of Germany was related to racial factors—that, not wishing to use it against Europeans, the U.S. "reserved" it for Asians. This is utterly false. The use of new techniques, such as incendiary bombing, against targets that included Dresden, in fact, killed as many or more than died at Hiroshima. Moreover, the men who built the bomb, including J. Robert Oppenheimer, had hoped to finish the bomb in time for its use against Germany. I have no doubt that had it been finished in time to be useful in shortening the European war, President Truman or President Roosevelt would have used it.

*A radio-station director who was temporarily assigned to the White House staff.

Second, a theory has frequently been advanced that one of the main reasons for the use of the bomb against Japan was to intimidate the Soviets. As recently as late 1989, Soviet Foreign Minister Eduard Shevardnadze repeated this charge in a speech in New York: "Militarily there was no need to drop the nuclear bombs on Hiroshima and Nagasaki. It was a political decision taken to intimidate us. This tragedy of the century must be brought to light and its perpetrators globally denounced."[1] There is no evidence to support this theory: never did I hear President Truman or any of his colleagues discuss the use of the bomb against Japan in terms of American-Soviet relations. In the summer of 1945, when a weary nation and its new President wanted nothing more than to end the Pacific War quickly and bring the rest of the troops home, considerations of postwar strategy and relations with Moscow were low on our agenda, and unrelated to the discussion of what to do with our new weapon.

Finally, the most highly debated question about the decision to drop the bombs on Hiroshima and Nagasaki: Why did the President not order a demonstration bomb dropped on an unpopulated area before using one on a populated area?

To President Truman the issue was not as complicated as it seems to many people today. He did not consider the idea of a demonstration bomb for several reasons. First, his scientists and military advisers, with only one test behind them, were not absolutely certain that the next bomb would perform properly, and they did not want to risk a publicized dud. Second, his advisers felt Japan would not appreciate its full destructive power unless it was used against an actual target. The fact that he was at Potsdam or on the heavy cruiser *Augusta* during the most critical period—between the flash in the New Mexico sky on July 16 and the flight of the *Enola Gay* on August 6—meant that he was never presented with a full-scale argument for a demonstration bomb. He told me later, however, that he had considered it, and came to the conclusion that a demonstration would not suffice after a war of such terrible carnage, that Japanese lives would have to be sacrificed to save many more American and Japanese lives.

In the end, what weighed most heavily on President Truman was the military estimate that enormous numbers of American casualties would be suffered in an assault upon the main islands of Japan. Only eight months earlier the American Army had suffered heavy losses in the Battle of the Bulge, against a German enemy thought to have been already defeated. The assumption was that the Japanese, deeply committed to their Emperor and on their own soil, would fight even more tenaciously than Germany, and everyone remembered that the Third Reich had resisted down to the last street in Berlin. In our conversations he mentioned this factor more than any other. The estimate that stayed in his mind was the total of 500,000, half killed in action, and half wounded.

Thus the decision was relatively simple in President Truman's mind, a choice between sacrificing a horrendous number of Americans or using a weapon which could shorten the war dramatically. Although later he spent considerable time defending his decision, he did not agonize over it at the time. Death and destruction on the most massive scale had been the hallmarks of both World War I, in which Harry Truman had fought, and the war whose conclusion was now in his hands. He wanted to end it as quickly as possible.

V-J DAY—AND STAYING ON

The pace of epochal events in August and September of 1945 was intense. President Truman and his entourage returned from Europe on August 7. Two days later, on the same day as the second atomic bomb was dropped on Nagasaki, President Truman reported to the nation on his trip and the atomic bomb. Five days later, the Japanese surrendered.

It was an unforgettable day, with excitement building as the nation waited for formal word that the war was over. A huge crowd gathered around the White House, creating the most joyous mood I have ever seen in Washington. Finally, in the late afternoon, word came through the Swiss government; the Japanese had surrendered unconditionally. At 7 P.M., I went outside to walk through the streets of the capital, in uniform as always. Everywhere people were dancing, celebrating wildly. Everybody was everybody's friend that night. It was a sweet time to be alive.

Although I did not know it at the time, Rosenman had talked about me to Vardaman during the long trip home from Europe, and the two men had agreed that it would be useful to have me stay in the White House as Assistant Naval Aide, in my spare time assisting Rosenman on various projects. They took their proposal to the President immediately, in order to prevent the Navy from calling me back to San Francisco. On September 13, 1945, barely a month after the Japanese had surrendered, I was officially transferred to the White House as Assistant Naval Aide. By order of the President, my "spot" appointment as a Lieutenant Commander, good only for the period of time that I was on temporary duty at the White House, was reissued as a permanent rank.

JAMES V. FORRESTAL

The formal responsibilities of the Assistant Naval Aide to the President were fairly limited, even when the President was in the White House. We used to refer to the job as being similar to a "potted palm" because one of its most important requirements, then and now, was to stand quietly in the background at social and ceremonial events, on the alert for some unescorted woman who needed to be helped to her seat, or to assist some lost guest in search of the White House washrooms. This aspect of the job, however boring, was central to its justification.

However, in the forties, before the development of the modern National Security Council structure and the elaborate system of communications that now exists between the President and the Pentagon, the Naval Aide had another, more important function: to act as the liaison between the Navy Department and the President on naval matters. This would bring me into contact with that remarkable and ultimately tragic man James V. Forrestal.

Forrestal was fifty-three years old. He had gone to Princeton, and then worked his way rapidly up to the presidency of the New York investment firm of Dillon, Read and Company. Unlike most of his Wall Street colleagues, he supported the New Deal. In 1940, he came to Washington as an administrative assistant to President Roosevelt, and later that year moved to the Navy Department, first as Undersecretary and then, in 1944, as Secretary of the Navy.

Given the strains between Vardaman and Forrestal, I was initially concerned that I would be caught between them; but in fact their mutual antipathy led both men to deal with each other through me rather than directly. Thus, almost from my earliest days at the White House, I was thrust into a close relationship with this fascinating and troubled man.

I approached my initial courtesy call on Forrestal with uncertainty; I was a newly promoted Lieutenant Commander working for a man Forrestal neither liked nor respected, and Forrestal was one of Washington's most powerful men. But to my relief he was cordial and made no references to his annoyance with Vardaman or the Navy's original opposition to my new assignment.

He had a wiry, coiled frame, and I was fascinated by his flattened nose, the result of a boxing match in his youth. I was struck immediately, and in all our subsequent meetings, with the extraordinary intensity and nervous energy of the man. Although we later became good friends and worked closely together, I always felt a bit uncomfortable in the presence of that intensity, which never let up. Over time another aspect of Forrestal's personality came to disturb me: he seemed virtually devoid of any sense of humor. I have always thought a sense of humor indispensable for people in high-pressure jobs, and Jim Forrestal not only lacked it, but increasingly—we were all to learn—found humor in others irritating. He was the opposite of Rosenman, who maintained an easy and relaxed demeanor even when dealing with affairs of great moment; Forrestal conveyed agitation and tension even when dealing with minor matters. This was true even in 1945, long before he began to destroy himself.

THE PRESIDENTIAL SEAL AND FLAG

Vardaman's first assignment to me, to oversee the redesign of the Presidential seal and flag, was an inadvertent consequence of legislation in December 1944, authorizing the armed forces to promote eight military officers from four-star to five-star rank, in order to give them a rank equal to British Field Marshals.*

After this popular piece of wartime legislation was passed, Franklin Roosevelt, an old Navy man with a love of detail, noticed that the Presidential flag and seal, with a star located in each corner, would have one less star than the five-star officers serving their Commander in Chief—so, at the end of 1944, Roosevelt decided he needed a new flag and seal. Sometime before Roosevelt's death, staff responsibility for this project was turned over to George Elsey.

Elsey worked with various heraldry experts, including Arthur DuBois, the chief heraldist of the Army, on possible designs. In mid-August, 1945, they showed me a splendid redesign, in which they had solved FDR's problem over the number of stars by a simple solution: surround the seal with forty-eight stars, one for each state, with the proviso that one star would be added for each new state that was admitted to the union. They suggested another change that especially appealed to me, one rich in symbolism appropriate at the end of the global war: the eagle's profile should be turned to face the olive branch of peace in the eagle's right talon rather than the arrows of war in the other. I enthusiastically approved the Elsey-DuBois design, and presented it to President and Mrs. Truman on Sunday, August 26, in a meeting in the family quarters of the White House—the first time I had ever visited the private area of the White House. The President examined the proposed changes carefully, decided that he liked them, and approved them. But he suggested one additional change: he wanted to have lightning emanating from the arrowheads in the left claw of the eagle as a "symbolic reference to the tremendous importance of the atomic bomb." We were able to talk the President out of this suggestion a few days later on the grounds that it would have made the flag and seal unattractive. This was the first time I heard the President talk about the atomic bomb, and I thought it told more than he publicly acknowledged about the impact the bomb had had on his thinking.

The President unveiled the new design on Navy Day, October 27, at the commissioning of the new aircraft carrier USS *Franklin D. Roosevelt*

*George Marshall, the most senior of the men to receive five-star rank, had vetoed the title of "Marshal" on the grounds that he did not want to become Marshal Marshall. Thus the American rank became either "General of the Army" or "Fleet Admiral." The original eight, already great national heroes then, and legends today, were: Army—Marshall, Douglas MacArthur, Eisenhower, and Henry "Hap" Arnold of the Army Air Corps; Navy—Leahy, Ernest J. King, Chester W. Nimitz, and William "Bull" Halsey.

at the Brooklyn Navy Yard. I was pleased the redesign was immediately accepted as an improvement over its predecessor, and remains to this day (with two added stars for Hawaii and Alaska) the official seal and flag of the President of the United States. Of course, in those pretelevision days, the Presidential seal was not as familiar to the American public as it is today, when it has become a sort of national logo, present whenever and wherever the President speaks, even displayed on matchbooks, cufflinks, tie clips, and stationery.

TWO IMPORTANT DEPARTURES

My work gave me growing satisfaction in the late summer and fall of 1945. I was spending less than a quarter of my time on my formal duties as Assistant Naval Aide. Once in a while, when Vardaman was away, I would fill in for him at functions that required the presence of the Naval Aide. The first time I sat in on high-level discussions was in November 1945, and the occasion was the first postwar summit, between President Truman and Prime Ministers Clement Attlee of Great Britain and Mackenzie King of Canada. The purpose of this meeting was nothing less than to develop a postwar policy for the international aspects of atomic energy. The impression it made on me—the sense of wonder at being present—is evident in a long, and somewhat wide-eyed, letter I wrote my mother:

> I had such an interesting weekend that I knew you would be glad to have the details. J.K. has been gone for a week so I had the opportunity to serve as Acting Naval Aide in his absence. It came at a most propitious time. The President invited me to the formal State Dinner which was held Saturday night for Prime Minister Attlee of England and Prime Minister King of Canada. There were fifty-five guests, and the table was arranged in the shape of a horseshoe in the State Dining Room. I attach a copy of the guest list and, if you will be patient and continue to read it long enough, you will ultimately come to the last name, which is that of your dutiful son. . . . The next day, which was Sunday, we proceeded to the Navy Yard where we boarded the [Presidential] yacht. . . . The group devoted itself to the discussion of the use of atomic energy and the world problems which had been brought into existence as the result of this terrifying discovery. . . . I have the feeling that it is one of the most important conferences in the history of the world, and I feel a great sense of gratitude that I was permitted to be present on such an epic-making occasion. The President is intelligent, forthright and reasonable and I felt very proud of him and the manner in which he represented our country on this occasion. I have developed a deep and abiding affection for him and hope and trust that I may be able to be of some small assistance to him. . . .

Exciting as such occasions were, they were very rare. But, with Vardaman's approval, Rosenman kept me busy on a growing number of projects, only a few of which had anything to do with military affairs. While most people in the government allowed events to set their agenda, Rosenman worked steadily toward clear objectives, minimizing diversions. I helped him draft messages for the President, organized research for him, and, always, learned from him about the government. In the closing months of 1945, he took me into the Oval Office for several meetings with President Truman. More important than my contribution to the issues under discussion was the fact that Rosenman wanted the President to start viewing me as more than a junior Naval Aide.

In those months the nation began the adjustment to peacetime conditions. For most people, this meant getting back to their prewar lives, or moving on to something new. The White House was no exception, and at the beginning of 1946, for different reasons and in different ways, both Vardaman and Rosenman left the White House. Their departures were to change my life decisively, and end my own personal plans to return to St. Louis.

Rosenman's departure had been expected. When he originally agreed to stay after Roosevelt's death, he told President Truman that for financial reasons he would have to return to New York City to practice law no later than the beginning of 1946. His White House salary never exceeded $12,000 per year. Although he was devoted to public service, he felt he owed it to his family to put them on a more secure financial footing. President Truman let Rosenman go only reluctantly, after extracting a promise that he would be available on a regular basis for special projects. His departure left a gaping hole in the White House structure.

Vardaman's departure, however, was more complicated. With the war over, he had had enough of the Navy and the job of Naval Aide. He did not want to return to St. Louis, at least not immediately. After looking around Washington, Vardaman decided that the perfect job for him would be as a Governor of the Federal Reserve Board.

Vardaman's abrasive and combative style, though, had created too many enemies in Washington. The flaw in J.K.'s personality, the very one which he knew had damaged his father's once-promising career in the Senate, hurt him as well. Forrestal had begun to complain to President Truman about Vardaman's behavior, charging that Vardaman was using his position to settle old scores with naval officers he did not like, and that he was ineffective as a liaison between the Navy and the President. In a choice between the Secretary of the Navy, a substantial figure on the Washington scene, and Vardaman, the President's choice would be all too clear.

Vardaman had another problem by this time, even more serious than his difficulties with Forrestal. He had antagonized Mrs. Truman, and within the Truman family he had begun to acquire a reputation, in the President's phrase, as a "prima donna." In her biography of her father, Margaret Truman described from the family's point of view the process which I could see unfolding in late 1945:

> In the White House Mr. Vardaman proceeded to stick his nose into almost every office and tell them how it should be run. Then he made the blunder of all blunders. He descended upon Mother's side of the White House and started telling *them* how to do the job. That was the end of Mr. Vardaman as Naval aide. Dad elevated him to the Federal Reserve Board, and he repaid him for this kindness by voting against every Truman policy for the next seven years. He also went around Washington spreading the nasty story that he was kicked out of the White House because he did not drink or play cards.[2]

On January 14, 1946, President Truman told his morning staff meeting that he intended to nominate Vardaman for a full fourteen-year term as a Governor of the Federal Reserve Board. He did not name a successor, and I became that odd Washington half-person, an "acting" Naval Aide.

But Vardaman's nomination caused a minor controversy and brought me into close contact with the President for the first time. The press went after Vardaman for several abuses of his position as Naval Aide, including the use of personnel from the Presidential yacht as occasional personal servants and a Navy painter to repaint his back porch and gate. These actions had undoubtedly been leaked by Navy officers seeking revenge against him. At the same time, some former business and banking associates of Vardaman's from St. Louis, primarily Republicans, indicated their readiness to testify against his appointment.

The hearings began in a special subcommittee of the Banking Committee under Senator George Radcliffe of Maryland on February 18, with Vardaman heatedly defending himself. After a month's adjournment, the hearings resumed on March 20 with testimony from two St. Louis businessmen, one a former head of the American Bankers Association, who charged that Vardaman was unqualified to be a Federal Reserve Bank Governor.

As the battle escalated, President Truman called me into his office for our first private meeting. He had an assignment: given my knowledge of both Vardaman and details of his St. Louis business career, he wanted me to take on responsibility for coordinating the confirmation of Vardaman. It was personally important to him, he said, that Vardaman be confirmed.

I had no previous experience in Congressional relations, and did not yet know any members of Congress well. In those more informal days, though, my assignment was not as unusual as it might seem today, when every President has a large office devoted entirely to working with Congress. The fight for Vardaman gave me my first lessons in the care and feeding of Congress. For six weeks in February and March 1946, I worked on the Vardaman nomination, conferring regularly with Senators in both parties. In the process we were able to demonstrate to the satisfaction of most Senators that his opponents were venting personal animosities which had no bearing on his qualifications for the Federal Reserve Board. Finally, on March 27, with Senate Majority Leader Alben Barkley personally presiding over a closed session of the Banking Committee, the appointment was approved by a 9–1 vote. On April 3, after three days and over thirteen hours of floor debate, the Senate confirmed Vardaman by a vote of 66–9.

NAVAL AIDE TO THE PRESIDENT

With the departures of Rosenman and Vardaman, obvious questions concerning my own future arose. Although I had been at the White House only seven months, there were rumors that I was being considered not only as Vardaman's replacement but as a possible successor to Judge Rosenman.

President Truman had made one last effort to get Rosenman to stay, arguing that there was no one available to replace him. Later, Sam Rosenman told me that he had immediately replied, "Mr. President, you have a fine replacement sitting right here in the White House, and he even happens to be from Missouri. His name is Clifford."

According to Rosenman, President Truman replied that I was too young and inexperienced to assume the authority and status that came with the title of Special Counsel, although he would assign to me many of the tasks previously carried out under Rosenman's direction. So while newspapers speculated that I would replace Rosenman, the President announced on January 24 that he simply would not fill the position; it was a "wartime emergency post" created for one man, the President said, and did not need to be filled "now that our enemies have surrendered."

This decision was greeted with relief and pleasure by several members of the White House staff who were part of the original Missouri team, especially the Military Aide, Harry Vaughan, who was soon to be promoted to Major General. Vaughan did not wish to see any threat to his intimate relationship with the President. They had been comrades since 1918, when, as young First Lieutenants, they trained together. More than anyone else, Harry Vaughan could relax and amuse his friend. Primarily to have Vaughan around, Harry Truman had created a new position, Military Aide to the Vice President, at the beginning of 1945, and

Vaughan had been with him from the first minutes after Roosevelt's death.

Unfortunately, like many other Presidential cronies over the years, Vaughan did not understand that a personal friendship between two people had to be different from a relationship, no matter how close, with a President. Neither I nor any other White House aide ever threatened Vaughan's personal association with Harry Truman; none of us wanted to interfere in an old and treasured fellowship of the very sort that every President needs in order to relax. But Vaughan thought that his old ties to Harry Truman gave him special authority in areas of substance and personnel.

Vaughan compounded his growing problems by a unilateral act of office imperialism. On his own authority, Vaughan took over Rosenman's spacious office. Washington has always been a city which pays special attention to such perquisites, and Vaughan's new office, with its proximity to the Oval Office, seemed to convey an increase in power. From it, Vaughan proceeded to attempt to spread his influence still further, and this led both Forrestal and Judge Robert Patterson, who had just succeeded Colonel Stimson as Secretary of War, to complain to President Truman.

Over the winter, Marny and I decided that my life in Washington held enough permanence for her to move from Massachusetts with our three daughters. Abandoning the Connecticut Avenue apartment I had shared with Dudley Orr, I rented a house in Chevy Chase, Maryland. Marny had visited Washington regularly during the months I had been working for Vardaman, but it was wonderful to have the whole family together again for the first time since I had left St. Louis.

My work was bringing me into ever-closer contact with the President, and I understood his reluctance to promote me over the heads of so many older White House aides who were closer to him. Nevertheless, on April 4, President Truman announced my appointment as Naval Aide, succeeding Vardaman. I had also received two rapid promotions in Navy rank, the first, in November, to the rank of Commander, the second, in January 1946, to the rank of Captain. The speed of these promotions, from a Lieutenant (junior grade) to full Captain in less than two years, was certainly unusual by any standards. My friends and others pointed out that I had never had any seagoing assignments. I was, as one of my friends said, the ultimate "dry-land sailor." Reading about my lack of seagoing experience, the famous humorist Robert Benchley, whom I had met during one of his visits to Washington, sent me a photograph of himself in an Admiral's uniform with *six* stars and eleven rows of decorations on his chest, and inscribed the photograph to "Clark Clifford, with whom I fought the war on the bottle-scarred banks of the Potomac."

The speed of my promotions, and the fact that I was doing a great deal of work unrelated to the Navy, began to attract press attention. I discouraged articles, which were certain to antagonize other people in the Administration, and might also be misunderstood by the President. For the first time, I came to the attention of *Time,* a magazine that would follow my career closely, and usually critically. In its April 22, 1946, issue, the magazine interspersed the lyrics of a famous Gilbert and Sullivan song with their own commentary to suggest parallels between my career and that of Sir Joseph Porter, the character in the operetta *H.M.S. Pinafore,* who had "served a term as office boy to an Attorney's firm":

> *Now landsmen all, whoever you may be,*
> *If you want to rise to the top of the tree,*
> *If your soul isn't fettered to an office stool,*
> *Be careful to be guided by this golden rule—*
> *Stick close to your desks and never go to sea,*
> *And you all may be Rulers of the Queen's Navee!*
>
> Last week 39-year-old Captain Clifford, who had stuck to his desk and never gone to sea, took over as President Truman's Naval Aide.[3]

4

A Little Gambling Among Friends

NAVAL INTERLUDES

As Naval Aide to the President, my most enjoyable function was arranging the President's cherished poker games, most of which were held on the *Williamsburg,* the Presidential yacht.

The change that has come over the Presidency in the last half century is illustrated by the casual candor with which the public, the press, and the White House itself treated the President's favorite way of unwinding. There was none of the public sanctimoniousness that exists today about such matters as a little gambling with the boys. When journalists asked what we were doing on the river, instead of presenting a false picture of a President hard at work, complete with rigged photo-opportunities showing him behind a stack of briefing books, President Truman simply would say, "Some of the boys and I were playing a little poker." If asked what we drank, the President would tell the truth: "Kentucky bourbon."

I am reminded of Harry Truman's refreshing candor when I see such examples of modern political hypocrisy as the answers given by the 1988 Presidential candidates. When asked what their favorite drink was, four out of the twelve candidates in the primaries said milk, and the rest, with the exception of Governor Bruce Babbitt of Arizona, chose some other nonalcoholic beverage. (Displaying great political courage, Babbitt admitted to enjoying a local Arizona beer.)

The President's yacht was a lovely 240-foot vessel, built in 1930 and reconfigured in 1945. It was said, even by my friends—or perhaps especially by my friends—that my seafaring career in the Navy was limited entirely to the *Williamsburg.* This may not have been entirely true, but it was close enough to amuse everyone, including President Truman. I was also ill prepared for another duty of the Naval Aide: to oversee the menus when the vessel transported the Commander in Chief. On one of the earliest cruises for which I was chief menu maker, I absentmindedly approved shrimp as an appetizer before both lunch and dinner for three straight days. The President found this both appalling and amusing, and after two days, turned to me and said, "I can't bear the sight of any more shrimp. I don't like shrimp. In fact, I've *never* liked shrimp!" From then on, President Truman often referred to the *Williamsburg* as "Clifford's Floating Shrimp Palace."

The poker games developed into one of the first important links between President Truman and me. The first few times I was on board the *Williamsburg,* he did not include me in the game; but about the third weekend he called on me to fill a vacant place at the table. Soon thereafter, President Truman asked me to assume responsibility for setting up the game. He loved an eight-handed poker game, and played with a core group of regulars, including George Allen, Stuart Symington, and Secretary of Agriculture (later Senator) Clinton Anderson. His favorite poker companion was Fred Vinson, his Secretary of the Treasury, and later Chief Justice of the United States. To this group he added other players on a rotating basis. Through the poker games I first met Averell Harriman, then Secretary of Commerce. Harriman, one of the wealthiest men in the country, guarded his chips as though he were on relief. A rising young protégé of Speaker Sam Rayburn, Congressman (and later Senator) Lyndon Johnson, also joined the game from time to time.

Johnson was not much of a poker player but was extremely pleased to be included. In fact, I realized quite soon that he was not really interested in poker at all; what excited him was the conversation. Political discussion enthralled him the way great music might move others. To Johnson, politics was more fun than anything else on earth. As he listened to men with greater experience than he discuss politics, he was learning about power in Washington. Although I did not realize it at the time, the *Williamsburg* poker games and the inevitable political discussions were part of a continuing seminar in the study of power.

The *Williamsburg* would usually depart late Friday afternoon, and return Sunday afternoon. The poker weekends were stag affairs: President Truman, while always courteous to women, was rarely relaxed and comfortable in their presence. With the exception of the President, everyone had to share a stateroom. Since I was in charge of these assignments, I tried, whenever possible, to share a room with Stu Symington.

The poker game could be fun—especially when I was winning. But, like Lyndon Johnson, I enjoyed most the long, leisurely meals when the President reminisced or talked about current affairs. Often breakfast or lunch would take two hours. More relaxed than he ever was in the White House, he loved to tell how he was chosen by Roosevelt to be his running mate, or recount, in impressive detail, important events in our country's history. It was on the *Williamsburg* that I first realized how much President Truman loved American history.

The game itself was for real money—not enormous amounts, but enough to make it interesting, and sometimes dangerous, for someone trying to live on a naval officer's salary. President Truman's theory on the stakes was simple: "I want to play for enough so that it is a good game with a lot of skill involved, but I don't want anyone to get hurt."

I bought a book on poker and studied it assiduously. I found that, if I played rather conservatively, over time I could actually generate a small, but useful, amount of additional income. As for President Truman, he enjoyed himself thoroughly, whether he won or lost. It was the fellowship and the release from White House pressure that made these trips so important to him.

The President asked me to be the banker of the poker game. Each Friday evening as we started out, I distributed a five-hundred-dollar stack of chips to each player. If he lost this stack he would receive another such stack. In my capacity as banker I would extract approximately 10 percent of each pot and put the chips in a silver bowl called the "poverty bowl." This would gradually amount to a rather substantial sum. If a player had lost his full thousand dollars I would supply him, free of charge, an additional one hundred dollars from the "poverty bowl." If he lost that stake he would be supplied with another one, and he could continue to dip into the silver bowl until he made his way back into the game. It kept everyone in the game, and the most a player could lose was nine hundred dollars.

President Truman was not an excessive drinker. In the relaxed privacy of the *Williamsburg,* however, where he went to unwind, he usually drank with his guests during and after the poker games, and this naturally affected the mood. Sometimes, like others on board, he showed the effects of a few drinks. He might express himself in language less restrained and more colorful than he would otherwise use, especially if he had faced a particularly difficult week onshore. He trusted the discretion of those he invited for the weekend, and this trust was never broken.

Many hours of poker lead, of course, to many stories—and like fishing stories they tend to get exaggerated over time. But one incident with Fred Vinson remained vivid for years afterward, and even had an aftermath involving that non–poker player, Dean Acheson.

President Truman had named Fred Vinson Chief Justice of the United States in 1946, but his status as the President's favorite poker companion did not change. A large and gentle man with a long, rather sad face (in the words of *Time,* he looked like "a tired sheep with a hangover"), he shared with President Truman not only a love for poker but a similar sense of humor. He had represented Kentucky in the House of Representatives for ten years before becoming a judge on the U.S. Court of Appeals in the thirties, and served Roosevelt as head of the Federal Loan Administration and Director of the Office of War Mobilization and Reconversion. When FDR died, President Truman, after letting Henry Morgenthau go, made Vinson Secretary of the Treasury.

In 1947 I suggested to the President that we combine a poker evening with a party on Vinson's birthday, and this became an annual event that usually took place at my house in Chevy Chase. After a festive dinner we would adjourn to a big round table for our poker game. Late at night one year, when my mother was by chance staying with us, we played a hand in which the pot in the middle of the table grew to about three thousand dollars. My hand was not strong enough to stay in, so, seated between the President and the Chief Justice, I dropped out to watch the action.

As the tension built, Vinson studied his cards. I could see that if he got any card from a jack down—this was a game of high-low, with most of the cards showing on the table—he would win at least half the pot. With the odds heavily in his favor, he turned to President Truman, who was dealing the cards, and said, "OK, Mr. President, hit me."

The President flipped the next card over. It was the Queen of spades. Without thinking, Vinson looked straight at the President and burst out, "You son of a bitch." There was a brief moment of shocked silence; no one ever called President Truman anything other than "Mr. President," even in the informal setting of the poker table. The hush was broken by the Chief Justice, stammering apologetically, "Oh, Mr. President, Mr. President. . . ." Never did President Truman, or the rest of us, laugh harder than we did at that moment; my mother, asleep upstairs, was awakened by the racket and said she had never heard a group of men laughing as loudly in her entire life.

Five years later, in the last week of the Truman Presidency, Dean Acheson gave a farewell dinner for President and Mrs. Truman. During the meal, President Truman asked me to describe, "leaving nothing out," the evening when, as the President put it, "the Chief Justice committed the grossest violation of common decency and conduct." Whereupon I recounted the tale—not for the first time, of course, because the President loved to have the story told and retold as a way of gently teasing his friend—in the form of an indictment of the Chief Justice for the crime, in Acheson's words, of "*lèse majesté.*" A mock trial thereupon took place, with the President acting as judge: the Chief Justice defended himself on the grounds that his comment was "ejaculatory only and not addressed to the President."[1] The President delivered his final judgment on the outburst: "not proven."

THE PRESIDENT'S MOTHER

As I came to know President Truman as a boss and a friend, I also came to know his mother and to see that this remarkable woman, born eight years before the Civil War, had been central in shaping her son's values. She took pride in him, not for being President, but for having character. For his part, I had the impression that President Truman was greatly pleased that his mother had lived long enough to see him become President, because then she would know that he had "amounted to something." Once, in 1946, he gave a small dinner for her in the upstairs family quarters at the White House. He wanted some of us to meet his mother. We chatted casually for a while, and then someone asked her, teasingly, if she wanted to share with us any secrets about her son. She lit up with pride, and said, in an utterly serious tone, that she would share with us a secret about Harry that the world did not know. We all leaned forward; I was literally on the edge of my seat. "When he was a boy," she said, proudly, "Harry could plow the straightest furrow in Jackson County." I looked at the President, who was beaming with pleasure.

He loved to tease her, ever so gently. One evening when she had just arrived from Missouri for a stay at the White House, the President made a small joke that played on his mother's Southern roots. "Tonight, Mother," he said, his eyes dancing, "we are going to give you a special treat, a chance to sleep in the most famous room in the White House, the Lincoln Room, and in the very bed in which Abraham Lincoln slept." There was quiet in the group for a moment, and Mrs. Truman—brought up on the myths of the Old Confederacy by parents who had owned slaves—looked at her daughter-in-law and said, "Bess, if you'll get my bags packed, I'll be going back home this evening." Led by the President, everyone in the room started howling with laughter. The President's mother, realizing that it was a joke, finally joined in.

SPEECH WRITING

My most frequent assignment in those early days was speech writing. Rosenman was gone, his talent with words gone with him. Unbelievably, there was no professionally qualified speech writer around the White House to fill the vacuum; but Rosenman had deliberately strengthened my position by bringing me into direct contact with the President at every opportunity, and assignments began to come my way. My association with the President at the poker table undoubtedly helped increase the flow of assignments toward me.

Notwithstanding the love of language instilled in me by my mother, I did not consider myself to have any special gift as a writer. Continuing a procedure that had developed over sixteen years of legal practice, I wrote slowly and laboriously in longhand, using a soft pencil, erasing and rewriting constantly. Even though he had suggested me as his successor, Rosenman himself understood my limitations in this area. He later commented, quite accurately, that I was "quite a pedestrian writer," but added that "Clifford was a great help to President Truman. I am delighted that I recommended him."[2]

No one would ever rank Harry Truman with Presidents like Lincoln, the two Roosevelts, and Kennedy as an outstanding orator, nor place his inexperienced speech writer in a class with great speech writers like Roosevelt's Robert Sherwood or Kennedy's Theodore Sorensen. But over time President Truman did develop a short, punchy style, one that came to reflect accurately his own homespun Missouri personality and values, in contrast to the very different phrasing and style of FDR. In this regard, Rosenman's departure had one important and unforeseen positive effect: Harry Truman stopped trying to sound like a substitute Franklin Roosevelt. After Rosenman's departure his staff gradually realized that President Truman was ready, and indeed wanted and needed, to move toward his own style. Despite my enormous respect for Rosenman, I felt strongly that President Truman must find his own style, and I worked assiduously toward this goal. The first reporter to note the evolution in Presidential style was Lester Markel of *The New York Times,* who, as early as March 16, 1947, described the process as follows:

> It is Clifford more than anyone else, as far as this reporter can make out, who convinced the President that he should not be Franklin Roosevelt, but Harry Truman, that he should no longer try to speak in Harvard accents, but with a Missouri twang; that in place of oratory he should offer his own brand of "common sense."

To review major speeches, President Truman would call a conference in the Cabinet Room. These sessions were always attended by his Press Secretary, Charlie Ross, and anyone with special knowledge of the subject. As the person responsible for preparing the master draft, I always sat directly opposite the President. He followed a procedure that was probably unique to him. First, he would read the entire draft aloud to get a feeling for it; sometimes he would also ask me to read the speech aloud, so he could hear how it sounded. Then he would review it paragraph by paragraph. He preferred short, basic sentences, and his own changes were always in the direction of making the speech simpler, more understandable, more direct.

SPECIAL COUNSEL

I served only nine weeks as Naval Aide to the President. After my role in the resolution of the railroad strike (see Chapter 5), the President decided that staying in the Navy while working on such issues not only made no sense but could create misunderstandings. He had not forgotten Sam Rosenman's original recommendation. Calling me into his office in early June, he said, without any drama or ceremony, that it was about time for me to get out of uniform and become Special Counsel in name as well as fact. After I had expressed my appreciation, he added, "You should also get out of the East Wing and be closer to my office. I want you and Vaughan to switch offices." Harry Vaughan took offense at this, and held me accountable for his removal to a distant and far more modest office in the East Wing, but at the time I did not foresee the problem this would cause—I was simply delighted at the sudden end of my naval career, and the new challenge that lay ahead. I retained only one duty of the Naval Aide: arranging the poker games.

No ceremonies marked my change in titles, which was announced on June 27—there was simply too much to do in my new job, and, in any case, my responsibilities had not really changed; more accurately, they had been formalized. The Navy, wasting no time, sent my separation orders to the White House the next day. Doris Fleeson, a rising Washington journalist, described the change in a column in the *St. Louis Post-Dispatch,* accurately headlined CLARK CLIFFORD'S NEW JOB MAKES EVERYBODY HAPPY, EVEN THE NAVY. In my new job, I was paid $12,000 a year, less than half of what I had been making in St. Louis, but between our family's savings and the proceeds from selling our house in St. Louis, we were able to cope.

To the inevitable question *What did a Special Counsel do?,* the simplest and most accurate answer was: Whatever the President wanted. The title of Special Counsel was grand, but the job had no power or authority other than that conferred by the President. In a pattern that was to continue throughout my career, my value was as an adviser or counsellor, and not as an administrator or bureaucrat.

A DAY AT THE OFFICE

Over time, a working pattern developed in the Truman White House. For me, the key events in each Presidential day were the first and the last—the morning staff meeting and, even more important, a private meeting that usually ended the working day. Shortly before nine each morning, the buzzer would sound on the desk of my main secretary, Mary Weiler, summoning me to the morning staff meeting. Walking through the anteroom, I would pass my secretaries, proceed down a short hallway for about twenty-five steps, and enter the Oval Office through the office of Matt Connelly, the President's Appointments Secretary.

On a typical day in the middle of the Truman years, the lineup around the President's desk for the morning staff meeting would include Charlie Ross, John Steelman, Connelly, Correspondence Secretary Bill Hassett, Harry Vaughan, and me. I usually sat along the wall, with the window behind me. These morning staff meetings had a casual air to them; today much of what took place in them would be handled by the White House Chief of Staff without the participation of the President. But President Truman did this work himself, sometimes in a haphazard manner. He began each meeting by going through the papers on his desk, handing them out to various members of the staff for action. Ross would raise any press or public-relations problems. After that, the rest of the staff would bring up anything they felt needed Presidential attention.

By the late summer of 1946, I had come to realize it would be most productive to visit with the President alone at the end of each day, usually between five and six P.M.; over time, it became accepted practice. Normally I would bring up items that needed immediate approval in the morning meeting, and saved for the later one those matters, which, while not necessarily urgent, required considered discussion. Nothing was off limits during our private discussions. It was the perfect time to reflect on the day and look ahead, and the President, who often had a bourbon and branch water as we talked, seemed to enjoy the interval between the working day and the evening. Those fifteen minutes were the most important of my day.

HOW TO ORGANIZE A WHITE HOUSE

There are many ways to organize the White House staff, and no single structure is right for every President. But the organization of the White House must start with the recognition that the President, like the rest of us, has his peculiarities, preferences, strengths, and weaknesses. Whatever system a President uses should, to be sure, reflect the nature of the job, but it must also reflect his individual character.

President Truman did not deliberately set one staff member against another, as Franklin Roosevelt had done and Lyndon Johnson would do later. Talking to Sam Rosenman about the contrast between Roosevelt and Truman, I concluded that the enjoyment Roosevelt took in watching members of his staff compete with each other was probably derived, in part, from the fact that because he was unable to engage in sports, because of his polio, he liked to play with people instead. Lyndon Johnson, a student of Roosevelt, also enjoyed intrastaff competition, but President Truman did not play this game.

The manner in which President Truman ran the White House evolved as time went on, but at all times it reflected his informality, his accessibility and openness, and his preference for rapid, intuitive decision making over careful, analytical staff work. His White House could best be visualized as a wheel with spokes: each spoke was one of his key aides, with different (but sometimes overlapping) areas of responsibility. Harry Truman would never have felt comfortable if access to him was controlled by a single person. No organization chart of the Truman White House ever existed, and no one except the President himself gave any of the senior staff a direct order. I was a major beneficiary of this unstructured system, but I must admit that the process of decision making sometimes dismayed me. Given my belief in exhaustive preparation, its casualness and frequent superficiality ran counter to my training.

LIBERAL VERSUS CONSERVATIVE

Sam Rosenman had taught me how to do my job and best serve the President, but I had not yet developed a personal philosophy of governance, or a clear sense of what the long-range, fundamental purposes of government should be. In confronting the challenges that lay ahead, I relied to a considerable degree on basic values formed in my youth. Facing the enormous range of postwar issues, I found the liberalism of my uncle, Clark McAdams, and the basic principles of character and compassion that my parents had tried to instill in me were the bedrock of my beliefs.

Despite the President's preference for harmony, an important struggle took place in his Administration between liberal and conservative factions. My values pulled me decisively toward the liberals in that confrontation over politics and policy. The President himself combined some contradictory attitudes, usually supporting specific New Deal or liberal policies when given a clear choice, but often appointing conservatives to high Cabinet positions. He had populist values which usually translated into liberal positions—but not without tension, for his simple style contrasted with that of many of the powerful intellectuals and ideologues of the New Deal, and he never felt comfortable with them. As he replaced them in the first two years of his Administration, the conservatives became stronger in the Cabinet, and Rosenman's departure robbed the liberals of their strongest voice inside the White House.

The leader of the conservative faction was John Snyder, a St. Louis banker who became Secretary of the Treasury in 1946 after Fred Vinson became Chief Justice. With Rosenman gone, Snyder became the dominant influence on domestic policy. I did not anticipate he would resent the fact that my rise had placed another liberal close to the President; we had been friends in St. Louis, and at first, with our offices close to each other in the East Wing before he transferred to Treasury, we worked together as colleagues. In January of 1946, for example, we exchanged friendly handwritten personal notes of encouragement and support; in mine to him, I offered the hope that the coming year would "bring more gratification" to him in his "difficult" job, and said I looked forward to our continued friendship and collaboration. But as I became more involved in policy, I came to the conclusion that Snyder and I would always differ on many basic issues.

In the early days of the Truman Administration, Snyder and Vaughan were probably his two closest friends—which meant that in almost every domestic policy discussion, President Truman would hear a conservative position, aggressively advanced. In one Cabinet meeting in late 1946, Snyder, annoyed at those who believed wages had to be allowed to rise after the war, even at the risk of inflation, burst out, "These people have enough. They wouldn't even know how to spend the money if they got any more!" This was typical of Snyder, who was openly probusiness and anti–New Deal on every issue. Snyder and I never argued in front of the President, but, as our differences sharpened, our relationship became quite formal and antagonistic. At times the situation resembled submarine warfare—almost constant, but conducted out of the President's view.

Most of the rest of the Cabinet was conservative as well. Snyder was usually supported by Clinton Anderson, a former (and future) member of Congress whom the President had appointed Secretary of Agriculture in the hope of improving relations between the White House and Capitol Hill. In addition, three other conservatives replaced more liberal Roosevelt Cabinet members: James Byrnes in place of Edward Stettinius at State, Lewis Schwellenbach for Frances Perkins at Labor, and Tom Clark of Texas as Attorney General (after the abrupt firing of the patrician from Philadelphia, Francis Biddle). Forrestal also spoke for a conservative point of view on any domestic issues that affected the military. Two Roosevelt holdovers, Harold Ickes at Interior and Henry Wallace at Commerce, remained in the first Truman Cabinet as advocates of liberal positions, but both were personally difficult and identified closely with Roosevelt. President Truman justifiably distrusted and rarely listened to them, and within a year, after much bitterness, both were gone.

By virtue of both his position and his great wealth, Wallace's successor as Secretary of Commerce, Averell Harriman, should have also been a stalwart conservative. But Harriman, the son of the builder of the Union

Pacific, had left the Republican party in 1928. A disciple of Harry Hopkins, Roosevelt's crusading adviser, Harriman had a strong sense of obligation toward the disadvantaged, instilled in him, he told me, by his parents and his sister. To my surprise and pleasure, he was a frequent ally in the battles of 1946 through 1948, generally supporting liberal positions, although he sometimes felt we were going too far. It was, for me, the beginning of a long and productive friendship, which was to reach its climax when we stood together in the great debate over Vietnam in 1968.

My other adversary on policy was a member of the White House staff, John Steelman. As time went on, our relationship became increasingly confrontational. To a certain extent, the Presidential staff divided into factions grouped around the two of us. Steelman, a large man with a convivial and engaging manner, had been a sociology and economics professor at Alabama College. His government career had begun in the New Deal under the tutelage of Frances Perkins, but he came to ally himself with John Snyder on domestic issues. Our differences went beyond ideology: they stemmed in part, I believe, from our very different styles. Like Vaughan, he disliked having an office in the East Wing, substantially further from the Oval Office than mine. He was determined to place himself above all other Presidential aides, although President Truman had often said he would not tolerate such internal ranking. By the end of 1947 Steelman allowed this drive for position to get so far out of control, that, to the surprise of his colleagues on the White House staff, he sent out Christmas cards signed "The Assistant to the President," and had special letterhead stationery printed with the same title. But the President made it clear that his senior assistants were all equal and that no one at the White House had seniority over the rest of the staff.

President Truman wanted Steelman around as a "conciliator," a link to labor who could work out compromises between contending factions. But, as President Truman told an interviewer after he left the White House, Steelman "wasn't a man to make decisions or judgments on his own and I didn't rely on him for that. I didn't want that."[3]

In theory, I concentrated on policy and planning, while Steelman focused on operations. Originally, he had primary responsibility for housing, education, surplus property disposal, strategic stockpiling, manpower, and labor, but he was supposed to stay out of foreign and defense policy entirely. In practice, of course, the line between policy planning and operations was very fine, sometimes nonexistent; often President Truman simply instructed me to handle a matter in an area which Steelman thought was properly his. This was bound to upset Steelman, and the friction between us eventually became common knowledge in Washington.

In those less complicated times the difference between liberals and conservatives seemed relatively clear-cut to me. Battles ranged over many issues, but the fundamentals usually boiled down to the difference between the welfare of the many and the privilege of the few. The conservatives believed the country had had enough of New Deal experimentation, and required retrenchment before anything else. Liberals like me thought the postwar world required us to address many long-deferred problems, from race to education to housing and better working conditions. In retrospect, it may seem simple; in fact, it seemed fairly straightforward at the time, and I was committed to the liberal agenda, although I approached strategy and tactics from a highly pragmatic point of view.

Foreign policy was a different matter. An enormous difference existed in the quality of the people on the President's personal staff and those working on foreign relations. Most of the men who had been drawn to Washington during the war had originally planned to return to private life, but many stayed on to serve Harry Truman, whom they gradually came to respect. Thus, the Truman Administration was served in the foreign policy field by the most remarkable group of men ever collected in the American government in peacetime. Some among them have become part of American history—men like Marshall, Leahy, Eisenhower, Bradley, Acheson, Harriman, Kennan, Lovett, Forrestal, Rusk, Bohlen, McCloy, Nitze, and Murphy—but there were others, less known to the public, who also served with distinction, including William Clayton, James Webb, Frank Pace, Robert Patterson, Frank Wisner, Llewellyn Thompson, Bromley Smith, Lucius Battle, Philip Jessup, George McGhee, and Carl Humelsine. It would be my pleasure and privilege to work closely with most of these men, both the famed and the forgotten. At the time I became Special Counsel, though, my involvement in foreign policy issues was limited, and I did not begin my new job with any thought that eventually my greatest involvement and satisfaction would come in this area.

MARGARET AND BESS TRUMAN

The factionalism in the White House unfortunately affected my relationship with the President's daughter, Margaret. She was the greatly beloved only child of an older father (Harry Truman was forty when she was born). At the time I arrived at the White House, she was only twenty-one years old, but she conducted herself with dignity and grace during her father's tenure as President. In this regard, I felt she was a welcome contrast to the Roosevelt children (and to many children of later Presidents), who constantly got their father into trouble by their high-handed and arrogant activities.

Although Margaret never was rude, I gradually became aware that in the White House factional intrigues she had sided with Harry Vaughan and John Snyder—men from Missouri whom she had known since she was a small child. Snyder and Vaughan had criticized me to Margaret, but I doubt she was aware that policy differences between liberal and conservative groups in the White House were the real cause of friction.

I did not realize how serious the problem was until Margaret sat next to Stuart Symington one night at a dinner party. Perhaps unaware of how close Stuart and I were, she criticized me in harsh terms. The next morning he called me: "I think I ought to tell you that Margaret really has her gun sights aimed at you. I got one hell of a speech last night about how since you came into her father's White House you've been getting all the good publicity." I was grateful for the warning, but there was nothing I could do about it. I worked for the President, and did what he wanted.

The coolness between Margaret Truman and me lasted many years. However, almost forty years later, she and John Snyder approached me to ask if I would serve as the chairman of the committee to celebrate the centennial of President Truman's birth in 1884. I was startled, but gratified—especially because the request had come from these two people. It meant a great deal to me, as did the respect and friendship with Margaret that followed. I think that she had come to understand that I revered her father.

Fortunately, my relations with Mrs. Truman were not affected by the strain with Margaret. Over the years our friendship grew, and I developed for her a very real affection and deep respect. Bess Truman was a pillar of strength to her husband, a person of sound judgment to whom he was devoted.

Because she was so retiring in public, most people did not realize how important her role was in President Truman's life. Harry Truman had given his heart to Bess Wallace years before she agreed to marry him. He told me more than once that he fell in love with her when they were in the fifth grade.

They made a splendid team. President Truman was not always analytical or sufficiently detached in evaluating the people around him. Mrs. Truman often had better insight than her husband into the quality and trustworthiness of the people who had gathered around him, and helped to steer him away from people whom he liked but who might have gotten the Administration into trouble.

One night at a small White House dinner with a few staff members present, the President began to tease his wife gently, but with great pride: "None of you probably knows this," he said, "but in her youth, my wife was a well-known athlete in Independence." This news did indeed surprise us; it hardly fit our image of Bess Truman.

"Now, Harry, that's enough," Mrs. Truman said, somewhat sharply.

"She had quite a distinction as an athlete," the President went on.

"Harry, I said that's enough."

"No, you hide your light under a bushel, dear, and I want to tell everyone about it. In her youth Bess was the high school shotput champion." Mrs. Truman continued to fuss, obviously thinking that being a shotputter was about the most unfeminine distinction a woman could attain—but she was also tickled at the way he had "boasted on her."

Bess Truman detested anything that had a trace of ostentation. On one occasion I saw her quash an effort by J. K. Vardaman to arrange a large motorcade of limousines for a Presidential visit to New York on the grounds that it was unseemly. She saw the ceremony and protocol of the White House for what it was, never let it turn her head, and was always ready to bring her husband back down to earth if she felt that he might take it too seriously.

People often remarked on the amount of time Mrs. Truman spent in Independence while her husband was President. Why wasn't she constantly at his side in the White House? Under today's more intense public scrutiny of Presidents, such prolonged and frequent absences by a First Lady would create a public-relations problem, and political necessity would force her to spend more time at the White House. But she genuinely disliked the pomp and ceremony of the White House, and preferred playing cards with her circle of old friends back home. To her, Washington was always just an interlude in her life; Independence was home. She was sincerely unaffected by being First Lady, and never tried to follow in the giant footprints of Eleanor Roosevelt, who had changed forever the boundaries of what a President's wife could do while her husband was in office.

President Truman genuinely missed her when she was away, and wrote her or spoke to her on the telephone every day. But they understood each other perfectly, and he accepted without complaint her stays in Independence. All in all, she was the most important person in his life, and played an immeasurable, but vital, role in the history of the Truman Presidency.

DISASTER: THE 1946 ELECTIONS

The turning point in the battle between the liberals and the conservatives for President Truman's heart and mind came unexpectedly; as often occurs in politics, a major disaster led to the turnaround. It was the first postwar, post-Roosevelt election, the Congressional elections of 1946. I accompanied President Truman to Independence, Missouri, where he and his wife voted. After voting, we began the trip back to Washington by train, playing poker with a group that included Charlie Ross and the two senior wire service reporters, Merriman Smith of the United Press and Tony Vaccaro of the Associated Press. The returns trickled in as we rode east. About the time the train passed Cincinnati we realized that the impossible had happened, and President Truman would face a Republican Congress for the next two years. Furious at a national beef shortage, scornful of many of the same homespun characteristics that were later to immortalize Harry Truman, and swept up in a simple and brilliant Republican slogan—"Had Enough?"—the voters wiped out the large Democratic majorities in both chambers, turning Congress over to the Republicans for the first time since 1928. It was one of the most decisive, sweeping expressions of voter sentiment in this century. As New Dealers fell across the country, a new generation of Republicans, including Richard Nixon and Joseph McCarthy, entered Congress. (Among the new Democratic faces in the House were the twenty-nine-year-old war hero from Massachusetts, John F. Kennedy, and the future Senate Majority Leader, Robert Byrd of West Virginia.)

The President showed little emotion and made few comments as the bad news continued to roll in. Our poker game continued until 2 A.M., and his only comment was that he regretted the result mainly because it would weaken his efforts internationally. I was amazed at how calm he seemed in the face of political disaster. We returned to Washington, to find Undersecretary of State Dean Acheson waiting alone on the platform at Union Station, an elegant symbol of loyalty at this political low point that President Truman would long remember.

The conventional political wisdom at that point was simple: Harry Truman was a caretaker President. In a proposal symptomatic of the President's weakened position, a promising young Democratic Senator from Arkansas named J. William Fulbright, who had been deeply impressed by the British parliamentary system from his experience as a Rhodes Scholar, suggested that President Truman appoint the senior Republican Senator, Arthur Vandenberg, as Secretary of State—which, with the Vice Presidency vacant, would make Vandenberg next in line for the Presidency.* Then, Fulbright suggested, President Truman should resign the Presidency in favor of Vandenberg. President Truman, in response to this strange proposal, thereafter forever referred to Fulbright as "Senator Halfbright."

On the afternoon of his return from Independence, President Truman called a staff meeting and told us the election debacle had filled him with a new sense of freedom. Although no one realized it at the time, the 1946 election also shifted the equation within the Administration in favor of

*This was in the days before the Twenty-fifth Amendment defined a formal procedure for filling the Vice Presidency whenever it is vacant.

the liberals. The conservatives had pushed a set of domestic policies that left the American public uncertain as to what sort of a President Harry Truman was. Until the 1946 election he seemed to be moving away from the New Deal. To me, the message of the election was clear: a Democrat must run as a Democrat, not as a warmed-over Republican.

THE MONDAY-NIGHT GROUP

Although the conservatives controlled the Cabinet, at the sub-Cabinet level there were still many liberals, either committed New Dealers or else a new generation of post-Roosevelt officials who felt that new circumstances required new solutions. They believed that the basic tenets of the New Deal should be adapted to the postwar environment, not abandoned. One of these men, Oscar R. Ewing, had an idea. At the end of 1946, he decided that the liberals within the Administration needed some sort of informal network to discuss issues and influence policy. Ewing, the acting Chairman of the Democratic National Committee and soon to become the Administrator of the Federal Security Agency,* invited a half dozen liberal sub-Cabinet officials to dinner at his apartment at the Wardman Park Apartments, and suggested they meet on a regular basis to further the liberal agenda.

I was not invited to the first of the Monday-Night dinners. Matt Connelly, a friend of Ewing's, attended, but decided the next day that he should not attend future meetings. He suggested I be invited instead, as I was more involved in policy issues than he was. Thus, almost accidentally, at the same time as I was looking for ways to encourage more liberal policies, circumstances and personalities combined to bring me into the most effective group of political activists with whom I have ever been associated.

The core members of the Monday-Night Group, in addition to our host, were: Leon Keyserling, Vice Chairman and later Chairman of the President's Council of Economic Advisors; C. Girard Davidson, Assistant Secretary of the Interior; Charles F. Brannan, Assistant Secretary and later Secretary of Agriculture; David A. Morse, the brilliant young Assistant Secretary of Labor who was soon to turn down an offer to become Secretary of Labor in order to become the Director-General of the International Labor Organization, a post he held for twenty-two years; and J. Donald Kingsley, soon to become Ewing's deputy at the Federal Security Agency. Keyserling was the intellectual of our circle, a respected but

*Later upgraded to become the Department of Health, Education, and Welfare, and now the Department of Health and Human Services.

refreshingly controversial economist; he was already in constant warfare with Snyder, Anderson, Steelman, and others over economic policy, and he welcomed the opportunity to build support for his views with the rest of us. President Truman was told by Ewing, Connelly, and me about the Monday-Night meetings, but he never attended or asked to meet with us as a group.

Starting at the beginning of 1947, we met every second Monday evening at the Wardman Park. The meetings followed a fairly set pattern: we would gather at 6 P.M. in Ewing's apartment for a drink, and within a half hour we were seated at the dining room table, eating a fine steak dinner. After dinner we moved into Ewing's spacious living room to continue the conversation. We kept no records or notes.

In the absence of a regular forum such as the one provided by Ewing, most of us would have seen each other only in chance meetings, and we would have never had an opportunity to develop and advance common positions. It was clear from the outset that the Monday-Night Group's effectiveness depended entirely on our ability to influence the President. Because I saw more of the President than anyone else in the group, it was agreed that I would be the conduit for our ideas. We also agreed that each of us would individually promote those ideas which represented a consensus of the group. We felt outnumbered by the conservatives within the Administration and misunderstood by most of the old New Dealers and ideological liberals on the outside. In consensus we saw strength, and we tried to work toward unified positions on key issues.

We did not include in the group "professional liberals," whose ardor and search for ideological purity outweighed their discretion and their judgment. This decision reflected the perennial struggle in government between the ideal and the possible, the perfect and the practical. There is no simple answer to this conflict; a government that represents all the people must balance many pressures. I have always respected the sincerity of those who commit themselves to the single-minded pursuit of an objective, but I am not one of them: to me, the question has always been, What is the most that can be achieved—in short, what is the best *possible* outcome?

I brought my own ideas to the Wardman Park to test them against the collective wisdom of the others. The Monday-Night Group helped shape my views and recommendations for a strong Civil Rights Act, desegregation of the armed forces, a special session of Congress in 1948, unification of the armed services and creation of the National Security Council, the veto of the Taft-Hartley Act (for which we invented the phrase, used repeatedly by President Truman, the "Slave Labor Act"), Social Security, and much of the strategy for the 1948 campaign. When I left the government in 1950, Charles Murphy, my successor at the White House, became a permanent member of the group; I continued to attend most of the meetings.

In the last three years of the Truman Administration, with the Korean War overshadowing other events, the group gradually lost its cohesiveness and drifted apart, meeting less and less frequently. Its participants, though, would always remember it with special emotion. More than forty years later, David Morse still felt, as he told me, that the Monday-Night Group made him "part of a brotherhood that gave us a larger vision of what the government should, and could, be." We all felt that way in those days when the postwar world was still so very young, and idealism—the dream that we could marshal the power and authority of the government for the benefit of all mankind—was still so high.

The memory of the group never died among its participants. From time to time we would reassemble, like aging veterans of some ancient war, to relive our special fellowship. The most memorable reunion was held over twenty-five years later, in 1973, as Leon Keyserling was battling terminal cancer. Everyone except Donald Kingsley, who had died, met at Keyserling's home for an immensely moving evening of laughter and remembering. After dinner, our host, who knew he would never see this group together again, handed out an "Ode to the Wardman Park Monday Night Steak Club" and asked each of the wives present to read a verse about the man on her right. As poetry it left something to be desired, but that evening had a special emotional impact. Mary Keyserling began by reading her husband's verse about Oscar Ewing:

When we gathered on Mondays with Oscar Ross Ewing,
It was certain that something momentous was brewing;
But of "side" and false pride he completely did lack,
So we called him by nothing more pompous than "Jack."

I received the following farewell from my old friend, who had taught us all so much:

The glamorous Clifford was much besides tall,
So his merit soon made him leader of us all;
Clark's key to successes with Harry S Truman
Was simply that both were so very human.

5

The Labor Wars of 1946

MY FIRST CRISIS

In 1946 two of the most important parts of the American economy—coal and the railroads—were almost simultaneously crippled by nationwide strikes. These strikes brought me into extensive contact with the President, and led to a sharp disagreement between me and some of my White House colleagues. In the end, the President sided with me, with far-ranging results for my career.

The crisis began with coal. Worker demands that had been deferred during the war could be contained no longer. On March 31, 1946, 400,000 miners went on strike. Then in May, two stubborn railroad union leaders defied the President. The result was a period of nine months in which Presidential leadership was tested as it had not been in the domestic arena since before World War II.

Railroads and coal were then what airplanes and oil are today, only more so. Coal was still king, providing the fuel for 95 percent of all locomotives, 55 percent of all industrial energy, and 62 percent of all electrical power. As for the railroads, in 1946 they still played a central role in American life, far more than it is possible to imagine today. Most Americans traveled by train rather than by car or airplane, and with interstate trucking still in its infancy, the rails carried most of the nation's freight. A railroad strike, especially if combined with a coal strike, could paralyze the nation.

The results of the coal workers' walkout were immediate: steel and automobile production dropped; railroad service was curtailed, and wartime dimouts to save energy were reinstituted in twenty-two states. The President ordered government seizure of the mines, placing them under the control of Secretary of the Interior Julius Krug. In late May the two sides reached an agreement that we thought would give us peace with the coal miners, and the President turned his attention to the railroads.

Wage negotiations between the railroads and the rail unions collapsed in April, 1946, just as temporary peace descended on the coal front. Eighteen of the twenty unions involved in the complex negotiations agreed to continue talking to management, but the two most powerful—the Brotherhood of Locomotive Engineers and the Brotherhood of Railroad Trainmen—flatly refused. The leaders of these two unions, Alvanley Johnston and A. F. Whitney, had been close political allies of President Truman; now, however, they refused his personal request to avert a national emergency. Instead, they called a general strike for May 18.

During the first twenty-five days of the thirty-day period until the date the unions had set for the strike, the President left the problem in the hands of his chief labor adviser in the White House, John Steelman. Still in uniform and housed in the East Wing, I was spending enough time in the West Wing to see firsthand the growing apprehension of the President and his advisers at the open defiance of the government by Johnston and Whitney.

In mid-May, President Truman called Johnston and Whitney to the White House, and in their presence signed an executive order, seizing the railroads in the event of a strike. At the same time, with the nation running low on coal, President Truman made his first move in the coal strike, ordering the Secretary of the Interior to seize the coal mines and force the miners back to work under federal supervision. But on May 23, after delaying the strike for five days, Johnston and Whitney sent President Truman a note brusquely rejecting any compromise. They ordered their men off the rail lines at 4 P.M. The greatest transportation tie-up in the nation's history had begun.

President Truman now faced a fundamental test of his Presidency. About one million workers were out on strike, including 164,000 coal miners who were still defying his seizure of the mines. Did he have the personal strength and political power to deal with American labor? If he did not, how could he deal with the darkening world situation, so graphically outlined by Winston Churchill in his "Iron Curtain" speech at Fulton, Missouri, only ten weeks earlier?

The President called a Cabinet meeting on Friday, May 24, 1946, to discuss the situation. Feeling oddly out of place in my naval uniform, I sat behind the Cabinet table in a chair along the wall, and witnessed

Presidential anger I could not have previously imagined. He had fumed overnight about the note from Johnston and Whitney. He said he wanted to speak to a special Saturday session of Congress the next day, May 25, and demand the toughest labor law in history. He would ask for the authority to draft strikers into the armed forces if the national security was threatened. He said he wanted to speak over a national radio hookup at 10 P.M. that evening to prepare the American public for his action. Then he pulled out of his jacket pocket a handwritten statement. "Here is what I want to say," he said, handing it to Charlie Ross.

It was surely one of the most intemperate documents ever written by a President. His opponents had "flouted, vilified, and misrepresented" his positions, the President wrote; Congress was "weak-kneed," lacked "intestinal fortitude," and was filled with "Russian Senators and Representatives." For his closing comment, the President had written an astonishing sentence: "Let's put transportation and production back to work, *hang a few traitors,* and make our own country safe for democracy." It was the sort of blunt "Trumanesque" language for which he later became famous, but if he spoke in this manner to the nation, the President would do himself immense damage, creating the impression he was losing control of both himself and the government.

As soon as the Cabinet meeting ended, Ross went to the Oval Office to see the President alone. A gentle, unassuming man who had been a friend of Harry Truman's since high school, Ross could speak to the President like no one else. He told him that this message would backfire. The President, feeling better after having let off some steam, recognized that Ross was right, and told Charlie to ask me to draft a message more moderate in tone but still tough enough to make the point.

At the time, the President's original handwritten message struck me as perilously out of control. I thought he had been saved from disaster only by the wise and firm intervention of Charlie Ross. Later, when I came to know the President better, I discovered it was not unusual for him to work off some of his frustration by putting his innermost thoughts on paper. We all have moments when we allow the deeper recesses of our minds to entertain delicious but private thoughts about the vicious things we would like to do to our adversaries. Harry Truman had the habit of writing some of these private thoughts down—some were shared with no one, others shown only to a few intimates. If he had not been President, they would have had little importance.* He expected his trusted inner staff to prevent him from going public with his fury.**

*The undelivered May 24, 1946, message on labor, for example, did not become public for over twenty years.

**This fail-safe system to protect him faltered once in a while—most notably when the President,

When Ross told me to draft a new message, only five hours were left until the President was scheduled to speak to the nation. This was the first time I ever worked in the White House under the time pressures that are both the glory and the burden of service to a President. Ideas and advice came in from my old boss, Sam Rosenman, who arrived late in the day at the President's request. Steelman, Ross, and Snyder later joined Rosenman and me in the Cabinet Room to review the draft. Skipping dinner, we produced a draft around 8 P.M. and I took each page into the President as we finished it.

I tried to express the President's anger in more moderate words with an opening sentence calling this "the greatest crisis in this country since Pearl Harbor." His anger of the night before had worked itself out, and the President, calm and focused, took that bit of hyperbole out, but left in the harsh sentence that followed: "The crisis of Pearl Harbor was the result of action by a foreign enemy, whereas the crisis tonight is caused by a group of men within our own country who place their private interests above the welfare of the nation."

The speech was put into final form only fifteen minutes before air time. I walked with the President downstairs to the room on the ground floor of the White House from which it would be broadcast, and watched him deliver it, standing, instead of sitting, in front of the radio microphones. As soon as the speech was over, the President, Ross, and I walked over to the East Wing, where he posed for the newsreel cameras. Then he met with members of the Cabinet to review the next steps. It had been a long and dramatic day, but the railroads were still not running, and the nation was heading for paralysis.

SATURDAY DRAMA

While Steelman was closeted with Johnston and Whitney at the Statler Hotel, I spent the morning working on the President's speech, scheduled for the highly unusual Saturday Joint Session of Congress. Pleased with the previous night's speech, the President asked me to draft this crucial speech.

About an hour before the speech, Steelman called. He said that Johnston and Whitney were feeling the mounting public pressure, and there was still a small chance for a settlement before the President addressed Congress. Rosenman and I wrote an alternative draft of portions of the

---

enraged at a bad review of his daughter's singing, fired off his famous letter to *Washington Post* music critic Paul Hume, mailing it himself in order to prevent his staff from trying to stop it. Fortunately, this was generally accepted as the act of a devoted father, and it actually enhanced his reputation.

speech with softer language, to be used if the strike was settled before the speech was delivered, and rushed both versions to the President.

The situation had reached fever pitch: the President delayed his departure for Capitol Hill, as I tracked Steelman down again at the Statler—there was nothing new, although he thought he was making progress. Then, running out of the office so fast that I left my cap behind (I was in uniform), I joined the departing Presidential motorcade, handing President Truman the final pages as I climbed into his car.

He went directly to the House chamber, where he received a tumultuous welcome reflecting the nation's frenzied mood and the anti-union sentiment raging in Congress. I peeled off from the rest of the Presidential party and went to an anteroom near the House floor to await a call that I hoped would come from Steelman.

Meanwhile, the President began his speech, attacking Johnston and Whitney for their "obstinate arrogance," and asking for emergency legislation which would give him broad authority to deal with the crisis. The legislation would permit the President not only to seize industries but to subject any labor leader to an injunction and contempt proceedings, and provide for criminal penalties for violators.

The telephone in the anteroom in which I was waiting rang. It was Steelman: "*We have an agreement!* The men are going back, on the President's terms." As Steelman talked, I wrote out a brief note: "Word has just been received that the railroad strike has been settled on the terms proposed by the President."

I ran into the House and handed my note to Les Biffle, Secretary of the Senate, who was sitting just below the podium. As I entered, President Truman reached the climax of his speech, a request for authority to draft "into the armed forces of the United States all workers who are on strike against their government." As the members of Congress thunderously applauded this proposal, Biffle handed the President my note. He smiled slightly, waited for the noise to die down, and then read it to Congress. The House chamber erupted in cheering—longer, louder, and more sustained than anything he had experienced before or was ever to experience again in Congress.

The railroad crisis had ended with a complete victory for President Truman. The scene was so dramatic that for a while some people thought it had been staged, as Senator Wayne Morse charged publicly, only to apologize after a talk with the President. For the first time since the end of the war, President Truman had shown strength and resolve under pressure. He had enraged big labor, but he calculated, correctly, that this would pass in time.

For my part, the railroad strike had an unforeseen consequence: the President promoted me to Special Counsel, and I left the Navy.

SHOWDOWNS—WITH JOHN L. LEWIS AND JOHN STEELMAN

Late in 1946, the President successfully faced another challenge to his authority, which changed his political fortunes and revived his spirits, and dramatically affected my standing and visibility within the White House. This was one of the greatest conflicts in American labor history, the celebrated showdown between President Truman and John L. Lewis.

A good crisis needs a colorful central character, and the coal strike of 1946 certainly had one in the person of John Llewellyn Lewis. For almost thirty years, Lewis had been the undisputed boss of his huge and powerful union. A former miner himself, Lewis had earned the unwavering loyalty of his rank and file over many years by fighting for much-needed reforms in working conditions and pay. Everything about him was dramatic; his personality and speaking style could not be duplicated in today's homogenized television era. I cannot improve on the portrait of him by Cabell Phillips of *The New York Times:*

> A figure of almost unbelievable power and picturesqueness . . . a man of ponderous and majestic bearing with a billowing crown of gray hair and dark, baleful eyes peering from under immense eyebrows. His scowl had an Olympian ferocity, and his speech the cavernous tone and the measured cadence of a nineteenth-century Thespian.[1]

On the eve of the 1946 elections, Lewis's monumental ego and ambition led him to demand the reopening of the entire contract based on a minor provision of the May accords. Lewis made an explicit threat: if we did not renegotiate the entire contract, he would bring the nation to a standstill.

For the first time I took an active role in a major policy debate as an *advocate,* not simply as a speech writer. In my view, President Truman had reached a turning point: Lewis's behavior constituted a direct threat to the President's political survival. If he yielded to Lewis he would have great difficulty governing for the next two years of Franklin Roosevelt's unfinished term and surely would not be elected on his own in 1948.

I was heavily outnumbered in the discussions that raged at the White House in the first two weeks of November 1946. Julius Krug and Attorney General Tom Clark sided with me in advocating a tough line, but, fearing Lewis's power, they were considerably more cautious. On the other side of the debate were John Steelman and his supporters. They advocated a policy of conciliation and compromise, arguing that President Truman could not win against the formidable John L. Lewis.

The battle lines on this issue later gave rise to the erroneous view in some Washington quarters that I was a conservative. While it was true that I had advocated a tough line against Lewis and in May had drafted the railroad speech, in policy debates within the White House I almost always favored labor's positions and objectives. In argument after argument with Snyder, Steelman, Anderson, and others, I was on labor's side—favoring a position, I felt, that would reduce inequality in American life. However, as Special Counsel to the President, I was a firm advocate for the powers and position of the President. It was my responsibility, as I saw it, to protect both the office and the man. I decided to weigh in heavily against compromise and retreat. Lewis's threats were directed at both the Presidency and Harry Truman personally. If he succeeded in breaking the agreement he had reached with the Administration only five months earlier, I saw no end to the erosion of Presidential authority.

The stage was thus set for my first open collision with Steelman, which took place late on Saturday night, November 16, 1946, after the annual White House News Photographers Association dinner. The President knew that events were coming to a head, and he asked Interior Secretary Krug, Attorney General Clark, Steelman, and me to meet him in the study on the second floor of the family quarters around midnight. Still in our dinner jackets, we debated our next moves until the early morning. The lateness of the hour, the intensity of the situation, the legacy of the election, and perhaps a certain amount of alcohol consumed by some people during the dinner all lent an odd air to the meeting. The combination of fatigue and tension made the meeting far more candid, and hence contentious, than would normally be the case.

Steelman, wanting to make a new deal with Lewis, argued that a strike could be averted with relatively small concessions. I argued strongly with Steelman, urging President Truman to stand firm and resist pressure for any further accommodation: the majority of the people were opposed to Lewis's grandstanding, and if the President held his ground, Lewis would be beaten in the court of public opinion. No one union or person can be bigger than the country, I argued, concluding somewhat dramatically, "*Mr. President, you have to take him on.*"

As our long and exhausting night of debate came to an end, the President made his decision. We would seek a court injunction against Lewis, and, if necessary, file civil and criminal charges for violation of contract and striking against the government. It would be, the President told us, "a fight to the finish with John L. Lewis." Steelman was openly furious at losing the President's support.

With the decision made, we showered, changed into casual clothes, and boarded the Presidential plane, the *Sacred Cow,* for the first of President Truman's many trips to his favorite vacation spot, Key West. Seething, Steelman did not join us, and instead left Washington for a hunting vacation.

We followed the situation closely by a special telephone hookup to Key West. Partly to show the nation that he was still Commander in Chief, however, the President included a remarkable (and somewhat hazardous) event in his vacation in which I participated: a dive to a depth of 440 feet aboard a captured German submarine. The superior quality of the German vessel, compared to our own submarines, greatly impressed both of us, but the President's security men were horrified at the risk he had taken.

On Monday, November 18, Attorney General Clark took Lewis to court, obtaining from a federal judge in the U.S. District Court an order directing Lewis to cancel his plans for a strike on November 20. Lewis thumbed his nose at the court order, and, on his original November 20 deadline, once more ordered his workers out on strike. After talking to the President, I asked Tom Clark to request the court to cite Lewis for contempt. In early December, the federal judge found the United Mine Workers guilty of contempt, slapping a whopping $3.5 million fine on the union and an additional $10,000 on Lewis personally. At our request, criminal charges were dropped. We did not want Lewis in jail; we wanted the strike settled.

Lewis was now in a quandary. The President and the courts were united against him, he faced an enormous fine, and jail remained a distinct possibility. To ease the pressure, he tried to call President Truman directly. I recommended that the President not take Lewis's call because a conversation might take the heat off Lewis.

This was a risky decision. The nation was running out of coal in early December, and people were—quite literally—feeling cold as coal supplies and "strikebreaker coal" ran short. Nonetheless, the President agreed not to speak to Lewis or any of his representatives while the UMW was still out on strike. For the rest of the crisis, we rebuffed every one of Lewis's increasingly frantic attempts to send negotiators to the White House.

The President's vacation had ended on November 23. We plotted strategy on the flight back to Washington, and upon my return, I set up a mini–command center in the Cabinet Room to coordinate the next steps. After careful consideration, the President instructed me to write a tough speech for delivery on Sunday, December 8. Our plan was to create unbearable public pressure on Lewis to capitulate. Both the President and I were acutely aware that this speech would come on the fifth anniversary of Roosevelt's Pearl Harbor speech, and we felt this symbolism would further strengthen his appeal to the nation.

December 7 was, like the Saturday of the railroad crisis six months earlier, a day charged with the excitement that surrounds a major confrontation—and the theatrical John L. Lewis gave it an additional drama that the railroad crisis had lacked. We made sure during the day that rumors of the tough measures we were planning to announce reached the UMW. In the Cabinet Room, I drafted a speech beginning with these words:

> I bring to you tonight a report on a major American disaster. By coincidence, it was just five years ago . . . that my predecessor spoke of another American disaster—Pearl Harbor. This present crisis has elements which make it just as ominous. The attention of every American—and, in fact, of cold and hungry people in countries all over the world—is centered on the coal strike which is paralyzing our entire nation. . . .

The speech was never given. By Saturday Lewis knew that his dilemma would only get worse if he continued to defy the President. At four o'clock that afternoon, he called a sudden press conference. As we listened over the radio in the Oval Office, Lewis spoke in wearied but measured cadences, ordering all his workers "to return to work immediately under the wages and conditions of employment in existence on and before November 20, 1946."

The Lord of Labor had capitulated. President Truman had succeeded where so many others, including FDR, had failed—he had trimmed the invincible Lewis down to size. He permitted himself a brief celebration in the Oval Office right after Lewis's surrender. As we celebrated, the President recalled what he felt was his toughest decision—to rebuff all Lewis's attempts to open a dialogue over the previous two weeks.

"The White House is open to anybody with legitimate business," he said, "but not to that son of a bitch."

AFTERMATH

It was, journalists and labor experts agreed, the end of an era in American industrial relations—and it was the beginning of a new era for Harry Truman. He was praised effusively by the same journalists and commentators who had dismissed him a few weeks earlier (and would write him off again in 1948). Arthur Krock, the Washington Bureau Chief of *The New York Times,* wrote that "the President has greatly regained stature as a national leader." Joseph and Stewart Alsop called it "the first break he has had in considerably more than a year."

The press became aware I had played an important role in the showdown with Lewis. The Alsop brothers, for example, said that I "deserved a large share of the credit" for the victory, and that the President had "ceased to consult John R. Steelman and the other advocates of appeasement." White House Press Secretary Charlie Ross joked to reporters, "All I do around here is answer questions about Clark Clifford."

A most embarrassing event took place soon thereafter, at the Gridiron Dinner, an annual event during which members of the Gridiron Club, all senior Washington journalists, entertain high government officials and other guests with irreverent skits. I have attended forty-six consecutive Gridiron Dinners since my first one in 1946, and have seen some memorable events at them. But only once, in 1947, did I wish deeply, with all my heart, that I was somewhere else. For on that night, with President Truman watching, one of the skits showed him as a ventriloquist's dummy sitting on the lap of a smug, heavily made-up Clark Clifford. I was profoundly upset, and spent a restless night wondering if the President had been offended. On Monday morning, I went into his office alone, and said, "Mr. President, I just want to express to you my deep embarrassment at the skit at the Gridiron. I wish neither of us had been there." He smiled for an instant, and said, "Clark, pay it no attention. That is what Washington is all about. Anyway, I am the target, not you, and they will always find something to use against me."

Newspaper articles about me began to appear, invariably following a standard pattern, describing me as a conservative because of my position in the showdown with Lewis and my strong views about the dangers of Stalinism. I did nothing to enlighten them as to my belief in liberalism, for I knew that if I publicly identified myself with any ideology, my efforts would only leave the impression that I had a personal agenda independent of the President's interests.

Part III

THE ORIGINS OF THE COLD WAR

6

Churchill at Fulton

A TRAIN RIDE AND A POKER GAME

In the history of the Cold War, the small college town of Fulton, Missouri, will always hold a special place of honor as the site of Winston Churchill's "Iron Curtain" speech. For me, however, the name of that town in central Missouri evokes first a train ride and a poker game—and only then the famous speech.

Winston Churchill's speech in Fulton was the result of the tenacity of one man and the inspiration of another. In October of 1945, Dr. Franc McCluer, the President of Westminster College in Fulton, read that Churchill, out of office since July, was planning to visit the U.S. early in 1946. McCluer, whose oddly shaped head had earned him the nickname "Bullet" McCluer, asked his old Westminster classmate Harry Vaughan to get President Truman to endorse an invitation to Churchill to speak at Westminster College.

The President considered Churchill "the first citizen of the world," but he hardly knew him. They had been together for a short time at the Potsdam conference, before Churchill was defeated in the British elections and had to leave the conference. Wanting to get to know him better, President Truman wrote: "This is a wonderful school in my home state. Hope you can do it. I'll introduce you."

Although we did not know it at the time, Churchill harbored deep reservations about President Truman, and, in his own later words, "loathed the idea of [Truman] taking the place of Franklin Roosevelt."[1] On the other hand, for some time he had wanted to make a major speech summing up his view of the world, especially of the growing Soviet threat. What better auspices for such a dramatic statement than a speech introduced by the President of the United States? He accepted at once. Thus "Bullet" McCluer, the dynamic but rather pedestrian self-promoter, had engineered not only one of the seminal speeches of the modern era but also its introduction by President Truman.

After some reflection, the President invited Churchill to travel from Washington to Fulton with him on the Presidential train, allowing them several days of close contact. With Vardaman fighting for confirmation, I was acting Naval Aide when, on March 4, Churchill came to the White House to meet President Truman. At breakfast that morning, I told my three young daughters, "Today your father is going to meet the number-one citizen of the world."

My eldest daughter, Margery, said, "Now, Daddy, remember exactly what Mr. Churchill says when you are introduced to him and tell us what it is, because that will be something important for our whole family to remember forever." I promised to report these words when I returned home.

When Churchill arrived, the White House staff lined up to be introduced to him. I did not rise in my daughters' estimation, however, when I gave them my report on Churchill's first words to me. As we shook hands he looked at me with cool, steely, gray-blue eyes, and said, "What was that name again?"

At midday we boarded the President's train for the trip to Fulton. President Truman had also invited Admiral Leahy (who had worked closely with Churchill during the war), Charlie Ross, General Harry Vaughan, and Colonel Wallace Graham, his personal physician.

As soon as the train pulled out of Union Station, President Truman had drinks served to his guests. As was his wont, Churchill drank scotch with water, but no ice, which he viewed as a barbaric American custom. Like everyone, I had heard of Churchill's reputation as a drinker, but it was my impression that he drank very slowly, nursing a single drink for hours. Holding his drink, Churchill leaned back and said, "When I was in South Africa as a young man, the water was not fit to drink. I have felt that way ever since about water, but I have learned that it can be made palatable by the addition of some whiskey." The President roared with laughter.

As we relaxed on the sofas and easy chairs in the President's private car, President Truman turned to his guest and said, "Now, Mr. Churchill, we are going to be together on this train for some time. I don't want to rest on formality, so I would ask you to call me Harry."

Bowing his head slightly and gracefully, Churchill replied, "I would be delighted to call you Harry. But you must call me Winston."

The President said, "I just don't know if I can do that. I have such admiration for you and what you mean, not only to your people, but to this country and the world."

Churchill, smiling broadly, settled the matter: "Yes, you can. You must, or else I will not be able to call you Harry." Clearly pleased, President Truman agreed, "Well, if you put it that way, Winston, I *will* call you Winston."

The President told Churchill, in confidence, that he was about to send the body of the Turkish Ambassador to the United States, Mehmet Munir Ertegun, back to Turkey on the USS *Missouri,* which was then the most powerful battleship in the world. Ertegun, who died in late 1944, had been interred at Arlington National Cemetery until his body could be returned to his homeland. Leahy added that the *Missouri* would be accompanied by a naval task force which would remain in the Sea of Marmara for an indefinite period in order to impress the Soviets with the importance America attached to Greece and Turkey.

Churchill was clearly pleased that this news was being shared with him even though he was, as he liked to put it, "a private citizen." He told us he considered this a "very important act of state," and said that he hoped it would help make Russia understand that "she must come to reasonable terms with the Western democracies." This show of force—which, it should be noted, came a year *before* the British decision to withdraw from Greece and Turkey, which led to the Truman Doctrine—fit precisely the theme that Churchill was about to enunciate at Fulton.

Churchill soon asked to be excused in order to work on his speech. His approach to speech writing was in direct contrast to almost every American politician I have known. For one thing, he wrote each speech, something increasingly rare even then in American politics. He attached the greatest importance not only to his general theme, but to the exact words with which he conveyed it. Churchill did not know if he would ever be returned to office, but he wanted to warn the world, and especially the U.S., about the dangers of Stalinism, just as he had warned in the thirties about Hitler. He knew that his only influence lay in the power of his words, and he intended this speech to take its place alongside the great wartime speeches with which he had rallied Britain in its moments of greatest peril.

President Truman had been in office less than a year. He was torn between a growing sense of anger at, and distrust of, the Soviet Union and a residual hope that he could still work with Stalin. Just days before we boarded the train for Fulton, Navy Secretary Forrestal had circulated to senior officials and hundreds of military officers around the world a lengthy telegram from the American Embassy in Moscow warning that the Russians, out of a combination of insecurity and age-old ambitions, would be a dangerous and destabilizing element in the postwar world. The message, which became known as the "Long Telegram," was probably the most important, and influential, message ever sent to Washington by an American diplomat. Its author, whom I had never heard of before, was soon to become famous: George F. Kennan, who, in the temporary absence of Ambassador Harriman, was running the American Embassy in Moscow.

Secretary of State Byrnes read a draft of Churchill's speech the day before the train left Washington and briefed President Truman on its contents. The President said he would not read the final text, in order to be able to say later that he had not endorsed or approved it in advance. Churchill's press aide handed out the final version of the speech to reporters on the train the night before it was delivered, though, and the White House staff also got copies. Reading it, I was deeply impressed with its sweep and sense of history; but the phrase that was to become a permanent part of our language did not leap out at me. As for President Truman, despite his earlier decision, he found he could not resist reading it.

It was a brilliant and admirable statement, he told Churchill, and would "create quite a stir." But it presented the President with a dilemma: he was not yet ready to endorse Churchill's view that we were entering an era of relentless confrontation with Moscow, even though his presence on the platform with Churchill certainly appeared to imply an endorsement. Still hoping to keep open channels of communication with Stalin, the President instructed me to put into his introduction of Churchill some positive words about Stalin that might make this possible.

After working on his speech, Churchill rejoined us for drinks and dinner. President Truman showed him the redesigned Presidential seal, which was on the wall of the car, and said, "This may interest you. We have just turned the eagle's head from the talons of war to the olive branch of peace." Churchill looked at the seal for a moment and said dryly, "I have a suggestion to make. The head should be on a swivel so that it can turn from the talons of war to the olive branch of peace as the occasion warrants." Churchill added, teasingly, that the berries on the olive branch looked more like atomic bombs to him.

During dinner, Churchill, who loved to play cards, turned to President Truman and said the magic words: "Harry, I understand from the press that you like to play poker."

"That's correct, Winston. I have played a great deal of poker in my life."

"I am delighted to hear it. You know, I played my first poker game during the Boer War. I like poker—a fine game. Do you think there is any possibility that we might play during this trip?"

"Winston, the fellows around you are all poker players, serious poker players, and we would be delighted to provide you with a game."

A few minutes later, with dinner completed, Churchill excused himself for a moment. The moment he had left, the President turned to us, and in total seriousness, said, "Men, we have an important task ahead of us. This man has been playing poker for more than forty years. He is cagey, he loves cards, and is probably an excellent player. The reputation of American poker is at stake, and I expect every man to do his duty."

Churchill returned to the dining room, dressed in his famous World War II zippered blue siren suit, which I thought looked a bit like a bunny suit. The stewards had put a green baize cover over the dining room table and six of us—the President, Churchill, Charlie Ross, Harry Vaughan, Wallace Graham, and I—sat down for the most memorable poker game in which I ever played.

The truth emerged quickly: however enthusiastic and proud of his poker skills, Churchill was not very good at the game. I learned later that, when playing his own card games in England, such as gin rummy and bezique, he was excellent. But in poker, with its bluffs and the value of deception and a certain code with which we were all familiar, he was, so to speak, a lamb among wolves. In addition, his terminology for the cards was foreign to us, and this required constant clarification, which only increased our advantage. He called a straight a "sequence," and the jack a "knave," a bit of routine British terminology so vastly amusing to Harry Vaughan that he could hardly keep from laughing aloud.

After about an hour, Churchill excused himself briefly. The moment the door closed President Truman turned to us, with a grave expression. "Now look here, men—you are not treating our guest very well." He looked at Churchill's dwindling stack of chips. "I fear that he may already have lost close to three hundred dollars."

Vaughan looked at his friend of thirty years and laughed. "But, Boss, *this guy's a pigeon!* If you want us to play our best poker for the nation's honor, we'll have this guy's pants before the evening is over. Now, you just tell us what you want. You want us to play customer poker, okay, we can carry him along all evening. If you want us to give it our best, we'll have his underwear."

President Truman smiled. "I don't want him to think we are pushovers, but at the same time, let's not treat him badly."

Those were our ground rules for the rest of the trip. Churchill "won" some splendid pots, lost some others. At one point, I dropped out of a hand of stud poker, and noticed that Charlie Ross, who was sitting next to me, had an ace showing and an ace in the hole. I watched Ross raise Churchill and raise him again. Churchill, with only a jack showing, stayed right with him. Then, at the end, Churchill bet a substantial amount of money, perhaps a hundred dollars, right into this ace. Charlie studied what he knew had to be a winning hand, with its two aces, looked over at the President, gave what I thought sounded like a sigh, and folded.

Finally, however, as the evening was drawing to a close, we moved in a little on our guest. When the dust had settled and we tallied up, Churchill had lost about $250. He had enjoyed himself thoroughly, but he had dropped just enough money so that he could not go back to London and, as Vaughan put it, "brag to his Limey friends that he had beaten the Americans at poker."

FULTON

Early on the morning after our poker game the train pulled into Union Station in St. Louis for a brief stop. Churchill stayed in his stateroom, but the President went onto the observation platform to greet the huge throng that had gathered. It was the first time I had seen President Truman greet crowds from the back of his train—and it was very effective. At the time, however, none of us saw it as a political device of such value that it would become the enduring image of the 1948 election.

Our train ride ended in Jefferson City, where we received an enthusiastic welcome before we drove the last twenty miles to Fulton. There we were greeted by McCluer, all puffed up for his great day. I found the entire scene at Fulton immensely exciting. In a small town in my home state, the greatest statesman of our age was about to make a historic speech. We filed into the gymnasium and onto the stage in academic procession, Churchill dramatic in scarlet robes, President Truman less imposing, robed in black. Admiral Leahy and I wore our naval uniforms. In front of us lay a remarkable scene, a small-town convocation in a gymnasium decked out with bunting, waiting with polite anticipation to hear a speech from the legendary man. The big windows of the gymnasium were open to let the warm spring air circulate. Professors in their academic robes, young clean-cut students, and well-dressed townspeople all squeezed together on wooden bleachers. Thrilled by the worldwide attention, the entire population of Fulton, as well as thousands of people from the surrounding area, turned out, filling up all three thousand seats, and spreading onto the green outside to listen to the speech, which was broadcast nationwide on the radio. Churchill had refused to permit a television broadcast of the speech, fearing that the heat of the lights would distract him and the audience, but a newsreel camera captured the event.

I was seated almost directly behind the rostrum. After the President's warm introduction, Churchill rose, put on his heavy glasses, and began to speak. From the point of view of high rhetoric, I had never heard anything like it before, and not since (although John F. Kennedy's Inaugural Address in 1961 and Lyndon Johnson's civil rights speech to Congress in 1965 moved me more because they came directly out of our own national experience). As a demonstration of the power of ideas when presented brilliantly by someone of global stature, it was an astonishing tour de force. He spoke for forty-five minutes, a long speech by present-day standards, but the audience was mesmerized. As I listened, I reflected on my mother's passionate attachment to the English language, and thought, *For this man, words are battalions, doing battle for his ideas.*

* * *

Churchill's grand theme was that the U.S. now stood at "the pinnacle of world power," with "an awe-inspiring accountability to the future."

Churchill discussed ways to strengthen the United Nations. He was particularly interested in creating an international air force and placing it under U.N. command, but he opposed sharing nuclear secrets with any nation except the United States, Great Britain, and Canada. He turned to the question of tyranny:

> A shadow has fallen upon the scenes so lately lighted by the Allied victory. Nobody knows what Soviet Russia and its Communist international organization intend to do in the immediate future, or what are the limits, if any, to their expansive and proselytizing tendencies. . . . It is my duty . . . to place before you certain facts about the present position in Europe.

Then came the words that became part of the history of our times:

> From Stettin in the Baltic to Trieste in the Adriatic, an Iron Curtain has descended across the Continent. Behind that line lie all the capitals of the ancient states of central and eastern Europe—Warsaw, Berlin, Prague, Vienna, Budapest, Bucharest, and Sofia, all these famous cities and their populations around them lie in what I might call the Soviet sphere, and are all subject, in one form or another, not only to Soviet influence but to a very high and in some cases increasing measure of control from Moscow. . . .

As I heard Churchill proclaim those words, in his peculiar, rumbling cadence, I felt their force much more strongly than I had when reading the text the day before—but even then none of us recognized the impact that this phrase would have. Indeed, the next day newspaper coverage focused more on Churchill's call for closer Anglo-American cooperation than on his description of the Soviet Union.

The audience had sat silently during the "Iron Curtain" passage. It interested me that Churchill's next sentence, taken out of context by the crowd—"I do not believe that Soviet Russia wants war"—evoked strong applause. He continued:

> What they desire is the fruits of war and the indefinite expansion of their power and doctrines. . . . I am convinced that there is nothing they admire so much as strength, and there is nothing for which they have less respect than for weakness, especially military weakness. For that reason the old doctrine of a balance of power is unsound.

For me, the most moving portion of the speech was a poignant personal passage near the end. It was to remain in my mind as I was drawn into the discussion and analysis of Soviet intentions and behavior later that year:

> Last time I saw it all coming and cried aloud, to my own fellow-countrymen and to the world, but no one paid any attention. Up till the year 1933 or even 1935, Germany might have been saved from the awful fate which has overtaken her and we might all have been spared the miseries Hitler let loose upon mankind. . . .

A TALK IN THE NIGHT

The speech delivered and the drama over, we were a relaxed group on returning to the train. We resumed the poker game, and after the game ended with the outcome desired by the President—another carefully calibrated loss by our guest—the President and most of the group retired for the night. But Churchill, in a convivial and mellow mood, stayed behind. Relaxed by a pleasant evening of poker and his address earlier in the day, which he said was the "most important speech of my career," Churchill felt like talking. Charlie Ross and I sat with him, listening to him with a sense of incredible privilege.

Ross, an old newspaperman, referred to Churchill's early career as a journalist. Churchill corrected him pointedly: "I was never a journalist. I was a war correspondent." We talked about how the design of our lives is shaped by the accident of birth. Suddenly, Churchill said, "If I were to be born again, I would wish to be born in the United States. Your country is the future of the world. You have the natural resources, the spirit, the youth, the determination, which will steadily increase your global influence. Great Britain has passed its zenith. We must adjust now to the enormous pressures in the world which have brought such dramatic changes. I believe your leaders must confront this responsibility head on, and it is my hope that you will assume the leadership of the free world." He added, with a smile and a puckish look, "I say this despite the fact that you Americans have some barbaric customs."

"Like what, Mr. Churchill?" Ross asked.

"For one thing," Churchill replied, eyes twinkling, "you stop drinking with your meals."

Churchill felt he had done something of great importance that day—laying out, as he had in the thirties, his view of an entire era. He was particularly gratified that he had done this in front of the President of the United States. Their appearance together in Fulton symbolized Churchill's view of the special relationship between the two countries. He passionately loved his island nation, but he knew that, after the extraordinary price it had paid in two great wars in less than thirty years, Britain would be unable to maintain the global role it had played for more than a century. Churchill wanted to accelerate the process by which the U.S. would assume leadership in the postwar world, and at the same time preserve a role for Britain as America's special partner.

Churchill took a broad, and highly personal, view of history. He was unafraid to reach grand, even romantic, conclusions, and believed deeply that the United States and Great Britain must maintain their unique wartime partnership not only to control their own destinies but to assure the ultimate triumph of Western civilization. In his hope for a fraternal association between the British Empire and the United States, which he intended as the main point of his Fulton speech, he was, of course, to be somewhat disappointed. But his acute sense of the danger posed by the Soviet Union was clear-eyed and unsentimental.

THE REACTION TO FULTON

There is a natural tendency to simplify history and give it more coherence than a detailed examination of the facts warrants. The Fulton speech is now treated as revelation and prophecy, a turning point in the evolution of policy and popular understanding of the Soviet threat. But initial reaction to the speech was divided, with the vast majority of editorial and public comment being, in Martin Gilbert's phrase, "almost universally hostile."

The White House watched American public reaction with great interest. *The Nation,* true to its left-wing ideology, said that Churchill had "added a sizeable measure of poison to the already deteriorating relations between Russia and the Western powers," and added that President Truman had been "remarkably inept" in associating himself with the speech in any way. *The Wall Street Journal* rejected Churchill's call for a closer relationship with Great Britain, saying that "the United States wants no alliance or anything that resembles an alliance with any other nation." Pearl Buck, then one of the world's most respected writers and a Nobel laureate in literature, told an audience that the world was "nearer war tonight than we were last night."[2]

President Truman gave considerable attention to the distinction between his relationship with Churchill and his reaction to the speech, which he admired but whose message he was not yet ready to embrace. On one hand, he recognized the power and insight of Churchill's speech and Kennan's Long Telegram; on the other, he still harbored the hope that some sort of agreement with Stalin would be possible. It was for this reason that President Truman told reporters on the train leaving Fulton that he had not read the speech in advance. President Truman did not feel he could take the same position as a former Prime Minister, who could speak unconstrained by the limitations of office. Much to our relief, Churchill, understanding perfectly the President's situation and deeply grateful for the gesture that the President had made in introducing him, did not contradict him.

Trying to distance the Administration slightly from Churchill's speech, the President instructed Undersecretary of State Dean Acheson not to attend a reception for Churchill the following week in New York, even though Acheson had dined with Churchill only a few days earlier in Washington. The President even sent Stalin a message emphasizing that he still held out hope for better relations. He issued an invitation to him to make a similar speech in Missouri, "for exactly the same kind of reception," and said he would introduce Stalin personally as he had Churchill. Stalin ignored the invitation, but the very fact that President Truman made the offer showed clearly that in the spring of 1946 the future was not as apparent in the President's mind as it was in Churchill's. He still hoped that the Cold War—a phrase not yet in vogue—could be avoided.

The situation would change rapidly in the coming months. Exactly how fast is illustrated by a letter Churchill sent Thomas E. Dewey in December of 1946: "If I made the Fulton speech today it would be criticized as consisting of platitudes." The same week, he sent a wonderfully triumphant message to another American friend: "Fulton still holds its own!"

Churchill was absolutely correct. Events in the latter half of 1946 and beginning of 1947 dramatically altered public perceptions of the Soviet Union. In the process of forging a new consensus on American policy toward the Soviet Union, I was to play a role which would bring me, for the first time, squarely into the arena of national security policy.

7

The Clifford-Elsey Report and the Firing of Henry Wallace

And if it should turn out to be the will of fate that freedom should come to Russia by erosion from despotism rather than by the violent upthrust of liberty, let us be able to say that our policy was such as to favor it, and that we did not hamper it by preconception or impatience or despair.

—GEORGE F. KENNAN, 1951

In the summer of 1946, as the nation turned its back on the outside world and returned to domestic priorities, two related events drew me deeply, for the first time, into foreign policy. Although a novice, I was given an assignment by President Truman which required me to take what amounted to a crash course with some of the nation's greatest experts on the issue that would dominate American foreign policy for almost half a century—American-Soviet relations. At the same time, I became deeply engaged in the epic confrontation between President Truman and the man he had succeeded as Vice President, Henry A. Wallace.

THE CLIFFORD-ELSEY REPORT: ORIGINS

The debate over American-Soviet policy brought relations between the President and Wallace to a crisis point; and while it was inevitable that Wallace would leave the Cabinet sooner or later, it was not inevitable that his departure would become such a fiasco for President Truman. Although it pains me deeply to say so, the manner in which Wallace left the Cabinet was one of the worst mistakes of the Truman Presidency.

In the summer of 1946, the President was not ready to proclaim the end of the era of wartime collaboration with the Soviets. He knew the American public was not ready to hear its President deliver the same bleak message that Churchill had made at Fulton. With the U.S. holding a nuclear monopoly, he felt there was no direct or immediate danger to the nation.

The Cabinet was split over the Soviet challenge. Henry Wallace, then Secretary of Commerce, saw no threat from Moscow, which, he said, "was offering a race with America in furnishing the needs of the common people without war or business crisis." He argued for continuation, even expansion, of our wartime cooperation with the Soviet Union—a position far beyond that of anyone else in the Cabinet.

On the other hand, Forrestal and Secretary of State James Byrnes were increasingly worried about Moscow. Forrestal, who saw himself as destined to awaken Washington to the Soviet threat, told me "we must prepare for war," and urged everyone he knew to read Kennan's Long Telegram.

Meanwhile, the first postwar confrontation with Moscow had presented itself in the area of northern Iran known as Azerbaijan, which adjoined the Soviet Republic of the same name. The removal of Soviet troops from the region had been agreed upon in principle during the meeting of Roosevelt, Churchill, and Stalin at Tehran in December 1943. At the end of the war, the Soviet Union formally agreed to pull its troops out of Azerbaijan no later than March 2, 1946. As that date passed without Soviet withdrawal, it became apparent that Moscow's objective was, in fact, to create a separate state in Azerbaijan, and then, presumably, later annex it to the Soviet empire. (The Soviets would finally withdraw from the area in October, after a series of increasingly tough warnings from Washington and London.)

The Soviet defiance of the United States and Great Britain during the spring and summer led directly to my first foreign policy assignment. During a staff meeting on July 12, 1946, the President began discussing his growing frustration with Soviet behavior. "The Russians are trying to chisel away a little here, a little there," he said. "If the Paris conference* busts up, I want to be ready to reveal to the whole world the full truth about the Russian failure to honor agreements." He turned to me and asked that I produce a record of Soviet violations of international agreements.

I was aware from the outset of the importance of this assignment, yet I knew I could not complete it and also carry out my other duties without assistance. Fortunately, the perfect person to help me was already in place: as always, I turned with confidence to George Elsey, who had spent the

*This was a reference to a twenty-one-nation peace conference that was supposed to forge a unified position on a peace treaty with Germany.

last four years watching the relationship among the wartime Allies from the secret confines of the Map Room.

The President had asked only for a review of those agreements the Soviet Union had broken. But as I discussed the assignment with Elsey, we decided to suggest a different process. We agreed that Kennan's Long Telegram was brilliant; but he had confined himself to analysis. Elsey suggested that we try to fill the gap between Kennan's analysis and policy recommendations by assembling the views of those senior officials most concerned with American policy toward the Soviet Union, to see what consensus, if any, existed. On July 16, 1946, I suggested this to the President, who immediately authorized me to expand the scope of the project, asking only that its completion not be delayed.

I did not realize it at the time, but I had received permission to begin what turned out to be the first peacetime interagency foreign policy review of American-Soviet relations. Within two years, a formal National Security Council system and a National Security Assistant would coordinate such studies. But the National Security Council did not exist in 1946, and the President turned to his Special Counsel.*

Elsey and I drew up a short list of people whose views we would solicit: Admiral Leahy, who spoke for the Joint Chiefs of Staff; James Byrnes and Dean Acheson at State; Secretary of War Robert Patterson; Forrestal; Attorney General Tom Clark; and Central Intelligence Group Director Sidney Souers. We made special use of George Kennan, who had returned to Washington, and, finally, we consulted Kennan's close friend and colleague in the Soviet field, Charles Bohlen.**

My first call, on July 18 to Admiral Leahy, taught me an early lesson in bureaucratic sensitivity. The five-star Admiral expressed surprise and a certain wounded pride that the project had not been assigned to him. Once satisfied, however, that the request came directly from the President, he offered his full cooperation. I showed Leahy a draft of a letter to the Joint Chiefs of Staff asking for their views on how to deal with the Soviet Union. Leahy, experienced in the ways of the military, insisted on restricting the request to "military policy" only, so that the Chiefs could not, in his words, "stretch it into an excuse to render a political opinion." I was struck by Leahy's loyalty to the interests of the President rather than the uniformed services, and the careful way he tried to prevent the President from getting undesirable pressure from the military outside

*The Joint Chiefs of Staff had written a memorandum a few months earlier addressing some of these issues from a military point of view, but their paper had not been coordinated with the State Department or the civilian service secretaries, and the President had not paid it much attention.

**Bohlen had been the President's interpreter at Tehran, Yalta, and Potsdam, and later served as Ambassador to the Soviet Union, the Philippines, and France.

their proper area of responsibility. It was a lesson I would remember when I dealt with the military as Secretary of Defense under Lyndon Johnson.

That afternoon, I made the short walk across West Executive Avenue and called on Secretary of State James Byrnes in his cavernous office in the State, War and Navy Building.*

Jimmy Byrnes was a difficult man to like. He had served in the Senate with Harry Truman, and the President felt, with justification, that Byrnes continued to treat him the way a senior Senator treats a freshman. Furthermore, Byrnes thought he had been cheated out of the Vice Presidential nomination in 1944. President Truman particularly liked to tell the story, which I heard many times, of how he had already agreed to place Byrnes's name in nomination at the 1944 convention when, at the last minute, President Roosevelt said he wanted Senator Truman as his running mate. Concerned that Byrnes not think that he was responsible for this unexpected event, President Truman asked Byrnes to become his Secretary of State. It was a nice gesture designed to bind up the party and soothe a disappointed compatriot. However, like Roosevelt's appointment of Henry Wallace to Commerce, it proved to be an act of misguided generosity: by the summer of 1946 he had concluded that Byrnes was trying to run the government behind his back, and he had decided to replace him with General Marshall. Marshall's appointment was supposed to remain secret until the completion of his mission to China, and the President did not wish Byrnes to leave at a time and manner that could weaken the Administration.

Byrnes reacted even more sharply than Leahy had to my request: annoyed that the assignment had not been given to State, he said he was not sure how much help he could be. With evident sarcasm, he went so far as to claim that he could not even be sure he was aware of "every agreement" Roosevelt had made with the Russians; some might be in Harry Hopkins's private papers, and others might be "buried" in Franklin Roosevelt's files.

I found Byrnes's statements about "lost agreements" both incredible and offensive. When I discussed them with the normally mild and careful George Elsey that afternoon, he exploded in anger at what he termed "a complete lie." Elsey had been in charge of filing the records of Presidential discussions and agreements during World War II, and on Admiral

*It is known today as the Old Executive Office Building. I always regretted that the growth of both the State Department and the White House staff forced State a few years later to exchange its ornate and imposing old home next to the White House for its pedestrian quarters in Foggy Bottom. When Dean Acheson recommended the move to George Marshall in 1947, he thought the only argument for staying put was sentiment and tradition.[1] I disagree: time and space impose their own logic on relationships, and proximity to the President is often the most valuable commodity in Washington. Secretaries of State lost something intangible but important when they could no longer reach the President's office with a two-minute walk.

Leahy's instructions had personally delivered every wartime agreement to Byrnes just before he became Secretary of State. Nonetheless, when Byrnes, nursing his resentment, later publicly repeated his statements about "secret agreements," he helped fuel the suspicion that FDR had made a secret deal with Stalin to sell out Eastern Europe—an erroneous but enduring myth of the American right wing.

HENRY WALLACE AND HARRY TRUMAN

The seeds of confrontation between the two former Vice Presidents were planted the moment Harry Truman became President. After all, had Franklin Roosevelt died only a few months earlier, Henry Wallace would have become President of the United States. As he awaited the new President with the rest of Roosevelt's Cabinet at the White House on April 12, 1945, he must have thought back to the summer of 1944, when, under conservative pressure, Roosevelt had dropped him from the ticket.

As Roosevelt's first Secretary of Agriculture, Wallace had championed the American farmer with flair and creativity. In the thirties, I regarded him as one of the genuine heroes of the New Deal, committed to what he later called "the common man." In 1940, Roosevelt picked him for the Vice Presidential slot on the third-term ticket; but in 1944, perhaps as penitence for dumping him from the ticket, Roosevelt did something quite strange—he offered Wallace the job of Secretary of Commerce in the fourth term. And to almost everyone's surprise, Wallace accepted.

President Truman told me once that he thought Wallace had been "the best damn Secretary of Agriculture we ever had." At first, he believed that their farm backgrounds and midwestern roots gave them something in common. In fact, though, the two men had little in common: Wallace's distinguished and proud lineage as the son of a former Secretary of Agriculture (under Harding and Coolidge) was in sharp contrast to Harry Truman's matter-of-fact, unpretentious background. Impractical and naïve, with more than a touch of arrogance, Wallace possessed a strange mystical streak in his makeup. While Secretary of Agriculture, he became involved with a charlatan named Dr. Nicholas Roerich, a Russian artist whom Wallace addressed in letters as "Dear Guru." Roerich enmeshed Wallace in several bizarre schemes for the salvation of China through Christianity, which vastly amused the public when their letters later surfaced. When watching Wallace's large, sad face and his unfocused eyes during a conversation I sometimes got the impression his mind had wandered off and left his body behind. Jim Forrestal, who enjoyed reading to me excerpts from Wallace's letters to Roerich, used to call this look "Wallace's global stare."

Our failure to come to terms with the dangers posed by Wallace stemmed, in part, from our own inexperience. But it was also based on a political reality. With the exception of Eleanor Roosevelt, Wallace was the leading liberal in the nation in 1946, the embodiment of the link between the Truman Administration and the New Deal. The new President determined that he would try to live with Wallace rather than alienate the large constituency he still retained among liberals and farmers.

A LETTER FROM HENRY WALLACE

On July 23, 1946, President Truman received a twelve-page single-spaced letter from Henry Wallace on the subject of relations with the Soviet Union. The next morning he tossed it at me across his desk. "Read this carefully," he said, "then come back and talk to me about it. It looks as though Henry is going to pull an 'Ickes.' " This reference to Harold Ickes worried me, for the firing in February 1946 of Roosevelt's cantankerous Secretary of the Interior, after a bitter public argument, had been nasty and politically damaging.

I asked Elsey to come to my office, and I began to read Wallace's letter aloud. Wallace charged that American actions since V-J Day, including the "large" $13 billion defense budget, the atomic tests at Bikini, and the continued production of B-29s and B-36s, "make it look to the rest of the world as if we were only paying lip service to peace."

"How would it look to us," he continued, "if Russia had the atomic bomb and we did not, if Russia had 10,000-mile bombers and air bases within a thousand miles of our coast lines and we did not?" Even in Eastern Europe, Wallace seemed unable to bring himself to condemn the trend of Soviet subversion:

> Our interest in establishing democracy in Eastern Europe, where democracy by and large has never existed, seems to [the Soviets] an attempt to reestablish the encirclement of unfriendly neighbors which was created after the last war and which might serve as a springboard of still another effort to destroy her. . . . We should ascertain from a fresh point of view what Russia believes to be essential to her own security. . . .

Wallace's letter should have forced the President to confront the problem posed by his continued presence in the Cabinet, but it did not. Wallace was preparing, I predicted to Elsey, for a public break with the President by positioning himself as a "man of peace." Yet after three days of internal discussions with the President, no decision had been made on how to respond. Instead, restating his distrust of Wallace, the President told me to show the letter to Byrnes before he left for the Paris Peace Conference.

When I look back, I am frequently struck by what a difference modern technology has made in the process of government. In those days before photocopying and fax machines, only one copy of a document or letter was available under normal circumstances, and in this case there were no other copies of the letter in the White House. To make sure Byrnes saw the letter, I had to deliver our only copy personally to him; and then to make sure we were not left without our only copy, I had to retrieve it myself from his secretary while bidding him good-bye the next day, just before he left for Paris. No one else, including the President, could study the Wallace letter until I got it back, while Byrnes could do little more than read it quickly in the course of many other last-minute preparations for his trip. Today's technologies—the photocopier, the word processor, and the fax machine—have changed our work habits, liberating us from many old tyrannies, but creating along the way the opposite problem—too many copies, too easily made, of almost everything, including sensitive documents.

A CRUISE AND SOME STAFF WORK

The President originally hoped to read my report during a vacation cruise starting August 16. But the expansion of its scope delayed its completion, and I left Elsey to toil away on it in Washington's summer heat while we vacationed—a point he noted half-humorously in several messages he sent to update me on his progress. The cruise was President Truman's first extended vacation on the *Williamsburg,* and it was characteristic of the way he enjoyed relaxing. Charlie Ross, Harry Vaughan, and I made the full trip; we were joined for portions of the trip by other staff members. Twenty-three reporters and photographers, a tiny number compared to the hundreds of journalists who follow a President's every move today, followed us on a separate ship

We did little work on this trip. We would swim or rest during much of the day, playing occasional games of fierce and noisy volleyball in which a medicine ball replaced the regular volley ball in order to avoid losing the balls in the ocean. These games greatly amused President Truman, who appointed himself umpire. By the end of the cruise, though, every medicine ball on board had been lost over the side, and the last few contests were conducted with special rope grommets which had been made by the crew.

Elsey spent August organizing the study, weaving together the different pieces we had gathered. He sent sections of the draft to me via the White House daily mail delivery as we cruised the waters of the Atlantic, and gave parts of it to Admiral Leahy and George Kennan for comments.

Kennan's extensive comments, covering six single-spaced pages, were particularly helpful, and we incorporated almost every one of his suggestions into the final report. Elsey offered to hand-deliver a portion of the study, saying plaintively that "it would cause me no pain at all to be allowed to fly down with the last pouch and deliver it in person." By the time Elsey's plea for a short vacation arrived, however, the President had decided to return to Washington early, thus preventing George from getting a richly deserved visit to Bermuda.

We played two last games of volleyball September 2 as the *Williamsburg* steamed up the Potomac accompanied by a growing number of small pleasure craft. Although relaxed and tanned, none of us was prepared for the rush of events that would dominate our agenda in the last four months of 1946: the Congressional elections, the showdown with John L. Lewis, and the next act of the continuing drama with Henry Wallace.

THE FIRING OF HENRY WALLACE

Less than three weeks after our return, the Wallace affair came to a dreadful climax, but because of a failure in the staff structure around the President, no one realized what was happening until it was too late.

Wallace had accepted an invitation to speak on September 12 at a Madison Square Garden rally opposing Thomas E. Dewey's bid for reelection as Governor of New York. He decided to use his letter about Soviet-American relations as the basis for his speech.

It was normal then, as it is now, for any member of the Cabinet to obtain approval in advance from the State Department for any speech on foreign policy. At the time, though, there was no formal mechanism for the clearance of such speeches, and in any case Wallace considered himself different from other Cabinet members. Without telling anyone what he had in mind, Wallace scheduled a meeting with President Truman for September 10, two days before the speech. The stage was now set for disaster.

The two men met alone. As he entered, Wallace handed the President a draft of the speech. The President told me later he asked, "What does it say, Henry?" Wallace ran quickly through it, page by page. The President's exact words when Wallace finished will always remain a matter of dispute, but they clearly constituted general approval for Wallace to give the speech. Not paying close attention, President Truman did not notice that Wallace's draft contradicted statements of other government officials, particularly Jimmy Byrnes.

No one else in the government, except Wallace's staff, saw the speech until the afternoon of its delivery, but late that morning, Wallace's office distributed an advance text of the speech to the press. The reporters quickly noticed that many of the views in the speech were in direct conflict with those of the Secretary of State. In one passage, Wallace said:

> The tougher we get, the tougher the Russians will get. . . . We have no more business in the political affairs of Eastern Europe than Russia has in the political affairs of Latin America, Western Europe, and the United States. . . . To make Britain the key to our foreign policy would, in my opinion, be the height of folly. . . . I am neither anti-British nor pro-British; neither anti-Russian nor pro-Russian.

Provocative as this passage was, what gripped the White House press corps was a sentence Wallace had added to the speech after his meeting with the President:

> And just two days ago, when President Truman read these words, he said they represented the policy of his Administration.

Wallace was already on his way to New York to deliver the speech when, wholly unprepared for the questioning he encountered, President Truman held a regularly scheduled press conference that afternoon:

> QUESTION: Mr. President, in a speech for delivery tonight, Secretary of State—I mean Commerce—Wallace [*laughter*] has this to say, about the middle of it, "when President—"
> ANSWER: [*Interrupting*] Well now, you say the speech is to be delivered?
> Q: It is, sir.
> A: Well, I—I can't answer questions on a speech that is to be delivered.
> Q: It mentions you, which is the reason that I ask, sir.
> A: Well, that's fine. I'm glad it does. What was the question. Go ahead. Maybe I can answer it. [*Much laughter*]
> Q: In the middle of the speech are these words, "When President Truman read these words, he said that they represented the policy of this Administration."
> A: That is correct.
> Q: My question is, does that apply just to that paragraph, or to the whole speech?
> A: I approved the whole speech.
> Q: Mr. President, do you regard Wallace's speech a departure from Byrnes's policy—
> A: [*Interrupting*] I do not.

Charlie Ross had been standing next to the President during this exchange, but he had not yet seen a copy of the speech, even though every reporter in the room had. Ross said to me later, "If only the President had stopped after saying he couldn't comment on a speech that hadn't been delivered. . . ." But the President had relaxed after the laughter and was then, in Ross's words, "betrayed by his own amiability into answering the question."

The reporters began filing stories saying that the President, by endorsing Wallace's speech, had broken with Byrnes and softened American policy toward Moscow. Still Ross did not see the full danger of the situation. Officials at the State Department first read the speech, obtained by a State official who had seen it lying on a press handout table at the National Press Club, around six o'clock. The acting Secretary of State, Will Clayton, called Ross to see if Wallace could be stopped, or, at a minimum, be ordered to remove from the text the sentence citing Presidential approval; Ross told Clayton it was too late to stop him. Undersecretary of the Navy John Sullivan, who had joined Clayton at the State Department for the discussion, grabbed the telephone out of Clayton's hands and told Ross very emotionally that if delivered as written, the speech would force the President to choose publicly between Wallace and Byrnes.

Ross was stunned. He recalled later it was the first time he realized "the magnitude of the President's mistake." But he had still not read the speech, and had no way of knowing whether Clayton and Sullivan were exaggerating. Because the President seemed unconcerned, Ross continued to underreact. In retrospect, it was clear he should have moved much faster and more vigorously, even at the last moment, to reduce the damage. Ross told the story himself in a note he made later:

> This was just a few minutes before the President was due to attend a party at Clark Clifford's. I told him that both Clayton and Sullivan were greatly alarmed over the Wallace speech and that Sullivan had suggested that something ought to be done to call Wallace off. It was then around 6:30 and Wallace was due to speak in an hour or so. The President did not appear alarmed. He said he had given Wallace permission to make the speech for its political effect in New York and while it might ruffle Byrnes, he did not think it would do any permanent damage. Anyway, he felt that it was too late to stop Wallace from speaking. I did not press the point, for, obviously, the damage had been done by the President's endorsement of the speech at his 4 o'clock press conference. . . .

The "party" was a poker evening. The President briefly mentioned concern in the State Department with a speech that Wallace was making that evening in New York, but added that it was "no big deal." Like the

President, I concentrated on the poker game, while in New York, Henry Wallace went ahead with his speech.

It was not until I opened the newspapers the next morning that I realized the gravity of the situation. The description of the rally at Madison Square Garden was vivid: after Wallace had made the opening speech, Claude Pepper, then a fiery left-wing Democratic Senator from Florida, roused the crowd with a sharp attack on the Administration's Soviet policy. Pepper was followed by the great black actor-singer Paul Robeson, who, to thunderous applause, denounced racism in the South and attacked British imperialism.

James Reston, then in the early years of his distinguished journalistic career at *The New York Times,* accurately captured the mood of an astonished Washington: "Mr. Truman seems to be the only person in the capital who thinks that Mr. Wallace's proposals are 'in line' with Mr. Truman's or Mr. Byrnes'. . . ."

The President began his morning staff meeting by saying he realized he had made a "grave blunder." After a heated discussion about whether or not to issue an immediate statement, he decided to wait another day and see if the problem would blow over. By the next day, the situation was only worse, with the press focusing on the mounting evidence of disarray between the President and two men who still aspired to his job, the former Vice President and the Secretary of State. We realized it was essential to issue a statement in time to make the first editions of the Sunday newspapers. Working in great haste, we produced a draft statement which the President approved. The President, Ross told the press crowded around his desk, felt that his original press comment

> did not convey the thought that I intended it to convey. It was my intention to express the thought that I approved the right of the Secretary of Commerce to deliver the speech. I did not intend to indicate that I approved the speech as constituting a statement of the foreign policy of this country. . . .

Ross and I harbored a small hope that this weak and misleading statement might stop the hemorrhaging, but we were quickly brought back to reality. Wallace, returning to Washington, told reporters, "I stand upon my New York speech . . . and I shall, within the near future, speak on the same subject again." This made Byrnes, in Paris, even more furious. The two equally aroused Cabinet members were still on a collision course.

The press laughed at our attempt to paper over what had happened. *Time* magazine called the President's explanatory statement a "clumsy lie." Even though I had helped draft it, I had to agree.

In this ugly atmosphere Wallace scheduled a meeting with the President on September 18. "I know I made a mistake," the President told me, "and it was a beaut"—but he was fed up with Wallace and expected him to resign. I could not have agreed more.

To the President's surprise, Wallace did not offer to resign when they met. Instead, he tried to engage President Truman in a serious discussion of American foreign policy. He was scheduled to make another speech shortly, he told an astonished President. After reading several passages of it aloud, he asked for authority to make the speech with a disclaimer that it did not represent the views of the President. President Truman said not only that this was impossible but that Wallace must stop speaking out on foreign policy.

I waited anxiously in my office for the end of their meeting. As soon as their tête-à-tête was over, I joined a heated discussion with the two of them about what to tell the press. After much argument, Wallace agreed only to say he would refrain from further statements on foreign policy until the end of the Paris conference. Asked by a reporter as he was leaving if he would stay in the Cabinet, Wallace answered, with a big smile, "Yes, I am."

The President was furious. Muzzling Wallace only until the Paris conference ended was, from the President's point of view, not much of a deal. He angrily told me that Wallace was a liar, a fool, and "one hundred percent pacifist."

Byrnes had no intention of continuing at State under conditions of near-anarchy. Since the crisis with Wallace had started, there had been no direct contact between Byrnes and the President. Now, from Paris, he angrily demanded to speak to him.

On September 19 we arranged a "secure teletype" conversation between the two men. Byrnes was fighting mad, and did most of the "talking." We read his deciphered words as they clattered out of the teletype machine in the Map Room:

> IF IT IS NOT POSSIBLE FOR YOU, FOR ANY REASON, TO KEEP MR. WALLACE, AS A MEMBER OF YOUR CABINET, FROM SPEAKING ON FOREIGN AFFAIRS, IT WOULD BE A GRAVE MISTAKE FROM EVERY POINT OF VIEW FOR ME TO CONTINUE IN OFFICE, EVEN TEMPORARILY.

As Byrnes "spoke," the President, Ross, and I exchanged scribbled suggestions. The President replied: "No speeches by anyone will be approved unless they are in accord with the foreign policy as it now stands." Byrnes replied, "Your statement makes me feel good."

President Truman was uncharacteristically depressed by the situation. That night, when he left the office, I asked him if he was going to take his regular swim in the White House pool. He replied that he didn't feel like swimming—he was going to the family quarters to do some thinking. He took with him the newspaper articles about the Wallace affair. As he reread them that evening, the President's anger boiled over, and he concluded that Wallace had embarked on a systematic campaign to weaken both the President and the Presidency itself.

When our staff meeting began the next morning, the President surprised us with the news that late the previous night, he had written an angry letter to Wallace demanding his resignation, and, without telling any of his staff, had sent the letter by messenger to Wallace's office. As the President spoke, he realized that the letter's intemperate tone could embarrass him if it became public. "Could you try to retrieve my letter?" he asked me. "It is not the sort of item we want in someone else's possession—especially Henry's."

I left the meeting and called Wallace: "The President has sent you a letter he wrote under most unhappy circumstances. He feels it unfortunate that he wrote this letter. We wondered if you would be willing to send it back." I was deliberately vague as to whether Wallace's dismissal was being withdrawn; the objective of my call was to get the letter back before he might use it to embarrass the President.

To my relief, Wallace immediately promised to return the President's letter by messenger—it was clearly a personal letter, he said. The letter promptly came back resealed, and the President destroyed it. I am aware of no one except the President and Wallace who ever read it.*

After the letter was returned, at about ten o'clock, the President called Wallace and, in calm and measured tones, repeated his request for Wallace's resignation. The former Vice President's resignation letter arrived at the White House almost immediately:

> Dear Harry:
>
> As you requested, here is my resignation. I shall continue to fight for peace. I am sure that you approve and will join me in that great endeavor.
>
> Respectfully yours,
> H. A. Wallace

Much-relieved at getting Wallace out of the Cabinet, the President ignored the breezy style and veiled threat implicit in his letter. I spent the morning with Ross, drafting the President's announcement. At noon President Truman told a packed press conference that he was firing Wallace. "I am sure that Mr. Wallace will be happier in the exercise of his right to present his views as a private citizen," he said.

*Wallace's own version of events differs from my account in one important detail: he wrote in his diary that he offered to return the letter on his own initiative so as not to embarrass the President.

With Wallace finally gone, President Truman told us that he wanted to "become a hermit for a while," and he went to the *Williamsburg* alone for the rest of the day and the evening. He seemed completely worn out. In one of those remarkable and revealing letters that he wrote throughout his Presidency to his beloved mother and sister back home in Missouri, he described the firing in bitter terms, and added this postscript:

> Charlie Ross said I'd shown that I'd rather be right than President, and I told him I'd rather be anything than President. My good counselor, Clark Clifford, who took Sam Rosenman's place, said, "Please don't say that." Of course, Clark, Charlie and all the rest of my friends are thinking in terms of [the election of] 1948—and I am not.[2]

This dreadful incident had four major consequences, two bad, two good. On one hand, it hurt the Democrats in the Congressional elections less than six weeks later, and it started Wallace on the path toward his third-party candidacy in 1948—which almost cost President Truman the election. On the other, it brought Averell Harriman back to Washington as the new Secretary of Commerce, and finally, it led to a major change in the way the White House functioned.

Two days after Henry Wallace was fired, Steelman, Connelly, and I met Charlie Ross in his office to discuss how we could avoid such problems in the future. Despite the messy way it had happened, we were all pleased that Wallace was gone, and we looked forward to the impending departure of Byrnes. We all felt strongly that the sooner Harry Truman replaced his former political rivals with his own men, the better; but we also agreed that the Cabinet could no longer be allowed to operate as a collection of independent fiefdoms, and the informal Roosevelt system could not continue without the risk of more disasters. We decided to recommend to the President a new way of conducting the business of the White House.

Two days later, on September 24, Ross, Connelly, and I met with the President. Ross led the discussion, making clear he was speaking for all three of us. We urged the President to allow us to prepare him carefully before each press meeting, and to try to refrain from his normal easy bantering and preliminary conversations with the reporters closest to him.

In regard to dealing with the Cabinet, I suggested that the President not see Cabinet members alone unless it was essential, and never approve anything brought directly to him—especially speeches or basic policy positions—until they had been reviewed by his senior staff and, if necessary, coordinated with other parts of the government. The President, much sobered by the Wallace affair, agreed to all our suggestions.

Such arrangements may seem obvious in hindsight, and variations of them have been in place in every adminstration since President Truman's. But in 1946, at the onset of the growth of the modern Presidency, Harry Truman and the men around him were just beginning to look for ways to strengthen the Office of the President. The Wallace affair dramatized the need for central control of the President's schedule, press relations, and speeches. As so often happens, a fiasco had led to essential reforms—in this case, reforms that became part of the modern White House structure.

THE CLIFFORD-ELSEY REPORT DISAPPEARS

Just as the Wallace drama reached its conclusion, Elsey and I finished our study of American-Soviet relations. In the September 24 meeting, after we had finished discussing Wallace's departure, I handed the President a printed, hardbound copy of our top-secret report, entitled simply "American Relations with the Soviet Union." Ross noted in his journal the next day, "Clark Clifford submitted his monumental top-secret report on our relations with Russia. This should be an extremely valuable source book. Only twenty copies have been prepared."

Noting the leaks during the Wallace affair, Ross said it was vital that even the report's existence be kept secret. As it turned out, Ross more than got his wish.

I left the office relieved at the developments of the day: the report finally had been delivered, and the Henry Wallace affair, messy though it had been, at least had led to a significant restructuring of the White House.

At about seven o'clock the next morning my telephone rang at home. I was surprised to hear President Truman on the other end of the line. "I stayed up very late last night reading your report," he began. "Powerful stuff."

"Thank you, Mr. President."

"Clark, how many copies of this memorandum do you have?"

"Twenty," I replied.

"Have any been distributed yet?"

"No, sir. They are all in my safe at the office."

"Well, please come down to your office now, and get all twenty copies. I want them delivered to me at once." The President offered no explanation for his surprising instructions, but I set out for the White House immediately, got all twenty copies out of my safe and took them to the Oval Office. "I read your report with care last night," the President said. "It is very valuable to me—but if it leaked it would blow the roof off the White House, it would blow the roof off the Kremlin. We'd have the most serious situation on our hands that has yet occurred in my Administration." Then the President took the reports from me, and neither I nor Elsey, nor anyone else, ever saw them again.

The report might have remained undiscovered indefinitely. But twenty years later, in 1966, Arthur Krock, the former Washington Bureau Chief of *The New York Times,* approached me. In the course of gathering material for his memoirs, he had interviewed former President Truman, who told him of the existence of a highly classified report that had been important in the evolution of Administration policy toward the Soviet Union. Krock, who had scored a huge journalistic coup in 1947 by revealing that George Kennan was the author of the "X" article, wanted to tell the story of "Clifford's secret report" in his memoirs, and asked me if I had a copy that I might show him. As it happened, I had kept a copy of the draft from which the final report had been printed, and since it was no longer sensitive, I showed it to him on what I thought was a background basis. But when Krock's memoirs appeared in 1968, the entire 26,000-word report was printed as a sixty-three-page appendix. To this day, it is the only complete version of the report that has been printed; the normally thorough and excellent official series, *Foreign Relations of the United States,* does not contain it, because it never entered the filing systems of either the State Department or the White House.[3]

THE CLIFFORD-ELSEY REPORT

What was in this report that caused it to disappear after one day, not to reemerge for twenty-two years? And how important was it to the evolution of President Truman's views on the Soviet Union?

The timing of the report was critical. It came halfway between Kennan's Long Telegram and the Truman Doctrine speech of March 12, 1947. While many of the observations in our report had already been made by Churchill, Kennan, and others, the report made a new point: it argued that as a matter of the highest national security the nation urgently needed to create an integrated policy and a coherent strategy to resist the Soviet Union. The report also carried a special authority because it showed, for the first time, that there was a consensus on Soviet relations among the President's senior policy advisers. As I noted in my letter transmitting the report to the President:

> I believe that the simultaneous definition by so many government officials of the problem with which we are confronted is in itself a forward step toward its solution. There is remarkable agreement among the officials with whom I have talked and whose reports I have studied concerning the need for a continuous review of our relations with the Soviet Union.

In three sentences near the beginning of the report, we suggested a new foreign policy for the United States:

> The primary objective of United States policy is to convince Soviet leaders that it is in the Soviet interest to participate in a system of world cooperation.
>
> Until Soviet leaders abandon their aggressive policies, the United States must assume that the U.S.S.R. may at any time embark on a course of expansion effected by open warfare and therefore must maintain sufficient military strength to restrain the Soviet Union.
>
> The United States should seek, by cultural, intellectual, and economic interchange, to demonstrate to the Soviet Union that we have no aggressive intentions and that peaceable coexistence of Capitalism and Communism is possible.

Today this may seem a self-evident summation of American policies during the Cold War under the nine Presidents from Harry Truman to George Bush, but in 1946 it was new. Others had warned of the Soviet threat, but no one had previously proposed a comprehensive American response to the Soviet challenge.

Much of the analysis paralleled that of George Kennan's Long Telegram, which we quoted at length. "I think the general tone is excellent," Kennan wrote me on September 16, after reading the last draft of our report, "and I have no fault to find with it." But the prescriptive sections of our report went considerably further than his famous telegram. He did not use the celebrated word "containment," or propose the concept that came to embody this policy, until his "X" article in *Foreign Affairs,* which appeared almost ten months after our report. Using a slightly different phrase, we outlined a policy very similar to that which Kennan would propose publicly the following year. The U.S., we wrote, "must maintain sufficient military strength to *restrain* the Soviet Union." Later, Elsey and I amused ourselves imagining that, had our report been circulated, future historians might have referred to the policy of "restrainment" instead of "containment."

We did not represent the views in the report as our own. Elsey and I agreed with most of the ideas and recommendations, but where we disagreed with what we had gathered, we still felt obliged to reflect accurately the views of the officials we had consulted. Thus, the report is a time capsule of high-level thinking six months before the enunciation of the Truman Doctrine. We stated the basic issue starkly:

> The gravest problem facing the United States today is that of American relations with the Soviet Union. The solution of that problem

> may determine whether or not there will be a third World War. Soviet leaders appear to be conducting their nation on a course of aggrandizement designed to lead to eventual world domination by the U.S.S.R. Their goal, and their policies designed to reach it, are in direct conflict with American ideals. . . . [Soviet policy] is based not upon the interests and aspirations of the Russian people, but upon the prejudices, calculations and ambitions of a . . . group of professional revolutionaries who have survived revolutions, purges and party feuds for almost thirty years. This small group of able men, headed by Generalissimo Stalin, possesses great practical shrewdness but it is isolated within the Kremlin, is largely ignorant of the outside world, and is blinded by its adherence to Marxist dogma. . . .
>
> The concept of danger from the outside is deeply rooted in the Russian people's haunting sense of insecurity inherited from their past. It is maintained by their present leaders as a justification for the oppressive nature of the Soviet police state. . . . The Soviet Union will tolerate no rival influence in [Eastern Europe] and it will insist on the maintenance there of "friendly" governments, that is, governments willing to accept Soviet domination. . . .

After a lengthy review of Soviet ambitions, we reached the most important part of our report, its final recommendations. They began on a positive note:

> The primary objective of United States policy toward the Soviet Union is to convince Soviet leaders that it is in their interest to participate in a system of world cooperation, that there are no fundamental causes for war between our two nations, and that the security and prosperity of the Soviet Union, and that of the rest of the world as well, is being jeopardized by the aggressive militaristic imperialism in which the Soviet Union is now engaged.

We attacked the concept, supported by Henry Wallace and others, that "hope of international peace lies only in 'accord,' 'mutual understanding,' or 'solidarity' with the Soviet Union":

> Adoption of such a policy would . . . only have the effect of raising Soviet hopes and increasing Soviet demands. . . . The Soviet Government will never be easy to "get along with." The American people must accustom themselves to this thought, not as a cause for despair, but as a fact to be faced objectively and courageously. *If we find it impossible to enlist Soviet cooperation in the solution of world problems, we should be prepared to join with the British and other Western countries in an attempt to build up a world of our own which will pursue its own objectives and will recognize the Soviet orbit as a*

> *distinct entity with which conflict is not predestined but with which we cannot pursue common goals. . . .*
>
> This government should be prepared, while scrupulously avoiding any act which would be an excuse for the Soviets to begin a war, to resist vigorously and successfully any efforts [at expansion by] the U.S.S.R. . . . It must be made apparent to the Soviet Government that our strength will be sufficient to repel any attack and sufficient to defeat the U.S.S.R. decisively if a war should start. [Emphasis added.]

We laid out a proposal that would reemerge as the core of both the Truman Doctrine and the Marshall Plan, and, eventually, Point Four:

> In addition to maintaining our own strength, the United States should support and assist all democratic countries which are in any way menaced or endangered by the U.S.S.R. Providing military support in case of attack is a last resort; a more effective barrier to communism is strong economic support. . . . The United States can do much to ensure that economic opportunities, personal freedom and social equality are made possible in countries outside the Soviet sphere by generous financial assistance.

Another proposal we made concerned the need for an effective information program overseas to counter Soviet propaganda. (Resurfacing later, this task was assigned first to the State Department, and later spun off into a new organization, the United States Information Agency, created in 1953.) Reread in light of the dramatic events of 1989 and 1990 in Eastern Europe, this section of the report turned out to be an accurate evocation of the power of the idea of freedom, although none of us could have imagined how long the effort to penetrate the Soviet darkness would go on:

> To the greatest extent tolerated by the Soviet Government, we should distribute books, magazines, newspapers and movies among the Soviets. . . . We should aim, through intellectual and cultural contacts, to convince Soviet leaders that the United States has no aggressive intentions and that the nature of our society is such that peaceful coexistence of capitalistic and communistic states is possible. . . . If this position can be maintained firmly enough and long enough the logic of it must permeate eventually into the Soviet system.

We strongly criticized the bureaucratic impediments to policy, especially the artificial divisions that existed within the State and War Departments:

> Our policies must also be global in scope. By time-honored custom, we have regarded "European Policy," "Near Eastern Policy," "Indian Policy" and "Chinese Policy" as separate problems to be handled by experts in each field. But the areas involved, far removed from each other by conventional standards, all border on the Soviet Union and our actions with respect to each must be considered in the light of over-all Soviet objectives.

Our summation gave a sense of where we felt American policy should go. It was prophetic; a succinct one-paragraph forecast of policies the nation would follow for the next forty years:

> In conclusion, as long as the Soviet Union adheres to its present policy, the United States should maintain military forces powerful enough to restrain the Soviet Union and to confine Soviet influence to its present area. All nations not now within the Soviet sphere should be given generous economic assistance and political support in their opposition to Soviet penetration. Economic aid may also be given to the Soviet Union [as well as] private trade with the U.S.S.R. . . . Even though Soviet leaders profess to believe that the conflict between Capitalism and Communism is irreconcilable and must eventually be resolved by the triumph of the latter, it is our hope that they will change their minds and work out with us a fair and equitable settlement when they realize that we are too strong to be beaten and too determined to be frightened.

AFTERMATH

Because the Clifford-Elsey report disappeared from sight the day after I delivered it to President Truman, because he did not mention it in either his diaries or his memoirs, and because its very existence was unknown to the public for more than twenty years, its role in the creation of policy is difficult to categorize and evaluate.

One important value of the report is indisputable: it gave President Truman—as well as modern readers—a precise picture of what the Administration's senior officials were thinking in that critical year, when our nation was suspended between the end of World War II and the beginnings of the Cold War. For the most part, they were far ahead of the American public in recognizing the dangers posed by the Soviet Union. Most of them supported a comprehensive policy of resistance to Soviet expansionism long before the formulation of the Truman Doctrine. Although the President felt it was too early to tell the public how serious the Soviet threat was, the report helped to prepare him for the challenge of the following year. If it were not for the farsightedness of the men who contributed to our report and fashioned policy in the late forties, I believe we would have been unprepared for the Soviet thrust into Eastern Europe, and our lack of preparedness would have, in turn, encouraged Stalin to press further.

There is no question that the report had a significant impact on President Truman. For one thing, he dropped completely the idea of a long-term low-rate loan to the Soviets comparable to the British loan extended earlier in the year—which, as recently as September 18, he had favored. After he read our report, he never mentioned such a loan again. The speed with which he buried the report did not indicate that he disagreed with it, but, recognizing its importance, he felt it was the wrong time to publicize such ideas.

President Truman focused on many other problems in the fall and winter of 1946–47—the fallout from Henry Wallace's firing, the Congressional elections in November, the confrontation with John L. Lewis and the coal miners—and deferred the Soviet issue, but he knew that our national security was his most important responsibility, and that he could not indefinitely defer dealing with the Soviet challenge. The report established the framework for his quick reaction the following February to the British decision to wash their hands of any further responsibility in Greece and Turkey. Our recommendations demonstrate that the policies created by President Truman between 1947 and 1950 were not simply a step-by-step response to specific events. Although the Truman Doctrine was a response to a specific problem in the spring of 1947, it was derived from thinking that existed in relatively specific form as early as the summer of 1946.

It was a short step from the report to the Truman Doctrine and the Marshall Plan. Those two fundamental elements, which represented the triumph of internationalism in America, survived every twist and turn of politics and history—including McCarthyism, Korea, Watergate, and Vietnam—until they finally emerged triumphant in 1989 with the collapse of communism in Eastern Europe. Anyone who played a role, even a small one, in the formulation of that policy has a right to say proudly, in Dean Acheson's grand phrase, that he was "present at the creation."

8

The Truman Doctrine and the Marshall Plan

I believe that it must be the policy of the United States to support free peoples who are resisting attempted subjugation by armed minorities or by outside pressures.

I believe that we must assist free peoples to work out their own destinies in their own way.

I believe that our help should be primarily through economic and financial aid which is essential to economic stability and orderly political processes.

—HARRY S TRUMAN, MARCH 12, 1947

Three quarters of the way through his speech to Congress on March 12, 1947, President Truman uttered three sentences that ended a century and a half in which American foreign policy had, in essence, consisted of reactions to specific events, and ushered in an era in which, for the first time in peacetime, we committed ourselves to continuous and active leadership in international affairs.

The policy set forth by President Truman took over forty years to succeed, was often controversial and expensive, and was at times misapplied—most notably in Vietnam. But a major war with the Soviet Union was avoided during a dangerous half century, and by 1989 it was clear that the Cold War was over. This was the direct, if long-delayed, result of the policies laid out in 1947 by Harry Truman and followed, despite all the political controversies at home, by every one of his successors. No President could wish for a grander legacy.

In late 1946, I had breakfast regularly with Secretary of the Navy Forrestal at his beautiful house on Prospect Street in Georgetown. At almost every breakfast he urged me to encourage the Administration to take a more active stand against the Soviet Union. I agreed with Forrestal's strategic assessment, but I told Forrestal such an effort could not be undertaken without strong personal leadership by the President. I knew the President understood the danger posed by the Soviet Union, and that in the near future he would step up to the challenge. However, the last few months of 1946 was not the time to begin the process, in the words of our report, of ensuring that "the American people . . . be fully informed about the difficulties in getting along with the Soviet Union." I urged Forrestal to be more patient—but patience was not one of his strong suits, and he continued to press his case.

The electoral disaster of 1946 changed the situation dramatically. Although we did not realize it at the time, it turned out to be easier to fashion a bipartisan foreign policy with a coalition of Republicans and conservative Democrats than with Democrats alone: they were still divided between liberals, who retained affection for Henry Wallace, and conservatives, who did not trust President Truman. To a surprising extent, these foreign policy alliances across party lines continued for the next forty-five years.

THE BRITISH NOTE

On February 21, 1947, the British Ambassador in Washington, Lord Inverchapel, asked to see Secretary of State Marshall to deliver an important message. It was a Friday, and Marshall had already left for the weekend, but his deputy, Dean Acheson, persuaded the Ambassador to deliver a carbon copy of the message informally, so that the State Department could consider it over the weekend.

The message from London was blunt and to the point: the British, having "already strained their resources to the utmost," wished to inform the U.S. that British assistance to Greece and Turkey would terminate on March 31, 1947—barely five weeks away. The British expressed the hope that the U.S. would assume their burden in both countries, which they estimated would be between $240 and $280 million for Greece, and about $150 million for Turkey. These sums, still substantial today, were staggering in 1947 dollars, totalling about 1 percent of a federal budget of only $41 billion.

I was alone with President Truman for our usual end of the day discussion when Acheson called to alert him to the contents of the British note. It was clear from listening to the President's end of the conversation that he was prepared for suggestions from Acheson to offer Greece and Turkey substantial aid, even though this would require support from Congress, since there were no funds allocated in the existing budget for Greece and Turkey.

Contrary to most accounts of the period, the news that the British were abandoning their aid to Greece and Turkey did not come as a complete surprise. We had received informal warnings from British diplomats in the last months of 1946, and we understood their special vulnerability. In the Clifford-Elsey report, we had singled out the area as particularly important and explosive:

> The Soviet Union is interested in obtaining the withdrawal of British troops from Greece and the establishment of a "friendly" government there. It hopes to make Turkey a puppet state which could serve as a spring-board for the domination of the eastern Mediterranean. . . . The long-range Soviet aim is the economic, military and political domination of the entire Middle East. . . .

Acheson's first set of recommendations arrived at the White House early the following week. He saw an opportunity to create a policy that went far beyond Greece and Turkey; but, wise in the ways of Washington, he did not unveil his long-range objective until he could get a clear picture of the degree of Presidential commitment and Congressional sentiment.

The answers to both questions began to emerge later in the week. In a crucial meeting with Congressional leaders on February 27, the President, Marshall, and Acheson outlined the need to give massive assistance to Greece and Turkey. I did not attend this meeting, which has been described by many of its participants,[1] but after the meeting ended, President Truman told me that the Republicans, led by Senator Arthur Vandenberg of Michigan, had showed willingness to support a request for massive aid if *and only if* President Truman personally argued the case for such aid, and linked it explicitly to the survival of the Western world. My reaction to this information was instantaneous: I told the President that I believed this was the time for him to make an effort to rally American support for a new policy along the lines of our September 1946 report.

Watching President Truman tackle this challenge, I felt he had come a long way since the messy Wallace affair and the loss of Congress to the Republicans barely three months earlier. His own spirits and self-confidence had soared with the victory over the coal miners in December. Now he seemed ready for what Senator Vandenberg told him was his "date with destiny." He was willing, he told me, to "lay it on the line" with the American people. He did not spend time, as most Presidents would have, studying "options papers." He simply wanted to see a speech draft before making a final decision.

ELSEY VOICES CONCERN

Despite Acheson's vision, those working on the crisis were not yet in full agreement. One of those who felt this was neither the right time nor the right issue for such a speech by the President was George Elsey, whose methodical mind rebelled against the pell-mell way in which the British note and the preliminary decision to give an "all-out" speech were now driving the policy. He wrote me a thoughtful personal memorandum outlining his views:

> 1. [There is] insufficient time to prepare what would be the most significant speech in the President's administration. . . .
> 2. There has been no overt action in the immediate past by the U.S.S.R. which serves as an adequate pretext for the "all-out" speech. The situation in Greece is relatively abstract; there have been other instances—Iran, for example—where the occasion more adequately justified such a speech and there will be other such occasions—I fear—in the future.
> 3. An "all-out" speech will have a divisive effect if delivered too soon. . . . For these reasons, I believe that next week's message should be limited in scope.

I considered Elsey's suggestions carefully. On one hand, it was unusual, indeed unnatural, for the normally unwieldy machinery of the American government to crank up a major policy in just a few days. Still, Congress would not approve aid to Greece and Turkey unless we justified it on larger grounds. Elsey's views only further convinced me that this was the moment to move forward. In any crisis there are always valid reasons to consider delay or inaction, but I felt it was high time to tell the American public the facts, as we had seen them for at least six months, and to ask for their support and understanding. Still, George's memorandum highlighted for me the importance of assuring that the speech contained no half-steps or ambivalent language, and I resolved to try to make the speech as strong as possible, both in style and content. "This speech," I told him, "must be the opening gun in a campaign to bring people to the realization that the war isn't over by any means." From that point on, Elsey, as always the consummate staff officer, worked brilliantly to improve the drafts that came from State.

THE DRAFTING

Despite its importance, the Truman Doctrine speech was prepared in much the same way as were routine Presidential speeches. The State Department prepared the first draft, and the rewriting and "Trumanizing" of it was done under my supervision at the White House.[2] By the time the final draft was ready, so many hands had touched it that, despite some claims to the contrary, no single person could assert paternity.

At first, State's drafting team was not sure if they were writing a Presidential speech or a legislative message. Within State there was disagreement, some of which reached our ears at the White House. The most notable dissenter was George Kennan, who wandered into the drafting process from his new position as Vice Commandant of the National War College and found, to his concern, that Greece and Turkey were being used to justify a global policy that he felt was out of all proportion to the situation in the eastern Mediterranean. Kennan's proposed alternative confined itself to the economic needs of the Greek people, somewhat along the lines of the suggestions made by George Elsey. It was oddly characteristic of this remarkable and lonely hero, soon to be famous for coining the word "containment," that he would become the first dissenter from its first application. Meanwhile, dissatisfied with the early drafts, Acheson took over the drafting process personally in the first few days of March, producing a statement stronger than any contained in the early drafts.

On March 2, as a heavy, wet snowfall brought Washington to a virtual standstill, the President went on a four-day state visit to Mexico—the first to that country by a sitting President. I stayed in Washington to keep in contact with State. On March 7, the morning after he returned from Mexico City, the President met with Acheson, Snyder, Leahy, and me, and made the final decision to move ahead as quickly as possible with a request for Congressional action. He also postponed his planned vacation to Key West. Then he led us into the Cabinet Room, where he informed the rest of the Cabinet of his decision and asked for advice on tactics. A consensus developed that the President should personally deliver a strong speech before a joint session of Congress, the position Acheson and I had both favored. The die was irreversibly cast for a speech instead of a message.

Until this point, the speech drafts had circulated only within the State Department. I asked Acheson to send the latest draft to me. My reaction was mixed: a great deal of work had been done on the message, but it simply was not crisp or tough enough for a Presidential speech. After the morning staff meeting on Saturday, March 8, I voiced my concern privately to the President, who told me to get more deeply involved immediately. The next five drafts were then revised under my direction. Each version marked another shift toward a tougher, more forceful statement.

Later that day, Elsey and I met with Joseph M. Jones, a State Department speech writer, and Carl Humelsine, the Director of the Secretariat at State. I told them that the speech still lacked focus and force, and did not build steadily toward a clear climax. I suggested substantially reorganizing the speech, building to a climactic request for Congressional action. As I suggested tougher language, Jones wrote on his copy of the draft: "Stronger peroration. 'This is a grim task we are accepting. Nothing to recommend it except [that] alternative is grimmer.' " Words very close to these would appear in the final speech.

I also made a number of specific suggestions, among them a major concern of Congress, that American aid money often got into the wrong hands: "The speech must emphasize American control of funds to avoid graft, the black market, and wastage." Furthermore, I said, we should mention the fact that the Greek government had also asked for American administrators and technicians. (In the final speech, this paragraph, ending with the words "each dollar spent will count toward making Greece self-supporting," would bring one of the rare rounds of applause the President received as he spoke.)

I urged that we explain clearly why the U.S. must undertake the task itself—"We must do it or it will not be done"—and that we must try to keep faith in democracy alive in Greece. Finally, I told Jones and Humelsine that it *must* explain clearly that we would not turn the job over to the U.N. because it would be too time-consuming and the outcome too uncertain.

I arrived early the next morning, Sunday, March 9, in the office. At 9:30, I received a new draft from Humelsine, with a short note saying it had been rewritten "in line with your suggestions" and constituted "an improvement over the original draft." Elsey and I spent a long Sunday in my office, taking turns reading portions aloud to each other, looking for ways to make it sound more like Harry Truman and less like a committee product from State. We made well over one hundred changes.[3] Elsey then produced a clean new draft, and early Monday morning, with the speech only two days away, we reviewed it again. I added a passage that, slightly modified, appeared in the final speech as follows:

> The seeds of totalitarian regimes are nurtured by misery and want. They spread and grow in the evil soil of poverty and strife. They reach their full growth when the hope of a people for a better life has died. We must keep that hope alive.

THE DOCTRINE

Despite all this work, I felt the speech still lacked a simple and coherent statement that would link the request for aid to Greece and Turkey to our larger foreign policy goals. It was our search for the proper way to characterize the policy that led to the three sentences that became famous as the Truman Doctrine.

These sentences were not in the State versions of the speech. One early draft contained a thought that had been culled from a report prepared at the midlevels of State, but it was written in a weakly worded, bureaucratic style which would have received no attention in a Presidential speech:

> It is essential to our security that we assist free peoples to work out their own destiny in their own way and our help must be primarily in the form of that economic and financial aid which is essential to economic stability and orderly political processes.

In the first week of drafting and redrafting, these thoughts were rephrased several times. In the March 4 draft, State tried restating the principles of the Atlantic Charter and the U.N. Charter—a reformulation that robbed the thought of any originality or dramatic punch. In the drafting session at State on March 5, Acheson made another change: he deleted much of the surrounding material concerning the charters and changed the statement from the past tense into a more forward-looking statement:

> I believe it must be the policy of the United States to give support to free peoples who are attempting to resist subjugation by armed minorities and outside forces. It is essential to our security that we assist free peoples to work out their own destiny in their own way, and our help must be in the form of economic and financial aid. . . .

This draft reached Elsey and me on March 9, and we tightened it in our Sunday drafting session—but neither of us was satisfied. I wanted something that was punchier, more dramatic, more memorable. We finished our long day's work without any solution, but early the next morning, Elsey had a simple and elegant idea: break the paragraph up into three single sentences, and begin each sentence with the same phrase: "I believe that . . ."* I liked this idea enormously, and immediately made it part of the draft we were preparing for the President. These sentences, which George and I called the "credo," finally seemed to leap out at the listener.

*The surviving drafts of the speech, available at the Truman Library, unfortunately disprove one of the enduring minor legends of the speech: that President Truman, as he wrote in his memoirs, "took my pencil, scratched out 'should,' and wrote in 'must.' "[4] (Truman, *Memoirs,* p. 105). Arthur Krock was one of the early purveyors of this story, writing in *The New York Times* on March 23, 1947, that "the important word 'must' (instead of 'should') which appeared in the master key to the Doctrine, was inserted at the President's express direction."

At noon on March 10 I took our latest draft to the President, while Elsey circulated it to key members of the White House staff. We then held the usual roundtable speech-drafting session in the Cabinet Room with the President, who read the speech for the first time. No one from State was present. After making a number of changes, the President it reflected what he wanted to say, but he wanted still more punch. I took a revised draft back across the street to show to Acheson.

Acheson accepted without comment almost all our suggestions, including the "credo,"[5] but objected to three of our proposed additions. The first two, concerning the Mideast, were relatively minor, and I dropped them immediately. The third deletion concerned a passage I had included in the March 10 draft with some misgivings, one that had been proposed by the conservatives in the Cabinet, led by my adversary on the domestic front, Secretary of the Treasury John Snyder. At the President's request, Snyder had convened a meeting of concerned Cabinet members in order to gather their suggestions. This group, which included Forrestal, Harriman, Patterson, Steelman, Schwellenbach of Labor, and Clinton Anderson of Agriculture, met only once, and recommended that the speech include a strong endorsement of the free enterprise system as essential to the preservation of both democracy and American aid. Acheson would not hear of this addition, saying it would put a dangerous limitation on the new policy. Did the existence of a Labour government in Great Britain mean that we could not give them assistance? he asked sarcastically. What mattered, Acheson said, was not the economic organization in a country, but whether its government was free and independent and wanted to remain so. I listened with quiet pleasure to Acheson's eloquent denunciation of Snyder's suggestions, which I deleted without further discussion. Thus did my final discussion with State on the speech end.

THE JOINT SESSION

On March 12, I rode up to Capitol Hill with the President, going over the speech one last time, underlining sentences that needed emphasis. Then he turned away from the history he was about to make, and talked enthusiastically about our plan to leave for that postponed vacation in Key West as soon as the speech was over.

I watched from the Executive Gallery with Mrs. Truman and Marny. The President spoke at a slower pace than normal, while the audience listened somberly, without any evident enthusiasm. Applause interrupted the speech only three times, and not at the most critical passages. For most members of Congress, this was not so much a historic occasion as another unfortunate foreign problem to confront when what the voters really wanted was housing, jobs, and meat.

As soon as the speech was over, we drove directly to National Airport, and boarded the President's plane, the *Sacred Cow,* for the flight to Key West, while Dean Acheson stayed in Washington, coordinating the effort to get Congressional approval for the President's requested aid.

Sometimes the true importance of historic events is not immediately recognized. This was not the case with President Truman's speech. *The New York Times* called the speech a "radical change [in American foreign policy] in the space of twenty-one minutes," and described Congress as "bewildered" and "much-shaken" as it faced "one of the toughest deadlines in modern history." James Reston said the speech was "comparable in importance" to the Monroe Doctrine. Senator Vandenberg issued a strong statement of support, which he had worked out in advance with Dean Acheson.

Curiously, the phrase "Truman Doctrine" was never uttered by any of the President's staff prior to the speech, nor was it used in any news accounts the following day. The phrase began to creep into the analytical stories a few days after the address. Despite the importance of the entire speech, it would not have achieved the status of a "doctrine" without its three key sentences, which immediately took their place among the most quoted—and misunderstood—sentences in the history of American foreign policy.

The criticism of the speech came from an unlikely combination of people, linked, I felt, only by their bitterness at not being part of the policymaking process. The most prominent early critics of the policy were Republican Senator Robert A. Taft, Henry Wallace, former Ambassador Joseph P. Kennedy, and Bernard Baruch. Taft, who thought himself "Mr. Republican," intended to run for the Presidency in 1948. He may have endeared himself to a generation of right-wing Republicans who interpreted his rigidity as adherence to principle, but as far as I was concerned he was simply obdurate. Because his rival, Senator Vandenberg, supported the Administration, Taft attacked, making the strange claim that the President was trying to "secure a special domination over the affairs" of Greece and Turkey similar to Russian demands for hegemony in her sphere of influence.

Taft's wild charge was matched by Henry Wallace, still embittered by the events of the previous year. The day after the speech, Wallace denounced it, predicting that if Congress approved aid to Greece and Turkey, "America will become the most hated nation in the world." As for Joseph P. Kennedy, who listened to the speech from the comfort of his vacation home at Palm Beach, his bitterness could not be contained: the new American policy, Kennedy told *The New York Times,* was wasting its money trying to save the "little nations" of the world, who were bound to be attracted by the bright promises of communism. Kennedy said that the U.S. should let communism spread, and keep our wealth at home to make our nation richer. It is remarkable, in light of Joe Kennedy's influence over his children in so many areas, how differently John F. Kennedy would approach these same issues a dozen years later.

Bernard Baruch, the legendary financier who was one of the most adept and relentless self-promoters of the century, joined Kennedy in attacking the new policy. When I asked the President how he wanted to respond to Baruch's attacks, he laughed: the only way to make Baruch happy, he said, was to consult him publicly. Harriman and others had suggested doing just that—but, said the President, "I'm not going to spend time listening to that old goat. If I see him, I've got him on my hands for hours and hours, and then it's *his* policy."

Because the Truman Doctrine was a success, such criticisms became mere historical trivia. But at the time, we viewed attacks from the likes of Kennedy and Baruch as very serious, even potentially fatal. President Truman had staked his reputation on one of the boldest changes in policy in American history, and he could not afford a defeat.

President Truman never intended his speech to be elevated into a doctrine. In March 1957, when I sent him a letter commenting on the public attention to the tenth anniversary of the Truman Doctrine, he wrote back, "I never was very much impressed that that policy was named the Truman Doctrine. Like the Marshall Plan, it was only a part of the foreign policy of the United States, and that is how history should refer to it." His assessment is characteristically Trumanesque, but I cannot agree: the speech was a seminal event in the history of our times, and, despite President Truman's admirable dislike of what he called "advertising," it deserves to be named after the man who had the courage and decisiveness to articulate it.

WHAT DID IT MEAN?

Ever since the speech was delivered, journalists, historians, and politicians have debated the meaning of its three key sentences. Were they intended to constitute a blank check for American intervention everywhere in the world? Were they misused by later Presidents to justify interventions that were never imagined? Were they an overstatement of American policy, as Kennan had feared?

As one of its drafters, I think I have an obligation to try to answer these questions. Obviously, the speech was not intended to establish a rigid doctrine that would apply equally in every corner of the globe. Testifying in support of the request for aid to Greece and Turkey only a few days later, Acheson made this cautionary note explicit: All aid requests will be judged, he said, "according to the circumstances of each specific case."

The same Senator who had insisted on a universal theme in the speech asking for aid to Greece and Turkey, Arthur Vandenberg, supported this narrower interpretation, saying, "I do not view [the policy] as a universal pattern but rather as a selective pattern to fit a given circumstance." The President had had no choice but to dramatize the situation with a broad and dramatic statement if he wanted Congressional approval; but, clearly, he did not intend it as a blank check.

Nonetheless, the President intended the speech to mark a historic departure from traditional American foreign policy. His modesty notwithstanding, he understood that he was asking the nation to engage actively in international affairs in a manner we had never before attempted in peacetime.

DEAN ACHESON

George Marshall was still Secretary of State, but Dean Acheson was now approaching the height of his influence. Even as Secretary of State two years later, nothing Acheson did would surpass his remarkable performance in the spring of 1947. He was not just "present at the creation"—he was, at that moment, the most important of an imposing collection of creators.

Everything came together for him that spring. First and foremost, he had General Marshall's full support. Nothing like the team of Marshall and Acheson will ever be seen again at the top of any department. As Stuart Symington liked to say, Marshall had President Truman's heart, and Acheson his mind.

An unlikely pairing it seemed at first, but it worked well: Harry Truman from a hardscrabble farm in western Missouri, with a high school education, and Acheson from the secure life as son of a distinguished Connecticut clergyman, educated at Groton and Yale. Acheson, who could be brutal and condescending, never made that mistake with President Truman, to whom he was unfailingly polite, patient, and deferential. In turn, the President recognized the great scope of Acheson's vision and respected him enormously. With Marshall as the third man of the team, temperament, intellect, values, and courage were combined in a unique way.

Acheson's loyalty and affection for President Truman were undoubtedly heightened by resentment over the way Franklin Roosevelt had treated him when he was Assistant Secretary of the Treasury. With his distinctly patrician style, Acheson seemed the very model of the Eastern Establishmentarian. This probably contributed to his distaste for the far more aristocratic squire of Hyde Park. "Roosevelt," he often told me, "made you feel like one of the peasants being called in by the lord of the castle. When I was with him, I felt I should be standing humbly at attention, turning my cap in my hand, reaching up to touch a forelock of hair while the great man gave me instructions."

It was ironic that Acheson felt this way about Roosevelt, since so many people felt something similar when in the presence of Dean Acheson. In a city filled with large egos, he was the most self-confident man I ever encountered. Fortunately, his intellect and his seriousness of intent justified his demeanor. His ego was not harnessed to an overwhelming personal ambition: when public service called, Acheson was usually available, but he did not seek high office, and indeed, had turned away from it several times in his career, under both Presidents Roosevelt and Truman—only to be called back in moments of national need.

I greatly admired the way Dean's mind worked. Most government officials spend much of their time on routine or unimportant matters, filling their days with meaningless internal meetings or ceremonies. This was never the case with Acheson. He had a clarity of vision, and the ability to separate the consequential from the trivial.

At the same time, his self-confidence was often interpreted, not without reason, as arrogance. Despite his intelligence in so many other areas, he was unable to conceal his feelings when dealing with someone he considered intellectually inferior. It was often said that he did not suffer fools gladly, but this was an understatement: he positively exuded an attitude that made other people feel belittled and scorned. He also had a certain contempt for the political process, which caused him difficulty, especially after the Hiss affair and the rise of Senator Joe McCarthy. Many of his appearances as a witness before Congress left behind bruised and offended Congressmen who would not soon forget the sarcasm and scorn with which he answered their questions.

The sense that he felt somewhat superior to the rest of his colleagues was reinforced by his unforgettable appearance. He was tall, imposing, and always impeccably dressed. Although he was in fact no special friend of Great Britain, many people thought from his appearance that he was either partly English or pro-British. This was due in large part to his famous mustache, which seemed to bristle with superiority. When friends tried to suggest that he consider shaving his mustache, he refused to listen, saying that on his personal appearance he would never compromise.

The supreme irony of Acheson's career, of course, was that he had to defend himself constantly against attacks from the far right that he was "soft" on communism. These attacks were wholly without merit—never did anyone see more clearly the dangers of communism and the Soviet threat, nor work harder to construct a policy to resist them. Before the end of his life, Acheson would be honored for his achievements, and consulted even by his old adversary Richard Nixon. But at the height of

Acheson's career, Nixon was among those who attacked him mercilessly, calling him the "Red Dean." Throughout the fifties, he was a constant target for Nixon, who lumped him with President Truman and Adlai Stevenson as "traitors to the high principles in which many of the nation's Democrats believe." In a famous remark which Nixon later tried to deny having made, the future President referred to "Acheson's College of Cowardly Communist Containment."[6] Others joined the assault: Senator William E. Jenner, Republican of Indiana, referred to Acheson and General Marshall as "joining hands once more with this criminal crowd of traitors and Communist appeasers who . . . are still selling America down the river." Senator Kenneth Wherry called Acheson a "bad security risk" and cried that the "blood of our boys in Korea is on [Acheson's] shoulders"; Robert A. Taft attacked Acheson's "pro-Communist group in the State Department."

Acheson bore these attacks with dignity, but they wounded him greatly. The injustice of the attacks and the unrelenting hostility directed against him was an enormous burden on both him and his wife Alice. Although his father had been the Episcopal bishop of Connecticut, Dean himself was not a religious man. Even ethical ideas seemed to bore him; he saw too much inherent ambiguity in them. From his father, he said, he had derived a strong sense of stoicism, and that was what he fell back on when he came under attack. Nonetheless, I feel that he never fully recovered from these attacks. Alice Acheson told me after Dean's death that she thought McCarthy had shortened her husband's life by ten years.

At the time we became friends, he had been in Washington for over twenty-five years, and I had just arrived. Our later relationship was one of relative equals, but in the early years, I was very much the novice. If he could have structured Washington to his own specifications, I think Acheson might have half-seriously considered eliminating from any serious involvement in policy everyone except himself and the President, and perhaps Marshall.* By the spring of 1947, however, Acheson knew I was sympathetic to his foreign policy views, and that I could help him with the President. Additionally, we were both lawyers, and Acheson, who was visibly uncomfortable with most of the President's Missouri friends, felt more at ease with me.

So a formal association gradually developed into a close friendship that lasted until his death in 1971. Like his friendship with other colleagues,

*This is sometimes reflected in his memoirs. His account of the crucial February 27, 1947, meeting with the Congressional leadership, for example, shows General Marshall faltering and Acheson stepping into the breach to save the day. Neither Senator Vandenberg nor President Truman remembered it that way; both gave Marshall credit for the presentation that led to bipartisan support for the Truman Doctrine. Similarly, in his account of the March 7 meeting in which President Truman decided to give his historic speech, Acheson mentions only himself and the President, omitting the fact that Admiral Leahy, Treasury Secretary Snyder, and I were also present.

including his friend at Groton and Yale, Averell Harriman, our relationship always bore elements of rivalry and competition—even a small matter, such as where to meet for lunch, could develop into a brief test of wills (conducted, in this case, through our secretaries). But I respected Dean Acheson as much as anyone I ever knew in Washington. We kept in close touch throughout the fifties and sixties, seeing each other regularly in both social and professional settings. Our paths would intersect one last time, during the dramatic events that followed the Tet Offensive in Vietnam in 1968.

THE MARSHALL PLAN

Acheson's crowning glory in that glorious spring of 1947 was the Marshall Plan. This farsighted program, while approved by the President, was almost entirely a State Department project. Acheson and many others have recounted how it was inspired, formulated, and presented to Congress. After the President's March 12 speech, Acheson and his colleagues, particularly Will Clayton, the Undersecretary of State for Economic Affairs, saw the need to expand the program to the rest of Europe, which was reeling under the twin threats of economic collapse and political pressure from local communist parties supported by Moscow.

The first opportunity Acheson had to lay out a new policy came almost by accident. At the request of Senator Theodore Bilbo of Mississippi, who was suffering from a terminal illness, President Truman had accepted an invitation to speak at the World Affairs Forum at Delta State Teachers College in Cleveland, Mississippi, on May 8—a commitment that Charlie Ross and I urged the President to back out of in a staff meeting on March 27. We noted that, in the aftermath of the victory over the coal miners and the success of the Truman Doctrine, the President's popularity was finally beginning to rise in the polls, with his positive rating in the most recent Gallup soaring to 60 percent. A speech as overtly political as one sponsored by Bilbo, one of the most notorious racists ever to serve in Congress, would set back the President's efforts to stay out of local politics.

Heeding our warning, he asked Acheson to replace him. To mollify the hosts, the White House announced that it would be "an important foreign policy speech." Certain that $400 million for Greece and Turkey was only a fraction of the amount of money that would be needed to save Europe, Acheson decided to use the Mississippi speech as the occasion, as he wrote later, "to sound reveille" and "awaken the American people" to the larger crisis that lay ahead.

The speech was drafted entirely within the State Department, reviewed quickly by me, and cleared without changes by the President. Then, in a crowded and steamy Mississippi gymnasium, the most proper of American diplomats had an uncharacteristic moment, rolling up his sleeves, removing his jacket, and delivering a speech that described "human dignity and human freedom" as being at stake. Without massive American help, he said, Europe might not survive.

Senator Vandenberg, always wary of Acheson, read about the speech and hit the roof. Vandenberg wanted to be seen in public as a great statesman, a shaper of history. In a meeting with the President and Marshall, he assailed Acheson's speech, saying it was, in effect, a commitment of funds without Congressional approval, and a violation of the bipartisan spirit of the Truman Doctrine.

Even as Vandenberg complained about Acheson's speech, a far more important speech was being drafted in the State Department, outlining the overall program. Watching this speech take shape in mid-May, I knew it would be one of the most important programs ever undertaken by an American government in peacetime. I suggested to the President that he deliver the speech himself, and that we name his proposal the Truman Concept or the Truman Plan.

President Truman smiled wryly at my suggestion and shook his head. "No," he said. "We have a Republican majority in both Houses. Anything going up there bearing my name will quiver a couple of times, turn belly up, and die. Let me think about it a little." A day or so later we returned to the subject. "I've decided to give the whole thing to General Marshall," he said. "The worst Republican on the Hill can vote for it if we name it after the General."

This exchange taught me a great lesson. Whatever my intent, I had been wrong, I realized, to propose that the program be named after President Truman. I was reminded of the old aphorism: "There is no limit to what a man can accomplish if he doesn't care who gets the credit."

Marshall gave the speech at the Harvard commencement on June 5, 1947. Although Acheson worried about including the Soviet Union and its allies in our offer of assistance, Marshall insisted on it: he did not want the U.S. to be the one to draw a line of division between East and West. Had Moscow accepted his offer, it is probable that Congress would never have approved the program, but, as Kennan had predicted during the discussion leading up to the speech, the Soviet Union was not about to join a European program on American terms.

It was a full year after Marshall's speech before all the pieces of the program were in place. Meanwhile, important changes were taking place at the State Department. Acheson, as he had longed planned, resigned and was succeeded as Undersecretary of State by his old Yale classmate, Robert Lovett. Kennan was recalled from the National War College to create a new division of the State Department, the Policy Planning Staff.

Vandenberg vetoed the President's idea of appointing Acheson as the head of the Marshall Plan, and President Truman asked Averell Harriman to resign as Secretary of Commerce in order to direct the program in Europe. Acheson had left the government, but his legacy was firmly in place. He would help us, from the outside, in selling the program to Congress, and return to State as its chief in 1949.

The phrase "Marshall Plan" has since become synonymous with a massive aid program to deal with a crisis: time and again, "a new Marshall Plan" is suggested to deal with some critical area of the world, or some pervasive problem such as the inner cities or drugs. But there will never be another Marshall Plan. The conditions that led up to it and made it successful cannot be re-created, and the scope of it defies modern budgets; it cost nearly $10 billion in 1948–49 dollars, the equivalent of more than $50 billion today. It was 16 percent of the federal budget, an inconceivable amount today, when interest on the national debt and defense alone take up 41 percent.

The most wonderful part of the story of the Marshall Plan is that it *worked.* Winston Churchill called it "a turning point in the history of the world"; the distinguished British historian Arnold Toynbee wrote, "It was not the discovery of atomic energy, but the solicitude of the world's most privileged people for its less privileged, as vested in Truman's Point IV* and the Marshall Plan . . . that will be remembered as the signal achievement of our age."

CODA 1990

In the summer of 1990, I addressed a group of Soviet historians at a joint American-Soviet conference in Washington on the origins of the Cold War. Point by point, I rebutted the long-standing official Soviet view that the blame for the Cold War lay with Washington. At the end of my remarks, the Soviet scholars, who had been forced for so long to twist history for political purposes, rose and gave a standing ovation—an expression of their partial liberation from the yoke of intellectual dishonesty under which they had worked. It was, I thought, a fine tribute to President Truman and the policies he had initiated in 1947.

*This was the technical assistance program announced by President Truman in 1949 (see Chapter 13).

9

The Birth of the National Security System

> *It must be remembered that there is nothing more difficult to plan, more doubtful of success, nor more dangerous to manage than the creation of a new system. For the initiator has the enmity of all who would profit by the preservation of the old institutions and merely lukewarm defenders in those who would gain by the new ones.*
>
> —MACHIAVELLI, *The Prince*

Given the way the American government was organized, President Truman liked to say, the U.S. was lucky—"damn lucky"—to have won World War II. "We must never fight another war the way we fought the last two," he told me more than once. "I have the feeling that if the Army and the Navy had fought our enemies as hard as they fought each other, the war would have ended much earlier."

Soon after he became President, he decided to reorganize not only the armed forces, but the entire national security structure—reforms that changed forever the way the American government worked. Consider his achievement: in less than three years, President Truman established the Department of Defense, the United States Air Force, the Central Intelligence Agency, the National Security Council, the position of Chairman of the Joint Chiefs of Staff, and the first foreign aid agencies. It was as if the nation had suddenly made the transition from horse-drawn carriages to the era of the automobile. When this surprisingly short period of explosive institutional creativity came to an end, it would become far more difficult for the U.S. to turn away from global responsibilities, as it had, with such disastrous results, following World War I.

It was no accident that governmental reorganization coincided with the development of the Truman Doctrine, the Marshall Plan, NATO, Point Four, and the policy of containment: these new policies required new machinery. For government officials, however, it was much easier to agree on major policy changes than on governmental reorganization—even minor changes could cause major bureaucratic battles. Today's national security structure was not the product of divinely inspired concept, rather, it was the result of compromises President Truman made as he fought a bitter struggle with Congress and many of his own civilian and military subordinates. That battle involved many of my friends and close colleagues, and would end with the tragic death, by suicide, of one of the men with whom I was then closest, James V. Forrestal.

THE NEED FOR REFORM OF THE MILITARY

President Truman began the struggle by proposing nothing less than the most radical reorganization of our armed forces in the nation's history. His goal—his impossible dream, as it turned out—was the complete unification of land, sea, and air forces. This seemingly rational goal was opposed by the Navy and the Marine Corps, and their supporters in Congress, until finally it had to be abandoned for plans which, while substantially less ambitious, still resulted in the creation of the Department of Defense as it exists today.

My own wartime service made it easier for me to understand the problem. I thought back to my own experiences in the Navy, especially our "liberation" of Army equipment through nefarious means near the end of the war. The Army and the Navy would communicate *only* if it was unavoidable, and genuine cooperation was not only rare, it was often actively discouraged by commanders in both services.

Even before the end of the war, a powerful group of generals—Marshall, Eisenhower, and Omar Bradley—all advocated a single, integrated military structure. Most important, the Army wanted a single commander, a Chief of Staff, to sit atop the entire command structure. They were willing to have this position rotate among the services, but they wanted the position to have real command authority.

The Army proposals provoked intense suspicion from the Navy and the Marine Corps, both of which feared that the Army would dominate the structure it had proposed. But the Navy was not without resources to defend itself in the bureaucratic wars. I have always been impressed by the importance of tradition in the Navy, which I attributed in part to the rituals that came with the isolation of service at sea. Those traditions struck a responsive chord among a powerful group of Congressmen, who gave stronger support to the Navy than the Army received from *its* Congressional friends. The most important of the Navy's supporters was Congressman Carl Vinson of Georgia, the legendary "Swamp Fox," who considered himself the father of the modern Navy. In the White House, we referred to Vinson, a plainspoken man from southern Georgia, as "Uncle Carl" or "Admiral Vinson." Uncle Carl was further strengthened by a close relationship with Senator Richard Russell, also of Georgia, whom President Truman probably respected more than anyone else in the Senate. The combination of Russell and Vinson was the most powerful legislative team in my entire experience in Washington.

THE PRESIDENT'S FIRST PROPOSAL

In the late summer of 1945, Judge Rosenman asked me to work with him on the issue of military unification. This assignment expanded into almost four years of work on the national security system. Until the 1948 campaign, no issue took so much of my time.

By the fall of 1945, we were demobilizing at the staggering rate of 1.5 million men per month. By 1947, the armed forces would decline from 12 million to 1.5 million, and the annual rate of military spending would drop from $90 billion to less than $11 billion. Despite the Soviet threat building in Eastern Europe, no one yet foresaw the possibility of new troop commitments in Europe, or the creation of a large standing peacetime army, or Americans returning to combat within five years. Each service anticipated a fierce scramble to keep its piece of a much smaller budgetary pie, and this was a major factor in the ferocity of the bureaucratic wars that were about to begin.

At President Truman's request, Secretary of War Robert Patterson submitted a proposal for military unification to the White House on December 17, 1945. It admirably fulfilled the President's desires, but I knew it would cause enormous problems with Forrestal and the Navy. At the time, I was still wearing the Navy uniform, and perhaps I was overly influenced by my relationship with Forrestal. I predicted to Elsey that the Navy would be "desperately unhappy with the small crumbs thrown its way."

But the President liked the Army plan, and on December 19, he sent it to Congress with a request for legislation "combining the War and Navy Departments into one single Department of National Defense." (At the same time, he also repeated his call for Universal Military Training.)

The plan called for the creation of a "Secretary of National Defense," a senior deputy, and three assistant secretaries who would head "coordinated branches of the Department of National Defense: one for the land forces, one for the naval forces, and one for the air forces." He also proposed the establishment of a single Chief of Staff who would oversee a commander for "each of the three component branches." The position of Chief of Staff would rotate among the three branches, and possess genuine command authority. By way of concession, the President's proposal allowed the Navy to retain its own aviation. He also agreed, reluctantly, to maintain the Marine Corps as a separate military branch within the Navy, instead of abolishing it, as both he and the Army desired. In his heart, he always felt that there was no need for a separate Marine Corps; over time, I reached the same conclusion. But the political power of the Marine Corps was overwhelming, as we were both to learn later.

In terms of true integration, the President's proposal went beyond what exists in today's Pentagon. Had it been approved in 1945 (with some modifications), the Pentagon would have been a much more efficient and less wasteful organization than it is today. But because the Navy and Carl Vinson were dead set against them, the President's December 19 recommendations never had a chance.

FORRESTAL FIGHTS BACK

Of all the President's proposals, Forrestal feared most the one recommending a single Chief of Staff as commander of all our land, sea, and air forces. He regarded this as an Army plot, spearheaded by Eisenhower, and he set out to fight it. Calling the President's proposal "completely unworkable," he told me it would be impossible for him and senior Navy officers to testify in favor of it.

Sam Rosenman and I discussed Forrestal's position with President Truman on the same morning he sent his message to Congress. I said it would be difficult to conceal the fact that the Navy and War Departments were digging in behind opposing proposals, and it would be futile to try to force the Navy to support the President's plan. Trapped by the situation, President Truman instructed me to tell Forrestal to allow "all witnesses [to] express their personal views on this subject without restraint."

The revolt of the Navy officers against the Army plan was understandable—but what was driving Forrestal, who fought even harder than the uniformed Navy did to retain its special status? This question would be asked often, by friend and adversary alike, as the puzzle of this extraordinary figure grew. Even though we were friends, I never felt I understood him, but I could see that by 1946 the Navy had become almost his entire life. His personal life was troubled: his wife, Josephine, a beautiful but difficult woman who had been an editor at *Vogue* before their marriage, was drinking heavily. Forrestal had left the Catholic Church, and was deeply guilt-ridden. Possessing great energy, but limited vision, he feared that the creation of a separate air force would make the Navy the odd man out in interservice fights, overwhelmed by the combination of the Air Force and the Army. "We are fighting for the very life of the Navy," he often told me in those early days, when he considered me a staunch ally.

A Senate committee, assisted by two senior military officers—Major

General Lauris Norstad and Vice Admiral Arthur W. Radford*—tried but failed to resolve the disagreement between the two branches and their supporters. The debate dragged on into 1946. On May 12, I told President Truman that I had concluded the Army's position might be correct on its merits, but was politically out of reach. Our real choice, I said, was between concessions to the Navy or no bill at all. To achieve progress, I urged the President to order Forrestal and Patterson to reach an agreement as quickly as possible. The next day, the President called the two men to the Oval Office and told them he was tired of their inability to reconcile their differences. He asked them to reach agreement promptly on a "mutually acceptable plan of unification."

Yet even this Presidential order was inadequate: within two weeks, the two Secretaries sent the President a joint letter listing four areas of continuing disagreement. "We regret our inability to bridge completely the gap between us," they said with massive understatement. When I presented this letter to the President, he all but snorted in annoyance and contempt. The four disagreements, the President observed, were over "the basic issues": whether to establish a separate air force, whether to allow the Navy to retain land-based aircraft to support certain naval operations, the role and mission of the Marine Corps, and above all, whether to unify the services under a single secretary.

Two weeks later, after further discussions with Leahy and me, President Truman attempted once more to force the issue. I drafted letters to Patterson, Forrestal, and the Congressional leadership in which the President offered his views on the four points still in dispute. First—his primary goal—he reaffirmed his support for a single military department and a single Cabinet-level secretary; he would agree to allow the civilian chief of each service to retain the title of "Secretary," although they would no longer be full members of the Cabinet. Second, he reluctantly agreed to three services—an army, a navy, and an air force, and he dropped the idea of a single Chief of Staff. Third, he gave the Navy the right to retain land-based aircraft. Finally, recognizing political reality, he put aside his own doubts about the need for a separate Marine Corps and accepted it as a separate entity within the Navy with its own air components.

In his letters, the President also called for the creation of a National Security Council, a Central Intelligence Agency, an agency for military procurement, a national security resources board, a research and development agency, and a military education and training agency. And although the organizations that were ultimately created bear a clear resemblance

*Norstad later became Commander of NATO, and Radford the Chairman of the Joint Chiefs of Staff.

to this farsighted set of proposals, at the time, the President's letters produced only further argument between Forrestal and Patterson.

Forrestal exploded at the President's letters. In a private talk with me, he referred to the Army in bitter and emotional terms. And again when we met with the President at a private meeting I arranged, with tight-lipped grimness, Forrestal accused the Army of "steamroller tactics" and said he was totally opposed to the idea of a single Department of National Defense. Then, for the first time, he suggested he might resign rather than support unification.

Threats to resign often present Presidents with genuine dilemmas. In this case, letting Forrestal go may have tempted the President, but it would have enraged the Navy's powerful supporters in Congress, further entrenched the rest of the Navy, turned Forrestal into a martyr, and doomed hope for military unification on *any* basis. Knowing this, the President began a slow, patient, and skillful strategy designed to move Forrestal as far as possible without losing him. The way to deal with the Navy, he felt, was to negotiate with Forrestal. It was the right strategy.

During this period, I remained closer to Forrestal than any other official except Stuart Symington, who had just been appointed Assistant Secretary of War for Air. However, a bitterly adversarial relationship developed between Symington and Forrestal as they defended their respective services, and the friction between them sometimes tested my friendship with Forrestal—which was built on our government service rather than the sort of deep personal fellowship that bound me to Symington. While my original sympathies had been strongly pro-Navy, and I retained great respect and affection for Forrestal, nevertheless I gradually began to feel he was showing excessive rigidity.

Looking back on his mental breakdown and death, one can surmise that his extremely emotional behavior, his obduracy, and his intensity were all early signs of the illness that would end his life. But at the time this was not apparent to me or to anyone else. Later, I recalled little occurrences that I had dismissed at the time as quirks, but appeared ominous in retrospect. When he and I played golf, for example, Forrestal did not engage in the casual conversation that makes golf such an enjoyable and relaxing pastime. Instead, he would practically run from shot to shot, pausing only a moment to line up the next effort. On a tennis court, where he was a scrappy competitor, he also rarely spoke. When he learned of the poker games on the *Williamsburg,* he asked me to invite him into the game; I did, but because he was unable to relax like the others around the green table, the President never let him become a regular.

Government was the only subject Forrestal ever seemed to want to discuss. He read voluminously, and loved to discuss ways to improve government service. He admired the British system of Cabinet government, and, like George Kennan, wanted to see the U.S. create a corps of civil servants who would staff the senior levels of the executive branch as a sort of permanent elite civil service. Forrestal lamented the endless turnover of top government personnel, and felt that the caliber of the average government official was inferior to his counterpart in private business. His most enduring dream, other than protecting the Navy, was to create a floating pool of talented people who would serve part of their careers inside the government and part in the private sector, always remaining on call for Presidents of either party.

While I listened with interest to Forrestal's views on government, I could never share his nearly obsessive passion for the bureaucratic wars. Except for those rare issues of the highest historical or moral significance, I have always tried to maintain a certain emotional detachment from my work. I believe strongly that a degree of detachment about one's work improves greatly one's ability to make the right decisions. Forrestal was the opposite: government and Navy had become life itself, and all detachment had been lost.

At our regular breakfasts, Forrestal repeatedly attacked the Army, predicting disaster if the President persisted in supporting a single Chief of Staff and a unified defense establishment. On September 7, 1946, he sent me a "private and confidential" memorandum that showed his obsessive fear of the Army:

> The Army is rigidly adhering to its conception of unification. . . . The Army is still wedded to the concept that a chart and "straight-line of command" will solve all problems as opposed to our belief that any plan, any chart, any system can only be as good as the men at the working level make them. . . . I send you these thoughts because they indicate the foundations for the great apprehension I would have if the President's bill were to follow the Army thinking on these lines. . . . These functions, as I have said, require a man of imagination on a bicycle with a dustpan—it will not get done by the simple drawing of a chart.

COMPROMISE—ON FORRESTAL'S TERMS

As the battle lines hardened, I spent as much time as possible with General Eisenhower, trying to gauge his willingness to compromise. Near the end of 1946, the Symingtons invited the Eisenhowers and Marny and me to their apartment at the Shoreham Hotel for a Sunday-night dinner. It was a pleasant evening; although well aware that he was a great national hero, Ike seemed unaffected by the extraordinary adulation. After dinner, while our wives chatted in the living room, Symington, Eisenhower, and I went into the library alone and talked until after midnight, mainly about the prospects for unification. After the difficulties he had encountered during World War II, Ike said, he believed in military unification with all his heart. He agreed with President Truman that it would be unconscionable to fight another war organized the way we had been in World War II; but, recognizing the Navy's power and determination, he said he was willing to accept substantially less than the Army position in order to get the reform process started.

Forrestal's emotional memorandum, which I shared with the President, convinced us both that we were losing ground as the battle lines were drawn ever more sharply between the Army and the Navy. Hoping to get the process started again, the President called a high-level meeting for September 10. It almost turned into a disaster.

The two adversaries arrived ready for battle: Patterson, outwardly relaxed and calm, and Forrestal, tight-lipped and intense. They were accompanied by an imposing trio of military men—Army Chief of Staff General Eisenhower, Chief of Naval Operations Admiral Chester Nimitz, and Admiral Leahy, all wearing their service ribbons. Noting the total of fifteen stars—five each—gleaming on their uniforms, I was relieved that I was no longer in the uniform of a lowly captain.

The President started the meeting with a blunt statement: he wanted an agreement immediately. After the meeting, he said, he would ask Admiral Leahy and me to draw up a new and final position, which would be submitted to Congress at the beginning of the next session. "Now," the President said, "let's let our hair down and express our true feelings about this."

This was the opportunity Patterson awaited. A former federal judge and holder of the Army's Silver Star and Distinguished Service Medal for heroism in World War I, he was widely respected for his controlled, judicious manner—and he showed it at that meeting. He offered an important concession: he was willing, he said, to have the law specify that a "Secretary of Common Defense" limit himself as much as possible to broad matters of policy and not interfere in the administration of the services.

Ignoring Patterson's gesture, Forrestal began his counter-attack. He started calmly, but as he proceeded he grew emotional. He proposed that an "Office of Deputy to the President" be created, to be headed by a "Secretary of Common Defense or what you will," but that his functions be strictly limited in scope, with no real authority over the services. Then, in unusually strong language, Forrestal said that, while he recognized the need for the President to have the support of the Cabinet, he could not agree to testify before Congress in favor of any bill "which did violence to my principles." If he could not support the President's position "with conviction and sincerity," he said, he would have to ask the President to accept his resignation.

I did not approve of Forrestal's tactics, but, as the intermediary between him and the President, I had already alerted the President to the depth of Forrestal's feelings. Well prepared to defuse this outburst, the President replied that he expected no such necessity would arise.

At this point, Eisenhower showed the qualities that had earned him a reputation in World War II for being an effective conciliator. He said he thought everyone present had accepted the concept of a "Secretary of Common Defense." The details, he said, could be worked out later.

At the time, Eisenhower was at the height of his prestige and authority. Forrestal, however, was clearly unimpressed with this effort to reassure the Navy. At that moment, as far as Forrestal was concerned, the great war hero was just another Army officer fighting for his service. Testily, he told Eisenhower that he could not go along with the Army's proposals. The President was displeased, but he understood there was no way to get a bill unless the Army position was modified still further. He asked me to try to get the two sides closer together.

The negotiations continued between the Army and Navy and their respective supporters for the rest of 1946, intensifying after the Congressional elections. In the first half of November, Forrestal held two lengthy meetings at his home, with Symington, Norstad, and Radford. Leahy and I attended the first meeting to dramatize the President's desire for an agreement before the new Congress convened. A compromise was agreed on the role of the Secretary: while he would have "full authority to take such action as required for effective coordination of the three Departments," his staff would be "sharply limited in number in order to make certain that he could not undertake any detailed administration."

During these meetings a procedural suggestion finally began to open up prospects for progress. Patterson had delegated authority to General Norstad for the technical discussions on unification, and Forrestal now offered to place similar responsibility in the hands of Admiral Forrest Sherman, the Deputy Chief of Naval Operations, whom he trusted completely. For the next two months, Norstad and Sherman worked together seven days a week, while Patterson, Forrestal, Symington, Leahy, and I monitored their progress.

On January 16, 1947, after Admiral Sherman and General Norstad finally produced a proposal acceptable to both the Army and the Navy, Patterson and Forrestal sent the President a joint letter offering the first real break in the logjam. The Patterson-Forrestal Agreement, as it came to be known, was possible only because Eisenhower and the Army dropped its insistence for a single Department, and accepted the creation of a loose organization under the overall direction of a "Secretary of National Defense." The Departments of the Army, Navy, and Air Force would function independently, and each service Secretary would have the right of direct access to the President. The flaws in this proposal were self-evident. It left real power in the hands of the services, and gave the Secretary of National Defense almost no real authority, but this was the best the President could get at the time, and he decided to accept it.

Like the President, I was ready to accept almost anything that the services agreed to, simply to get the process started. But Forrestal continued to express suspicion that the Army would try to change the terms of the deal during the drafting sessions, warning me the day after the Patterson-Forrestal Agreement was announced that "We are going to have to watch them very carefully."

Forrestal's suspicion notwithstanding, for the next six weeks Army and Navy representatives met to draft the legislation. When possible, I sat in on these discussions to urge them to meet the President's deadline. It took eight different drafts and countless hours of discussion—most taken up with minutiae, but finally, on February 26, 1947, the legislation was ready to be sent to Congress; the President was "heartily recommending" passage, and the Marines and the Navy were still very unhappy.

CONGRESSIONAL PASSAGE; THE MARINES FLEX THEIR MUSCLE

Just as the battle between the services reached its most intense level in the spring of 1947, the Administration unveiled the Truman Doctrine and the Marshall Plan. But even the Soviet challenge did not end the bureaucratic and political infighting over military reorganization.

One of our biggest problems came from the smallest service, the Marine Corps. The Commandant of the Marine Corps, General A. A. Vandegrift, criticized the President's bill so ferociously that I called Forrestal on April 17: furious at Vandegrift's insubordination, I suggested that Forrestal rein in the Marines. He responded angrily that the Marines were only reacting to provocative testimony before Congress by General Eisenhower. The next day, in order to give me a lesson in the political power of the Marine Corps, Forrestal invited me to lunch in his office with several powerful Senators, including the patrician Republican from Massachusetts, Leverett Saltonstall, and Democrats Millard Tydings of Maryland and A. Willis Robertson of Virginia.

The Marines wanted specific language added to the bill to protect their special status. When I tried to explain why this was both unnecessary and in contravention of the Patterson-Forrestal Agreement, Saltonstall interrupted me: "The Marines occupy a unique and singular place in the hearts of the people," he warned, in his gentle, understated style. "Don't fool around with them." Tydings, whom I had expected to be an ally, chimed in, "This is not a matter of logic but emotion. You can't win this one. These are the boys who took Mount Suribachi"—referring to the bloody assault on Iwo Jima. "The American people will never forget them or let them down."

I knew when my case was hopeless. Later that day I called Norstad and Sherman and told them that "unless some additional concession is given to the Marines, the whole bill could blow up in our face." I had compromised to save the bill, but I never felt the Marine Corps position had merit. To this day, no major politician of either party can say so publicly, but in my view—and the private view of many military experts—there is no reason to continue to maintain a separate Marine Corps. I hold the achievements and bravery of the Marines in the highest regard, but it is politics that keeps the Marines in existence as an independent military force. The Army, restructured to work more effectively with the Navy in amphibious operations, could do the job with less command confusion.

President Truman felt the same way. During the reorganization debate, he kept private his attitude toward the Marine Corps's behavior. But his true feelings slipped out a few years later in a characteristically candid letter to a Congressman who advocated a separate seat on the Joint Chiefs of Staff for the Marine Corps Commandant: "The Marine Corps is the Navy's police force and as long as I am President that is what it will remain. They have a propaganda machine that is almost equal to Stalin's."[1] Public outrage forced the President to "clarify" his remarks almost at once, but he had said what he really believed. (The Marine Corps eventually won the argument, obtaining a Congressionally mandated seat on the Joint Chiefs.)

THE "NME"

With the Marines finally satisfied, the Senate passed the bill on July 9, 1947. The Navy however, still had not finished protecting itself: Vinson pushed through the House a bill substantially more favorable to the Navy than the Senate version. In the joint Senate-House conference, the relentless and effective Vinson obtained additional language weakening the authority of the Secretary of Defense, as the new position had been renamed. On July 26, just as Congress was about to adjourn for the summer, the final version of the National Security Act of 1947 passed both Houses of Congress.

Its defects were serious: there was no Chairman of the Joint Chiefs of Staff, leaving the Chiefs to quarrel among themselves with no one but the President to settle their differences. The Secretary of Defense had no deputy and almost no staff: he presided over an organization that was not even called a Department—it was given the awful-sounding designation, "National Military Establishment," immediately shortened by Washington bureaucrats to "NME."

Patterson, Eisenhower, Norstad, and Kenneth C. Royall, who was about to become Secretary of the Army, all expressed disappointment to me about the final bill and their private disgust at the behavior of the Navy. Royall summed it up: the new organization, he told me, "will not save money, will not be efficient, and will not prevent interservice rivalry." Nonetheless, everyone recommended signing the bill. Both the President and I felt it was the best we could get under the circumstances and constituted an improvement over the system with which we had fought World War II. "Maybe we can strengthen it as time goes on," he said.

In this hope President Truman was prescient. Despite its flaws, the National Security Act contained tremendous innovations, and remains one of the most important pieces of legislation passed since World War II. The bill not only formally established the Joint Chiefs of Staff, it also created the Air Force, the position of Secretary of Defense, and civilian secretaries for all three services. In addition, it created the Central Intelligence Agency and the National Security Council. Much remained to be done, though.

The Marshall Plan was still being debated in Congress, and to show the world our determination, the President wished to sign the National Security Act immediately—despite unusual and trying circumstances. His beloved ninety-four-year-old mother had fractured her hip in a fall in February, and was not recovering. The President worried constantly about her and had visited her in Missouri four times. As Congress went through a final night of deliberations on the bill, his mother's condition deteriorated. He prepared to fly home for a final visit, but he wanted to sign the bill before he left. The next morning, he waited impatiently at the White House while we expedited the paperwork needed to prepare a bill for his signature. Finally, to save time, he went out to the airport and waited in the cabin of his airplane. Shortly after noon, I raced to the airport with the bill, and he signed it as the plane's engines started up.

As I began to leave with the papers, President Truman turned and handed me one of the pens with which he had signed the bill—the first such gesture he made toward me—and asked me to give the other pens to Patterson, Forrestal, Royall, and Symington. Then he left hurriedly for Missouri; but as his plane passed over Cincinnati, the President received word that his mother had died.

THE FIRST SECRETARY OF DEFENSE

For the same reasons that he signed the National Security Act as soon as it passed, the President wanted to announce the name of the first Secretary of Defense without delay. The leading contender was Patterson, but he had made it clear early in the process that, after six years in Washington, he was financially pressed and wished to return to private law practice in New York. This left the choice wide open; we discussed the subject frequently during the summer. Finally, the President decided to choose the man who had most opposed creating the position, and who had succeeded in weakening it, James Forrestal. The President's motives in choosing Forrestal were simple: if Forrestal remained Secretary of the Navy he would make life unbearable for the Secretary of Defense; if, on the other hand, *he* was the Secretary, he would have to try to make the system work. It was a brilliant tactical decision that was to have a profound effect on the future of the Pentagon; but it was also to contribute to Forrestal's tragic death.

Despite his original opposition to the creation of the position, Forrestal accepted immediately. I think he sensed his dilemma as soon as he was offered the position; he now had to deal with the problems he had done so much to create. When I congratulated him on his appointment, he showed no joy or excitement. And to a friend, the playwright Robert Sherwood, he wrote, "This office will probably be the greatest cemetery for dead cats in history."[2] To the President he sent a letter of thanks the day after his appointment. It included a sentence that reflected, I thought, a slight sense of guilt over his relentless lobbying for the Navy: "With the exception of Clark Clifford, I know probably more than anyone else how much restraint you had to exercise under trying and sometimes provoking circumstances."

The same day, Forrestal also sent me a note. It was generous in its praise, but I did not read it as an endorsement of unification itself:

> My dear Clark:
>
> The fact that we have Unification, or to put it more formally—the National Military Establishment—is due largely to your continuing tact, intelligence and persistence. In other words, you have taken a vital part in one of the historical legislative achievements in our history. Put this in your records. Someday your children may derive some satisfaction from looking at it and by it you may be able to persuade them that the old man really did amount to something.

THE CREATION OF THE DEPARTMENT OF DEFENSE

James Forrestal was sworn in as the first Secretary of Defense on September 17, 1947, in an atmosphere of urgency, drama, and tension. President Truman, who had wanted to officiate at the swearing-in, was four days away from Washington on the battleship USS *Missouri,* returning home from a trip to Rio de Janeiro, where he had signed the first formal collective security treaty in American history. Today commonly referred to as the Rio Pact, it was another milestone in America's postwar security arrangements, embodying for the first time a concept that would reappear in other postwar treaties: an attack against any signatory would be treated as an attack against all. I had accompanied the President on the trip to Rio, but returned to Washington early.

In the first two weeks of September, American intelligence reported that Yugoslavia—still regarded as strongly pro-Soviet because Stalin and Tito had not yet split—might seize Trieste, an Italian city near the border, occupied by American and British military forces. Any such move by Yugoslavia would have created a major crisis. Forrestal felt that his ambiguous status, confirmed by the Senate but not yet sworn in as Secretary of Defense, might signal indecision to Moscow. At his request, I sent a suggestion to President Truman on the *Missouri* that Forrestal be sworn in immediately by Chief Justice Fred Vinson, without waiting for the President's return to Washington. The ceremony, ironically, took place in the very seat of opposition to the new position, the Navy Department. The next day there were two more ceremonies: the swearing-in, at the Pentagon, of Stuart Symington as the first Secretary of the Air Force, and John L. Sullivan as Secretary of the Navy. Kenneth Royall, who had become Secretary of War, automatically became the first Secretary of the Army. The National Security Act of 1947 was now operational, and the new team was in place.

But we were, in fact, only at the midpoint in the long road toward unification. Once again, the central figure was Forrestal. He should have been pleased, for he had won a decisive victory over the Army and had created a structure that fully protected the Navy and the Marines. Moreover, positions he had long advocated toward the Soviet Union were gradually becoming American policy. He was, at that moment, equal in stature to anyone else in Washington other than the President and George Marshall.

Forrestal viewed himself as a policymaker, not an administrator, and he kept his office staff small. "My concept of this office is that it will be a coordinating, a planning, and an integrating rather than an operating office," he told a press conference in November. But it could not work that way, as Forrestal was about to learn. Even though his new job put him atop the largest and most costly agency in the government, he was neither happy nor satisfied.

FORRESTAL SEES THE LIGHT

In more than forty-five years in Washington, I know of no more dramatic metamorphosis than the one James Forrestal underwent in 1948. To put it simply, he realized that he had been wrong, and publicly admitted it. It was a brave but enormously costly decision for him, alienating many of his closest friends in the Navy, and it added enormously to the strain under which he was already working.

The process began almost immediately upon his moving to the Pentagon. Forrestal had to operate under the constraints on which he himself had insisted—a tiny staff, no deputies, and a very limited mandate. Understaffed and overworked, he had to do everything himself, relying on a few talented but overworked personal aides. As early as March 1948, after a three-day meeting with the Joint Chiefs of Staff in Key West, Forrestal asked the President to issue an executive order modifying his original job description.

In our regular private breakfasts, Forrestal began to express increasing frustration at his inability to do his job. Then, in the summer of 1948, less than ten months after taking office, Forrestal made a startling statement to me: "Clark, I was wrong. I cannot make this work. No one can make it work." I knew how difficult it must have been for him to make this statement, even alone to a friend. "You have done the very best you could, the best that anyone could have done," I replied. "You should go see the President and discuss with him what might be done to improve the situation."

But before Forrestal was ready to see the President, he convened a series of evening meetings in his office at the Pentagon with high-level officers, asking them to suggest ways to improve the NME. I participated in some of these discussions and also kept myself informed through Forrestal, Symington, Eisenhower, and others. For the first time, Forrestal told me, he was finding that he trusted some senior Army generals more than his former Navy colleagues; Eisenhower and Omar Bradley, in particular, had risen in his estimation. After these meetings, Forrestal said he was ready to see the President.

The meeting, delayed because of a long campaign trip by President Truman, took place on October 5, 1948. It was a remarkable moment: Forrestal told President Truman that he had been wrong in 1946 and 1947, and that because neither he nor anyone else could make the existing

National Security Act work, he was ready to support its revision. His mood struck me as a strange combination of suppressed emotion, courage, and a sense of defeat.

President Truman accepted Forrestal's change of heart in a matter-of-fact manner, with no gloating. With the election only a month away, Forrestal, who had already told me he believed Dewey's victory was certain, may have regarded his discussions as academic. But the President asked him to head up a new legislative drafting team, and asked me and Frank Pace, Jr., the Director of the Bureau of the Budget, to work with Forrestal. We were assisted by Marx Leva, the most impressive of Forrestal's young assistants, and George Elsey.

After the election, I accompanied President Truman on his vacation at Key West, where Forrestal visited us. But his attention was not so much on the reorganization as it was on his relationship with President Truman, which had become strained for a variety of reasons—disagreements over Israel, the reorganization battle, and rumors that Forrestal had been in secret contact with Dewey during the campaign. The President added to Forrestal's sense of alienation by seeing him at Key West only in the company of local politicians, thus avoiding a serious private conversation. Forrestal was deeply disturbed by this snub; what he did not realize was that the President was beginning to view him as indecisive and weak.

Our assistants produced a draft memorandum that Forrestal, Pace, and I reviewed, modified, and sent to the President on February 10, 1949. We proposed that "the present National Military Establishment [be converted] into a single executive department," and the Secretary of Defense be provided with "sufficient authority to exercise effective direction and control" over the armed forces. We proposed an eleven-point legislative program, including the creation of a Deputy Secretary of Defense and—finally!—the position of Chairman of the Joint Chiefs of Staff. We also recommended removing the three service secretaries' direct access to the President and downgrading the services from independent executive departments to subdepartments within the new Department of Defense. Looking at our new proposal, Symington wrote me, "It is remarkable how close the President's message of December 19, 1945, conforms to what we now want."

President Truman was delighted with our proposals. He accepted every recommendation save one: he rejected our suggestion to create a single Chief of Staff for all the services on the grounds that Forrestal, the Navy, and Uncle Carl still opposed it strongly. The concessions to Vinson and the Navy, while probably unavoidable under the circumstances, significantly weakened the position of Chairman of the Joint Chiefs. Only in 1986, thirty-seven years later, did Congress pass legislation—opposed, as usual, by the Navy—that made the Chairman of the Joint Chiefs an independent military adviser to the President, rather than the representative of the other Chiefs (the Goldwater-Nickles Bill).

Forrestal led off the administration testimony in favor of the new bill on March 24. "My position on the question," he said with massive understatement, "has changed." Predictably, Carl Vinson tried to kill the new reforms, but this time he succeeded only in watering down a few provisions. On August 10, 1949, President Truman signed the bill, renamed the Reorganization Act of 1949. "We have finally succeeded," he said to me after the signing ceremony in the Oval Office.

THE CREATION OF THE NATIONAL SECURITY COUNCIL

James Forrestal's legacy to the nation also included the creation of the National Security Council, although not in the form he originally wanted. He had long advocated an interagency group to coordinate foreign and defense policy, and he quickly converted me to the idea. We worked together to ensure its inclusion in the final version of the 1947 bill on unification. Forrestal wanted the National Security Council to be part of the Pentagon, but after examining the issue I came to favor a National Security Council staffed primarily by civilians, responsible directly to the President.

When the Army submitted its first unification plan in December 1945, I sent Judge Rosenman, who was in charge of drafting the President's message, a memorandum which took issue with the Army draft because it "does not provide for the needed comprehensive relationship between the military services and the State Department. . . . The [Navy recommendation] with which I agree most strongly, is the creation of a National Security Council."

After the President's first unification proposal died in early 1947 because of Navy opposition, President Truman decided to include Forrestal's idea in the next version of the bill. First called a "Council of National Defense," and later redesignated the "National Security Council," it included all three service secretaries, the new Secretary of National Defense, and the Secretary of State. In this first version of the NSC, neither the President nor the Vice President were members.

* * *

In the spring of 1947, Forrestal had an idea for a "Cabinet Secretariat" along the lines of the Private Office that was a central part of the British structure. In March, he invited Acheson, Harriman, Patterson, Budget Bureau Director James Webb, Agriculture Secretary Clinton Anderson, and me to lunch at the Navy Department to discuss this idea; but he was unable to muster much enthusiasm for his idea, another manifestation of his admiration for the British system. After the luncheon, he called to suggest that I create an informal secretariat and add it to my other duties. I knew such an action would be deeply resented by others in the government, and politely ignored the idea until it faded away.

The President chose Admiral Sidney Souers as the first Executive Secretary of the NSC. A successful businessman from St. Louis whom I had known before the war, Souers was a quiet, undemonstrative man with good common sense. He had risen rapidly through the ranks of Naval Intelligence during the war, and served for six months as the first Director of Central Intelligence before assuming his National Security Council duties. As his deputy he chose a career civil servant with extensive intelligence background, James Lay. Souers and Lay were cautious men, and restricted themselves to coordinating formal policy papers, leaving to me most of the sensitive functions of liaison with the Departments of State and Defense.

Forrestal, who saw himself as the creator of the NSC, sought control over Souers and Lay. To head Forrestal off, they drafted a memorandum of instructions from the President to themselves, and asked me to obtain Presidential approval of it. I believed that Souers and Lay were correct in seeking complete independence from the Pentagon. This meant another disagreement with Forrestal, which I regretted, but the stakes were high, and it was impossible to avoid choosing sides.

I reviewed the draft memorandum while the President was still on the high seas on his way back from the Rio Conference. Although we knew that it would upset Forrestal, we decided to discuss it with him right after he had been sworn in. The meeting, on September 17, was a star-studded affair with all three service secretaries and the Chiefs of Staff, including Eisenhower and Nimitz. As we had expected, Forrestal insisted that the NSC report to him, and said that his decisions should be final, and binding on the executive secretary. Forrestal also wanted the entire NSC staff to be headquartered in the Pentagon, and staffed almost entirely by military officers.

I had no choice but to disagree with my friend in the meeting. I said the new NSC system should not be used to circumvent the State Department or diminish the President's role. The State Department had to be centrally involved in decision making, and the process had to be placed directly under the control of the President. I also opposed locating the NSC staff in the Pentagon; the NSC staff should be located near the White House, I said, and not within the confines of any existing Department. After the meeting, I asked Charles Murphy, a White House assistant who worked closely with me, to find space for Souers's staff in what is now the Executive Office Building. The NSC staff is still housed there today.

Forrestal was unhappy. When Elsey edited Forrestal's diary after his death, we learned that immediately after the September 17 meeting he had written:

> It is apparent that there is going to be a difference between the Budget [Bureau], some of the White House staff and ourselves on the National Security Council—its functions—its relationship to the President and myself. I regard it as an integral part of the National Defense setup.

REFLECTIONS ON THE NSC

The National Security Council was thus born, almost as a byproduct to military reorganization. President Truman wanted a small NSC staff under his direct control, with its role restricted to coordination. When the Korean War began, this role expanded, but he still resisted a large staff, preferring to deal directly with his senior Cabinet officials. Over the next forty years, I watched the Executive Secretary of the National Security Council evolve into the National Security "Adviser," and become a rival for power to the Secretary of State. This was clearly not our original intention, but it was an inevitable consequence of the growth of government, the desire of some Presidents to run the national security structure personally from the White House, and the personal ambitions of several men.

President Truman had a clear sense of how the American government should work, and his words still serve as an admirable guide for Presidents:

> Like the Cabinet, the [National Security] Council does not make decisions. The policy itself has to come down from the President, as all final decisions have to be made by him. . . . Forrestal for some time had been advocating our using the British Cabinet system as a model in the operation of the government. There is much to this idea—in some ways a Cabinet government is more efficient—but under . . . our system the responsibility rests on one man—the President. To change it, we would have to change the Constitution, and I think we have been doing very well under our Constitution. We will do well to stay with it.[3]

THE CREATION OF THE CIA: DONOVAN LOSES ROUND ONE

An aura of mystery and controversy has surrounded the Central Intelligence Agency for most of the last forty years. Because its creation was a small part of the National Security Act of 1947, the struggle over the structure and mandate of the CIA was obscured, in the public eye, by the noisy battles over the unification of the services and the NSC. But the CIA did not come into being without fierce disagreement; for four months between September 1945 and January 1946, a battle raged in Washington within the tightly knit but highly competitive intelligence community. This struggle drew me into my first involvement with the world of intelligence, an involvement that was to resume later in my career.

President Roosevelt had given General William Donovan authority during the war to create the most romantic of all wartime organizations, the Office of Strategic Services, or OSS, but "Wild Bill" Donovan went beyond the legends he did so much to originate. His role in the creation of the modern American intelligence system cannot be overstated. In person, Donovan was not the dashing daredevil of legend, at least not when I came to know him. What he possessed in great measure was charm, and effectiveness in bureaucratic warfare. Even before the end of the war he proposed the creation of a permanent new intelligence agency, independent of both State and the military, and answerable only to the President.

Predictably, Donovan's plan enraged the State, War, and Navy Departments, all of which felt it threatened their existing intelligence units. J. Edgar Hoover, who had feuded with Donovan throughout World War II, objected strongly to the creation of a permanent rival to the FBI; Donovan replied that no existing organizations possessed the talent or the mandate to meet the needs that would arise after the war. Even though Donovan was correct, his enemies won the first round, when Hoover leaked a copy of Donovan's plan to two of the leading conservative newspapers in the nation, the *Chicago Tribune* and the New York *Daily News,* which called it the "Spy Director's Secret Plan" to create a "U.S. Gestapo."[4] Amid the controversy, Donovan's plan foundered.

For reasons I never fully understood, President Truman never liked Donovan. Perhaps he regarded Donovan as a self-promoter. On September 20, 1945, just days after the Japanese surrender, President Truman prematurely, abruptly, and unwisely disbanded the OSS. He had been persuaded by a bitter critique from Army intelligence that was inspired by jealousy. Months of bitter argument within the intelligence community about whether, and how, to replace the OSS, were about to begin.

STATE VERSUS THE MILITARY

By early 1946, President Truman was becoming increasingly annoyed by the flood of conflicting and uncoordinated intelligence reports flowing haphazardly across his desk. Greater coordination of intelligence was essential. In addition to Donovan's proposal, President Truman had on his desk a revision of a proposal the wartime Chiefs of Staff had submitted to Franklin Roosevelt in late 1944, for a coordinating organization called the "Central Intelligence Agency." The military plan vested joint supervisory authority in the Secretaries of State, War, and Navy.

The State Department responded to this plan at the end of 1946 by proposing a "National Intelligence Authority," or NIA. It recommended that State be designated the sole conduit of intelligence reports to the President. The State Department casually brushed aside the question of covert operations and clandestine activities as needing further study: "If [covert operations] are to be conducted, [they] might well be under a central agency." The single word—*if*—conveyed as much about the mood and assumptions of that more innocent time as volumes of historical analysis. Most people, including some professional intelligence officers, thought covert operations would be, at most, a minor part of peacetime foreign policy.

The President asked Admiral Leahy to review and compare the State Department and military proposals; but because he was preoccupied with unification of the services, Leahy asked me to assume responsibility for coordinating the process within the White House. I had neither worked with the intelligence services during the war nor come into regular contact with the world of intelligence, but Leahy's request thrust me unexpectedly into the debate that created our modern intelligence structure.

SIDNEY SOUERS AND THE FIRST INTELLIGENCE DIRECTIVE

Seeking advice I turned first to the man I knew best in the intelligence community, my friend from St. Louis, Rear Admiral Sidney Souers. He objected strongly to the State Department plan on the grounds that it lacked safeguards for military intelligence operations. He supported the military approach, adding a recommendation that the Director of the "Central Intelligence Agency" be chosen by the President. This was a significant change from Secretary of State Jimmy Byrnes's suggestion that the head of the National Intelligence Authority come from State.

The President listened to these conflicting views, and rejected them all. He agreed only to set up a loose coordinating group. He was not ready to create a new intelligence agency. Following his guidance, I prepared an executive order establishing an NIA and a Director of Central Intelligence, which the President signed on January 22, 1946. It was the first postwar Presidential directive on intelligence. *Time* magazine called it the end of our "historical innocence" in international intelligence.

Under this executive order, a Director of Central Intelligence (DCI) would coordinate a Central Intelligence Group (CIG). We defined the CIG's functions so as to minimize friction with the other departments: the "correlation and evaluation of intelligence relating to the national security," as well as the protection of foreign intelligence "sources and methods."

We addressed directly the longest-standing and most important controversy in American intelligence: operations within the U.S. The directive I drafted stated flatly, "No police, law enforcement or internal security functions shall be exercised under this directive. . . . Nothing herein contained shall be construed to authorize the making of investigations inside the continental limits of the United States. . . ." This prohibition made temporary allies out of President Truman and J. Edgar Hoover, who wanted to keep all domestic intelligence activities completely under the control of *his* F.B.I.

Despite Souers's disclaimers, Leahy, Forrestal, and I agreed that he would be ideal as the first Director of Central Intelligence. The day after the directive was issued, Souers reluctantly agreed to the President's request that he become the first Director of Central Intelligence, but only on the condition that he would be released from the job after six months.

President Truman kept his word: on June 10, 1946, Souers was allowed to leave, but, as already noted, he agreed to stay on in Washington as the first Executive Director of the National Security Council. At his own recommendation, Souers was succeeded as Director of Central Intelligence by Army Air Force Lieutenant General Hoyt S. Vandenberg, one of the most glamorous of the young aviators who had emerged from World War II. In a city then filled with war heroes, Vandenberg was clearly marked as a star of the next generation. Only forty-seven at the time and strikingly handsome, he carried extra weight as the nephew of the powerful Republican Senator from Michigan, Arthur Vandenberg. It was taken for granted that he would be Chief of Staff of the soon-to-be-created Air Force.

I first met Vandenberg through his friend and ally, Stuart Symington. A man in a hurry, he viewed his appointment as Director of Central Intelligence as a brief stepping-stone in his career—though he also wanted to make something of the job. Less than a month after taking over, Vandenberg sent me a far-ranging recommendation that the President ask for legislation creating a separate Central Intelligence Agency. Elsey and I studied Vandenberg's suggestions carefully. I did not doubt that a great nation with international responsibilities had to have a serious and effective intelligence service. But at the same time, I was concerned with the vagueness of some of the language in his draft legislation. Accordingly, on July 1, 1946, I sent Vandenberg a memorandum outlining my concerns with his draft, expressing dismay at his "failure to distinguish between 'intelligence' and 'foreign intelligence,' [which would] raise a serious question in many minds as to . . . the real intent of the bill." I noted that the proposed bill

> provides for several programs which embrace *all* existing intelligence activities of the Federal Government, both foreign and domestic. I fear that this will lead to the suspicion that the "National Intelligence Authority" and the "Central Intelligence Agency" will attempt to control, with the powers granted to them in this bill, the F.B.I. and other [domestic] intelligence activities.

This was not simply a question of semantics; it went to the heart of my belief that the line between foreign intelligence and activities within the U.S. must be sharply drawn. It was essential to create a *foreign* intelligence organization which could not conduct operations against American citizens.

Four days later, Elsey and I met with two members of Vandenberg's staff, James Lay and Lawrence Houston, who had drafted the proposed legislation. "Has your experience," I asked Houston and Lay, "convinced you that the CIG concept laid out in the executive order will not work?"

The two men, both highly responsible civil servants who were in the early stages of lengthy careers, laid out in detail why they believed the CIG could not work. "We do not have the power to hire anybody, fire anybody, or assign anybody," Houston said. "We are nothing but a stepchild of the three departments we are supposed to coordinate." I found their description of the limitations of the CIG and the NIA quite persuasive. It was clear to me that the brief era of the CIG had run its course, and something new was needed. I told Lay and Houston that I would recommend the creation of a new, permanent intelligence agency—but only if they agreed to make four changes in the proposed legislation: exclude the new intelligence agency from any involvement in domestic affairs, keep the CIA and the FBI completely separate, keep the FBI outside the control of the Director of Central Intelligence, and preclude the CIA from activities directed against Americans.

President Truman accepted my recommendations: he felt he had given the CIG concept a fair test, and it had failed. He cautioned me, however, that the first priority was still to get the squabbling military services together behind a unification bill. For his part, he did not wish to complicate the fight for unification by sending legislation on the subject of intelligence to Congress prematurely.

Shortly after the 1946 Congressional elections, Vandenberg sent me a revised bill, incorporating my suggestions. He wanted to press forward immediately with the legislation. But this was the period during which Secretaries Patterson and Forrestal were trying to meet President Truman's January deadline for finding a compromise on military unification. I told Vandenberg several times during December and January to slow down, stressing that we could not address the intelligence issue until the first order of business—the war between the Army and the Navy—had been settled. On January 8, 1947, quite agitated, he came to see me. He said that since my meetings with Lay and Houston in July, he had been under the impression that the President and I were both in favor of his plan. Perhaps emboldened by the Republican victory in the Congressional elections, which had just made his uncle Chairman of the Senate Foreign Relations Committee, Vandenberg expressed disappointment, verging on outrage, that the President was not going to recommend the creation of the CIA in his 1947 State of the Union message, which Elsey had just completed drafting under my direction.

I was sympathetic to Vandenberg's objective, but his approach would have risked our higher priority, military unification. I told Vandenberg that we had to await progress in the Army-Navy negotiations. A week later, Forrestal and Patterson reached their compromise on military unification, and I told Vandenberg that we could finally add to the bill a section creating a central intelligence agency.

Section 102 was now added to the National Security Act. It abolished both the NIA and the CIG and established the CIA. The Director of the CIA continued to hold the additional title of Director of Central Intelligence (DCI). In this capacity he would not only oversee the CIA but also have authority over the rest of the foreign intelligence community within the American government. But in practice, the military intelligence services resisted taking directions from the DCI rather than from their own chain of command, and to this day, the DCI's oversight of the intelligence community falls far short of our original intent.

Covert operations were placed under the new National Security Council with a carefully phrased "catchall" clause (Section 102 (d) (5)), which provided that the CIA shall: "perform such other functions and duties related to intelligence affecting the national security as the National Security Council may from time to time direct."

I reviewed this sentence carefully at the time, but could never have imagined that forty years later I would still be asked to testify before Congress as to its meaning and intent. The "other" functions the CIA was to perform were purposely not specified, but we understood that they would include covert activities. We did not mention them by name because we felt it would be injurious to our national interest to advertise the fact that we might engage in such activities. We intended that these activities be separate and distinct from the normal activities of the CIA, and expected them to be limited in scope and purpose—thus the important limiting language, "affecting the national security."

The National Security Act of 1947 remains to this day the statutory authorization for covert activity. In light of the continuing controversy over the role and activities of the CIA, it bears emphasizing that it was by act of Congress that the CIA was established and exists today, and it was by act of Congress that covert operations were authorized.

During the six years in the sixties that I sat as a member and then Chairman of the President's Foreign Intelligence Advisory Board, I often reflected on the complexities of this problem. A great nation must have the capability to defend its own interests, and this includes a first-rate intelligence service. I believed that a limited number of covert programs, tightly controlled by the President and the NSC, would be a necessary part of our foreign policy. But over the years, covert activities became so numerous and widespread that, in effect, they became a self-sustaining part of American foreign operations. The CIA became a government within a government, which could evade oversight of its activities by drawing the cloak of secrecy around itself.

My concern over this trend reached its height during the Iran-*contra* scandal of the Reagan years. I came to the conclusion that we must reassess the very idea of conducting covert operations. Testifying before the House and Senate in 1987 and 1988, I expressed my concern:

> If we are to continue with [covert operations] and gain any benefit from them, we must find a way to keep them consistent with the principles and institutions of the Constitution and our foreign policy. If we determine that this cannot be done, then I again say we are better off without covert activities entirely than with them out of control.[5]

Some people mistook my statement for opposition to covert operations. But in fact I was simply supporting legislation (unfortunately opposed by the Reagan Administration) designed to prevent the recurrence of the outrageous, and I believed unlawful, activities of the CIA in the Iran-*contra* affair. On the advice of the CIA and the Justice Department, President Reagan, ignoring existing laws, did not keep Congress informed of the CIA's covert activities in Iran and Central America. To avoid a repetition of this lamentable event, I supported legislation that tightened the requirements for the President to consult and inform the Congressional Intelligence Committees. I urged that teeth be put into the law in a way that everyone could understand: criminal penalties for "knowing and willful" violation of the law.

This was not the first time I testified on the subject of covert operations. Twelve years earlier, in 1975, when I appeared before the Senate Select Committee to Study Governmental Operations with Respect to Intelligence Activities—the so-called Church Committee*—to discuss the Nixon Administration's covert activities, I said:

> The lack of proper controls has resulted in a freewheeling course of conduct on the part of persons within the intelligence community that has led to spectacular failures and much unfortunate publicity. A new approach is obviously needed, for it is unthinkable that we can continue to commit the egregious errors that have caused such consternation to our friends and such delight to our enemies.

It is shocking that these obvious defects in our system have still not been corrected. Covert and clandestine operations should be limited to those deemed essential to the national interest by the President, and information about them shared with the small number of members of Congress who have oversight responsibility. The risks of leaks are real, but they can be minimized, and should not be used as an excuse for excesses.

THE TRAGEDY OF JAMES FORRESTAL

The strain on Forrestal had increased steadily during 1948. The debris of his personal life added greatly to the pressures building up on him. The Forrestals seemed to live separate lives, and his wife's personal behavior increasingly mortified him, and as time went on, her condition became an open secret around Washington. At one dinner they gave, in honor of Randolph Churchill, Josephine did not come downstairs for over an hour after the first guests had arrived. Finally, she appeared, after too much to drink, at the top of their magnificent staircase, and, looking down at the guests, said, loudly, "Good Lord, what in the world do all you people have to say to each other?" Randolph Churchill, who enjoyed drinking as much as anyone, found this remark amusing, but Forrestal felt humiliated.

On another occasion, I asked Forrestal if he would act as host on short notice for the President's poker game—something he felt greatly honored to do. Throughout that day, I learned later, Forrestal, worried that she might appear during the evening and create an incident, tried to persuade

*Named after its chairman, Senator Frank Church of Idaho.

his wife to go to New York, on the grounds that the Presidential poker evenings were stag affairs. When she refused, Forrestal became nearly frantic with apprehension at what she might do. Finally, just before the guests arrived, he convinced her to go upstairs and not greet the guests. Throughout the evening, he was in fear that she would emerge without warning and repeat her performance at the Churchill dinner.

Forrestal also became a target for some powerful journalists. For months, Drew Pearson and Walter Winchell, the two most widely read columnists of the time, had been attacking him as a tool of Wall Street. He was not a man who could put a quarrel behind him and move on—an important ability for longevity in Washington—and he was deeply upset by the charge, after his opposition to Israel became known, that he had "cared more for oil than he did for the Jews."

The attack that upset him the most was an accusation by Pearson that Forrestal had fled in fear during a holdup of his wife outside their Manhattan townhouse in 1937; the truth was that he had been asleep upstairs and unaware of the incident until after it was over. He expressed great bitterness about this assault on his honor and personal courage; I could see the former Princeton boxer in him erupting with anger and frustration as he described the incident. Finally, there were rumors in Washington that Forrestal, assuming a Republican victory in 1948, had been in secret contact with Dewey in the hope of staying on as Secretary of Defense. I never knew if these stories were true, but they were conveyed to President Truman by Harry Vaughan, who despised Forrestal and was campaigning to have him replaced by Louis Johnson, President Truman's chief fund-raiser in 1948 and a former Assistant Secretary of War.

Work had become Forrestal's life, or perhaps the sanctuary from the rest of his life, but by the end of 1948 it too had begun to deteriorate. He was worn out from trying to make the 1947 act work. Often unable to sleep, he began calling his friends in the middle of the night just to talk. When he called me, I listened carefully, but with increasing puzzlement. Like most people in the forties, my understanding of mental disorders was quite limited, and I was unaware how serious an illness depression can be.

After he died, I remembered only one glimpse into the bottomless darkness of his internal crisis. Sitting directly behind him during a Cabinet meeting near the end of 1948, I noticed that he had scratched raw a spot on the top of the back of his head with his fingernail. As the meeting progressed, he continued to scratch until it was the size of a half-dollar. I watched in silent horror as blood slowly oozed from the spot.

In the course of working together in 1947–48, Symington and Forrestal had argued bitterly over the size of the Air Force budget. In those days

Symington was a tenacious defender of air power, and he had given Forrestal a difficult time, adding to Forrestal's distress. In 1949, Symington, too, caught a glimpse of Forrestal's anguish. Forrestal called to ask for the name of a good lawyer because, he said, he needed to change his will right away. Puzzled at the urgency of the request, Symington recommended Paul Porter, one of Washington's most prominent lawyers. A few days later Porter called Symington and said, "This man is crazy, he is raving—he doesn't know what he wants." Despite our friendship, Symington did not tell me about this incident until later, when it was too late. Something in our backgrounds, some combination of respect for Forrestal's privacy and our inability to recognize the danger signals, kept us—and, it turned out, everyone else—from comparing notes and coming to his aid.

Forrestal apparently confided the extent of his distress to no one, not even Marx Leva and John Ohly, the devoted aides with whom he spent almost every waking moment. Had the roots of his distress been understood, his departure would, of course, have been handled differently—but at the time even his closest friends thought that he was simply exhausted.

Because the Presidential election had become my overwhelming preoccupation, I saw less of Forrestal in the second half of 1948. Our private breakfasts were no longer as frequent. Forrestal was not the sort of person, like Symington, with whom one could disagree on issues without any effect on a friendship, and we had disagreed frequently enough that it had strained our friendship.

The President respected the courage it had taken for Forrestal to admit that he had been wrong on military unification, but he was increasingly disturbed by Forrestal's indecisiveness. "Jim has trouble making up his mind," the President said to me. Even Treasury Secretary John Snyder, a friend of Forrestal's, told the President that Forrestal was acting strangely. Vaughan's continued intrigues succeeded in raising doubts in the President's mind about Forrestal's loyalty during the 1948 campaign. For all these reasons, as well as the President's sense it was time for a postelection reorganization of the Administration, in March 1949 he asked Forrestal to resign, and offered the job to Louis Johnson.

At a ceremony the day after Forrestal left office, the President presented him with the Distinguished Service Medal. Unable to respond to the President's generous words of praise, Forrestal was led, speechless, from the podium. It was suddenly clear to everyone that something was very wrong.

Lovett and Symington arranged for him to fly to the secluded resort of Hobe Sound, Florida, to rest. But demons were inside him, and rest could not quiet them. As Lovett recounted it to me later, he met Forrestal at the airport, prepared to take his mind off Washington with golf and swimming. Forrestal immediately pulled Lovett aside: "I must talk to you," he whispered. "The Russians are after me, the FBI is watching me, the Zionists are after me." Lovett was stunned. At Lovett's house, Forrestal searched the closets and looked under beds for hidden microphones.

The famed psychiatrist Dr. William Menninger was flown to Hobe Sound to examine Forrestal. He saw immediately that the man was desperately ill, and advised immediate professional attention. Too sick to make decisions for himself, Forrestal was flown back to Washington on a military plane. In a tragic error of judgment, the Navy, concerned that he might blurt out national security secrets to the wrong people, vetoed suggestions to send him to the Menninger Clinic or another private facility specializing in mental disorders. With Mrs. Forrestal's assent, they placed him in the Bethesda Naval Hospital, a military facility that lacked both the staff and the understanding to deal with his illness. Once there, he was assigned to the VIP suite of rooms on the sixteenth floor.

I never saw him again. During his stay at Bethesda, the Navy would not let him receive visitors. Only President Truman and the new Secretary of Defense, Louis Johnson, were permitted to penetrate, briefly, the curtain the Navy and its doctors had drawn around Forrestal.

After a month at Bethesda, his friends were told that he appeared more relaxed and was recovering—but in the middle of the night on May 22, 1949, Jim Forrestal jumped out of an unguarded hospital window. On the desk in his room lay an anthology of poetry, with a red bookmark at the "Chorus from Ajax" by Sophocles, in which Ajax, about to commit suicide, describes the comfort of death. Next to the book lay some hospital memorandum paper, on which Forrestal had copied most of the poem just before leaping to his death. It contained these searing lines:

Worn by the waste of time—
Comfortless, nameless, hopeless save
In the dark prospect of the yawning grave . . .
Better to die, and sleep
The never waking sleep, than linger on
And dare to live, when the soul's life is gone.

10

J. Edgar Hoover and the Loyalty Program

It is one thing for a nation to take basic counter-espionage and security measures necessary to protect its existence. That it must do. It is another thing to urge or tolerate heresy hunts at every stump and crossroads to smoke out and punish non-conformists of every shade and stripe of opinion different than that of the majority. I'm afraid we are moving increasingly in that direction.

—MEMORANDUM FROM CLARK CLIFFORD TO THE PRESIDENT, APRIL 29, 1949

As I look back on my career in government, my greatest regret is that I did not make more of an effort to try to kill the loyalty program at its inception, in 1946–47. I did not pay enough attention to this misguided and pernicious effort to eliminate "subversives" from the government, and by the time the full dangers of the program were evident, it was too late: the Korean War had started, McCarthyism had begun to flower in America, and the Administration had lost its chance to control the issue.

The program's beginnings came at a time when the Soviet challenge was moving to center stage. As the Administration proclaimed the dangers of communism abroad, conservative politicians, encouraged by FBI Director J. Edgar Hoover, claimed to have found evidence of a subversive communist threat on the domestic front. The search for "the enemy within" was not confined, as it should have been, to the search for Soviet spies—a legitimate and important function of the FBI and American counterintelligence; rather, it spread into a twentieth-century witch-hunt for "disloyal" Americans. Riding the crest of this issue, a new generation of right-wing politicians, dominated at first by Senator Joe McCarthy, began its rise to national prominence; two future Republican Presidents, both from California, would use this issue as their launching pad into national politics.

At first the President and his senior advisers paid insufficient attention to the politics of this issue because more urgent and serious matters constantly demanded our attention. This is an explanation, however, not an excuse, for what happened.

To be sure, the nation needed to protect itself against Soviet espionage, as we had pointed out in the Clifford-Elsey Report. This was a real problem—as was made clear by the frequent discovery of Soviet spies within the American, Canadian, and British governments. President Truman supported FBI and CIA efforts toward that end. But J. Edgar Hoover believed the national security was threatened not only by Soviet agents, but by anyone who expressed views that might be characterized as "leftist" or "socialist" or "procommunist." He sought authority to dismiss from public service anyone whose views were politically suspect. The Truman Administration resisted Hoover's efforts to control the process throughout the entire federal government, but unfortunately, created a different structure, loosely called the Federal Loyalty and Security Boards. The intention was to prevent the concentration of power in the hands of the FBI and its political allies, but the result was an unhappy one: the Administration compromised with its critics, creating a poorly conceived and poorly executed program that satisfied neither the conservatives, who wanted a far more aggressive hunt for subversives, nor the liberals, who believed that any loyalty program was an infringement of the First Amendment.

J. Edgar Hoover was fifty-two years old in 1947. He had served in the FBI and its predecessor, the Bureau of Investigation, since 1917, and had been the nation's chief domestic intelligence officer since 1936. His hatred of communism was genuine, and he felt that everyone else in the Truman Administration was a novice compared to him—especially on this issue.

Thus began the "attack of the primitives," as Dean Acheson aptly called them: an irresistible opportunity for Hoover and his allies in the Congress, including a young first-term Congressman from California named Richard M. Nixon.

Unfortunately, the Attorney General, Tom Clark, gave Hoover general support. Clark had risen through the ranks of the Justice Department before being appointed to the top post in Justice in 1945 at the urging of his fellow Texan, House Speaker Sam Rayburn. He was cautious, quiet-spoken, and conservative. President Truman enjoyed Clark's company, although their relationship would collapse later, after Clark was appointed to the Supreme Court and voted against the President's 1952 seizure of the steel mills. I developed a cordial personal relationship with

Clark, which allowed us to work together even when we differed, as we frequently did.

In their submission to the Clifford-Elsey Report, Clark and Hoover included a paragraph that hinted at the rationale for a loyalty program, although we did not realize it at the time:

> The Soviet Government, by utilizing the membership of the Communist Party in the United States, has thousands of invaluable sources of information in various industrial establishments as well as in the departments of the Government. In this regard, it must be remembered that every American Communist is potentially an espionage agent of the Soviet Government, requiring only the direct instruction of a Soviet superior to make the potentiality a reality.

American communists, the report added, were poised to "engage in industrial espionage" and "promote left-wing sentiment among soldiers . . . in order to prepare for sabotage in the event of war with the Soviet Union."

In retrospect, this was the most unfortunate section of the Clifford-Elsey Report. Most members of the American Communist Party had joined out of misplaced idealism or naïveté. Although their views were misguided and served Moscow's political interests, only a small number ever consciously acted against their own government, and even fewer would ever have accepted "direct instruction of a Soviet superior." There was no proof for the FBI's statement that the government was riddled with Reds, but because it represented the deeply held views of Clark and Hoover, Elsey and I included it in the final report with only one change: an additional comment suggested by George Kennan, referring to similar subversive communist activities in Spain.

President Truman, a great optimist about his nation and its resilience, paid little attention to the threat of internal communist subversion. He concentrated on what could be done to defeat communism in those areas overseas where it might take root unless America took action. His attitude, and mine, could be summed up in a phrase that was to become common around the White House as the "primitives" grew louder in the next two years: communism was a threat *to* America, but not a threat *in* America.

EXECUTIVE ORDER 9835

The Republican sweep in the 1946 Congressional elections not only weakened President Truman, it emboldened Hoover and his allies. From that point on, they treated the Administration as a group of very lame ducks. Within days after the election, Hoover pressed for a tough line on the issue of loyalty in the government, and shamelessly leaked information to his favorite columnists, especially Walter Winchell. The incoming Speaker of the House, Joseph Martin, set the new tone in his maiden speech on January 3, 1947, when he declared that "there is no room in the government of the United States for any who prefer the Communistic system." Federal employees "who do not believe in the way of life which has made this the greatest country of all time," Martin said, "should be—they must be—removed."

President Truman was in a trap. He did not like Hoover, but in 1947 the FBI director was widely regarded as a genuine American hero, protecting the nation against gangsters and Nazis. To a certain extent, these were skillfully manufactured public-relations myths, but they prevented the President from even thinking about getting rid of Hoover. Meanwhile, Attorney General Clark constantly urged the President to expand the investigative authority of the FBI.

On November 25, 1946, the President yielded to pressure from Hoover and Clark, and accepted a recommendation from the House Un-American Activities Committee to establish a Temporary Commission on Employee Loyalty. The commission, chaired by an Assistant Attorney General who was Hoover's stooge, was told to come up with recommendations for a permanent program.

The result was Executive Order 9835, issued on March 21, 1947, nine days after the Truman Doctrine speech, establishing the Loyalty Program. It authorized the Civil Service Commission to conduct a loyalty investigation of every new federal employee, and set up loyalty boards in every department and agency empowered to recommend "the removal of any officer or employee . . . on grounds relating to loyalty." This executive order was drafted by the FBI and the Justice Department and passed through my office before it was approved by the President. Hoover wanted both investigatory and review power vested in the FBI, but I supported the recommendation that the Civil Service Commission, rather than the FBI, be placed in charge.

Although Executive Order 9835 was subsequently criticized by liberals for failing to protect the civil rights of government employees, the first assault on it came from the right, which raged at its "weakness." Hoover was infuriated, and concluded that the President was not serious about domestic subversion. He was particularly angry at what he regarded as two deliberate insults to the FBI: assigning the Civil Service Commission responsibility for examining new government employees, and leaving each agency in charge of its own loyalty review of its employees. Both tasks, Hoover felt, should have gone to him. Almost immediately, he publicly criticized the Administration in fiery testimony before the new Chairman of the House Un-American Activities Committee, J. Parnell Thomas of

New Jersey. From that point on, Hoover continually sought full control of the program.

Our efforts to resist Hoover's grab for power diverted our attention from the real defects of Executive Order 9835. The first problem was inherent in the word "loyalty," which was vague and suggested the wrong intent; since communist espionage and subversion was the stated objective of the program, it should have been called a "security program." While "security" could be defined, loyalty is an intangible quality, defined differently by different people. As one perceptive scholar put it later, loyalty "by definition relates to qualities of heart, mind, and character, and covers many differing ideas. [It is a] word from which all content, save the emotional, may readily be drained."[1] The problem was evident in the sloppily worded preamble to the executive order:

> WHEREAS it is of vital importance that persons employed in the Federal service be of complete and unswerving loyalty to the United States; . . .
>
> WHEREAS maximum protection must be afforded the United States against infiltration of disloyal persons. . . .

The second problem with the program was more specific. An official charged with disloyalty was granted the right to an "*administrative* hearing before a loyalty board in the employing department," but the executive order allowed the loyalty boards to keep secret the charges against the individual if it wished to do so for security reasons. Furthermore, no specific finding that the individual was a security risk was necessary for dismissal; all that was required was the government's view that "*reasonable grounds* exist for belief that the person involved is disloyal to the Government of the United States" (emphasis added).

A few days after the President had issued it, I saw David E. Lilienthal, who had just weathered one of the first assaults of the "loyalty" era, and been confirmed by the Senate as the first Chairman of the Atomic Energy Commission. During the confirmation hearings a month earlier, Republicans had accused Lilienthal of "coddling" communists during his tenure as head of the Tennessee Valley Authority. At a point when his confirmation seemed problematic, Lilienthal told me that he would withdraw if at any time his nomination was viewed as a political liability. Moved by Lilienthal's typically self-effacing modesty, I told him that "the President was in the fight to the finish." Lilienthal then responded to his accusers in the Senate with an extemporaneous statement of his unshakable belief in free speech. His opening line—"This I believe, Senator"—became famous, and he instantly became a hero to liberals.

When I asked the newly confirmed Lilienthal whether he thought the

Loyalty Program would have an effect on the Truman Doctrine, he said we should keep the two matters as separate as possible so as not to weaken our foreign policy. Then he added a perceptive warning: while he recognized that the President had resisted pressure from the House Un-American Activities Committee and the FBI to go further, Lilienthal expressed deep concern that the order would subject service in the government to the constant risk that some "malevolent or crazy person might accuse you of being a leftist." The discretionary power delegated to the individual review panels was immense. Lilienthal noted that, in effect, the executive order reversed the usual rule in the U.S. that people are presumed innocent until proven guilty.[2]

"AN AMERICAN GESTAPO"

In late April and early May, 1947, as Marshall and Acheson drafted the Marshall Plan and we fought to salvage the National Security Act from Congressman Vinson and the Navy, the backstage struggle between the Civil Service Commission and the FBI over control of the loyalty program burst into open warfare.

The issue over which the battle was waged was the one central to so many Washington power struggles, the funding process. At least two million incumbent federal employees had to be fingerprinted, checked, and investigated. Normal turnover in the government would require an additional annual review of some half-million new employees each year. Because of the enormous size of this program, a supplemental budgetary request was necessary. After careful study, we decided to request $24.9 million, two thirds for the Civil Service Commission, and the remaining one third for the FBI. Hoover objected to the FBI's allocation, and demanded that his agency take over primary responsibility for the program. He pointed out that the FBI was the only existing agency staffed and qualified to carry out the investigations and the follow-up, and that the Civil Service Commission lacked both background and staff to do the job assigned to it. Hoover's assault was clever, because both his points were technically accurate; he *did* have better resources to carry out the program, as I noted in a memorandum to the President.

But President Truman felt Hoover had pushed him far enough. On May 1, 1947, as Elsey and I worked on the response to Hoover's latest attempt to grab power, the President came into my office twice to discuss the issue. Presidential visits to my office were highly unusual. The second visit was memorable: "Let's be sure that we hold the FBI down," the President said. "If we leave them to their own devices and give them what they want, they will become an American Gestapo." His message was clear: he did not want the Loyalty Program to fall under Hoover's control.

He sent the funding request to Congress without turning the program over to the FBI, as Hoover had demanded.

The FBI fought back. Over the next few months, Hoover worked behind the scenes to gain control of the Loyalty Program. On May 23, 1947, I sent the President a memorandum reporting that both Hoover and Clark wanted the FBI's portion of the program and its funding increased, but I recommended that he reject the FBI's request. He returned my memorandum with a handwritten note scrawled across it showing that he knew exactly what he was up against, and the likely outcome:

> Clark: You have properly diagnosed the case. But J. Edgar will in all probability get this backward-looking Congress to give him what he wants. It's dangerous. H.S.T.

The President's prediction was all too accurate. After three months of lobbying by Hoover, Congress reversed the ratios in the funding, granting the FBI $7.4 million and the Civil Service Commission only $3 million for the remainder of 1947. Hoover had won a big battle for the FBI. On August 17, the FBI began fingerprinting incumbent employees, and on October 1, 1947, the Loyalty Program was officially launched.

THE LOYALTY PROGRAM

Thus began an era in which every aspect of a person's private views on political issues suddenly seemed open to public scrutiny. The Loyalty Program gave rise to a myriad of similar programs, run with even less justice or justification, in the private sector. One of the most famous, in Hollywood, led to the blacklisting of many prominent members of the film community, and brought Ronald Reagan into his first important involvement in politics. Even people's reading habits could be cause for their dismissal, and an accusation—even unproven—of attendance at a meeting sponsored by a leftist group could destroy a person's career. The State Department witnessed many of the most dramatic and memorable battles of the era, including the tragic destruction of the careers of John Stewart Service, John Carter Vincent, John Paton Davies, and others. Not one of these men was a communist, but each had made the mistake of reporting frankly on the reasons why communism was gaining strength, especially in China.

President Truman abhorred what was happening, but events took the issue out of his hands. The defection of a Soviet code clerk, Igor Gouzenko, from the Soviet embassy in Canada, generated enormous interest in the U.S., and his testimony about Soviet espionage in the U.S. spurred the right wing on. The Alger Hiss affair began its long voyage through American history. In October 1949, China fell to Mao. Less than five months later, Senator Joe McCarthy made his infamous speech in Wheeling, West Virginia, charging that the State Department was harboring communists. Five months after that, the Korean War began. With each passing month more fuel was thrown on the fire, and the right-wing assault on civil liberties that we now call McCarthyism began to rage.

The trend had begun to alarm President Truman well before the start of the Korean War. After the 1948 election, he indicated to me his growing dissatisfaction with both Hoover and the developing atmosphere. Never once, though, did he indicate that he thought the Loyalty Program had either contributed to the problem or was a mistake; in his eyes, the program had been designed to prevent the excesses which were taking place, and would not have become a problem if Hoover had not perverted it. He felt that without the Loyalty Program, the political pressures would have been much greater, and more difficult to resist. At the time, I agreed with him; later I would come to a different conclusion.

After the battle over responsibility for the loyalty program, President Truman and Hoover never trusted each other. But at the time, Hoover's prestige in the nation was at its highest point, and an uneasy truce was the best the President could manage. So deep was Hoover's contempt and hostility for the Truman Administration that, barely a year after President Truman left office, the FBI Director testified openly against his former boss before the Senate Internal Security Subcommittee, saying, "He was blind to the Communist menace and used very bad judgment."[3]

When Hoover and I were together we maintained a surface cordiality. On one occasion we were seated together as someone's guests at a memorable boxing match between Rocky Graziano and Tony Zale. After the battle over the funding of the Loyalty Program, however, Hoover made no further effort to ingratiate himself with anyone in the White House; he merely sent us his reports, usually through Harry Vaughan, whom he viewed, correctly, as his best friend in the President's inner circle.

There has probably been no one, in my years in Washington, who amassed and abused power more shamefully than J. Edgar Hoover. As the disclosures of recent years have shown, his agenda for the FBI was highly personal, and included vendettas against Martin Luther King, Jr., Robert F. Kennedy, and a host of other people whose views or behavior had somehow offended him.

In the forties, we could only suspect the dimensions of his megalomania; by the seventies, evidence was beginning to emerge about his activities. But even today, I am sure there is a great deal we do not know about the uses to which J. Edgar Hoover put his vast array of agents, networks, and resources. He was very close to being an American fascist, and it is unfortunate that the new FBI headquarters on Pennsylvania Avenue in Washington still bears his name.

A FINAL MEMORANDUM

After the 1948 election, I became increasingly aware of, and disturbed by, abuses of the civil liberties that were taking place in the name of national security. Several bills introduced in Congress had been directed against the Communist Party of the United States and its front organizations. The most prominent of these was the Mundt-Nixon Bill, submitted by Senator Karl Mundt and Congressman Nixon on March 9, 1949.

At the beginning of April 1949, Max Lowenthal, who had played such a useful role in the decision to recognize Israel, sent the President a memorandum that compared the Mundt-Nixon Bill and others like it to the Alien and Sedition Acts of 1798–1799. The President asked for my views. In reply, I summed up my views on civil liberties in great detail in a memorandum dated April 29, 1949. I recommended that the Administration oppose "legislation such as the Mundt, Nixon, or [Homer] Ferguson bills." Instead of these bills, I suggested the President submit alternative legislation based on the Civil Rights Commission proposals of 1947, requiring "all groups which attempt to influence public opinion to disclose the pertinent facts about themselves through a systematic registration process." This was a futile attempt to substitute a mild requirement for disclosure for the sort of legislation Mundt and Nixon had proposed.

I warned that we were watching "an ominous trend in the United States toward the increasing curtailment of freedom of expression and opinion through economic and social intimidation," and continued:

> With the possible exception of the days of John Adams and those of A. Mitchell Palmer, the situation is becoming more dangerous today than at any other period in American history. This situation of course plays into Soviet and Communist hands in several ways (aside from the obvious one of moving us in the direction of the very totalitarianism we oppose). . . . There are quite a few people around today who could take counsel from Dr. Sam Johnson's famous comment, "Patriotism, sir, is the last refuge of a scoundrel." As Boswell observed, this was a startling statement, but Johnson did not mean a real and generous love of our country. Rather, he meant that pretended patriotism which so many in all ages and countries have made a cloak for self-interest.

I ended my memorandum with some strong words. I believe that they are equally valid today:

> We gambled more than one hundred and fifty years ago, by writing the First Amendment into the Constitution, that in a free market place of opinion, the truth would prevail. . . . Reliance upon hysteria and repression as our weapons against totalitarian movements is self-defeating. . . . Irresponsible persons who make it a practice to attack every person or group with whom they disagree, as "Communist," have thereby actually aided their supposed enemies. . . .

But the tide was running too strongly for anyone, even the President, to turn it back. When Congress passed a revised version of the Mundt-Nixon bill as the Internal Security Act of 1950, better remembered today as the McCarran Act, the President promptly vetoed it, only to see it passed over his veto by an overwhelming margin. But in defeat, the President had taken the right stand. His veto won him new respect, and allowed him to stand for civil liberties even at the height of the Korean War and McCarthyism.

Part IV

THE MIRACLE YEAR

11

1948: The Beginning

History will always treat Harry Truman's "whistle-stop" campaign by train across America as the dramatic highlight of his stunning upset victory over Thomas E. Dewey, but it did not seem so at the time. In fact, there was nothing romantic or exciting about it. I remember it as a miserable, ceaseless, and exhausting treadmill. Months after the 1948 campaign was over, I still woke occasionally in the middle of the night with nightmares that I was trapped on that train. Only later would we learn that those of us who rode the rails with Harry Truman in 1948 had been participants in a mythic event—the centerpiece of the greatest political upset in American history, and the last Presidential election conducted before television, jet travel, political consultants, modern polling, and communications changed politics forever.

What an incredible year 1948 was! Those train rides were just a small part of it: the communists took over Czechoslovakia, Israel was born, Stalin lay siege to Berlin and the Airlift saved it, Whittaker Chambers confronted Alger Hiss, and Harry Truman defied the predictions of every political pundit and expert in the nation—except himself.

To appreciate what whistle-stopping was really like let us look at a fairly typical day, September 30, 1948. We already had been on the train for fifteen straight days, sleeping in cramped and unstately staterooms—except for the rare and treasured night that we slept in a hotel in a major city. On this particular day we stopped, and the President spoke, in Mount Vernon, West Frankfort, Herrin, Carbondale, Marion, El Dorado, and Carmi (all in Illinois), Mount Vernon and Evansville (Indiana), and Henderson, Owensboro, Hawesville, Irvington, and Louisville (Kentucky)—fifteen speeches in all, twelve from the back of the train and three on quick visits into larger towns. Every stop required something new, something local, something to satisfy the politicians who usually boarded the train a stop ahead of their hometown. And without telephones on board, almost every stop, no matter how short, was also a frantic race to call Washington to see if there was any business requiring Presidential attention. And so it went, for well over 250 speeches.

In the year before the election, as my relationship with President Truman grew closer, I had been drawn gradually into the campaign. I was already the President's chief speech writer, but I had never participated in a Presidential election (except as a voter)—and Washington was filled with Democrats who, having participated in Franklin Roosevelt's four victories, were, or thought they were, political experts.

Many Democrats did not want or expect President Truman to run, and considered him an unelected usurper of FDR's mantle with no chance against the Republicans. But those of us who met at Jack Ewing's apartment on Monday evenings wanted him to run, even though his national campaigning thus far had been limited to an unremarkable run for the Vice Presidency in 1944. Like everyone else, however, we were not sure he could win.

In the end, nothing would ever give him greater satisfaction than being elected in his own right. But in 1947 he was apparently not so sure he would run, for in great secrecy he sent word to General Eisenhower that he would step aside if Eisenhower wanted the Democratic nomination. Neither President Truman nor anyone else had the slightest idea of Eisenhower's political views, and in the luminous aura that surrounded the war hero, no one had bothered to ask. Although Eisenhower declined President Truman's suggestion, the "Ike factor" was to cast a continual shadow over the campaign until the very eve of the Democratic Convention. Curiously, the Republicans showed almost no interest in Eisenhower in 1948; there were simply too many eager Republicans already in the field.

Of the President's secret offer to Eisenhower I knew nothing at the time. I am sure President Truman knew I would have tried to dissuade him from such an action, so he simply did not tell me. The only occasion on which I saw the two men discuss politics was during a luncheon Eisenhower, then Army Chief of Staff, gave President Truman at the Pentagon in early 1946: in a lighthearted manner, President Truman turned to Eisenhower and said, "General, if you ever want to go into politics, come to me and I'll sure endorse you." Ike just laughed and smiled his famous smile, and the conversation moved on.

The obstacles to President Truman's election were staggering. Roosevelt's coalition was fragile and in danger of breaking up. Both Houses of Congress were in Republican hands. Part of the South would follow Strom Thurmond, then a Democratic Governor from South Carolina, in a regional revolt against the Democrats, and Thurmond would run on the States' Rights, or Dixiecrat, ticket. And Henry Wallace, still smarting from his firing in 1946, would run as a left-wing third-party candidate.

If Harry Truman was confident of victory, he did not wholly succeed in convincing the person closest to him. One September afternoon, as we raced through another one of those days that seemed to be without end, Bess Truman pulled me aside. This was unusual in itself; she was a fine, intelligent and gracious woman, devoted to her Harry, and very kind to me, but she and I rarely had conversations on serious matters. On this day, conditions seemed especially bleak. The newspapers were full of articles about the hopelessness of the situation, and our opponent was confidently picking his Cabinet. "Do you think that Harry really believes he is going to win? He certainly acts that way," she asked me. So even Mrs. Truman was not sure what was going on in her husband's mind! My reply was simple: "Yes, I believe he does." But in my own heart, I was not really sure.

Did I think Harry Truman could win? I have been asked that question so often in the years since then that I am no longer sure exactly what I did think, and when. As the campaign unfolded, my hopes went up and down. At times I thought the President was either fooling himself or putting forward a brave front to keep *our* spirits up. But our job was to stay at it, no matter how hopeless things seemed—we did not have time to sit around and analyze our chances. This is the way campaigns always are: while the rest of the world argues over who is leading, at the center of the enterprise the staff staggers on, worrying only about the next event, counting down the days until, win or lose, it is finally over.

THE MEMORANDUM

My role in the 1948 campaign really began in November 1947, with a memorandum that has been praised by some historians for its foresight in laying out how events would evolve. It grew, in part, from discussion at our Monday-Night Group.

By the summer of 1947, we knew we were heading into difficult and uncharted waters. We lacked any plan or overall strategy for the campaign. As we talked over our steak dinners at Jack Ewing's apartment, I felt the need for a comprehensive approach to the election. But no one in our little group had the time to write it.

Enter James Rowe, one of the most brilliant political thinkers of the

New Deal era. Rowe had been an administrative assistant to Roosevelt, and was devoted to his memory. He had left the government in 1945 to become a partner in the law firm headed by the legendary Roosevelt aide, Thomas Corcoran. In the early days of the New Deal, Corcoran had perfected the use of the deliberately ambiguous phrase, "I'm calling from the White House . . ." as a device for prodding people into action by implying that his call was being made at Presidential direction. Of course, this was rarely the case, but Corcoran's ploy worked so well that over fifty years later it is still used—one might say, abused—by members of an ever-expanding White House staff, few of whom deal directly with the President.

Rowe's close association with "Tommy the Cork," as Corcoran was universally known, was a major liability in the Truman White House. Notwithstanding Corcoran's undeniable cleverness and charm—he was a particularly prized guest at Washington parties, where he often entertained after dinner by playing the accordion—questions had been raised about his commitment to the New Deal in the years since he had left the White House. By the time I arrived on the scene in 1945, he had been functioning as a part-time lawyer and full-time Washington wheeler-dealer for five years. Although I appreciated his intellectual agility, I questioned both his style and ethics.

President Truman disliked Tommy the Cork intensely. This natural animosity was heightened when a series of Corcoran's comments denigrating the Administration reached President Truman. At the time I did not know the source of the President's information, but from the specific nature of his references to Corcoran, I suspected J. Edgar Hoover was feeding to the Chief Executive confidential information about his political rivals derived from wiretaps. In the eighties, it was revealed that Hoover tapped Corcoran's telephone between June 1945 and May 1948, and sent selected excerpts of Corcoran's conversations to President Truman through Harry Vaughan. Even though President Truman normally disliked this sort of activity, he was not immune to the attraction of inside information about a political adversary.

When Harry Truman disliked someone, he would often extend that hostility, in the spirit of old Missouri feuds, toward his enemy's associates—and that most definitely included Tommy the Cork's partner, Jim Rowe. As for Rowe, although he had no great affection or respect for Harry Truman, he desperately wanted the Democrats to extend their hold on the White House for another four years. This could be done, he decided, only if President Truman ran as a liberal, reassembling the key elements of Franklin Roosevelt's New Deal coalition. As it happened, for the past two years I had been defending the same view against the conservatives in the Administration, who wanted President Truman to abandon the New Deal.

That summer, Rowe told James Webb, the Director of the Bureau of the Budget, he had some thoughts on the 1948 election. Webb suggested Rowe write a memorandum, which Webb said he would give to President Truman. But when, late in the summer, Webb offered it to the President and identified it as the work of Jim Rowe, President Truman waved it aside, and told Webb to "give it to Clifford." Webb asked a trusted aide, Richard E. Neustadt,* to hand-carry Rowe's memorandum to me with a note that said simply, "The President asked me to give this to you for the appropriate action."

I read the memorandum at home over the weekend, and then shared it with the people I trusted most in Washington. The Monday-Night men were unanimous: the Rowe draft was consistent with our views and contained the core of a very perceptive strategy for the 1948 election. We felt it should be used as the basis for a memorandum to the President, so I set out to revise and update it.

In the following weeks I talked to political experts around Washington about the 1948 election. Of particular value were several long conversations I had with Leslie Biffle, the no-nonsense Secretary of the Senate, a powerful Washington insider who liked to travel around the country incognito in his old beat-up car, taking informal soundings of the popular mood.

After rewriting the memorandum and reviewing it once more with the Monday-Night Group, I handed it to the President. He would have dismissed it again if it was associated with Rowe, so I did not mention Rowe's role in its drafting. There was nothing unusual about this process, although for many years afterward, Rowe incorrectly thought the President had received and read his original memorandum. Asked about the origins of the memorandum in 1981, Jim Webb said, "If Clifford had told the President he was sending him a memorandum primarily prepared by Jim Rowe, it would not have had the same effect as the memorandum Clifford wrote."[1]

What arrived on the President's desk on November 19, 1947, was a forty-three-page memorandum, offering seven major predictions about the coming campaign and suggesting a strategy for victory. Its first paragraph made clear its ambitious scope:

> The aim of the memorandum is to outline a course of political conduct for the Administration extending from November, 1947 to

*Later a Professor of Government at Harvard, my close associate during the 1960 transition, and the author of one of the most influential books ever written on American government, *Presidential Power.*

> November, 1948. . . . The basic premise of this memorandum—that the Democratic Party is an unhappy alliance of Southern conservatives, Western progressives and Big City labor—is very trite, but it is also very true. And it is equally true that the success or failure of the Democratic leadership can be precisely measured by its ability to lead enough members of these three misfit groups to the polls on the first Tuesday after the first Monday of November, 1948.

In the light of history, phrases in this document that seemed unexceptional in 1948 take on a different ring, with suggestions that foreshadowed sea changes in American politics cropping up casually. I am struck now by both what we got right—and what we got wrong. Our predictions were, as these things go, surprisingly accurate: six out of seven right, enough on which to base a winning strategy.

Our most serious error was taking the South for granted. We did not anticipate the Southern revolt that would lead to Strom Thurmond's fourth-party candidacy. I can only smile ruefully when I reread my assessment of the South: "As always, the South can be considered safely Democratic. And in formulating national policy, it can be safely ignored."

Since Reconstruction, black Americans had favored the "party of Lincoln," but FDR had broken the Republican lock on the black vote, and it was up for grabs in 1948. Anticipating a major effort by Dewey to win black votes, we recommended "a determined campaign to help the Negro* (and everybody else) on the problems of high prices and housing. . . . Unless there are new and real efforts . . . the Negro bloc, which, certainly in Illinois and probably in New York and Ohio, *does* hold the balance of power, will go Republican."

What a sense of the passage of time these words evoke! In recent times, it has been the black vote that the Democrats have taken for granted, while white voters in the South have usually voted overwhelmingly Republican in Presidential campaigns. We did not realize how quickly Southern whites would abandon the President if he supported equal civil rights for all Americans.

With that important exception, the memorandum was surprisingly accurate. We called "the Winning of the West" our "Number One Priority," and planned a special campaign targeted at farmers. This turned out to be a critical decision: it was President Truman's success in the farm belt that provided him with the cushion he needed to withstand the shock of the loss of the South.

*Where more appropriate to the context than the more recent term "black," I will sometimes use the term "Negro," which was the terminology of the time. Although now outmoded, the use of this word, including the habit of capitalizing it, may help the modern reader understand the changes since 1948.

We foresaw Dewey's nomination over his rivals—a fairly easy prediction. More important, the memorandum forecast Henry Wallace's third-party candidacy: "The humility which was once [Wallace's] dominant characteristic has decreased to the vanishing point. There is something almost Messianic in his belief today that he is the Indispensable Man." I described him as surrounded by "Party-liners . . . political opportunists . . . and gullible idealists" and recommended criticizing him for being an unwitting tool of the Communist party.

The memorandum identified several groups, in addition to farmers, who would require special appeals. These included independents, progressives, labor union members, Catholics, Italians, Jews, and "liberals." This last group was up for grabs between Wallace and the President. While numerically small, we wrote, the liberals were "far more influential than mere numbers entitle them to be. The businessman has influence because he contributes his money. The liberal exerts unusual influence because he is articulate. The 'right' may have the money, but the 'left' has always had the pen."

I assumed the key foreign policy issue would be American relations with the Soviet Union—which would get worse, we predicted, strengthening the President, who was "comparatively invulnerable to attack because of his brilliant appointment of General Marshall" as Secretary of State. But the major issue of the 1948 election, we predicted, would be the high cost of living, heightened by the continuing housing shortage. This led to the most important recommendation of the memorandum:

> The Administration should select the issues upon which there will be conflict with the majority in Congress. It can assume it will get no major part of its own program approved. Its tactics must, therefore, be entirely different than if there were any real point to bargaining and compromise. Its recommendations—in the State of the Union Message and elsewhere—must be tailored for the voter, not the Congressman; they must display a label which reads "no compromises."

In this brief and blunt passage the glimmerings of a strategy for the campaign first emerged. The President would run not against his opponent, but against the Republican Party's record in Congress. It was to prove the most important strategic decision of the entire campaign. I recognized that "this may mean the end of 'bipartisan cooperation' on foreign policy," but I assumed election politics would be highly partisan regardless of the international situation. In any case, the key elements of a bipartisan foreign policy had already been put into place the year before, and I did not think they would be affected by the campaign. This judgment proved to be correct.

Style is always a vital part of campaigning. We urged the President to adjust his own to reflect a stronger sense of personal leadership. Harry Truman was never comfortable with actions that seemed self-serving or phony, and often let members of his Cabinet claim the limelight when some major announcement was made. I felt that this tendency, while admirable, was not the stuff of election politics. We outlined how he could be presented more effectively to the public, including a suggestion that was to develop into the whistle-stop campaign:

> The public has a tremendous interest in its Chief Executive and is invariably hungry for news about him. . . . The press *must* print news of the President—so he controls his publicity by his own whim. . . . A President who is also a candidate must resort to subterfuge—for he cannot sit silent. He must [hold regular meetings with key labor leaders and prominent Americans] to stay in the limelight and he must also resort to the kind of trip which Roosevelt made famous in the 1940 campaign—the "inspection tour."

While he agreed with most of our conclusions, he vehemently rejected the idea that he call in labor leaders or people (names like Albert Einstein and Henry Ford were put forward) for publicized "nonpolitical" meetings. "It's phony," he said, "and anyway, I especially don't want to spend any more time with those labor leaders than I have to." However, he was willing to test our suggestion for an early "nonpolitical campaign trip."

In conclusion, I wrote, "The campaign of 1948 will be a tough, bitterly fought struggle." Of this I had no doubt. Things did not seem as bleak, however, in November of 1947 as they were to become by the middle of 1948, and as I gave him the memorandum, I had no idea of how tough and bitter the campaign would in fact become. The President liked the memorandum, and kept it in his desk drawer throughout the campaign for handy reference.

THE STATE OF THE UNION

As the memorandum had indicated, the State of the Union Message offered a prime opportunity for the President to lay down a strong challenge to the Republican Congress and set the framework for the rest of the year. However, he himself and several staff members were not sure that he should even deliver the message in person. In a series of staff meetings in late December, and in private, I argued that the State of the Union Message was an ideal vehicle with which to begin putting the onus for the nation's economic woes squarely on the shoulders of the Republican Congress. Finally, President Truman agreed.

We produced a draft which we thought was bold and challenging, and aimed the speech at the nation, not Congress, even though the speech was delivered in the middle of the day (the idea, now routine, of making such a speech in the evening hours in order to reach a larger audience was as yet unheard of). The programs we proposed in some ways foreshadowed the sweeping efforts that Lyndon Johnson would make almost two decades later, although, of course, there was no chance that the Republicans would approve President Truman's proposals in 1948—whereas in 1964 President Johnson had the power and Congressional support to enact the Great Society. But President Truman was not insincere; these programs in housing, conservation, public power, and so on were ones in which he really believed. He also called for an appropriation of $6.8 billion for the first fifteen months of the Marshall Plan—an enormous sum by any standards, a stunning 18 percent of the 1949 budget, and over 2.5 percent of the nation's gross national product. Figures like this would be out of the question today, but in that immediate postwar atmosphere, Americans were willing to be generous in helping other nations when they also saw it as being in their own interest.

At 1:30 P.M. on January 7, 1948, the President traveled up Pennsylvania Avenue to deliver what we had planned as the opening blow of the campaign. I rode up to the Congress with him to go over last-minute changes. I was looking forward to the opening gun of the election year. But even before he could enter the House chamber there was a troubling sign of the Congressional mood. As we waited in a holding room, we heard a long and sustained roar from the floor, occasioned, we learned, by Secretary of State Marshall, who, arriving late, had sat down in the wrong seat. When he moved to his proper place at the head of the Cabinet row, the entire chamber rose to its feet in tribute. "Old-timers on the Hill said that they had never seen anything like it," reported *The Washington Post* the next day. While Marshall deserved such an accolade, there was no question that it was also intended as a demonstration of preference, an implicit rebuke of President Truman, whose applause, a moment later, was noticeably milder.

Typical of the early Truman speeches, the President crisply and matter-of-factly put the facts forward with almost no rhetorical flourishes: "Food costs too much. Housing has reached fantastic price levels. Schools and hospitals are in financial distress. . . . Worst of all, inflation holds the threat of another depression."

As one of the drafters of the speech, I was pleased—but the response of the Congress, the press, and the national radio audience was not favorable. There were no interruptions for applause until more than halfway through the forty-minute speech. James Reston's reaction the next day, in a front page story in *The New York Times,* was fairly typical:

> The finished product is not a speech but a catalogue, and not a report on the state of the Union, but a commentary on a state of mind. . . . Clark Clifford, the President's aide, was given the task of selecting, rejecting, and providing the pattern for Mr. Truman's approval. After all this work, however, the extraordinarily chilly reception of the speech created the impression that many who heard it decided that, after all the sewing and basting, Mr. Truman was long on rags and tatters and short on pattern.

EVERYONE LIKED IKE

The months following the State of the Union Message were a period of mounting difficulties for the Administration. On the international front, the communist takeover of Czechoslovakia made it easier to maintain a bipartisan front on foreign policy. But on the domestic side, there was a sense in Washington that events were slipping out of the President's control. This was heightened by President Truman's delay in announcing that he would run for election, thus allowing other Democrats free rein in urging the party to dump him for Eisenhower or some other candidate.

Ironically, the leading liberal organization in the country, Americans for Democratic Action, was leading the effort to replace President Truman. Just as he was proposing the most far-reaching civil rights legislation in American history (see Chapter 12), this group proposed to replace him with General Eisenhower, whose political views were completely unknown, and who, when he finally surfaced four years later, turned out to be a conservative Republican. It may seem hard to believe today, but the ADA's Committee to Draft Eisenhower was strongly backed in 1948 by such influential Democrats as FDR's three sons, Franklin, Elliott, and Jimmy;* Alabama's two Senators, John Sparkman and Lister Hill; Florida Senator Claude Pepper; the courageous leader of the United Automobile Workers, Walter Reuther; and a promising young mayor from Minneapolis named Hubert H. Humphrey. This was serious business: it seemed clear that if Eisenhower made himself available, he would be nominated and elected in 1948. But Ike, who was then President of Columbia University, knew himself well and deftly deflected the pressure while concealing his own political views and long-term ambitions.

The President watched Ike's actions anxiously and closely. When Eisenhower issued a statement on January 23 that temporarily closed the door on the race, the President was so pleased that he called me into his office simply to read to me a newspaper account of Eisenhower's statement. Then, with evident enjoyment, he handed me the newspaper and

*To Jimmy Roosevelt, President Truman wrote an angry note: "Here I am trying to carry out your father's policies. You've got no business trying to pull the rug out from under me."

listened as I read Ike's statement back to him. But despite this statement, the "draft Ike" movement was still not dead.

IT'S NOT ALWAYS AN HONOR TO BE ON *TIME*'S COVER

Ike was not our only problem. Washington, in the late winter and early spring of 1948, had decided to write Harry Truman off. "If Truman is nominated," wrote columnists Joseph and Stewart Alsop in a typical comment, "he will be forced to wage the loneliest campaign in history."[2] The Gallup Poll showed the President with a 36 percent approval rating, down sharply from the fall and continuing to drop; in sample match-ups he lost decisively to Governors Dewey and Stassen, Senator Vandenberg, and General Douglas MacArthur. The President seemed outwardly unruffled throughout this period, but I felt it was getting to him. He told me that he did not read stories about his political weakness, but it was impossible for a man in his position to avoid all of them. Like vultures, all of Washington awaited the belated end of the Age of Roosevelt. At the White House, we felt beleaguered, surrounded by enemies closing in from all sides.

In Washington, external threats do not always produce internal unity. When the ship of state rides through troubled seas, its crew all too often gets into fights. Such was the case in the first few months of 1948, as Democrats blamed each other for the crumbling Administration. There was nothing surprising in this—it had happened before, it would happen again. But it was a rough time for everyone. In this atmosphere, it was inevitable that the press, so often Washington's weapon of choice, would become part of the battle. And so, without warning, I suddenly found myself the target of a first-class press assault.

In the second week of March, *Time* magazine ran a cover story on me. Although I had been interviewed by a *Time* reporter, I did not know that such an honor was coming my way. For an instant, upon seeing the cover, my reaction was not entirely negative, since the painting of me seemed quite accomplished. But behind my portrait was a rather sickly looking ghost reading a murky crystal ball, and once I read the story, my moment of vanity vanished entirely. *Time* wrote that "the country appeared to be getting ready to dump the whole Truman Administration." President Truman's performance was "awkward, uninspired and above all, mediocre." He was "listening to the wrong people and . . . getting bad advice from people who did not know the score." The President's friends, said *Time,* blamed one person in particular: "Presidential Adviser Clark Clifford, who was strictly an amateur politician and a stranger to the President's old friends. . . . Like his boss, he is a political accident."

Time laid responsibility for most of what it regarded as the President's long list of political blunders on me. In other circumstances I might have regarded the list as a badge of honor, but that was not *Time*'s intent. According to *Time*, I had prevented a "gracious surrender" to John L. Lewis during the 1946 coal strike, written "the ill-advised, intemperate" message on the railroad strike, and erected "a barrier between the President and the professional politicians." But my greatest alleged crime was to have pulled President Truman toward the left:

> Whenever [the President] opened his mouth to deliver one of the messages prepared by Clifford, the President talked like a New Dealer. And Adviser Clifford was kept busy scribbling. He wrote the tax vetoes; the Taft-Hartley veto; the October 1947 call for a special session; the State of the Union message last January; this year's Jackson Day dinner speech and the civil-rights message. There was no real difference between what these messages said and what a generation of New Dealers had said before. But in Mr. Truman's monotonous twang and Clifford's primer sentences, they just sounded dull.

Later, after the President's victory in November, I took a certain perverse enjoyment in going back and rereading *Time*'s article—but that was not my initial reaction. The article was a clear signal that knives were being sharpened within the White House and on Capitol Hill. I was upset. I was supposed to be helping the President, not hurting him. Nevertheless, I resolved not to show my concern. With the exception of George Elsey and Charlie Ross, I did not discuss the article with anyone, and tried to ignore it.

President Truman's own reaction bound me more closely to him, in an emotional sense, than ever before. The day after it appeared, he simply dismissed it: "I read that mean piece about you. Don't let it concern you." And as he always said when one of his aides was under attack, "It's me they're after, not you." That was that; we never discussed the article again.

I examined it for clues as to who the anonymous "old cronies" and friends quoted in the article might be. The article had combined the words of pro–New Deal Democrats and conservatives in order to attack the President from both the left, for failing to fulfill the promise of FDR, and from the right, for moving too fast on civil rights. I assumed that *Time*'s sources included senior Congressional leaders who were shaken by the civil rights message, and White House staffers who were more concerned with power politics within the Executive Mansion than with the substance of policy. Among these, I thought first of White House Assistant John Steelman, described by *Time* as my "rival in the antechamber."

But, regardless, there was no rationalizing the one inescapable message of the article: as long as the campaign seemed to be going badly, I was going to be an easy target for the President's critics.

A SHAKEDOWN CRUISE

One of the problems we faced in 1948 was the President's speaking style. He generally read poorly from written texts, his head down, words coming forth in what the press liked to call a "drone." The contrast with the brilliant and compelling style of his predecessor made the problem all the more serious.

We had tried various devices to improve his speaking style, which even he knew was uninspiring. One, in late 1947, was particularly memorable to me. I thought perhaps the President's style would improve if he read from large cue cards that we would place just out of sight of the cameras. I brought several large cards, about three feet by four feet, to a staff meeting in October. With a few staff members looking on, the President cheerfully agreed to try out the idea. He read the cards with interest when I placed them on his desk, but as soon as I moved them just three feet away he told us that he could not read them, even with their huge lettering. "My eyes have been like this since I was a boy," he explained—and that was the end of that experiment.

Ross, Murphy, and I returned to the problem in the weeks following the unsuccessful State of the Union message, and finally hit upon a more successful approach—having the President speak extemporaneously. He agreed to try speaking without a text on April 17, to the annual convention of the American Society of Newspaper Editors in Washington. This experiment went well, and he agreed to do the same thing with three other speeches. He was reluctant at first to make a radio speech without a text, but we insisted that it was important to convey greater informality on the air, and he finally agreed to do this also, addressing the National Conference on Family Life on May 6 using notes only. With this new approach, Harry Truman's natural, down-to-earth style emerged, complete with an informal ease that prepared texts did not permit.

The President had shown interest in the idea of "nonpolitical inspection tours," based loosely on the Roosevelt model. In the spring, I arranged for one of my Monday Night Group cohorts, Undersecretary of the Interior Oscar Chapman, to arrange a plausible excuse for a cross-country tour: an invitation to deliver the commencement address and receive an honorary degree at the University of California.

Most people still traveled by train in 1948, but President Truman preferred to fly. Now, however, he agreed to go to California by train, stopping frequently as he crossed the country to make five major speeches and about forty minor ones—all ostensibly "nonpolitical." It would be treated as an official trip, paid for out of the President's annual travel allowance of $30,000. He asked me to prepare drafts of the major speeches; the short talks from the back of the train platform would be given in his new off-the-cuff style.

We pulled out of Union Station just after 11 P.M. on June 3, 1948. Most of the Cabinet, including General Marshall, saw us off. The President was in a very good mood. We each had a bourbon and branch water as the train started out, and then went to bed—the President to his quarters in the Presidential car, I to my berth in a stateroom in the adjoining car, where I was to spend far more time than I could ever have imagined in the coming months.

Our shakedown cruise was marked by confusion, poor coordination, and plain dumb mistakes. But we learned a great deal about how to conduct a campaign—and these lessons were to serve us well when the final round began in September. Without that June trip, I doubt the whistle-stops would have succeeded in the fall. In speech after speech as we rode slowly toward California, President Truman followed a similar script, joking about the "nonpolitical" nature of his trip, making references to the area in which he was speaking, and then lambasting the Republicans. There were some successful moments along the way—such as the parade in Omaha, when the President jumped out of his car and marched for half a mile with his old World War I buddies from Battery D—but mishaps occurred with alarming frequency. That same day, poor advance work resulted in a nearly empty hall for a major speech, wiping out the pleasant image of the President with his wartime comrades. Local Democratic politicians were often inadvertently barred from getting on the train or not given enough time with the President because of our efforts to avoid making the trip seem too overtly partisan. Meanwhile, the Republicans charged that the trip was, in the words of the Chairman of the Republican National Committee, as "nonpolitical as the Pendergast machine."

In the small town of Carey, Idaho, every politician's nightmare took place. Asked to dedicate the new airport, the President understood it to be named after a local war hero, and was deep into a celebration of the wartime bravery of Wilmer Coates when he was loudly interrupted by a woman who informed him that it was her daughter Wilma, a victim of a civilian airplane crash, after whom the airport was being named.

A more serious incident took place June 11 in Eugene, Oregon, when the President made what would become a much-quoted comment about Stalin: "I like Old Joe." He went on to describe the Soviet dictator as

> a decent fellow [who] is a prisoner of the Politburo. . . . [Stalin] can't do what he wants to. He makes agreements, and if he could, he would keep them; but the people who run the government are very specific in saying that he can't keep them.

The uproar caused by this remark was immediate, sustained, and understandable. From Washington, Lovett and Forrestal both called me to urge that the President repudiate his comments. Ross, Elsey, and I discussed the situation frankly, and came to the conclusion that we had to provide the President with notes to guide him whenever he spoke extemporaneously; otherwise there was too great a chance he might create additional difficulties for himself. We also realized we needed to strengthen our research staff, and, at my request, the Democratic National Committee set up a special unit to prepare the President for all future campaign appearances.

We had an immediate and delicate task facing us: to talk to President Truman about his comments. This was the moment that anyone who has ever worked for a President most dreads: telling the boss he has made a mistake. Unlike some Presidents, though, Harry Truman took criticism well, at least if it came from someone he trusted. In this case, the duty fell to Charlie Ross and me. The day after the incident, we sat down with him and told him that we had a serious problem. Ross led off: "Mr. President, we just have to tell you, frankly, that your 'I like Old Joe' remark is not going over well. We are going to get hammered for it, we know you understand, and we know you will not want to repeat that phrase." I then summarized the calls from Lovett and Forrestal.

The President listened to us quietly. After a moment, he said, rather quietly, "Well, I guess I goofed," and from then on there was no more affectionate talk about Stalin.

But what lay behind his famous remark? Did he really believe that Stalin was a prisoner of the Politburo? The answer is oddly elusive. This President, under whose leadership the foundation for more than forty years of American foreign policy was established, understood the dangers the Soviet system posed to the West; he had, after all, already produced the Truman Doctrine and the Marshall Plan. Nevertheless, he retained a surprisingly warm personal memory of his only meeting with Stalin, at Potsdam in July of 1945. Stalin had been on his best personal behavior at Potsdam; he wanted to establish a relationship with the new President, and spent time talking about subjects like farming, in which he knew Harry Truman had a personal interest. Moreover, the last important holdover from the Roosevelt White House, Admiral Leahy, also had told President Truman he thought Stalin was controlled by the Politburo. I had heard the President make similar statements privately a few times before Oregon.

After the criticism that followed the Oregon incident, it was never a problem again—in great part because his view of Stalin was to harden over the next year. He came to see that Stalin was the ruthless leader, not a prisoner, of the Soviet system for which he had always had such distaste.

If we made our share of mistakes on the June trial run, a more costly one was made by one of the leading contenders for the Republican nomination, Senator Robert A. Taft of Ohio, who gave us and the English language a phrase that would endure. After we had been on the road for about a week, Taft attacked the President for "blackguarding Congress at every whistle-stop station in the West." We decided to try to turn Taft's derisive phrase around to convey a feeling of friendly neighborliness, in contrast to the cold, unfeeling attitude of the Republicans. With an unusually quick reflex, the Democratic National Committee promptly sent wires to most of the towns where the President had spoken, asking for local reaction to Taft's reference to them as "whistle-stops." Of course, the smaller towns were furious at the implied condescension, and the cities thought it silly. By the time we rolled into Los Angeles on June 14 and were greeted along the route to the Ambassador Hotel by an astonishingly enthusiastic crowd estimated at close to one million people, we knew that Robert Taft had given the President a priceless gift. "Los Angeles is the biggest whistle-stop," President Truman said triumphantly in his speech that night. I was delighted when that line, which we were tentatively field-testing, got an enormous roar of laughter. Some of the weight from the "I like Old Joe" fiasco three days earlier began to drop from our shoulders.

Pleased as we were with this response, none of us could have imagined then that we had turned Taft's mistake into an enduring phrase in American politics. The expression, unknown in a political context before 1948, became part of the language, defined in Webster's Third New International Dictionary, for example, as "a brief personal appearance especially by a political candidate usually on the rear platform of a train. . . ." Almost every subsequent campaign trip by train has been called a "whistle-stop" by the press, always in an affectionate way, evoking the now-legendary days when Harry Truman discovered a campaign style that suited both him and the times perfectly.

12

Civil Rights and the Desegregation of the Armed Forces

It is hereby declared to be the policy of the President that there shall be equality of treatment and opportunity for all persons in the armed services without regard to race, color, religion, or national origin.

—EXECUTIVE ORDER 9981, JULY 27, 1948

In the first two months of 1948, the President sent to Capitol Hill a barrage of specific legislative proposals designed to keep the pressure on the Republicans. For a while the staff slogan at the White House was "hit 'em every Monday," in honor of the President's preference for sending proposals up at the beginning of each week. I was put in charge of this effort, assisted by Charles S. Murphy.

THE CIVIL RIGHTS MESSAGE

On February 2, 1948, as part of this process, the President sent up the most significant of these messages, probably the only one of enduring historical value. It concerned civil rights. In the November 1947 memorandum, I had recommended that he "go as far as he feels he possibly could in recommending measures to protect the rights of minority groups," adding that even if we had "difficulty with our Southern friends, that is the lesser of two evils." But the civil rights message was far more than a campaign stratagem: it committed the Democratic party to a historic enterprise from which there was no turning back, the quest for equal rights for all Americans. At the same time, the identification of the Democrats with the struggle for civil rights would be the primary factor that drove the South into the Republican column in most subsequent Presidential elections.

Despite his immense prestige and power, Franklin Roosevelt had never done anything remotely comparable in terms of redressing racial inequality in the nation, beyond creating a *temporary* Fair Employment Practices Commission during the war. He had avoided the problems of segregation in the federal government and the armed forces. He had never pressed Congress for the passage of the antilynching bills considered during his Presidency, bills that Senator Truman had twice supported. But FDR was a master of symbolism, and together with his wife Eleanor they created an impression of action and commitment, while avoiding an open break with the Southerners in Congress. He won every Southern state every time he ran.

President Truman's 1948 proposals grew out of a Commission on Civil Rights, established in December 1946 with Charles E. Wilson, the president of General Electric, as chairman. The Wilson Commission's report, the first serious government-sponsored report on civil rights, entitled "To Secure These Rights," was submitted to the President in October 1947. In early December, he asked me to prepare a comprehensive civil rights program for submission to Congress, in consultation with Attorney General Tom Clark, based on the recommendations of the Wilson Commission.

This was a truly exciting assignment. I believed in it, and knew how strongly President Truman felt about it. When I went to Attorney General Clark's office to ask for help, though, I encountered a notable lack of enthusiasm. Although he would later be part of the unanimous 1954 Supreme Court decision ruling school segregation unconstitutional, Clark warned me in 1948 that we were moving much too fast. He particularly opposed including any antilynching and desegregation provisions in the Presidential message, and told me that segregation was a "social matter" best handled by the individual states. After that meeting, it was clear the program would have to be drafted entirely within the White House.

I asked Elsey to coordinate the drafting of the civil rights message; he had both professional knowledge and strong convictions on the issue. We called on Professor Robert Carr of Dartmouth, who had served as executive secretary of the Civil Rights Commission, to assist us. It was examination time at Dartmouth, so Carr was able to spend a few weeks working with us in January.

Elsey and I took our draft message to the President on Sunday, February 1. He read through it rapidly. When he saw it was consistent with his basic objectives, he instructed us to send it to the Hill the next day. It was typical of the loose and informal style of the Presidency in those days (true also, in general, of his predecessors) that the President approved such a momentous and controversial message without further analysis, meetings, or Congressional consultations—a style of Presidential decision making that would be virtually inconceivable today.

In fact, the civil rights message of 1948 was not President Truman's first statement on the subject; he had spoken out as early as the Fourth of July, 1946, from Thomas Jefferson's home at Monticello, Virginia. He had been the first President ever to address the National Association for the Advancement of Colored People, speaking from the steps of the Lincoln Memorial in June of 1947, sixteen years before the famous speech by Martin Luther King, Jr., from the same spot.

Despite the President's commitment to his proposals, he was under no illusions as to how they would be received. With a combination of resignation, detachment, and determination he wrote in his diary on February 2: "I sent the Congress a Civil Rights message. They no doubt will receive it as coldly as they did my State of the Union message. But it needs to be said."

Even today the Special Message on Civil Rights makes impressive and stirring reading; it resonated with fundamental principles. In often moving language, the President urged Congress to close the "serious gap between our ideals and some of our practices" and ensure "that equal protection under the laws of the land is not denied or abridged anywhere in our Union." He asked for legislation that would enact into law the main recommendations of the Wilson Commission. By any standard, the scope and ambition of the President's sweeping ten-point agenda was impressive:

1. Establish a permanent Commission on Civil Rights, a Joint Congressional Committee on Civil Rights, and a Civil Rights Division in the Department of Justice;
2. Strengthen existing civil rights statutes;
3. Enact an antilynching law;
4. Protect everyone's right to vote;
5. Create a *permanent* Fair Employment Practices Commission;
6. Prohibit discrimination in interstate transportation facilities;
7. Grant home-rule and suffrage in Presidential elections for the District of Columbia;
8. Grant statehood for Hawaii and Alaska, and greater self-government for our island possessions;
9. Equalize the opportunities for all residents of the U.S. to become naturalized citizens;
10. Settle the evacuation claims of Japanese-Americans.

In addition to these farsighted proposals, President Truman also made two important personal pledges: he would issue executive orders to enforce an end to discrimination in the federal government and segregation in the armed forces.

That he was ahead of his time is evident when one looks at the dates on which the proposals he made in 1948 were finally enacted into law: statehood for Alaska and Hawaii in 1959–60; civil and voting rights in 1964 and 1965; immigration reform in 1965 and 1986; Presidential voting for the District of Columbia in 1961; and compensation for Japanese-Americans interned during World War II not until 1988—an astonishing forty years later!

It was highly significant that such bold proposals and messages on civil rights would come from the grandson of a Missouri slave owner. Harry Truman was born less than twenty years after the end of the Civil War, and had grown up surrounded by veterans of that conflict. His early attitudes were shaped by that environment; words that would be unacceptable in today's world were very much a part of the language with which young Harry Truman grew up. Some observers later recalled, not inaccurately, that many of the jokes told when President Truman was relaxing with "the boys" had a racial flavor; nor was the White House an equal opportunity employer—there were, for example, no black staff members or black secretaries in the White House. However, President Truman had grown up with black people, lived with them, and understood the hopelessness of their lives. Down to his very core he desired to raise the level of blacks in this country. He had seen the cruelty and stupidity and wastefulness of discrimination back home in Jackson County—it was time, he felt, to begin to put an end to over seventy years of officially condoned discrimination, intimidation, and segregation. He saw as well that leadership on this most difficult of all domestic issues could come only from the President. The position he took was unexpected and courageous for a man born in rural Missouri in the nineteenth century, but he felt strongly that our system could not have two classes of citizens. He had heard the voices of caution and concern, including those of the conservatives within his own Administration—and he had rejected their advice.

Working on President Truman's seminal message remains one of the most satisfying experiences of my career. Race relations had been a cancer eating away at our nation since before the Civil War, and would continue to sap our national strength for the rest of the twentieth century. Delay in addressing the problem had only made its consequences worse. President Truman's actions did not solve the problem, but they were a long-overdue admission that these problems had to be addressed, not simply to help black Americans, but to help the entire nation.

To me, this was service in the government at its very best. Successful "crisis management" is usually thought of as the most memorable part of public service, and there is truth to this: one usually remembers the high drama of confrontation longer than the slow process of policy formulation. But no matter how exciting and memorable it is to live through the eye of a hurricane, the highest form of public service comes when one helps change the course of history by tackling a seemingly intractable and fundamental problem.

THE SOUTHERN BACKLASH

However, we badly underestimated the reaction of the South to the civil rights message, and it almost cost President Truman the 1948 election. The message produced an immediate explosion of anger in the South, and set into motion the Dixiecrat revolt. Had we foreseen the Southern counterattack, the President might have adjusted his timing and tactics, but he still would have pursued his basic objectives.

We did not need to wait long to see how the South felt. The most important annual event on the Democratic party's calendar was the Jefferson-Jackson Day dinner. When Marny and I arrived at the Mayflower Hotel on February 19, 1948, for the dinner, we found a crude but cleverly executed rebuke of the President by South Carolina Senator Olin Johnston. Unbeknownst to anyone at the White House, Johnston had bought an entire table directly in front of the Presidential dais, which he left vacant in silent but ostentatious censure of the President. That same evening, in Little Rock, Arkansas, four hundred people listening over a radio hookup rose en masse as the President spoke and filed from the room. We began to realize that we were facing a nastier time with the South than we had expected—but how much nastier we still could not imagine.

Four days later, we began to sense the larger dimensions of the situation. A group of Southern Democratic governors, led by Strom Thurmond of South Carolina,* called on the Chairman of the Democratic National Committee, Senator J. Howard McGrath. Thurmond demanded that the President withdraw "this highly controversial civil rights legislation, which tends to divide our people." When McGrath told Thurmond and his colleagues that this was out of the question, the meeting broke up, and Thurmond went outside to announce to the press that "the present

*Men often try to change their image in response to the flow of history, and Thurmond, by 1991 the senior serving United States Senator and a Republican for over thirty years, later worked hard to develop a different image—but in 1948 he led a political movement based openly and almost entirely upon racism.

leadership of the Democratic party will soon realize that the South is no longer in the bag."

At first, we thought Thurmond was bluffing, but we were to learn differently. Immediately, letters began to pour in from all over the South charging that President Truman was breaking up the Democratic party. Most of the letters were bitter, and many of them contained ugly or obscene racial slurs directed at the President, his family, and some of his staff, including me. Arkansas Governor Ben Laney branded the civil rights message "distasteful, unthinkable, and ridiculous." Mississippi House Speaker Walter Sillers went even further, attacking the civil rights proposal as "damnable, communistic, unconstitutional, anti-American, anti-Southern legislation." To my dismay even Ralph McGill, the editor of *The Atlanta Constitution,* one of the most courageous liberals in the South, called the proposed legislation too radical for the region.

DESEGREGATION OF THE ARMED FORCES

Of the goals contained in the President's civil rights message, only desegregation of the armed forces and equal opportunity in the federal government could be achieved by Presidential action alone; every other objective required legislation. Knowing that a Congress controlled by Republicans and conservative Southerners would not move promptly on the rest of his program, President Truman took action during the summer of 1948 on the two issues that lay entirely within his purview.

His action was not without controversy, especially from some of the leaders of the military—but the results since 1948 speak eloquently for the decision. Black men and women, once a rarity in the armed forces, and long confined to secondary positions, have risen to positions of the highest authority and importance. In 1989, President George Bush appointed Army General Colin Powell Chairman of the Joint Chiefs of Staff, fulfilling another part of the promise begun with President Truman's belief that separate was inherently unequal.

The facts spoke eloquently of this inequality. In 1948, the Army and the Air Force had only one black Colonel each, and no one of higher rank. The Navy had a grand total of four black officers, the Marine Corps only one. While 10.7 percent of all Army enlisted men were black, in the top enlisted grades the percentage dropped to about 5 percent.

President Truman believed segregation in the armed forces undermined American values and acted against the nation's best interests. He thought it was outrageous that men could be asked to die for their country but not be allowed to fight in the same units because of their color. He knew that in the military, where arguments over equipment and privileges were a way of life, white soldiers inevitably took precedence over blacks.

I had seen the effects of segregation in the Navy. Discrimination went far beyond anything that could be imagined today; I thought the Navy at times resembled a Southern plantation that had somehow escaped the Civil War. Blacks swabbed the decks, shined shoes, did the cooking, washed the dishes, and served the food. Virtually no other jobs were open to them. The Army, after establishing a postwar board of inquiry into the "utilization of Negro manpower," had established a quota for black Americans in the Army of 10 percent—a policy Army leaders actually thought of as progressive. They trained with white troops but lived in segregated barracks, shopped at segregated stores, rode on segregated trains, and served in separate units.

The President's pledge had been issued in February, yet as the summer began, no action had been taken. The delay had not been caused by his ambivalence about the rightness of the cause; rather, once the civil rights issue threatened to split the Democratic party on the eve of the convention, President Truman hesitated. Some of his advisers urged him to postpone the implementation of his pledge until after the election. Southerners and conservatives seeking to prevent a wider split in the Democratic party argued strongly for an indefinite delay, while the delay caused liberals and black leaders to question the President's sincerity.

The battle lines on this issue within the Administration were not entirely predictable. Of the three services, the Army, which would be the most immediately affected by desegregation, showed the greatest opposition to a Presidential order. The Navy, normally more conservative, was less concerned, probably because there were so few blacks in their service. The Air Force, under Stuart Symington, seemed ready to support an announcement. But in fact, none of the military services could be called enthusiastic—and it is unlikely they ever would have taken the lead in advocating such a profound change in their own private universe. On March 12, 1948, I called on Secretary of Defense Forrestal to ask him to take the lead on this issue. But Forrestal, although personally sympathetic, hesitated. He felt he could not impose his views on the three services. The next day, I sent Forrestal a memorandum elaborating my views: "I think we are all fully aware of the difficulties and the fact that the world is not going to be changed overnight, but I also think the time has come when we must make a start." Still, Forrestal, struggling to make sense of his job, hesitated.

External pressure changed the equation. Early in the year, the President had sent to Congress another request for Universal Military Training, and proposed a revival of the draft. Black leaders, led by the union leader, A. Philip Randolph, saw the legislation as a golden opportunity to press for military desegregation.

Randolph took his case public in testimony before the Senate Armed Services Committee on March 31, 1948. Black Americans, he warned, would refuse to serve if segregation continued, even if this risked charges of treason. "We are serving a higher law than the law which applies to the act of treason to us when we are attempting to win democracy," he told the committee. Despite Randolph's warning, the Senate passed the Selective Service Act without adding an antisegregation clause. Randolph promptly announced the formation of a League for Non-Violent Civil Disobedience Against Military Segregation, with the stated objective of persuading the President to desegregate the armed services by proclamation before the new act went into effect in August. In forming this organization, Randolph was one of the first people to bring to the civil rights movement the precepts of nonviolent resistance that Gandhi had used to bring independence and worldwide attention to India less than a year earlier.

Randolph's actions were widely attacked in the press, but in my mind, they strengthened the argument for acting quickly, and I pushed hard for the immediate issuance of a Presidential proclamation. In early July, I asked Phileo Nash, a White House staff officer, to return early from his annual vacation at his cranberry farm in Wisconsin to help draft two executive orders on civil rights. Nash, who worked for David Niles on minority affairs, had made this issue his personal crusade; this would be his finest hour in the government. Working rapidly, he sent me two draft executive orders by mid-July. The first established a "fair employment practices" policy for the entire federal government and banned "discrimination because of race, color, religion, or national origin." Each department would be required to hire personnel solely on the basis of merit, and a Fair Employment Board would be created as part of the Civil Service Commission. Ingrained habits and prejudices die slowly, and we knew that much more would be necessary to ensure equality in the federal bureaucracy. Nonetheless, this was an important first step.

The second document Nash sent me was a draft of Executive Order 9981. While it applied only to the armed forces, it marked a turning point in the long struggle of black Americans for equal treatment under the law. With Nash's draft in hand, I sought the agreement of Forrestal and his service secretary colleagues. When I saw him, Forrestal made one important request: eliminate any reference to a specific timetable or deadline for compliance. He said each service had to work out its own method of compliance, and insisted that the order simply call for progress "as rapidly as possible." I felt that, under the circumstances, Forrestal's suggestion should be accepted in order to break the logjam. I felt the White House would be able to push for rapid action once the order was issued. The longer the President delayed the order, the closer the election would be, and the more vulnerable he would be to charges that his actions were politically inspired. I recommended that he issue the order with the change Forrestal requested.

The order, issued on July 27, 1948, caught almost everyone off guard. Reaction was rapid, and reinforced the divisions already developing in the Democratic party: the Dixiecrats had nominated Strom Thurmond as their Presidential candidate the previous week. Nineteen of the twenty-two Southern Senators, led by Russell of Georgia, stated that they were "fixed in our purpose to . . . use every resource at our command" to stop an upsetting march of the federal government into their way of life. Russell condemned the executive orders as an "unconditional surrender . . . to the treasonable civil disobedience campaign organized by the Negroes."

In the end, of course, the major beneficiaries of President Truman's order were the armed forces themselves, but at the time they did not welcome the change. One of the giants of World War II, General Omar Bradley, the new Army Chief of Staff, epitomized this view at a meeting the day after the order was issued: the Army, he said, "is not out to make any social reforms. The Army will put men of different races in different companies. It will change that policy when the nation as a whole changes it." Realizing his mistake immediately, Bradley wrote President Truman that he had "had no intention whatsoever of embarrassing you. . . . At that time I had not seen the Executive Order." He did not, however, retract the views ascribed to him.

Black leaders were still unhappy. As far as they were concerned, the order still fell short of the President's pledge; they focused particularly on the phrase on which Forrestal had insisted, "as rapidly as possible." They pointed out, quite accurately, that the order did not prohibit segregation immediately.

Randolph considered continuing his planned nonviolent resistance movement, but for once the political calendar worked in favor of restraint. He saw that further pressure on the Administration would hurt President Truman's chances in November. Finally, the President defused further pressure at a press conference in early August. Asked if his order was based on the long-range objective of ending all segregation in the armed forces, he gave a simple one-word answer—"Yes"—and dispelled any further thought by Randolph of a civil disobedience campaign.

AFTERMATH

President Truman appointed former Solicitor General Charles Fahy as the head of a special committee to assure implementation of his executive order. The committee worked through 1949 to remove institutionalized roadblocks to equality in the armed forces. They made the greatest initial progress in the services with the worst previous record, the Navy and the Air Force. The Army, with the highest percentage of black personnel by far, set up one obstacle after another to progress. Forrestal's successor as Secretary of Defense, Louis Johnson, confined his support of desegregation to empty rhetoric, and fought the very existence of the Fahy committee throughout the summer of 1949.

I strongly supported Fahy in his fight with Johnson, appealing several times to President Truman. On October 1, 1949, the President gave a major speech reaffirming his commitment to Executive Order 9981 and the Fahy Committee. However, incredible as it may seem today, the Army refused to abandon its 10 percent enlistment quota for blacks. Finally, just days after I left the White House, the President took a step I had urged for a year: he ordered the Army to abolish the quota. Over time, the service initially most reluctant to integrate, the Army, did the best job.[1]

Whatever the limitations of Executive Order 9981, it was a milestone in American history, similar to Jackie Robinson breaking the color barrier in baseball the previous year. "As a result of Truman's order," wrote a scholar forty years later, "the military became one of the first major American institutions to desegregate and routinely place blacks in positions of authority over whites."[2]

That point was illustrated in the most dramatic fashion when General Powell became Chairman of the Joint Chiefs of Staff in 1989. Powell had an outstanding thirty-one-year career in the Army, with service in Vietnam, Korea, West Germany, and the White House (where he was National Security Assistant to President Reagan). A natural leader and a man of great intelligence and strength, Powell was ideally qualified to be the top military officer in the U.S. He also happened to have been born in Harlem, the son of black immigrant laborers in Manhattan's garment district. As I watched him standing next to President Bush on the day of his appointment, I thought back to 1948, and another President who had ignored words of caution from many of his advisers and the Pentagon itself because he felt that it was time to take action. I could not avoid a feeling of pride that the long road started by President Truman had reached, if not its end, an important new plateau.

13

Upset

PREPARING FOR PHILADELPHIA

The 1948 Presidential election was the last campaign in which television was not a central factor. Politics was about to change more than anyone could imagine, but the campaign was conducted in a style that still echoed earlier times. Television did gain a concession from the parties, however, the first of an endless number they would extract from politicians over the next four decades: all three parties—the Democrats, Republicans, and Henry Wallace's Progressives—agreed to hold their conventions in a single city, Philadelphia, in order to facilitate the experimental coverage. But the number of television sets in the country was still small, and we paid little attention to the new medium.

Even in a pretelevision age, however, the President's speaking style still presented a problem. His tone was monotonous and wooden, and he waved his right hand up and down as if he were chopping wood. So for his convention acceptance speech, we again urged him to speak only from an outline. Many politicians would have considered this too risky, but he agreed, and asked me to pull together the materials, with the assistance of Sam Rosenman, who came down from New York to join the speech-drafting team. It was good to have his wise, calm judgment available again, and it reassured President Truman to see him there.

I had returned from the President's trip to the West in June convinced something dramatic would have to be done to reverse his situation. On

June 29, shortly after the Republicans had nominated Dewey and California Governor Earl Warren, I gave the President a memorandum based on discussions with our Monday-Night Group and others:

> This election can only be won by bold and daring steps calculated to reverse the powerful trend now running against us. The boldest and most popular step the President could possibly take would be to call a special session of Congress early in August. This would: (1) focus attention on the rotten record of the Eightieth Congress . . . (2) force Dewey and Warren to defend the actions of Congress . . . (3) keep the steady glare of publicity on the Neanderthal men of the Republican party, which will embarrass Dewey and Warren; (4) split the Republicans on how to deal with such major issues as housing, inflation, foreign policy, etc., and (5) give President Truman a chance to follow through on the fighting start he made on his western tour. This course may be hazardous politically, but we cannot shut our eyes to the fact that President Truman faces an uphill fight to win the coming election.

Disturbing currents beset us as we prepared for the convention. Over the Fourth of July weekend, Jimmy Roosevelt, Chairman of the California Democratic Committee, sent a telegram to each of the 1,592 convention delegates, inviting them to come to Philadelphia two days early for a special caucus to choose "the ablest and strongest man" for the nomination. Everyone knew that he meant General Eisenhower.

Despite Ike's earlier denials of interest, President Truman remained concerned. Shortly before the convention opened, during one of the regular political "bull sessions" the President held at the White House, he asked what the chances were that Eisenhower might be nominated. While most of those present doubted this could happen, Secretary of the Army Kenneth Royall said bluntly it not only could, but would, happen if Ike's name were permitted to reach the floor. The President asked Royall, John Snyder, and me to stay behind after the meeting. Once the others had left, he said to Royall, "I agree with you about Ike. What can we do to prevent this from happening?" Royall offered to talk to Eisenhower about the need for an unambiguous restatement of his unavailability. He and I then drafted a statement that Royall asked Ike to send to Claude Pepper, the Senator most actively opposing President Truman's nomination.

Eisenhower knew he must now close the door definitively or risk letting himself be pushed into running. "No matter under what terms," his cable to Pepper read, "I would refuse to accept the nomination." Thus ended, finally, the Eisenhower boom of 1948.

Never the retiring sort, Pepper promptly announced that he was the only man who could fill FDR's shoes. His minicandidacy lasted just two days, but was typical of the bleak and chaotic mood in Philadelphia as the delegates began to arrive. Two campaign buttons seemed to me to sum it up: I'M JUST MILD ABOUT HARRY and TO ERR IS TRUMAN.

We needed something to bring the convention to life and put pressure on the Republicans. As we discussed alternatives, the proposal to recall Congress for a special session still looked best to me. Although the idea had been raised in a few newspaper articles, the fact that we were seriously considering it had not leaked—thus giving the President the opportunity for a genuine surprise announcement.

As Elsey, Murphy, Rosenman, and I sat around the big table in the Cabinet Room on Monday, July 12, working on the President's acceptance speech, the convention got under way in Philadelphia in an intense heat wave. We kept the radio tuned in to the convention as we worked. The sluggish first session was brought to life in the evening by a rousing keynote address from Senator Alben Barkley of Kentucky, the Senate Minority Leader. At seventy, Barkley seemed to be nearing the end of a long career, and he had been asked to speak as a way of recalling the golden days of FDR, when Barkley had twice given the convention keynote speech.

THE SEARCH FOR A VICE PRESIDENT

Barkley's speech was to have an unexpected consequence—the Vice Presidency of the United States. He was not Harry Truman's first choice, but he had made a popular speech, and the President's first choice—and mine—had just turned the job down.

Two weeks before the convention, the President had invited roughly a dozen people to the White House to discuss the question of a running mate. A curious aspect of this meeting was the participation of the Chief Justice of the United States, Fred Vinson. Today the participation of any member of the Supreme Court, let alone the Chief, in such a political discussion would provoke intense criticism, but in those days it received hardly a thought. At the time, I saw nothing improper in Vinson's presence; the meeting had no bearing on any matters pending before the High Court, and Vinson was a close friend whose views President Truman respected. There were also precedents for close relationships between Presidents and members of the Supreme Court, most notably between Herbert Hoover and Harlan Fiske Stone, and Franklin Roosevelt and Felix Frankfurter. Later, Lyndon Johnson would consult Abe Fortas regularly on a wide range of matters.

My views on this subject have changed in the forty years since Fred Vinson joined us at the White House and the twenty years since Abe

Fortas and I last sat together with Lyndon Johnson. What seemed routine then seems unacceptable now: there is simply too much at stake in our system of government to permit the risks and temptations that can arise in such circumstances. Discussions with the President inevitably involve the Justice, at least subconsciously, in the President's political fate—and this could affect his opinions on a variety of issues before the Court. To put it most simply: one cannot be both a Presidential confidant and a Supreme Court Justice. If a President chooses to appoint a close friend and adviser to the Court, he had better be prepared to lose that person as an adviser. If he wants to keep him as an adviser, then the President should not appoint him to the court.

As the group assembled by President Truman discussed names for the Vice Presidency, many names were suggested, but my first choice, and the President's, was another member of the Court, William O. Douglas, the brilliant liberal from Washington.

Still only fifty years old, Bill Douglas was intelligent, forceful, and dynamic. At forty-one, he had been the youngest appointee to the Supreme Court in American history. He was eminently qualified to be Vice President; indeed, I believe he would have made an outstanding President. I thought his selection as the Vice Presidential candidate would help the President with blacks, labor, and the West, and cut into Henry Wallace's appeal to liberals.

Knowing that Douglas and I were close friends, President Truman called me a few days later and asked me to find out if Douglas was interested in joining the ticket. I tracked him down in the remote mountain cabin in the state of Washington where he loved to retreat every summer. He and I had already talked privately about the Vice Presidency before he left for vacation, and he had expressed uncharacteristic ambivalence. Douglas wanted to be President, of that I had no doubt: he had admired Franklin Roosevelt enormously, and had told me often of his disappointment that FDR had passed him over for the 1944 Vice Presidential nomination. But he regarded Harry Truman as an unlikely and accidental Chief Executive and was not enthusiastic about giving up a seat on the Court in order to run on a ticket he assumed would lose.

Douglas asked me to give him three more days to think about it. I called Mrs. Roosevelt and asked her if she would try to persuade Douglas to join the ticket. With her characteristic graciousness and efficiency, she immediately said she would be happy to try—but even her efforts produced no movement from the man in the woods. Douglas waited until Monday, the day the convention opened, to turn the offer down. Although he told the President he had decided not to go into politics, his rejection was based, in my opinion, almost entirely on the assumption that the Democratic ticket had no chance to win in November.

With only two days left in which to chose a running mate, the President and his inner team considered the options. No one stood out, although Governor Mon Wallgren of Washington, another close friend of the President, openly sought the spot. At this precise moment, Alben Barkley made his rousing speech to the delegates in Philadelphia. Urged on by Secretary of the Senate Leslie Biffle, Barkley called President Truman to make it clear that he was available for the position. By Tuesday morning none of us could see a better alternative, and time was running out. I did not yet know Barkley well, although within a year I was to play a major role in his life—but I liked what I knew of him. I thought he would help the ticket with liberals, although not nearly so much as Douglas. A tall and portly man with a wonderful sense of humor who loved to tell stories, he was very popular in Washington, especially on the Hill. Barkley had that rare and invaluable gift of being able to disagree with someone on an issue without losing his friendship or affection. I told the President that under the circumstances, we had no better choice available. We sent word to the convention that the President "would be most happy to welcome [Senator Barkley] as his running mate." In the glow following his keynote address, Barkley was a popular choice—in dramatic contrast to the President, who was about to get caught in a historic confrontation over civil rights.

WALKOUT!

We had known for a month we would face problems from two opposing groups on the civil rights plank of the platform: the Southerners, still enraged over the February civil rights message, wanted the weakest possible plank, while the militant liberals wanted the strongest statement possible. The clash between these two groups was to change the Democratic party—and American politics—forever.

Party platforms often generate a great deal of heat before a national convention, but they are almost always rapidly forgotten. They are not binding on the nominee, nor do they have much to do with policies after the election. The President had already declared himself on civil rights in February, and he planned to do so again in the campaign. But with the party already coming apart and President Truman's chances considered poor to hopeless by most delegates, our main concern at the convention was to hold the party together—not to engage in empty gestures which would do nothing for civil rights.

The militant liberals, led by young Hubert Humphrey and a former Congressman from Wisconsin, Andrew Biemiller, were well intentioned, and I admired their tenacity and support for a cause to which I felt equally committed. But there are times in politics when the best is the enemy of the good. What the liberals wanted was an even stronger restatement in the platform of the goals of the President's February message. In my view, this was the wrong time, the wrong place, and the wrong way to further the civil rights cause. It could only hurt President Truman's chances.

The President and I discussed this delicate situation frequently before the convention opened. He felt I was exaggerating the threat of a Southern rebellion, and he made clear he wanted a civil rights plank endorsing his proposed legislation.

Our strategy was to let the platform committee hold hearings in Philadelphia while we drafted the actual document in the White House with assistance from Bill Batt and his research team at the Democratic National Committee. Although I remained concerned we would provoke a crisis with the South, we drafted the civil rights platform plank as the President requested. When our work was completed, I sent Elsey to Philadelphia in secret on Thursday, July 8, to deliver it to the chairman of the platform committee, Senator Francis J. Myers of Pennsylvania.

On Saturday afternoon, two days before the convention opened, I slipped up to Philadelphia on the train to get a feeling for the mood of the delegates. I met with Myers, who described the difficulties we faced over the platform and urged that the President soften the civil rights plank. As I returned to Washington on the train Sunday, I came to a difficult decision: I would make an attempt to convince him that we should soften the civil rights section of the platform.

I went directly to the White House to discuss the situation with the President. Reluctantly he agreed—but only, he said, to keep peace in Philadelphia. His acceptance of my suggestion did not indicate in any way, he stressed, a diminution of his commitment on the issue.

We sent Senator Myers a revised, more moderate plank with which the South could live; but because our compromise no longer called for specific legislation, it created a firestorm of protests among many militant liberals. In fact, the words to which the liberals objected were hardly a betrayal of the civil rights movement; they should have been sufficient to hold the party together through the convention:

> We again state our belief that racial and religious minorities must have the right to live, the right to work, the right to vote, the full and equal protection of the law, on a basis of equality with all citizens as guaranteed by the Constitution. We again call upon the Congress to exert its full authority to the limit of its constitutional powers to assure and protect these rights.

I felt we were at the crossroads where the future of the Democratic party, the election of Harry Truman, and the world of real politics met.

And in their zeal, Humphrey and his colleagues were jeopardizing the first two. Of course, almost all of them had supported the "draft Ike" effort, and the platform battle was in part a continuation of that fight. As the battle over the plank escalated, tempers flared. Humphrey charged the administration with a "sellout." Senator Scott Lucas, one of our key spokesmen on the platform committee, responded by calling Humphrey a "pipsqueak."

On Tuesday night the liberals met in private caucus. After a dramatic all-night session, they decided to propose an alternative plank. At 5 A.M., after great personal agonizing, Humphrey decided to support the liberal alternative, provided that it contained an additional sentence praising President Truman's "courageous stand on the issue of civil rights." This was hardly a tribute we wanted or needed at that time, but there was nothing we could do about it.

On Wednesday, July 14, the lobbyists for both sides were out in force in Philadelphia. David Niles worked the floor for the White House. But Niles and his team were facing a convention brought to life by the excitement of a powerful cause and a dynamic new leader. At the age of thirty-seven, Hubert Humphrey was about to make a dramatic entrance on the national scene. Some of his friends had warned him that he was risking a brilliant political future by leading the civil rights fight, but he felt strongly on the issue, was under great pressure from his own supporters, and—as we all came to know when Hubert later emerged as a major Washington figure—he liked to talk. Besides, like almost everyone else at the convention, he thought that President Truman would lose, and he was therefore less concerned than he might otherwise have been about the fact that he was about to challenge the national leadership of his party.

His speech was high rhetoric—beautifully crafted, eloquent, memorable. It further weakened our position at the convention, as Northern delegates were stirred both by the strength of Hubert Humphrey's conviction and his oratory. "There are those who say to you we are rushing this issue of civil rights. I say we are a hundred and seventy-two years late," he cried. "The time has arrived for the Democratic party to get out of the shadow of states' rights and walk forthrightly into the bright sunshine of human rights."

Within the hour, most of the big-city bosses, thinking President Truman was a "gone goose," and wanting to save the rest of the party in the North by carrying the black and liberal vote, swung into line behind the Humphrey-Biemiller plank. In a stunning rebuke to the President, the liberal plank on civil rights was approved by the delegates in a floor vote. Seeing the rising anger in the faces of the Southern delegates, Sam Rayburn, the convention chairman, quickly gaveled the afternoon session to a close, and sent word to the White House that it was time for the

President to accept the nomination. Just before 7 P.M. the President's party, including Marny and some other wives of White House officials, boarded the Presidential train for Philadelphia—and perhaps the strangest evening of politics I ever witnessed.

Judge Rosenman, Murphy, and I worked with the President as the train carried him north toward the most important political speech of his career. He spent the ride going over our outline, committing sections to memory. Meanwhile, we strained to catch the news, over a poor radio connection, of yet another disaster unfolding on the convention floor in Philadelphia.

Shortly after we pulled out of Washington's Union Station, the chairman of the Alabama delegation, Handy Ellis, rose on a point of "personal privilege." Alabama's electors, he announced, had pledged "never to cast their vote for a Republican, never to cast their vote for Harry Truman, and never to cast their vote for any candidate with a civil rights program such as that adopted by the convention." Then, with the famous cry, "we bid you good-bye," Ellis walked out, followed by half the delegates from Alabama, and the entire Mississippi delegation. The remaining Southerners stayed glumly in their seats.

THE ACCEPTANCE SPEECH

Our train pulled into this cauldron of political fever and confusion shortly before 10 P.M. Unlike most recent national political conventions, where events are carefully scheduled to attract the largest possible television audience, the 1948 Democratic Convention was a chaotic affair, run not by the White House but by Rayburn and various party officials. President Truman had expected to go directly to the convention hall to deliver his speech—in what would today be referred to as prime time—but the Southern walkout delayed it. As the fractious convention kept him waiting and the hour grew late, the national radio and television audience dwindled. Offered a room at a nearby hotel in which to wait, President Truman, underestimating the length of the delay, said he preferred to wait at the convention. As a result, we were ushered into a small makeshift office which, in my memory, resembled the Black Hole of Calcutta. There we waited for almost four hours in the sweltering heat as the delegate voting process inched along. I worried about the President's energy level, and feared for his white linen suit, wilting in the humidity. Unknown to all but a tiny handful of the people around him, he had been suffering for some hours with a gastrointestinal upset, adding greatly to his discomfort. Finally the heat became so unbearable that he and Senator Barkley went outside and sat on a ramp near the stage entrance overlooking the railroad yards.

Almost an hour after midnight, Harry Truman was finally nominated by the Democratic Convention, with 947 ½ votes. In a final insult to President Truman, those Southerners who had not walked out with Handy Ellis mounted a last-minute effort to nominate Georgia's Richard Russell, and garnered 263 votes—another indication of the crisis we now faced in the South. No one even moved that the nomination be made unanimous, the first time this traditional courtesy was denied to an incumbent Democratic President.

It was about 1:30 A.M. by the time Barkley was formally nominated. Rayburn suggested that the convention adjourn for the night and hear the President's acceptance speech the next day, but some instinct in Harry Truman told him that he should seize the moment, despite the lateness of the hour, to deliver some fighting words to this deeply wounded convention and party. He told Rayburn he wanted to go on immediately.

I was gravely worried for the President. The evening had been truly draining. At 1:45, Harry Truman and Alben Barkley came out on stage. I followed them out into the vast crowd, taking a seat next to Sam Rosenman just below the speaker's platform. Then occurred the incident I often looked back on later as the low point of the year: just as Rayburn was beginning his remarks, a rather large national committeewoman from Pennsylvania named Emma Guffey Miller—she would be described as "matronly" by reporters the next day—bustled over to the microphone and interrupted Rayburn. With an air of great importance, she said she had the honor to present the President with a surprise tribute from the host city, a huge Liberty Bell made out of flowers.

It was a surprise all right. Inside the floral arrangement was a flock of forty-eight white pigeons, or, as Emma Guffey Miller called them, "doves of peace." As she presented the Liberty Bell to the President, the birds—or at least those still alive—were suddenly liberated from the stifling quarters in which they had been cooped up all evening. At this point, the birds did exactly what one would expect birds confined to a tiny space for a long time to do—they went wild, flying into the rafters, getting caught in the bunting, swooping and dive-bombing the President and others on the platform. Worst of all, although the press delicately did not mention it the next morning, Emma Guffey Miller's doves of peace began, not surprisingly, to drop the inevitable product of their hours of imprisonment on any delegate who had the bad luck to be underneath them. Farmers in the crowd shouted, "*Watch your clothes!*" and, after the long hours of tension and animosity, the hall seemed united in the childish glee brought on by the absurdity of the moment. Standing on the floor just below the speaker's platform, I saw one pigeon land on a large fan, where it looked as if it was about to be skewered. To gasps and cheers, "Mr. Sam" snared it and threw it back out toward the crowd. Directly in front of me, I saw Marny struggling to calm down one of the birds, which had landed in her lap. She eventually fashioned what she later described as "a dove diaper" out of the text of one of the speeches to protect herself. Even as President Truman accepted his party's nomination for the Presidency a few moments later, I could still see a few birds that had evaded capture circling above us in the harsh spotlights.

After Mrs. Miller's ludicrous pigeons of peace, I thought I was ready for almost anything. But I was not prepared for the effectiveness of President Truman's speech. Facing an exhausted audience at 2 A.M., Harry Truman unveiled a new and dynamic speaking style. Using some of the notes we had given him but ad-libbing over half his speech, punching the air with a high-pitched staccato instead of his usual droning style, President Truman roused the sluggish audience, which, to my amazement and pleasure, roared its approval and gave him a prolonged standing ovation at the end.

In President Truman's tone and manner that night I thought I saw the beginning of a new and different sort of leader, a man who, finally nominated in his own right to head the party of Franklin Roosevelt, was ready to come into his own, win or lose. Never once referring to his opponent, he focused his fire entirely on the Republican Congress, as we had proposed in the November memorandum.

In the middle of the speech, President Truman unveiled his secret punch—the special session of Congress for which I had been lobbying. In urging him to proceed, I had said we were on our own one-yard line, and needed some "razzle-dazzle" to break out of our defensive position. I think that it was the disastrous events of the day that finally convinced him that he somehow had to seize the initiative—and this was the best available idea.

He added a highly personal touch to his surprise announcement, a homespun phrase that took him back to the Jackson County farm where he had plowed such a straight furrow:

> On the twenty-sixth day of July, which out in Missouri we call "Turnip Day," I am going to call Congress back and ask them to pass laws to halt rising prices, to meet the housing crisis. . . . Now, my friends, if there is any reality behind that Republican platform, we ought to get some action from a short session of the Eightieth Congress.

President Truman later took pleasure in explaining that he had in mind an old Missouri saying, "On the twenty-fifth of July, sow your turnips wet or dry." (Since July 25 fell on a Sunday in 1948, the special session actually began the following day.)

President Truman was greatly pleased with his reception in Philadelphia. On the train back to Washington, although it was now early morning, he talked with enthusiasm about how he was going to surprise everyone, especially Dewey, once the campaign got under way. Our spirits lifted, we arrived in Washington at 5:30 A.M. After a short nap, I went back to work.

The call for a special session was a masterstroke. The Republicans charged it was blatantly political, that not since 1856 had an emergency session of Congress been called in a Presidential election year, and that *never* before had a special session been announced at a party convention—but they were trapped. It took Dewey's team five full days to figure out how to respond, and when they did, it was with a weak two-sentence statement by Herbert Brownell, Dewey's campaign manager, that rejected in advance any possible merit or hope of achievement in the special session.

THE "TURNIP SESSION"

The "Turnip Session," as it inevitably came to be called, turned out exactly the way we had hoped. On July 27 the President went to the Hill to tell Congress that his highest priorities were to stop inflation and solve the housing shortage. The Republicans were not about to do anything on either issue; indeed, so angry were they that some of them refused to stand when the President arrived in the House chamber—an uncommon act of discourtesy, but one that merely emphasized the point we were trying to make about the negative attitude of the Republicans. For the next two weeks, the Republicans attacked every proposal that President Truman sent up. A few minor items got through, including a slight liberalization of credit terms for housing, but they were not politically significant.

This was what we hoped the Republicans would do; our greatest concern had been that they might pass two or three bills during the special session, and try to take the issue of a recalcitrant Congress away from us. I later heard that Senators Arthur Vandenberg and Hugh Scott had proposed doing just that, but were overruled in a Republican leadership conference by Senator Robert Taft, who had said, in his blunt and arrogant way, "I'm not going to give that fellow [Truman] anything." It was a serious error: the President had gambled that they would not try to pass any significant legislation, and, thanks to Taft, he proved to be right.

When the session was over, I prepared a detailed list of all the proposals Congress had not enacted. We released this list in conjunction with a press conference on August 12 in which President Truman used for the first time an expression that we thought had staying power, and was to become part of the American political language. The "Turnip Session," the President said, had been a "do-nothing" session—part of a "do-nothing Congress."

TWO MORE PARTIES JOIN THE FRAY

As months in politics go, July of 1948 was unique. In addition to the Democratic Convention and the "Turnip Session" of Congress, two other political parties nominated Presidential candidates—each a defector from the President's party. At the same time, the President was confronted with the enormous challenge posed by the Soviet blockade of Berlin, which began on June 24. His dramatic and inspired response, the Berlin Airlift, would save Berlin—but American politics does not stop, not even for one of the Cold War's most dangerous moments. Two days after the end of the Philadelphia convention, rebellious Democrats from the South held a convention in Birmingham, Alabama, under the banner of states' rights and nominated Strom Thurmond of South Carolina for President and Governor Fielding L. Wright of Mississippi for Vice President. The Dixiecrats, as they were called, were not very subtle about their racist views, stating that "we stand for the segregation of the races and the racial integrity of every race." Their strategy was to try to get enough electoral votes in the South to throw the election into the House of Representatives—the same strategy that George Wallace would attempt twenty years later, in 1968, running on a similarly racist platform. In both cases, they almost succeeded.

Less than a week later, on Friday, July 23, the Progressive party took over the hall in Philadelphia to nominate Henry Wallace. Fortunately for President Truman, Henry Wallace was not only a difficult man, he was not very smart politically. Time after time during the campaign, he failed to repudiate positions that identified him with Soviet aggression, or Stalin, or the openly pro-Moscow Communist Party in the U.S. It was never clear to me how aware he was of the uses to which the Communist Party was putting him, but whether he knew it or not, he was following the communist line, serving communist ends, and betraying those Americans who supported him as a serious alternative to the two main candidates.

As event after event demonstrated the ruthless nature of Stalinism, Wallace had repeatedly failed to disassociate himself from Moscow. When challenged on the issue of communist support, he replied, "I will not repudiate any support which comes to me on the basis of interest in peace." In February, testifying before the House Committee on Foreign Affairs, Wallace attacked the Marshall Plan. Even more astonishing were his comments following the Soviet coup in Czechoslovakia, which he said proved that a tough American policy "only provokes a 'get tougher' policy" from Moscow. He said the coup had been provoked by a Soviet desire to prevent a right-wing revolution fomented by the American Ambassador to Czechoslovakia, Lawrence Steinhardt. He finally topped all his previous statements with one that appalled almost everyone and, in a perverse way, amused President Truman: "I would say that the communists are the closest things to the early Christian martyrs." After one of Wallace's many self-destructive remarks, President Truman commented to me, "Poor Henry. He doesn't know what's happening to him."

These statements and Wallace's decision not to repudiate the communists eroded his support and were a great political gift to President Truman. In early 1948, before the invasion of Czechoslovakia and the Berlin Blockade, Gallup polls showed Wallace holding 7 percent, or over 4 million votes. Had he actually won anything close to that, he would have not only drawn enough votes away from President Truman to give victory to Dewey, but he might have also laid the groundwork, as was his original intention, for another Presidential run in 1952, by which time he hoped to split the Democratic party in two. But on Election Day, Wallace would receive only 1.15 million votes, almost half of them in New York. In the end, the Wallace vote threw only three states to Dewey, far fewer than we originally feared.

THOMAS E. DEWEY

At the time of the campaign I had never met Tom Dewey. Later, when I came to know him personally, even spending a pleasant golfing weekend with him in California once in the sixties, I found him a decent and moderate man, although without much of a sense of humor. In 1948, though, he ran an amazingly poor campaign, behaving as if the purpose of his campaign was merely to ratify an outcome that was not in doubt. This was exactly the sort of arrogance which the American electorate does not like, and it gave us an easy chance to poke fun at the stately procession toward the White House which Dewey thought he was leading.

The President almost never attacked his opponent personally. Dewey had been a decent Governor, with an outstanding reputation as a prosecutor of organized crime. But since Dewey did not emphasize that record, the President was able to ignore it as well. At the same time, Dewey chose not to counter President Truman's highly effective attacks on the "do-nothing" Eightieth Congress.

Dewey's speaking style was soporific, and his speeches, carefully prepared through a cumbersome staff process structured more for an incumbent President than a candidate, were bland. By contrast, President Truman's speeches became steadily more aggressive and animated as the campaign progressed. Dewey opted for fewer days on the campaign trail than President Truman because he wanted to spend time in Albany as

Governor. President Truman ran as the underdog and outsider, as he sought to erode the image of inevitability that the press had woven around Dewey. A visitor from another planet might reasonably have concluded that Thomas Dewey was the incumbent, Harry Truman the challenger.

ON THE TRAIN

As I prepared drafts of the President's speeches, George Elsey, as always, worked at my side, bringing to his task both his scholarly background and a zest for battle. In addition, William Batt's young men at the Democratic National Committee sent us drafts and ideas. With the Deep South lost, we focused on four groups: labor, farmers, blacks, and veterans (which in today's terms would mean, to a considerable extent, consumers).

This strategy had been recommended in a memorandum submitted to the President during the relative quiet of August. Our primary objective, I wrote, was "to win a large majority of the 15,000,000 independent voters who overwhelmingly followed the liberal leadership of the Democratic Party in the last four elections." In regard to the black vote, I urged him to "speak out fully on his Civil Rights record. . . . His record proves that he acts as well as talks Civil Rights. The Negro votes in the crucial states will more than cancel out any votes the President may lose in the South."

I recommended several long train tours of the nation, targeting specifically those states that had been most closely contested in 1944, especially California, "the home of the extremely popular Governor Warren." I respected Warren so much that I paid him the ultimate compliment and suggested that the President refer to him "as really a Democrat [who] would be most useful to the people in the Governor's mansion in California rather than as a helpless occupant of the Vice President's chair in an administration which would be controlled by men who differ strongly from Warren on every important point."

I also reviewed the main lessons we had learned during the "nonpolitical" June trip. We needed advance men at every stop at least a day ahead of the President; this was a technique that was to become a routine part of all campaigning but was used then only for major occasions. We did not want any more empty halls or confusion. Spring training was over, I thought; this is the big leagues now.

The first full-scale whistle-stop trip got underway on the morning of Friday, September 17. George Marshall and Alben Barkley saw us off at Union Station. As we pulled out, Barkley yelled out, "Mow 'em down, Harry!" The President smiled and yelled back, "I'm going to give 'em hell."

The train on which Harry Truman was to make history had sixteen cars. The President's car, the *Ferdinand Magellan,* had been built for Roosevelt by the Association of American Railroads. It was a massive, armor-plated affair, containing luxurious main sleeping quarters for the President and his family, including a bath, dining room, and wood-paneled sitting room. On the rest of the train, we had converted one dining car into staff office space, and a second into a traveling newsroom. We slept in cramped quarters, and, as in June, how and when to get our laundry done became something of an obsession.

Over time, we developed a pattern for the typical stop. The President would emerge at the back of his car, make a few nice remarks about the town he was in, and then launch into an attack on the "do-nothing Eightieth Congress." He would ask the crowd, "How would you like to meet my family?" and wait with his head cocked for the response. Then he would introduce Bess Truman, always referring to her as "the Boss." After that he would present his daughter Margaret (in the border states, "Miss Margaret") "who bosses the boss." Then, as the train started to pull away, Margaret would toss a red rose to someone in the crowd.

My role during these short stops varied. Sometimes I worked frantically to communicate with Washington about a breaking news event, but I often left this to Elsey and wandered through the crowd to overhear what was being said about the President. We were not organized well enough to have a claque positioned at every stop, so this subtle assignment of stirring up crowd enthusiasm sometimes fell to the President's physician, Brigadier General Wallace Graham, and me. The show we put on so amused one observant journalist, Richard Rovere of the *New Yorker,* that he described the two of us as "carnival shills" in a political version of the carnival that used to wander through small American towns. Of all the things I ever did in government, this may have been the least dignified—but, after all, we were shorthanded on the train, and very far behind in the polls. And, to tell the truth, I rather enjoyed it.

"GLUTTONS OF PRIVILEGE"

We had always considered the farm vote critical, but now an extraordinary piece of good fortune fell in our laps. In June, almost unnoticed, the Congress had passed legislation prohibiting the Commodity Credit Corporation from acquiring any new storage bins for grains. In the absence of government-supplied facilities, those farmers without their own means of storage—which meant most farmers—would have to sell their surpluses immediately into the market at prices that would be depressed if the harvest was good.

The political implications of this situation first came to my attention from an unusual source: McNeil Lowry, the Washington correspondent of *The Dayton Daily News.* By early August, while big-city journalists ignored the story, Lowry had written a series of articles under headlines such as CONGRESS ACTS TO FORCE DOWN FARMERS' PRICE AT BEHEST OF GRAIN LOBBY. Then the outraged Lowry went further; unbeknownst to his editors, he came to my office in order to make sure the White House understood the political opportunity presented by the situation. Lowry did not stop with keeping me informed; he even secretly helped draft a key section of the President's farm speech.

Such legislation would normally have had little political importance, but the weather smiled on Harry Truman—literally. The year was a banner harvest, especially for corn, wheat, and oats. When the result was a shortage of storage space, exactly as Lowry had predicted, the farmers were indeed forced to sell their bumper crop at less than the support price, and the issue began to have real bite in the Farm Belt.

We decided to launch a preemptive attack on Dewey in the Farm Belt before he could get there, with a speech that would set the tone for the entire campaign. Skillful scheduling by our advance team had brought the President to Dexter, Iowa, on September 18, in time to address a crowd of eighty thousand gathered for the annual National Plowing Contest. The latest Gallup poll showed Dewey leading Truman 54 percent to 40 percent, with Wallace at 5.5 percent, but the President ignored the polls as he addressed the vast throng in the scorching heat with energy and enthusiasm.

I cringe a bit at the memory of some of the President's comments at Dexter, but the truth is that I had co-authored those well-remembered phrases—and would not hesitate to do so again, under similar circumstances. "GOP," he said, stood for "gluttons of privilege," a party that had "stuck a pitchfork in the farmer's back." Closing on a high emotional note, the President exclaimed, "I'm not asking you just to vote for me. Vote for yourselves! Vote for your farms! . . . Vote for your future!"

The huge crowd listened quietly and gave the President polite applause. I wandered across the fairgrounds trying to gauge the reaction, wondering if we needed to tone the message down. Many journalists critized the Dexter speech as too harsh, but I thought it effective; it showed voters that Harry Truman was a fighter, not a quitter, and it raised serious concerns about the policies the Republicans would follow if they recaptured the White House.

Dewey got off to a slow start. He had scheduled the official opening of his campaign a few days after the President. On the very day President Truman spoke in Iowa, Dewey gave us a glimpse of his style in a meeting with farm editors at his home in Pawling, New York. He told the editors, *The New York Times* reported as its lead, that he hoped to have "much closer relations with Congress than now prevail." Although we did not know it then, it was typical of the way Dewey would campaign—vague, general, and away from the issues of concern to the voters.

From Dexter, our long train trip continued, covering 8,300 miles. The President delivered at least 126 speeches—no one could ever determine the exact number—in sixteen states and did not return to Washington until October 2. We estimated that about three million people had seen him, a degree of direct contact between a candidate and voters which will never be repeated again. Day after day the President presented his themes, sometimes even going to the rear platform of his train in his pajamas in the middle of the night so as not to disappoint people who had gathered to greet him.

We paid particular attention to Texas. With the Deep South probably lost to Thurmond and the Dixiecrats, the Lone Star State was essential to victory. We made a special stop in Uvalde, Texas, at the ungodly hour of 5 A.M. on a Sunday—normally a day on which he felt it inappropriate to campaign—to obtain the endorsement of Franklin Roosevelt's "other" Vice President, John Nance Garner. This stop turned into a real political coup when the seventy-nine-year-old conservative gave his old friend a warm public endorsement, followed by an enormous, Texas-style breakfast. The next day, September 27, in San Antonio, our train picked up that occasional participant in the *Williamsburg* poker games, Congressman Lyndon Johnson, who one month earlier had won a much-disputed Senate primary race against former Governor Coke Stevenson. Most politicians would stay on the train for only one leg of the trip, but Johnson stayed with us the whole day, talking to everyone he could corner. The forty-year-old Johnson towered over almost everyone else on the train. But his normal hurricane-force energy had been diminished by exhaustion from his grueling campaign against Stevenson, and he looked ill. He was understandably tense, for it happened to be a critical day in Lyndon Johnson's career: he had won the Democratic primary by only eighty-seven votes out of almost one million cast. Court challenges initiated by Stevenson, which would determine Johnson's political future, had started that very day in both Washington and Texas. Although serious questions were being raised about Johnson's primary victory, the Truman Administration strongly favored Johnson over Stevenson, a conservative Representative of old Texas. At stop after stop, the President took Johnson out on the platform at the rear of the train and told the crowds, "Go to the polls on Election Day and send Lyndon Johnson to the Senate." After the trip, Johnson sent me a letter thanking me for my assistance, and adding that the "Texas electoral votes are safe now, I do believe."[1]

I returned to Washington at the end of the whistle-stop tour so exhausted that I actually fell asleep at least once while standing up at a reception, much to Marny's horror. It was then that I began to have my recurring nightmare of being trapped on the train. Marny told me later that she had feared for my health.

Our opponent made no effort to match our pace. With a staff twice as large as the President's, Dewey left Albany on September 19, allowing himself only six weeks to campaign. Reporters who traveled on both trains told me Dewey's campaign was much better organized, especially in regard to such critical details as laundry and luggage. His speeches were prepared well in advance, and loudspeakers were installed on the press car of his train so that reporters could hear the candidate's remarks without having to go outside. This sort of efficiency eluded the Truman team throughout the campaign. Yet Dewey's campaign lacked any spontaneity, and on a typical day he made about half the number of stops that President Truman did.

DOMESTIC COMMUNISM

One of the few issues on which Dewey generated a strong audience response was his pledge that "we won't put any communists in the government." With the Berlin Airlift underway, it was not surprising that the Republicans, urged on by J. Edgar Hoover, would try to create an issue by alleging that the President was oblivious to a comparable domestic menace. It was the year of Elizabeth Bentley and Whittaker Chambers, both of whom testified before Congressional committees about communist penetration of the government. In August, Chambers accused Alger Hiss of being a Soviet spy, and Hiss had dramatically confronted Chambers before the House Un-American Activities Committee to deny the charges. These events had created a sensation.

During a press conference on August 5, the President inadvertently allowed a politically costly phrase to enter the vocabulary of the era. In response to a reporter's question—"Mr. President, do you think that the Capitol Hill spy scare is a red herring to divert public attention from inflation?"—he replied, "Yes, I do." When the Republicans and Hoover began attacking him for the use of the expression "red herring," he unnecessarily defended it in another press conference a week later. Over the next two weeks, reporters repeatedly pressed the President to retract or modify the phrase, but he refused, saying, "I am not going to back down on that because it is a fact, and I will prove it before the campaign is over."

Elsey sent me a note calling domestic communism the "Administration's most vulnerable point," and warned that "our hopes this issue will die are ill-founded. There is paydirt here, and the Republicans have no intention of being diverted by appeals from anguished liberals who see the

Bill of Rights transgressed." I was convinced the so-called internal threat was bogus and posed no threat to the nation, but that "domestic communism" would develop into a major political issue if we did not stop the Republicans quickly. In August, I met several times with Attorney General Clark and other members of the Justice Department to discuss whether or not the President should respond personally to these attacks. Up to that point, Dewey had left the rougher attacks to his supporters, notably Senators Hugh Scott and Karl Mundt, and Congressman Richard M. Nixon. There was much to be said for responding through surrogate speakers as well.

The situation changed after Dewey attacked the Administration in a major appearance in the Hollywood Bowl September 24, after he received endorsements from Gary Cooper, Jeanette MacDonald, and Ginger Rogers. It was one of Dewey's few effective assaults on the President during the campaign, and we knew we had to counterattack quickly. (In the battle of the Hollywood stars, a liberal Democrat named Ronald Reagan endorsed President Truman that year, and we met briefly on the platform before a Presidential speech in Los Angeles September 23.)

Because the issue seemed to hurt the President most in the Midwest, we recommended that he respond during a stop at the state fairgrounds in Oklahoma City on September 28. He decided that, given the importance of the issue, the speech should be broadcast live on a national radio hookup. With a last-minute contribution by a liberal businessman from New York, Abe Feinberg, the Democratic National Committee was able to produce the funds for the broadcast, the first of the trip. With air time reserved and paid for, we courted disaster by arriving in Oklahoma City forty minutes late. Ignoring the crowds waiting to see the President, we raced through the streets at an alarming speed and reached the fairgrounds less than a minute before the scheduled air time.

Much criticized later, the Oklahoma City speech was designed to preempt the Republican attempt to portray the Truman Administration as inattentive to domestic subversion. No issue presented greater difficulty for the President, for he really did feel that the issue had been blown out of all proportion by Hoover and the right wing. Yet Dewey and his surrogates had to be answered. In this regard, there was an unanticipated dividend from Henry Wallace's participation in the race; his attacks on President Truman for being too *tough* on communists helped protect the President from Republican charges that he was too soft. We decided that the best way for the President to handle the issue was to seize the middle ground between his two main opponents by an attack on Henry Wallace for *his* closeness to the communists.

We prepared a blunt and direct draft for the speech in Oklahoma City. Warning that the Republicans were diverting attention from the real danger—Soviet expansionism—the President charged that they had hindered the efforts of the FBI, failed to produce "any significant information about communist espionage," "recklessly cast a cloud of suspicion over the most loyal civil service in the world," and "trampled on the individual freedoms which distinguish American ideals from totalitarian doctrine."

"The truth is," he continued, "the Democratic party has been leading the fight to make democracy effective and to wipe out communism in the United States." The communists, by backing Henry Wallace's Progressives, were hoping to elect a Republican President "because they think that its reactionary policies will lead to the confusion and strife on which communism thrives." He continued, in words I had drafted:

> I ought to know something about communism. I have been honored by its bitter enmity and its slanderous statements. . . . That is because I have been fighting communism not merely here where it is a contemptible minority in a land of freedom, but wherever it is a marching and menacing power in the world. The great danger to us does not come from communism in the United States. . . . The Democratic party is for free government and against totalitarianism. We are for free enterprise and against communism. . . . There is nothing that the communists would like better than to weaken the liberal programs that are our shield against communism. . . .

President Truman's reply defused the issue politically for the rest of the campaign, but our fears about the potential danger of the issue were justified: McCarthyism's flowering was less than two years away.

THE VINSON MISSION

After four days of rest we went back on the train again. President Truman was bouncy and increasingly cheerful; the rest of us felt as if we were drowning. In the midst of this second major whistle-stop of the campaign, though, the President made a mistake which could have cost him the election—had Dewey exploited it.

Two aggressive young campaign staffers in Washington, concerned with the growing confrontation with the Soviet Union over Berlin, made a private and informal suggestion to Appointments Secretary Matt Connelly that the President should send Chief Justice Fred Vinson to Moscow for private conversations with Stalin. Despite the safeguards we had agreed on after the Henry Wallace affair, in the confusion of the campaign Connelly passed the suggestion directly to the President, who liked the proposal the moment he heard it. Later, the President tried to defend the Vinson mission as a way to "expose the Russian dictator to a better understanding of our attitude as a people and of our nation's peaceful aspirations for the whole world. I had a feeling that Stalin might get over some of his inhibitions if he were to talk with our own Chief Justice."[2]

As soon as we heard the proposal, Elsey and I argued against it with great vigor—but with no effect. The President ignored our objections. During the four days he spent in Washington between whistle-stop trips, he spoke to the Chief Justice, who, with a mixture of pride and reluctance, agreed to make the trip.

As sometimes happens during campaigns, chaos then took command. Anxious to get Vinson to Moscow, the President asked Charlie Ross to arrange network time to announce the mission. When Ross met with representatives of the networks on October 5 to ask for free air time for a nonpolitical speech, the networks, understandably suspicious, demanded to know what subject would justify free air time so close to the election. In confidence, Ross told them of the Vinson mission, and the networks, realizing that this was real news, agreed.

In his enthusiasm for the idea, though, the President had neglected to mention it to the man it affected the most, the Secretary of State. George Marshall was at that moment in Paris, locked in a difficult round of meetings with Soviet Foreign Minister Molotov and his British and French counterparts. When Lovett, at the State Department, heard of the impending announcement, he insisted the President discuss it with Marshall immediately. Marshall, understandably, objected strongly: such a trip, he said, would undercut the united front the Western powers had agreed to maintain as long as the Soviet blockade of Berlin continued.

The moment he talked to Marshall, President Truman realized he had made a serious error, and he instructed Ross to cancel the request for air time. But the networks had been told, and it could not remain secret for long. It leaked on October 8, as the Presidential train worked its way through upstate New York. The next day we returned to Washington so that the President could confer with Marshall, who had been recalled from Paris to soothe his feelings. We issued a statement carefully designed to obscure the events of the previous week by explaining that Marshall, having been consulted by the President on October 5, had warned about the "possibility of misunderstanding," after which President Truman had "decided not to take this step."

This was the worst mistake of the Truman campaign. I was astonished that Dewey did not exploit it—but, apparently feeling that the election was wrapped up, he said virtually nothing about it beyond a few vague references.

Not knowing I had strongly opposed the scheme, *Time* magazine struck again, opening that week's issue with a wildly inaccurate story attributing the idea of the Vinson mission to me:

> In view of the political debacle facing the Truman Administration, it was hard to understand how handsome Mr. Clifford could look so happy and knowing. He looked like a man who had something up his sleeve. In fact, he had. . . . Jubilantly, Mr. Truman approved of the idea.

There was an amusing coda to the incident. *Time*'s article provoked a great deal of hostile mail. For about a week, my secretary, Mary Weiler, who was not used to such missives, would come into my office each morning and say, "Well, we have another dozen letters today, all critical." Finally, she came into my office one morning much cheered, and said, "We had a friendly letter this morning."

"Well, by all means get it in here and let's look at it," I replied. It was on lined paper and written in crayon:

> Dear Mr. Clifford,
> I have read the article in *Time* magazine. I am familiar with what you have been doing. I do not agree with *Time* that you have been playing fast and loose with the peace of the world. I think you honestly felt that Justice Vinson could help in our relations with the Russians. I agree with you and I support you.
> Jonathan Witherspoon
> P.S. Please excuse the crayon, but I am not permitted any sharp instruments.

When we checked the return address we discovered, sure enough, that it had come from a mental institution in Illinois.

THE *NEWSWEEK* POLL

Most of the major public opinion surveys had stopped polling because, in light of Dewey's large lead, further surveys seemed unnecessary. Roper stopped his sampling in early September—one of the classic errors in polling history. The Democrats did not have enough funds to conduct their own polls, and the Republicans saw no need for any more.

Instead of an expensive national poll, *Newsweek* magazine decided to query fifty of the leading political journalists in America, and run the results in their October 11 issue. We awaited this article anxiously, since it included some of journalism's brightest names, men like columnists

Marquis Childs of *The St. Louis Post-Dispatch,* Arthur Krock of *The New York Times,* and Raymond Moley, former New Dealer turned *Newsweek* columnist.

Early on the morning that the issue of *Newsweek* was due on newsstands, I slipped off the train at the first stop and found it. I opened the issue and found a big black headline: ELECTION FORECAST: 50 POLITICAL EXPERTS PREDICT A GOP SWEEP. That Dewey would be favored hardly surprised me, but the shocker was the vote: fifty to *nothing.* Not even one pundit out of fifty was willing to buck conventional wisdom and predict a Truman victory.

I had to pass through the President's car to get back to my own cabin. He was sitting on a sofa reading a newspaper, so I tucked *Newsweek* into my jacket and tried to slip by, but he stopped me. "What does it say, Clark?" he asked.

"What does what say?" I said, trying to look innocent.

"What have you got under your coat, Clark?"

"Nothing, Mr. President."

"Clark. I saw you get off the train just now and I think that you went in there to see if they had a newsstand with a copy of *Newsweek.* And I think maybe you have it under your coat."

I hated to be the bearer of bad news. Reluctantly I handed it over. He looked at the article for a while, and then handed the magazine back to me, seemingly unperturbed. "Don't worry about that poll, Clark," he said. "I know every one of those fifty fellows, and not one of them has enough sense to pound sand into a rathole."

THE FINAL STRETCH

The days and nights blurred into an endless march toward November 2. We were on the train from October 11 to October 16, in Washington for one day, out again for two days, and then back in Washington for three, before setting out for a marathon final week.

The train trips seldom offered any chance for escape, but on the big mid-October trip, I had a memorable—and painful—evening. The President had finished a tough day of campaigning across Wisconsin and Minnesota with a major speech in St. Paul. Having worked all day on the speech, I decided I deserved the evening off and, abandoning the Presidential entourage, I went to dinner with some old friends who lived in Minneapolis. By 1948, I drank quite rarely—I had learned over the years that alcohol did not agree with me—but that night I felt that if I did not give myself a break I might explode from the pent-up pressure and strain. We had a few drinks before dinner and then listened to the President's speech on the radio while we ate and drank some more. Suddenly the

President was no longer speaking, and I realized if I did not get back to the St. Paul railyards quickly I would miss the train. Driving wildly, we made it to the station just in time, but as I lingered, making prolonged and fond farewells about fifty or sixty feet from the train, it began to pull out. Running directly behind it on the tracks, I clambered onboard at the last possible moment, in full view of several amused and cheering local reporters. If the President was aware of the incident, he never mentioned it.

How was the campaign going? On one hand, I could not help but be impressed by the unanimity of professional opinion that the President still had no chance. On the other hand, I noticed that his crowds were getting bigger and more enthusiastic as his train moved back and forth across America, and I mentioned this observation to several people, including Marny. The erosion in Henry Wallace's support was evident, and Dewey's bland campaign was beginning to bore voters, especially in the Farm Belt. The Dixiecrats also looked as if they would carry fewer states than they had originally hoped, although it still seemed certain that they would cut significantly into the President's Electoral College totals.

Before I left Washington for our last trip, Marny pressed me as to how I really thought we were doing. I still did not quite dare to draw the full implications of what I was sensing, so I replied, "If we had one or two more weeks, I think we would be able to catch Dewey. But we are running out of time and I don't know if we can make it."

During that brief stay in Washington I had lunch at the Mayflower Hotel on October 20 with Arthur Krock. When I expressed the view that a Truman victory was not impossible, Krock laughed, and pressed me for a state-by-state analysis. Wearily, I took an envelope out of my pocket and wrote down the states I thought President Truman would carry. I was not convinced I was right, but I had begun to glimpse a scenario that could give the President victory. Krock took notes on what he called my absurd predictions; we would both refer back to them later with a combination of amusement and amazement.

The reporters traveling with us also noticed that President Truman's crowds were getting larger, but they refused to believe it could change the outcome. "I think the President's message is getting through," I would say to the regulars traveling with us, trying to stimulate coverage of the growing crowds. They would reply, "Well, certainly something is happening. It's too bad for you guys that it didn't start earlier." To the end, not one reporter traveling with us believed that Harry Truman would win. They were as exhausted as we were, and, with far less motivation, they were just going through the motions until the campaign was over.

On October 30, 1948, the train reached St. Louis, where the President made a brief speech from the rear platform of the train and then went to Kiel Auditorium for his last major address of the campaign. After taking a nap on the train—something that he had not done on any previous leg of the trip as far as I was aware—he made one last slashing attack on the Republicans, and ended with a flat prediction of victory:

> I have been all over the United States from one end to another, and when I started out the song was—well, you can't win; the Democrats can't win. Ninety percent of the press is against us, but that didn't discourage me one little bit. You know, I had four campaigns here in the great state of Missouri, and I never had a metropolitan paper for me that whole time. And I licked them every time!

With our work finally done, I parted company with the President for the first time in the campaign. On Saturday night I bid a warm farewell to him, Mrs. Truman, and Margaret as they boarded the train for their hometown of Independence, Missouri. He was relaxed and smiling. I had mixed emotions as I said good-bye to them, but on one point I was not nostalgic: watching the *Ferdinand Magellan* pull away and knowing that I did not have to be on it, I felt a wave of joyous relief, as though a prison sentence had been lifted.

That was the end of the campaign, except for final radio addresses on Monday night by both candidates. There was no campaigning at all on the last Sunday before the election, something that would be inconceivable today. But in 1948, given the political strength of those who felt that the Lord's Day should be respected, active campaigning on Sundays could still create a backlash.

I stayed in St. Louis to vote. In addition, I wanted to spend some time with my mother. On Tuesday, November 2, she and I got up early and cast two votes for Harry Truman. Then I caught an early plane back to Washington so I could be with my family on election night. For the first time in months I was out of the cauldron, and for a few precious hours, I was alone on an airplane with nothing left to do.

POLITICS AS A PROFESSION

I had been at the President's side almost every day, with the exception of a few Sundays, for more than two months. Our relationship had developed into one of great closeness and intimacy during the intense days on the train.

Harry Truman had brought me into the world of practical politics at the national level for the first time. I had found it simultaneously fascinating and horrifying, uplifting and boring, noble and trivial. I had thrilled to the dimensions of the endeavor, to the importance of the stakes for which we were fighting. To play a useful role in the struggle to capture the greatest office on earth had been exhilarating, and, having no doubt that Harry Truman would be a better President than his opponent, I was convinced his election was a historical necessity. Thus everything I contributed to the campaign, no matter how minor, was directly linked in my own mind to the noble quest for the highest honor to which an American may aspire.

Yet at the same time I had found most of the actual work of a campaign tedious or inconsequential. My training as a lawyer had helped me master the inordinate detail required during the marathon we had just run, but I preferred the challenge of grand strategy to the dubious honor of involvement in every operational detail. I had learned an immense amount about politics, and did not regret a moment of it—but I also knew that life as a politician was not for me. I simply did not enjoy or need the constant superficial interaction with a myriad of people. I knew many politicians who gained a sort of physical strength or energy from such interaction—one thinks of Lyndon Johnson "pressing the flesh" or Hubert Humphrey joyously revitalizing himself from endless contact with the voters—but I knew I preferred to work with greater deliberateness, in private, with time for careful preparation. Whatever moved people to seek political office did not move me, and I knew then that while I hoped to retain an involvement in public affairs for the rest of my life, I would never be tempted personally by the call to run for public office. I respected those who subjected themselves to the trials and hurly-burly of elections—this group would include many close friends and even our own daughter Joyce, who in 1976 was elected to the County Board of Supervisors in Suffolk County, New York—but I knew it was not for me.

THE UPSET OF THE CENTURY

It used to be said of an earlier generation that they could remember exactly where they were on three days in their lives: Pearl Harbor Day, the day Franklin Roosevelt died, and the night that Harry Truman beat Thomas E. Dewey. (A tragic fourth day—the worst of all—was added to that list on November 22, 1963.) I spent the afternoon of Election Day in my office, where I received a telephone call from Bob Lovett, asking me if I would work with him on an orderly transition if Dewey were elected, so that the Soviet Union could not benefit from conditions of "terrible uncertainty" during the interregnum. Lovett, I learned later, had been told that he was under serious consideration to become Dewey's Secretary of Defense.

Almost everyone expected the result to be settled early. The Democratic National Committee was so pessimistic that it had not even bothered to reserve a ballroom at the traditional site for such affairs, the Mayflower Hotel. I listened over the radio with Marny and my daughters to the early, inconclusive returns, but by eleven, when it was clear the election would be much closer than anyone expected, Marny and I went to the home of a friend, Jay Hayden of *The Detroit News.* The Haydens were among the first people in the neighborhood to own a television set, and together we settled down to watch the first television coverage of an election night.

We had planned to stay only about an hour, but as the election hung in the balance, we could not tear ourselves away from the Haydens' new toy. Behind the commentators on the screen the numbers, written on chalkboards, indicated an incredibly tight race. Twice during the night Dewey's campaign manager, Herbert Brownell, came down to the ballroom in New York's Roosevelt Hotel to claim victory for his candidate, but the race was not over; it was going down to the wire in four states that held the key to the outcome—Ohio, Michigan, Illinois, and California. From Truman headquarters at the Muehlebach Hotel in Kansas City, no claims were made. At the nearby Excelsior Springs, the President, in one of the most remarkable examples of inner serenity that I ever heard of, ate a sandwich, drank a glass of milk, and went to bed early. He waked around midnight, and, as he was to recount many times, heard over the radio the gravelly voice of the famous commentator H. V. Kaltenborn saying that, although the President was 1,200,000 votes ahead, Dewey would win when the farm vote came in. President Truman went back to sleep, and waked again at about 4 A.M. to hear Kaltenborn *still* predicting a Dewey victory.

We stayed at the Haydens' most of the night, transfixed by the drama. Around 5 A.M. I decided to go home and get some rest, but after less than an hour in bed I waked again, drained yet transfixed, turned the radio back on, and started making telephone calls seeking more information. One of my calls was to our headquarters in Kansas City, where the staff told me that the President had not yet arrived, but it looked like we had won. Then, shortly after 9 A.M., I got the most gratifying telephone call of my life. It was President Truman, just arrived at the Muehlebach. With great jubilation he told me that Illinois and Ohio were going into the Democratic column. The victory was his.

* * *

As it turned out, the analysis I had given Arthur Krock in October was too conservative. My predictions had added up to 278 electoral votes for the President, considerably less than the 303 votes he actually won. Of the four states that hung in the balance all night long, three—Ohio, Illinois, and California—fell to the President; Michigan held for Dewey, who ended up with 189 electoral votes. Thurmond won only the four Southern states in which, through complicated legal maneuvering, the Dixiecrats had been permitted to run as the Democratic party—Alabama, Louisiana, Mississippi, and South Carolina, with 38 electoral votes in all. (Thurmond would pick up one additional electoral vote from a Tennessee elector who refused to vote for President Truman.)

Henry Wallace had faded in the home stretch, carrying no states, but his votes still cost the President victory in New York, Maryland, and Michigan. Had Wallace done a little better in California and not been kept off the Illinois ballot through a legal challenge, President Truman would have lost both states to Dewey, and the election would have been decided by the House of Representatives. This would have been a nightmare, but, based on the control of the House delegations on a state-by-state basis—which is how the Constitution provides for the selection process to work if no one has a majority of the Electoral College—the Democrats presumably would have chosen Harry Truman President by virtue of their control of twenty-five state delegations, compared to twenty for the Republicans, and three evenly divided. However, selection by such a method would not have constituted the kind of mandate that a true victory at the polls did, and left an unfortunate political legacy for the future.

WHAT HAPPENED?

The endless postmortems began the day after the election and have continued ever since. James Reston, who had dismissed the State of the Union address in such disparaging terms ten months earlier, and whose newspaper had predicted a 345 to 105 electoral vote victory for Dewey, attributed the victory to four factors in a *New York Times* news analysis the day after the election:

1. The ideas of Franklin D. Roosevelt's New Deal and Woodrow Wilson's New Freedom.
2. The faith of President Truman in these ideas and his courage in basing his campaign on them.
3. The political tactics of Clark Clifford, which won the admiration of the electorate, if not of Mr. Truman's other associates in Washington.
4. The organization of the labor movement, which acquired strength from the middle and the right by shedding the support of the ideological left.

Reston went on to identify, with considerable accuracy, the tension that had always existed within the Truman team over how liberal a campaign to wage:

> Many times in the forty-four months since the death of Franklin Roosevelt, Mr. Truman had been a dubious and even wavering supporter of many of the New Deal measures of the past, but in identifying himself in the end with these issues, he gained a response which was greater than anybody on his campaign train imagined. Almost alone among the White House advisers, Clark Clifford supported and added to this strategy. . . . [The President's] faith was greater than that of almost any other member of his official party with the exception of his handsome young secretary and political tactician, Clark Clifford.[3]

What can explain an outcome so unexpected and so stunning? Certainly Dewey's arid personality and his passive, overconfident campaign gave President Truman an easier target than anyone anticipated. The defections of both Wallace and Thurmond also gave President Truman an unexpected opportunity to present himself as the true heir to FDR—but at great cost. The good weather and the grain storage shortage helped him in the Farm Belt. Organized labor, after initial ambivalence and internal bickering, had helped organize a massive effort on Election Day to get out the vote. Black Americans rallied to the Democrats in record numbers, and actually provided the margin of victory for the President in several key states. In short, the pieces of the puzzle had for the most part fallen into place in November of 1948, much as we had hoped when preparing the strategy memorandum a year earlier.

But one factor clearly transcended all others—Harry Truman himself. Without question, it was his tenacity, his indomitable spirit, his ability to keep himself and his supporters going through the bleak and seemingly hopeless campaign, and his unwillingness to give up that rallied the nation. As he fought overwhelming odds he gained America's respect. That respect turned into affection, and the affection turned into votes. He was no longer the man sitting in Franklin Roosevelt's chair. He was the *elected* President of the United States. He had already created the outlines of the modern postwar world and the system which preserved the peace for over forty years. Yet without the victory he had earned for himself, he would never have been able to come out from under the shadow of FDR. The satisfaction he felt was richly deserved.

Part V

WASHINGTON IN THE FIFTIES

14

Last Year at the White House

FIRST THOUGHTS ABOUT DEPARTURE

The victory of 1948 was, without question, the most satisfying political event of my life. And yet, even as we celebrated the President's triumph, I was beginning to wonder how much longer I should stay in the government.

Five years had elapsed since I had made the trek to the top floor of the Missouri Pacific Building in St. Louis to join the Navy. The price paid by my family had been high. I wanted to spend more time with my wife and three daughters, who were growing up without me.

I was also facing growing financial pressures. Until the fall of 1949, when it was raised to $20,000 per year, the annual salary of the Special Counsel to the President was $12,000 a year. The savings I had when I entered the Navy had been used up, and the money from the sale of our St. Louis house was gone.

There was a third factor—less tangible, but equally important. I was reaching the point of diminishing returns in my government service. I was worn out, not the simple weariness that a week or two in Key West or some other vacation spot could cure, but that penetrating fatigue that comes when one's intellectual resources have been depleted. I had always liked fresh challenges, but I could feel the excitement oozing out of the job. I felt that my speech drafts for the President all began to sound alike.

The election had also altered the way I was perceived within the

Administration. I had grown even closer to the President during 1948, but the campaign had unavoidably involved me in frequent battles with other members of the Administration, creating friction and jealousy. Even with the President's continued support, which I felt I could count on, I could forsee a concerted effort by some of those with whom I had disagreed to weaken my position. I did not wish to expend my remaining time and energy simply defending my position and convictions.

What I felt intuitively in 1948, I now believe to be a basic rule. After four or five years of service in the same position at the higher levels of government, one begins to lose effectiveness. The time comes to either move on or move out.

Late in the campaign, I told the President that, when the contest was over, I would have to consider leaving his Administration and returning to the practice of law. I told him of the heavy financial pressure I felt, and how much I wanted to spend more time with my daughters before they reached college age. To both concerns he was very sympathetic: he understood the financial issue completely, and he also knew, and was very fond of, my daughters, especially the youngest, Randall.

He made only one request—that I remain at the White House for at least one more year. He anticipated major changes in the Cabinet, and he wanted me to stay until they were completed. He also asked me to coordinate two more cycles, for 1949 and 1950, of the three major messages on which I had always worked, the State of the Union, the budget message, and the economic report. Of course I agreed.

VACATION AT KEY WEST

After the election, the President took a few staff members to Key West for a vacation. I celebrated his victory by not shaving for a week. Wandering around barefoot in a tattered pair of old slacks, I looked so much like a bum that the President called me "Jeeter" throughout the vacation, after a scruffy-looking character in the thirties hit play, *Tobacco Road.*

This Key West vacation was one of the few times when government service was just plain fun. Each morning at breakfast, the President read aloud from letters and various newspapers some of the lame excuses politicians and journalists were offering for their inaccurate election predictions. His favorites were letters from people who sent him campaign contributions that they claimed had been mailed late through some unfortunate secretarial error. We spent the mornings on the beach, and returned to the "Little White House" for luncheon. If there was work to be done, we tried to compress it into the afternoon. The President walked through the little town wearing his famous garish sports shirts, which had caused a stir among some Americans who felt that a President should dress in a more formal manner. But he loved those shirts and did not care what other people thought of them.

Key West had not yet become a famous resort. It was run-down, and filled with the kind of cheap bars, heavily frequented by sailors, that one associated with Hemingway stories or a Humphrey Bogart–Lauren Bacall film. It seemed as far as one could get from Washington and still stay in the U.S., and after those endless days and nights on the train, we loved it.

* * *

Still, Washington was filled with serious issues awaiting President Truman's return. At the top of the list was the need to lay out his domestic and foreign agenda in the two major speeches he would have to make in January—the State of the Union Message and the Inaugural Address.

There had been a brief discussion of this in the only Cabinet meeting the President held before going to Key West. He wished, he told the Cabinet, to set forth his entire legislative program in the State of the Union Message, and then use the Inaugural Address to summarize its high points. Because of the length of his legislative program, President Truman wanted to send the State of the Union Message to the Congress in writing instead of delivering it in person. In private, I told him that I hoped he might reconsider; even in a year when it is overshadowed by an Inaugural Address, I felt the State of the Union Address should be delivered in person and carry a ringing message.

I asked Elsey to collect ideas for both the State of the Union and Inaugural speeches. On November 16, he sent me a memorandum suggesting that the President devote his State of the Union Message to domestic affairs, while "reserving for foreign policy issues" the Inaugural Address. "The circumstances of the President's re-election [*sic*] thrilled the free world," he wrote, "and the dramatic occasion of his inauguration on January 20 will insure world-wide attention to whatever the President may say."

During the vacation I undertook to persuade President Truman of the merits of this approach. By the time we returned to Washington on November 21, he had accepted the idea; but with this simple structural approach approved, we needed to find a strong theme for each speech. Our search was to lead to two memorable concepts—the Fair Deal and Point Four.

THE FAIR DEAL

I had felt for some time, and told the President during our relaxed conversations at Key West, that he should not always let credit for every idea go to his Cabinet. I was not suggesting that Harry Truman change one of his most attractive traits, his innate modesty and distaste for self-promotion; rather, I thought he deserved to be identified more personally with some of the Administration's major achievements.

As I reviewed the suggestions we had received from the Cabinet departments for the State of the Union Message, three main themes emerged: full human rights for all Americans, expansion of the economy, and a permanent peace. But we still lacked a phrase or concept that would tie everything together. Finally, as we sat around the Cabinet table in one of our drafting sessions, the President wrote on his own copy of the draft an additional sentence: "Every segment of our population and every individual has a right to expect from our Government a fair deal."

This time, we did not wait around for the phrase to emerge, as had been the case with the "Truman Doctrine." We had learned far more about dealing with the press, and pointed them toward the phrase "Fair Deal." I was particularly pleased that, in the age of the speech writer and the manufactured slogan, the phrase which would forever encapsulate the Truman Administration's domestic values was coined by the President himself. For the first time since 1945 the public had a phrase to supplant Roosevelt's "New Deal." It had a certain simple brilliance to it, representing a delicate balance between continuity and change. The Fair Deal was neither a continuation of the New Deal, nor a break with it; it was, I explained to reporters in many background briefings, a consolidation of those parts of the New Deal which had survived the testing of the last sixteen years. I sometimes compared politics to war: the Fair Deal was to the New Deal much like the point where the army, having stopped after the long and constant advance, brings its supply train and communications lines up to the front, reorganizes, reevaluates, and then starts a new offensive under a new banner. The new offensive would move more slowly, but it would, I hoped, move steadily, with emphasis on civil rights, housing, and education.

POINT FOUR

Rarely can a great idea be traced directly to the mind of one man—especially someone working in the midlevels of a large bureaucracy—but such was the case with one of President Truman's most widely acclaimed proposals: the program to provide technical assistance to poorer nations. Known as Point Four, it became the godfather to a host of American foreign assistance programs, including the Peace Corps, which followed in the next four decades.

Point Four was an unbureaucratic response—out of channels—to a request I made to the State Department to provide us with some ideas for an Inaugural speech that would, I said, be "a democratic manifesto addressed to the peoples of the world, not just to the American people."

My memorandum received little serious attention from the higher levels of the State Department, but it stimulated the thinking of a young and idealistic public-affairs officer named Benjamin Hardy. Neither George Elsey nor I had ever heard of Hardy, but we—and the world—would soon be deeply in his debt.

During the war, Hardy, a former reporter for *The Atlanta Journal,* had served in Brazil as a representative of the Office of the Coordinator of Inter-American Affairs. Familiar from his native Georgia with the way new technologies could help a backward economy, he realized that many of the lessons of the New Deal were applicable to Brazil, where the U.S. had supported a modest technical assistance program.

When Hardy saw my request for ideas in late November, he sent a memorandum to his boss, Francis H. Russell, Director of the Office of Public Affairs, which proposed elevating technical assistance into a major new component of American foreign policy. Hardy suggested converting the small program that already existed in Latin America

> into a dramatic, large-scale program that would capture the imagination of the peoples of other countries and harness their enthusiasm for social and economic improvement to the democratic campaign to repulse Communism and create a decent life for the earth's millions.

With Secretary of State Marshall in Walter Reed Hospital for kidney surgery (the President would reluctantly accept his resignation within a few days), Hardy's proposal went to Bob Lovett, who sent it back to Russell with a note that the idea needed more study.

The idea surely would have died at this point, if it had not been for Ben Hardy's resolve. This relatively junior official believed passionately in his idea. Convinced it would appeal to President Truman too—if only it could somehow be brought to his attention, he determined not to let it disappear inside the State Department.

In mid-December 1948, Hardy decided upon a bold course of action. Going outside—way outside—normal governmental channels, he picked up the telephone, called George Elsey, whom he had never met, and asked to see him right away. Assuming the request concerned some official matter, George agreed to see Hardy.

To Elsey's surprise, though, Hardy immediately launched into an eloquent exposition of his view that technical assistance was the missing part of American foreign policy. He said the State Department intended to "smother the idea with planning groups and bureaucracy," and added that there was no chance it would emerge from State in the foreseeable future unless the White House rescued it.

Elsey thanked Hardy, and, promising not to give him away to the State Department, brought me Hardy's paper as soon as the meeting ended. One reading convinced me that it was the right idea at the right time. This was the solution to our dilemma: while we had a speech in search of an idea, Hardy had an idea in search of a speech.

Hardy knew he was risking his career by going outside official channels. Some persons in Washington play bureaucratic games of this sort routinely as a means of self-promotion, but this clearly was not the case with Hardy. To protect Hardy, Elsey told State that the President wanted to consider making a proposal in his Inaugural Address to expand American scientific and technical aid to the poorer nations. We asked State for an immediate reply.

To my astonishment, there was no response. After about ten days of silence, Hardy reappeared in our offices, carrying with him an unsigned memorandum labeled DRAFT NUMBER 5. Leaving this parentless paper in our hands, Hardy told us it had been blocked in State by Lovett and Paul H. Nitze, a rising young expert in strategic issues who had succeeded Kennan as Director of Policy Planning. Their excuse was, once again, "insufficient preparation and analysis"—in other words, they hoped to bury it through inaction.

On January 10, 1949, with only ten days left until the Inaugural Speech, I asked Elsey to begin drafting a speech that would highlight four points. The first three were not new: unwavering support of the United Nations and support for the new nations that were just beginning to emerge from colonialism; a commitment of full support to the Marshall Plan; and a version of a security system for Europe that would soon become the North Atlantic Treaty Organization. The fourth point—hence Point Four, the accidental nickname that was to excite the world—was referred to at first simply as "Hardy's idea." I told Elsey to include it in his drafts, no matter what State said.

As State continued to oppose inclusion of the idea, Hardy became a clandestine member of our drafting team, alerting us to State's positions. This process consumed most of the week before the speech; finally, less than forty-eight hours before the Inauguration, we sent a last version of the speech to the State Department. Lovett and Nitze again objected to the fourth point. The President, thoroughly fed up, simply told us to ignore them.

As the Inauguration approached, I met frequently with Dean Acheson, who would succeed George Marshall as Secretary of State on January 20, to help prepare him for reentry into the Administration. Later, a myth developed that Acheson first learned of Point Four while listening to the President's speech, but this was not true. Acheson had read the entire speech, including Hardy's idea, in a draft I handed him on January 16, 1949. After working on it late into the night, he replied the next day with a series of suggestions. In a handwritten postscript to his letter he wrote: "Aside from these suggestions, I think that the address is splendid."

Acheson's recommendations did not mention Point Four; they were, however, revealing of an interesting difference between himself and the President. Acheson wanted to delete two sentences on which as it happens, President Truman and I had worked closely:

> Communism is based on the belief that man is so weak and inadequate that he is unable to govern himself, and therefore requires the rule of strong masters. Democracy is based on the conviction that man has the moral and intellectual capacity, as well as the inalienable right, to govern himself with reason and justice.

Brilliant but highly pragmatic, Acheson saw the struggle between the United States and the Soviet Union primarily in strategic, rather than ideological, terms; he felt uncomfortable with such sweeping moral distinctions and judgments. But President Truman, who rejected Acheson's suggestion and retained the two sentences, regarded them as perhaps the most succinct statement on the fundamental differences between communism and democracy that he ever made, and he referred to the speech later with great pride.[1]

* * *

The first time Harry Truman had taken the oath of office, inside the White House in 1945, he was almost dazed. Now, on a beautiful cold winter day, under a dazzling sun and almost cloudless skies, with over one million people attending the celebration, he took the oath of office again. Police said it was the largest Inaugural crowd in history, and it certainly was one of the most boisterous.

The public reception to his Inaugural Speech exceeded our hopes, but it was the overwhelming response to Point Four that most gratified and surprised me. The President's proposal tapped a deep wellspring of altruism and idealism within the American people. We had already committed ourselves through the Marshall Plan and the emerging network of security relationships and alliances, notably NATO, to assist Europe. But nothing had been done to help the poorer peoples of the world. Point Four was the first global program that addressed the knowledge gap between the developed world and what was later to be called the Third World, and foreshadowed a myriad of technical assistance programs and U.N. programs.

Over the decades since Point Four was unveiled, much foreign economic aid has been wasted, lost to corruption or inefficiency. Some technical assistance has suffered from the misapplication of Western techniques or values to traditional cultures or societies. Yet I am convinced that Point Four and its offspring remain one of the noblest commitments our nation has made in this century. While these programs have generally been unpopular with the Congress, they represented a large return from a small investment, especially compared to the hugely wasteful amount of funds spent on foreign military assistance and overseas deployments of American forces. I have always believed that economic progress and education were the strongest bulwark against the spread of communism and military dictatorship. I was convinced, in fact, that we should commit more resources to the worldwide struggle against such problems as illiteracy, malnutrition, poor irrigation and primitive farming techniques, and overpopulation. My strongest criticism of our programs in this area is that we should have put more emphasis on self-reliance—President Truman's own Missouri-bred value—from the beginning.

Whatever the limitations imposed by Congress and the State Department, Point Four was a turning point in American foreign policy. In the words of Jonathan Bingham, who worked for the Technical Cooperation Administration before a distinguished career as a Congressman, "Never before in the history of the world had a government launched a large-scale effort to help peoples to whom it was bound by no special ties other than a common interest in the world's peace and prosperity."[2]

POINT FOUR: THE AFTERMATH

At Acheson's insistence, State was assigned responsibility for implementing Point Four—even though they had opposed the program. In the first year after the speech, State did almost nothing. The Foreign Service looked down on activities that were not purely diplomatic. Yet at the same time, State opposed the creation of any rival foreign affairs agencies, a self-defeating position: by taking positions like these, State contributed greatly to its own decline in influence and power.

Greatly concerned at the lack of action, I urged the President to set up a separate agency for Point Four, at first to no avail. He did not wish to overrule Acheson, who continued to oppose such a new agency. Over a year later, by which time I had left the White House, Elsey asked me to intervene again with the President on this issue. Elsey was blunt: Point Four, he wrote me, was

> never going to reach the expectations that you and I had for it at its inception so long as initiative for the program remains in the Department of State. It seems to me that a "bold new program" is necessary to get our bold new program out of the mud.

I talked to the President again in the spring of 1950; finally, he agreed something had to be done. On June 5, 1950—more than a year after the Inaugural Address, and less than a month before the outbreak of the Korean War—he signed into law the Act for International Development. A Technical Cooperation Administration (TCA) was established, but in a concession to Acheson, it was located within a still-reluctant State Department. The TCA was administered by a genial and inspiring educator from Oklahoma named Henry Garland Bennett. Nelson Rockefeller, an energetic and enthusiastic supporter of technical assistance, chaired the Point Four Advisory Board.

Ben Hardy never publicized himself, but he was justly proud of his role in the birth of Point Four. At Dr. Bennett's request, he joined TCA "in order to do what I can," and became its chief information officer. He had told his wife that, to get his dreams past the naysayers of State, he had been ready to risk his career. On December 23, 1951, at the age of forty-five, this gentle idealist paid the ultimate price when he, Henry Bennett, and several other TCA officials died in a plane crash in a heavy storm north of Tehran. They were planning to spend their Christmas holidays discussing Point Four with the Iranians.

I PLAY MATCHMAKER

Washington is not usually thought of as a romantic place, but in the summer of 1949, I found myself unexpectedly playing matchmaker in what Jack Anderson later called "the most tender love story of the decade"[3]—the courtship of the Vice President of the United States.

It began innocuously enough. My best friend in St. Louis, since college, had been Carleton S. Hadley. We had been best men at each other's weddings, and our wives were close friends. Suddenly, in February 1945, at the age of forty-two, Carleton died of a massive heart attack. I was on Navy assignment when the shocking news reached me.

Carleton's widow, Jane Hadley, was a bright and spirited woman of great beauty, then in her mid-thirties. She took a job as a secretary to a senior officer at the Wabash Railroad Company, and kept in close contact with Marny and me. In April of 1949, in reply to a suggestion I had made that she visit us in Washington, she wrote me a touching letter: "For some time now," she said, "I have been so desperately unhappy that

I am wondering if perhaps my best bet would be to get out of this town. . . ."

I replied immediately that we would be delighted to have her visit us whenever it was convenient, and she made plans to come to Washington in early July. To welcome her, Marny and I reserved the President's small day cruiser, the *Margy,* for a dinner party in her honor on July 8. Among those we invited was one of Washington's most enjoyable dinner guests, Vice President Alben Barkley.

Barkley's demeanor belied his seventy-one years. A beloved figure in Washington, he had a zest that made younger men seem burdened by their cares. He also had a great sense of humor, disdained the pomp and protocol that goes with the Vice Presidency—and loved a good party.

Jane, Marny, and I stood together on the deck of the *Margy,* greeting the guests as they came up the gangplank. Barkley was one of the last to arrive. After I had introduced them, he and Jane talked a great deal. Nothing seemed unusual about that; Barkley was well known for enjoying the company of beautiful women. He told me later, though, that he had fallen in love with Jane the moment he saw her.

The next morning Barkley called me to ask what Jane Hadley was doing that night. When I told him we were taking her to a party at the home of Gwen Cafritz, one of Washington's leading party-givers, he thanked me and called Mrs. Cafritz to invite himself to the party. That night, he talked to Jane so long before dinner that, because protocol required no one be seated until the Vice President had entered the room, the rest of us shuffled behind our chairs awkwardly for ten or fifteen minutes until Mrs. Cafritz could persuade them to come to the table. Alben Barkley could not have cared less—he was smitten.

The next day, Sunday, the Vice President arrived at our house in the middle of the afternoon with a bottle of bourbon for us and a box of chocolates he had picked up at a corner drugstore for Jane. Then we all went out to dinner together.

On Monday morning, ever jovial, he came into my office: "What's on our schedule today, Clark?" he boomed. I did not need to ask what he meant. Meanwhile, Marny sat down with Jane and said to her, very simply, "You know, the Vice President is falling in love with you."

Jane did not know what to make of this whirlwind. She felt greatly attracted to Barkley, she told us, but she was confused by the attention, by the drama of being courted by the Vice President, and, above all, by the thirty-three year difference in their ages. After less than a week in Washington, she returned to St. Louis. She had seen the Vice President every day during her brief trip.

The day after she left, Barkley came into my office again. Looking back on the conversation after he had left, I thought, this must have been one of the oddest talks any White House assistant ever had with a Vice President.

He came right to the point: "I have something serious to discuss with you," he said. "I have fallen in love with Jane Hadley."

This news did not exactly surprise me.

He went on: "I must ask you a question. While Jane was here, I permitted myself the luxury of thinking about spending the rest of my life with her. I am seventy-one, she is thirty-seven. I want you to look me straight in the eye and tell me if I am a damn fool."

I looked directly at him. "Alben," I said, "you are certainly not a damn fool. I would suggest that you continue to think about this, and see what may develop."

"But what did she think of me?" he asked.

"She thought you were charming."

"What else did she say?" he asked, sounding like a teenage boy.

"She liked you, Alben. She really did."

"What should I do next?"

"Call her. Tell her that you would like to see her again. Say you will visit her the next time you are in the Midwest. Then, if things are going well, square your shoulders, bring up 'the subject' and see what kind of a reaction you get."

That same day, Marny and I, feeling very much like two conspiratorial Cupids, called Jane to alert her to the situation. Choosing my words carefully, I said, "You know, Alben is very serious about his regard for you. He will be in the Midwest for some speeches and would like to see you. Is that all right with you?"

Jane said she would be delighted to see him again. Later in the month, he made a swing through the Midwest, which had been hastily put together to suit his deeper purpose. The press erupted with rumors of a May-September romance, and Barkley's stop in St. Louis received intense coverage. Jane, very much the proper woman of her era, made sure their meetings were all chaperoned, but this only made them more visible. Alben, meanwhile, was enjoying every minute of it. When crowning the queen of a local celebration in Virginia a few days after his visit to St. Louis, he quipped, "One of these days, I am going to crown a queen of my own—and keep her." His comments received national attention.

Finally, Alben asked Jane to marry him. She asked for a few days to think about it, he told me when he called excitedly the next morning. He was hopeful, because he knew she cared about him, but he was still worried about their age difference.

Jane called Marny the same day. She had decided to marry Alben, she said. We were delighted, and watched with pleasure as the nation shared the couple's happiness. It was big news. When they announced their engagement, on a Sunday evening in October, an announcer even broke into the immensely popular Edgar Bergen–Charlie McCarthy show to tell the nation. NBC carried live coverage from outside the church during their wedding that November in St. Louis, something quite unusual in the early days of television.

The only discordant note was the reaction of one of Alben's daughters, Laura.* She resented Jane, who was one year younger than her new stepdaughter, and she never forgave Marny and me for what she believed was an arranged romance. I was not sympathetic to Laura's jealous reaction to her father's obvious happiness. For our part, every time we saw the Barkleys together after their marriage, we thrilled again at how happy they were together. Their marriage lasted seven years, and ended under the most dramatic circumstances, during a speech in 1954 by the former Vice President, who had been elected once again to his beloved Senate by the people of Kentucky. He had just finished saying, "I would rather be a servant in the House of the Lord than sit in the seats of the mighty," when he gasped, clutched his head, and fell down, mortally stricken by a heart attack, as Jane watched helplessly from the front row. Sadly, in 1964, at the age of only fifty-two, she died from heart disease.

AN UNPLEASANT ASSIGNMENT

Sometimes President Truman would ask me to do something genuinely unpleasant that he did not wish to do himself. One such assignment was to tell a Cabinet member that he had to resign. The person in question was Julius Krug, the pleasant but ineffectual Secretary of the Interior who had replaced Roosevelt's famous curmudgeon, Harold Ickes, in March 1946. At thirty-eight, Krug was the youngest member of the Cabinet, and had been generally thought to have a brilliant political future—but his ineptitude soon became evident. In 1948, he made a serious mistake: assuming a Dewey victory, he did not bother to campaign for the President. Then, the following year, he became involved in some politically and financially questionable offshore oil leases.

In the fall of 1949, having tried to ignore the problem for some time, the President finally decided that he had to get rid of Krug. Perhaps because I had long advocated this, the President asked me to tell Krug privately that it was time to resign. On November 3, 1949, I called on Krug in his office at the Interior Department to suggest that perhaps it would be better for everyone if he offered the President his resignation.

Krug could not believe his ears. He asked me on whose authority I was

*Laura was already married to General Douglas MacArthur's nephew, Douglas MacArthur II, a Foreign Service officer who was later Ambassador to Japan and several other countries.

speaking. When I assured him I was speaking on behalf of the President, something unexpected happened; he began to cry. This, I must admit, unnerved me more than almost anything else that I had experienced in dealing with high-level members of the government.

Over the next few days, Krug tried, without success, to get the decision reversed. Finally, the President asked me to tell Krug that if he did not announce his resignation, the White House would. That day Krug announced his departure in a graceless twelve-word statement: "I am leaving. I have wanted to leave for a long time."

"MR. JUSTICE CLIFFORD"?

Over the years rumors occasionally circulated that I had been offered a seat on the Supreme Court by both Presidents Truman and Johnson. It will not surprise students of Washington that the facts are somewhat less clear cut.

In the summer of 1949, two Justices, Frank Murphy and Wiley Rutledge, died. One day that summer, while we were talking about whom he might nominate for one of the vacancies, President Truman asked me an uncharacteristically indirect question: "Have you ever given any attention to making a career of service on the Supreme Court?" I was forty-two at the time, and, as I told him, the thought had never seriously entered my mind.

"Well, I do not know how this is going to develop," he said, "but I thought at least that I would bring it up with you. How would you react if your name were to be placed under consideration?"

I did not hesitate for a moment: "Mr. President, I will always remember with the deepest sense of gratitude that you even discussed this matter with me. I know that nothing might ever come of it, but I thank you so much for even raising it with me. But I have never considered this a possibility, as I look forward to the rest of my career."

"Why is that?" he asked. "Isn't this the great prize for all lawyers?"

"That's certainly right, Mr. President," I answered, "but I feel I am best cast as an advocate, not a judge. My training is as an advocate. I wish to be down there in the pit where the action is, and not sit up above the struggle and attempt to judge disputes. I do not think it is the right kind of career for me."

President Truman seemed both intrigued and a bit relieved. He made not the slightest effort to persuade me to reconsider, and said something to the effect that he not only understood my view but agreed completely with it. He never raised the subject again with me, and I never knew whether he was serious about it, or just probing to find out what I thought.

I had been influenced to some extent toward this view by watching my friend William O. Douglas, a great Justice who was continually restless on the Court. I thought of how often Douglas would watch some great domestic debate, and say wistfully, "Damn it, I wish I could get into this one, but I can't; I'm on the Court."*

As for Lyndon Johnson, he never offered or discussed with me a seat on the Court, as was reported in the press. He did make several efforts to persuade me to join his Cabinet as Attorney General—but that is another story.

A DINNER WITH LILIENTHAL

From the time I began to think about leaving, I talked to only a few people about my personal situation. One of them was George Elsey, who had to make plans of his own in the event of my departure and deserved to know what I was thinking.** Another with whom I shared my private thoughts was David E. Lilienthal. Because he was a highly intelligent and observant loner, and had never sided with any faction in the White House, I could talk to him more frankly than I could to most of my colleagues in the Administration. On December 10, 1948, shortly after our return from Key West, I went to Lilienthal's house for a quiet dinner with him and his wife Helen. In his private journals, Lilienthal wrote an account that captured the mood of our discussion:

> Clark seemed tired and very thoughtful. He spoke in a worried tone—quite unusual for him—about the conflict within the President's own family about future policy, between the conservatives and the "forward-lookers." He said he was "tired, awfully tired, not physically, but emotionally, psychologically." Felt that the life that came from doing new things, of learning, is no longer there. He spoke of the awful exhibition one sees around the White House of self-seeking, etc., and seemed rather depressed by it, not as if it were something new but that he was getting his fill of it. I was struck by the way he spoke of the dangers of being in the midst of such great power and influence, and its effect on people, adding, "Every once in a while I notice it in myself, and I try to drag it out in the open." . . . It was his thought that he get out of Government in the reasonably near

*The two vacant seats went to Attorney General Tom Clark, and former Senator Sherman Minton of Indiana. Clark served until 1966 when he resigned to make possible the appointment of his son, Ramsey Clark, as Attorney General.

**Elsey took leave from the White House in February 1949 to assist Professor Samuel Eliot Morison in his monumental official history of the Navy during World War II. He returned to the White House in August 1949, with a promotion to the rank of Administrative Assistant to the President. In December 1951 he became Executive Assistant to Averell Harriman, who had been appointed coordinator of all foreign aid programs.

> future. Financial reasons were important—he had about used up what he had saved, and had a girl about to enter college. But he said, "If I returned to St. Louis, almost none of the rare experience I have had in the past few years would be of any particular value to me." I knew what he had in mind: he wanted me to comment on whether it would be proper for him to practice [law] in Washington. I said of course he shouldn't go to St. Louis, that the fact that others had been greedy and not too principled in how they practiced law didn't mean that he needed to, nor would he.[4]

I also consulted Dean Acheson. Over dinner at his house in late 1949, I told him of my plan. Acheson, who had been a partner since 1921 in one of Washington's premier law firms, Covington & Burling, reacted bluntly and sardonically: "I must now completely revise my opinion of you. Until now, I thought that you had reasonable intelligence. But now I can see that you are quite dumb. The idea of going out and starting a new law firm here where there are so many already"—and then he ticked off the names of about ten Washington law firms. "That's simple-minded. Just plain simple-minded. There is not enough business for another firm. What you ought to do is come over to Covington & Burling. Someday I'll go back there, and we can have a whale of a time together."

I respected Covington & Burling, but it was, by the standards of the time, a big firm, with over sixty lawyers. I was well aware of the competition in Washington for law business, but I wanted to set out on my own. I was willing to take a chance. Acheson simply could not understand it; even years later, he still seemed offended by my decision, and never even hinted at any acknowledgment that he might have been wrong.

When I talked to Symington, he joined with some of our mutual friends in St. Louis in urging me to return to St. Louis and rejoin my old firm there—and to run for the United States Senate. I was flattered at the suggestion, but I never took it seriously. Running for public office was not what I wanted to do with my life.

One day, near the end of 1949, I brought up the matter of my successor with President Truman. I would have liked very much to have recommended George Elsey for the position, but unfortunately he was not a lawyer. Over the previous year, in much the same manner that I had started working with Rosenman four years earlier, another White House assistant, Charles Murphy, had offered his services to me whenever I needed extra help. He was thorough and able, with an orderly and trained legal mind. He also had the knack of communicating well with the President—a vital attribute for any Presidential aide. President Truman liked Murphy, and as with so many Presidents after they have been in office a few years, continuity was an important factor. He was delighted that he had someone competent inside the White House who could move into the Special Counsel's job.

In fact, everyone liked Charles Murphy. His loyalty and commitment to President Truman were unquestioned. He had worked in Washington for fifteen years, and had been a New Dealer when I was still back in St. Louis. One major difference concerned foreign policy: Charlie was comfortable only in the domestic field, and did not have close ties to State and Defense. Thus, for the first time, a clear division between those working on domestic and national security affairs began to emerge in the White House, a division that would widen over time.

We planned to announce my departure early in 1950, but the news leaked on November 21, 1949, and was confirmed by the White House the next day. A week later, I accompanied the President on his vacation to Key West. For the first ten days of the vacation, Mrs. Truman and Margaret were part of the Presidential party, which gave the vacation a different rhythm from that of the President's all-male vacations. Margaret participated energetically in the daily volleyball game, and Mrs. Truman sometimes joined us for the early morning Presidential walks. The women left Key West on December 7, and we settled into the old routine for the next two weeks, mixing rest with preparations for the State of the Union Message.

I cannot fully explain it, but I have never been one for sentimental or nostalgic farewells. I did not spend time dwelling on the fact that this would be my last vacation with President Truman as a member of his staff, nor did I feel particularly nostalgic or sentimental about leaving. When we returned to Washington on December 20, I resumed work as if I would be around for years to come. On my last day at the White House, I worked late cleaning up some loose ends, and then left without any ceremony except a farewell call on President Truman. He shared my aversion to displays of emotion at such times. Our last meeting was routine, as if we both wanted to act as if nothing was changing. But we both knew that was not the case.

We exchanged letters of farewell. In mine, I expressed, in highly personal terms, what it had meant to me to work for President Truman. He replied with two letters—one a short handwritten note dated on my last day at work:

> Of course I regret your leaving, but a man has responsibilities he must meet. I understand what yours are. Hope you are successful and that you'll keep your contacts here at the House. You're still a member of the "Palace Guard."

After I had left the White House, a second, more formal letter arrived from him. To this day I regard it as the most treasured document in my possession.

> Dear Clark:
>
> I have now to take a step which from the bottom of my heart I wish could be indefinitely deferred. In acquiescing in your wishes I am moved by circumstances with which I have long been familiar. Reluctantly, therefore, and with deep regret I accept, effective at the close of business on next Tuesday, January thirty-first, the resignation which you tender in your letter of January twenty-sixth.
>
> It would be difficult to overstate the value of the services which you have rendered your country. . . . Through six years of public service—and those potentially among the most fruitful of your professional life—you have devoted your talents and superb abilities exclusively to your country's welfare. That is a long time for you to be away from the practice of the law. The urgency of your need to return is readily understood.
>
> For all that you have given we owe you a debt impossible to pay. You had much to contribute as Special Counsel to the President because you brought to your work such great resources of legal learning and experience as a practicing lawyer. Besides this you had foresight and courage. Your reports on the various problems on which I asked for your advice were models of lucidity and logic. In the marshaling and presentation of facts your method reflected your days before the jury. Quick in the detection of spurious evidence and alert always in detecting the fallacious in the arguments of our opponents, your final opinions were always models of brevity and accuracy, as well as clarity and strength.
>
> I shall miss you—we shall all miss you. My regret at your departure is tempered by the knowledge that you are to remain in Washington and the assurance that I can call upon you as occasion requires. In going you carry with you every assurance of my personal gratitude and appreciation. You have also earned the thanks of the Nation which you have served so selflessly.
>
> Sincerely,
> Harry S Truman

15

A Washington Lawyer

The morning after I left the White House, I began work at my new law firm, Clifford & Miller, located at 1523 L Street in northwest Washington, only four blocks from my former office. Instead of commuting to work in a White House limousine, I used a city bus, which I later replaced with my own car. My desk was clean, with no appointments, no clients, and uncertain prospects.

I started out, intentionally, with only one partner. After some thought, I had asked Edward H. Miller, whom I had known in St. Louis before the war, to join me. As a Justice Department lawyer, Miller had done an outstanding job directing the antitrust case against the tobacco companies, and had then become Attorney General Clark's special assistant. I thought Miller's expertise in the antitrust field would complement my own broader knowledge of the government. A tall and slender man with a serious attitude toward his work, Miller was enthusiastic about the opportunity to become a "name partner" in a new firm.

I brought with me from the White House only one person: my secretary, Mary Weiler, who had worked with me at Lashly, Lashly, Miller* and Clifford, before the war. The most devoted of people, she was to work with me for fifty-two years, in St. Louis, the White House, my law practice, and the Defense Department, before retiring in 1980 and returning to St. Louis.

*The Miller of Lashly, Lashly, Miller and Clifford was not related to Edward H. Miller.

In that first week, I received two telephone calls that resulted in long-standing client relationships. The first came from Phillips Petroleum Company of Bartlesville, Oklahoma. I had met its chairman, Kenneth Stanley Adams, known to everyone as "Boots," through our mutual friend, Senator Robert S. Kerr of Oklahoma. My relationship with Phillips was to prove the longest of my legal career, continuing to this day. Later in our relationship, Adams invited me to join the Phillips board, which I did, enabling me to acquire an understanding of the oil industry.

THE MOST UNFORGETTABLE CLIENT I NEVER MET

The second telephone call began what proved to be the most unusual relationship I ever had with a client. He called me himself, with no prior warning, no introductions, and no intermediaries, although I later learned from one of his aides that he had investigated me extensively. He opened the conversation with the briefest of personal introductions, and then went directly to the purpose of the call: "Mr. Clifford, this is Howard Hughes calling you from California. I have followed your career with interest, and we all thank you for the contribution you have made to the nation. I understand you have gone into private law practice. I find that as time goes by we have more and more problems and legal matters in Washington. I have three corporations that need representation and legal advice in Washington—Hughes Tool Company, RKO Motion Picture Company, and Trans World Airlines. Would you be willing to represent them?"

By now I was listening closely. In 1950, everyone knew about Howard Hughes: his business empire, stretching from aviation to movies, made him one of the wealthiest and most powerful businessmen in the world; and his dashing personal style, already eccentric but not yet completely reclusive, made him the object of intense and continual curiosity.

"Mr. Hughes," I said, speaking slowly in order not to appear too enthusiastic, "I believe that establishing a Washington legal presence, as you are considering doing with me, is going to become a major trend of our times for major American firms. There are a great number of legal matters that require the specialized abilities of a Washington law firm."

"I will ask you to give us advice and legal assistance on a number of problems," Hughes said. "You will usually hear from me. Occasionally, you may hear from my main assistant, Noah Dietrich." His voice took on a harder edge. "Do not, *under any circumstances,* accept anyone as representing my views except me and Dietrich."

Before the conversation ended, I gave Hughes a well-rehearsed little speech that I had prepared for use with all prospective clients. In a refined form, I was to give it so many times over the next forty years that my younger associates liked to joke that they could recite it along with me.

"Mr. Hughes," I said, "I look forward to our association. But before we proceed, there is one point I must make clear. I do not consider that this firm will have any influence of any kind here in Washington. I cannot, and will not, represent any client before the President or before any of his staff. If you want influence, you should consider going elsewhere. What we can offer you is an extensive knowledge of how to deal with the government on your problems. We will be able to give you advice on how best to present your position to the appropriate departments and agencies of the government."

Hughes said he understood my point completely. What he wanted was advice and legal help, not influence or special access—he was quite confident of his own abilities in that regard, he said. On this pleasant note, the conversation ended.

The relationship with Hughes and his three companies lasted over twenty-five years, gradually phasing out in the seventies. Most of our work was of the ordinary legal variety: advising TWA in presentations to the Civil Aeronautics Board concerning the awarding of air routes, assisting Hughes's companies with complicated tax-related matters, and the like.

But long before that, Howard Hughes achieved a unique status in my legal career. In my more than sixty years before the bar, he was the only client I never met.

At first I did not make much of this. After all, Hughes lived in California, I was in Washington—a city he hated, especially after his much-publicized argument in 1947 with the Congressional committees investigating war production. We dealt with each other on the telephone, but as time went on, I realized this was more than a question of convenience and logistics; it was an aspect of this very strange man. Hughes chose the oddest times to call me, usually calling after midnight, and frequently between two and four A.M.. Marny, who usually answered the telephone in our house, began to refer to Hughes as my "midnight caller."

As it turned out, an old friend from St. Louis knew Hughes quite well, and offered me some insights into this strange man. General Elwood "Pete" Quesada had married the daughter of Joseph Pulitzer II, my uncle Clark MacAdams's boss at the *St. Louis Post-Dispatch.* He served as a military aide to Eisenhower during World War II, and became a White House special assistant on aviation affairs, and later Administrator of the Federal Aviation Administration during Eisenhower's Presidency. Hughes made several efforts to hire Quesada. They were unsuccessful, but resulted in some marvelous Howard Hughes incidents that Quesada shared with me.

In one, Hughes asked Quesada to fly to Los Angeles, take a certain suite at the Beverly Hills Hotel, and wait there. Hughes arrived in Quesada's suite at the appointed time, alone, wearing shabby clothes, dirty tennis shoes, and no coat. Immediately, he got down on his hands and knees and looked under the beds and chairs, and inspected every closet in the suite to make sure they were alone. Then, sitting awkwardly on the edge of the bed, Hughes tried to persuade Quesada to come to work for Hughes Aircraft. When Quesada refused, on the grounds he was satisfied with the position he held at Lockheed, Hughes was astounded: in his world, the vast amount of money he had offered Quesada should have been sufficient to persuade anyone to defect from his current employer.

Hughes pursued Quesada by telephone, and insisted that they meet the next night on a specific street corner in a run-down part of Lost Angeles. At the appointed moment, an ordinary-looking Chevrolet passed Quesada once, circled, and pulled up next to him. The door opened, and Hughes, behind the wheel, ordered Quesada to get in. Then they drove around in circles while Hughes tried again to persuade Quesada to leave Lockheed.

When it became clear Quesada would not leave Lockheed, Hughes stopped circling and drove directly to a private industrial airport, where he pulled up to a parked plane. A man climbed out of the cockpit and silently disappeared into the hangar. Hughes got out of his car, grabbed some papers from the glove compartment, and, without any words of farewell, climbed into the cockpit, started up the engines, and disappeared into the night. Not quite sure what to do, Quesada waited a moment, and then drove Hughes's car back to the Beverly Hills Hotel and left it with the doorman.

My own relationship with Hughes never reached such a level of weirdness, but as time went on, it was clear, even over the telephone, that Hughes's obsessions were gaining control of his acute business and aviation skills. He had been a genuine pioneer in the aviation industry, and a visionary in the field of future technologies. Gradually, through, his talents were overwhelmed by his deep and uncontrollable fears. A former FBI agent named Robert Maheu replaced Dietrich as my only direct contact with Hughes, and behaved as if he were guarding dark and dangerous secrets about his boss. Maybe he was.

Meanwhile, the telephone calls would continue to come in sporadically, almost always in the middle of the night, about increasingly odd matters. In one such call, in the early fifties, Hughes asked for assistance in a field in which I had absolutely no qualifications: "I need a complete rundown on some British character who is pursuing Elizabeth Taylor. His name is Michael Wilding." I told Hughes that I could not help him, but I was fascinated by his call. It was clear that Hughes was upset at the idea of Taylor dating Wilding, whom she later married.

As the years went on, he began to deal with people almost entirely through his trusted Mormon aides. Our legal work for his companies continued, but my contact with this fascinating, but ultimately sad and tormented, man gradually came to an end.

THE SUPREME COURT

Although exotic clients and difficult cases are what make the law exciting, there is no greater honor for an attorney than to argue before the Supreme Court. My first opportunity came on November 17, 1959, in a complicated tax case in which I represented the Phillips Petroleum Company. As always when I appear in court, I rose extremely early in the morning and rehearsed my presentation while I prepared for the day. This time, however, I put on my formal morning clothes, honoring a sartorial tradition that had once been obligatory when appearing before the court, but which now has been discontinued except for the Solicitor-General.

At precisely 1 P.M., the clerk called the Court into session, and the nine black-robed Justices settled into their high-backed chairs. The Justices of the Warren Court, one of the most influential courts in American history, sat above me—Earl Warren, Felix Frankfurter, Hugo Black, William O. Douglas, William Brennan, and their colleagues.

I argued that Phillips had been denied equal protection under the Fourteenth Amendment. The questions were not unfriendly. Three months later, the Court issued a unanimous decision in favor of Phillips, ruling the taxation a "substantial and transparent . . . discrimination against the [federal] Government and its lessees," and reversing the ruling.[1]

A 1969 appearance before the Supreme Court was particularly memorable. I had just left my post as Secretary of Defense when Chief Justice Earl Warren asked me to represent before the Supreme Court a Missouri prison inmate, Robert Ashe. The case raised a fundamental question regarding double jeopardy that the High Court wanted to examine.

The circumstances were these: Nine years earlier, six men had gathered for an evening of poker in a basement of a home in Lee's Summit, Missouri. Late that night, several masked gunmen crashed the party and stole four thousand dollars in cash and jewelry. Hours later, policemen arrested Ashe, a small-time drifter with a long criminal record, as he walked along the highway near the abandoned getaway car.

In the first trial, the prosecution failed to establish Ashe's identity as one of the gunmen, and the jury found him not guilty of robbing one of the players. Unhappy with the verdict, the State of Missouri decided to put Ashe on trial again—this time for the robbery of a different player in the same poker game. In the second trial, a witness who had been unable to identify Ashe at the first trial recognized his voice because of its "unusual" quality, and a deputy sheriff not called at the first trial testified he had found money stashed in Ashe's shoe. The second jury returned a guilty verdict, and Ashe, because of his previous criminal record, received a thirty-five year sentence.

In prison, Ashe honed his skills as a jailhouse lawyer, appealing the verdict on the grounds that the robbery was all one crime and that being tried the second time constituted double jeopardy, thus violating the Fifth Amendment's provision that no person "shall be subject for the same offense to be twice put in jeopardy of life or limb." Ashe's appeal was rejected in two lower courts, but the Supreme Court agreed to review it in early 1969.

When I entered the case, I received a handwritten letter on prison stationery from my new client, which read:

> Dear Mr. Clifford:
>
> Received notice from the Supreme Court of the United States, that you have been appointed to serve as counsel for my defense! Mr. Clifford it is hard for me to express my feelings, at receiving this news. Certainly want you to understand that I am *most satisfied* with the courts choice, along with being overwhelming greatful for your help.

Seven months later, I appeared before the Supreme Court, headed by its new Chief Justice, Warren Burger. In my oral remarks, I challenged Ashe's second prosecution as unconstitutional, arguing that the state had improperly made my client "run the gauntlet again." On April 7, 1970, the Supreme Court reversed Ashe's conviction, extending the doctrine called *collateral estoppel* to criminal prosecutions at the state as well as the federal level. This was an important victory for individual legal rights: henceforth, once an issue of fact has been determined by jury verdict, that issue could not again be tried by the state. Associate Justice Potter Stewart, writing for the majority, noted that it meant that when someone was tried on a criminal charge, the trial could not be regarded as "a dry run for [a] second prosecution."

Ashe served out the remainder of a separate prison sentence for larceny, and was released in 1971. Seven years later, I received a short letter from the lawyer who had represented him in Missouri, informing me that Ashe had been found dead in a Kansas City boardinghouse with two bullet wounds in his back. "The poor fellow," I wrote back, "never had a chance."

PRACTICING LAW

For the rest of my career, with the exception of my service as Secretary of Defense, my private practice—Clifford & Miller or its successor, Clifford & Warnke—was to be my base. I would work with Presidents, undertake foreign and domestic assignments for the executive branch, accept appointments from the Supreme Court to argue cases, and find myself involved in ten more Presidential campaigns. But my job—except for my part-time service in the 1980s as chairman of a banking corporation, First American Bankshares—was the practice of law.

I have always been proud of my profession. I know of no other work in the private sector that offers a greater challenge, more potential rewards, and greater variety than the practice of law. But I am speaking of the law as I knew it over the last sixty years—not necessarily the kind of work done by so many young lawyers in large firms today.

The firm that Miller and I envisioned was smaller than the law firms that dominate the legal profession today. At almost any time since the early sixties, we could have created a firm to rival in size some of Washington's or even New York's larger firms, but I felt strongly that such a firm was not for me, and I have resisted pressure to build a large firm. Small firms retain the personal flavor and style I believe produce the best working conditions and the greatest job satisfaction.

Large law firms are undeniably necessary in this age of multibillion dollar transactions and complicated legal proceedings. I have worked closely with many of these giant firms, including Wachtell, Lipton, Rosen & Katz, the New York firm specializing in mergers and acquisitions. Martin Lipton, who heads the firm, and I have argued the issue in a good-natured way over the years as we worked together on many cases. One of the most creative legal minds of our era, Lipton has made a persuasive case for the necessity of large, specialized firms in the modern world.

Lipton likes to point out that when I entered the law over sixty years ago, an individual lawyer or a small law firm like Lashly, Lashly handled everything from general litigation and corporation law to contracts and wills for individuals and businesses. Lawyers were regarded as pillars of society, and were often addressed as "Counsellor," a term which was used as a mark of respect. Outside of New York City, lawyers rarely specialized until fairly recently. Lipton agrees that as individuals, lawyers benefited greatly from the well-rounded and varied experience that they obtained in the small, multipurpose law firm, but he points out that in today's world, successful lawyers must specialize early in their careers.

I recognize the validity of Lipton's argument, although it saddens me that young lawyers today will have to choose their career paths so early. My years defending criminal cases gave me invaluable trial experience. Today, one must choose early between civil and criminal law; the chance to do both and thereby hone one's courtroom skills is unlikely to be available to most young lawyers, unless they spend a period of time in a prosecuting attorney's office at the beginning of their careers.

A central aspect of practicing law is the art of persuading others of one's point of view. Arguing before a judge or jury—the act of *advocacy,* of trying to convince others of the merit of your case—is, to my mind, the very essence of being a lawyer. Even years after one's last courtroom appearance, memories of early courtroom experiences remain a valuable asset for those fortunate enough to have experienced it. To get the best possible training, I believe a young lawyer should, ideally, spend the first few years of his career clerking for a judge, working for an assistant district attorney, serving as a legal aide to a public defender, or working in a government agency with the opportunity to get into court. This may mean sacrificing income at the beginning of one's career, but there is no substitute later on for the experience gained working in the courts.

I often discussed the changes in the legal profession with another lawyer—one of the greatest courtroom lawyers of the century—Edward Bennett Williams. I first met this extraordinary man in 1950, when we were both starting out as Washington lawyers. Williams had just started his own firm, and it took us both a while to overcome the sense that we were cast as potential rivals in the small Washington legal world of the fifties. After we had worked together on a few matters, our relationship evolved into a deep friendship that lasted until his death in 1988.

Had I ever needed a lawyer myself, I would have turned to Ed Williams. A massive, physically impressive man, he was one of the smartest and most determined practitioners of the law in the nation's history. "The country's best criminal lawyer," as *Time* magazine once called him, he worked diligently on his clients' behalf right up to the last day of his life. He often took on unpopular causes, defending such men as Jimmy Hoffa, Frank Costello, Congressman Adam Clayton Powell, Jr., John Hinckley, Jr., Michael Milken, and Oliver North. In 1954, Ed was denounced publicly as a "fascist" for defending Senator Joe McCarthy and as a "Red" for defending several Hollywood writers who had been blacklisted for alleged communist activities. He earned enormous fees from his corporate clients, but he also represented worthy causes and friends who were unable to pay.

Williams defended his unpopular clients on the grounds that, under our system of government, every person had a right to the best defense within the existing laws. Every defendant had a right—and his lawyer an *obliga-*

tion—to test the law to its limits to get the best possible outcome from the courts. That was what made the law work. To the lawyer, there was no such thing as a loophole; if a law was flawed, the legislative branch could change it—but unless and until they did, it was the law, and applied equally to all. Ed respected, indeed loved, the law. It was, he and I both believed, what kept us a civilized nation.

Williams resisted creating a large firm until late in his life, but his long and courageous fight against cancer, which lasted eleven years and included seven operations, convinced him that he either had to expand his firm or see it disappear after his death. He chose to expand it to a size which, he told me, made him feel uncomfortable in some ways but which he felt would be best for the future of his partners and associates.

As a friend and fellow lawyer, I miss Ed Williams more than I can say. Over the years, we consulted each other regularly when confronted with serious problems, and we never lost a case that we worked on together.

* * *

By the late spring of 1950, just when it seemed clear that the firm of Clifford & Miller would prosper, Ed Miller, who was only forty-three years old, suffered a massive heart attack. He survived, and began his recuperation at his home in northwest Washington, D.C.; everything seemed encouraging, and we both anticipated his return to work in a few weeks, when he suffered a second, fatal attack. It was a stunning and tragic end to a career which had held such bright promise.

After much thought, I concluded that the success of the firm justified a bold step, and I decided to ask John J. McCloy to become my new partner. At the time, McCloy was fifty-five years old, one of the main links between World War II and the postwar world. A Wall Street lawyer and a Republican who had come to Washington at the beginning of the war, he had served as Assistant Secretary of War alongside his friend Bob Lovett. At the beginning of the Berlin crisis, President Truman had asked McCloy to go to Germany as High Commissioner.

I respected McCloy's legal abilities and his calm, unemotional way of working his way through problems—and I knew he wanted to leave Germany. When I approached him, he seemed enthusiastic. He liked Washington, he said, and the idea of developing a legal practice with me appealed to him. Before we could begin a detailed discussion, though, I needed to check with one special person. So, on August 25, 1950, I went to Blair House to see the President. I did not wish to recruit such an important public servant without his prior approval.

The President agreed McCloy would make a splendid partner. However, he said he intended to ask him to stay in Germany for another year to demonstrate our continuing commitment to NATO despite Korea.

Would I wait one year before formally asking McCloy to join me? I replied that I would, of course, do whatever the President wanted. The next day, I received a handwritten note: "Will let you know what I'll do about that man in Europe as soon as I can."

A few weeks later, McCloy agreed to stay in Berlin. A year later, when he was ready to leave Germany, I renewed my offer, but was easily outbid when he was offered the chairmanship of the Chase Manhattan Bank. Although we occasionally talked afterward of what it might have been like to form our "dream law firm," it was to remain a dream. With McCloy unavailable, I decided not to replace Ed Miller. Instead, I brought in two younger lawyers, Carson Glass and Samuel D. McIlwain, as associates and later as partners, and began to expand slowly.

16

The Years Between: 1950–1960

My departure from the White House did not mean the end of my relationships with friends in the Congress and the executive branch. They stayed in touch with me, and often asked for advice or assistance on matters political, personal, or legal. Thus a pattern of great importance to the rest of my life gradually developed: I became, for better or worse, a practitioner in the arcane art of advising some of the nation's leaders and would-be leaders. This led to close relationships with many fascinating people, including two future Presidents, John F. Kennedy and Lyndon B. Johnson.

After I left the White House, President Truman and I still kept in close touch. He invited me to join him on some of his Key West vacations. He relied on his staff heavily for day-to-day assistance, and I was no longer part of it, but I continued, at his request, to arrange the poker sessions on the *Williamsburg* or at private homes.

My seat on the sidelines did not dissatisfy me. I did not wish to become part of that large and frustrated Washington subculture composed of former high officials who second-guess their successors and dream of a return to government. If a problem arose on which, drawing from personal experience, I could be helpful to the President or some other government official—on a personal basis, not as a lawyer—I would be available. But I loved the law and the challenge of setting up a new firm; and, despite some speculation to the contrary, I did not feel any yearning to return to the government.

KOREA

By sheer chance, the timing of my departure turned out to be crucial. Barely nineteen weeks after I had left the White House, the North Koreans attacked South Korea. Had I still been in the Administration on June 24, 1950, it would have been impossible for me to leave before the end of President Truman's term.

On that day, President Truman was relaxing with his family in Independence, Missouri, when Dean Acheson called to inform him that the North Koreans had launched a surprise attack. By the time the President had returned to Washington the following day, he told me later, he already knew he would have to respond. The North Korean action was a fundamental test of the Truman Doctrine, the U.N., and the depth of America's commitment to its friends and allies. Coming only nine months after the communists had taken over the mainland of China, and with the French deeply embattled in Indochina, the attack appeared to be part of an attempt to use force to expand communist power throughout the world, especially Asia.

Once again, as in 1947, Dean Acheson strode to the fore as the President's chief adviser. The two men never hesitated in their decision to respond to the crisis under the U.N. banner. The President had been deeply influenced by the League of Nations' failure in stopping the rise of Hitler. As he confronted the challenge in Korea, he told me, he was determined not to let the U.N. go the way of the League.

I fully supported the President's decision to intervene in Korea; but I felt strongly that the American effort should not be unilateral, and I expressed this view in a letter of support I wrote the President on June 29. The war "should be made to appear what it is," I wrote, "a contest between one aggressor nation and the rest of the peace-loving world."

Sometimes history takes a while before deciding whether a policy was right or wrong, but there can be no doubt as to the correctness of President Truman's actions in Korea. In my view, in the Truman years it was second in importance only to the use of the atomic bomb against Japan. Had we not acted immediately, South Korea would have fallen within days under the control of a North Korean regime which ranked at the time as perhaps the most repressive on earth. The survival and success of modern-day Korea demonstrates, as clearly as anywhere else on earth, the high purpose of America's immediate postwar foreign policy. I can think of no other nation on earth which would have gone to war halfway around the globe in defense of an idea, rather than the preservation of an empire.

Unfortunately, the Administration made an unnecessary and serious error in not seeking a formal authorization of war from Congress. The decision not to ask Congress for its formal support, as Republican Senator

Robert A. Taft had recommended, had two unfortunate consequences. First, it made it easier for Taft and other Republicans to criticize the Korean War in 1952 and turn it into a domestic political issue.

A second, and more serious, consequence was the precedent it established. President Johnson emulated it in Vietnam, arguing that the Tonkin Gulf Resolution in August 1964 and the annual military appropriation, constituted de facto Congressional approval of his policies in Vietnam. By 1973, Congress had had enough of this argument, and passed the War Powers Act, intended to define more precisely the President's obligation to involve the legislative branch when American troops are sent into combat situations.

* * *

The Korean war changed forever the character of the Truman Administration. Priorities were suddenly reversed, as the nation and its leaders once again had to put a faraway war ahead of domestic needs. Inexcusably, desegregation of the armed services was slowed down by the war—the Army argued that it should not be required to change its procedures and traditions under wartime conditions. Alerted by George Elsey, I brought these delaying tactics to President Truman's attention. I did not see any reason why Korea should slow down desegregation, and urged President Truman to instruct the Army to carry out the executive order regardless of the situation in Korea.

SENATOR ROBERT S. KERR

While my work in the White House had brought me into close contact with many members of Congress, that interaction was governed by the fact that, even in a social setting, I was an advocate for the President and his policies. Once I left the Administration, though, I found it easier to develop real friendships with many members of Congress. Among the most memorable of these was the one that developed with Robert S. Kerr, the Democratic Senator from Oklahoma. We had become friends while I was still at the White House, and the friendship deepened after I left.

From the outset, I was fascinated by Kerr, a strange combination of rough-and-tumble pirate and devout, teetotaling Baptist. He was the only politician I ever met who was born in a log cabin—literally—an event that took place in 1896, on his parents' small farm in what was then the Indian Territory of Oklahoma. He worked his way through college and became a lawyer in Oklahoma after World War I. In 1926 came the big break of his life: he and his brother-in-law borrowed thirty thousand dollars to buy two oil drilling rigs, and established a company that later grew into Kerr-McGee Oil Industries. As his company prospered, Kerr, by now a rich man, moved into politics. In 1942 he became the first native-born Oklahoman to be elected Governor of the state, and six years later he entered the United States Senate.

He accumulated vast power by adroitly combining a charming and gregarious personality with a rough, practical political style. Six days a week he was a very tough politician, but on Sundays, he was as devout a person as one could imagine. He had taught what he proudly told me was the largest Sunday school class in Oklahoma City; I thought it typical of Kerr that, if he taught a Sunday school class, it would have to be the biggest in town.

Kerr vigorously protected his own interests and those of his state. In 1950, the President had vetoed Kerr's attempts to deregulate natural gas for independent producers—a bill which would have clearly benefited Kerr personally. Yet, when President Truman dismissed General MacArthur in 1951, creating an enormous national uproar, Kerr was virtually the only Democratic Senator to come to the President's defense—thereby earning the President's lasting gratitude.

Kerr made a disastrous run for the Presidency in 1952 and discovered what so many others have learned the hard way: that Washington power does not translate easily into votes in primaries. For the next ten years, until his death of a heart attack in 1963, he was one of Washington's most powerful Senators, feared and courted by politicians of both parties; but he knew that he could never shake his image as a representative of big oil.

Even though most of his colleagues in Congress drank regularly and tended to distrust teetotalers, Kerr was utterly sincere in his opposition to the consumption of alcohol. He would not serve beer or wine in his home. He and his wife, Grayce, were militant "drys," a circumstance that led to the most uproarious dinner party I ever attended in Washington.

Not too long after becoming a Senator, Bob Kerr asked me for a favor. "Clifford," he said, "the time has come for Grayce and me to give a dinner party. I do not want to make it a big affair, but I thought we would get some friends together for a Sunday supper. That will be more relaxed and less formal than a party during the week. I want your help in putting together the guest list."

We drew up a list that included a number of prominent Washingtonians, including Stuart and Evie Symington. Stuart knew the Kerrs would not allow any alcohol in their home, and that did not sound like much of an evening to him—so, after obtaining from me a list of those who had accepted, Stuart called each guest himself. "Listen," he said, "you're not going to get a drink at the Kerrs' Sunday. If you want one, come on over to our place first."

Almost everyone showed up at the Symingtons'. That evening, I made an interesting sociological discovery: the realization that there would be no drinks served at the Kerrs' turned every guest into a much heavier drinker than he or she normally was. Those who usually drank one drink had three before leaving the Symingtons', and those who normally had two drank four or five. By the time we arrived at the Kerrs', the group that had started the evening so sedately at the Symingtons had a tail wind of about a hundred miles an hour.

We swarmed raucously into the Kerrs' house, slapping our hosts on the back with booming joviality. The Kerrs got out orange juice and soft drinks, and were pleasantly surprised to see how rapidly everyone started drinking them—though there was a remarkable amount of spillage.

At some point in this riotous proceeding, Speaker Rayburn rose unsteadily to his feet and called for silence. "You may not know it," he thundered, "but I was the valedictorian of my high school." There were loud cheers and cries of "What's the matter with Sam?" and "He's all right." Then Mr. Sam recited a hackneyed poem by Longfellow that children used to be required to memorize in school. When he finished, he was helped back into his chair, and sat beaming at his triumph. His stellar performance sifted through the fog surrounding Connecticut Senator Brien McMahon, who was known in Washington as "Mr. Atom Bomb" because of his authorship of the Atomic Energy Act. He rose, with some assistance. "I want to make a confession," he said. "When I was a young man I had to make a very difficult decision, should I become a famous Irish tenor or a United States Senator."

"You made the wrong choice, Brien," somebody yelled.

"I had a glorious voice," McMahon said sadly. "My mother always said, 'Brien sings like an angel.' "

Somebody else yelled, "That's enough build-up, Mac. Let's have a song." McMahon launched into "When Irish Eyes Are Smiling." After the first few words, everyone was joining in, quite loudly and off-key. In the momentary lull that followed this musical extravaganza, Senator Alan Frear of Delaware got the floor, and announced, "I had a very unhappy childhood." The rest of his life story was lost amidst exclamations of concern and sympathy and a surge of guests wanting to offer him comfort and solace.

The evening continued in this extraordinary way for some time. Other people of normally sober mien also offered maudlin confessions of a youth misspent or dreams denied. Finally, around 10 P.M., the crowd began to leave. "Great party, Bob. Great party, Grayce," everyone said as they piled out of the Kerr home.

Out in the street, somebody said, "Let's all go back to the Symingtons' and have a nightcap."

Stuart and Evie Symington looked genuinely alarmed. "The hell you are," he said. "We are not going to have this gang of drunks in our house."

So everyone went home.

About eight the next morning, Kerr called. "Clifford," he said, "how do you think it went last night?"

"Oh, Senator," I replied, "it was superb. It was an absolute bull's-eye. It was the best party ever given in Washington. Everyone had a wonderful time."

I could almost hear Kerr beaming with pleasure at the other end of the line as I laid it on. "Well, Clifford," he said, "it just goes to show—you don't have to serve liquor to have a good time."

THE NEW YEAR'S DAY PARTY

In the early fifties, our family began a tradition that lasted for a decade. This was the annual New Year's Day Open House, to which we invited our friends. Over the years, the party grew in size until attendance exceeded two hundred guests, including many of Washington's leading citizens, and other friends who came from as far away as St. Louis and California.

What distinguished this party was the entertainment, which was provided entirely by the family Clifford. At first, we restricted ourselves to a few songs, with others joining in, but we gradually expanded the singing into a full-fledged show, complete with skits gently lampooning public figures and recent events. It was, in short, a sort of miniature Gridiron Dinner, although we modestly thought it far superior to the original in talent and wit.

The most memorable party took place in 1956, when Lyndon Johnson came for a short while; it was his first appearance at a Washington social event since his heart attack during the summer. The following year, he stayed for the entire program, sitting with Sam Rayburn on straight-backed chairs against the wall, while Lady Bird, in a bright red dress, sat on the floor with the other guests, including, most improbably, Dean Acheson. People were jammed into every corner of the living room; some, including Supreme Court Justice Stanley Reed, would arrive early and stake out a good spot each year so as to have an unimpeded view of the proceedings.

The program we offered had been prepared with great care over the previous months. My daughters, who had lovely singing voices, and one of our sons-in-law, who had been a semiprofessional singer, sang a variety of popular songs, which had been given new lyrics for the occasion. I sang as well, always including in my repertoire a favorite from my St. Louis days, "The Tattooed Lady." Each year, as I sang this song, a chorus of catcalls and cheers met its quaintly suggestive lyrics:

I paid a dime to see the tattooed lady
Tattooed from head to toe;
It's quite a sight, you know;
And on one thigh was a British Man O'War
And across her back was the Union Jack
Now, who could ask for more?
And up and down her spine
Was the Boston Red Sox nine;
And in a certain spot,
Was a blue forget-me-not;
And over on one kidney
Was a bird's-eye view of Sydney.
But what I liked best
Right across her chest
Was my home in Tennessee.

The program became steadily more elaborate. In 1957, I solemnly sang an old-fashioned, moth-eaten song with lyrics from the poem *Invictus,* while two of my sons-in-law slowly and methodically wrapped me from toe to head in a wide bandage, and, just as I completed the song, carried me out of the room. In 1959, I offered a spoof of Eisenhower's State of the Union Message, playing on his famously convoluted syntax. In 1961, we gave our most impressive performance, with all three daughters—Gerry, Joyce, and Randall—performing, along with Gerry's and Joyce's husbands, Bill Lanagan and Dick Barrett. We kidded the incoming Kennedy Administration, some of whom were present, with a peek inside the new White House kitchen, where a menu was being prepared consisting of Oysters Nelson Rockefeller; "a real turkey from California, Richard Nixon;" and "Boston Cream Pie in the Sky." I closed with a review of the year that included such lines as: "Half the people think the Eisenhower Administration has been excellent, the other half thinks it has been terrible—but everyone is proud of Ike for not getting mixed up in it."

The 1961 party proved to be our last. Our daughters had moved from Washington, and the effort had simply become too great to sustain. We were having increasing difficulty keeping the number of guests small enough to fit within our house. That last year we had to remove all the furniture in order to cram 225 people in, and we had to wire it for sound. The effort our family was putting into the performance was getting larger and larger, and we all felt that if we did not end the program, it would consume us. After 1961, we continued to invite people to share New Year's Day with us, and we often sat around the piano singing, but never again did we put on a full-fledged program. Still, almost thirty years later, people who were there come up to me and recall those parties fondly. So do I.

PROBLEMS IN THE WHITE HOUSE

Almost from the moment of his appointment to replace James Forrestal, it was apparent that Louis Johnson was not qualified to serve as Secretary of Defense, especially in wartime conditions. At best he was unsuited for the job; at worst, as Acheson believed, he had mental problems. In a private meeting on August 24, 1950 (the same meeting in which I told the President I hoped to ask John J. McCloy to become my law partner), the President told me the growing hostility between his Secretaries of State and Defense made it extremely difficult to manage the Korean crisis, then only eight weeks old. I told him that, in all candor, Johnson was widely viewed in Washington as dangerously unfit for such a sensitive position. (Averell Harriman, then the President's Special Assistant, told me later he had shared similar views with the President.)

The President said he was considering asking General Marshall to replace Johnson as Secretary of Defense, an astute way to extricate himself from a potentially disastrous situation. The day after the meeting with President Truman, I sent him a note:

> I was greatly encouraged by your decision to make the change you spoke about. I feel so strongly that it is correct that, if by any chance, you should wish me to perform the same function that I did in the Krug case, you have only to call upon me.

President Truman sent back a handwritten reply:

> Your good note hit me in a soft place. Thanks very very much for your offer. It looks as if I'll have to do this one *myself.* Terrible to contemplate, isn't it?

Despite his note, the President delayed taking action, and, as so often happens in government, the decision leaked to the press before it could be discussed with Johnson. After the leak, the President summoned Johnson to the White House, and asked him to resign immediately. Marshall's appointment was announced at the same time, on September 12, 1950, swamping the news of Johnson's departure.

Seven months later, the pressures on the President reached a crescendo following his dismissal of General Douglas MacArthur as commander of our forces in Korea and Japan. The President was unquestionably correct in his decision to remove MacArthur, whose insubordination had reached such a level that to leave him in command would have been unthinkable. It was, nonetheless, a painfully difficult decision to make, unleashing, as he knew it would, a firestorm of protests and attacks—not only from Republicans but, for a time, many Democrats.

Two weeks after MacArthur's dismissal, with the nation still in the emotional thrall of the General's famous farewell address to Congress—"Old soldiers never die, they just fade away"—the President sent me a letter remarkable for its uncharacteristic tone of self-pity, a trait I almost never saw in President Truman:

> There have been only two or three Presidents who have been as roundly abused and misrepresented in certain sections of the press as I have. I call your attention to Washington, Jefferson, Jackson, Lincoln and particularly to Grover Cleveland. I have just finished going through McElroy's life of Cleveland[1] and I don't think there ever was a President as thoroughly misrepresented by the press as he was, and I don't think there ever was a more honorable man in the Presidency, although he followed the program of going straight ahead with his policies when they were as unpopular as they could be.

One last member of the Cabinet, Attorney General J. Howard McGrath, had to be dismissed early in 1952, after a scandal within the Justice Department. This completed the series of unpleasant departures from the Cabinet which were a disturbing but recurring feature of the Truman Administration. I had been involved, directly or indirectly, in many of them—Henry Wallace, James Byrnes, James Forrestal, Julius Krug, Howard McGrath, and Louis Johnson—and had missed several others, including Henry Morganthau, Harold Ickes, and Francis Biddle, all holdovers from the Roosevelt Administration. Even if one makes allowance for the fact that several key departures had been Roosevelt appointees whose style was incompatible with that of President Truman, the number of Cabinet members whose exits were handled poorly may seem striking to the contemporary observer.

In every Administration some Cabinet-level appointees do not live up to expectations, and have to be replaced, but in most Administrations, departures have been handled with less confusion and less public attention than was the case during the Truman Presidency. There is no question that these departures could have been handled better, but President Truman's famed honesty and bluntness were quite real, not part of a manufactured public image. These strengths could also be his weaknesses. He regarded public relations with a combination of revulsion and contempt. There were many benefits from his admirable traits, but there was a cost as well; an impression of confusion was sometimes left as a result of minor, and avoidable, errors. On great policy issues, when it mattered, President Truman performed in an outstanding manner; moreover, he appointed some of the greatest public servants in American history, including Marshall (twice), Acheson, Harriman, Forrestal, and Lovett, as well as a distinguished group of sub-Cabinet officials. On some lesser domestic appointments, however, those standards were not always maintained. As for dismissing his own appointees, he was always reluctant to do so; his compassion for friends usually took precedence over the needs of government unless or until he felt he had been deceived or misled. Then he could be quite unforgiving and dismiss someone abruptly.

1952: TO RUN OR NOT TO RUN

If President Truman could have chosen his successor, he would have chosen Chief Justice Fred Vinson. In his eyes, Vinson's experience in all three branches of government made him uniquely qualified for the Presidency. Moreover, President Truman had always liked Vinson's down-to-earth, unpretentious style, and was grateful for his constant support through good times and bad since 1945. As early as 1950, he had told Vinson that if he did not run again he hoped he would be his successor.

Few others shared the President's extraordinarily high assessment of the Chief Justice. Fred Vinson was a decent and amusing person whose friendship I valued greatly, but he had hardly shown special leadership qualities as Secretary of the Treasury or as Chief Justice. In addition, at age sixty-two, he was not in good health.

On October 11, 1951, the President invited me to dine with him and Vinson at the Blair House. He promised Vinson his full support if he would run. Flattered by the offer, Vinson listened, but three days later he informed the President that he was not interested in becoming a candidate. I was greatly relieved.

What about Ike? The President still had a warm spot for General Eisenhower, and had Ike run as a Democrat, President Truman would have been delighted. Neither the President nor I realized at the time that Eisenhower had no intention of running as a Democrat because he privately disagreed with much of both the New Deal and the Fair Deal. When Ike finally entered the political arena in January, 1952, it was as a Republican: using Senator Henry Cabot Lodge of Massachusetts as his main intermediary, he made clear both his party preference and his availability for a draft. President Truman felt tricked by Eisenhower's skillful evasions over the years, and he spoke to me of his new distaste for the General. Thus began a deterioration of relations between President Truman and General Eisenhower which was never repaired, and which caused all of us around Mr. Truman much anguish. It was to explode before the end of the 1952 campaign in a particularly ugly manner.

With Vinson uninterested and Eisenhower a Republican, President Truman had no candidate to back. He had told his staff in late 1951 he would not run again, but once Vinson bowed out, the issue was reopened. Vinson, ironically, led the effort to convince him to run again.

I was clear on my own feelings on this issue: I loved President Truman, and I would have done anything he asked me to do. But I did not think it was in either his interest, or the nation's, to seek another term as President. I thought it likely that the tide which he had so brilliantly turned back in 1948 would sweep over him. More important, I felt his Administration had run out of steam. He had led the nation through eight of the most tumultuous years in American history. He was wearier than he knew, and he deserved and needed a rest.

On February 18, 1952, President Truman invited six advisers—Fred Vinson, Sam Rosenman, Bill Hassett, Charles Murphy, John Steelman, and me—to a dinner meeting that lasted until almost midnight. Vinson began with a strong statement that the President should run again: while he did not believe in the theory of the "indispensable man," Vinson said, he did not see how he could refuse another term. Rosenman said much the same thing. Murphy and I disagreed, and suggested that the Democratic party should start looking for other candidates.

In March, the President went to Key West to rest and make a final decision. On the morning of March 21, apparently on an impulse, he called me from a telephone on the beach, and asked if I could join him immediately. I left by plane for Miami, then drove through the night, arriving in Key West at 2 A.M. The next morning, we had breakfast together, walked to the beach, and went through the usual ritual of volleyball, swimming, and relaxation. Early on the afternoon of March 23, President Truman and I sat down alone in the gardens behind the Little White House. Without permission, his name had been placed on the New Hampshire primary ballot, and he had been beaten handily by Senator Estes Kefauver of Tennessee. I warned him that the longer he waited, the harder it would be for any other Democrat to mount an effective effort against Kefauver, whom the President neither liked nor respected. And the longer he waited, the weaker the party would be—whomever they nominated—in the November election. Furthermore, I argued, he risked weakening himself in his remaining months in office if he left his status unclear. I told him frankly I hoped he would withdraw his name from contention as soon as possible.

President Truman was concerned about the effect his withdrawal would have on the war in Korea—to which I pointed out that the war's course had long been established. He then said that he would make a withdrawal announcement at the next appropriate opportunity, and enjoined me to silence. He talked about the possibility of running for the Senate from Missouri after leaving the White House, an idea that I found intriguing.

(Mrs. Truman squashed that idea the moment he raised it with her: she wanted to return, once and for all, to Missouri.)

The next morning, my mission completed, I flew back to Washington. Six days later, on March 29, 1952, the President wrote a surprise ending into a speech he was to deliver at a Jefferson-Jackson Day dinner:

> I shall not be a candidate for reelection. I have served my country long and, I think, efficiently and honestly. I shall not accept a renomination.

The parallels to the withdrawal of Lyndon Johnson, exactly sixteen years and two days later, would be striking. Both men inherited the Presidency, and left office during an Asian war that was dividing the country, after suffering a political setback in New Hampshire. And both men made the right decision.

THE 1952 CAMPAIGN

With President Truman out of the race, the search for a Democratic nominee accelerated. There were several Democrats who wanted the nomination, but each of them carried some disabling liability. Alben Barkley, at seventy-four, seemed too old. Averell Harriman wanted to be President, but, never having run for public office, he had neither a national base nor practical political experience.* Kefauver was distrusted by party regulars and labor for both personal and professional reasons. Robert Kerr, whom I would accompany to the Democratic Convention in Chicago, still hoped for the nomination, but he had no real chance of getting it; my assistance to him was more in the nature of meeting an obligation to a friend rather than a commitment to a viable candidate.

The strongest Democrat now available seemed to be the Governor of Illinois, Adlai Stevenson. President Truman spent some time in the early months of 1952 trying to persuade Stevenson to run—but after each meeting his opinion of the Governor declined. President Truman was plainspoken and direct, a nineteenth-century man of strong and simple values. Stevenson was almost the exact opposite: wealthy, divorced, cosmopolitan, elegant, even eloquent. The more the President pressed Stevenson, the more frustrated he became with Stevenson's elusiveness. I thought I saw in the Governor's style a deliberate pattern: he enjoyed the chase, and the leisurely, self-indulgent, slightly self-satisfied attitude that came as others told him what a fine President he would make. For President Truman, though, this act wore thin rather quickly, and it was

*He later became Governor of New York.

to lead to a lifelong feeling on his part that Stevenson was simply too weak and indecisive to be President. I had more respect for Stevenson's intellect than President Truman did—but, like my old boss, I became frustrated with a man who insisted on playing Hamlet in the face of such great issues. In normal circumstances, Stevenson's ambivalence would have denied him the nomination, but 1952 did not thrust up a natural candidate.

The race for the 1952 Democratic nomination was an exception to my general experience. Normally, the Presidential nomination goes to those who single-mindedly seek it, without ambivalence or uncertainty. Those who tiptoe up to the race, who temporize or agonize about it, are invariably left in the dust by those who pursue it without hesitation. Hence the triumphs of such otherwise dissimilar men as John F. Kennedy, Jimmy Carter, Richard Nixon, Ronald Reagan, and George Bush—all of whom focused obsessively on the great prize for years. By contrast, American politics is littered with the bones of men hailed by Washington as future Presidents, but who were not ready to make the enormous personal sacrifices necessary to stay the course.

When the convention opened in Chicago in July, President Truman announced he would back Vice President Barkley. He simultaneously blessed Averell Harriman's entry into the race as a favorite son from New York—both actions designed to stop Kefauver. But the labor union bosses eliminated Barkley as a candidate, partly because of his age, and Harriman was never a serious possibility. This left Stevenson. In the first and second ballots, Kefauver led Stevenson, with Harriman holding over one hundred delegate votes. President Truman came to Chicago intending to participate in the process, and after discussions with a number of people, he sent Charles Murphy to ask Harriman to withdraw in favor of Stevenson. Harriman promptly did so, thereby assuring Stevenson the nomination.

If President Truman expected Stevenson to be grateful, he was mistaken: Stevenson did not wish to be presented as the choice of President Truman, and he immediately made a series of statements which irritated the President. The President began to resent the way Stevenson was treating him, and talked to me about it several times that summer. Years later, some remarkable letters that he wrote, but never sent, to Stevenson surfaced, showing how angry he was. In one he wrote, "Cowfever could not have treated me any more shabbily than you have."[2]

Fortunately, President Truman's inner anger never became public, and he soon gave public support to Adlai Stevenson, stimulated, in part, by several incidents that were to destroy relations between President Truman and General Eisenhower forever.

The first of these incidents occurred in August, when President Truman offered both candidates a White House briefing from CIA Director Walter Bedell Smith, Eisenhower's former Chief of Staff during World

War II. Eisenhower refused the offer. Deeply offended, President Truman wrote Eisenhower a bitter personal note saying that, in suggesting the meeting, he had merely sought to ensure "a continuing foreign policy. You know that is a fact, because you had a part in outlining it." Rather regretfully, the President closed, "I am extremely sorry that you have allowed a bunch of screwballs to come between us. . . . From a man who has always been your friend and who always wanted to be!"[3] In rejecting the briefing, Eisenhower had been influenced by John Foster Dulles—once again, as in 1948, the senior foreign policy adviser to the Republican candidate.

Most of the time, campaign enmity recedes after elections—such was the case, for example, in the relationship that developed between Jimmy Carter and Gerald Ford in the eighties, as their initial hostility gradually turned into joint projects. But any chance for a postelection reconciliation between Presidents Truman and Eisenhower was doomed forever by the second incident, a dreadful mistake Eisenhower made in early October. For the rest of his life, whenever Ike's name came up in conversations, it was to this incident that President Truman would turn.

Senator Joe McCarthy had attacked General Marshall several times in the previous year, charging him with, among other things, responsibility for the fall of China to the communists. While campaigning by train with the Senator in McCarthy's home state of Wisconsin on October 3, Eisenhower, in deference to McCarthy, deleted from a prepared speech a paragraph praising General Marshall. In the face of continued attacks by McCarthy on Marshall, some delivered in his presence, Eisenhower remained silent.

President Truman's fury at Eisenhower for what he regarded as an act of political cowardice was unrestrained. He felt that Eisenhower owed Marshall, who had chosen him as Supreme Allied Commander in Europe in World War II over many more senior Generals, a special loyalty. When Eisenhower failed to stand up for his old boss, the President's reaction was immediate: "I never thought the man who is now the Republican candidate would stoop so low" as to abandon his "great friend and benefactor." Had Eisenhower stood up to McCarthy, it might have resulted in McCarthy's defeat in the Senate race, which McCarthy won by far less than Eisenhower's margin in Wisconsin.

EISENHOWER AND THE 1952 NONTRANSITION

The rancor this incident caused also made transition arrangements between the Truman and Eisenhower Administrations difficult, indeed, almost nonexistent. There was virtually no cooperation, nor even serious discussion, between the outgoing and incoming teams. Only one meeting between the President and the President-elect took place, on November 18, and it was marked by what President Truman remembered as Ike's "frozen grimness."

President Truman's feelings about himself and Eisenhower were quite evident in a revealing handwritten letter he wrote me on February 7, 1953, barely two weeks after leaving office. Even a man as modest and unassuming as President Truman can take comfort from evidence that he is still appreciated, and his letter described, in touching detail, the size and enthusiasm of the crowds that greeted his train as he returned to Independence. The affection of ordinary people had moved him most deeply: "You'd thought I was the President instead of an ex." Recounting Mrs. Truman's reaction to the five thousand people who had gathered to welcome him home, he wrote, "Well, the missus said the thirty years of 'hell' was worth such a welcome." He continued,

> Thursday night the Mayor of Independence gave us a welcome home dinner. Seats for 650 and 6500 wanted to come! The mayor said he could have sold ten thousand tickets. . . . The old man [i.e., himself] gave ten minutes of Ozark talk that seemed to please. Had at least a hundred favorable editorials and columns. Why you've never seen such crow eating, feathers and all, in your life. If you gentlemen [the poker players] of the "class in education" don't do something to keep me in practice, I'm going to be an easier mark than ever.

At the end of this letter, President Truman's bitterness toward his successor spilled out again, in a caustic postscript prompted by a wild accusation from some right-wing Republicans that the Democrats had struck a deal with the Chinese communists:

> P.S. What do you think of Gen. Demigod [Eisenhower] now? "Secret Treaties" protecting Mao's China against a horse that can't get up! Oh my! Oh me! O tempore! O mores! Mr. Cicero on Cataline [*sic*].

The lesson of the transfer of Presidential power in 1952 was an important one for me. When John F. Kennedy asked me eight years later to oversee the transition from Eisenhower, my overriding objective was to avoid a repetition of the nontransition of 1952.

EISENHOWER

I had liked Eisenhower. During the years in which we worked together on military unification and other issues, he and Mrs. Eisenhower had come to our house a few times for dinner. On at least one occasion they joined a group of friends around our piano, singing old songs, and once or twice, when Ike was traveling overseas and Marny was at our summer house in Nantucket, I escorted Mamie Eisenhower to Saturday-afternoon parties our mutual friend George Allen gave at Pimlico Racetrack in Maryland.

During our work together on the unification of the armed services, I found Eisenhower a reasonable and thoughtful man. When he was nominated in 1952, I felt that, of all the possible Republican candidates, he was undoubtedly the best. If the Democratic era was going to come to an end, it seemed better to me that it end with Eisenhower than anyone else.

Looking back on the fifties today, I still feel that way. Eisenhower had the stature for the Presidency, both at home and abroad. He was what the nation wanted, and perhaps needed, at that time. He left behind some solid accomplishments—and did not create any major international crises.

Yet I was disappointed with his tenure. Although he was skilled in personal politics, I do not think he ever understood the potential or the dynamics of the Presidency. To be fair, it was unlikely that he would have: he had spent his entire life in the military, and taken little interest in national political issues. I felt he allowed the nation to drift, and that, given his enormous popularity and the capacity it gave him for positive leadership, he took far too passive a stand on several key issues, especially civil rights and McCarthyism.

In any case, we saw relatively little of each other during his Presidency. I shared President Truman's feeling that he had behaved badly during the campaign and afterward, not only toward General Marshall but also toward his predecessor, and we made little effort to maintain contact with each other. He asked me to serve on the Franklin D. Roosevelt Memorial Commission, which was established to consider what permanent memorial should be established in Washington in honor of FDR—but that was my only official involvement with the Eisenhower White House.

17

McCarthy and His -ism

How dangerous is it that this man goes loose!
—HAMLET, IV, iii

In the spring of 1954, as much of the nation was glued to television sets watching one of the first major national events to be carried live on television, the Army-McCarthy hearings, I waited to be called as a witness. Speaking of dark plots spearheaded by "Sanctimonious Stu"—as he referred to Senator Symington—and Symington's "friend . . . Clifford, the chief political advisor of President Truman at the time when they were most vigorously fighting my attempts to expose Communists in the last administration," Senator Joseph McCarthy repeatedly demanded that I be subpoenaed.[1]

But each time the subcommittee met in executive session, Senator McCarthy opposed calling me as a witness. Up to the last day of the hearings, he demanded my appearance in public and opposed it in private. By waiting for the summons that never came, I lost an opportunity to take McCarthy on in public; but, to my immense pride and pleasure, my friend Symington *did* challenge McCarthy, making an important contribution to the termination of a dreadful era. Symington, who had been elected to the Senate from Missouri in 1952, sat on both the Armed Services Committee and the Senate Subcommittee on Investigations—Senator McCarthy's infamous committee. Angered at McCarthy's behavior, especially his wild attacks on the Army, Symington decided to take him on.

To people too young to have lived through the period, McCarthy may not seem so dangerous in retrospect. On old films, his heavy five-o'clock shadow, his nasty, whiny speaking manner, and his frequent interruptions of other Senators on a "point of order" sometimes appear comical. It seems hard to believe that anyone ever took him seriously. One might conclude that he was not a serious person, that his sloppy preparation for battle and reckless personal behavior were not only self-destructive but damaging to the cause to which he professed adherence.

There is some truth in such a description: in appearance and behavior, McCarthy was the kind of demagogic thug whom, in a television age, one hopes to have as an opponent. It is easy to make light of McCarthy today, when even conservatives use the word "McCarthyism" to mean unfair political smear tactics—but the harsh fact, which must never be forgotten, is that until he destroyed himself during the Army-McCarthy hearings, Joe McCarthy literally terrorized Washington and much of the nation. His popularity was growing steadily in the national polls, and the Eisenhower Administration lay passive and supine before his depredations. When McCarthy decided to take on the Army, he had a rating in the polls of 50 percent favorable, 29 percent unfavorable, 21 percent no opinion—very strong numbers for someone so controversial.

Behind McCarthy lurked his chief counsel, Roy Cohn, a cold-blooded, manipulative, and opportunistic man who saw in the Senator a vehicle for his own limitless lust for power. Cohn had serious weaknesses, including his personal life, and was without the slightest sense of ethics or morals—but he was indispensable to McCarthy's success. I often thought, as I watched them, that if McCarthy was ugly, crude, and self-destructive, Cohn was as close to a genuinely evil man as I have ever seen in American political life.

The fifties would be littered with the names of those whose careers had been damaged or destroyed by McCarthy or the score of imitators that he spawned at every level of American society. Throughout the last three years of his term, President Truman looked for ways to stop, or at least slow down, McCarthy. On the evening of February 28, 1951, the President invited me to join a group at Blair House which included several Senators and Attorney General McGrath to discuss what might be done about McCarthy. McGrath said that a "thick and devastating dossier" had been assembled that would blow McCarthy sky high—it even contained details of McCarthy's bedmates over a number of years. Someone suggested that it be leaked to the press.

By chance, the Pulitzer Prize–winning writer John Hersey attended this meeting as background for a magazine article on President Truman. I cannot improve upon Hersey's eyewitness account of the President's reaction:

> The flat of his hand came sharply down on the table. His third person self spoke in outrage: the President wanted no more such talk. Three

pungent comments of Harry Truman's on the proposal that had just been made have stuck in my mind ever since:

> You must not ask the President of the United States to get down in the gutter with a guttersnipe.
>
> Nobody, not even the President, can approach too close to a skunk, in skunk territory, and expect to get anything out of it except a bad smell.
>
> If you think somebody is telling a big lie about you, the only way to answer is with the whole truth.[2]

How different politics has become today, in the age of John Tower and Gary Hart! The line between personal and public behavior has shifted so often that no one can quite define where it is. Whether a liberal or a conservative, a man with the personal behavior of Joe McCarthy would now be mercilessly exposed by the press or his political opponents.

THE LIBERAL DILEMMA

There was great irony in the situation faced by the Truman Administration. Since 1946, we had sought to rally the nation to resist communist expansion. We never felt any need to justify our anticommunism to anyone, least of all to such a mountebank as McCarthy. We knew, and had repeatedly told the nation, that communism was a pernicious and dangerous political force, and we did not need instruction from the likes of Joe McCarthy or J. Edgar Hoover. As liberals, we saw ourselves as the true internationalists, the Americans who best understood the dangers of both communism and fascism, while conservatives, many of whom came out of an isolationist background, saw the world in grossly simplified terms.

At the same time, the "attack of the primitives" left a mark on liberals which survives even today. In their attempt to make anticommunism their exclusive province, the right wing often succeeded in placing anticommunist liberals on the defensive. On the other hand, liberals felt it was intolerable to watch the First Amendment freedoms, the most precious ones bestowed upon us by the Founding Fathers, trampled by know-nothings masquerading as patriots. In the course of defending those freedoms for people whose political views were left wing, liberals often became targets for the "guilt by association" tactics of McCarthy and the far Right. Even today, some right-wing politicians continue the effort, not far removed from original McCarthyism, of deliberately confusing liberals with "leftists" and describing them as "weak on communism," unpatriotic, or worse. I find such tactics contemptible, a departure from normal political give-and-take.

McCARTHY TARGETS THE ARMY

In Eisenhower's first year as President, Joe McCarthy, riding very high, began to aim not simply at leftover targets from the Democratic era, but at the Eisenhower Administration itself. He charged it with "continuing to send perfumed notes [in] the style of the Truman-Acheson regime" and failing to reverse the "shining, whimpering appeasement" of the Democrats. As Eisenhower refused to respond, McCarthy chose still another target: the United States Army.

Only nine years after the end of World War II, most Americans still held the Army in near-heroic regard. It is hard to understand why he and Cohn chose such an uninviting target at a moment when they were riding so high. I believe two factors were dominant: first, the two men had reached such heights of power that they had lost touch with reality; second, they were both deeply, irrationally angry at the Army for failing to give special treatment to a close and special friend of Roy Cohn named G. David Schine, who had been drafted despite their best efforts to prevent it.

McCarthy and Cohn singled out for attack a highly decorated veteran of the Battle of the Bulge, Brigadier General Ralph W. Zwicker, then commanding the Army training center at Camp Kilmer, New Jersey. His alleged misdeed was astonishingly trivial: the promotion, and later the honorable discharge, of an obscure Army Reserve dentist from Queens named Irving Peress. McCarthy and Cohn thought Peress's promotion involved a cover-up of the dentist's earlier membership in a left-wing organization, and they pulled out all the stops to exploit what they viewed as a golden opportunity.

SYMINGTON'S FINEST HOUR

On February 18, McCarthy held a closed hearing of his subcommittee in New York, at which General Zwicker, under orders from the Army, denied the Senator any further information concerning Peress. Raging out of control, McCarthy charged Zwicker with "shielding traitors," adding that he was "not fit to wear that uniform."

Unaware that McCarthy and Cohn were berating General Zwicker in New York at that very moment, Army Chief of Staff Matthew Ridgway and Secretary of the Army Robert T. Stevens called on Symington in his Senate office on February 18. Stevens, an old-line New Jersey Republican from the family that had founded the J. P. Stevens textile company, had been a friend of Symington since they attended Yale together in the twenties. Symington told Stevens and General Ridgway that he was not going to allow McCarthy to try to destroy the armed forces he loved so much. He wanted to let both men know that he was available at any time if he could be of assistance to the Army. "Little did I realize," Stevens said later, "that within twenty-four hours I would take advantage of his offer."[3]

When he heard the next day what McCarthy had subjected Zwicker to, General Ridgway ordered Zwicker not to appear again before McCarthy's subcommittee. Meanwhile, Stevens went to see Symington again; they met alone in the early afternoon on February 19, 1954. When Stuart called me before Stevens arrived to discuss the situation, I urged him to use his personal relationship with Stevens to cut across party lines and create a backlash against McCarthy. But everything depended, I said, on Stevens: Was he ready to stand up to McCarthy, in public if necessary? Symington asked me to stand by in my office in case I could be of help to Stevens.

Everything in Symington's background had prepared him perfectly to play an important role in the confrontation that now loomed between the Army and Joe McCarthy. Stuart had splendid bedrock values and the highest personal integrity; McCarthy had neither. Symington would never compromise those values, and he was willing to slug it out with McCarthy if necessary on a matter of principle. As a former Secretary of the Air Force, Stuart felt a strong personal commitment to the armed services. He believed deeply in the importance of keeping the military out of politics, and hated the way McCarthy was dragging honorable military officers like Zwicker into the political arena.

Stevens arrived in Symington's office, greatly agitated over McCarthy's behavior. "You need a lawyer's advice, Bob," Symington told Stevens. "Let me ask Clark Clifford to join us." A few minutes later, I was in Symington's Senate office with the two men.

Stevens was an extremely pleasant man, but inexperienced in politics. He had never been close to anything like the situation he now faced. The immediate issue confronting Stevens was fairly simple: How should he respond to McCarthy's call for more hearings on communist subversion in the Army? If he stood up to McCarthy without support from the Administration or other Republican Senators, he might be out on a limb; if he did not, the integrity of the institution he was supposed to head would be threatened. He appreciated the support of Democrat Symington, but where were Stevens's fellow Republicans? What did they want him to do? He was deeply confused.

On February 21, 1954, while Symington was visiting American troops in Europe, Stevens came to see me. He said he was under great pressure from the Senate Republicans not to engage in a war with McCarthy. With McCarthy's public support at an all-time high, no one on the Republican side, including President Eisenhower, wanted to take him on.

If McCarthy wanted to hold hearings, they said, Stevens would have to appear.

I reminded Stevens that McCarthy had been conducting an unfair and dishonest campaign against the Army. I felt McCarthy's insistence on hearings provided Stevens a unique opportunity for a direct confrontation with the demagogue. In such a confrontation he could support the Army and at the same time point out how unjust and unfair McCarthy had been. I said McCarthy was vulnerable to such an attack, and I hoped he would take advantage of this opening. He listened with care, and, I thought, reacted well. When he left the office, I felt hopeful, even confident, that he would take a strong position.

Three days later, however, Stevens caved in, under extraordinary pressure. Senator Karl Mundt had summoned him to a secret luncheon with Republican members of the subcommittee, including McCarthy. Vice President Nixon also attended. During this remarkable session, later labeled the "chicken luncheon" by the press, McCarthy pressured Stevens into an agreement to produce for his subcommittee all individuals related to the Peress case, and to make Zwicker available for testimony. After the luncheon, McCarthy boasted publicly that Stevens could not have submitted "more abjectly if he had got down on his knees."

Shaken and near tears, Stevens called to tell me he had felt obliged to agree to appear before the McCarthy subcommittee if requested to do so. I told him I thought he had made a mistake, but, recognizing the immense pressure that he was under, I wished him well and told him I would be available if he needed me.

Left to fend for himself by the White House, Stevens had caved in to inexcusable bullying and badgering by the Republicans. Symington told me later that upon hearing the news reports of his "surrender" Stevens had broken down and cried, and called the White House the next day to say that he wanted to resign. He was talked out of the idea by White House aides who understood that Stevens's departure would only further strengthen McCarthy.

I made no effort to contact Stevens again. My advice would not be useful after he had been bludgeoned by his own party into such ill-conceived concessions. Meanwhile, on March 3, President Eisenhower made a press conference statement in which, while calling for "fair play" in investigations, he never mentioned McCarthy by name, and declared that this was his "last word" on the subject. Sensing Eisenhower's reluctance for combat, McCarthy immediately issued an astonishingly patronizing statement that same day which included the following sentence: "Apparently, the President and I *now* agree on the necessity of getting rid of Communists." At the end of this tumultuous day, it was clear

McCarthy had once again defied President Eisenhower, and in a particularly insulting manner.

On March 11, after days of silent seething, the uniformed leadership of the Army took steps to defend itself, leaking stories that charged McCarthy and Cohn with forty-four separate attempts to obtain special treatment for Cohn's friend, G. David Schine. The next day, claiming he was the target of political blackmail, McCarthy made the most serious miscalculation of his career: he demanded public hearings to settle his differences with the Army. The stage was set for a showdown, which the Senate Minority Leader, Lyndon Johnson, wisely insisted be covered by television.

The hearings opened on April 22, 1954, with a cast of characters destined to take their places in the history of our times. At the outset, McCarthy dominated the hearings, leaving his opponents in despair. I talked to Stuart Symington several times each day, urging him to do whatever was necessary to expose the real Joe McCarthy—crude, vulgar, dishonest, and unfair. Symington agreed; he would challenge McCarthy on every point, and try to reveal his true nature to the American public.

In this task, Stuart was, of course, not alone. Stevens had finally realized that in this fight, only one man—either he or McCarthy—could emerge intact. One decision was to serve Stevens particularly well: the selection as the Army's counsel of a sixty-three-year-old Republican lawyer from Boston named Joseph Welch. As the hearings continued, the verbal battles between Symington and McCarthy increased steadily in intensity. McCarthy charged Symington with using the hearings as a base to run for President, labeled him "an alleged man," and called him "unfit" to serve in the Senate.

McCarthy also tried to bully Stuart into silence. As his messenger, he used the subcommittee's minority counsel, John F. Kennedy's younger brother Robert, who hated Cohn, but had relatively cordial relations with McCarthy. McCarthy gave Bobby Kennedy a message for Symington: "Tell Stu that unless he takes it easy I will put his criminal record on television."

Kennedy had no idea what "criminal record" Stuart Symington might possess, but he delivered the message to Symington, who called me immediately, vastly amused. We decided to explain the facts of this story to Bobby at a breakfast at Stuart's home in Georgetown. Abe Fortas, already one of Washington's most respected lawyers, joined us.

What Stuart told Bobby Kennedy and Fortas was this: Sometime around 1916, when Stuart was still a teenager in Baltimore, he and a few of his friends, all from prominent Baltimore families, had borrowed a neighbor's car for a "joyride" around town. Having had a few beers, the boys did not drive very well, and the car ended up wrapped around a tree. Stuart's father, a stern disciplinarian, wanted the kids to learn a lesson, and he insisted that they go before a judge, who convicted them on a misdemeanor charge and gave them a lecture and a suspended sentence.

That was all there was to it. Symington's opponent in his 1952 Senate race had raised the matter and Stuart had asked me to handle it. After an investigation, we located the owner of the misappropriated car, who, at our request, issued a statement that he had long since forgiven Stuart and the others for a boyish prank. Now Symington told Bobby to tell McCarthy that if he wished to pursue the matter in the hearings, Symington would be delighted to "confess" again to his youthful mistake. Needless to say, nothing more was heard about Stuart's criminal past, and the hearings continued without McCarthy's pathetic threat ever becoming public.

With Symington's "criminal record" out of the picture, McCarthy searched for a new issue, and on June 4, he decided he had found it in my unexplained role in advising Symington and Stevens. That day, my name arose for the first time:

> MCCARTHY: A point of personal privilege, and a very important one. . . . We now find that the man that was advising Mr. Stevens was Mr. Clark Clifford.
>
> SYMINGTON: You didn't mind that. I told you that. You came up and asked me and I told you.
>
> MCCARTHY: . . . In common decency, Mr. Chairman, in common honesty, [Senator Symington] should have given these facts to this committee. He can't conceivably sit here as a fair judge after he has said to Mr. Stevens, "I will get you a top Democrat lawyer."
>
> SYMINGTON: Well, Mr. Chairman, I have listened carefully to this diatribe of the Senator from Wisconsin and in my opinion it is just another diversion. Now, because he brings up the name of Mr. Clark Clifford, a private attorney, I think it is in order for me to say how Mr. Clifford got into my conversations, and I would also like to say—
>
> MCCARTHY: Why don't you say that under oath, Mr. Senator?
>
> SYMINGTON: I will always go under oath for anything I say, because I always tell the truth. As I was saying before being interrupted by that strong voice, Mr. Clark Clifford is my friend. The Secretary of the Army came to me . . . and he asked me for help. . . . He asked me if I knew a good lawyer, and I said, "Yes, I did. I knew some good lawyers." And I recommended to him Mr. Clifford. That is the way he got into this case.

My position from the outset was simple: I would testify if asked to. I told Stuart I would welcome an opportunity to testify, and thought that it might strengthen his own hand by exposing the ludicrousness of McCarthy's position.

When the hearings resumed on June 7, McCarthy asked for the floor. The sharpest exchange of the entire first six weeks of the hearings then occurred:

> MCCARTHY: Mr. Chairman, I would like to now request that the Chair subpoena a witness, a witness whom I consider absolutely essential if we are to present evidence on the Cohn-McCarthy side. . . . The man I want is mentioned on page 5295 of the testimony taken on June 4, mentioned in one of the monitored calls of Mr. Symington. At that time, Mr. Symington was talking to Mr. Stevens as to how Zwicker could be prevented from coming to testify; testify, that is, about who was responsible for the fifth-amendment Communists. He said, "I will get into that with Clifford."
>
> SYMINGTON: A point of order, Mr. Chairman.
>
> MCCARTHY: I will not yield for any point of order.
>
> SYMINGTON: A point of order, Mr. Chairman. . . .
>
> MCCARTHY: Point of order, Mr. Chairman.
>
> CHAIRMAN MUNDT: We will have to go into one point of order at a time.
>
> MCCARTHY: Point of order that this is not a point of order.

I was watching this theater of the absurd on television, along with much of the rest of the nation. If it had not involved me, I might have found it laughable. But I watched with intense interest as the tempers of both Symington and McCarthy flared:

> MCCARTHY: I will not yield to the Senator from Missouri. I know he may be rather uncomfortable—
>
> SYMINGTON: I never was more comfortable in my life, Senator. If you have any point to make, you worry about what you are thinking and not how I feel.
>
> MCCARTHY: . . . We now find that Mr. Symington—and I can't say whether he is running for the presidency or not, many papers say he is, we find—and this is no reflection upon him, that is a right of any American—we find that Mr. Clark Clifford is also the advisor of Mr. Symington, and without the knowledge of this committee, the advisor of the Republican Secretary of the Army. That makes it very important, Mr. Chairman, that we have him here. . . . Clark Clifford, the chief political advisor of

> President Truman—and I assume the chief political advisor of a man who would be President on the Democratic ticket in 1956—is doing the advising [of Stevens], charging Mr. Cohn, Mr. Carr, and myself with almost everything except murdering our great-great grandmother. . . . It may seem very clever to Senator Symington at this time that he got Clark Clifford to mislead a fine, naive, not too brilliant Republican Secretary of the Army. . . . I will ask the Chair tonight to immediately subpoena Clark Clifford. . . .

It was now exactly 5:30 P.M., and a long day of hearings was about to be adjourned. Symington was told by Mundt to answer in two minutes. His friends and family always looked back on his reply to McCarthy as one of the great moments in his career:

> I want you to know from the bottom of my heart that I'm not afraid of anything about you or anything you've got to say any time, any place, anywhere. . . . That is all I have to say tonight, Mr. Chairman, except I believe in America, every bit of me believes in America. You will always find a rotten apple in a barrel, but that doesn't mean that there is anything wrong with the United States of America, and that is the basic difference between the junior Senator from Wisconsin and the junior Senator from Missouri.

Up to that point in the hearings, no one had taken McCarthy on in this manner, and the audience in the packed caucus room erupted in cheers. Senator Mundt gaveled the session closed.

Although Symington had been severely criticized by McCarthy loyalists, he and I felt encouraged by the reaction against McCarthy's behavior. Still, the pressure was immense—he and his wife Evie were the target of obscene and threatening telephone calls.

The next day, June 8, Democratic Senator Henry "Scoop" Jackson made a motion in executive session to call me as a witness; McClellan, the senior Democrat on the subcommittee, seconded the motion. McCarthy replied, "I am going to continue urging that he take the stand." Then, to the astonishment of the Democrats, he proposed and got passed by a straight party vote of 4 to 3 a substitute amendment calling for the subcommittee to stick to its original list of witnesses and *not* to call me to the witness stand!

When the open hearings resumed, Jackson asked for the floor and made public this odd reversal. Symington demanded that Chairman Mundt explain the Republican behavior. Mundt lamely replied that the Republicans wanted to limit the number of witnesses.

And so it went. Hours were consumed in both public and private session with some of the most preposterous posturing that the Senate chamber, no stranger to theater, had ever seen. In the afternoon session on June 8, McCarthy called Symington "Sanctimonious Stu," at which point Symington, both amused and indignant at the same time, objected and suggested that McCarthy go to a psychiatrist.

Stuart and I met late that evening at my house. I considered issuing a statement simply stating that I was available as a witness, but decided that, since this was self-evident and had been asserted in the hearing by Symington, it would look like self-promotion. We decided to wait, since both Stuart and I still assumed I would be called.

The charade continued: the next day, Senator McClellan repeated that it was unfair not to ask me to testify after dragging my name into the proceedings. Again, the Republicans found reasons to object.

I realized it was quite possible I would not be called after all. In such circumstances both Stuart and I felt it was important to explain clearly what had actually transpired between the two of us and Stevens. On June 10, Symington asked to speak in executive session and gave a lengthy explanation of the events that had brought me into the situation. Stuart explained that when Stevens asked for the name of a good lawyer, Symington had first suggested William Rogers, a Republican who would later become Eisenhower's Attorney General (and years later, Nixon's first Secretary of State). When Rogers was unavailable, Stuart said, "I suggested, to my now great personal regret, my friend and my personal lawyer, Mr. Clifford." Symington added that the situation had caused me "unfavorable publicity," and stated again that I was "entirely available at any time."

On June 17, Mundt's gavel closed the Army-McCarthy hearings. Everyone, myself included, had become bored with the repetitious and fruitless argument over my role, but it had contributed to the picture of McCarthy as a bullying and tendentious person—a picture that had been fixed forever in the minds of Americans when Joseph Welch had asked him the famous question, "At long last, have you left no sense of decency?"

The Army-McCarthy hearings were one of the most appalling, sloppiest, and worst-conducted events in the long history of the United States Congress. Senator McClellan called them "deplorable, . . . one of the most disgraceful episodes in the history of our government." I agreed completely with him, but, at the same time, the hearings had served a vital, higher purpose, which was not apparent on the day they ended.

The hearings marked the end of Joseph McCarthy as a political force in America. Republicans, even conservatives, now found him an embarrassment, and avoided him, both personally and politically. Roy Cohn left the Senator's service that summer, leaving him without the man on whom he had become almost totally dependent.

On December 2, 1954, the Senate passed a resolution which "condemned" McCarthy's behavior as having been "contrary to senatorial ethics" and designed to "obstruct the constitutional processes of the Senate and to impair its dignity." Within three years McCarthy was dead, having literally drunk himself to death.

Symington, true to his character, never saw the battle with McCarthy as a personal vendetta. He never felt personally hostile toward the Senator, despite the harsh words they had exchanged at the hearings. As McCarthy slid toward oblivion in his last years in the Senate, Symington even found time for a gracious gesture toward Joe's wife, Jean McCarthy. One day, when he saw her enter a hearing room looking for her husband, Stuart stopped the hearing, got up, and escorted her to a seat. That evening, he received an unexpected call at home from Joe McCarthy, thanking him for the courtesy shown earlier that day toward his wife. Then McCarthy surprised Stuart by asking if the Symingtons would join the McCarthys for a barbecue dinner some time. I am not sure whether or not Stuart would have accepted the invitation out of sympathy for McCarthy's personal decline, but Evie Symington ended the issue swiftly: under no circumstances would she dine with Joe McCarthy.

Part VI

JOHN F. KENNEDY

18

The Beginning, 1957–1960

The first observation I would add to the enormous amount written about John F. Kennedy is that while he was alive no one imagined that he would, after his death, become a mythical figure in American culture and history.

When we first met he was a young man of immense charm and political promise, the son of an overbearing, and to my mind, dictatorial, father. First we were acquaintances, then I was his lawyer, and finally, as a result of all we went through together, Jack Kennedy and I became friends.

As our relationship developed, Kennedy called on me for advice on a broad range of political, governmental, and personal matters. I knew Kennedy well, and I think I understood his character. As his lawyer, I saw him in situations of extraordinary professional and personal stress, and nothing that I ever encountered or learned made me question his fitness or capacity to be a superb President. In some of the matters I handled for him, the constraints imposed by the lawyer-client relationship still apply today. Like matters concerning other clients on which I feel similarly constrained, they will not be discussed in this work.

When I think of Jack Kennedy today, I remember first his incomparable grace. This rare quality, hard to define but easy to recognize, was undoubtedly innate, but he enhanced it through his great political skills. He knew how to win friends and charm people as well as anyone who has ever practiced the art. But behind his appeal and elegance lay a very retentive mind, a quick intellect, and a pragmatic and useful cynicism regarding events and people. Unlike most politicians, he did not respond well to the excessive and empty flattery that is such a large part of normal political intercourse, and he looked for deft ways to deflate or deflect it. His wit, much of it highly sardonic, was justly celebrated.

Another quality, equally important, has been less remarked upon: his ability to approach events, even those directly involving himself, with both an uncommon objectivity and something rare and valuable in politicians—a sense of irony. He brought more genuine intellectual curiosity into decision making than any other President I have known, perhaps more than any other President in this century. Where Harry Truman usually reacted spontaneously and Lyndon Johnson, Richard Nixon, Jimmy Carter, and George Bush personalized almost every situation, Kennedy approached people and decisions with cool detachment and calculation. Where both Presidents Johnson and Nixon took North Vietnamese attacks on Americans as personal challenges, for example, President Kennedy saw such events as part of the dangerous game of international power politics; something to respond to, but not to take personally.

Kennedy was unusually successful in maintaining objectivity under pressure. I felt at times that, as he dealt with personal or professional crises, he was able to step away from himself and look at a problem as though it involved someone else. Sometimes, watching him during a discussion on some contentious issue, I felt as if his mind had left his body and was observing the proceedings with a detached, almost amused air. Something within him seemed to be saying, "This may seem supremely, even transcendently important right now, but will it matter in fifty years? In one year? I must not permit myself to become involved to the point where my judgment is suspect."

This attitude may also have run through his personal relationships. Between him and the large number of men and women who were devoted to him and considered themselves to be his special friend, I believe there was a deeply impersonal factor at work. Perhaps this was no more than a protective layer accumulated as a result of the unusual difficulties in his early life—his older brother's death in World War II, his own near death in the Solomon Islands and his recurring medical problems, the death of one older sister in an airplane crash and the mental retardation of another, the influence of his cynical and power-hungry father—but (aside from his unique relationship with his brother Bobby) I felt he kept a very tight rein on his personal emotions, enjoying immensely the company of many people from all walks of life, but never allowing intimacies to go beyond a certain point, and never losing control of his own emotions.

WHAT SHOULD A VICE PRESIDENT DO?

After he entered the House of Representatives in 1946, I met Jack Kennedy socially on many occasions—but while we were friendly, we were not close. This was probably my fault: in the forties and fifties I associated him with his father, whose public opposition to the Truman Doctrine had offended me and struck me as particularly inappropriate for a former ambassador to the United Kingdom.

By coincidence, Marny had a slight acquaintanceship with Jack Kennedy's maternal grandfather, John "Honey Fitz" Fitzgerald, the first Irish-American Mayor of Boston. In about 1924 on a vacation from boarding school, she was visiting friends in Palm Beach. One evening she went to a dinner at a local club where the legendary Honey Fitz was her dinner partner. Asked by some of the guests, as he frequently was, to sing his theme song, "Sweet Adeline," he turned to Marny and asked her if she could sing. When she answered yes, a little, he told her to stand up because, he said, "I don't like to sing alone." Surprised but willing, Marny stood and joined Honey Fitz in a rendition of the song with which he was so identified.

In January 1956, Kennedy and I had our first extended professional contact, over an issue that had always interested me—the role of the Vice President. I was asked to testify on the subject before the Senate Subcommittee on Reorganization. There was irony in the fact that I was finally testifying before the committee whose summons I had awaited in vain two years earlier during the Army-McCarthy hearings—but this time the Democrats controlled the Senate, and the man in the chair was the junior Senator from Massachusetts, John F. Kennedy.

My testimony was a direct response to that of former President Herbert Hoover, who had recommended the establishment of a new position—Administrative Vice President of the United States—to help the President run the government. It was characteristic of this good and conscientious man, who had never understood politics, that he would make such a well-intentioned but unworkable proposal, one that would have fundamentally changed the nature of the executive branch, in effect creating an American version of a prime minister and weakening the Presidency. President Truman immediately wrote Senator Kennedy a letter objecting to Hoover's proposal. This placed the only two ex-Presidents then alive in open disagreement. President Eisenhower sent the Senate a deliberately ambiguous message that, while he did not need such a position, he would have "no objection if the Congress should decide to make such an office available to the President for his use."[1]

I objected strongly to Hoover's suggestion, and recommended instead that the Vice President be given greater standing and specific responsibilities within the executive branch, in order to reduce the work load on the President and prepare the Vice President for the Presidency. At that time, the Vice President played almost no part in the operations of the executive branch, spending most of his time on the Hill in his capacity as President of the Senate, and otherwise doing very little. I suggested that additional duties for the Vice President would result in "a great deal more thought [being] given to the selection of the Vice President . . . than has been given in the past."[2]

Senator Kennedy showed substantial interest in the hearings. Symington, who liked Kennedy, told me that while his father, Joseph P. Kennedy, was the dominant force in family affairs, Jack Kennedy thought for himself and reached his own conclusions on political and international issues. That he was intelligent and had a promising future seemed clear, although if I had been asked I would surely have said that, because of his religion, it was very unlikely that he could reach the Presidency. Up to that time, Catholicism had been an absolute block to Presidential ambitions. In any case, at thirty-nine, he seemed far too young for national office.

PROFILES IN COURAGE

On Monday morning, December 9, 1957, Kennedy called and asked to see me immediately. When he arrived, very unhappy, he said he needed immediate assistance. "Did you see *The Mike Wallace Interview* Saturday night?" he asked. When I told him that I had not, he described to me an exchange between Wallace, whose program, broadcast nationally on ABC, had already established him as America's leading television interviewer, and Drew Pearson, the most widely read political columnist of his time. The following discussion had taken place:

> PEARSON: Jack Kennedy is . . . the only man in history that I know who won a Pulitzer Prize on a book which was ghost written for him, which indicates the kind of public-relations buildup he's had.
>
> WALLACE: Do you know for a fact, Drew—
>
> PEARSON: [*speaking over Wallace*] Yes, I do—
>
> WALLACE: . . . that the book, *Profiles in Courage,* was written for Senator Kennedy—
>
> PEARSON: I do.
>
> WALLACE: . . . by somebody else—and he has never acknowledged the fact?
>
> PEARSON: No, he has not. You know, there's a little wisecrack around the Senate about Jack, who is a very handsome man, as you know. Some of his colleagues say, "Jack, I wish you had a little bit less profile and more courage."

Kennedy had come to me, he said, with the full knowledge and concurrence of his father, who was even angrier than he was. "I cannot let this stand," he said. "It is a direct attack on my integrity and my honesty." If Pearson's charge was not dealt with, Kennedy could see further consequences, including a possible withdrawal of the Pulitzer Prize.

I replied that he could sue Wallace, Pearson, and ABC for libel or slander. But that would be a lengthy process, with court proceedings and substantial publicity—which in itself could be damaging to him. The best solution, I said, would be to obtain a quick retraction from everyone involved, before the story grew and developed a life of its own.

Kennedy asked me to represent him with ABC. As we were discussing how to proceed, the telephone rang. It was Ambassador Kennedy, who, either by prearrangement or coincidence, had found his son in my office. I could hear the old man screaming at Jack. Very calmly, Kennedy said, "I will let you talk to Clark, Father."

I got on the telephone. Before I could even say hello, Joe Kennedy said: "I want you to sue the bastards for fifty million dollars. Get it started right away. It's dishonest and they know it. My boy wrote the book. This is a plot against us."

"Mr. Ambassador," I said, "I am preparing at this moment to go to New York and sit down with the people at ABC."

"Sit down with them, hell! Sue them, that is what you have to do, sue them!" he shouted into my ear. His son watched me with a faint air of amusement.

"Well," I said, "we may have to do that, but first we want to try to see if there isn't some other solution."

This did not soothe Joe Kennedy. He continued to demand that we sue ABC, Pearson, Wallace, and anyone else in sight. But watching Jack Kennedy's calm countenance, I could see that he understood the desirability of a more restrained course of action. When I got off the telephone, he said to me, "Well, that's just Dad. Let's deal with this thing."

I asked Jack to assemble everything that he could find concerning the writing of *Profiles in Courage*—handwritten notes, notebooks, records, comments by anyone who had seen him working on the book. After he left, I set up a meeting with Leonard Goldenson, the Chairman of ABC, for Thursday, December 12, in New York.

The materials we needed to deal with ABC were assembled by a young man I had not met before, Kennedy's closest aide and adviser, Theodore C. Sorensen. One of the most thorough and precise men I ever met, he did a splendid job of collecting every scrap of paper that could be located on such short notice, plus a list of possible witnesses who had observed Kennedy working on the manuscript.

Major snowstorms tied up all airplane traffic along the Eastern corridor between New York and Washington the next day. In order to assure that I reached the ABC offices on time, I took a slow, much-delayed train to New York the afternoon before the meeting, arriving to find the city paralyzed. In the middle of the snowstorm, with the temperature dropping below zero, the worst subway strike in New York's history and wildcat bus strikes had converted Manhattan into one enormous traffic jam. I stayed at a hotel near ABC's headquarters, and the next morning slogged through the city streets to ABC. Sorensen stood by at the hotel, in case he was needed, while Kennedy and I plunged into a lengthy and difficult day of meetings at ABC. We had agreed we would stay there as long as necessary to get what we needed.

Many people have observed that one of the few matters on which one could never joke with John F. Kennedy was the question of the authorship of *Profiles in Courage.* In the face of ABC's attempt to back up Pearson, Kennedy remained outwardly cool, but he was still angry. We met first with Goldenson, who passed us on to his lawyers and other officials at ABC. Mike Wallace was noticeably absent. We produced portions of Senator Kennedy's handwritten drafts, plus statements from the editor of the book, Evan Thomas, who said he "personally saw Mr. Kennedy writing parts of the manuscript in longhand while in the hospital," and Arthur Krock, who had seen Kennedy in Palm Beach "lying flat on his back on a board with a yellow pad on which he was writing the book, and had read enough of those pages at the time to know that the product was his own." I insisted that ABC issue a retraction the following Saturday on Mike Wallace's program.

In our presence, the ABC executives and lawyers called Drew Pearson. Although he had been unable to recall the name of the "ghostwriter" on the air the previous Saturday, Pearson now remembered it clearly. Theodore Sorensen, he said, had written *Profiles in Courage.* We were, of course, fully prepared for this charge, and pointed out that in the preface of the book, Kennedy had acknowledged his "greatest debt" to his "research associate, Theodore C. Sorensen, for his invaluable assistance in the assembly and preparation of the material upon which this book is based." Kennedy also admitted that the publisher had paid royalties totaling six thousand dollars directly to Sorensen, but I stressed that this did not constitute an admission that Sorensen had written the book.

I offered to have Sorensen furnish a sworn statement that he was not the author of the book. ABC asked first to interrogate Sorensen, who rushed to ABC from the hotel, and, well prepared, rebutted efforts by ABC's lawyers to break down his story.

We had reached the moment that occurs in any serious confrontation, when each side has to decide if the other is bluffing. Many negotiations have broken down in misunderstanding because of imprecision at this moment. We sensed that ABC was not happy with the bind in which Drew Pearson had placed them; after all, it was not their correspondent who had made the statement, nor could anyone at ABC prove it, even if they believed it to be true. ABC wanted, if possible, to avoid both a retraction and a lawsuit; obviously, that would not satisfy Kennedy.

I made our offer: in return for a complete retraction and apology at the beginning of the next Mike Wallace show, Senator Kennedy would drop all further claims against ABC, Mike Wallace, and ABC's advertisers arising out of the interview. We would deal with Drew Pearson separately, and not hold ABC responsible for his behavior. If ABC did not accept our offer, we would be obliged to start legal proceedings.

The ABC officials and their lawyers withdrew to discuss our offer, and presumably to consult Goldenson. After a considerable time they returned with the news we wanted to hear: they had accepted our offer. I wrote out in longhand the statement that we wanted read on the air, which ABC accepted later in the day with only minor changes. ABC's lawyers prepared a document renouncing all claims against them, which I signed for Kennedy.

At the beginning of *The Mike Wallace Interview* Saturday evening, December 14, Oliver Trayz, an ABC vice president, read my statement:

> This company has inquired into the charge made by Mr. Pearson and has satisfied itself that such charge is unfounded and that the book in question was written by Senator Kennedy. We deeply regret this error and feel it does a grave injustice to a distinguished public servant and author and to the excellent book he wrote, and to the worthy prize that he was awarded. We extend our sincere apologies to Senator Kennedy, his publishers, and the Pulitzer Prize Committee.

Mike Wallace himself continued to object to ABC's agreement with Kennedy and disassociated himself from the apology. Almost thirty years later, he still felt that it "was a craven gesture and an insult to Pearson." ABC, he said, should have had the "fortitude to call [Kennedy's] bluff."[3] Looking back on this incident today, one can see how much television has changed: a retraction with such strong wording would be almost inconceivable, and any retraction or correction at all by the major networks would be far more difficult to obtain.

I suggested to Kennedy that, after things cooled down a bit, he invite Pearson to his office for a private chat to see if he could take the venom out of Pearson's dangerous and influential sting. Pearson's diary entry for the meeting, which took place January 14, 1958, gave a fine picture of the impact of John F. Kennedy's dazzling personality and charm on even a cynical journalist:

> Talked to [Kennedy] for about an hour. He showed me his original notes, and unquestionably he did conceive the idea of his book *Profiles in Courage*. . . . Sometimes I'm a sucker for a nice guy who presents an appealing story. He didn't ask for a retraction, but I think I shall give him one. He got a whale of a lot of help on his book. I'm still dubious as to whether he wrote too much of it in the final draft himself. . . . But he also showed enough knowledge of the book, had lived with the book, made the book so much a part of him, that basically it *is* his book. . . . "Ted [Sorensen] did an awful lot of work," he said.[4]

Pearson's final judgment as to where the credit lies for the book was, in my opinion, pretty close to the mark. Kennedy had help, and plenty of it—but the book was his.

True to his word, Pearson inserted a small item in his column about a month later crediting Kennedy with authorship of the book. Kennedy was delighted, and even his father indicated later that we had followed the right course—which was as close as the old man ever came to an admission of error. The Kennedys commented afterward that they were particularly grateful that I had fought the poor weather to get to New York.

This success on his behalf changed my relationship with Kennedy, and he soon told me privately why he and his father had pursued ABC with such unusual vigor. He had, he said, definitely decided to seek the 1960 Democratic nomination, and he felt that if the question of authorship of his book were not laid to rest immediately he would have to deal with it continually during the campaign. "It could have destroyed my candidacy," he said.

THE GRIDIRON DINNER

Only weeks later, I received a letter from Jack Kennedy with what seemed to be an oddly urgent tone for a seemingly minor request:

> While I am reluctant to add to your burdens, I would be most grateful for a personal favor you are uniquely qualified to perform. I am slated to give the Democratic address at the Gridiron Club next month. Not only did I hear some years back about the excellence of your address to the club, but I have been advised by several members to seek your assistance as Washington's best wise-crack artist. . . .

Those not familiar with Washington might be surprised at the importance that Kennedy attached to the Gridiron Dinner. Other events, such as the annual White House Correspondents Dinner, compete for similar guests and prestige, but the Gridiron Dinner stood, and still stands, as the most important single testing ground for politicians. In this off-the-record setting, before a large number of journalists, other politicians, and businessmen from around the nation, politicians have often found ways to establish or reshape their images or reputations. Kennedy viewed the 1958 Gridiron speech as, in effect, his launching pad into Presidential politics.

Having weathered the embarrassment of the 1947 skit that had portrayed President Truman in such unflattering terms, I had been asked to speak on behalf of the Democrats at the members' dinner at the club in December 1955. It was this speech to which Kennedy referred in his letter. Among the lines at that dinner was one that has survived and is quoted from time to time by chroniclers of the Gridiron tradition: my teasing rebuttal of its traditional boast that "the Gridiron glows, but it never burns."

"I have heard that statement many times but I still don't believe it," I said. "The Gridiron glows, but it never burns—any member of the Gridiron Club. Year after year, I have seen more casualties carried out of this hotel than occurred during the Great Fire of London."

The intense preparations for Kennedy's appearance indicated the way he would approach the 1960 campaign. For weeks in advance Ted Sorensen gathered ideas from Kennedy's Gridiron "team." We even held meetings to analyze various jokes. At one session, Sorensen kept a careful running scorecard as five of us—Fletcher Knebel of *The Minneapolis Tribune,* Marquis Childs of the *St. Louis Post-Dispatch,* Senator Kennedy, his father, and I—voted on each of 112—yes, 112!—jokes and humorous suggestions. Our session, combining hilarity and fatigue in almost equal measures, went on for hours. And at the center of it all was the young Senator, just forty years old, amused and detached on one hand, totally intense and focused on the other. He knew how bizarre these Washington rituals were; but he also knew how important for him this one was going to be.

Finally, the great evening arrived—March 15, 1958. Almost everyone in official or journalistic Washington was there, with the exception of President Eisenhower, who hated the Gridiron Dinners and in his second term saw no reason to subject himself to any more of them. Kennedy's opening line was a classic that became part of his legend. His father had been lampooned in the preceding sketch as planning to buy the election for his son. Reaching into his breast pocket, he read a "telegram" that he said he had just received from his "generous Daddy": "Dear Jack," it read, "Don't buy a single vote more than is necessary—I'll be damned if I'm going to pay for a landslide."

Although Gridiron Dinner speeches are off-the-record, this joke was widely printed around the nation within days. Authorship for jokes is a particularly tricky matter, but my memory is that this one had originated with Sorensen.

Few political jokes last very long, but one contribution of mine that Kennedy used that night was remembered for a while, especially by Senator Lyndon Johnson:

> I dreamed about 1960 the other night, and I told Stuart Symington and Lyndon Johnson about it yesterday. I told them how the Lord came into my bedroom, anointed my head, and said, "John Kennedy, I hereby anoint you President of the United States." Stu Symington said, "That's strange, Jack, because I had a similar dream last night in which the Lord anointed me President of the United States *and* outer space." Then Lyndon Johnson said, "That's very interesting, gentlemen, because I, too, had a similar dream last night—and I don't remember anointing either one of you!"

Watching the enthralled reaction of the Gridiron audience that night, I knew a new star had begun to rise in Washington.

SYMINGTON AND KENNEDY

I have been told that supporting Stuart Symington over Jack Kennedy for the Democratic nomination in 1960 was the biggest political mistake of my career[5]—but I never felt that way. Stuart Symington had been my friend for twenty-five years, and when he asked for my support, I never hesitated.

At the end of 1958, after winning reelection to the Senate by a stunning margin, Stuart began thinking seriously about the 1960 Presidential election. He and his wife Evie joined us for dinner one night in January, 1959, and afterward, Stuart and I talked well past midnight. The evening was exploratory for both of us, but I stressed that there was nothing easy about a campaign for the Presidency, and that it would require a total commitment from both him and his wife beyond anything with which either of them was familiar. I was thinking of the nightmares I had endured during the whistle-stop campaign of 1948.

Stuart gradually expanded the circle of people consulted until eight of us—all with Missouri roots—were involved. We took preliminary soundings around the country, and discovered that while Stuart Symington was well liked by those who had heard of him, he was relatively unknown outside Missouri, despite the brief flurry of the Army-McCarthy hearings. To the extent he was recognized, Symington was regarded as a one-issue man. Ever since his days as the first Secretary of the Air Force, Symington had been viewed by many as the "Big Bomber Boy."

On Sunday, September 6, 1959, Symington and his senior advisers met at my house. We outlined the difficulties of his candidacy, but added that no one appeared to have a lock on the 1960 Democratic nomination. A deadlock between Kennedy, Humphrey, and Johnson was a distinct possibility, and if Symington were part of that game, he could well end up as the nominee.

Everyone liked Stuart, but he was not the sort of person who commanded intense loyalty, like Kennedy, or controlled people through raw power, like Johnson. Traveling around the country, he found most people wishing him well, telling him that he had a lot of unfocused secondary support, and offering to back him if the front-runners faltered or deadlocked. Thus developed the phrase that hung around Stuart's neck, for better or worse, throughout the campaign: "everybody's second choice."

While Stuart's many attractive qualities combined to make him one of the most appealing politicians of his time, Theodore H. White's assessment of the Symington campaign in his classic *The Making of the President 1960* had more truth to it than I would have liked to admit at the time:

> Deep, deep, in the approach of Symington's managers was a conviction—almost naive for such seasoned politicians—that ability alone could sell a man for the Presidency. The kind of ability Symington possesses is caviar to the general; his is a personality that either in Germany or in Britain guarantees a brilliant parliamentary career but that in the brawl of American politics usually fails. . . . Since Symington could hope for a friendly audience from the power brokers and friendly appreciation of his abilities through the intercession of Harry Truman; and since, further, his hope lay in a deadlocked Convention; and since, even further, at the Convention he must emerge as the compromise candidate with the acquiescence of his rivals, the bitter fratricidal war of the primaries was a condition he must avoid. Thus Symington and Clifford in the summer of 1959.[6]

Given my growing friendship with Kennedy, I knew that sooner or later I would be faced with a difficult choice between two men I liked a great deal—three, in fact, if Lyndon Johnson were also a candidate, as seemed probable. Finally, in the summer of 1959, Kennedy asked if I would support his bid for the Democratic Presidential nomination. "Jack," I replied, "I respect you and I believe you would make an excellent President. But I have been a friend of Stu Symington's for twenty-five years. If he does run, and I think he will, I am bound to him by our friendship. If he does not run, then I will be more than delighted to support you."

Kennedy's reply, graceful as usual, endeared him to me for life: "I understand entirely. If you and Stu have known each other for twenty-five years, I would not think you were much of a friend if you didn't support him. I would expect the same from my friends."

The most remarkable aspect of this incident was that Kennedy continued to use me as his personal lawyer after he knew I was supporting Symington. For his part, Stuart was aware of my lawyer-client relationship with Kennedy but never once questioned me about it. This curious conjunction of relationships—in which I supported one man for the Presidency while acting as lawyer to one of his rivals—remains one of the most unusual experiences of my sixty years before the bar.

On July 1, 1960, shortly before the convention, Kennedy asked me to have breakfast with him at his Georgetown house. By this time he was close to the nomination, but he was concerned that if he failed to win on the first ballot, he would gradually lose support to other candidates. Lyndon Johnson was now in the fight, and there was a growing effort by liberals, led by Eleanor Roosevelt, to resurrect their sentimental favorite from 1952 and 1956, Adlai Stevenson.

Kennedy told me that his own delegate count showed him with about 600 delegates, out of the 761 needed for the nomination. The delegates Symington controlled—by most counts, between 100 and 150—could put him near or over the top. Would Stuart, Kennedy asked, withdraw before the first ballot and support Kennedy?

Kennedy went on: "Stuart has run a clean and decent campaign, and I'd like to talk with you about having him on the ticket." This did not amount to an offer, and, under the circumstances, it sounded more like the baiting of a hook than a real proposal. Kennedy then settled back, as though he had all the time in the world, and asked me to describe the way that President Truman had won, against all odds, in 1948. It was Kennedy at his charming, intellectually curious best.

After speaking to Stuart, I gave Kennedy Symington's formal reply: as long as there was still a chance of a deadlock, Symington was not ready to walk away from the fight. "Stuart knows he is not going to be nominated on the first ballot," I said, "but he believes he has strong secondary strength among delegates who will switch to him if no one wins on the first ballot. He also feels obligated to his supporters to have his name put before the convention. That is Senator Symington's strategy, and I think it is a good one."

Kennedy smiled. "It is not only a good strategy, it is his *only* strategy," he said. "Nonetheless, I would appreciate it if you and he would continue to consider what I said, because with his strength, I think I can make it on the first ballot."

Symington and I politely ignored the talk of the Vice Presidency; we assumed that Kennedy was dangling the same bait in front of others as well.

19

The 1960 Campaign

This race is a contest between the comfortable and the concerned, between those who believe that we should rest and lie at anchor and drift, and between those who want to move this country forward. . . . War and peace, the progress of our children, jobs for men and women who want to work, the development of our resources—the symbolic feeling of a nation, the image the nation presents to the world, its power, prestige and direction—all ultimately will come to rest on the next President of the United States. . . . I run for the Presidency because it is the center of action. . . .

JOHN F. KENNEDY,
BOSTON, NOVEMBER 7, 1960

The Democrats gathered in Los Angeles on July 11, 1960, to pick the next President of the United States. As Marny and I moved into a suite at the Biltmore Hotel next to the Symingtons and one floor above Senate Majority Leader Lyndon Johnson, I felt a sense of excitement at the prospect of a new era in American politics. What united everyone at the convention was a dislike of Richard Nixon and the desire to restore the Democrats to power. But doubts persisted about the front-runner, Senator John F. Kennedy; some thought him too young, some feared his religion, and others worried that he was not a true liberal.

Stuart Symington's inner circle understood by the eve of the convention that his only chance for the nomination—a deadlocked convention—was becoming more and more remote as Kennedy's efficient forces picked up delegates. Lyndon Johnson also had more delegates than Symington; although his chances for the nomination seemed slim because of Northern and Western opposition, he was playing a much tougher hand in Los Angeles than Symington. I had the impression that, in an effort to slow Kennedy down, Johnson was secretly encouraging Adlai Stevenson.

In American politics the great prize usually goes to those who will subordinate every other consideration to its pursuit. Once a politician has reached the Senate or other high office, he inevitably begins to hear—from his old friends, from acquaintances, from sycophants—that he would make a fine President. This is music to any politician's ears, but it conceals a dangerous virus not yet identified by the medical profession—the Presidential bug. Watching politicians caught in its grip, I have often thought that this ailment has but one cure—embalming fluid.

But Stuart Symington was remarkably free of that virus. I believe that in his heart of hearts, he never craved the Presidency the way so many others do. To be sure, he wanted to be President, but he was not willing to go to any and all lengths to achieve his goal. He knew his chances at Los Angeles were low, but he seemed perfectly relaxed, almost detached, about his situation.

Yet Stuart could be stubborn. The night before the convention opened, he rebuffed still another request from Kennedy to withdraw—because he felt he had to allow his name to be placed in nomination as a tribute to those who had fought the long, hard fight at his side.

As it turned out, Kennedy did not need Symington's delegates. After two days of furious maneuvering, Kennedy's forces pulled together enough votes to win a first-ballot victory on the evening of July 13. Kennedy ended up with 806 delegate votes, Lyndon Johnson with 409, and Symington with 86.

ALMOST SYMINGTON

Because the events of the next thirty-six hours were to have an enormous effect on American history, they have been recounted scores of times. Yet confusion and debate still exist as to how John F. Kennedy chose Lyndon Johnson as his running mate.

It is well understood that Johnson was chosen after a long night of argument within the Kennedy camp. Part of the night of July 14–15, 1960, was spent with a group of powerful Southerners—men like Sam Rayburn of Texas and Richard Russell of Georgia—who joined with some big-city professionals from the North to argue that without Johnson on the ticket, Kennedy could not carry Texas, and that without Texas he could not win. Other advocates of a Kennedy-Johnson ticket included the acerbic columnist Joseph Alsop and Philip Graham, the brilliant and memorable publisher of *The Washington Post,* who was a close friend of both Kennedy and Johnson. Meanwhile, the liberals and most of the Kennedy inner circle remained adamantly opposed to putting Johnson on the ticket, leaving a legacy of bitterness that was to explode after LBJ became President.

To the best of my knowledge, these stories converge on the truth about a chaotic night whose final outcome is virtually the only fact not in dispute. I cannot vouch for them personally, since I was not in the Kennedy suite during that long night, and only heard the tales later—from Phil Graham, who was my friend, from others in the room, and from Senator Kennedy himself. Johnson told me later that he would not have accepted Kennedy's offer without the approval and urging of Speaker Sam Rayburn.

But there was another part of the story not told in any of the major histories or memoirs of the time and which is still little-known today: the offer made to and withdrawn from Stuart Symington during that historic night.

Late on Thursday afternoon, July 14, Kennedy's personal secretary, Evelyn Lincoln, called to ask me to meet her boss in his private hideaway suite. When I got there, Kennedy was relaxing with a drink, acting as though he did not have a care in the world. He praised the dignified way in which Symington had conducted himself, and then, to my surprise, told me he wanted to offer the Vice Presidential nomination to Symington: "Find out if Stuart will accept and let me know right away."

I walked back to Symington's suite deep in thought. Kennedy had to announce his running mate the following day. This was an unequivocal proposal from the candidate. Symington had always said that he was not interested in the Vice Presidency. Still, this was a real offer. . . .

Stuart's initial reaction was characteristic of his excellent values. He wanted the advice not of professional politicians, but of his own family. Over dinner in his suite, a family council, attended by his wife Evie, his two sons, and their wives, and Marny and me, debated Kennedy's offer. Stuart's sons were devoted to him, and were fairly new to politics. Jim, who went on to a distinguished career as a Congressman from Missouri, Chief of Protocol of the United States, and a successful Washington lawyer, was then thirty-two years old. Stuart, Jr., known as "Tim," who practiced law and was involved in New York City politics for many years before returning to St. Louis, was thirty-five. They were reluctant at first to see their father give up his Senate seat, which was probably safely his for life, in exchange for a few years of "presiding over the Senate." At that time, the Vice President still played almost no role in the executive branch. Of course, no one in the room even considered the possibility that the youngest man to run for the Presidency in over half a century might not survive his first term.

Jim and Tim argued strongly against accepting Kennedy's offer. "You didn't come here to hold someone else's coat for four or eight years," Jim said. "You're in the prime of life, you've got a lot of legislating to do, and you don't want to be muzzled by the obligations of loyalty to the President." Evie and Marny both expressed reservations as well, although in tones more muted than those of the boys. Stuart listened to the discussion, limiting himself to a few questions. Then he turned to me.

I had thought hard about this question ever since it first seemed a remote possibility. I wanted to pull back from the emotions of the moment and see where we were, and how we had gotten there. Jim told me afterward that he always remembered this conversation as "the education of Jimmy Symington."

"We have nominated this courageous young man to be President of the United States," I began. "He is running against Richard Nixon"—I came down as harshly as I could on Nixon's name to emphasize our common view of the Republican nominee. "Senator Kennedy will have many requests to make of many Democrats. He will need the support of every single one in order to have a chance to win. As I go over it in my own mind, I am asking myself whether or not there is any more important question he could ask of any Democrat than 'Will you be my running mate? Will you go with me in this venture?' "

For maximum effect, I turned toward Stuart's sons. "As I understand it, your answer is, 'No, I won't do that. We will do other things if you ask, but not that.' Is that right? Is that what you are saying?"

Stuart took me into the bedroom alone for a moment. "I hate to disappoint the boys," he said, "but you can tell Jack I will accept his offer." He then added what proved to be the most prescient comment of the entire day: "But I will bet you a hundred dollars that no matter what he says, Jack will not actually make me his running mate. He will have to pick Lyndon." I lightheartedly accepted Stuart's bet and left to call Kennedy with the news that Symington would be honored to join the ticket.

As far as I was concerned, the deal was closed, and would be announced the next morning. The convention was filled with rumors of a Kennedy-Symington ticket, and speculation along these lines had begun to appear on television.

In the morning, I received another call from Evelyn Lincoln summoning me to Kennedy's private room. "Clark," he said when I arrived, in an uncharacteristically weary tone, "I must do something I have never done before in my political career. I must renege on an offer made in good faith. During the night I have been persuaded that I cannot win without Lyndon on the ticket. I have offered the Vice Presidency to him—and he has accepted. Tell Stuart that I am sorry. I would greatly appreciate his and your understanding. I hope to call on both of you for help during the campaign." Kennedy added that no one in his whole family liked Lyndon Johnson; there had been a "family ruckus" about his selection, he added, but he saw no alternative, no matter how painful the choice.

I was stunned by the sudden reversal, but I realized it made political sense. Texas was far more important to the ticket than Missouri. I replied that I understood the situation completely, and that I was sure Stuart would as well.

I returned to the Symington suite with the news. True as always to his nature, Stuart took it with good grace. His sons, having argued against acceptance of Kennedy's offer, were now angry, at least momentarily, at Kennedy for thinking that there was anyone better than their father for the ticket. But they quickly recovered.

Stuart himself never complained about the might-have-beens of history. Not once in the remaining twenty-nine years of his life did I hear him talk about how close he had come, through succession, to the Presidency. In fact, after the incredibly close results of the November election, in which Texas did prove to be critical,* both of us recognized that Kennedy and the advisers who had pressed for Johnson had been right—that without Johnson on the ticket the Democrats probably would have lost.

Later, Stuart laughed about the evening he almost became Vice President: "At least I made a hundred dollars out of it," he said, after I paid off on our wager.

THE TRANSITION ASSIGNMENT

I did not have to wait long to hear from the Democratic Presidential nominee again. In the first week of August, he asked me to breakfast with him at his home on N Street in Georgetown. He was not very interested in the losing campaigns of 1952 and 1956; he said: "Tell me about the last one we won." We had another detailed discussion of the 1948 election and the forthcoming campaign.

Kennedy said he wanted to use me in various ways during the campaign. Near the end of our conversation, he made a request that had no precedent in American politics, one that was to set a pattern for future transfers of Presidential power. "Clark," he said, "I've been thinking about one matter where you could be of special help to me. If I win, I don't want to wake up on the morning of November 9 and say to myself, 'What do I do now?' I want to have a plan. I want someone to be planning for this between now and November 8." Would I, he asked, undertake the task of preparing a memorandum—"a plan of takeover"—to be ready on Election Day if he won, outlining the main tasks for the new Administration?

A week later, Kennedy called and said he had learned of a study done by the Brookings Institution, a respected Washington think tank, which criticized the poor transitions between past Administrations, focusing

*The Kennedy-Johnson ticket carried Texas and its 24 electoral votes by only 2 percent.

especially on the appalling sloppiness of the 1932 and 1952 transfers of power. Brookings had formed a group to discuss the transition, and Kennedy asked me to represent him on it.

ROBERT F. KENNEDY

Two weeks after the convention Robert F. Kennedy asked to see me. I met alone with him in his brother's Senate office for a sandwich lunch, to discuss what role I might play in the campaign, which he was going to run.

From that time on, almost every aspect of my relationship with Bobby would be clouded with tensions and disagreements. Although there were times when we were on the same side of issues, I found all too often that we seemed destined—almost programmed—to be advocates for opposing points of view. I was told by mutual friends that Bobby regarded me with suspicion because of my age and my association with the Truman Administration—for which neither he nor his father had much respect. But I believe that at the heart of our difficulty was my close association with his brother, which remained an intimate one through every other twist and turn of the last years of his life.

As President, John F. Kennedy deliberately brought me into meetings with himself and Bobby, by then Attorney General, in which my role was to offer my own opinion on some important matter, usually involving the Justice Department. This often put me into conflict with Bobby on issues of substance and questions of law. In explaining my role, President Kennedy said that while he loved and respected his brother, he was conscious of the fact that Bobby had never practiced law, while, by 1960, I had been a practicing lawyer for thirty-two years.

My relationship with Bobby Kennedy would reach a climax in the great drama of 1968, when he and President Johnson each faced the most critical political decision of his life—one considering whether to enter the race for the Presidency, the other whether to withdraw—and I became the intermediary between them (see Chapter 29).

In our meeting July 29, I told Bobby that in my experience people running the campaign on a day-to-day basis sometimes got lost among the many details of the operations. I suggested organizing a small group of persons, acceptable to both Kennedys, who would meet regularly and make their own independent assessment of the campaign, which would be shared with no one except the candidate and his brother. Bobby showed no enthusiasm for the idea.

The next day, I received a letter from Senator Kennedy asking me to meet with his brother-in-law, Sargent Shriver. Kennedy wrote that he thought he was "in pretty good shape for August and September," but that by October "I am concerned that our people may be running out of gas." Shriver would discuss with me the need to "come up with new plans for programs and policy, ideas and speeches for the last four weeks." When Shriver visited me two days later I repeated my suggestion for a separate "campaign review group." Shriver, a volatile man with an open mind and great energy and enthusiasm for almost everything, was visibly more enthusiastic than Bobby had been.

KENNEDY AND TRUMAN

Another early problem on which Kennedy asked my assistance concerned former President Truman. As early as the spring of 1960, even though I was still actively assisting Symington, Kennedy asked me to try to moderate the former President's hostility toward him, especially insofar as it touched on the extremely delicate issue of religion.

In June, somewhat constrained because I was supporting Symington, I met with Dean Acheson and urged him to join me in communicating with Truman on the need for party unity. In several letters which he shared with me, Acheson gently urged upon "the Boss" a list of suggested "don'ts" for the coming election, starting with "Never say any of [the other Democratic candidates] is not qualified to be President." Acheson also addressed Kennedy's religion: "Do you really care about Jack's being a Catholic? I never have. It hasn't bothered me about de Gaulle or Adenauer . . . so why Kennedy?" Furthermore, Acheson added dryly, "I don't think he's a very good Catholic."

But our efforts had only limited success. On July 2, just before the convention, Truman lashed out at Kennedy in a remarkable and unfortunate manner. "Senator," he asked, in a public statement that rocked the Kennedy camp, "are you certain you are quite ready for the country, or that the country is ready for you in the role of President in January 1961? . . . May I suggest you be patient?"

Even though the former President went on to reiterate his endorsement of my candidate, Stuart Symington, I was embarrassed: such an attack was misguided in substance, and could only help the Republicans. I felt that he had been badly advised by friends in Missouri, who were not serving the interests of Stuart Symington well either. Kennedy, though, recognized that Truman's attack offered him an opportunity: with a technique he was to repeat later in regard to the far more explosive "religious issue," he used the attack as an excuse to raise, and then put to rest, one of the issues on which he felt most vulnerable—his youth. "If fourteen years in major elective office is insufficient experience," he said, "that rules out all but a handful of American Presidents, including Wilson, Roosevelt, and Truman." It was an effective performance, and it defused the issue.

After he was nominated, Kennedy asked me to obtain public support from the former President. In a handwritten postscript scrawled across a letter to me on another subject, Kennedy wrote, "Lyndon said the President [Truman] is in a difficult mood. Perhaps you could intervene as I should like to see him." He felt it would be particularly helpful with Baptists and Masons (Truman was a Thirty-Third Degree Mason)—two groups who seemed most disturbed by the idea of a Catholic President.

Accordingly, Lyndon Johnson, Acheson, Governor Abraham A. Ribicoff of Connecticut, and I all pleaded Kennedy's cause—and the cause of party unity—with Truman. Ribicoff, an unusually gentle and subtle politician, visited Independence as Kennedy's personal emissary. After some grumbling, the former President agreed to see the Democratic nominee, and the meeting was finally arranged for August 20 at the Truman Library in Independence. Leaving Stuart Symington, who had accompanied Kennedy, on the steps of the Truman Library, the former President pulled Senator Kennedy into his office with the words, "Come right on in here, young man. I want to talk to you." Forty minutes later, when they emerged with the announcement that Truman would campaign for the ticket, he was badgered by journalists about his earlier statements that Kennedy was too young to be President. With characteristic bluntness, he dismissed them: "The convention nominated this man," he said, "and I am going to support him—and what are you going to do about it?"

THE GORE GROUP

On August 31, just before the traditional Labor Day start to the final phase of the campaign, Kennedy and I dined alone at his home in Georgetown. Relaxed and tanned after his vacation, he did not show any of the cares one normally associated with candidates under pressure. With his brother running the campaign, and a team of skilled and loyal people, he was able to leave most details to them and concentrate on larger strategic issues—and on his opponent.

Many candidates have not understood that the candidate must never try to be his own campaign manager; rather, he or she must leave the operational details of the campaign—television ads, scheduling, even tactics—to his chief lieutenants. His time is far too precious to be wasted on anything other than grand strategy, the presentation of his message to the voters, and, to the extent that it has become unavoidable, fund-raising. Kennedy did understand this fundamental rule, as had Truman.

Kennedy said he had been intrigued by the suggestion I had made to Shriver for a senior political advisory group, and he wanted to hear my rationale. After I had repeated my arguments, Kennedy said a second set of opinions from a group of respected outside advisers would fit well into his detached style.

He asked me to form such a group immediately, and we discussed who should be included. Kennedy and I both greatly respected the political acumen of Tennessee Senator Albert Gore, Sr., a dynamic, forward-looking example of the new Southern political leader whom we hoped would replace the old guard as they began to fade. We decided to ask Gore to act as leader of the group. For his foreign policy knowledge, intelligence, and general thoughtfulness, we settled on Arkansas Senator J. William Fulbright, the new Chairman of the Senate Foreign Relations Committee. Kennedy suggested I ask Missouri Congressman Richard Bolling, one of the up-and-coming new leaders of the House. Kennedy also asked that one of his bright young campaign aides, Frederick Dutton, who had until recently served as Chief of Staff to California Governor Edmund "Pat" Brown, join us as a sort of recording secretary. Dutton, whom I had never met before, was particularly valuable because of his knowledge of the West.

Kennedy insisted on only one rule: the very existence of the group must remain private. If it leaked, he would never stop hearing complaints from those who had not been invited to join it. Mentioning the Monday-Night Group that had met from 1946 through 1948 without a leak, I assured Kennedy I agreed entirely with him about the importance of confidentiality.

The next day, Ted Sorensen and I went over the formation of the group and discussed the transition assignment, then went together to Kennedy's office to discuss the campaign. Sorensen, my old associate from the *Profiles in Courage* fight, was cordial to me, but I felt he was troubled by the transition assignment. The youngest and, in my opinion brightest of the Kennedy men, Sorensen was then thirty years old; I was fifty-three. Having myself been the youngest of President Truman's senior advisers, I was, for the first time in my life, working with a generation of men younger than I, including the candidate himself. To them, I must have seemed like someone from another era, a survivor of some ancient war. But Kennedy made it clear he wanted me around precisely for this reason: I brought to events a different, and broader, perspective.

On September 2, as the nation prepared for the long Labor Day weekend, I had breakfast with Senator Gore at the Fairfax Hotel. Gore was enthusiastic about the political advisory group, and volunteered to host the meetings at his apartment at the Fairfax in order to avoid public attention. Gore combined a fine understanding of practical politics with a high idealism about public service. When, ten years later, he lost his Senate seat to Bill Brock, he did so in the most admirable fashion imaginable, over principled stands on two issues of transcendent importance—

the war in Vietnam and civil rights. Today, his son, Albert Gore, Jr., sits in the United States Senate, carrying on the family tradition with intelligence and vision.

The Gore Group met three times a week, usually for breakfast, throughout the rest of the campaign. Bobby Kennedy joined us on several occasions. As a group, we saw the candidate only once, but he frequently called Gore or me from the road to check our reactions to events as they unfolded. Sometimes he listened to us, other times he did not, but he never doubted the value of a second group of advisers, outside the operational structure of the campaign and reporting only to him.

THE CAMPAIGN

As he had said during the convention, Kennedy also wanted to involve Stuart Symington in the campaign, and this led to another assignment for me. In mid-September, Kennedy asked Symington to head up a special Committee on the Defense Establishment.

In subsequent campaigns such advisory committees or task forces have become so routine that they have lost almost all their political value, but in 1960 it was still a relatively new technique. Like so many of Kennedy's political innovations, it seemed quite creative at the time and received favorable public attention.

By late October my involvement in the campaign was extensive, almost obliterating my law practice for about a month. In addition to the Symington Defense Committee and the Gore Group, I participated in the preparations and strategy sessions for the first televised debate between Nixon and Kennedy. On September 30, I flew to Hyannisport for two days of meetings, capped by the longest political strategy meeting that Kennedy held between the convention and the election, a grueling five-hour affair involving his father, pollster Lou Harris, and his inner circle of advisers—Pierre Salinger, Ted Sorensen, Kenny O'Donnell, and Larry O'Brien. Still unknown to the general public, they would soon be celebrated as the "New Frontiersmen."

The first televised debate proved to be a historic moment in American politics. Nothing like this debate had ever happened before, and excitement was far higher than it would ever be again. Today the televised debates are almost taken for granted and both sides have learned the art of punching and counterpunching in short television-sized "sound bites." Much of the drama is gone, and the chances for a decisive "win" are much diminished. But in 1960 there were no precedents, no guidelines or previous tapes to study. Every nuance, every gesture and comment was scrutinized by commentators and replayed by the networks. Although on the issues the two candidates were fairly even, there was no question about the political effect of their joint appearance. It eliminated the "experience versus youth" issue that had originally seemed to favor Nixon. I urged Kennedy not to allow Nixon to repeat his effort, made several times in the first debate, to portray the two parties as alike in goals, differing only in method. There were real differences between the philosophies of the two parties, and in their attitudes toward everything from the working man to foreign policy. "Nixon must not be permitted to create the illusion that you and he are working toward the same end," I wrote in a private memorandum to Kennedy.

As I reflect on this advice today, I find an ironic reversal has taken place in the intervening thirty years. After three straight Republican Presidential victories—five out of the last six—many Democrats seem to feel today that the way to win the Presidency is to run as Republicans. I do not agree: Democrats must run as *Democrats,* emphasizing what they stand for as a party. Times have changed enormously since the New Deal and the New Frontier, and policies must change with them, but the traditional Democratic values of equal rights, fairness, compassion, economic growth, and internationalist foreign policy do not need to be abandoned, only updated. John F. Kennedy did just that in 1960—brilliantly.

THE ELECTION

In the final days before the election, I absented myself from the campaign, which was running on its batteries by that point and needed no further outside advice. It was time to concentrate on my assignment to prepare for a possible takeover of the government. Even as I prepared my memorandum, Professor Richard Neustadt was working on the same subject. At first, I assumed Kennedy and Neustadt knew each other, but in fact they had never met before "Scoop" Jackson took Neustadt to Kennedy's house at the end of August, 1960, to discuss the problems of the transition, a subject that interested Neustadt. Kennedy told him to work independently of me, saying he wanted two sets of advisers. But Neustadt and I were old friends and colleagues from the Truman White House, and we kept in touch throughout the campaign. Neustadt had just published one of the most important and insightful books ever written on the Presidency, *Presidential Power.* Like me, he believed in a strong Presidency. We would work independently, and present Kennedy—if he won—with two separate memos; even if they differed on details or emphasis, I knew that their overall thrust would be the same, urging measures to assure strong Presidential control of the executive branch. Based on our experience in the Truman White House and observation of the Eisenhower Administration, we shared the conviction that if a President did not control the bureaucracy, the bureaucracy would control him, and little would be accomplished in a four-year period. To avoid this, Kennedy would need to pick the right team of senior personnel, get off to a fast start, and place the White House at the center of the executive branch.

I spent election night, November 8, at home in Washington, waiting for the final results. The popular vote count at first showed a substantial margin for Kennedy, but as the night progressed his lead dwindled steadily and alarmingly. When I finally went to bed very late that night, victory seemed to be in Kennedy's grasp, but by no means assured. He had run one of the longest, toughest, most grueling, and brilliantly executed campaigns in American history. If he held on to win, he would have done it by such a narrow margin that one could truthfully say that if any one of dozens of events had gone differently, he might have lost; but, he and his advisers had approached the campaign with boldness, decisiveness, and nerve. As I reflected on the campaign, I could not think of a significant error that they had made.*

Around 10 A.M., as I tried to catch up on my sleep, I was awakened by a telephone call. It was Kennedy, calling from Hyannisport. "Clark," he calmly began the conversation, as if he was making the most routine request in the world, "could you send that takeover memo of yours up here right away? It looks like we're going to need it." And that was how I learned that John F. Kennedy would be the next President of the United States.

*The final result was astonishing, closer even than 1948—less than a 120,000 vote margin for Kennedy out of nearly sixty-nine million votes cast. Kennedy's electoral total turned out to be exactly the same as Truman's, 303.

20

The Transition

The transition memorandum that President-elect, or, as he preferred to be called until Inauguration Day, Senator Kennedy wanted from me was ready, bound in stiff covers, and running thirty-one pages. Within hours a Secret Service courier came to my office to pick up the copies and take them to Hyannisport. The arrival of the Secret Service reminded me instantly of the enormous changes that come over a man the moment he is elected President. Soon it would no longer be "Jack," but "Mr. President," even to his closest friends, and no matter how informal a relationship he tried to maintain, a curtain would descend between the President and everyone else. The following day, November 10, Senator Kennedy met with his advisers at the Cape. They reviewed the memorandum from me and the one from Dick Neustadt, and discussed what to do during the seventy-two days remaining until the Inauguration.

Most historians view the 1960 transition as a dramatic change from all previous transfers of the Presidency. While this is true, it is also often described as setting the pattern for subsequent transitions. This statement is incorrect. Current transition practice is quite different from that of 1960.

In 1960, no public funds were available for either the transition or members of the incoming Administration. Many of those who came to Washington early to prepare themselves, at Kennedy's request, could ill afford the out-of-pocket expense. Later, when President Kennedy became aware of the problem, he asked Congress for a small appropriation for future transitions. Thus was born the Presidential Transition Act of 1963.

I strongly supported this act, but I never had in mind the vastly oversized "transition teams" that have become a periodic but permanent part of the Washington scene—and a sorry example of the government's penchant for self-indulgence at the taxpayers' expense. The Presidential Transition Act unintentionally spawned a form of life that could originate only in Washington—a seventy-day monster that springs up overnight once every four years, has no purpose except its own existence, feuds with itself, and then suddenly disappears on January 20, leaving behind nothing except empty cardboard boxes. In recent transitions—1976, 1980, and 1988—large temporary bureaucracies have set up shop in Washington, with advance teams from the new Administration moving into each of the departments and agencies. The transition has become The Transition—an end in itself for *thousands* of suddenly unemployed campaign workers, most of whom are seeking permanent places in the new Administration. In 1980, for example, the Reagan Administration spent the full two million dollars appropriated by Congress for the transition, plus more than an additional one million it had raised out of private funds: its ten-story headquarters was a "blizzard of task forces, committees, and teams."[1] This is not merely a waste of money, it is also a diversion for the President-elect and his senior advisers when they should be concentrating only on the most critical matters—especially the all-important task of selecting the right people for the top jobs.

The transfer of power from one President to another is a solemn and important task which is vital in setting the tone of a new Administration. It should not be trivialized by useless commotion. In no way should what we did in 1960 be associated with these recent transitions.

THE TRANSITION MEMORANDUM

My 1960 memorandum to President-elect Kennedy was based on a very simple premise: never again should a transition be handled as poorly as those of 1932 and 1952. I foresaw a far easier transition than in 1952. "Much of the 1952–53 experience is irrelevant," I wrote, because "the Kennedy Administration will not be suspicious of or hostile to the Federal bureaucracy." Nonetheless, I stressed the importance to the President-elect of "consolidating the reins of power and leadership as soon as possible, and not merely relying on good will and experience." The new President would inevitably encounter "pockets of resistance" in Washington, and I urged him, as his top priority, "to get off the mark quickly with the New Frontier program."

A key question on which both Neustadt and I agreed was that a White House Chief of Staff was not desirable for an activist, hands-on man like

John F. Kennedy. Such a system had fit well the military style of Dwight D. Eisenhower, but, I concluded,

> A vigorous President in the Democratic tradition of the Presidency will probably find it best to act as his own chief of staff, and to have no highly visible majordomo standing between him and his staff (and, incidentally, between him and the public).

If the structure I suggested resembled that of the Truman White House it was no coincidence; I felt this was best suited to Kennedy's style and personality. But times and the government have changed, and today, given the size of the White House, I believe that any President, regardless of personal style, would need a Chief of Staff. With dozens of people carrying such once exclusive titles as "Assistant to the President," the White House has become a government within a government, trying to oversee and manage most of the rest of the executive branch. I still would prefer a lean and fast-moving White House, but I recognize how difficult it would be to eliminate most of the positions created over the years to work with special constituencies. The White House has become a separate agency of the government, the President's machine to control or circumvent the rest of his own bureaucracy. Revealingly, most of this "White House" operates from offices physically located outside the White House itself. In these circumstances, I recognize, although reluctantly, the need for a single senior person to coordinate the rest of the White House.

In an earlier memorandum, dated August 5, 1960, remembering the 1946 Henry Wallace affair, I had warned Kennedy:

> It is almost impossible to avoid being inundated by yes men in the White House. No matter how much a staff member wishes to help, the awesome power of the presidency overwhelms him. . . . One of the greatest opportunities for errors arises when the President hears but one side of an issue. Often times a cabinet member will present an issue to the President and ask for authority to act. It is best to have the Cabinet member submit the matter in writing so it can be analyzed by the President's staff and, if there are two sides to the question, one of the staff members can be the advocate for the opposition.

Similar thoughts were to pass through my mind again a few months later, when the Kennedy Presidency was nearly wrecked by the disaster at the Bay of Pigs.

THE SYMINGTON DEFENSE STUDY GROUP

During the campaign, Symington's defense study group met in both Washington and New York several times. It made its recommendations to Kennedy a month after his election. We went much further in the direction of unification of the services than was politically feasible, but this was deliberate: both Symington and I, remembering the brutal battles of 1946–1949, felt that a group as tangential to the process as ours could make an impact only if it consciously overstated its recommendations. To get half a loaf, as I suggested in our first meeting, we needed to ask for a whole loaf.

Our objective was to restart the engines of reform, stalled for several years, and strengthen the positions of Secretary of Defense and the Chairman of the Joint Chiefs of Staff. We were partially successful in the first objective, because the man eventually selected by the new President as Secretary of Defense, Robert S. McNamara, wanted such changes. The military services still resisted significant changes in the structure of the Joint Chiefs, though, and even McNamara did not wish to take them on at that time. Recommendations as bold as doing away with the separate departmental structure for each service—a reform I have always believed would be in the national interest—were rejected without serious discussion. During the Vietnam War, the failure to move toward a more unified military structure was a costly one. A reform like Goldwater-Nickles (1986) should have been passed a generation earlier.

A PRESIDENTIAL ASSIGNMENT

Just before noon on Thursday, November 10, the President-elect called me from Hyannisport. President Eisenhower had just phoned him to urge the appointment of a liaison with the White House for the transition. "Clark," he said, "I feel that you are qualified to handle this. Would you accept?"

I said that I would be happy and honored to do so—on one condition: "I want you and your entire staff to know that my only function will be to assist you in the takeover of the government. After that I will fade from the picture."

"Why is that?" he asked, genuinely surprised. "There will be a lot of tugging and pulling around you for jobs," I replied. "I think I can be of more service to you if everyone around you knows I am not their competitor or enemy. It will be easier for the members of your staff to work with me if they know we are not in competition in any manner whatsoever."

Kennedy was silent for a moment. "Well, that makes a good deal of sense," he finally said. "I will pass the word on to my staff. I am not sure, however, that I am prepared to agree that I will let you fade out of the picture entirely," he said with an amused tone. *He doesn't believe that I am serious,* I thought, but I was: I had no desire to return to full-time government service, but I was ready to be helpful in any other way. I was well aware that my utility during the transition would be compromised if Kennedy's own aides saw me as a potential competitor, rather than as a facilitator. Dick Neustadt, who had the same reaction, enlisted my assistance a short time later in convincing the Kennedy staff that he too would refuse any position offered. This was in sharp distinction to later, less disinterested "transition teams," where most participants were active job-seekers.

Kennedy also wanted to review the initial round of appointments. Ted Sorensen would be his Special Counsel, a job and title that, he said, he knew meant a great deal to me personally. I approved completely: Sorensen had exactly the right combination of intellect and integrity, and a close relationship with the President. Sargent Shriver would take charge of the delicate and politically charged job of personnel selection in the initial phase of the takeover of power, assisted by Larry O'Brien. All three men would wish to consult with me, Kennedy said.

He then asked for my views on the retention of two important Eisenhower Administration officials, CIA Director Allen Dulles and FBI Director J. Edgar Hoover—two decisions that would take on great significance, primarily in retrospect.

In light of Kennedy's narrow margin of victory, these decisions were neither controversial nor difficult to make; any other choices would have provoked a partisan debate that the President-elect did not need at that time. I told Kennedy I thought it appropriate to retain both men *"for the time being."* Dulles, I said, was eminently qualified for his job. As for Hoover, although I had despised and distrusted him since the Truman years, I never seriously considered recommending that he not be asked to stay on. He might leave later, as I had implied, but not then.

Historians have searched for hidden meaning in the reappointment of Dulles and Hoover, questioning the wisdom and rationale for both decisions. Retaining Dulles would be cited as contributing to the disaster at the Bay of Pigs five months later; the reappointment of Hoover viewed by some as a result of compromising information the FBI Director had on Kennedy. One theory is that Hoover had evidence that Chicago Mayor Richard J. Daley had "stolen" the election in Illinois, which went to the Democrats by a margin of only 8,850 votes, by fixing ballots in Cook County, and that Hoover threatened to use this information if he were not kept on. Another set of theories revolves around the idea that Hoover knew something of an embarrassing nature concerning Kennedy's personal life.

I see no merit in either charge. Only the hindsight of history makes either decision controversial. With respect to Dulles, had he been replaced at the CIA, I doubt it would have changed the situation at the Bay of Pigs; the agency as a whole was committed to the operation, as was the military, and Kennedy would have gotten the same advice regardless of who was DCI.

The decision to keep Hoover after winning by such a tiny margin was dictated by the politics of the situation, and to a certain extent, perhaps, by Joseph Kennedy's admiration for Hoover. In fact, Hoover was the only real choice we thought we had at the time. *The Washington Post* accurately captured this attitude when it editorialized the next day: "It has become a ritual to request J. Edgar Hoover to continue as Director of the Federal Bureau of Investigation; what would be news would have been silence [yesterday] on the part of Mr. Kennedy."

Even without Illinois's 27 electoral votes, Kennedy would still have carried the Electoral College by 7 votes more than the minimum required for election. Moreover, Hoover's reappointment was announced by Kennedy immediately after the election, well before any information on what had actually taken place in the disputed Cook County vote (and the Republican strongholds in southern Illinois, where the vote count was equally suspect) could have been used by Hoover.

Kennedy decided to announce my transition assignment immediately, together with the reappointments of Dulles and Hoover. Kennedy asked if I could come to Palm Beach the following week to spend some time with him and his staff to discuss the structuring of the White House.

FIRST CONTACTS AT THE WHITE HOUSE

While I was sorting out my new responsibilities, the Assistant to President Eisenhower, Major General Wilton "Jerry" Persons, called me from the White House. President Eisenhower had named Persons as my counterpart, and he wanted to meet as soon as possible.

Persons was a fortunate choice. I had known him for years, and respected him as a thorough, careful, and nonpartisan military officer, with an easygoing and attractive manner. After the powerful White House Chief of Staff Sherman Adams had been forced to resign in a scandal, President Eisenhower had selected Persons as Adams's replacement. Dealing with Adams, a taciturn and flinty politician, would have been much more difficult; someone said at the time that Persons and Adams were "as different as mellow bourbon and hard cider."

Entering the White House, I was stopped at the gate by a guard. Fishing around in my wallet, I found a ten-year-old White House pass, which he accepted—something that could never happen in today's more security-conscious world.

Our first meeting was cordial and set a tone of low-key cooperation that was to last through the transition period. Persons began by outlining the defects, from his point of view, of the 1952 transition. We both recognized our obligation to do better this time around, and we agreed we would have no press conferences or interviews, either on or off the record, during the transition. We agreed to set up a meeting between President Eisenhower and Senator Kennedy in early December. I asked that a daily intelligence briefing from the CIA and the State Department for the President-elect begin immediately, requested a special procedure for expedited FBI clearances for key personnel as they were selected, and asked that clearance procedures begin immediately for Ted Sorensen and Larry O'Brien. President Eisenhower's one concern was that "a substantial influx of Kennedy men might disrupt the work of the departments and agencies" before January 20. He requested that all contacts with the executive branch be coordinated through Persons and me.

Persons had only one piece of advice for the incoming Administration: they should make their key appointments as early as possible, especially the critical position of Director of the Bureau of the Budget. I agreed with him, and asked to meet with Maurice Stans, the Eisenhower Budget Director, to discuss the matter further.

There was no tension, no fireworks, no ego problems. I was to meet regularly with Persons for the next two months, and speak with him on the telephone on a daily basis, without ever encountering a single difficulty.

After meeting with Persons, I called on J. Edgar Hoover to ask for a special procedure to speed up security clearances for incoming personnel. He was cooperative during this meeting. I kept my personal feelings about him hidden, and he kept to himself whatever his private thoughts were about having to deal with me again. He designated Assistant Director Courtney Evans as the contact point within the FBI for the clearance of all new appointees.

Names began to appear for key White House staff jobs. Some of the new appointees would soon become celebrated as the New Frontiersmen, but they were still unknown. Kenneth O'Donnell became Appointments Secretary, Pierre Salinger was named Press Secretary, and Larry O'Brien was given responsibility for Congressional relations. I noticed that the primary factor in making these assignments was the men themselves, rather than any attempt to create a coherent and rational White House structure, but this did not surprise me; the inevitable jockeying for position around the new President had begun, and as always, friction would arise first among the people who had so recently shared the same trenches in the campaign.

As each person was designated for a position, I requested the FBI to begin a top-priority security check. I met with most of the new appointees individually before arranging meetings for them with their counterparts in the executive branch. They were a competent and dynamic group, younger than the Truman or Eisenhower staff men. From the start, however, I was disturbed by one aspect of their general demeanor: with the exception of the President-elect himself, they behaved as though history had begun with them. They regarded both Eisenhower and Truman (and their own Vice President) with something bordering on contempt. Their new leader, the first President born in the twentieth century, was going to be *different.* Franklin Roosevelt carried more relevance for the Kennedy men, because he had set the same dynamic tone that they hoped to establish. But with three notable exceptions—the President himself, Sorensen, and Arthur Schlesinger, Jr., the distinguished historian whom Kennedy was to bring into the White House as a special assistant—no one seemed to have much of an interest in history.

I regarded this as a form of arrogance. They were undeniably able and utterly devoted to their chief in a way that transcended the normal loyalty of a White House staff—a valuable quality that would carry them far. But knowing what one doesn't know is important, and respect for the lessons of history is essential. Looking back on my own experience starting in 1945, I felt that as a White House newcomer I had learned a great deal from wise men like Sam Rosenman and many others, including Jim Forrestal, Dean Acheson, Bob Lovett, Jim Rowe, and George Elsey. Kennedy's men were making a serious mistake in undervaluing such an essential part of the learning process.

PALM BEACH

Meetings now took place almost around the clock. For a few weeks, my law offices became one of the centers of the new Administration, host to a steady stream of Kennedy appointees and would-be appointees. Sorensen, Neustadt, and O'Brien stopped by frequently. Bobby Kennedy, his future in the Administration still unresolved, visited as well. A few times, Kennedy asked me to shield him from outside pressure groups. On November 21, for example, while in Palm Beach, I met with an angry group of Southern legislators protesting court-ordered desegregation, and politely listened to their howls of protest, informing them gravely that I would convey their views—which I found repellent—to the President-elect.

On Sunday, November 20, I flew to Palm Beach for three days of meetings with Kennedy and his inner team. I stayed at his father's seaside house. There was a relaxed but purposeful air as we sat around the pool. Once, we enjoyed a round of golf, a game he rarely played. The object of the trip though, was not relaxation. The atmosphere was brisker, with a far more competitive edge, than the Truman vacations at Key West had been. The men around Kennedy were not entirely happy with my arrival in their midst; it only complicated their relations with their boss. I was glad, and not for the first time, that I had stipulated I would not take any position in the new Administration.

Before I arrived in Palm Beach, Kennedy's personnel team, led by Sargent Shriver, had begun the search for what Sorensen later called "a ministry of talent."[2] A vast array of people had been consulted during this process. As we reviewed the names on Shriver's lists, Kennedy said he wanted to dismiss all consideration of the past political affiliations of the people under discussion. At one point, when Larry O'Brien mentioned that someone should be disqualified because he was a Republican, Kennedy said, "I don't care if the man is a Republican or a Democrat or an Igorot. I just want the best person available for the job." This attitude may have disturbed some of his political advisers, but it appealed to me—a President should be self-confident enough to seek the very best people for his government, and not worry about whether or not they had supported him in the past.

Kennedy took his time. Eisenhower had selected his entire Cabinet by December 1, but it was not *until* that same day that Kennedy announced his first Cabinet member, Abraham Ribicoff as Secretary of Health, Education, and Welfare. By the time I arrived in Palm Beach, the press was starting to comment on the slowness of the appointment process, but Kennedy was unconcerned: he knew that personnel selection was 75 percent of the work of a transition, and he wanted to do it right.

As we worked our way slowly through a review of names, Kennedy turned to the group and said, wryly, "You know, I thought this would be the fun part of the job, but it is damn hard work." The meetings went on all day long, with shifting groups of people, and on late into the Florida night. Lists were drawn up and refined, names added and dropped continually.

BOBBY KENNEDY

It was always clear that Bobby Kennedy would receive a major job. He had performed brilliantly during the election campaign, and he was the person closest to the new President. Yet at the same time, suspicions about him remained in many quarters: some people, having felt his wrath, saw him as ruthless and difficult, while others worried about his early association with Joe McCarthy. Larger questions of nepotism also came into play: many people, including me, simply did not like the idea of concentrating too much power in the hands of a single family.

I had heard rumors from staff members that Bobby Kennedy might be offered the post of Attorney General. At first I could not believe it, since the idea seemed so farfetched. In a session with the President-elect around the pool, I made a little speech about the special role of the Attorney General, without mentioning Bobby. I said that in several earlier Administrations, including those of Ulysses S. Grant and Warren G. Harding, politically selected Attorneys General had rendered terrible disservice to the Presidents and left lasting stains on the history of those Administrations. In the Truman Administration, I noted, Howard McGrath had moved from Chairman of the Democratic National Committee to the Justice Department, and that mistake had been rectified only with McGrath's painful departure. Eisenhower had likewise appointed a Republican National Committee Chairman, Herbert Brownell, as Attorney General, and I felt that had also been a mistake. Such appointees had come to the Justice Department with political commitments that could compromise their integrity as the top law enforcement officer of the United States.

Later that day, Senator Kennedy took me into the house for another private meeting. "Let me tell you about the Attorney Generalship," he said. "My father wants me to appoint Bobby. My concern is that Bobby has never practiced law. Bobby says he does not want the job—he thinks it will hurt me. I would rather put him into the Defense Department as the number-two man, and then let him succeed to the top after a while—or keep him around the White House to help me out. I have told my father that Bobby would create a real problem as Attorney General."

I listened in amazement as he continued, in a grave, low, intense voice. "My father said, 'That doesn't make any difference. I want Bobby to be Attorney General. He's a lawyer, he's savvy, he knows all the political ins and outs and can protect you.' I agree with what you have said about the job; so does Bobby. I think my father might listen to you. He speaks highly of your contribution to the campaign and the family, and you have good standing with him. I'd like you to go to New York and talk to him about this. But don't tell anyone else about it."

"Of course," I said, but I thought, *this* was truly a strange assignment—the President-elect asking a third party to try to talk to his father about his brother. Only the Kennedys!

A few days later, I called on former Ambassador Kennedy in New York. The meeting started pleasantly, with a discussion of the splendid occurrences of recent months. I steeled myself for the main event.

"Mr. Ambassador, there is an important matter that the President-elect has asked me to raise with you," I finally said. "That is the question of the appointment of Bobby to be Attorney General." Joe Kennedy said nothing and looked at me with total concentration. I made a carefully prepared presentation of why it was not in the interests of the new President, the Kennedy family, the entire Administration, and Bobby himself to take the post. "Bobby is very valuable," I concluded. "He is young. He has time—start him somewhere else, perhaps number two at Defense. Give him the chance to grow. He will be outstanding."

I was pleased with my presentation; it was, I thought, persuasive. When I had finished, Kennedy said, "Thank you very much, Clark. I am so glad to have heard your views." Then, pausing a moment, he said, "I do want to leave you with one thought, however—one firm thought." He paused again, and looked me straight in the eye. "*Bobby is going to be Attorney General.* All of us have worked our tails off for Jack, and now that we have succeeded I am going to see to it that Bobby gets the same chance that we gave to Jack."

I would always remember the intense but matter-of-fact tone with which he had spoken—there was no rancor, no anger, no challenge. He did not resent my presentation or my opposition to the appointment, he was simply telling me the facts. For a moment I had glimpsed the inner workings of that remarkable family, and, despite my admiration and affection for John F. Kennedy, I could not say I liked what I saw.

LOVETT TURNS US DOWN

When I called the President-elect to report my conversation with his father, he was not surprised. Perhaps he had already heard from him directly. But he was not ready to give up entirely on his idea of appointing his brother to the number-two job at Defense. His last effort would involve my old friend, Robert Lovett.

Before I left for New York and my lesson in Kennedy family politics, the President-elect asked me to see Lovett during the trip and try to persuade him to serve as Secretary of Defense. When I said I doubted his health would permit a return to such a taxing job, Kennedy asked me also to offer him the top post at Treasury.

Lovett and I had maintained a close friendship during the Eisenhower years. At sixty-five, he was still the delightful, gracious, and charming man I remembered from the forties. As we talked over a leisurely lunch, I thought that no one would get along better with Kennedy than this wise and gentle man. But, Lovett said with a grin, he could never keep up with "a bunch of forty-year-old touch-football players." I urged him not to refuse the new President outright, even on health grounds, without talking to his doctors again. "I am sure we agree that no one should lightly turn down an opportunity to be of service at a time like this," I said. "You offer a unique package and your obligation to the government has not yet been fully discharged." Laughing, Lovett agreed to consult his doctor.

As soon as I left, Lovett went to Presbyterian Hospital to see his doctor, who expressed serious reservations about Lovett's health holding up under the rigors of full-time government service. Lovett called me the next morning to turn down Kennedy's offer. Even so, I asked him to come to Washington for a personal meeting with Kennedy. They met on December 1, and, after Lovett had charmingly dodged what he later called "a rather shifty end-run by Caroline Kennedy," Kennedy gently pressed him one last time to reconsider, adding that he would welcome Lovett at State, Defense, or Treasury—a remarkable, but well-deserved, tribute to this great public servant. Lovett, so deeply touched that "I found it difficult to put my appreciation into words," nonetheless declined again.

After that meeting, Kennedy called me. He had been deeply impressed with Lovett, whom he had not known well before their meeting. Even now, he had not given up on bringing Lovett into the government. What did I think of asking him to head Defense for just one year? Bobby Kennedy could be his deputy, and then replace him. This idea might have been sufficient to stop even Joe Kennedy from his master plan for Bobby, but I was sure that Lovett would still decline, and said so. Kennedy thought of asking Eisenhower's Defense Secretary, Thomas Gates, to stay on for one year with Bobby as *his* deputy, then promote Bobby to the top post. I objected to this idea; it would be unseemly, I said, to keep Gates after the campaign debate on defense issues, in which Kennedy had criticized Eisenhower and Gates for weakening our national defense and creating the "missile gap." He discussed making Bobby a secretary for one of the services and then, in his words, "jumping him to Defense Secretary after a year or so," but this idea died before it received any serious consideration. There would be no job for Bobby Kennedy at Defense.

On December 16, the President-elect announced Bobby's appointment as Attorney General. To my pleasant surprise, Bobby was to perform well in that position, although I would still object to such an appointment if a similar situation were to arise again, on the same grounds. As usual, President Kennedy was able to defuse much of the criticism of the appointment with perfectly timed humor. Noting that his brother had never practiced law, he made a celebrated comment at a dinner the day after the Inauguration: "I can't see that it's wrong to give him a little legal experience before he goes out to practice law. Every lawyer has to start somewhere."

ROBERT S. McNAMARA, AND OTHERS

Lovett's decision not to return to Washington led to the most important appointment of the new Administration. During our luncheon in New York, he had suggested a new candidate for the Defense portfolio: the president of the Ford Motor Company, Robert S. McNamara, whom Lovett had known as an able, bright, young executive in the War Department near the end of World War II. I had never heard of McNamara before, but I brought his name back to Washington and mentioned it to Kennedy. When he checked McNamara's name with Sargent Shriver, he found it was on a large list Shriver's team had compiled in their nationwide search for new talent. Given Lovett's strong endorsement, McNamara clearly deserved a close look. Thus began the emergence of one of the dominant figures of the sixties in Washington.

Another appointment I favored strongly was that of David Bell to head the Bureau of the Budget. Bell was only forty-one, but he had served with distinction in the Truman Administration, and both Neustadt and I agreed he would make an excellent choice for this critical spot. When Kennedy met him, there was instant rapport, and the appointment proved to be an eminently successful one. Neustadt and I both felt the Budget Bureau should have substantially expanded responsibilities and should serve, not just as a sort of gigantic accounting office, but as one of the President's key tools for controlling the federal government. As this new approach to the budget process emerged in the sixties, the job became one of the most important in Washington, and the office was renamed the Office of Management and Budget in 1969 to reflect this change.

DEAN RUSK

For Secretary of State, Kennedy consulted a large number of people, and considered a wide variety of candidates. He looked at Averell Harriman, whom he rejected because he felt that, at sixty-nine, Harriman was too old; Senator Fulbright, who was eliminated because of his voting record on civil rights legislation; and Ambassador David Bruce, who withdrew himself from consideration. It was ironic that Harriman was eliminated because of his age: once he got a hearing aid the following year, this veteran of the Roosevelt and Truman era became one of the great workhorses of the Kennedy and Johnson Administrations, serving with great distinction in a variety of important jobs just below Cabinet rank. (As he approached ninety he would still be active, assisting President Carter on several important matters involving U.S.-Soviet relations.)

The job finally went to Dean Rusk, then president of the Rockefeller

September 25, 1968: One of a series of intense discussions as the Vietnam drama nears its climax

In the office of the Secretary of Defense, behind the Pershing desk. The portrait on the left is of the first Secretary of Defense, my friend James V. Forrestal.

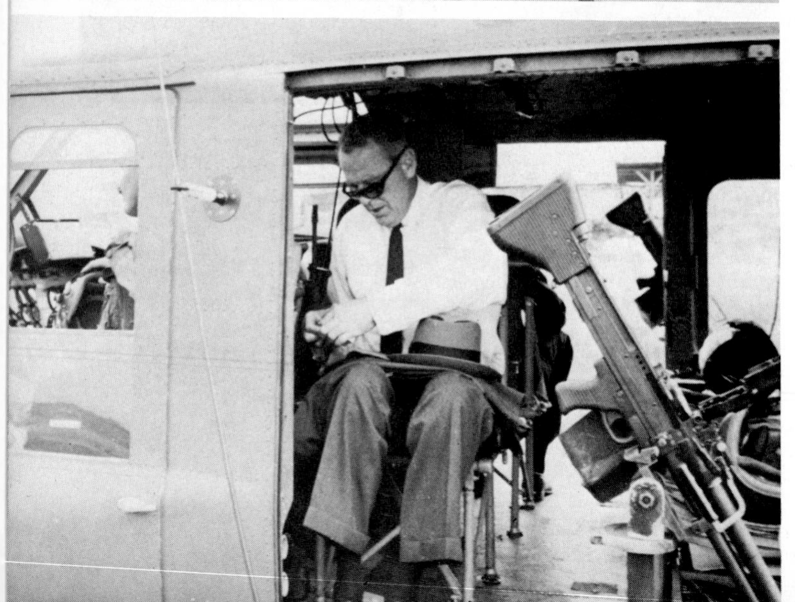

Visiting the field in Vietnam by helicopter

July 6, 1979: The "domestic summit" at Camp David. Seated between President Carter and me, left to right, are Hamilton Jordan (behind table), AFL-CIO President Lane Kirkland, former HEW Secretary John Gardner.

January 31, 1980: Conferring with Prime Minister Indira Gandhi of India at Government House, New Delhi

February 6, 1980: With President Carter at a joint press conference in the Oval Office upon my return from a Presidential mission to India

State Dulles, and the Chairman of the Joint Chiefs of Staff, who had even advocated the use of nuclear weapons.* But on his last day in office, he was taking a far tougher stand than at any time during the previous eight years.

The tone of the old soldier—on his last day of public service, half a century after entering the United States Military Academy—had a powerful effect on Kennedy, Rusk, McNamara, and me. None of us had been prepared for the seriousness Eisenhower attached to Southeast Asia. I did not then have enough knowledge of Southeast Asia to challenge Eisenhower's assessment of the situation, even if I had had the inclination to do so.

In retrospect, I believe that President Eisenhower, while sincere, did a disservice to the incoming Administration. This new line in Southeast Asia—far tougher than he had taken on his own watch—cast a shadow over the early decisions of the next Administration. Its consequences, moreover, affected Vietnam and even Cuba. In the first two months of his Administration President Kennedy, as one of his staff later noted, "probably spent more time on Laos than on anything else."[3] Sixty days after he became President, the Laos obsession reached its height with a remarkable, nationally televised press conference. Standing before three maps of Laos designed to illustrate the advance of the communist guerrillas, President Kennedy consciously echoed the theme we had heard from Eisenhower in the Cabinet Room on January 19: "Laos is far away from America, but the world is small. Its own safety runs with the safety of us all. . . ." Eisenhower himself had never said anything that strong in public about Laos.**

. . . AND A FEW WORDS ON CUBA

Before that January 19 meeting broke up, Eisenhower turned briefly to Cuba. He said we must support "to the utmost" anyone who opposed Fidel Castro. Without going into details, he added that the U.S. was helping train anti-Castro guerilla forces in Guatemala. It was the new Administration's responsibility, he said, "to do whatever is necessary" to make their efforts succeed. This understated version of the CIA's efforts to overthrow Castro was the first time I was even dimly aware of the preparations for what was later to become the Bay of Pigs disaster.

Finally, the outgoing President offered Kennedy best wishes. He wanted us to know he would support, or at least not criticize, the new

*This was the proposal to intervene on behalf of the French at Dienbienphu.

**Six years later, President Johnson, searching for ways to show that the origins of the American involvement in Southeast Asia included the Republicans and particularly the war hero–President, paid special attention to this meeting, and asked me for a personal memorandum on it.

Administration in the area of foreign policy. There was only one issue on which he would take an absolutely clear position in advance: China. If Kennedy recognized commnist China, as some liberal Democrats urged, Eisenhower said he would attack the decision and try to rally public opinion against it. Kennedy did not comment, but I had no doubt that Eisenhower's warning had its desired effect.

The meeting broke up and we went outside into a heavy snowfall that had started while we were in the Cabinet Room. By the next day, it would blanket all of Washington, adding chaos and an air of special beauty to the spectacle of the Inauguration. By then, John F. Kennedy would be responsible for the problems we had just discussed, and for everything else as well. The transition was over.

21

The Presidency and Foreign Crises

INAUGURATION AND THE ALFALFA CLUB

Thoughts of Laos and Cuba were far from my mind the next day, as John F. Kennedy took the oath of office. Watching from the stands behind the new President, with most of the loudspeakers facing away from us, bundled up against the freezing weather, Marny and I probably had less of a sense of the occasion, and the brilliance of his Inaugural Address, than most Americans watching at home on television. But it was a glorious day to revel in the pomp and ceremony of a great event, and what seemed to everyone present to be a transition of power to a new generation of Americans.

We joined the Kennedys and their other guests on the reviewing stand in front of the White House for the Inaugural parade. Mercifully, the stands were heated, and although the parade seemed to go on forever, there was a congenial quality to this moment, suspended in time, as it were, between the old and the new. We were seated three rows behind the President, and in the middle of the parade, he invited us to join him in the front row for a while.

The day ended with the usual round of Inaugural balls, made especially unforgettable by the beauty and confusion caused by the heavy snowfall. Even though it snows almost every year in Washington, the nation's capital has always thought of itself as a Southern city in which snow is a rarity; hence, a small snowfall in Washington causes more problems than a heavy one in a city better prepared for it. And nothing ever tied Washington up more than the combination of the snow and the Inauguration. Women in long dresses struggled through snowdrifts to get to the parties; a dreamlike quality suffused the scene.

The next night, one of Washington's most cherished rituals took place, the annual dinner of the Alfalfa Club. The Alfalfa Club is similar to the Gridiron Club, but its members are businessmen, politicians, and private citizens rather than journalists. Its distinguishing feature is that each year, amid much ribbing of the politicians present, it nominates an "Alfalfa Party candidate" for President.

In 1961, the Alfalfa Club chose me as its candidate for President. Bob Hope was asked to make the traditional "nominating" speech. Among the guests that night were President Kennedy, former President Truman, most of the Supreme Court, Vice President Johnson, and almost the entire new Cabinet. I sat next to Hope just below the head table, looking up with pleasure at a scene that I had long hoped to see, Presidents Truman and Kennedy, seated side by side, chatting pleasantly with each other.

The evening began with Bob Hope's nominating speech. Glancing at President Kennedy from time to time for added effect, he said: "You don't hear of Clifford running around nights. You don't hear of Clifford stealing. You don't read about Clifford in *Confidential* magazine. That's what I like about Clifford. He never gets caught. He has the combined virtues of a Truman and an Eisenhower—he plays the piano like Ike and swings a golf club like Harry." Hope commented on my political astuteness in 1960: "Before the convention Clifford personally endorsed Johnson, Symington, Stevenson, and Kennedy."

In reply, noting that the Alfalfa Club had nominated outstanding men for forty-seven straight years and they had all lost, I pledged to run a tough race. "I say to hell with this business of being a good loser," I said, "let's be a lousy winner for a change."

When President Kennedy spoke at the end of the evening, he made a joke that I would always treasure:

> Clark Clifford is a wonderful fellow. He was enormously helpful during the campaign. After I was elected, he handled the transition. He picked the Cabinet, set up the command posts in the old Administration, and even rode a buffalo in the Inaugural parade. But after the election, when everyone else was seeking a reward for their contributions to the Democratic victory, he didn't ask me for anything. So I said to him, "Now, Clark, you've done so much for me. What can I do for you?" And Clark said, "Nothing, Mr. President.

> You can't do anything for me. But if you insist, the only thing I would ask is to have the name of my law firm printed on the back of the one-dollar bill."

In the first few weeks after the Inauguration, everything seemed to go as well for the new Administration as that opening evening had. The First Couple seemed to float on air, above and beyond the reach of mere mortals, even other Presidents. I watched with pleasure as Jackie Kennedy blossomed in her new role as First Lady. It was, as Arthur Schlesinger would later write, "the hour of euphoria."

A JOB OFFER

As I had suspected, President Kennedy did not believe I had been serious about not seeking a position in his Administration. Four days after he had taken office, he called me from the White House, where he was meeting with Secretary of State Rusk and John McCloy, then serving as his disarmament adviser. The President wanted me to become chief disarmament negotiator with the Soviet Union, commuting between Washington and Geneva. There had been no arms agreements under Eisenhower, but President Kennedy said he was determined to make a fresh start. He wanted to announce my appointment the next day, in his first press conference since taking office.

I told the President I was honored to be considered for this assignment, but at the same time I questioned whether I could accept. I said that I would reply within a day, after consulting McCloy.

In fact, I did not seriously consider this offer. First of all, to accept a full-time job would obviously have cast the sincerity of my original disclaimer into doubt. I wanted to set a precedent for future transitions, and going back on my word would make that impossible. Second, while it was an important and interesting assignment, it was not one to which I would bring any special skills. I had no expertise in the field of arms negotiations, and I did not think this was a task in which my presence would make a real difference. When I informed the President the next day that I was not available, I commented that there were other people with much better qualifications for the job.

FIRST CRISIS: THE BAY OF PIGS

In the early months of the Kennedy Administration, I saw relatively little of the President. This lack of contact came to a quick conclusion after a ceremony in the White House Rose Garden in the early spring, when the President approached me and said, in a slightly teasing tone, "Clark, am I off your list?" Taken aback, I replied, "I don't understand, Mr. President. It never occurred to me that the President would be off anyone's list."

"But the last two times that I asked to see you, I didn't hear from you," he said.

"I'm sorry, Mr. President, but I have had no call from the White House advising me that you wanted to see me."

He gave me a penetrating look. "In the last two weeks you've had no requests that I wanted to see you?"

"No, Mr. President. If you have Mrs. Lincoln call me, she always reaches me." From that time on, he always contacted me through the totally reliable Mrs. Lincoln, and the problem ceased. Neither the President nor I ever said another word about who had prevented communication between us, or why. But it was fairly clear that someone in the tightly knit group around President Kennedy had intentionally failed to contact me when requested to do so.

Our conversation was fortuitous, because it reopened communication on the eve of the greatest disaster of his Administration, the American-sponsored invasion of Cuba at the Bay of Pigs. Launched on the morning of April 16, 1961, it was poorly planned, poorly executed, and heavily infiltrated by agents of Fidel Castro. Almost the entire invasion force was captured or killed.

The Bay of Pigs changed the course of the Kennedy Administration. He would never again accept anything that resembled conventional wisdom or bureaucratic momentum without intense questioning. He might make mistakes in the future, but they would be *his* mistakes, not someone else's. It had taken a catastrophe to turn the rhetoric about a new beginning into a harsh reality, but it had happened.

The moment I entered the Oval Office for the first time after the Bay of Pigs I could see a change in the President. His mood was somber, his normal grace buried in a shell of regret, anger, and distress. I had never seen him so depressed. As he had already publicly stated, he accepted the ultimate responsibility as his own. But he was angry, and he wanted to prevent such a tragedy from ever recurring.

"Let me tell you something," he said. "I have had two full days of hell—I haven't slept—this has been the most excruciating period of my life. I doubt my Presidency could survive another catastrophe like this."

He did not dwell on the details of the disaster. He knew that, like the rest of the country, I was well aware of what had happened: contrary to CIA predictions, the people of Cuba had not rallied in support of the invasion force, air cover for the invasion had not been planned properly, Castro's agents had infiltrated the invasion force in advance, the American role in the invasion was going to be fully revealed, and the whole operation had been ill conceived from the outset.

He analyzed his predicament in precise, biting, angry words I would long remember: "I made a bad decision. The decision I made was faulty because it was based upon the wrong advice. The advice was wrong because it was based upon incorrect facts. And the incorrect facts were due to a failure of intelligence."

I listened as he continued: "You were one of the main drafters of the legislation that created the CIA, and watched it develop since its birth. I want you to join a Presidential board to oversee the operations of the intelligence community. You turned down the arms control job because of the commitment you made when you went to work on the transition, but this is not a full-time job, and I consider it important that you participate as a member of this board."

I accepted the invitation immediately, and wrote him on May 9, 1961, that I considered a "comprehensive investigation" of the CIA, going far beyond General Taylor's Bay of Pigs study, essential. I was convinced, I wrote,

> that such an investigation will reveal such basic shortcomings to require immediate Presidential action. . . . [T]he Agency's activities are inherently dangerous and embarrassing when not conducted with consummate skill. . . . An inquiry will probably reveal that there are certain present Agency operations in which U.S. involvement is being concealed no better than it was in the Cuban effort. . . . [Our] objective should be to provide a comprehensive set of recommendations to insure that the intelligence system becomes an effective tool in the hands of the President rather than a constant source of personal embarrassment and national concern.

THE PFIAB

Thus began almost seven years of service on one of the least known and most sensitive organizations in the U.S., the President's Foreign Intelligence Advisory Board (PFIAB)—first as a member, then, for almost five years beginning in April, 1963, as Chairman.*

Its origins lay in a prior organization, established by President Eisenhower in February 1956, known as the President's Board of Consultants on Foreign Intelligence Activities. Ironically, one of the original members appointed by President Eisenhower was Ambassador Joseph P.

*When I became Chairman of PFIAB, Allen Dulles, the retired director of the CIA, sent me a copy of his book, *The Craft of Intelligence,* inscribed, "To Clark Clifford, who worked on the organization of the C.I.A. in 1947 and fifteen years later became chief among its 'watchdogs.' "

Kennedy—who, for unexplained reasons, resigned only five months after being appointed. President Kennedy originally planned to abolish it, along with so many other committees and commissions that he and his team felt were superfluous—"bureaucratic obstructions," he once said, "to a vigorous, activist foreign policy." The Board of Consultants was lying moribund and ignored, waiting for its formal termination, when the Bay of Pigs staggered President Kennedy's confidence in Allen Dulles and the CIA. Kennedy recognized immediately that he needed a separate group of advisers on intelligence activities who reported directly to him.

Rather than create a new group, President Kennedy "reactivated" and upgraded the Board of Consultants and renamed it. As its Chairman, he chose the same man who had headed the Eisenhower Board of Consultants, James R. Killian, Jr., the President of the Massachusetts Institute of Technology.

We met with President Kennedy for the first time on May 15, 1961. Before the meeting with him, I repeated to the Board his haunting words to me right after the Bay of Pigs: "I doubt my Presidency could survive another catastrophe like this." Kennedy was blunt in telling us what he expected of the PFIAB, and what its mandate would be. We would have access, he said, to every aspect of the activities of the intelligence community.* In addition, our group would be expected to follow up on any recommendations that he approved and to make sure they were fully implemented.

THE PFIAB IN ACTION: "TECHNICAL MEANS"

I found the PFIAB to be one of the most rewarding governmental activities in which I was ever involved. We met regularly, and reviewed hundreds of issues ranging from satellite reconnaissance to every form of scientific and human intelligence. We made 170 formal recommendations to President Kennedy in the space of only twenty-nine months, most relating to intelligence activities within the Department of Defense, the rest in the Department of State and the CIA. He approved 125 of these recommendations, disapproved two, and deferred action on the rest. At the time of his death, eighty-five of the 125 approved recommendations had been implemented; the rest were completed under President Johnson, and we continued to make recommendations at about the same pace throughout Johnson's tenure.

President Kennedy wanted the PFIAB to reflect a balance between

*Despite the President's statement, there were several important matters about which the PFIAB was never told, including the assassination plots against foreign leaders later revealed during the Church Committee hearings in 1975–1976.

technicians and generalists. One member, General Maxwell Taylor, stayed on the Board only a few months before the President recalled him to active military service and appointed him Chairman of the Joint Chiefs of Staff. (When I became Secretary of Defense in 1968, Taylor, who had returned to the Board in 1965, succeeded me as Chairman.) The other generalists were an impressive group: Jimmy Doolittle, the legendary Air Force General who had led the raid over Tokyo during World War II; Harvard historian William Langer; former Undersecretary of State Robert D. Murphy, at that time the president of Corning Glass International; President Eisenhower's national security assistant, Gordon Gray, and Frank Pace, President Truman's Secretary of the Army.

To me the most valuable members of the PFIAB, though—the men who introduced me to the brave new world of modern technology—were two brilliant scientists, Edwin Land, the inventor of the Polaroid Land camera, and William Baker, the President of Bell Labs. They were to play an immensely important, and much underappreciated, role in the development of our nation's intelligence capability. As they fought for the modernization of American intelligence, they gave me the equivalent of a graduate course in modern technology. Dr. Baker served on the PFIAB until 1990, a record without parallel: for over thirty years he campaigned with single-minded determination and effectiveness to assure that American intelligence technology remained ahead of the rest of the world, especially in the field of satellite and electronic technology.

The tutelage of Drs. Baker and Land turned all of us into missionaries for intelligence collection by "technical means": that is, electronic, photographic, and satellite espionage. To this day, I firmly believe that the U.S. should vastly increase its commitment to the finest state-of-the-art technologies in these fields.

Baker and Land not only showed us what technologies already existed; they forecast, with prescience and accuracy, the trends of the next two decades. I would never forget the day they brought to a PFIAB meeting some of the first ultrahigh-resolution photographs taken from a satellite. Today such photographs seem commonplace, but we were awed and amazed as we gazed for the first time upon photographs taken of a tennis court from one hundred miles above the ground, with resolution so clear that one could clearly see a tennis ball lying on the court!

I felt that the era of cloak-and-dagger operations had more or less run its course. To be sure, there was still a role in the world for the daring agent operating inside another government or in a closed society such as the Soviet Union. We did not advocate any curtailment of such activities, but we felt that Allen Dulles, an aging veteran of the clandestine world and a hero of some of the most daring exploits of World War II, was insufficiently alert to the importance and possibilities of collecting intelligence with new technologies.

THE PFIAB: ITS VALUE TO PRESIDENTS, FROM KENNEDY TO BUSH

The value of such an organization to the President depends, of course, on how he uses it. In the last thirty years, President Kennedy used the PFIAB the most, and got the most benefit from it. He met with our Board at least twelve times for lengthy sessions in which we reported to him on a wide variety of issues, and in addition he regularly called individual members to ask their opinion or advice. In April 1963, when he asked me to become its chairman, he told me that the PFIAB was more useful to him than any other Presidential advisory board.

Other Presidents have used the PFIAB in different, and, I believe, less effective ways. President Johnson met with the Board less frequently, but relied as much on individual members, sending us on special missions to various parts of the world. (On my first trip to Vietnam, in 1965, I would travel as the Chairman of PFIAB.) Under President Nixon, the Board continued to meet regularly but had less contact with him. Gerald Ford expanded membership on the Board and appointed as Chairman Leo Cherne, the dynamic president of the International Rescue Committee—but Ford did not listen to it carefully.

To my regret, President Carter took the advice of his Director of Central Intelligence, Admiral Stansfield Turner, and abolished the Board. Like most DCIs, Turner felt the Board encroached on his prerogatives. When he abolished the PFIAB, President Carter did not realize he was denying himself an important tool in the execution of his duties. Ronald Reagan reestablished the PFIAB, but he was wholly uninterested in its activities, and made some of the most undistinguished appointments imaginable, mixing a few qualified people with some of his friends and social cronies.* In 1989, President Bush considered once again abolishing it.[1] As a former Director of Central Intelligence himself, President Bush undoubtedly was reacting to the Board in the same way that Admiral Turner and most other DCIs have done.

Presidents, though, should desire a strong and effective PFIAB for precisely the same reason that DCIs do not want it to exist—to provide, in the words of President Kennedy's letter appointing me as its Chairman,

*Ironically, one of President Reagan's appointees to the Board, Zbigniew Brzezinski, had issued the orders for its abolition in 1977, while serving as President Carter's National Security Assistant.

"an independent review and assessment of the objectives and conduct" of the intelligence community.[2] Bush eventually recognized this fact, and reconstituted the PFIAB with former Senator John Tower as its Chairman, and one of the nation's most experienced and brilliant intelligence officers, retired Admiral Bobby Ray Inman, as its Vice Chairman.

The greatest failure of the PFIAB over the years was not that it delved too deeply into the activities of the intelligence community, but that it did not delve deeply enough—as in the Iran-*contra* scandal, which the PFIAB was prohibited from examining by the Reagan Administration. I believe as strongly today as I did in 1947 in the importance of a strong and effective intelligence service, but many of the activities of the CIA over the years have been misguided or wrong, going far beyond the needs of the nation, and serving only the narrow bureaucratic interests of the very agency in the American government least susceptible to oversight. The Congressional intelligence oversight committees cannot be asked to fulfill a role that properly belongs within the executive branch. Were I to make recommendations today to an incoming President, I would urge that the PFIAB be upgraded and strengthened—a strong and independent PFIAB is in the President's interest, no matter what the CIA says.

THE PFIAB: TURF WARS WITH THE DCI

Tension had existed between Allen Dulles and the old Board of Consultants, but since Dulles knew after the Bay of Pigs that he would be leaving the CIA, he did not spend much time worrying about the PFIAB. But a fierce struggle soon broke out between the PFIAB and Dulles's successor, John McCone.

In the summer of 1961, President Kennedy raised with me the idea of my replacing Dulles as DCI. Upon discussion, we quickly agreed that this would be inappropriate; I felt that my commitment not to join the Administration still applied, and in any case I was not the right person to run the American intelligence community. In the fall of 1961 the President chose a Republican businessman from California, John McCone. A deeply ideological anticommunist, McCone had a quiet but blunt speaking manner, and did not submerge his strong personal opinions inside official assessments in the manner of most senior intelligence officials.

From the beginning, McCone looked with suspicion upon the PFIAB. He found meeting with us a nuisance and continually delayed providing us information that we regarded as essential. He made an early run at the PFIAB, suggesting to the President that the PFIAB become *his* advisory group, instead of the President's. Needless to say, we rebuffed this attempt to incorporate the organization into the CIA.

One of the outstanding issues between Allen Dulles and the PFIAB was one that had existed since 1947—that of the dual role of the DCI as head of the CIA and overall chief of all American intelligence agencies. We believed that the DCI should oversee the entire intelligence community; Dulles had ignored the rest of the intelligence community, while keeping everyone else ignorant of his activities. When McCone took over, the PFIAB urged McCone to choose a professional intelligence officer as his deputy to run the CIA, and focus on the larger intelligence community. Although the President endorsed every recommendation the PFIAB made on this matter, McCone made only a perfunctory, and unsuccessful, effort to coordinate the entire community.

The friction between us reached a crescendo at the end of 1962, shortly after the Cuban Missile Crisis. McCone had repeatedly tried to prevent the PFIAB from obtaining material and information. I found this intolerable and so informed the Board: if McCone was going to set himself up as a censor of what the PFIAB could and could not see, I said, then the Board's functions and rationale would be destroyed. It was up to us, not the DCI, to decide what material we wished to see, and if McCone prevailed, I would not want to continue on the Board. When he heard of my concern, President Kennedy instructed McCone to be more responsive to our requests. This was done, but a breach had been opened with McCone that remained to the end of his tenure.

From time to time, President Kennedy called on the PFIAB to investigate the performance of the intelligence community. He wanted a case study by the PFIAB of major intelligence failures, and he hoped such studies would reduce the number of times we were surprised by events. In this last hope Kennedy, and the nation, would be sorely disappointed, but he nonetheless deserved praise for his efforts.

The most notable examples of events which we were asked to reexamine during my tenure on the Board were the Berlin Wall, which stunned the West when it was started without any warning, in August 1961; the Soviet attempt to deploy missiles in Cuba in October 1962; and the Israeli strafing of the USS *Liberty* during the Six-Day War in 1967, in which thirty-two Americans died. Each of these important benchmarks in the history of American foreign policy—one of them the only nuclear confrontation in history—had its own special attributes.

THE BERLIN WALL

From 1961 until its dramatic dismantling in 1989, the Berlin Wall was the ugliest of all the symbols of the Cold War. It took twenty-eight years for the Wall to come down, but America's strong stand in Berlin, in both 1961 and 1948, was critical in stemming the spread of Soviet power in Europe.

The world was stunned when it went up. The Soviets apparently made the final decision to build it only a week earlier—probably in a secret meeting of Warsaw Pact leaders in Moscow—and no messages concerning it were picked up over those channels most accessible to electronic intelligence. Materials for permanent construction were brought into Berlin only *after* an initial barrier of barbed wire had been hastily put up overnight.

Still, we in the PFIAB felt that the intelligence community should have been more alert to the possibility. We found that the American Ambassador to the Soviet Union, Llewellyn Thompson, had warned in March that the East Germans might try to close the border. We noted also that on June 15, 1961, East German party boss Walter Ulbricht, in one of his rare press conferences, had answered a question with an unnecessarily specific answer: "I understand your question to imply that there are people in West Germany who would like to see us mobilize workers of the capital for the purpose of building a wall. I am not aware of any such intention." No one paid attention to Ulbricht's statement at the time, but the intelligence community studied it carefully later. Why did Ulbricht refer to "building a wall" when the questioner had not mentioned it? Finally, there was a particularly tragic aspect of the affair: the CIA's best agent in the Soviet Union, Colonel Oleg Penkovsky, learned of the decision on August 9, but either failed or was unable to notify his handlers in the West. He was later caught and executed by the KGB after sending information concerning the next, and greatest, crisis in East-West relations.

THE CUBAN MISSILE CRISIS

The PFIAB had no role in the Cuban Missile Crisis until a few hours before President Kennedy's speech to the nation on Monday, October 22, 1962, when I called several of its members asking that they be prepared to fulfill their responsibilities to the President on a moment's notice. Our mandate did not involve us in operational matters, but I assumed that we would be asked to review the intelligence aspects of the crisis when it was over. This was indeed the case. Thus, a few words on the intelligence aspects of the situation are in order, especially because it was intelligence—first the lack of it, then its conclusive nature—that determined the timing and nature of our response.

The PFIAB had discussed Cuba repeatedly since the Bay of Pigs, seventeen months earlier, that had led to our formation. On September 28, 1962, McCone discussed Cuba with us at length, in an atmosphere affected by a series of speeches that New York Senator Kenneth Keating and others were making, charging that the Soviet Union was putting offensive missiles in Cuba. (Subsequent examination showed that Keating's sources were untrained civilians unable to distinguish between offensive and defensive missiles, but Keating's speeches were of considerable political importance.) In that meeting, McCone reviewed with us the most recent satellite photography, taken on August 29: it showed surface-to-air missile (SAM) sites and a cruise-type missile on its launch pad, but no offensive missiles. McCone expressed his personal view—not shared by his own intelligence officers—that what we were looking at was part of a phased operation in which medium-range ballistic missiles would be put in place after our reconnaissance aircraft had been denied access to airspace over the island by the deployment of Soviet MiG 21's.

When the PFIAB reviewed the intelligence on November 9, after the crisis, we were faced with a dilemma: we did not wish to criticize the President, who had handled the crisis brilliantly once the Soviet missiles had been positively identified by American intelligence, but we felt the length of time it had taken to discover the missiles was dangerously and inexcusably long. We were particularly disturbed that there had been no overflights of Cuba between August 29 and October 14 despite public charges that offensive missiles were being installed. Although the matter was delicate, I felt it was our responsibility to bring our views to Kennedy's attention—especially since his critics were publicly charging him with a failure to act on their early warnings.

What we found caused still more friction between the PFIAB and McCone—which was ironic, since McCone was the only person in the intelligence community to predict what the Soviets were going to do. But his warnings had been couched in highly emotional and impressionistic terms, and he never pushed the intelligence community into making a more intensive effort to corroborate his beliefs. Part of the reason for this was, in my view, highly personal: McCone, a widower, had remarried in 1962, and he spent a crucial portion of September on his wedding trip in France. From France he sent strongly worded personal messages—the so-called honeymoon cables—repeating the views that he had expressed to the PFIAB in September, but he still did nothing to speed up the pace of air reconnaissance.

When we examined the reasons for the six-week delay in reconnaissance flights, everyone pointed the finger at someone else. McCone and his agency blamed the delay on bad weather and limitations imposed at a high level on the use of the U-2. I felt that there was another factor: a state of mind within the intelligence community, encouraged by the negative results of the August 29 photography, which rejected the possibility of offensive missiles in Cuba.

In late December, the PFIAB returned to the same subject. When we reviewed McCone's report of his own agency's performance, I noted that, not surprisingly, the report downplayed the shortcomings of intelligence. Unimpressed, I bluntly called the report a "snow job" that confirmed many of my doubts concerning the intelligence community. I found it preposterous, for example, that the national intelligence estimators had declared that there were not likely to be offensive missiles in Cuba on September 19—at the exact moment when the DCI, in his "honeymoon cables," was predicting the opposite. *It was clear that the estimators had limited themselves to preconceived notions.* I was also critical of the excessive "delicacy" with which the question of scheduling overflights of Cuba had been handled, and I expressed surprise at the failure to analyze the charges made in the speeches of Senator Keating.

I asked my fellow boardmembers a direct question: If a situation similar to Cuba were to be encountered again, and our intelligence were about the same, would anyone in the room be satisfied? In the ensuing silence, I said I would not be, nor did I think that the President should be. He deserved better intelligence, and the successful outcome of the Missile Crisis should not lull us into a false sense of comfort over what had happened. The Republican National Committee had made a preposterous charge against President Kennedy: he had deliberately withheld information on the missiles in Cuba until just before the Congressional elections in November in order to influence the outcome. The facts proved otherwise, I commented, and showed that the delays had been caused by decisions made within the intelligence community for internal reasons.

We continued our discussion in subsequent meetings. In March 1963, Ambassador Robert Murphy told McCone that the entire Board had reached the conclusion that there had been a significant intelligence failure, and it was our duty to report our views to the President. When McCone responded angrily that Murphy had misstated the facts, we enumerated thirty-five specific failures, of which McCone conceded only seven.

Thus began the struggle to control the history and assessment of the Cuban Missile Crisis. I was concerned that the President would be hurt by the CIA's efforts to protect itself, but my major objective, expressed repeatedly in PFIAB meetings, was to strengthen the intelligence efforts in any future crises. I discussed both of these matters with President

Kennedy in the spring of 1963, shortly before he asked me to succeed Killian as Chairman. Over the next two decades, the failure of every subsequent President to make the intelligence community perform better was to add immeasurably to our nation's problems in many parts of the world, including Korea, Vietnam, Cambodia, Iran, Afghanistan, Nicaragua, Libya, Lebanon, and, most recently, Iraq.

In April 1963, I succeeded Killian, who was resigning as Chairman of the PFIAB for health reasons. Approval was not unanimous. Ignoring my role in the drafting of the 1947 legislation setting up the CIA, and my subsequent involvement in military and intelligence matters, *The New York Times* criticized my appointment in an editorial, saying that

> Mr. Clifford has a brilliant mind, but as a Democratic trouble-shooter for the Democratic party, he is inextricably associated with partisan politics. . . . The selection is at best unfortunate. It is bound to give the impression that our intelligence activities will be monitored—not by a chairman who is an expert in the field—but by one who is essentially a politician.[3]

I felt that this criticism was unfair: my interest in government vastly exceeded my interest in politics, and I had always tried to keep the two separate. Jim Killian wrote a gracious letter to the *Times* after the editorial appeared, supporting my appointment and adding that if his health had permitted him to stay on the Board, he "would be happy to serve under [Clifford's] chairmanship."

22

The Presidency, Closer to Home

JACQUELINE KENNEDY

As his lawyer, I had been much closer to Jack Kennedy than to Jackie while he was a Senator, but at the beginning of 1961 a series of matters came up on which I began, at the President's request, to work closely with her.

At first glance, little would seem to be left to say about Jacqueline Kennedy Onassis. Over the last thirty years, more words have probably been written about her than about any other woman in the world. Although she has not given an on-the-record interview during the entire period of time since she left the White House, her every public appearance receives international attention, and each anniversary or milestone—her children's graduations, her own birthdays, anniversaries of her husband's death—bring her back into the public consciousness.

The curiosity about her is understandable. She is both intensely private and also the most dramatic of public people. She is beautiful and conducts herself in public in a regal manner. Above all, her very presence or appearance, no matter what the occasion, evokes a nearly primordial national memory of that terrible weekend that began in Dallas and ended at Arlington National Cemetery, when with faultless dignity and unbearable grief she embodied the pain and sorrow and sense of loss that the entire nation felt at the death of its young President.

One could not have foreseen such an outcome for the young girl whom

I first met prior to her marriage in 1953. She was only twenty-three at the time, and her husband-to-be, whose health was still seriously endangered by injuries sustained during World War II, was thirty-six. They seemed on the surface to be a perfect couple. But marrying into the Kennedys was an extraordinarily difficult undertaking: they were very close-knit, but competitive and outspoken among themselves, an exuberant group of outgoing touch-football players. Jackie did not seem to me to fit in well with them, especially in the early years, and I am not sure she ever really felt that she was part of the group. She was quiet, graceful, and introspective, drawn to the aesthetic and social rather than to politics or sports—except for horseback riding. Strains seriously threatened the Kennedy marriage during the late fifties, but once the great quest for the Presidency began, Jackie involved herself heavily, earning respect and credit from the entire family.

When her husband reached the White House, Jacqueline Kennedy truly came into her own. Neither he nor Jackie had expected that, almost overnight, she would become internationally famous. I could see the respect and regard that he held for her increase steadily. Recently, writers have chosen to concentrate on the difficulties in their relationship, but there was another side to their marriage. When, for example, they traveled together to France for the visit in which the President memorably introduced himself as "the man who accompanied Jacqueline Kennedy to Paris," the pride and pleasure he took in his wife seemed to me to be genuine. Under the most intense pressure, this thirty-one-year-old woman performed flawlessly. So many other political wives have come apart or disappeared from view under less pressure, but Jackie Kennedy never faltered as First Lady.

The first two assignments that brought me into closer contact with Jackie concerned real estate. Such transactions are not always as easy for Presidents to manage as they might be for ordinary people—as proved to be the case here.

The Kennedys' Georgetown house had quickly become famous as the television backdrop for many of the President-elect's public statements and announcements during the transition. After the election, the Kennedys put it up for sale, and received an immediate offer of $102,000—a nice profit on the $78,000 they had paid for it in 1957. Jackie agreed to the offer, and the President-elect, while in Florida, indicated his acceptance of the offer, but before he signed the contract of sale, another potential buyer came forward with an offer of $110,000. Jackie, who wished to accept the higher offer, asked me if they were bound by the first. I told her the prospective sale of their house had been a transaction under discussion but was not binding. After several months of publicized negotiations, the house was sold to the original bidder for the higher price, satisfying both him and the Kennedys. One aspect of this minor transaction particularly amused me: while I represented the seller, the eventual buyer was represented by Dean Acheson. The press, which had followed the sale and nonsale of the Kennedys' house carefully, had fun with the idea of the two of us doing the legal work on a simple real estate matter. But, of course, everything about the Kennedys was big news, and 3307 N Street was no longer an ordinary house.

At about the same time we were negotiating the sale of their Georgetown house, the Kennedys asked an old family friend, the painter Bill Walton, to scout the Virginia hunt country for a quiet weekend place they could either buy or rent. Walton soon located a beautiful four-hundred-acre estate called Glen Ora, near Middleburg, less than an hour by car from the White House. A perfect spot for the Kennedys, it provided privacy and seclusion, and a chance to relax in secure surroundings. There was only one problem: its owner, Gladys Tartiere, did not wish to sell or rent to the Kennedys. She abhorred the idea of the Secret Service setting up shop in her house, and nothing Walton said to her made any difference.

Faced with this impasse, Jackie Kennedy called me. Apologizing for bringing up such a minor problem, she said, "Jack thinks you are the only one who might be able to talk this woman into letting us have the house." I said I would do my best to "establish a relationship" with Mrs. Tartiere.

I called on Gladys Tartiere at once. She and her husband, Raymond, had bought Glen Ora in 1940, and after his death, she continued to use it. She said that she had nothing personal against the Kennedys, but she repeated to me her concern about damage to the house. I listened and asked if she would please think it over. When I returned to see her, I assured her that the house would be kept in perfect condition, and would be returned to her in the same or better shape than when she had rented it. She turned me down again.

I informed Jackie of my first two calls. She told me how much it would mean to her and her husband if they could rent it. I decided to make one last try. I appealed to Mrs. Tartiere on what amounted to national security grounds, saying that one should not refuse a President such a reasonable request, especially if it would help ease the great burdens of his office. This time, Mrs. Tartiere very reluctantly agreed, although only for a period of two years. When I described to President Kennedy my presentation to Mrs. Tartiere, he said he thought that I had gone about as far as anyone could go in applying the national interest to a real estate transaction. Jackie was delighted. A few days after the deal was completed, I received by messenger from the White House the most treasured "payment" I ever received from a client: a charming pencil and crayon drawing by Jackie entitled "The Legal Profession." It showed a man with wavy yellow hair, carrying a lawyer's briefcase in one hand and a bunch of flowers and a bottle of champagne in the other, walking up a footpath toward a formidable-looking woman peering angrily out the front window of a large house. Underneath this scene, in a flowery script, Jackie had written, "Establishing a Relationship."

Our next collaboration was of far greater interest, and lasting value.

"I WANT TO MAKE THE WHITE HOUSE THE FIRST HOUSE IN THE LAND"

The first time Jackie saw the family quarters of the White House, escorted by Mrs. Eisenhower shortly after the 1960 election, she was surprised at its run-down appearance. The White House contained almost nothing of historical value or importance. "Everything looked like it came from B. Altman," she said, referring to a now-defunct New York department store. Jackie set out to make the White House beautiful again. The project was a logical extension of her own personality and values. Her sense of style, taste, and tradition were to serve her and the nation well. First she read everything she could find about the Executive Mansion, going through old books and files supplied by the Library of Congress. As she proceeded, she realized that her efforts should go far beyond the family quarters. She decided to try to turn the public rooms in the White House into a sort of national home, something which would make all Americans proud.

When President Kennedy realized the scope and ambition of his wife's plans, he called me. He remembered the furor and bitterness that President Truman had encountered when he added a second-floor balcony to the South Portico of the White House in 1947–1948, and he knew that I had lived through that event. Although today the Truman Balcony looks like it was part of the original White House, at the time it and its designer-President were criticized so severely for tampering with the structure that President Truman told me that he sometimes felt as if he had been accused of interfering with the natural order of the universe. President Kennedy did not want a repetition of this incident, and asked me to join him and his wife for lunch on February 6, barely two weeks after the Inauguration, to discuss her ideas.

As we ate, I described the way the White House had looked before and after the 1949–1952 renovation. President Truman had been disappointed in the rebuilding effort, calling it "tacky and inferior" to the prerenovation White House. With his strong sense of history, he had wanted to redecorate it in a way that matched the tradition of the White

House with furnishings that were equally historic—but funds had not been available, and the result was the somewhat pathetic and shabby air the building had acquired during the Eisenhower years.

"How many people do you think come through the White House every day?" Mrs. Kennedy asked me. I had no idea, but, upon checking, found that on most days the number ran into the thousands. "We must make this building something that they will be proud of," she said. "I want to make the White House the first house in the land."

Some have suggested that Jackie and I disagreed over the restoration of the White House. This is not true: I saw the merit in Jackie's idea and supported it strongly. I did warn her and the President, however, that in proceeding with her dream the greatest care had to be taken not to offend the American people. "The White House," I said, "is a sacred cow to the American people and woe to any President who touches it without preparing the groundwork."

I reminded the Kennedys that the White House was government property, occupied only temporarily by whomever was President, and cautioned that the legal groundwork had to be prepared carefully so as to avoid any political problems. At President Kennedy's request, I created, with my law partner Carson Glass, an airtight legal framework for Jackie's work in the White House. On February 23, 1961, only a month after the Inauguration, Jackie unveiled the first result of our efforts, the Fine Arts Committee for the White House, established for the purpose of locating "authentic furniture of the date of the building of the White House and the raising of funds to purchase this furniture as gifts for the White House."

Mrs. Kennedy became honorary chairman of the Fine Arts Committee for the White House; I was its legal adviser. When the committee met for the first time, we discussed how donors might be approached, and we laid out simple guidelines to accept gifts. We expected a few gifts, but nothing prepared us for the response. Within a few weeks after the announcement almost seventy-five thousand letters poured into the White House, offering to donate or sell an astonishing variety of items. Of course, over 99 percent of this odd assortment had to be declined. Most of it, predictably, was undistinguished, and much was offered for personal profit. Still, it was clear that once again, what interested Jacqueline Kennedy interested millions of other Americans.

Meanwhile, she set her sights on obtaining some of the very best furniture and paintings still in private hands in the U.S. When necessary, Jackie herself would take on the task of soliciting objects. I doubt anyone was ever able to turn her down. One day, for example, she decided that the White House needed a valuable painting of Benjamin Franklin by David Martin, which was owned by Walter Annenberg, the wealthy publisher from Philadelphia who was later to serve as President Nixon's Ambassador to the United Kingdom. One day, she used her magic over the telephone with a man she had never met: "Mr. Annenberg, today you are the first citizen of Philadelphia," she told him in her whispery, almost breathless voice, "and in his day, Benjamin Franklin was the first citizen of Philadelphia. That is why, Mr. Annenberg, I thought of you. Do you think that a great Philadelphia citizen would give the White House a portrait of another great Philadelphia citizen?"

Annenberg hardly knew what had hit him. He did not tell her that the painting had cost him over $250,000—a substantial sum for an American painting in those preinflationary days. He did say he would like a few days to think it over, but less than thirty minutes later he called back to say yes—and the painting was shipped to the White House within a few days.

I was not immune to Jackie's charm and determination. On January 15, 1962, in a handwritten letter asking my assistance in finding legal ways to raise money for the acquisition of works of art without creating a political problem for her husband, Jackie wrote me, using her characteristic punctuation:

> You always come to the rescue whether it is Profiles in Courage or the Blaufeld [*sic*]* case—so I would be eternally gratified if you would keep me out of debtor's prison and make this work—which is so worthwhile and has done so well so far—possible to continue. Jayne Wrightsman—my friend who works the hardest—said we should say we were trying to raise 2 million—Jack and I agree that figure sounds awful. It could be politically used against us—"palace of the Caesars" etc.—that Congressman Oglethorpe** used against Van Buren. . . . On Feb. 16 there will be an hour CBS show of me showing what we have done so far here. Jack thinks the [fund-raising] drive should come as soon as possible after that.

In May 1962, some reporters started investigating a report of a potentially questionable deal between an antique dealer and an employee of the Smithsonian, which involved an expensive piece of furniture. The issue was not serious, and faded from sight quickly; but Jackie was worried and sent me a note with some suggestions of what I might say to Alfred Friendly, the managing editor of *The Washington Post,* if his newspaper pursued the story. She was unusually sharp:

> Dear Clark,
>
> I wrote this on plane—points for you to bring up with Friendly—

*See below, this chapter.

**Jackie was thinking of Congressman Charles Ogle of Pennsylvania, who used this phrase in the "Tippicanoe and Tyler Too" Presidential campaign of 1840.

> to his tired old song "The public has a right to know." Tell him the public does know—its all been printed—why hasn't he read it—and its being done for the public. Why doesn't he think nice thoughts once in awhile and go take a running jump. . . . No other 1st lady tried and no future one will if this is the way her efforts are received.
>
> Your friend!
> Jackie

To her letter she attached a series of "talking points" she thought I might use with reporters, which she had written partly in the third person. They contained some unusually revealing comments about herself:

> Sometimes she got very depressed when she couldn't get big sums of money from strangers but she stuck to the difficult task of finding donors among friends—or friends of Fine Arts Committee members. . . . If [Friendly] thinks this has been a shady operation, that is most unfair of him and he knows it. I have spent 1½ years of working to the bone to make the W.H. what it should be—because I cared, not for kickbacks—and I know perfectly well he realizes that—and everyone who gave did so because they shared my feelings. . . . Ask him if he wants to be on my committee and see what drudgery is really like!

From the outset, we had viewed the Fine Arts Committee of the White House as only part of the solution. Both Jackie and I also wanted to establish a nonprofit organization, which would have far greater leeway to operate than a White House committee. This was the genesis of the White House Historical Association, an organization that was incorporated on November 3, 1961, with John Walker, the director of the National Gallery of Art, David Finley, chairman of the Commission of Fine Arts, and me as its initial incorporators. The White House Historical Association, on whose board I have sat ever since, evolved into a well-established organization with offices near the White House and a distinguished record of publications. At the end of 1961, however, it was simply a name with neither funds nor personnel. To raise money for it, Jackie suggested selling postcards of the White House. I objected to the idea as too commercial for the dignified White House, and Jackie came up with another, superb idea: a White House guidebook.

It was an inspired concept. The original White House guidebook blossomed into a cottage industry of books published by the Historical Association; five are now in print, produced as a public service by the National Geographic Society, including revised versions of the original *Historic Guide.* These books have been an enormous success; close to eight million copies have already been sold, and the proceeds from their sales have funded both the Historical Association and the continued acquisition of historical furnishings and works of art for the White House. They even pay for the official portraits of the Presidents and First Ladies that hang in the White House. In addition, the White House Historical Association now also publishes a series of prints, reproductions of artworks from the White House collection, slides, and—my initial objection having long since been overruled by others—postcards.

On November 3, 1963, in preparation for the next meeting of the White House Historical Association, Jackie sent me a handwritten letter which, in its detail and controlled passion, showed how much the beauty of the White House would owe to the personal drive and vision of this remarkable woman:

> I just wanted to tell you two things so you wouldn't worry and so that you could tell the Association at the next meeting. One is that I will be very economical this year—until we are out of the red. . . . There are two projects ahead that I really care about—and then . . . the White House will be all I ever dreamed for it. These 2 projects are
>
> 1) New curtains for the East Room
>
> 2) New curtains for State Dining Room.
>
> The present East Room curtains have been there since at least 1952 and are falling apart. As they are tied back in the daytime, when they are closed at night they are full of horrible wrinkles and I am always ashamed of them at State Dinners. The new ones are to be the same color—yellow damask—the valences in the same Nineteenth century spirit as these but so much prettier. I am ashamed to confess that the silk for them is already being woven, but you know how Jansen is and we can pay on the installment plan. About the State Dining Room—it still has the ugly yellow curtains when the room was dentist office green.
>
> You know we got a new rug—patterned after a priceless Bessarabian. It is a strip carpet which means that when one part wears out, you can replace it with a strip instead of the whole carpet. The room is white and I have approved the designs for the most beautiful white curtains with a pinkish red tasselled fringe—to pick up that color in the rug.
>
> But the go-ahead signal has not been given on the State Dining Room and won't be until we have the money—but if we are no longer in the White House—could you try to see that it gets done—as it will make the whole first floor you can really be proud of if you are an American wondering how the White House strikes foreign visitors—or just be proud for ourselves.
>
> If you asked me what else there is to do—I would say only this—a decent pair of chandeliers for the ground floor foyer (by movie room) where tourists come in. These shouldn't cost much and I have told

> the curator to scout for them. And some day a beautiful china service for State Dinners . . . but maybe we'll never get around to that and I'll have to look for someone to donate it. I seem to have used up all donors I know.
>
> It would just finish that room off when it is done, and de Gaulle would be ashamed at Versailles in comparison—yet it is not ornate. Versailles isn't the right word to use, I never wanted this house to look like a house, but just what it is—the state rooms used by the President of the United States—with all the best we have had on view.
>
> Thank you dear Clark.
> Jackie

Three weeks after she sent this letter, she would no longer be the First Lady.

A CRISIS FOR EDWARD M. KENNEDY

In September 1961, the President asked my help on another family problem, this one involving his youngest brother, Edward M. Kennedy. As usual in these personal matters, the story began with a call from Evelyn Lincoln requesting, without explanation, that I come immediately to the Oval Office.

When I arrived, President Kennedy was with Bobby. They had been discussing whether or not Ted should run the following year for the Senate seat held until the beginning of 1961 by Jack Kennedy. For just such an eventuality, when John F. Kennedy had left the Senate to become President, the seat had been given by the Democratic Governor of Massachusetts to a Kennedy family friend, Ben Smith, who had promised to fill it only until the next election.

There was, however, an unexpected problem. Unbeknownst to the public, ten years earlier Teddy Kennedy had been asked to withdraw from Harvard College for cheating on a Spanish examination. The President and Bobby wanted my judgment as to its effect on their brother's possible candidacy, and recommendations as to how to deal with it publicly if the family concluded that he should make the race. A few days later, I received a letter from Ted, enclosing some background material and offering to come to Washington at my convenience to discuss the matter further.

From the documents Kennedy had sent me, I learned that during his freshman year at Harvard, a classmate, William A. Frate, had taken two Spanish-language examinations posing as Ted Kennedy. The two boys got away with the first deception; on the second, in June 1951, they were both caught, and admitted their guilt immediately. On June 12, 1951, Harvard asked them both to withdraw from the college. Considering the incident in light of his previous "good record" and a favorable report from his instructor, who felt that he "has shown some regard for the truth regardless of consequences in the unpleasant questioning that followed the examination," Harvard decided against the more severe punishment of dismissal. The distinction was crucial: it meant, in the words of Harvard's letter to Ted, that Harvard was "not crossing you off the books as hopeless," leaving open the question of readmission "if you can convince [the administrative Board] that you are worthy of it."

In my first meeting with Ted Kennedy, I listened carefully as he outlined the incident. As Ted understood fully, there were no extenuating circumstances. He knew that he and Frate had made a huge mistake. He had immediately thereafter enlisted in the Army for two years, during which he had received several commendations for superior service. He was readmitted to Harvard in the fall of 1953, and graduated in 1956 in the second quarter of his class. As I looked at his academic record, I noticed that his grades had gone up each year at Harvard.

When he came to see me, I was struck by how different Ted was from his brothers. He was much bigger than Jack or Bobby, with the build of a professional football player. He was only twenty-nine, and the age difference had created a certain separation between him and his two older brothers. While they obviously loved him, they treated him very much as a kid brother. Ted had immense charm and a boyishness I found appealing. Next to him, the President and the Attorney General no longer seemed quite so young.

After meeting with him, I flew to New York to meet with William Frate, who confirmed every detail of Ted's story. I then met once more with Ted to go over some details, and drew up a balance sheet on the incident in order to make my report to the President.

I did not think this was so serious a problem as the challenge to Senator Kennedy over the authorship of *Profiles in Courage.* Ted had responded properly to his crisis, and, after honorable military service, had returned to Harvard as a good student. If it were not for the fact that the man in question was the youngest brother of the President, it would not have been much of a problem. Accordingly, I sent the President a letter on November 27, 1961, in which I said,

> I have reached the firm conclusion that the occurrence in question will not adversely affect Teddy's chances in a Senate race. If Teddy and his Massachusetts political advisors feel that this is the opportune time for him to run, then he should do so.
>
> Teddy made a mistake in 1951. However, it was over ten years ago

> and he was only nineteen years old at the time. . . . Mistakes in judgment are not uncommon in boys in their teens, and I dare say there is hardly a man who has not committed some similar type of blunder in his youth. I have the conviction that the citizens of Massachusetts, and in fact, the American people, will not hold this against Teddy.
>
> I know of your affection for your brother. I have, however, endeavored to be as objective as possible in submitting my independent views in this regard.

At the President's request, I also sent Ted a letter outlining how I thought the matter should be handled publicly:

> Your attitude on the matter should be frank and forthright. Any attempt at concealment or half truths will lead only to further questions and possible concealment. . . . I believe you should not bring up the incident in the form of a prepared public statement. Your position on the occurrence should be stated, either in answer to a question at a press conference, or it should appear in an article written by a reporter as the result of a question by the reporter.

By early December, it was clear that Teddy Kennedy would indeed seek the nomination for the Senate seat in Massachusetts. His main opponent in the Democratic primary would be Edward J. ("Eddie") McCormack, a favorite nephew of Congressman John McCormack, who had just become Speaker of the House upon the death of Sam Rayburn. A battle between the two leading political powers in the state was shaping up. The President decided that Teddy should follow the suggestion I had made to surface the matter through an interview with a friendly journalist. The man chosen, Robert Healy of *The Boston Globe,* wrote the story on March 30, 1962. The story received national attention, but had no discernible effect on the election. Teddy swamped Eddie McCormack in the Democratic primary, and in the general election defeated George Cabot Lodge, the son of Henry Cabot Lodge, his brother's 1952 opponent for the same seat.

I maintained cordial relations with Ted Kennedy over the next three decades, watching him grow into an outstanding Senator. He demonstrated an indominability of spirit that I found admirable and impressive. We were never as close, however, as I was to President Kennedy, and Ted understandably developed his own set of advisers as time went on.

THE BLAUVELT AFFAIR

In January 1962, Evelyn Lincoln called once again with those words that always somehow seemed to imply an emergency, without actually saying so: "The President would like to see you right away." Ten minutes later, I was alone with President Kennedy, who began the conversation by saying, "You won't believe this one." Thus began my involvement in one of those silly and bizarre incidents that can happen to almost any public official—the wholly inaccurate story which takes on a life of its own. The "Blauvelt Affair" is a remarkable example of how time-consuming it sometimes can be to deal with a complete fabrication.

President Kennedy told me that a story had been circulating that he had been secretly married when he was younger to a woman named Durie Malcolm. The rumors were based upon a privately printed book, a genealogy of all the descendants of a seventeenth-century Dutch Hudson Valley settler named Blauvelt; it had been compiled over twenty years by a retired General Electric toolmaker in New Jersey named Louis L. Blauvelt, who finished his work in 1957, and died two years later at the age of seventy-nine. Fewer than one thousand copies of the book had been printed, but one was on file at the Library of Congress. In the late summer of 1961, an unknown person had photocopied and mailed to several reporters page 884 of this obscure book, which contained the following passage:

> (12,427) DURIE, (KERR), MALCOLM. . . . She was born Kerr, but took the name of her stepfather. She first married Firmin Desloge IV. They were divorced. Durie then married F. John Bersbach. They were divorced, and she married third, John F. Kennedy, son of Joseph P. Kennedy, one time Ambassador to England.

At first, in the summer of 1961, President Kennedy and his staff had tried to deal with the matter by ignoring it; but when the rumor continued to circulate and then surfaced in a few minor periodicals, the President called me. When I asked him what the facts were, he replied, "All I know is that some years ago, I knew very briefly a young woman named Durie Malcolm. I think I had two dates with her. One may have been a dinner date in which we went dancing. The other, to my recollection, was a football game. Those were the only two times I ever saw her. My brother Joe also dated her a few years earlier. I remember that she was quite attractive."

My response startled him, as I knew it would: "I'll go further than that, Mr. President. I think she was one of the most attractive women I ever met."

"What are you talking about?" he asked, genuinely puzzled.

"Well," I replied, "I have known Durie Malcolm for a long time. Some years ago, one of the heirs of a wealthy family in St. Louis, a young man named Firmin Desloge, met this charming girl—my recollection is that she was from Chicago—and brought her back to St. Louis as his wife. Her name was Durie Malcolm. They were a good deal younger than my wife and me, but we saw them quite often socially. She had a great deal of spin and vitality. Firmin Desloge was a nice fellow, but not right for Durie and she left him after a while. Later, she married a man I knew slightly named Tommy Shevlin, a social fellow and a good amateur golfer, and they moved to Palm Beach."

He was amused at this striking coincidence, but he was less amused at the fact that the extract from Blauvelt's genealogy was beginning to circulate widely among right-wing and anti-Catholic circles throughout the nation—with several hundred thousand copies of the item being distributed by bigoted opponents. So far it had not appeared in print in any serious or responsible publication. But the President showed me a "blind" item from a recent issue of *Roll Call,* a publication for Capitol Hill employees, that asked, "Who is the former Senator, now in high public office, who is concealing his former marriage?" The President asked me to deal only with him, his brother, and Press Secretary Pierre Salinger.

I went to the Library of Congress that same day to see for myself the Blauvelt genealogy. It was a tiny item in a huge book that contained virtually nothing but names. There was no evidence that the author had noticed that the man mentioned in the item about Durie was already a United States Senator at the time of publication.

Next, I located Durie Malcolm Desloge Shevlin in Palm Beach and called her up. She was surprised to hear from me again. It had been a long time since we had last seen each other in St. Louis, but she said she had followed my career from time to time. I said I needed to talk to her about President Kennedy: "I want to read to you an item from a book about the genealogy of the Blauvelt family that states that you and President Kennedy were married."

I could hear her laugh. "Good God," she said, "imagine being married to President Kennedy. That's a laugh."

"Durie," I said, "as a lawyer, let me ask you some very formal questions. One, were you ever married to John F. Kennedy?"

Again, she laughed. "No."

"Did you know John F. Kennedy?"

"Yes, I knew him and his brother Joe. He was young and attractive. I believe that it was before he was in the Congress. My recollection is that we had two dates. We may have had dinner in New York and the other time we went to a football game."

"Durie, we are old friends. Let me ask you the sixty-four-dollar question. Was there anything serious between you and John F. Kennedy?"

"Absolutely not," she replied, quite emphatically. "We hardly even knew each other. There were those two casual dates. We did not seem to click and that was all there was to it. How in the world that stuff could have gotten into that genealogy, I do not know. I come from the Blauvelt family, but the genealogy is wrong."

I told her I would report all this back to the President, and we would look for ways to stop the story from spreading any further. She said she did not wish to deal with reporters and would refuse to take their calls, but that we were free to state that she had denied the story if we wanted to do so. I asked her if she would sign an affidavit stating that she had never been married to John F. Kennedy, and she readily agreed.

Throughout the rest of the year, the story continued to circulate without appearing in a major publication. In May 1962, *The Thunderbolt*, which described itself on its masthead as "the official white racial organ of the National States Rights party," ran the item from Blauvelt's book, and accused the national press of suppressing the story. A right-wing business executive in Massachusetts mailed copies of the story to a list of selected "patriots."

In growing numbers, letters began arriving at the White House, asking about the story. The White House replied with a form letter pointing out several gross errors of fact in the genealogy. But, hoping not to give the story any further dissemination, the President and Salinger resisted making any public statement.

Rumors, however, do not have to be true in order to survive. On September 2, 1962, *Parade*, the nationally distributed Sunday newspaper supplement, printed a letter from a reader in its widely read column, "Walter Scott's Personality Parade," written by Lloyd Shearer, asking if the rumor that the President had been married before was true. In telling his readers that the story was false, "Walter Scott" was, of course, disseminating it widely for the first time. And on the same day the British press reported the story.

These two press items convinced the President that he had to take rapid action. In order to "control" the story, he invited his closest friend in the press corps, Benjamin Bradlee, then the *Newsweek* bureau chief in Washington, to print the story in the form of a false rumor revealed, denied, and hopefully buried. At the President's request, I recounted to Ben my involvement in the story. *Newsweek*'s story, in the September 24, 1962 issue, said that the magazine had been aware of the rumor since August 1961, and had found it completely false, but that it had created an "acute" problem for the President as it continued to be widely circulated "by extremist groups . . . for political purpose."

The *Newsweek* story was picked up by the rest of the national press, and was the talk of Washington for a week or so. As the Kennedys had hoped, though, once the falsehood had been exposed to public light, it was reduced to a curious footnote to the Kennedy legend. I remain to this day convinced that the entire affair was nothing more than the result of an error made by an old man who was not careful in checking his facts. I doubt that it would ever have received much attention had it not been for the intense interest and continual rumors swirling around the personal life of President Kennedy and the entire Kennedy family.

THE SUPREME COURT

In the spring of 1962, Justice Charles E. Whittaker resigned from the Supreme Court. It was President Kennedy's first opportunity to nominate someone to the Court, and he asked for my advice. Sitting alone with him in the Oval Office, I delivered what I felt later was a rather ponderous speech about the chance to set a tone for his Administration with a truly outstanding appointment. I told him that, notwithstanding my enormous admiration for President Truman, I felt that one of the weakest aspects of his Presidency had been his appointments to the Supreme Court. The appointments of Presidents Roosevelt and Eisenhower, I said, had been far more distinguished.

As I spoke, I knew that Robert Kennedy was supporting the selection of William Henry Hastie, a Harvard Law School graduate whom President Truman had appointed in 1949 to the Circuit Court, the first black judge to be appointed to such a position. Bobby wanted his brother to be the first President to appoint a black to the Supreme Court. But Chief Justice Earl Warren and William O. Douglas had objected privately, on the grounds that Hastie would probably vote with Frankfurter and the conservative wing.

After researching Hastie's record, I concluded that his qualifications were shaky. He was hardworking and steady, but I felt his opinions did not demonstrate the caliber of excellence the Court required, and I was concerned his appointment would be regarded as politically motivated. I felt that the first black to be appointed to the Court would be scrutinized far more closely than other appointees, and would have to possess the strongest credentials. I told President Kennedy that I felt it would demean both the Court and the civil rights movement if he made an appointment which appeared to be based solely on the grounds of race. I was sure, I told him, that he would have a chance later to appoint a qualified black to the Court.

He asked if I had any personal desire to serve on the Court, adding with his characteristic frankness, "I do not want to suggest by this question that I am considering you for the Court. I just want to know the extent of your personal interest." I replied, with equal frankness, "I made that decision back in the Truman Administration. I am an advocate, not a judge."

I recommended Paul Freund of Harvard, considered by many to be the leading constitutional scholar in the nation. Freund's name had already been raised in press speculation. Some were opposing him on the grounds that he was Jewish, and with Frankfurter still on the Court, the "Jewish seat" was filled. I considered this argument ridiculous, but there were several other problems with Freund. Bobby Kennedy worried that the Administration was already overly identified with Harvard, and some of the President's advisers wondered if Freund was liberal enough.

Faced with this dilemma, the President surprised almost everyone except Bobby. On March 30, 1962, ten days after our meeting, President Kennedy announced he was appointing Byron White, the Deputy Attorney General. At the time of the appointment, the President told Arthur Schlesinger that he fully intended to appoint Freund, Hastie, and Arthur Goldberg to the Court before his tenure ran out.[1]

THE WAR WITH BIG STEEL

In the spring of 1962, President Kennedy had his celebrated showdown with the steel companies. Because of the relationships I had built up as a lawyer with many leading businessmen, Kennedy called me for help. The crisis began on April 10, when the President of the U.S. Steel Corporation, Roger Blough, told the President that his company was about to announce an increase of six dollars per ton in the price of steel. President Kennedy reacted with disbelief and anger. It violated an understanding he thought he had reached with Big Steel—as the powerful steel giants were called—that if he helped hold down wage increases in the latest round of wage negotiations, management would not raise prices. Blough's announcement was sure to start an inflationary cycle in the economy. One year, almost to the day, after the Bay of Pigs, the President did not want to lose a public struggle that would reveal him to be weak and ineffectual. The moment that Blough left the Oval Office, the President set into motion one of the most intense efforts in American history to influence a domestic business decision. That afternoon, he called and asked me to activate any channels to businessmen which might put pressure on U.S. Steel to rescind the price increase.

Whatever the facts as to the understanding between the two parties—Blough denied there had been an understanding on prices, and he stated that he had come to Washington as a "courtesy" to the President—

Blough's action was uncommonly stupid. The President appeared to have been double-crossed. Within hours other big steel companies followed Blough's lead, exacerbating the problem and suggesting collusion.

On the first full day of the public showdown, the President blasted U.S. Steel in a nationally televised press conference, charging them with undermining "our national security in this serious hour in our nation's history when we are confronted with grave crises in Berlin and Southeast Asia."* I made some telephone calls to business friends and clients, telling them that Blough's actions were certain to create a negative climate toward business everywhere. I told my business friends I was convinced a very determined President was not going to yield or compromise.

The next day, Thursday, April 12, I was pulled into the center of the negotiations. All day long, Arthur Goldberg, the experienced labor negotiator who had become Secretary of Labor, tried to bargain with the chairman of U.S. Steel's finance committee, Robert Tyson. When it was clear the negotiations had gone nowhere, Tyson prepared to return to New York.

The President realized that Goldberg's past history as a representative of labor made him a highly adversarial figure in the eyes of the steel executives. From a State dinner that he was giving, the President sent word to me through Charles Bartlett, a close and trusted friend who was a guest, that he wanted me to meet secretly with Tyson before he returned to New York. The talks with Goldberg "had run out the string," Kennedy told Bartlett.

The meeting had to be kept completely secret. After some discussion, Tyson and I agreed to meet aboard the U.S. Steel airplane, which was parked at the small, remote Butler Terminal at National Airport reserved for corporate and private planes. We met around eight o'clock that evening. It was an eerie setting for a meeting of such importance. We were alone, except for a crew member who served us drinks and a light snack. Beyond us, other planes took off and landed in the dark, oblivious to the aircraft parked in a deserted part of the airport. Tyson reviewed the entire story from the point of view of U.S. Steel, continuing to maintain that they had not violated any understanding with the President. When Tyson had finished, I said that no matter what he and Roger Blough thought, the President saw it differently: he would continue to keep the pressure on Big Steel until the price increase was completely rescinded.

Tyson suggested a number of compromises. Perhaps the President would accept a smaller increase? I replied that he would not. If they

*The President ended his opening statement with a stunning piece of rhetoric: "Some time ago I asked each American to consider what he would do for his country, and I asked the steel companies. In the last twenty-four hours we had their answer."

rescinded the entire increase, I was prepared to say that the President would not pursue U.S. Steel with all means at his disposal. However, if U.S. Steel persisted, the President would use every tool available to turn the decision around. Already he had ordered the Defense Department to switch orders for steel away from those companies which had increased prices, even if this meant taking business overseas.

Kennedy and I talked late that night, after the State dinner. He was encouraged by my report. It seemed to both of us that U.S. Steel and the other steel companies which by then had followed its lead were feeling the heat from the immense public pressure that President Kennedy had mobilized. The President decided to keep the channels open. The next morning, before setting out on a trip to Norfolk to witness naval maneuvers, he asked me to go to New York with Goldberg on a military jet to confer directly with Blough. "You stay as long as you have to," he said, "whether it's one hour or one week. Just stay there until the job is done."

At Blough's suggestion, we met on neutral ground at the Carlyle Hotel, famous at the time as President Kennedy's favorite hotel. On the way to New York, I filled Goldberg in on my talk with Tyson. I was concerned that Goldberg, a proud man, might be offended by my role in the discussions, but he seemed to accept that I had been brought into the matter to strengthen him, not to replace him.

A former Wall Street lawyer, Blough was a balding, heavily built, fairly tall man with large black glasses. Although he was not a typical business villain, as he appeared in much of the press at the time, he was extraordinarily inept in politics and public relations. He simply could not understand what he had done wrong, or why he was suddenly the focal point of a national crisis.

He and Tyson began our meeting by suggesting ways to compromise, but our instructions from the President were clear: no compromise. I outlined the wide range of actions the President was already setting in motion to use the full power of the Presidency to divert contracts from U.S. Steel and the other companies. I mentioned that he still had several actions in reserve, including tax audits, antitrust investigations, and a thorough probe of market practices. I also pointed out that public opinion was heavily supporting the President.

Blough alternated between angry bluster and more suggestions for compromise. At times the conversation was quite rough, at others we talked as though we were colleagues. Occasionally, Blough and Tyson consulted in private. At times one of them would leave the room; I was sure that they were calling the other major steel companies to report on our conversations. I had felt all along that the confrontation between President Kennedy and Blough had been so sharp that it would be extremely difficult for U.S. Steel to make the first move. I hoped that if they continued to hold the line, one of the other major companies would give in on behalf of the industry.

This is exactly what finally happened. As we were nearing exhaustion, the news arrived by telephone: Bethlehem Steel had rescinded its price increases. That was the end of it, and Blough began looking for a way out; by midafternoon, under immense pressure, he capitulated. He seemed almost relieved that it was over. Goldberg and I tried to call the President while he was still at sea but were unable to reach him before he received the first news report through Navy channels. When I finally talked to Kennedy by telephone as he cruised off the Virginia coast, he sounded genuinely elated.

I had been a useful tool in talking to Blough in language that he could understand, but the primary reason for the retreat of Big Steel was the skillful manner in which President Kennedy had mobilized every resource at his command, focused on a specific target, and used the public stage to maximize the effect of his every action. Having dazzled the public from the outset with his style and glamour, he was showing an ever-increasing awareness of how to use that special style for political effect.

DALLAS

On the morning of November 22, 1963, I chaired a meeting of the President's Foreign Intelligence Advisory Board. The major subject that morning was how to improve the CIA's image. John McCone was present, and blamed the CIA's image problem on hostile journalists, singling out, of all people, James Reston of *The New York Times*—one of the most responsible and respected journalists in the city—as being determined to destroy the CIA. At 1:30, we adjourned and most of us walked over to the White House mess to have luncheon. Someone came into the mess, quite agitated, and said that the President had been shot and wounded while in a motorcade in Dallas, but that the wound was not serious. It seemed incredible to us that anyone would want to shoot this enormously popular President, but for a brief moment we felt gratified that the wound was not serious. In a few minutes, however, we heard the awful, irreversible news.

Sometimes the most memorable events are hardest to recapture. Words cannot convey the sense of emptiness and horror—for the President, his wife, and the nation—that I felt. For a few minutes, I did not know what to do. Finally, I decided to reconvene the Intelligence Board in executive session. We needed the strength that comes from coming together, from going on with the routine of one's work, even though that work no longer seemed to have any meaning. I declared the session of the past two days to be at an end: it would be inappropriate for us to present our recommendations for a broad overhaul of the intelligence community, which were being formulated at President Kennedy's request, to the new President at this time. I said I would convey to the new President our readiness to be of assistance in any way, but also cautioned that he might not wish to use our Board in the same manner as President Kennedy had. I asked everyone to be available on short notice.

In reality, we were just spinning our wheels—nothing made any real difference. We were just looking for something to keep us busy in the aftershock of this dreadful tragedy. Not only our own lives, but the course of history would change forever. Like the rest of the nation, and the world, I sleep-walked through the next four days, attending the funeral and memorial services for the President in a state approaching numbness.

Shortly after President Kennedy's funeral, I was having dinner at home when a telephone call came from Jackie through the White House switchboard. I took it in the kitchen. Jackie, wreathed in the tragedy whose horror could still hardly be comprehended, asked for some personal advice. We started on the most mundane subject, a real estate transaction that I later handled for her. Gradually, she began talking, at first calmly and then emotionally, about her husband and his Presidency. I felt an unutterable loneliness descending on her. I offered whatever help and solace I could, but there was an unreachable gulf between us, imposed by events. Worlds were closing around her.

AN ASSESSMENT

How will history ultimately view the Presidency of John F. Kennedy? On one hand, he offered vast promise to a new generation of Americans. He inspired the nation with a heroic vision of the Presidency as the center of action in American life. No President during my lifetime, with the exception of Franklin Roosevelt, matched Kennedy in creating a sense that the Presidency was the center of our national life, the place from which we could solve our nation's most pressing problems.

On the other hand, in the thousand days that he was President there was not enough time to fashion a full record. The substantive and legislative legacy he left behind was incomplete, and it is difficult to measure him without taking into account the achievements of his successor, especially in the domestic area, and the difficulties, especially in Vietnam.

Because in many ways the drama of his Presidency outweighed its achievements, John F. Kennedy may grow more elusive to Americans as time passes. Already an entire generation has been born since that dreadful day in Dallas. As those who were alive during his Administration grow older, the memory of his charm and grace will fade, and he will slowly recede until he becomes a dim and distant figure, and finally a nearly mythical part of our collective memory, like Abraham Lincoln. People may look back and wonder what Camelot and the New Frontier were all about, and remember the Kennedy Presidency more for its awful end, or for gossip about the family, than for its record.

But President Kennedy was an inspirational leader, and he left an enduring legacy. Even if he had done nothing else in his thousand days, he would deserve to be remembered for at least one major accomplishment: his handling of the Cuban Missile Crisis, which changed the nature of the Cold War forever.

It often has been noted that the Cuban Missile Crisis was the only direct confrontation between the two nuclear superpowers, but this truism tells only half the story: Moscow never tested the U.S. directly again. Having failed in his dangerous gamble in Cuba, Nikita Khrushchev was ousted within two years, replaced by the more cautious Leonid Brezhnev. During his eighteen years in power, Brezhnev built up Soviet military capabilities, and there were many areas of serious American-Soviet dispute, in Afghanistan, Central America, and the Mideast. After October 1962, however, the leaders of both sides, having experienced the bitter taste that comes from thinking the unthinkable, shied away from any repetition of that experience. The Missile Crisis had served the same function as an inoculation against a dread disease: there was never another confrontation as dangerous as that nuclear face-off between the two superpowers, which taught both sides how dangerous it was to go to the brink face to face, eyeball to eyeball.

The Cuban Missile Crisis marked the beginning of a long, slow trend away from the threat of nuclear war. War games, crisis planning, and a massive (and wasteful) military buildup on both sides would continue for another quarter century, but after the Missile Crisis, even though the two sides continued their worldwide competition, neither side again flirted with a direct nuclear showdown.

To have reduced measurably the threat of nuclear war; to have presided with skill and precision over the most dangerous moments of the entire Cold War; to have established a workable system of communication with the Soviet leadership during times of great danger—these are enduring achievements. Although it took almost three more decades, by its strong actions in Berlin and Cuba Kennedy's Presidency was instrumental in creating the conditions that led the Soviet Union to abandon its postwar goals of controlling Eastern Europe while trying to destabilize Western Europe. As I watched the opening of the Berlin Wall in November 1989, my thoughts went back to the summer of 1961, when it was built, and American and Soviet tanks faced each other across Checkpoint Charlie. It was no accident, I thought, that at the time the Berlin Wall was pulled down every television program showed President Kennedy's stirring *"Ich bin ein Berliner*" speech at the Wall the summer before he died. Even a quarter century after his death, there was still no better spokesman for our nation than John F. Kennedy.

IF KENNEDY HAD LIVED . . .

Some questions, even though they can never be answered, constantly recur and deserve attention. Such is the case with a question I have been asked repeatedly since Dallas: Would Kennedy have handled Vietnam the same way Johnson did?

Obviously, this question has no answer, only intensely personal surmises. History does not allow us to test alternatives; one must rely on one's instincts. Here is my own answer:

The two Presidents had the same advisers and would have confronted the same situation. It is safe to assume they would have gotten the same advice. One can argue that, for these reasons, Kennedy would have followed the same policies as Johnson did in Vietnam. That is my conclusion in regard to the main events of the election year of 1964, when I believe President Kennedy would have done more or less what President Johnson did. Those actions—continuation of the advisory buildup, the effort to improve the South Vietnamese Army, the attempt to stem the infiltration from the North, and the effort to encourage political stability—all were consistent with the policies followed in 1963 by the Kennedy Administration. Even the controversial Tonkin Gulf incident in August 1964 might have unfolded in much the same manner, given the fact that Robert McNamara, as Secretary of Defense, would have interpreted events in the Gulf the same way for either President.

But I do not believe that John Kennedy would have followed the same course as Lyndon Johnson in the all-important year of 1965, when the major decisions to escalate the ground war and start bombing North Vietnam were made. On the basis of personal intuition and a knowledge of both men, I believe that because of profound differences in personality and style, Kennedy would have taken a different path in his second term.

I often saw President Johnson personalize the actions of the Vietcong, interpreting them as somehow aimed personally at him. He reacted by thinking, *They can't do this to Lyndon Johnson! They can't push me around this way!* On the other hand, I believe President Kennedy would have treated the attacks strictly as an international problem—not something aimed at him personally. In reacting to the same events, I believe he would have thought, *I don't like the looks of this. I don't like the smell of it. Sending more troops may just increase the costs—let's hold off for awhile and see what happens. I'm not going to get us more deeply involved.*

Confronted with the decision either to send American ground troops at work, you will have to call upon your friends more and learn to be satisfied with something short of perfection." At that moment, it seemed improbable that Johnson would ever again be the hurricane force that he had been.

But nothing, of course, was ever to change Lyndon Johnson's essential character and style—not even a heart attack. When, in early November 1955, Senator Kerr and I flew to the LBJ Ranch, we found Lyndon Johnson impatiently awaiting permission from his doctors to leap back into the Washington fray. I was astonished at the speed of his recovery, and even more at the zest with which he looked forward to returning to the battle. Some people, faced with such undeniable signs of their own mortality, reassess their lives and decide to change their priorities. As far as I could tell, though, his heart attack had only made Lyndon Johnson feel more impatient, as though he now feared that he might be felled by another before he could achieve his goals. By the end of the year, he was back in Washington, where, as already noted, his first social outing after his heart attack was our family's annual New Year's Day party.

THE COMMITMENT TO FULL EQUALITY

Controversy will always swirl around Lyndon Johnson; it was inherent in the nature of the man. But I resent that his commitment to civil rights and full equality for all Americans has been cast into question recently by some writers, who have interpreted it as part of a cynical quest for power.

Of course Lyndon Johnson sought political power—it was the central, driving force in his life—as it is with most politicians. But the safe route to power hardly included fighting for the rights of black Americans. Lyndon Johnson was a member of the Southern caucus, yet he stood for civil rights for black Americans long before it was politically acceptable for a Texan to do so. Consider:

- In March 1949, just weeks after entering the Senate, he spoke of racial discrimination in words not at that time part of the litany of the Southern politician: "Racial prejudice is dangerous because it is a disease of the majority endangering minority groups. . . . For those who would keep any group in our nation in bondage, I have no sympathy or tolerance."
- Five years later, in 1954, Johnson was the only Senator from the states of the old Confederacy who refused to sign the famous "Southern Manifesto" protesting the Supreme Court's decision to desegregate the public schools. Senator Richard Neuberger of Oregon, one of the Senate's most liberal members, called it as "courageous an act of political valor as I have seen take place in my adult life."

· In the summer of 1957, after a bitter battle with his friends in the Southern caucus, including Richard Russell of Georgia, Senator Johnson steered through the Senate the first important civil rights bill since Reconstruction. Persuading three other "new Southerners"—Estes Kefauver and Albert Gore, Sr., both of Tennessee, and Ralph Yarborough of Texas—to join him, Johnson forged a fragile alliance between liberal Democrats and Republicans to beat down the conservative coalition that had thwarted change for generations. Deeply impressed with Johnson's skill and commitment during this historic legislative battle, I wrote at the time that "no one else could have [kept] our party from splitting irretrievably."

Moreover, Lyndon Johnson's Senatorial record on civil rights—the best of any Southerner since Reconstruction—was only the backdrop for his great achievements as *the* civil rights President of the century.

THE 1960 CAMPAIGN

By the time Johnson belatedly entered the 1960 race for the Democratic Presidential nomination, my support for Stuart Symington was well known. Like Kennedy, he understood my personal ties to Stuart; while the race was on, though, he and I did not maintain the same close relationship that Kennedy and I had kept.

After he was nominated for the Vice Presidency, Johnson and I worked together on matters pertaining to President Truman, and a few other relatively minor issues, but the bulk of my time was spent working directly with the Kennedys. While he was Vice President, we kept in contact, but as Johnson became aware of the amount of time I was spending with President Kennedy, he withdrew still further from me, as if to avoid appearing to encroach on the President's turf.

It has been widely reported that his Vice Presidential years were the unhappiest of his career. Lady Bird told me once that she thought of them as "Lyndon's quiet years, out of the arena." Many of the Kennedy people—but not the President himself—treated Vice President Johnson with almost open disdain and contempt, ignoring him and mocking his Texas manners. Some of the fiercely loyal men around President Kennedy worked hard to deny Johnson access to the President, and to make sure he was as far from the action as possible.

Johnson also saw real or imagined slights everywhere. He told me that on one occasion, while he was sitting in the small room outside the Oval Office waiting to see President Kennedy, Bobby Kennedy walked rapidly through the room and entered the Oval Office without even acknowledging or greeting him. Whatever the facts of this story, it rankled the proud

House Historical Association. Accordingly, I set up a meeting with Jackie on February 28, 1964. The two women, so different in style and background, treated each other with great mutual respect and deference, but it was never possible that they would work together closely, given the circumstances. Later, Lady Bird asked Jackie if she would allow the garden behind the Oval Office to be named the Jacqueline Kennedy Garden, but Jackie, with her customary sensitivity, immediately said she felt it was inappropriate to have parts of the White House named after individual First Ladies. Thus the garden continued to be known as the Rose Garden.*

Lady Bird was devoted to her husband, and loved him deeply. In turn, he needed her—as friend, as confidante, and sometimes as a punching bag. Although his affection for her was obvious, I was sometimes appalled at the way he treated her. At one small family dinner we attended, he decided that Lady Bird was wearing the wrong dress for the occasion. From the moment she appeared, he began attacking the dress, mockingly asking why she was wearing that "dreadful yellow thing." Finally, almost in tears, Lady Bird left the room before we sat down to eat, returning a few minutes later in another dress. The rest of the evening went on as though nothing had happened. As Marny and I drove home that night, we could not contain our anger at his treatment of Lady Bird. Nothing justified such behavior, we felt. Yet Lady Bird understood Lyndon Johnson like none of the rest of us, and saw him through every up and down in his stormy career.

One evening at another small dinner, following a particular accomplishment by Lady Bird, I felt that she deserved some words of appreciation. I tried to lighten the mood by suggesting that she should be "canonized" so we would have a Saint Lady Bird. Other guests laughed, and Lady Bird smiled, but President Johnson just glared at me, and changed the subject immediately. I realized as I looked at him that he felt if anyone was going to be canonized, it should be Saint Lyndon. He wanted at all times to be the center of attention, and he was offended because he thought I was implying that it must be difficult to be married to Lyndon Johnson—which, in truth, it was.

Lady Bird combined elements of nobility and dignity. She never postured or promoted herself. Her campaigns for beautification and for wildflowers have made a real contribution to the nation. Yet while staying in the background, she gained a deep national respect that continued to grow long after her husband's death in 1973.

*In 1965, with Jackie's permission, Lady Bird did name a small flower garden off the East Wing of the Mansion the Jacqueline Kennedy Garden.

VISITING THE RANCH

To those who did not know him, many of the stories about Lyndon Johnson sound like Texas fables, but for the most part, they are true. The trips to the LBJ Ranch while he was President were particularly memorable. The visit I remember most vividly, not at all like my first visit in 1955 when he was recovering from his heart attack, was a full-fledged Presidential initiation—A Visit. For me, its most memorable moment was a drive in an open convertible around the Ranch. The President was at the wheel, driving dangerously fast and drinking a Dr. Pepper, as we careened across something I came to think of as "Lyndonland"—an airspace totally dominated by Lyndon Baines Johnson in much the way he would have dominated the entire world if it had been possible.

At one point, our car reached the top of a hill and started accelerating rapidly downhill toward a lake. Johnson seemed unable to slow the car down. Suddenly he said, in a very loud voice, "The brakes have failed." The car hit the water, and seemed to bounce, coming to a bobbing rest about ten feet out from shore. Water started seeping in, and Marny and I leaped up onto the back of the seat, preparing to dive into the water.

The President seemed to be struggling with some mechanism. Just as I was about to abandon ship, he turned to me and said, rather calmly, "Clark, what's the matter—are you afraid you're going to get wet?" As I started to reply that I was thinking about going for a short dip, he leaned down and pushed a button, and we shot forward in the water—the car was amphibious! As it proceeded back to the shore under its own power he joyfully recited the names of visitors who had abandoned their Commander in Chief in wild jumps for safety.

ABE FORTAS

> He was an outsider who played the consummate insider. His contemporaries viewed him as an elder, but he remained boyishly playful. He was relentlessly ambitious, but he was remarkably loyal to friends and clients. He seemed to think only of himself, but he often willingly sacrificed for others. He was a committed reformer, but he often seemed more a technocrat than an idealist. He wanted to do good, but he was equally interested in making good. He was an actor, lawyer, and musician; a devoted social reformer who reminded some of Sammy Glick and others of the prototypical bureaucrat.[3]

Abe Fortas was far closer to Lyndon Johnson than I was. For many years, Johnson had relied heavily on Abe for a first opinion on almost everything; he consulted me in a more limited way, when he wanted another point of view. Over the years preceding his Presidency, a pattern had developed, which continued during his Administration: he would ask the two of us to come to his office or invite us to dinner with our wives, and he would raise a problem, asking for our views. If Fortas and I agreed, he would be comforted; if we disagreed, he settled back to watch with evident enjoyment, as Abe and I used whatever skills we possessed to persuade him of our point of view.

Fortas had a splendid legal mind and great intellectual self-confidence. He was a genuinely committed New Dealer, and fought hard for liberal causes throughout his life. Many stylistic differences separated us, and we were never intimate friends, but over the years we worked together without the slightest friction or competition. Contrary to Washington belief at the time, we did not coordinate our positions with each other before seeing President Johnson, rather, we became an informal sounding board for him, operating outside official channels. He valued our advice partly because he felt it was unencumbered by the pressures that bureaucracies exert on Cabinet members. In addition, he knew that we were reliable in an area with which he was obsessed—leaks to the press. Although there were occasional rumors, some of them accurate, about the advice that Fortas and I gave the President, on the most sensitive matters, with the exception of Vietnam, our views always remained private.

BOBBY KENNEDY AND LYNDON JOHNSON

On a few occasions, Lyndon Johnson talked of not running in 1964. Lady Bird even sent him a touching and shrewd personal memorandum, urging him to run. If he withdrew, she gently warned him, she could see "nothing but a lonely wasteland for your future [while] your friends would be frozen in embarrassed silence and your enemies jeering." I think, though, that he was only going through the motions of getting reassurance before setting out on the quest for legitimacy in the job he had wanted all his life. He knew he would never feel comfortable in the Presidency until he had won it in his own right.

My first discussion with President Johnson about the 1964 campaign came in late February of that year. I told him I felt the transition from the Kennedy Administration was over; the American public was now beginning to judge him on his own merits. He wanted to keep as many Kennedy men as possible through the 1964 election, including Kenneth O'Donnell, whose political skills he felt would be particularly valuable with the various state Democratic organizations. He also valued the services of Larry O'Brien very much, whom he felt had been the most loyal of the Kennedy holdovers since the assassination. McGeorge Bundy had performed ably and impeccably as National Security Assistant, and could remain as long as he wished.

For the first time, we discussed the special problem of the Attorney General. I had known from the beginning that there was simply no way that Lyndon Johnson and Bobby Kennedy could ever get along with each other. Their relationship was filled with bitterness, misunderstandings, and real and perceived slights and snubs. The two men went through the motions of working together, with a surprising degree of civility and consideration, but neither could refrain from revealing his true feelings about the other to close friends and associates. Johnson called Kennedy a "liberal fascist" because of Kennedy's association with Joe McCarthy; for his part, Kennedy regarded Johnson as crude and overbearing. After Dallas, when Bobby Kennedy looked at Lyndon Johnson, he saw a usurper in the Oval Office; when Johnson looked at Bobby, he saw a pretender to the Presidency. It was inevitable that some of their remarks would reach Washington's ever-active rumor mills, and even find their way into print. The relationship was doomed.

In the late afternoon of June 11, 1964, Bobby Kennedy came to my law office. He told me he had just sent President Johnson a letter, offering to take the place of the retiring Henry Cabot Lodge as the American Ambassador in Saigon. This remarkable offer was, I believe, an utterly sincere act from a man still deeply depressed over his brother's death. Perhaps Kennedy also felt some sense of guilt over Vietnam, the single most intractable issue that his brother had bequeathed to his successor, and, as he told me, "obviously the most important problem facing the United States." Kennedy said he wanted me to know that this was not a political ploy. After discussions with Rusk, McNamara and me, the President rejected the offer on the grounds that Kennedy's personal safety could not be ensured in the war zone, given the fact that he would be a special target and would probably take greater risks than an ordinary Ambassador. Although I feel President Johnson was correct in turning down Kennedy's offer, it is interesting to speculate on how events in both Vietnam and the U.S. might have developed if Bobby Kennedy, with his youth and intelligence, had gone to Saigon. Instead, Johnson asked the Chairman of the Joint Chiefs of Staff, General Maxwell Taylor, to replace Lodge.

In late July, in one of the ugliest and most divisive conventions ever held, the Republicans nominated Arizona Senator Barry Goldwater for President. President Johnson and I had anticipated Goldwater's nomination; in fact, at a family dinner early in the year when I had offered him four-to-one odds that Goldwater would be the nominee, he laughingly refused the bet because he did not want to lose. Victory over such an extreme candidate might prove easier than against a more broadly based opponent like Governor Nelson Rockefeller of New York, but Goldwater's supporters were filled with a hatred and passion which, especially in the wake of John F. Kennedy's death, we all found alarming.

Meanwhile, public pressure had been building on the President to choose Bobby Kennedy as his running mate. Among many others, Mayor Daley of Chicago, the most powerful city boss in the nation, made clear that he wanted Kennedy on the ticket. Increasingly, President Johnson feared that once the delegates to the Democratic Convention heard Bobby Kennedy's speech, certain to be the emotional high point of the convention, they would nominate him by acclamation for the Vice Presidency.

The President, however, was absolutely firm on this matter: he was not going to have Bobby Kennedy on the ticket with him. If Bobby became Vice President, the President told me, he would forever be sandwiched between the two Kennedy brothers, unable to govern or command public support for his programs. In this assessment of his own situation I felt he was correct. The relationship between a President and his Vice President has always been a complex one; there was no chance that a Johnson-Kennedy team could function effectively; if it was attempted, a crisis was inevitable. With Robert Kennedy as Vice President, President Johnson would be treated almost as a lame duck for the entire four years of his elected Presidency. Yet the problem remained: how to eliminate Bobby Kennedy as a possible running mate with a minimum of public outcry? The President discussed this problem with me at great length during the month of July, as the Democratic convention approached.

Finally, on July 22, he asked me to draft a talking paper for him to use with the Attorney General. I sent it to him the next day, and, in his own words, he "literally read it" to Bobby Kennedy in a dramatic meeting on July 29, 1964.* I had listed several reasons why Kennedy would not be the right running mate in 1964, leaning heavily on the need for someone with strength in the border states and the Midwest to balance a ticket against Goldwater. In a sentence that must have evoked bitter memories for Bobby Kennedy, the memorandum said, "I am sure that you will understand the basis of my decision and the factors that have entered into it, because President Kennedy had to make a similar type of decision in 1960." The memorandum added that Kennedy had a "unique and promising future in the Democratic Party," and asked him to consider serving as the American Ambassador to the U.N. Bobby, bitterly disappointed,

*President Johnson reprinted the entire memorandum in his memoirs, a revealing insight into the importance he attached to this incident.[4]

rejected the offer and said, "Mr. President, I could have been of help to you."

Kennedy had assumed that the meeting would remain confidential, but the next afternoon, Johnson, vastly relieved that everything had gone according to plan, could not resist telling three correspondents about it in an off-the-record meeting. Using his considerable talents for mimicry, the President even showed the reporters how Kennedy had "gulped" when he got the news.

Washington thrives on political gossip, and this was top quality. Predictably, news of the President's meeting with the reporters reached Kennedy within a few hours; he was understandably furious. When he called the President to protest, Johnson said he hadn't told anyone about the meeting, and Bobby bluntly called him a liar. Johnson retreated a bit, saying, well, *maybe* there was a conversation he had forgotten—but he would have to check his records. On that note, with the story about to leak, Johnson called me back to the White House. A public announcement that same day was now essential, and time was short.

As we talked, I noted that recent press speculation had included Secretary of Defense McNamara and Secretary of Agriculture Orville Freeman as possible running mates. The name of Kennedy's brother-in-law, Peace Corps Director Sargent Shriver, had also surfaced. Our amusement at these journalistic fantasies led me, almost inadvertently, to a rather simple suggestion: why not announce that *no one* from the Cabinet or of Cabinet rank (i.e., Shriver) would be selected as the Vice Presidential nominee? It might not fool anyone, but perhaps it could help reduce speculation about a personal feud between Johnson and Kennedy. The President asked me to draft a short statement immediately. I wrote it out in long hand and gave it to his secretary, Juanita Roberts. At 6 P.M., President Johnson called an astonished White House press corps back to make an announcement:

> In reference to the selection of a candidate for Vice President on the Democratic ticket, I have reached the conclusion that it would be inadvisable for me to recommend to the convention any member of the Cabinet or any of those who meet regularly with the Cabinet. . . .

He went on: "Because their names had been mentioned in the press," he had personally informed Dean Rusk, Bob McNamara, Bobby Kennedy, Orville Freeman, Adlai Stevenson, and Sargent Shriver of his decision.

Sometimes in politics a cosmetic covering, even a transparent one, serves the purpose of softening an action that has become unavoidable. Such was the case with the public explanation we devised for eliminating Bobby Kennedy from consideration as a Vice Presidential candidate—a ploy that made life easier for everyone involved. There was much amusement at the idea that apolitical men like Rusk were included in the list, but it worked well enough to defuse the risk of a big story about a war between Johnson and the Kennedys. Bobby, in fact, had the last word: "I'm sorry," he quipped a few days later, "that I took so many nice fellows over the side with me."

THE CONVENTION AND ELECTION

President Johnson invited me to fly to the Democratic Convention in Atlantic City with him and his family. Watching the convention, I realized that from his point of view, it had been essential to eliminate Bobby Kennedy from consideration. Bobby's speech was everything that Johnson had anticipated and feared, an electrifying moment which could have swept the delegates away and forced the President's hand.

The President held the decision about his running mate to himself, hoping for maximum surprise. I had the impression that Lady Bird preferred the *other* Minnesota Senator, Eugene McCarthy, while Johnson deliberately fueled speculation about Senator Tom Dodd of Connecticut to give the convention a little suspense. In the end, Senator Hubert Humphrey of Minnesota was Johnson's choice. Although I thought in 1948 that Humphrey's civil rights speech to the Democratic Convention was a tactical mistake, I had long since come to respect and like this irrepressible and exuberant man, and I strongly supported the choice.

In retrospect, the 1964 election itself seems anticlimactic, but any campaign, even the easy ones, are all-consuming events—and, since 1948, no candidate has ever dared to rest comfortably on a lead in the polls. So Johnson and his team, including me, worked constantly on tactics, speeches, and strategy. The President used a highly personal system of campaigning, with one set of advisers running the daily campaign, another group mapping out strategy and tactics, and a third group second-guessing the first two groups. Theodore H. White later described this third group, which was composed of Abe Fortas, Jim Rowe, and me, as "a senior court of review . . . cast as presiding appellate judge for any major speech, any major appearance, any major television show, any decision of policy."[5]

To the extent that he could, the President kept the war in Vietnam out of the campaign. When it did surface, he used it to emphasize his own restraint as contrasted to his trigger-happy opponent. Two incidents in early August apparently involving North Vietnamese gunboats and American Navy patrol boats in the Tonkin Gulf offered the President a chance to forge unified bipartisan support for his policies in Vietnam with the Tonkin Gulf Resolution, which Congress passed by an overwhelming vote. No one could foresee how controversial and divisive these incidents would later prove to be.

THE TRAGEDY OF WALTER JENKINS

The campaign was proceeding smoothly when tragedy struck. I got the first word shortly before 10 A.M. on October 14, 1964, when Abe Fortas called me. "Walter Jenkins is here with me," he said. "He needs our help." Fortas said he could not discuss the matter on the telephone, and asked that I meet him in front of my office in ten minutes. As I waited for him, I tried to imagine what the problem might be. I knew of no crisis in the campaign. On this day, President Johnson, with a huge lead over Goldwater in the polls, was campaigning in New York City with Robert Kennedy, who was running for the Senate. And I knew of no problem with Walter Jenkins, the President's closest aide for twenty-five years.

Fortas was driving himself so that we could talk freely. "We have to see the editor of *The Washington Star* right away," he said. "Let me fill you in while we drive over there"—and he told me a story that I could not believe. Jenkins was, at that moment, at Abe's house, in a distraught state. He had told Fortas that a week earlier, he had been at a party celebrating the opening of the new Washington office of *Newsweek,* that he had had a number of drinks—and was not too sure what had happened next. He talked vaguely and incoherently of an arrest, of "another man," and an inquiry from a reporter on *The Washington Star.*

It had to be a mistake, I said to Fortas, it couldn't be the same Walter Jenkins we both knew, the hardworking, dedicated staff member and devoted family man. No, Abe said, something *had* happened, although the details were unclear. We agreed to ask the *Star* to consider withholding the story unless there was clear proof of wrongdoing on Jenkins's part.

Abe and I also decided not to tell anyone in the White House, including the President, what we were doing so that they could be in a position to disown us if our efforts to protect Jenkins's privacy failed or proved to be an embarrassment to the President. Despite a widespread impression later that Abe and I were trying to protect the President, our thoughts at that moment were primarily of Walter Jenkins.

Quiet, competent Walter Jenkins, the most devoted of Johnson's aides. Except for Army service and an unsuccessful run for Congress in 1951, he had served Lyndon Johnson continuously since 1939, available to his demanding boss twenty-four hours a day. Born in Texas, a devout Catholic, he had six children—including one named Lyndon. He was a somewhat chunky man with graying hair, and he gave the impression at times of being nervous. I thought he was shy, but I admired his incredible dedication to his boss, his thoroughness, and his precision. Self-effacing both in public and private, until the crisis he was the staff person closest to the President, as evidenced by the fact that he had long served as the treasurer of the Johnson family corporation, a position of unique importance and sensitivity to the Johnsons. He was the indispensable aide, utterly reliable as a barometer of Lyndon Johnson's views and moods, totally accurate in conveying his boss's exact words and wishes.

All this was swirling through my mind as Fortas and I went to see the *Star*'s editor, Newbold Noyes, Jr. We told him the story as we knew it. We asked the *Star* not to print the story until further investigation revealed whether it was true or not. Noyes asked us if we were sure we knew all the facts of the case.

As it turned out, we did not. Later on, when the full story had been pieced together, both Fortas and I understood the depths of Jenkins's despair. What actually transpired was far more serious and tragic than Abe had initially understood.

What had happened may seem astonishing in today's permissive world, where some members of Congress have even acknowledged homosexuality and retained their seats. But in 1964, homosexuality was still a dark, illicit corner of American life—illegal in most states and in the District of Columbia. Jenkins had gone from the *Newsweek* party to the basement of the old YMCA building near the White House, a gathering spot for Washington homosexuals. About thirty minutes after Jenkins had left the *Newsweek* party, two morals plainclothesmen waiting in the Y arrested him. (There was no evidence that they were there, as Lyndon Johnson later believed, to trap Jenkins.) After being booked at the police station that night, Jenkins posted a fifty-dollar bond, which he later forfeited, and was freed. Amazingly, he went back to the White House and worked at his desk until midnight.

Nothing more happened for six days. But on October 13, an anonymous tip reached the *Star,* and shortly thereafter, other newspapers and the Republican National Committee, that there was something interesting on the District of Columbia police blotter for the night of October 7. Early the next morning, the *Star* sent two reporters to the police station, and found the entry for Jenkins's arrest. A policeman mentioned to one of the reporters that Jenkins had been arrested on a similar charge in 1959.

Noyes, watching our reaction to the information he was providing, was sympathetic. He said he understood that this was a human tragedy as well as a potential news story. He said his newspaper did not ordinarily publish articles on such cases, and would hold off on this story if no one else printed it. We thanked Noyes and set out for *The Washington Daily*

News, Washington's other afternoon newspaper. The *News* had the same information and was preparing to run a story in a few hours, but after hearing our plea, they too agreed to withhold the story. Our final stop was *The Washington Post*, where we met with the editor, J. R. (Russ) Wiggins. The *Post* had not yet heard about the story, and Wiggins withheld any commitment not to publish until he had time to assess the matter.

Abe and I had done all we could with the press. Even at the outset, we knew that the chances of stopping publication permanently were slim to none. But we thought that even a short delay, which would permit Jenkins to resign his White House post and receive proper hospitalization before the story was reported, was worth trying to obtain. Still, even though we were criticized later for trying to suppress the news, I never regretted our effort. I always felt comfortable with the knowledge that our primary motive was to try to ease the pain for Walter Jenkins and his family.

I went directly to the White House, while Fortas returned to his house on R Street, where Jenkins was resting with his doctor. As Fortas told Jenkins about the darkening situation, Jenkins came apart completely. His doctor gave him a sedative and took him to George Washington University Hospital.

At the White House, I discussed the situation with Bill Moyers, a rising young Presidential aide. Then only thirty years old, Moyers would take over most of Jenkins's duties after October 14. At about 4 P.M., calling from Moyers's office, Fortas and I reached the President, who was about to call on Jackie Kennedy prior to giving a major speech that evening. When we told him the news, he was struck dumb. "Oh, no, not Walter," was all he could say. Like us, he simply could not believe it. A series of frantic telephone calls followed over the course of that difficult afternoon, before the President reluctantly agreed to let Fortas go to the hospital and obtain Jenkins's resignation.

At 6 P.M., the Chairman of the Republican National Committee, Dean Burch, issued a cruel and cryptic statement: "There is a report sweeping Washington that the White House is desperately trying to suppress a major news story affecting the national security." Burch's statement was carried by the two wire services shortly after 6 P.M.; within minutes, the wire services were also carrying the first report of Jenkins's hospitalization, and inquiries began pouring into both the White House and the President's suite at the Waldorf. In New York, White House Press Secretary George Reedy, weeping openly, confirmed that his old friend had been hospitalized.

President Johnson wavered between despair and anger. Although he had a huge lead in the polls, he was concerned about the effect on the election: no scandal involving homosexuality in the White House had occurred before, and we were at the climax of the campaign. He was worried that the Republicans would try to turn it into a national security story, as Burch's initial statement had implied.

As it turned out, the story of Walter Jenkins was instructive for entirely the opposite set of reasons than those that President Johnson had feared. While Washington talked of nothing else for ten days, the Walter Jenkins story *had no effect whatsoever* on the election. Not for the first time, the American public was well ahead of Washington in its attitude toward such matters. The voters understood that this was a personal tragedy, not a public matter. Perhaps it marked the beginning of a new era in which the American public began to show a greater tolerance and understanding of homosexuality.

For his part, Lyndon Johnson never spoke of Walter Jenkins again: his faithful retainer became a nonperson. But Lady Bird Johnson issued a beautiful statement that spoke directly to the issue that had concerned me. It began:

> My heart is aching today for someone who had reached the end point of exhaustion in dedicated service to his country. . . . I know our family and all of his friends—and I hope all others—pray for recovery. . . .

LANDSLIDE

Lyndon Johnson's landslide victory over Goldwater in 1964 was a moment of great personal triumph for him: he felt he was finally President in his own right, out from under the shadow of the Kennedys. President Truman had faced a similar situation after Franklin Roosevelt's death, but he had confronted it quite differently. Like Johnson, he was elated when the electorate gave him their approval in 1948, but, unlike Johnson, he had not been inhibited or impeded, prior to his own victory, by the fact that he was not yet an elected President. President Truman's attitude was simple: whether people liked it or not, he had the job, and he would do it as well as he could. President Johnson, on the other hand, worried about his mandate—his "legitimacy," although he never used such a term—and deferred most difficult decisions until after the 1964 election. Now, freed in his own mind from the constraints of an inherited Presidency, he could turn his colossal energies to the problems, especially Vietnam and civil rights, he had postponed for over a year. He possessed the legislative skills, personal drive, and Congressional majority to accomplish his noble domestic goals—provided Vietnam did not derail him.

24

Vietnam: The Drama Begins

History is, in fact, the fragmentary record of the often inexplicable actions of innumerable bewildered human beings, set down and interpreted according to their own limitations by other human beings, equally bewildered.

—C. V. WEDGWOOD
History and Hope

I come now, with a sense of almost infinite sadness, to the most painful, tormenting event of my years in public service. For me, it did not begin until the late spring of 1965, when President Johnson asked that I participate in what proved to be the most important foreign policy debate since the U.S. entered the Korean War. Thus commenced my involvement in Vietnam.

In the debate during the spring and summer of 1965, I argued as forcefully as I could against the massive escalation of our involvement being proposed by Secretary of Defense Robert McNamara and the American military. I amassed whatever lawyerly skills I had, argued my case—and lost, in a face-to-face debate with McNamara in the unlikely tranquility of a summer weekend at Camp David.

Vietnam was not only tragic, it was also a cauldron in which good and able men of high integrity, acting out of solid and well-reasoned motives, went terribly wrong. The success the leaders of the government had just achieved, and the danger they had just faced, in the Cuban Missile Crisis were still fresh in their minds. Above all, the communist menace was palpable. Memories of Munich and appeasement were also still fresh, especially in the minds of Dean Rusk and Lyndon Johnson.

The essence of American policy, despite years of domestic debate, was still variations on the theme of containment. I had been a participant in the creation of that policy in 1947, but I did *not* believe it applied to Indochina, and, when first consulted, I opposed our involvement. Even though the odds were heavily against preventing an escalation that was supported by the top three members of the Cabinet, the entire military establishment, and most of the Congressional leadership, I felt there was no alternative but to tell the President that I foresaw a calamity for the nation if ground troops were sent to Vietnam. To a large extent my conclusions were instinctual, based on my conviction that American troops should not be committed to combat except when the national security is clearly at stake. I did not believe that we were threatened by the internecine war in Vietnam, and I was deeply concerned that our chances of success were far too low to justify the risks and costs the undertaking entailed.

I did not oppose the early commitment to help the South Vietnamese with military and civilian advisers. The initial strategy—assisting a new and small pro-Western, anticommunist government to resist subversion—seemed a logical and appropriate extension of earlier policies in Europe and Korea. Looking back on 1965, I wrote in 1969,

> We had seen the calamitous consequences of standing aside while totalitarian and expansionist nations moved successively against their weaker neighbors and accumulated a military might which left even the stronger nations uneasy and insecure. . . . We had reason to feel that the fate averted in Korea through American and United Nations military force would overtake the independent countries of Asia, albeit in somewhat subtler form, were we to stand aside while the communist North sponsored subversion and terrorism in South Vietnam.[1]

From its beginning, though, we were constrained by the fact that our South Vietnamese allies were corrupt, inefficient, and poorly motivated. This was critical: in the final analysis, American objectives in Vietnam depended more on the capabilities of our allies in Saigon than on our own efforts. And the more we did for them, the more dependent and ineffectual they became. It was on this very point that our policy would ultimately fail—although I did not realize it at first.

It has sometimes been said that Vietnam was the "liberals' war." Since many of the most critical decisions were made during the Kennedy and Johnson Administrations, there is a certain small truth lurking in this observation; but understanding of the tragedy is not advanced by viewing events through a political prism. Every President from 1950 through 1975—three Democrats, three Republicans—made mistakes in Indochina, and the Congressional leadership of both parties supported almost every key decision.

THE KENNEDY ADMINISTRATION

My own involvement in Vietnam was minimal during the Kennedy years. Though the PFIAB received occasional briefings on the situation in Southeast Asia, we concentrated on intelligence methods and organization rather than the situation in the field. Our last discussion during the Kennedy years took place on September 12–13, 1963, amidst a fierce debate over whether or not to encourage a military coup against the increasingly unpopular South Vietnamese government headed by the rigid Catholic strongman, Ngo Dinh Diem. I had not been following the situation in Vietnam closely, and I was startled by our briefing from the normally cautious and conservative CIA Director, John McCone. The situation in Vietnam had deteriorated so badly, he told us, that we might simply have to pull out entirely. Diem had lost all popular support except from his fellow Catholics, and could not win the war against the communist guerrillas, who were steadily gaining ground. Asked about press reports that the CIA was supporting a coup, McCone told us that while the CIA was in contact with senior Vietnamese Generals, we were not encouraging them. I do not know whether in making this statement, which later turned out to be false, McCone was misleading us, or whether he was inadequately informed by his own subordinates about CIA activities in Saigon—especially the actions of Lucien Conein, a legendary CIA agent with a long career in Southeast Asia, who was already secretly working with General Duong Van Minh ("Big Minh"), the leader of the coup that took place only six weeks later. Certainly, McCone should have known what was going on in Saigon–and if he did, he had an obligation to tell us.

One area we failed to investigate during those early years of the American buildup was the growing gap between the optimistic reports of progress that were coming in through the official chain of command, and the increasingly skeptical reporting by some of the journalists covering the war, notably *New York Times* correspondents Homer Bigart and David Halberstam, Neil Sheehan of United Press International, and Malcolm Browne of the Associated Press. Even though these skeptical reports were based in part on the views of many junior American officers serving as advisers to the South Vietnamese Army, these reports were viewed by the Administration as a public-relations nuisance, rather than something that needed to be looked at carefully. The PFIAB should have examined this early indication of what was later called the "credibility gap," but neither I nor my colleagues suggested we consider this question. It was a serious oversight on our part.

1965: THE YEAR OF DECISION BEGINS

A few days before he left for his Inauguration in Washington in 1913, President-elect Woodrow Wilson remarked to a Princeton friend, "It would be the irony of fate if my Administration had to deal chiefly with foreign affairs."[2]

Wilson's comment could have applied equally to Lyndon Johnson: he was not well prepared for Vietnam, and he did not want it to divert him from his domestic priorities. Yet it consumed him and became his nemesis, just as surely as World War I and the fight for the League of Nations devoured Wilson. Although President Johnson had an excellent understanding of the political trap he was in, he never understood the war itself.

With the notable exception of the Tonkin Gulf Resolution in August 1964, President Johnson's personal imprint on Vietnam did not begin to emerge until he had won the 1964 election. He had a strong sense that there was a difference between the unexpired term of John F. Kennedy and the term he had won on his own. Although long advocated by the military and some civilians, the bombing of North Vietnam began only two weeks after his Inauguration. On February 7, 1965, after a bold Vietcong attack on the American installations near the central highlands city of Pleiku, he authorized a retaliatory air strike against North Vietnam. Within a few days, the original idea of carefully calibrated *retaliatory* strikes against the North was replaced by a program of sustained bombing long sought by the American military. Its code name was "Rolling Thunder."

No connection between bombing the North and sending American ground troops was recognized and discussed *before* the bombing began. Historians have largely ignored this aspect of the decision, but here was the greatest failure in the entire decision-making process. History sometimes turns not on what was considered, but on what was *ignored.* Such was the case in February 1965.

In none of the discussions leading up to Rolling Thunder was the President told, either by the Joint Chiefs of Staff or his Secretary of Defense, that once bombing of the North began, the military would require, and demand, American combat troops, first to protect the American air bases from which the bombing was launched, and then, inevitably, to begin offensive operations against the enemy.

It later became evident that at the time Rolling Thunder began, most senior military planners already believed that only American ground troops could avert Saigon's defeat; but, fearing that the President would be more hesitant to start sustained bombing of the North if he knew that American ground troops would also be required, they did not inform him of this essential fact. Thus the February debate, restricted simply to the question of whether or not to bomb the North, had, in retrospect, an air of unreality. Later, the American military would complain bitterly about civilian interference in such military decisions as the timing and targeting of the air war against North Vietnam. But they themselves committed a far more fundamental error in failing to tell their Commander in Chief that the bombing of the North would inevitably lead to requests for ground troops.

For their part, the President and his senior civilian advisers, especially those in the Defense Department, should have been more persistent in questioning the American military. The respect the military deserves for its patriotism and courage should not blind civilian leaders to the biases and vested interests which are part of the military system and style. Three years later, as Secretary of Defense, when it was my responsibility to consider a request for more troops in Vietnam, I tried not to repeat the same mistake.

FIRST INVOLVEMENT; THE MAY 17 LETTER

At the beginning of April, I was drawn, for the first time, into the debate concerning the next steps in the war.

By this time a curious—and temporary—alliance had sprung up, including, on one hand, those who saw the bombing of the North as a way to avoid sending ground troops to Vietnam (Rusk, McGeorge Bundy, McNamara), and on the other, the military, which had begun to ask for a limited number of ground troops to protect our airplanes and other American installations.

An influential voice arguing for a tough response to Hanoi was former President Eisenhower, whom President Johnson consulted during this decisive period. As he had with President Kennedy in January 1961, Eisenhower advocated a variety of strong actions which he had never taken when he was President: "As long as the enemy are putting men down there, do what you have to do! We are not going to be run out of a free country that we helped to establish."[3]

A handful of people opposed any escalation at all. This small, outnumbered group included some "old Asia hands" at the State Department, notably Paul Kattenberg and Louis Sarris, and a few people on the fringe of the debate, like John Kenneth Galbraith, our former Ambassador to India, and Senate Majority Leader Mike Mansfield. But the opponents of escalation had only one strong voice inside the Administration with access to the President—Undersecretary of State George Ball.*

With the exception of Bob Lovett and Dean Acheson, two of his

*The title of the position Ball held, the number-two job in the State Department, was later changed to Deputy Secretary of State. His memoir, *The Past Has Another Pattern* (New York: W. W. Norton, 1982), is one of the most graceful and valuable memoirs of the period.

predecessors as Undersecretary of State, I can think of no sub-Cabinet official who ever operated with greater prominence and distinction than George Ball during this period. A unique combination of factors gave him near-Cabinet stature. First, Ball clearly had the presence, and intellect to serve at the Cabinet level. A lawyer from Chicago and Washington who had long supported Adlai Stevenson, Ball was also closely associated with Jean Monnet, the legendary Frenchman who had devoted his life to creating what is now the European Economic Community, and whose dream was a United States of Europe. A large, tall man with great style and self-assurance, Ball was extremely articulate and utterly fearless in expressing his own opinions. I liked and admired him, though we were not close friends.

One key to Ball's unusual role was the great latitude he was given by his superior, Dean Rusk. In an arrangement virtually without precedent, Rusk not only allowed but even encouraged Ball to advocate a position on Vietnam entirely different from his own. To his credit, Rusk often took Ball to major policy discussions with the President, where the two men would disagree, politely but firmly. Later, when Ball's private dissents became public, the White House tried to describe his status as that of a "devil's advocate," but this was not true. Ball was not role-playing, he was presenting his beliefs. He thought the commitment in Vietnam was wrong. He argued his case with courage, clarity, rare prescience, and eloquence, but with no other high-level support. Soon he would have what he later called "support from an unexpected quarter"—me.[4]

The situation in Vietnam continued to deteriorate during the spring of 1965, despite the bombing of the North. But President Johnson had substantial public support for his policies. Before Pleiku, about 41 percent of the American public approved of his Vietnam policy, and after the air attacks, his support soared to 60 percent; the bombing itself was supported by a staggering 83 percent, and 79 percent supported the goal of "keeping the communists from taking over all of Southeast Asia."

In this atmosphere, General William C. Westmoreland, the new American military commander in Vietnam, obtained approval for deployment of the first American ground troops—sent ostensibly to protect the air base near Da Nang—with comparatively little debate. On March 8, 1965, two battalions of Marines, dressed in full battle gear, waded ashore on the beaches south of Da Nang. To the amusement of everyone except themselves, they were greeted by pretty young Vietnamese girls in bikinis, local Vietnamese officials, and a few U.S. Army advisers holding up a sardonic sign reading WELCOME TO THE GALLANT MARINES. Official spokesmen in Washington and Saigon stated that the Marines would simply defend the Da Nang air base, but, in fact, plans were already being made for offensive operations.

On April 1, Ambassador Maxwell Taylor, on a trip home from Saigon, attended a meeting of the intelligence board. He remained unshaken in his commitment to save South Vietnam, but I learned at the meeting that he had taken one unexpected position: he had opposed sending American combat troops to Vietnam. Taylor argued in several top-secret cables that if we sent combat troops to Vietnam, the Vietnamese would simply "seek to unload other ground force tasks upon us." Once we started down that slippery slope, there would be no stopping, Taylor said. He went on to state his belief that the American soldier "is not a suitable guerilla fighter for Asian forests and jungles."[5] If we cross the Rubicon, he argued, there will be no turning back. In putting forward this case, Taylor was directly opposing his own protégé, General Westmoreland. Taylor's view, a surprising reversal of recommendations he had made in 1961 to Kennedy, had a considerable impact on me.

The day after Taylor met with the PFIAB, I saw President Johnson to discuss the search for a successor to John McCone at the CIA. I suggested Richard Helms, a professional intelligence officer for whom I had developed a high regard, but he was passed over in favor of Admiral William "Red" Raborn, the builder of the first nuclear submarine. Raborn was not experienced in the intelligence field, and after an unhappy year he was replaced by Helms, who had been serving as his deputy.

In the same meeting, President Johnson asked me to start following the situation in Vietnam more closely. He wanted my observations added to the recommendations now pouring in from every direction. During the next month I looked carefully at Vietnam for the first time, with the assistance of PFIAB Executive Director Patrick Coyne, who was to act as my channel for information on the war for the next two and a half years.

On May 11, President Johnson handed me a private letter he had received from McCone and asked for my reaction to it. Clearly concerned that the letter could, if leaked, add to the pressure he was already under, he enjoined me from discussing it with anyone or even keeping a copy of it for myself.

I returned to my office to study McCone's letter. He argued that rapid and dramatic steps were necessary to prevent defeat: "As we deploy additional troops, which I believe necessary, we [should] concurrently hit the north harder and inflict greater damage." If we were not ready to do this, McCone said, we should not send ground troops to Vietnam at all.

The powerful internal logic of McCone's arguments helped clarify my own thinking. In a certain sense, he was right: if Americans were going to take over the ground war in the South, they should be fully backed by heavier bombing of the North. A limited war would be hard for the American people to accept for more than a brief period of time, as we had learned in Korea.

But as I studied McCone's suggestions, I reached a conclusion exactly opposite to his. If the only way to avoid defeat was by the massive escalation that McCone was suggesting, then we should not escalate at all. The level of bombing McCone advocated would shock and horrify the entire world, and even he admitted there was no guarantee we would prevail. I saw far more disadvantages in following his all-out strategy—worldwide opposition, high risk of failure, great loss of life on all sides, an open-ended commitment—than in looking for a way out before the costs of failure went any higher. As for the middle course—the one pushed by McNamara and Rusk, among others—it seemed at that moment to carry the worst of both other scenarios: too little to turn the tide, but enough to involve us more deeply. Furthermore, I believed that the U.S. should send troops to fight *only* if our national security truly was at risk. I had believed this to be the case in Korea, but I was not persuaded that it was so in Vietnam.

Thus, for the first time, I came to a personal conclusion about Vietnam: we should start looking for a settlement, even if it did not meet our original objectives. I sent my reply to the President on May 17, 1965. It was the first time I had written about Vietnam, and I phrased my letter carefully, weighing every word:

> Dear Mr. President:
>
> I am returning herewith the letter of the Director of Central Intelligence, dated May 8, 1965, together with enclosures.
>
> I wish to make one major point.
>
> I believe our ground forces in South Vietnam should be kept to a minimum, consistent with the protection of our installations and property in that country. My concern is that a substantial buildup of U.S. ground troops would be construed by the Communists, and by the world, as a determination on our part to win the war on the ground.
>
> This could be a quagmire. It could turn into an open ended commitment on our part that would take more and more ground troops, without a realistic hope of ultimate victory.
>
> I do not think that situation is comparable to Korea. The political posture of the parties involved, and the physical conditions, including terrain, are entirely different.
>
> I continue to believe that the constant probing of every avenue leading to a possible settlement will ultimately be fruitful. It won't be what we want, but we can learn to live with it.
>
> Respectfully Yours,
> Clark M. Clifford

I did not get a reply.

WITH LBJ AT THE RUBICON

Nine weeks later, Bob McNamara returned from a visit to Vietnam with a recommendation for a huge increase in American ground troops. At 3 P.M. the next day, July 21, President Johnson's secretary, Juanita Roberts, called and said that the President wanted me to come to the White House immediately to join a meeting on Vietnam. It was particularly urgent, she said—the meeting was already in progress. I walked rapidly across Lafayette Park and into the most remarkable series of meetings that I had attended since the showdown with General Marshall over Israel in 1948. As an assistant to the President in 1948, I had known exactly what my role was; this time I had only a small sense of what was going on, and no idea at first of what role I should play.

As I entered the Cabinet Room, President Johnson waved me to an empty seat at the table. He was flanked by Secretary of State Rusk on one side and Secretary of Defense McNamara on the other. Next to McNamara sat the Chairman of the Joint Chiefs of Staff, General Earle Wheeler. Around the room were other senior members of the Administration: National Security Assistant McGeorge Bundy, Undersecretary of State Ball, Assistant Secretary of State for Far Eastern Affairs William P. Bundy, CIA Director Raborn and Deputy CIA Director Helms, former Ambassador to South Vietnam Henry Cabot Lodge, U.S. Information Agency Director Carl Rowan, Deputy Secretary of Defense Cyrus Vance, and two White House aides, Press Secretary Bill Moyers and Special Assistant Jack Valenti.[6]

These men had been deeply influenced by the lessons of the Cuban Missile Crisis, especially the value of "flexible response" and "controlled escalation." Their success in handling a nuclear showdown with Moscow had created a feeling that no nation as small and backward as North Vietnam could stand up to the power of the U.S. These men were not arrogant in the sense that Senator Fulbright and others later accused them of being, but they possessed a misplaced belief that American power could not be successfully challenged, no matter what the circumstances, anywhere in the world.

Still, everyone in the room seemed deeply aware that we were facing—belatedly, in my opinion—a momentous decision. Westmoreland had requested thirty-two additional American combat battalions—100,000 more men by the end of the year, *more* in 1966, plus an intensification of the bombing of the North and a partial mobilization of the National Guard and the Reserves. McNamara, once the advocate of bombing the North, in part to avoid deploying ground troops, supported this request. Taylor had also changed his position, and now supported Westmoreland, thinking it too late for the nation to turn back.

When I entered, George Ball was speaking. "We can't win," he said, his deep voice dominating the Cabinet Room. "The war will be long and protracted, with heavy casualties. The most we can hope for is a messy conclusion. We must measure this long-term price against the short-term loss that will result from a withdrawal."

Producing a chart that correlated public opinion with American casualties in Korea, Ball predicted that the American public would not support a long and inconclusive war. World opinion would also turn against us. Ball said he knew that withdrawal was difficult for a President, "But almost every great captain in history at some time in his career has had to make a tactical withdrawal when conditions were unfavorable." He compared the situation to that of a cancer patient on chemotherapy: we might keep the patient alive longer, but he would be fatally weakened in the long run.

Looking straight at Ball, the President said—not harshly, but with deep concern, bordering on anguish, I thought—"Wouldn't all these countries—Korea, Thailand, Western Europe—say Uncle Sam is a paper tiger? Would we lose credibility by breaking the word of three Presidents if we give up as you propose? It would seem to me to be an irreparable blow, but I gather that you don't think so."

"If we were actively helping a country with a stable, viable government, it would be a vastly different story," Ball replied.

One by one, the other senior members of the Administration lined up against Ball. McGeorge Bundy argued, in his usual crisp style, that Ball's views constituted "a radical switch in policy, without any evidence it should be done." Ball's arguments, he asserted, went "in the face of all that we have said and done."

"It will not be quick," he added. "No single action will bring victory, but I think it is essential to make clear that we are not going to be thrown out—"

Ball interrupted: "My problem is not that we will get thrown out, but that we will get bogged down and won't be able to win."

Since I had entered the room, Dean Rusk had been silent. I was curious to see where he would come out. Now he spoke, in the calm, lucid, methodical manner that gave his words such authority: "I am more optimistic about the situation in Vietnam than some of my colleagues. . . . We should not worry about massive American casualties when the military says, at the same time, that we cannot find the enemy. I don't see great American casualties unless the Chinese come in. Vietnam is a testing ground of us by the Russians and the Chinese. Certainly we have had setbacks in Vietnam, just as we had setbacks in Korea. We may have more. But Vietnam must be an example for the entire Free World."

Henry Cabot Lodge joined the discussion. This tall, slender, and attractive man with his curious upper-class Boston intonations and manners was not noted for his intellect, but his position would carry extra weight with President Johnson for two good reasons: he was a prominent Republican,* and he had just agreed to return to the most difficult assignment in the American diplomatic service—the Ambassadorship in Vietnam—at an age when most men had already retired. "There is a greater threat of World War III if we don't go in than if we go in," he said. "I cannot be as pessimistic as George Ball about the situation in Vietnam."

Bob McNamara joined in, with his usual precision and air of certainty: "Our national honor is at stake. Our withdrawal would start further probing by the communists. We would lose all of Southeast Asia. I feel that the risks of following my program have been vastly overstated by George Ball."

I took careful notes, but said nothing. Shortly after 5 P.M., the meeting adjourned, and I returned to my office deeply troubled by the magnitude of the McNamara request.

We resumed the discussion at noon the next day, July 22, with the Joint Chiefs of Staff presenting their formal position on the need for the buildup. Although it had a slightly ritualistic air, this meeting was an essential part of the process. The President could not address an issue of such importance without giving the Chiefs a chance to present their views. In addition to the President and the Chiefs, the three service secretaries—Stanley Resor for the Army, Paul Nitze for the Navy, and Harold Brown for the Air Force—were also present. The only others there were McNamara, Vance, McGeorge Bundy, and me.

The President opened the meeting by listing three options: we could leave—an "elegant bug-out," as he put it; we could maintain our current force levels and lose slowly; or we could add 100,000 men to our force levels in Vietnam, recognizing that this may not be enough to achieve our objectives, and that we might have to add more next year.

One by one the Chiefs gave their views. Although they all favored escalation, none offered assurance of success. Admiral David McDonald, the Chief of Naval Operations, said, "More troops are needed to turn the tide. Otherwise, we'll lose slowly." The President looked at him for a moment then asked, "But you say you don't know if a hundred thousand more men will be enough. What makes you conclude that, if you don't know where we are going, and what will happen, that we shouldn't pause to find out?"

McDonald replied, "I believe that sooner or later we'll force the enemy to the conference table. We can't win an all-out war."

"Is this a chance we want to take?"

*By coincidence, Johnson and Lodge had been opponents in the 1960 Vice Presidential race.

"Yes, in my opinion," Admiral McDonald responded, "when we view the alternatives—get out now or pour in more men."

And so it went. Repeatedly, the President asked the military the same questions. The answers varied little. Nitze said that putting in more men would give us about a "sixty-forty chance to turn the tide." He suggested giving Westmoreland more troops than he had asked for in order to increase the chances of success. But McNamara, clearly annoyed at the questioning of his position by Nitze, disagreed; the levels he and Westmoreland had requested, he said, were the most that South Vietnam could absorb. McNamara estimated the cost of the buildup at $12 billion in 1966—a low estimate, as it turned out.

President Johnson showed pain at the choices he faced. Turning toward McNamara he said, "Westmoreland's request means that we are in a new war. This is going off the diving board."

McNamara replied with the most extreme version of the domino theory that I had ever heard: "Laos, Cambodia, Thailand, Burma, Malaysia are all at immediate risk. For two or three years, communist domination would stop there, but the ripple effect would be great—in Japan, and India. We would have to give up some of our bases. Ayub Khan [of Pakistan] would move closer to China. Greece and Turkey would move to neutralist positions. Communist agitation would increase in Africa."

Air Force Secretary Harold Brown* agreed that all the alternatives are "dark," but said that "the chances of losing are less if we move in."

Someone mentioned a recent Gallup poll showing substantial public support for a hard line with Hanoi. The President understood that the polls meant little so early in the war: "If you make a commitment to jump off a building, and you find out that the building is too high, you may withdraw the commitment."

I had remained silent; as the sole private citizen in the room, present only as a personal friend and adviser to the President, I felt I should express my opinions privately to him before discussing them with anyone else. But near the end of the meeting, without commenting directly on McNamara's proposals, I asked General Wheeler a simple question: "If the military plan that you propose is carried out, what is its ultimate result if it is 'successful'?" Wheeler answered that, in all likelihood, we would be able to withdraw most of our forces, but there was a chance that we would have to stay for a long time with a smaller number of troops to help secure a stable government. Shortly after our exchange, the meeting adjourned and the Chiefs left.

When we resumed the meetings after luncheon, the President made an emotional statement, reflecting his growing frustration, I thought, with

*Later Secretary of Defense in the Carter Administration.

the State Department's failure to produce a peace plan. "This war is like a prizefight," he said. "Our right hand is our military power, but our left must be peace proposals. Every time you move troops forward, you should move diplomats forward too. I want this done. The Generals want more and more from me. They want to go farther and farther. But State has to supply me with something, too." There was no reply from Dean Rusk.

GEORGE BALL'S "UNEXPECTED SUPPORTER"

The meetings had depressed me. The pressure on the President for escalation was overwhelming. As we left the room, George Ball whispered that he wanted to speak with me privately. We walked down the hall a few yards to the Roosevelt Room. Once we were alone, Ball asked me if he was correct in assuming that I had deep doubts about the war and McNamara's proposals. I told him that not only did I have such doubts, but I had sent the President a letter stating my concerns in May.

"Then you and I are in total agreement," he said enthusiastically. "I have been looking for support for a long time. I think your influence with the President is tremendously important. I want to put into your hands a series of memoranda which I have sent to the President. Can you handle them? They are highly classified."

I reminded Ball that, as a member of the PFIAB, I had the necessary clearances and a safe at my house. "Have the memos hand-delivered to me," I said, "and I will see that they are properly cared for."

As I started to leave the White House, a guard said the President was looking for me. I returned to the small anteroom adjoining the Oval Office to find Johnson and McGeorge Bundy waiting for me. The President wanted to know my reactions to what I had heard over the past two days. I replied that I needed more time to reflect on what I had heard, but I had some preliminary reactions. "The way the military acted today reminded me of the way they dealt with President Truman during the Korean War," I said. "Some of what General Wheeler said today was ridiculous." I quoted from my notes. " 'The more men we have, the greater the likelihood of smaller losses. And if they infiltrate more men into the South, it will allow us to cream them.' These are disturbing statements. I don't believe they are being straight with us."

"I am bearish about this whole exercise," I continued. "I know what pressure you're under from McNamara and the military, but if you handle it carefully, you don't have to commit yourself and the nation. If you overplay the decisions now under consideration, the nation will be committed to win a ground war in Asia. I asked myself two questions today as I listened to McNamara and the Chiefs. First, can a military victory be won? And second, what do we have if we do win? Based on what we have heard, I do not know the answer to either question."

The President listened in silence, and Bundy jotted down a few notes. When I finished, Johnson said he wanted to talk to me again in the next few days, when I had had time to reflect more on the meetings that I had attended.

PREPARATIONS FOR A SHOWDOWN

Shortly after I returned to my office, an aide from Ball's office arrived with a thick bundle of documents, the memoranda that Ball had been writing since October of the previous year, arguing against each stage of the escalation. I took them home and stayed up until almost 2 A.M. reading them and taking careful notes. They were everything that I would have expected—forceful, fearless, and, to my mind, convincing. They amplified and gave historical context to the presentations that I had heard him make to the President. I realized as I read them that George had been fighting his lonely battle so long that, to a certain extent, the President was probably no longer paying Ball the close attention he deserved. Perhaps I had been brought into the discussions by the President in part because he wanted a new voice to argue against McNamara, Rusk, and the Chiefs.

On Friday, July 23, I called George and told him that the documents he had sent me were impressive and persuasive. He was, he said, "elated" to have me as an ally. He was going with Rusk to the White House for another meeting and would call me as soon as he got back.

Ball called again after the meeting. It had involved a much smaller group—Rusk, McNamara, Wheeler, Moyers, and McGeorge Bundy. George was convinced that my talk with Johnson the previous evening had had a "salutary effect."

I was less hopeful: I told him I had just finished talking on the telephone to "another source" and, based on that conversation, it appeared that President Johnson had virtually made up his mind to support McNamara and Westmoreland. My informant had been another participant in the meeting—Bill Moyers, who sympathized with Ball and me, but felt he could not play an open role in policymaking because his job as Press Secretary constrained him from active policy formulation. Moyers told me it would take a miraculous effort to change the President's course—requiring not only a change in Johnson's mind, but also Rusk's, McNamara's, and Bundy's.

Ball told me he understood the difficulties, but he felt I was the only person who had even the slightest chance to stem the rush toward disaster. I promised to have "a very hard and long talk" with the President, but I cautioned him against false hope. "Individuals sometimes become so bound up in a certain course," I said, "that it is difficult to know where objectivity stops and personal involvement begins."

According to Ball, the President was not much concerned with the opposition from students and the Left, and my presentation would have to deal primarily with his fear of a right-wing backlash. Ball repeated a comment that President Johnson had made to him: "George, don't pay any attention to what those little shits on the campuses do. The great beast is the reactionary elements in this country. Those are the people we have to fear."

Just before 7 P.M., the President called to invite Marny and me to come to Camp David on Saturday. Bob and Margie McNamara would be there, he said, along with a few other people. We would relax, and we would have a chance to talk privately about Vietnam. The stage was now set for the final argument. I knew Moyers was correct: it would be very difficult, perhaps impossible, to stop the rush toward escalation. Could the President reject the advice of his three top national security advisers—all inherited from Kennedy—as well as the unanimous advice of the Joint Chiefs of Staff and the Ambassador in Vietnam, himself a former Chairman of the Joint Chiefs of Staff? Could he change a policy that had the support of a substantial majority of the American public? Would he risk going down in history as the first American President to lose a foreign war? The answer seemed likely to be negative.

On the other hand, Lyndon Johnson had just won an overwhelming victory in a campaign built around the theme of his restraint versus Goldwater's extremism. The next election was as far away as could be, and if the economy did not deteriorate, there would be ample time to repair any political damage inflicted by the Right. The effect on our position in Asia of a withdrawal from Vietnam would be difficult to predict, but I believed it could be contained and minimized. And the support of the American public was clearly based on a belief that the conflict would be short in duration; if the war dragged on, we all agreed this support would erode.

In thinking about the meeting about to take place at Camp David, I thought particularly of Bob McNamara, who had been playing a dominant role in the government during an extraordinarily difficult period, and who was now leading the support for a policy that he would have opposed six months earlier. Although Rusk, Bundy, Taylor, Lodge, and the Chiefs all were important, McNamara held the key; his formidable intelligence and reputation were the critical variables in the process driving the President toward approval of Westmoreland's request. Bob's mastery of facts and his analytical skills had led him, I felt, into a logical fallacy, but his reputation for personal integrity and the force of his personality were carrying the case against those few voices calling for a different course.

I had liked and respected Bob McNamara from the moment we had first met in 1960, and it pained me that we would be cast into advocating opposing points of view. As in almost every such disagreement in my life, I determined to do my best to keep the argument totally impersonal. Bob had his views, I had mine—I thought he was wrong, but I did not question his motives or his professionalism. We would present our views to the President and let him decide.

JULY 25, 1965: CAMP DAVID

Marny and I flew to Camp David Saturday afternoon, sharing a helicopter with Bob and Margie McNamara and their son Craig, the Johnsons' daughter Luci, and her husband Pat Nugent. On the beautiful twenty-five-minute flight from Washington to Camp David, we chatted in the most friendly fashion. Vietnam was never mentioned, and an observer would never have guessed that a major confrontation was about to take place between two of the passengers on the plane.

We spent the afternoon relaxing in the glorious surroundings of Camp David. Each guest or couple was assigned a separate cabin. The accommodations, contrary to public perception, were not opulent, but they were extremely relaxing. Because the cottages are dispersed, the guests could keep to themselves much of the time, play golf or tennis, or stroll around the Presidential retreat.

Supreme Court Justice Arthur Goldberg, who was going to be sworn in as the Ambassador to the U.N. the following day, was another guest at Camp David, as were Indiana Senator Birch Bayh and his wife, Marvella. Two important members of the White House staff—Horace Busby and Jack Valenti—joined us, and we ate dinner with the Johnsons. Despite the informal and friendly environs, the President was more subdued than normal.

On Sunday morning, I went over my notes one last time. From Ball's memoranda and my own thoughts, I had assembled the strongest case that I could against McNamara's proposals and had structured it as though I was arguing in a courtroom, with McNamara as the opposing attorney and the President as the judge. My case boiled down to a few fundamentals. I knew that the President had heard them before, but I hoped that, if properly assembled, they would shake McNamara's certitude, impose their own logic on the President, and lead to a new conclusion.

At 5 P.M. on Sunday, President Johnson asked me to join him and Bob McNamara at Aspen Lodge. From the large, glassed-in living-dining room looking out over a beautiful panoramic view, I could see, through the large windows to the right, the little golf course that Ike had installed, and straight ahead, the lovely green hills called the Catoctin Mountains. In sharp contrast to the subject we were about to discuss, the sylvan setting gave a seemingly relaxed air to the conversation; from a distance, one would not have imagined that the subject under discussion was a decision that would change American history.

Aspen Lodge was decorated as a hunting lodge, with unassuming furnishings surrounding a large fireplace on one side. On the left side of the living room was a rectangular dining-room table, around which President Johnson often held conferences and late-night meetings. It was here that we sat to discuss Vietnam.

The President sat at the head of the table with his back to the fireplace. I sat on his right, directly across from McNamara. To his left sat Arthur Goldberg, and to my right sat Jack Valenti, who took notes, and Horace Busby. As we talked, two Filipino stewards served drinks. The President drank Fresca, I sipped club soda.

The President began, primarily because of Goldberg's presence, by mentioning a proposal to take the Vietnam issue to the U.N. He asked for my views, and I quickly dismissed the idea, saying that the risks far outweighed the potential gains at the U.N.—then I moved into the broader discussion for which I had prepared myself.

"We must not create an impression that we have decided to replace the South Vietnamese and win a ground war in Vietnam," I began. "If the decisions about to be made are interpreted as the beginning of a permanent and long-range policy, it will severely limit the flexibility which the President must have."

"What happened in Vietnam is no one person's fault," I continued, trying to reduce President Johnson's overpersonalization of the situation. "The bombing might have worked, but it hasn't. A commitment like the one that we have made in Vietnam can change as conditions change. A failure to engage in an all-out war will not lower our international prestige. This is not the last inning in the struggle against communism. We must pick those spots where the stakes are highest for us and we have the greatest ability to prevail."

McNamara listened without showing the slightest emotion, but I put more passion into what I was saying than in any presentation I had ever made to a President:

> I hate this war. I do not believe we can win. If we send in 100,000 more men, the North Vietnamese will match us. If the North Vietnamese run out of men, the Chinese will send in "volunteers." Russia and China don't intend for us to win the war. If we "won," we would face a long occupation with constant trouble. And if we don't win after a big buildup, it will be a huge catastrophe. We could lose more

> than 50,000 men in Vietnam. It will ruin us. Five years, 50,000 men killed, hundreds of billions of dollars—it is just not for us.

I paused for a moment, then went on:

> For the time being, Mr. President, let us hold to our present course, without dramatic escalation. You will probably need to send some additional men now for this strategy, but not many. At the end of the year, after the monsoon season, let us probe, let us quietly search with other countries for an honorable way out. Let us moderate our position in order to do so, and lower our sights—lower the sights of the American people—right away. Let the best minds in your Administration look for a way out, not ways to win this unwinnable war. I can't see anything but catastrophe for my country.

I did not know, at the time, that Jack Valenti, the President's chief assistant, had kept a permanent record of my remarks. However, many years later, as we went through files at the Johnson Library, we came across the notes that he had written. It is interesting to see what impressed him the most. His entry reads as follows:

> CLIFFORD: "Don't believe we can win in South Vietnam. If we send in 100,000 more, the North Vietnamese will meet us. If the North Vietnamese run out of men the Chinese will send in volunteers. Russia and China don't intend for us to win this war. If we don't win, it is a catastrophe. If we lose 50,000 men it will ruin us. Five years, billions of dollars, 50,000 men, it is not for us. At end of monsoon, quietly probe and search out with other countries—by moderating our position—to allow us to get out. Can't see anything but catastrophe for my country."

After I had finished, President Johnson turned to McNamara, who replied forcefully that he did not agree with my premises or my assessment of the chances for success in Vietnam. He repeated arguments he had made earlier in the week, but added nothing new. Without more American troops, he said, South Vietnam would fall, and this would hurt the U.S. throughout the entire world. The buildup was essential if we wanted to avoid a rapid defeat.

I was prepared to debate McNamara on every point, but to my disappointment the President wanted to end the discussion. Perhaps he sensed the futility of further debate. The lines were drawn clearly; he had heard the arguments on both sides, and there was little else to say. He told us that no one wanted peace more than he, but he did not discuss the details of my position.

When the meeting ended, we returned to our respective cottages. While we waited for dinner or word that we were going home, the President did something quite unusual. He drove around the Camp David area alone for an hour; then, for another hour, he walked around the grounds, also alone. It had been a lovely day, and the soft summer light lasted late into the evening.

During his lonely drive and walk, I assume that he reviewed all that he had heard in the previous week and made up his mind. When he returned to the Aspen Lodge, we ate another family meal with some other friends whom he had invited to Camp David, but never once did he refer to the debate between McNamara and me. We returned to Washington with President and Mrs. Johnson shortly before midnight for a short night's sleep before the final meetings.

ACROSS THE RUBICON

We resumed shortly after noon on Monday and continued, with a break in the afternoon, until 7 P.M., but the meetings had a different tone than those of the previous week. Johnson shifted the discussion toward important but secondary, matters—the exact number of men to be sent, the timing of the deployments, the public and Congressional aspects of the announcement, and so on.*

The President asked me to repeat the presentation I had made the previous evening at Camp David. So, for the first time, I stated to a larger group my objections to the escalation and my dark fears for the future. After I had finished speaking, George Ball slipped me a note that I saved with pride:

> Clark—
> I'm glad to have such an eloquent and persuasive comrade bleeding on the same barricade. I thought your statement was great.

But both George and I sensed that the battle was over. I felt the President had asked me to repeat my arguments in the larger group only to show that he had listened to both sides before granting the massive troop increase.

In the evening on July 26, the same group—now in effect a war council—returned to the White House to discuss whether or not to attack

*In *The Vantage Point,* President Johnson cites these meetings on Monday as the ones in which he finally made up his mind. But almost everyone else involved in the process believed that the decision was made over the weekend, as evidenced by the fact that William P. Bundy had already sent a telegram to key embassies around the world telling them how to explain the new policy to their host governments.

the surface-to-air missiles recently installed in North Vietnam. Given the fact that American pilots were risking their lives daily in raids over the North, I argued strongly that we should take the SAMs out with whatever means were available. It was the first, but not the last time, I would argue for a tough position on a question of military tactics. Once the President had committed us in Vietnam, I would generally support actions that I hoped would shorten the war or minimize American losses.

Ironically, the one minor success Ball and I had during the debate actually worked *against* our larger purpose. We both had argued that we should "underplay" any public announcements so as to maintain maximum flexibility for future withdrawal, while arguing, of course, against any escalation at all. In the actual event, the President turned down our strategic objective, but handled the public announcement in a manner consistent with our suggestion. Instead of a nationally televised speech in prime time, the President simply disclosed the buildup during a midday press conference on July 28. Even though he had already secretly approved an increase of 100,000 men by year's end, with the possibility of another 100,000 in 1966, he referred only to an increase of 50,000 men, and told reporters that the additional troops did "not imply any change in policy whatsoever." Thus, in our last-ditch efforts to stop the escalation, Ball and I had unintentionally encouraged a major Presidential deception that added significantly to the emerging "credibility gap."

25

On the Team

When friends heard that I was preparing my memoirs, the question they asked most often was, "How will you explain your change from hawk to dove on Vietnam after you became Secretary of Defense?" Most of those asking the question were unaware of my opposition to the buildup in 1965, but even those who knew of it, like George Ball and Cyrus Vance, still wanted to know why I had supported the war in 1966 and 1967. They asked, "Did you deliberately fool LBJ?," "Were you a secret dove?," and "Why and when did you change your mind?"

Here is the answer.

The years of Vietnam were just beginning. I was constantly invited to the White House, often accompanied by Abe Fortas, for private discussions with the President, covering every conceivable subject; increasingly we focused on the war. At the same time, I continued to decline the President's invitations to join the Administration. I knew Lyndon Johnson paid more attention to those who maintained their independence. I would surely lose some of my freedom to speak my mind, and be of less value to Johnson, if I worked directly for him. I preferred to remain outside the system, a private adviser, available whenever he called.

I have been asked many times, what is the role of an outside adviser? How should Presidents use them?

My answer is simple: even if he ignores the advice, every President should ensure that he gets a third opinion from selected and seasoned private citizens he trusts. (The second opinion should come from Congressional leaders.) Though Cabinet members and senior White House aides often resent outside advisers, a President takes too many risks when he relies solely on his own staff and the federal bureaucracy for advice. Each has its own personal or institutional priorities to protect. An outside adviser can serve the role of a Doubting Thomas when the bureaucracies line up behind a single position, or help the President reach a judgment when there is a dispute within the government. They can give the President a different perspective on his own situation; they can be frank with him when White House aides are not.

For years, I resisted any and all suggestions that I join the Johnson Administration, just as I had with President Kennedy. However, the relationship I had with each man was quite different. When Kennedy called on me, it was usually to play a clearly defined role on a specific problem—from the aftermath of the Bay of Pigs to the Steel Crisis. Johnson, on the other hand, wanted my advice or observations on almost anything that might confront him. Kennedy rarely asked me for political advice; Johnson constantly did. Johnson also asked me to participate in important national security meetings which otherwise involved only government officials, something Kennedy never did. In these meetings, I would say little unless asked to comment by the President—and even then I shared my views with him later, only in private.

ON THE TEAM

Nineteen sixty-five was perhaps the year of greatest legislative productivity in American history: Lyndon Johnson's dream, the Great Society, seemed to be coming true. But on another front, he had to deal with the fact that our allies in Saigon were facing military and political defeat unless we substantially increased our involvement in the war.

His July 1965 decision constituted an enormous gamble that the infusion of American combat troops could win the war before the American public tired—as it inevitably would—of the conflict. I opposed the decision initially, yet once he made it, I supported it, and for the next two years I looked for ways to make it succeed.

My colleague in opposition, George Ball, had told the President and Rusk that he would not criticize the decision publicly. Nonetheless, his opposition to the July decisions became public, and his October 1964 memorandum to the President was later printed in its entirety, creating a sensation. By contrast, my own opposition to the buildup remained confidential, since I felt it inappropriate to discuss personal conversations with the President with anyone else—even Stuart Symington, who complained to mutual friends after he became a leading opponent of the war in 1967 that he could no longer talk to me about Vietnam.

The period from the summer of 1965 to the end of 1967 was a critical time for the U.S. in Vietnam. Our troop strength there grew from 75,000 to 485,000. Casualties grew even faster, from about 400 killed in action before July 1965 to more than 16,000 by the end of 1967. Domestic controversy over the war effort also grew dramatically, with a handful of campus teach-ins giving way to massive demonstrations in front of the Pentagon. Gradually some newspapers and Congressmen who had supported the war switched to antiwar policies. Growing casualties and television coverage of the war—the first "living-room war," in Michael Arlen's fine phrase—began to create pockets of opposition to the war throughout the country, including areas far from the universities and big cities.

I continued to believe we did not have a major national security interest in Vietnam, but, having lost the argument over escalation, I felt it my duty to support any actions that appeared to offer a chance to bring an end—any end—to our involvement. Thus, within months, I was widely viewed in Washington as a leading "hawk." That the President often met alone with me and Abe Fortas, who was a deeply committed hard-liner on Vietnam, certainly added to that perception. Three main reasons led me to take these positions, controversial then, and criticized later:

- I had never considered myself to be an expert on the situation in Vietnam. Many of those who had opposed Ball and me had greater experience and familiarity with the problem, and presented their views with certainty and conviction. Everyone else represented a department or agency of the government, with his own channels of information from the field. My opposition to the buildup had been based to a considerable extent on intuition; I had no firsthand knowledge or sources of information from Southeast Asia to place against the confidence and detailed knowledge of the supporters of the war.

- I was also influenced, starting in 1966, by a steady stream of optimistic briefings (many to the PFIAB) coming from the military, the White House, and even the CIA. Although the CIA later claimed that their reports were more cautious than those of the military, nothing in their analyses suggested that the basic American objective was unattainable; they stressed only that the war might take longer than the military forecast. The military briefings, and the picture painted with relentless optimism by Walter Rostow, who had replaced McGeorge Bundy as President Johnson's National Security Assistant, emphasized that we were headed for success if we persevered. General Westmoreland predicted that communist casualties would soon exceed Hanoi's replacement capability—the "crossover point," as he called it—and the communists would either negotiate or withdraw ("fade away," as Ambassador Lodge liked to put it). Messages from the embassy in Saigon described the steady strengthening of the South Vietnamese government in glowing terms. These assessments supported a belief that we could find our way out of Vietnam by following the policies advocated by General Westmoreland, the Joint Chiefs, Bob McNamara, Maxwell Taylor, Ambassadors Henry Cabot Lodge and Ellsworth Bunker, Dean Rusk, and Walt Rostow. When I later took a firsthand look at the situation, I discovered that much of the information from the embassy and the military command in Saigon was either inaccurate or irrelevant. I should have acted earlier on the warning signs, but I did not begin to realize how inaccurate these official reports were until my trip to Southeast Asia in the late summer of 1967. Until then, I was so anxious to find a way out of Vietnam that I accepted them as accurate, and I supported the military requests for more troops as the best way to end the war quickly.

• A final reason for my position from 1965 to 1967 resulted from my relationship with President Johnson. Once the President had set the basic course, I felt that what he needed was support, not more criticism. I had opposed the buildup in 1965, and lost. But once the course had been set, I looked for ways to make it succeed, instead of continuing to argue an issue that had been decided. I felt my responsibility was to help him to achieve the objective he had laid out.

FIRST TRIP TO VIETNAM

In mid-September 1965, at the end of a relaxing Sunday-afternoon cruise on the Potomac, the President asked me to return to the White House, where we talked about Vietnam until almost midnight. He was increasingly worried that the buildup and the bombing were not having the effect on the enemy predicted by the military. I mentioned that the PFIAB was concerned about the poor performance of the intelligence agencies in the war zone. He responded, "Why don't you go out there and get a firsthand look at the situation?" I was delighted with the suggestion, never imagining at the time that the trip itself would be overshadowed by its aftermath—the angriest exchange I ever had with Lyndon Johnson, caused by an incident involving a Harvard professor named Henry Kissinger.

After briefings in Washington, I left on the morning of October 21, 1965, for Tokyo, Taiwan, Hong Kong, and Saigon. My discussions with intelligence officials were highly classified, and remain so to this day, as they dealt with the intelligence community's most tightly guarded secrets, sources, and methods. Much attention was focused on a "target" then considered one of the highest priorities in the world, the People's Republic of China. There was concern in Washington that Chinese "volunteers" might enter the war, as they had in Korea, and intelligence methods designed to warn us of this possibility were a high priority in my discussions.

I arrived in Saigon late on October 26, and went directly to the residence of Ambassador Lodge, a lovely old French colonial villa near the edge of town. With its tree-lined streets and broad boulevards, the city still retained vestiges of its days as a colonial capital. Yet it showed signs of the growing American presence as well—heavy military traffic, hastily constructed headquarters and barracks, and numerous young American soldiers in the streets and bars of the city.

Lodge was an exuberant and amusing man, to whom a cheery surface optimism was second nature. In an era when crisp presentations and crisper analysis was the most highly prized Washington commodity, Lodge's casual, meandering style stood out in sharp contrast. But his willingness to return to this most difficult of all foreign postings for a second tour had won him great gratitude in Washington. Even after his first tour, he knew very little about Vietnam, and at the age of sixty-three was unlikely to learn; consequently, he was dependent on his own instincts and his staff. At the time, when the war seemed to most observers to be going well, his limitations seemed unimportant compared to the value of having him in Saigon. Lodge's wife had left Saigon with the rest of the American dependents for safety reasons, and he enjoyed having company. He also had another houseguest at the time, a Harvard professor I had not previously met named Henry Kissinger, who was there as a consultant to Lodge. He and I had different missions and schedules, and saw only a little of each other.

The intelligence effort in Vietnam was as confused as Maxwell Taylor had warned me it would be. My assistant Pat Coyne and I made up another of the endless lists of "action items" designed to improve the intelligence effort there. Upon my return, I submitted it to the President, who approved its recommendations and sent them back to the field. They had little effect.

In private, Lodge, Westmoreland, and other senior American officials expressed a combination of concern and optimism over the political situation in Saigon. Nguyen Van Thieu and Nguyen Cao Ky were running the government in an uneasy alliance, with Thieu as Chief of State and Ky as Prime Minister. But the political turmoil in Saigon was still diverting attention from the all-important task of building the government's presence in the countryside.

These problems were admittedly serious, but they dismayed neither Lodge nor Westmoreland. While Lodge thought the task of "nation-building" would be long and slow, he was utterly convinced that we were on the road to success. Even more important, Westmoreland gave very upbeat presentations during a private meeting as well as our formal briefing. We were prevailing, he said, the enemy was weakening, with their casualties mounting at a rate so great that soon they would no longer be able to replace their losses. Westmoreland said he needed greater authority to make decisions "in theater," without recourse to Washington or his superior in Hawaii, the Commander in Chief, Pacific Area Command (CINCPAC). One of his strongest complaints was Washington's incessant second-guessing of his selection of bombing targets for B-52's. I sympathized with Westmoreland on this matter; one cannot run a war at the tactical level from ten thousand miles away, through a lengthy and cumbersome chain of command. When I returned to Washington, I took Westmoreland's case up with McNamara, and the interference in selecting B-52 bombing targets was substantially reduced, to Westmoreland's relief.[1] I was less successful in freeing Westmoreland from the requirement to report to Washington through the headquarters command at CINCPAC in Hawaii: opposition from the Navy prevented such a reorganization, even though it made sense.

I made one field trip in Vietnam, traveling by helicopter to Army bases at Bien Hoa and Vung Tau. Just north of Saigon, Bien Hoa, once a small provincial town, had been turned into a mammoth American Army headquarters. I remembered my days at the Western Sea Frontier Command in 1944, when the Army and the Navy fought for limited supplies, and I marveled at what, by comparison, seemed real luxury. It was only weeks before Thanksgiving, and I was told proudly that every American in the country, even those manning the most isolated and dangerous outposts, would get Thanksgiving dinner, complete with yams and cranberries—thanks to the ubiquitous helicopter. What a perfect symbol of the American presence in Vietnam was the helicopter, an indispensable tool in our effort to defeat an enemy that possessed no aircraft and, at that time, only a small number of motorized vehicles, but controlled a network of trails and tunnels under the triple-canopy jungles of Indochina.

Vung Tau, which had been a peaceful and popular French seaside resort, was now an important Army logistics base east of Saigon. It also was the site of a training center for rural pacification workers ("cadre," in the jargon of Vietnam), which had been set up by the CIA. This idea seemed particularly promising to me; instead of relying on American firepower forever, field workers trained in political organization would counter the Vietcong at the village level, where the war would ultimately be won or lost. Later, the idea, though well conceived, went the way of so many American efforts in Vietnam; a victim of bureaucratic infighting and corrupt management, it failed to live up to its early promise. At the time, though, my American hosts were confident that the cadre program would cut deeply into Vietcong strength. I was impressed with the energy of the Americans at both Bien Hoa and Vung Tau; they represented, I thought, the best America could send abroad. But in my enthusiasm for the dedication of the young Americans briefing me, I did not see that the Vietnamese role in their own war was declining—or the danger this posed for both countries.

A PROBLEM WITH KISSINGER, A BLOW-UP WITH JOHNSON

I returned to Washington late in the evening on October 31, exhausted from what seemed an almost endless trip from Hong Kong to Tokyo to Seattle to Baltimore's Friendship Airport. I did not find out for some weeks that my fatigue was not simply due to jet lag; I had contracted hepatitis and when it erupted a few weeks later I would be hospitalized for several weeks.

Two days after I returned to Washington, I picked up *The Washington Post* to read a front page article by Jack Foisie. It began:

> SAIGON—Recent emissaries from the White House are reporting that there is an almost total lack of political maturity or unselfish political motivation among the current leaders of the South Vietnamese government.
>
> Although they themselves are not talking, these are known to be the findings of Prof. Henry Kissinger, the noted political scientist, and Clark Clifford, the Washington lawyer and advisor to Presidents—both of whom have been recent visitors to Saigon. Clifford and Kissinger were sent here by President Johnson to make independent appraisals of the direction American political policy should take in South Vietnam.

My name did not appear again in Foisie's long article, which described in detail Kissinger's purported views of Saigon's political immaturity, and said that the White House was awaiting his report.

I was stunned. I had not met with the press at any point during my trip to Asia, nor had I discussed my views of the political situation with anyone outside a small circle of officials in Saigon—Ambassador Lodge, General Westmoreland, political counsellor Philip C. Habib, and the CIA station chief. I was even more astonished when a very concerned Bill Moyers called from the White House to tell me the President was "off the wall" about Foisie's article. He made it clear it would take some doing to calm the President down. And did I know, he added, that Jack Foisie was Dean Rusk's brother-in-law?

I told Moyers that Foisie's story was a complete mystery to me. Not only did I not know of his connection to Rusk, but I had never even met him—and, furthermore, I did not see what difference it made *whose* brother-in-law he was.

I liked and respected Moyers. He owed his entire career to Lyndon Johnson, having worked for him since the age of twenty-five, yet he never lost himself completely in Johnson's strange and overpowering world, as so many others had. One of Moyers's great skills was his ability to transmit accurately the President's mood, while subtly detaching himself from what he was conveying. Some of his colleagues in the Johnson White House may have thought Moyers was not always completely loyal to his chief, but I felt he served the President all the better by retaining a degree of independence of thought.

Moyers suggested that while he tried to calm the President down, I write a letter to him explaining my position. When asked about the views ascribed to Kissinger and me in his press conference the next day, Moyers deliberately separated us:

> Those views are not Mr. Clifford's views. Whatever Professor Kissinger's views are, his views are not those of the government's. . . . I don't know what he [Kissinger] was doing over there. The President didn't know about it.

There was one minor, but unfortunate, aspect to what the White House said about my trip. Moyers was instructed to say that my trip to Asia had *not* been made at the President's request. Since there were higher matters at stake than this unnecessary but small misstatement of fact, I accepted it as part of the price of working with President Johnson.

My letter, drafted in close consultation with Moyers, went to the President November 4 and was released by the White House two days later. It contained a flat denial of Foisie's article "insofar as the references to me are concerned." I still had not talked to the President. Moyers told me that despite my letter, he remained upset. Although he himself was a major source of information to the press—as the saying goes, "The ship of state is the only vessel that leaks from the top"—President Johnson had a nearly pathological hatred of leaks by others.

On November 11, I flew to the LBJ Ranch, where the President was recuperating from gall bladder surgery a month earlier. Before I could even inquire as to his health, he began to berate me about Foisie's article. Ignoring the fact that Moyers had, in his name, absolved me of any connection with the article, Johnson asked me, in the most caustic terms, why I would go and say such stupid things to a reporter—and to Dean

Rusk's brother-in-law, of all people, which in Johnson's eyes gave the story added credibility.

I was as angry as the President, and told him again that the story was wrong.

"Well, I read it in the paper," he said.

This was the last straw. "You are a great one to talk about reading something in the newspapers," I said, with unfeigned anger. "You constantly state that the papers never report accurately what you say, that they put words in your mouth. Now you are doing the same thing to me that you charge the papers with doing. I am telling you flat out, once and for all, that there is no truth to the Foisie story as far as it deals with me. That is all there is to it, and I must add that I deeply resent your questioning my word in this manner."

Surprisingly, this ended the discussion—he simply did not respond. He never mentioned the incident again, and, if anything, our relationship grew closer. I learned later that Moyers also told the President he was sure I had not talked to Foisie.

All this activity, of course, left Professor Kissinger out on a limb. What, if anything, had he said, and to whom had he said it? Kissinger had served as a consultant in both the Kennedy and Johnson Administrations. He did not wish his relationship with the government threatened.

Called by the Associated Press, Kissinger said the Foisie article was "wholly in error." He then called me and told me that he had had nothing to do with the article. I expressed my appreciation for his call, but I questioned his denial: had he not met with a group of reporters in Saigon, including Foisie, the day before the article had appeared?

Kissinger said he had indeed, but that the meeting had been off the record. Within a few days a letter containing a detailed version of events arrived from Harvard:

> Dear Mr. Clifford:
>
> . . . I do not recall when an incident has dismayed me more. Because it involves fundamental issues of honor and propriety, I am taking the liberty of summarizing the relevant facts on this my first day after my return from Vietnam. . . .
>
> On my next-to-last day in Saigon I reluctantly agreed—at the urgent request of Barry Zorthian, the Embassy Public Affairs Officer—to meet with some selected newsmen. . . . I said, to all practical purposes, nothing and listened instead to an often passionate debate among the newsmen. No White House connection on my part was either stated or implied. . . . Your name was never mentioned by me and it did not enter the conversation in any way within my hearing.

> . . . The views ascribed to me are wholly at variance with the trend of my conversations with Vietnamese officials as contained in official Embassy reports or with my many informal talks with Ambassadors Lodge and [William] Porter* and with Phil Habib, the head of the Political Section. They will confirm, I am sure, my strong belief in governmental stability. . . .
>
> I do not know whether Foisie was riding his own hobby-horse or whether some Embassy official was using the occasion of your visit (and mine) to urge a point of view outside of channels. Perhaps an ambitious Saigon politician was trying to exploit the dislike of the press for the existing Saigon regime in order to undermine it.
>
> We will probably never know. I can only say that I am deeply sorry that our names became linked in such an unfortunate way. I am depressed and shaken that my effort to be helpful to the Administration and to Ambassador Lodge has ended so ignominiously. I have tortured myself these past few days to decide what I could have done otherwise and I still cannot understand what happened.

Years later, Barry Zorthian explained to me that Foisie had arrived late at the luncheon with Kissinger, and was unaware of its off-the-record ground rules. He then wrote a story which reflected, according to Zorthian, many of the comments Kissinger had made that day. Neither Zorthian nor anyone else could explain how my name had been dragged into the story.**

The Kissinger incident would have died the death of most press flaps except for two special factors. It had led to the most serious argument I ever had with Lyndon Johnson, and it put Kissinger in an exceedingly difficult position at a time when he hoped to become more deeply involved in diplomatic affairs—and when several Administration officials thought he could be of value as an adviser on Vietnam. For a while the Foisie incident so infuriated President Johnson that it threatened to make Kissinger unemployable even as an adviser, let alone a go-between in sensitive diplomatic matters. This problem was overcome through the passage of time, though, and Kissinger was to continue his involvement in Vietnam during the Johnson years—including a role two years later as an intermediary in a secret negotiating channel.

Kissinger himself remembered the incident with regret. "It was my first real exposure to the press," he said twenty-five years later, "and I was totally unprepared for it." It was a mistake he rarely made again.

*At the time Deputy Ambassador in Vietnam. Porter later became Ambassador to Saudi Arabia and Undersecretary of State for Political Affairs.

**When contacted during the preparation of these memoirs, Foisie, now retired, said that Kissinger was the source of the views ascribed to him in the article. He could not, however, remember why or how my name came to be included in the article.

THE CHRISTMAS BOMBING PAUSE BEGINS

When the President and I finally cleared the air and got down to business, I told him I had been deeply impressed by the dedication and energy of the Americans in Vietnam, and it was clear that the American buildup and bombing had prevented the defeat of our South Vietnamese allies in 1965. Unfortunately, the North Vietnamese responded to the American buildup with a counterescalation of their own, which neither our bombing nor our ground troops seemed able to cut off. I said our combined forces could not defeat the Vietcong by eliminating them or driving them into North Vietnam—perhaps we could achieve our objectives, I said, if we made it absolutely clear to Hanoi that the U.S. would sustain a prolonged and major military effort in South Vietnam. Over the next few weeks, I gave a similar assessment to Dean Rusk, Bob McNamara, and McGeorge Bundy.

This was the situation when McNamara returned from another one of his periodic trips to the war front in November 1965 and presented the President with a new and extraordinarily difficult pair of choices. Westmoreland asked for a staggering increase in American troop strength, to at least 400,000 and perhaps as many as 600,000 troops by 1967. McNamara supported Westmoreland's request, but on the air attacks against North Vietnam, he and Westmoreland disagreed sharply: McNamara recommended that the bombing be suspended for at least three or four weeks prior to the beginning of the next phase of the military buildup in an effort to start negotiations. Westmoreland wanted air attacks against the infiltration routes to be increased sharply and immediately.

The battle over the new troop buildup and McNamara's recommended bombing pause was to have repercussions affecting the epic debate of 1968. When I first heard about it at a small meeting in Dean Rusk's office on December 6, 1965, I expressed my concern in strong language: "*Where the hell are we going?* I have the feeling we are getting further and further into this war with no prospect of a return. We are fighting the kind of war that Mao Zedong would have us fight. I agree we must do the job—I am sure of that. But couldn't we use air power while holding our ground troops in more defensive positions? Can we avoid sending six hundred thousand men to fight in these jungles? We *must* try to get the job done with less costly means."

My opposition to the Christmas bombing pause became one of the primary factors in the emergence of my reputation as a hawk. Later, my reasoning was forgotten and my position reduced to one simple point—that I had opposed a bombing halt. Yet I felt then, and still feel today, that my reasons for opposing a temporary bombing pause were consistent with my fundamental desire, which never changed—to find the most rapid way out of the quagmire.

On December 18, 1965, the President began two days of highly emotional meetings in the Cabinet Room. The group consulted was smaller than it had been in July—only the President, Rusk, McNamara, McGeorge Bundy, George Ball, Jack Valenti, Undersecretary of State for Political Affairs Alexis Johnson (who had just completed a tour as Deputy Ambassador in Saigon), and me. One other outsider joined our meetings, Justice Fortas. When the fact of the meetings became public the next day, neither my name nor Fortas's was released to the press.

McNamara linked his proposed pause to the forthcoming Christmas season. He argued that even if it failed to produce a response from Hanoi, it was important to show the world that the U.S. had "walked the last mile" for peace before announcing any further troop increases. Rusk said that while the chances a bombing pause would produce a meaningful response from Hanoi were about "one in twenty," he now supported McNamara's proposal as the best way to show the American public and the world that we had "done everything that could be done for peace."

Visibly annoyed at the suggestion anyone might question his peaceful motives, the President interrupted Rusk, asking, "Haven't we already demonstrated this?" Rusk skillfully defused his anger: "To my satisfaction, but not to that of the American people."

After giving several reasons why he favored the bombing halt on political and diplomatic grounds, McNamara added a comment that surprised me: "Moreover, a military solution to the problem is not certain—I estimate it to be one out of three or one out of two. Ultimately, we must search for a diplomatic solution."

The President fixed his mournful gaze on McNamara: "You mean that no matter what we do in the military field, you think there is no sure victory?"

For the first time in my presence, McNamara hinted at an inner doubt, but he masked it with his usual tone of crisp authority and precision. "That's right," he said. "We have been too optimistic. One in three or one in two is my estimate." Rusk broke in, presumably to take the edge off McNamara's pessimism, "I'm more optimistic than that, but I can't prove it."

McNamara persisted: "I'm saying that we may never find a military solution. We need to explore other means. Our military approach is an unlikely route to a successful conclusion."

I asked why we would be considering massive troop increases if military victory was so unlikely. McNamara tried to explain:

> I know this may seem like a contradiction. I recognize that I have come to you for a huge increase in Vietnam, to at least 400,000 men, yet at the same time our actions may lead to counterescalation by the North Vietnamese and some undesirable results. Therefore, I am simply suggesting that we look for other alternatives first.

Just before the meeting adjourned for lunch, the President warned, in very strong language, about the danger of leaks. McNamara's response seemed unusually personal: "The greatest danger of leaks is here in this room. You can't discuss this sort of thing even with your wife. I can visualize stories about all this, and I am concerned with our being embarrassed. Please, let us discuss this with no other human beings outside this room."

The meeting continued for hours after lunch without a decision. Once again, as in the Camp David meeting in July, I was opposed to McNamara—although this time I also disagreed with George Ball, whose disengagement strategy, given the course on which the President had already embarked, was no longer within the realm of what the President would consider. I knew McNamara would have the greatest influence on the President; his very unpredictability probably increased his leverage. But I felt that his recommendations did not constitute a coherent strategy. When the President asked for my views, I responded:

> The arguments for a bombing pause and a troop buildup have been well presented. But even if I accepted them, I would feel deep concern over this move. I want to end the war. I have tried to envision the circumstances under which North Vietnam would talk. I think they will talk only if they believe they are not going to win the war in South Vietnam. I don't believe they are at that stage now. . . . They believe that ultimately the United States will tire of the war and go home and North Vietnam will prevail. . . . Given this situation, I believe the President and our government have talked enough about peace at this time. I don't believe such talk will do any good in the present circumstances. . . . When the time comes to resume the bombing—and it will resume, because the chances are only one in twenty or one in fifty that the bombing halt will produce a response—the U.S. Government will come under even more intense pressure from those who want to extend the pause on one hand, and those who will argue that its failure requires us to escalate still further. I do not like the President to take a position that is so clearly unproductive. Finally, I am deeply concerned that a bombing pause will be viewed as a gimmick. The time may well come when a bombing pause would be valuable. If there is a chance that it would be successful, then I would favor it. But not now.

When I finished, President Johnson wrote a note and pushed it across the table to me. Its tone was different from the note George Ball had passed to me in the same room a few months earlier, but the sentiment—phrased in a uniquely Johnsonian manner—was similar:

> *Magnificent—*
> *To sum up—*
> *As Abraham Lincoln said—*
> *"You can't fertilize a field by farting thru the fence"*

The next day, in a much shorter meeting, the President revealed his final decision: a bombing pause of unspecified determination, during which he would send high-level emissaries around the world to plead the cause of peace, and a tentative approval of another large troop increase, the exact number to be determined later. Once again I had presented my views and lost.

THE CHRISTMAS BOMBING PAUSE ENDS

As soon as the bombing pause began, the American military launched massive ground force operations supported by heavy air attacks *inside* South Vietnam. From a military point of view, such action was justifiable on the grounds that everything possible had to be done to prevent the North Vietnamese from "taking advantage" of the pause, but the American offensive also had the effect of negating whatever message McNamara and the President intended with the bombing pause. It was an incomprehensible combination of mixed signals, I thought, that we were sending to Hanoi.

Nonetheless, the entire world watched—and hoped, against all reasonable expectations—for some response from Hanoi. Finally, in late January, following his standard pattern, the President convened his advisers to discuss the situation, prior to a smaller meeting in which he made his final decision. As in the December meetings, I attended the first of these sessions, on January 28, 1966. The President invited three other outsiders—John McCloy, Allen Dulles, and our Korean War negotiator, Arthur Dean. In his record of the meeting, Bundy, elegant as always in the use of the English language, referred to McCloy, Dulles, Dean, and me as "The Wise Men"—a name that, applied later to a larger group of advisers, became a part of the Washington vocabulary and even a book title.*

*See the White House memorandum of the meeting of January 28, 1966. The phrase has been used many times in many different contexts; starting in the Bible. In its present form it apparently

"We should resume carefully controlled bombing," McNamara began. "I don't think that the American people will long support a government which will not back up four hundred thousand of its own troops with bombing." At the same time, he said, he doubted that resuming the bombing would affect Hanoi's will to fight: "No matter what bombing we do, we will need more men. There is a chance that doubling our force over a period of six months might be sufficient to break their will."

When the President asked me to comment, I stated simply, "I want to get out of Vietnam," and followed with a deliberate paraphrase of the closing section of the Clifford-Elsey Report of 1946: "The only way to get out of Vietnam is to persuade Hanoi that 'we are too strong to be beaten and too determined to be frightened.' If we are to pursue our present course, we must make the war more costly to Hanoi. I want to resume the bombing. I don't want to get trapped by a phony peace bid which immobilizes our ability to resume the bombing. We must fight the war where we are strongest—in the air."

The die was cast: the next day, Johnson and his advisers did not debate resuming the bombing, which was decided, but discussed its timing and the nature of the targets to be hit. At 10 A.M. on January 31, even as Air Force planes were already streaking north once more, the President announced that the bombing had begun again.

The thirty-seven day bombing pause left a particularly unfortunate legacy; its memory was a significant factor in the President's doubts about another pause in 1968—even though by then a full bombing halt was the appropriate course to follow.

In 1965, I had underestimated Hanoi's willingness to resist, no matter what the costs. Based on the best intelligence then available, I believed Hanoi would change its objectives if faced with massive airpower and an iron will. Like many of my colleagues, I did not realize Hanoi would outlast us both politically and on the battlefield, even if outgunned at every turn. But I did not appreciate the fallacy in my judgment until several years later.

---

originated with Bundy. The phrase was enshrined in Walter Isaacson-Evan Thomas's work, *The Wise Men.*

26

The Years of the Hawk

JOB OFFERS

At times, President Johnson's efforts to bring me into the Administration seemed quite casual and even roundabout, as in 1965, when he asked Marny if she thought I might be interested in succeeding Adlai Stevenson, who had just died, as the American Ambassador to the U.N. Marny, startled at both the idea and the President's use of her as a go-between, answered that she had no idea what my reaction would be, and relayed the suggestion to me.

It was relatively easy to avoid an offer—if one could even call it that—made in such an indirect, but characteristically Johnsonian, manner. When I next saw the President, I raised the matter, saying I was not the right man for the post. Similarly, I was able to reject, before it reached the status of a formal offer, hints from President Johnson that he might like me to become his National Security Assistant upon McGeorge Bundy's departure, or Director of Central Intelligence when it was clear that Admiral Raborn was unsuitable for the job. Again, as with the U.N. suggestion, there was no real offer, no real rejection.* This was the way Lyndon Johnson liked to operate. He hated to be rejected, and this indirect method allowed him to maintain that since he had not made an offer, he had not been turned down.

*The President chose Arthur Goldberg for the U.N., Walt Rostow as his National Security Assistant, and Richard Helms as DCI.

There were three other occasions when he asked me to join his Administration, and by a curious coincidence, they all were connected to the career of Nicholas deB. Katzenbach.

Katzenbach had served as Robert Kennedy's deputy in the Justice Department and became Acting Attorney General when Bobby resigned in September 1964 to run for the Senate from New York. A large man with stooped posture that was the result of slow-acting bone deterioration, Katzenbach was subtle, low-key, and possessed of a wry and delightful sense of humor. He had one of the most brilliant and creative legal minds I have encountered, and approached public service with total seriousness. At the same time he saw the ironic side of service in Washington—the endless games some people play, the petty deals that are often necessary in the pursuit of objectives of great purpose. Speaking of a senior White House aide, Katzenbach once observed, "The problem with that man is that he thinks government is just a game. He doesn't care about the consequences of his actions." One of Nick's greatest strengths, something lacking in most Washington policymakers, was an uncanny ability to listen to two fiercely contending sides in a dispute, each unalterably opposed to the other, and devise a compromise acceptable to both.

Nick Katzenbach deserved to become the next Attorney General, but his close association with Bobby Kennedy gave rise to unjustified suspicion in the eyes of Lyndon Johnson. Undecided as to how to proceed, Johnson simply left Katzenbach in the top post as Acting Attorney General. At first, Katzenbach regarded the situation as awkward but acceptable; finally, however, in early January 1965 he informed the President that it was not in anyone's interests for him to continue to function as the nation's chief law enforcement officer unless his status was resolved before the new session of Congress got underway.

Late in 1964, the President had asked me, in his usual indirect manner, to become Attorney General. Responding in kind, I said I was completely happy as a private lawyer. I hoped the conversation would prevent a formal offer.

It did not: in mid-January, after Katzenbach asked to have his status resolved, the President raised the idea again with me. I said that, while I was deeply flattered, presiding over the Department of Justice, with its many divisions and administrative responsibilities, was not an effective use of my services. The truth was that as a lawyer, I liked the freedom of practicing on my own, and, in addition, I did not wish to give up the ability to speak frankly to the President, something I could do more effectively as an outside adviser than as a member of the Cabinet.

I thought the subject closed, but on January 28, 1965 (one week after his Inauguration and less than two weeks before the beginning of the bombing of North Vietnam), Johnson invited me to luncheon in the family quarters of the White House with Abe Fortas, Lady Bird, and the two Johnson daughters. At the end of our meal, presumably by prearrangement, the three women left, and Fortas and Johnson began telling me why I should become Attorney General. It was not easy to say no to Lyndon Johnson without getting him mad, but I managed it, using the same arguments I had used before. He finally decided that since I was adamant in my refusal, he would offer Katzenbach, on a permanent basis, the position that he was already carrying out so admirably. The next day, the President nominated him as Attorney General.

Johnson's next serious attempt to bring me into the Administration took place after George Ball decided to leave the State Department in the summer of 1966. President Johnson, again backed by Abe Fortas, asked me to replace Ball. It was not hard to turn this offer down: I pointed out that it would seriously undercut the Secretary of State if a person known to be a close personal friend and adviser of the President became Undersecretary of State. He accepted this reasoning, but said meaningfully that he was not through trying to bring me into the Administration.

The President then asked Katzenbach if he would step down from the Cabinet to succeed Ball. Challenged by the opportunity to work on foreign policy, Nick agreed without hesitation. This reopened the top post at Justice, and would lead to the most memorable of Lyndon Johnson's attempts to bring me into the Administration, which came after we had returned from the President's summit conference in the Philippines and his whirlwind visit to the troops in Vietnam.

THE MANILA SUMMIT

On October 18, 1966, President Johnson called from Hawaii, and asked if I would join him in the Philippines for his summit conference with Asian leaders. Two days later, I flew with Dean Rusk and his party to the Philippines. Reaching Manila on the evening of October 21, we went directly to the famous but faded Manila Hotel, where General MacArthur had lived before World War II.

The Manila summit was conceived as a meeting of the leaders of all the nations with troops in Vietnam, and brought to the Philippine capital not only Thieu and Ky from Saigon, but also President Park Chung Hee of South Korea, and Prime Ministers Thanom Kittikachorn of Thailand, Harold Holt of Australia, and Keith Holyoake of New Zealand. Our host was the new President of the Philippines, Ferdinand E. Marcos.

At the time, Washington viewed Marcos as the great democratic hope of Asia. He had won a relatively honest election as President in January 1966, and his naked seizure of "emergency" powers under martial law was still six years away. A classified briefing note prepared for me by the State

Department illustrates the euphoria with which Washington regarded Marcos in those early years: he was "the most skilled, vigorous, and attractive leader the Philippines has produced since Ramón Magsaysay more than ten years ago. . . . [His] leadership represents a 'last chance' of the Philippines to achieve a peaceful transition to modernism under democratic processes."

I watched Marcos and his wife Imelda with fascination during the conference. Both had been educated in an American school system while the Philippines had been an American colony, and they were far more attuned to American culture than any of the other leaders at Manila. It was clear that the Marcoses, especially Imelda—a former beauty queen who in 1966 still had a youthful figure and a dazzling smile—had charmed Lyndon Johnson.

Although I was a private citizen, the President formally designated me the third-ranking member of the official American delegation, after himself and Dean Rusk—an unusual arrangement that fueled speculation that I might soon be entering the Administration. Rusk took this in stride publicly, but he made no effort to engage me in serious conversation during our travels. At the end of each day during the trip, I joined President Johnson in his hotel suite. In those private talks, Johnson was impressive and moving. He had, in his own words, grown up "in a section of the country [that] regarded Asia as totally alien in spirit as well as nationality." He talked not about the war, but about his desire to extend the benefits of the Great Society to Asia. Johnson's vision of Asia's potential was accurate, even visionary, but, as it turned out, his dreams of regional cooperation and economic development could not be achieved until the war was over.

As a public-relations exercise, the Manila summit proved to be successful, leaving the impression, as intended, that the U.S., in the words of a *Washington Post* editorial, "did not stand alone."[1] As a way of improving the situation in Vietnam, though, it was close to worthless: little could be accomplished in such a setting. The plenary meetings were composed of lengthy statements, not dialogue. An honest review of the political and military difficulties confronting the allies was avoided.

One visual memory remained long after Manila. On the last night of the conference, our hosts gave a large buffet dinner at Malacanang Palace. Each of us was given a *barong tagalog,* a loose-fitting off-white silk shirt worn outside one's trousers. Ideally suited to the tropical heat of Manila, it tends to look less graceful on a large American than on most Filipinos, and it seemed only to add to Lyndon Johnson's considerable bulk.

After dinner, everyone, from the seven chiefs of state down to junior staff officers, moved to an open veranda alongside the Manila River, where the hot, muggy atmosphere was made even more oppressive by a low ceiling and the body heat of a vast throng of people. As patrol boats tooled along the river in front of us, a band played American dance music of the forties and fifties.

I thought the scene already surreal enough, but it held one more surprise. I wandered over to a group of people standing silently in a large circle near the middle of the dance floor: there, in the middle of the crowd, were Lyndon Johnson and Imelda Marcos, dancing. Moving slowly in a sort of shuffle, he towered over her, his face mournful, his eyes looking unseeingly beyond the gaping crowd, his mind seemingly far from Manila and his dance partner. Imelda, radiant in her trademark Filipino dress with butterfly shoulders and tight waist, was smiling up at Johnson, smiling at the cameras, smiling in total triumph as her friends and retainers looked on in awe and amazement.

The scene would later become world-famous, and was turned into a clever and cruel drawing by David Levine, but at that moment, as I sweltered in the Southeast Asian heat, the scene carried no symbolism for me. I merely thought to myself, *Poor Lyndon. He really looks miserable.*

THE COONSKINS OF CAM RANH BAY

On October 26, the day after the end of the Manila summit, President Johnson made his celebrated secret trip to Vietnam. A heated debate had taken place during the days leading up to the surprise visit as to whether or not the risks to the President were too great. Dean Rusk, Henry Cabot Lodge, and I favored a trip, but the main advocate was General Westmoreland, on whose shoulders the burdens of security and logistics would fall. So tight was the secrecy—the President having said that for security reasons the trip would be canceled instantly if it leaked—that when I was summoned by Bill Moyers to a midday meeting in the Manila Embassy on the twenty-sixth, I was unaware that the decision had actually been made.

The deception and security were the greatest I ever encountered. When I arrived, I was closeted with several other members of the Presidential party. Meanwhile, the White House press corps was summoned to a special briefing at the Embassy, while the rest of the correspondents covering the summit were diverted on a three-hour boat trip with Lady Bird Johnson to the World War II battle site of Corregidor. After the White House press corps had filled the room, Moyers locked the doors, closed the curtains, and told them that they were going to Vietnam. To add to the security precautions, the American Embassy "pulled the plug" on all direct communications between the Philippines and the outside world for several hours.

The visit to Cam Ranh Bay was one of the emotional high points of the Johnson Presidency. It was the first trip by a President to American troops in a war zone since Franklin Roosevelt had visited GIs during the Casablanca Conference in January 1943, and it lasted only two hours and twenty-four minutes—but the impressions lingered for a long time. It is hard to describe the emotions that came from seeing the Commander in Chief with his troops in the combat zone. Hearing the National Anthem played by a military band as the wind whipped in from the South China Sea, feeling the strange energy that comes from men at war, seeing the President moving among soldiers carrying M16s or lying in hospital beds, no one—hawk or dove, for or against the war—could remain unmoved.

President Johnson made a quickly forgotten speech to the troops, but the remark which became part of the Johnson legend came near the end of an informal talk he gave senior officers in a packed officers' club. I stood in the back of the overcrowded room next to Rusk, sweltering in the heat, listening to one of the most emotional statements that Lyndon Johnson ever made: "You will get everything you need," he said, almost shouting. The phrasing was artful—"everything you *need*," not "everything you *want*"—but it offered room for further misunderstanding between the military, which believed it needed *everything* it wanted, and Johnson, who thought it needed *only* what he gave it.

Then, warming to his audience, hoping words could somehow shorten the war, Lyndon Johnson reached back to his Texas roots and, speaking with unfeigned emotion, told the officers to "go out there and nail that coonskin to the wall." The phrase stuck: for the rest of the war, people joked about "nailing that coonskin to the wall."

The trip to Cam Ranh Bay had an unfortunate effect on the President. Having pressed the flesh with the soldiers in Vietnam, having visited the wounded in the field hospital, having seen the war—or so he thought—firsthand, his emotional commitment to the struggle increased exponentially. He was sincere when he told people at the time, and wrote later, that he had "never been more moved by any group I have talked to, never in my life."[2]

As 1967 began, I still believed that if we persevered, Hanoi would have to reconsider its war aims and its strategy. Every official assessment reaching Washington supported this view. In the spring of 1967, the CIA's top Vietnam expert, George Carver, told the PFIAB that within a year, the situation would show a "dramatic improvement." I was impressed by such predictions, but not totally convinced. One of the best reporters of the era, Chalmers Roberts of *The Washington Post,* recorded in his memoirs a fairly typical comment of mine from that period: while the commitment in Vietnam was a "great decision," I added, "We will go through hell before it is over."[3]

ANOTHER JOB OFFER

Two weeks after we returned from Asia, the President checked into Bethesda Naval Hospital for surgery to remove a throat polyp, and to repair scarring caused by the gall bladder operation of the previous year—an operation made famous by his public display of his surgical scar. While in the hospital, he asked to see me.

His hospital suite had been decorated with oil paintings of the LBJ Ranch, and his familiar three-screen television set had been placed in the room so he could watch all three network news broadcasts at once—a habit that many of his aides and friends found maddening. When I entered, I saw he had needles and tubes in his arms. He motioned me to pull a chair close to his bed. When I had done so, he whispered, "I very much appreciate your coming out because I have a very important matter to take up with you."

His voice was weak and hoarse. "I am an old man," he said, ignoring the fact that I was a year and a half older than he. Grabbing my arm, he reached over with his other hand to hold mine. "I know you're going to come through for me on this, Clark. I'm laid low here, I've got a tough time coming up. I want you to become my Attorney General." Then the stopper, with which Johnson had snared so many people: "So often have I called on you in the past, maybe sometimes you might have been reluctant, but you always wind up doing what I ask you to do. Do this for your President."

"Let me think about it, Mr. President," was all I could manage.

The pressure increased the next day, when, for the first and only time in our long relationship, Lady Bird involved herself in a substantive issue between her husband and me. "Lyndon feels so strongly about this," she said. "He is so sure that you are going to accept, and I am too. It is really important to him. I hope you will do it for both of us."

Lady Bird made it tougher, but nonetheless, I still intended to refuse. The next day, I returned to the hospital. The President was convalescing from his throat surgery, and he was temporarily unable to speak. He communicated by writing on a notepad; as Lady Bird told the press, she had never seen her husband speechless before, "and we are going to make the most of it."

"Mr. President," I began, "I want to do my best to have you understand why I must again turn down your request that I become Attorney General. For a man to go into a job it must be a job in which he is deeply interested, one in which he feels that he has a very real contribution to make. With the Justice Department at this particular stage of its existence, it is very clear to me that I'm not the right man. I would not have my heart in it, and it isn't what I ought to be doing. My background and training in government falls heavily within the national security and foreign policy field, and that is where my interest lies."

I thought that the President's feelings were probably hurt by my comments, but, of course, he could not speak. Perhaps he accepted my explanation; in any case, I am sure he saw the finality of my decision. Taking out his pad, he simply wrote on it, "Who should I select as A.G.?" I knew that he was considering Katzenbach's deputy, Ramsey Clark, and I asked for more time to think about it. He wrote that if he chose Clark, "then Tom resigns and Thurgood is up"—a reference to the fact that Ramsey's father, Tom Clark, would have to resign from the Supreme Court, leaving a vacancy for Johnson to fill. Johnson wanted to be the first President to appoint a black Justice, and had long hoped to appoint Thurgood Marshall, who had successfully argued the case for school desegregation before the Court in 1954. Johnson knew that Ramsey Clark's appointment to Justice would speed that process by forcing a vacancy on the Court.

Everything eventually went according to Johnson's typically complicated plan. Clark's nomination was announced on February 28, and on the same day his father made public his intention to retire from the High Court. Thurgood Marshall was nominated to succeed Tom Clark on June 13, 1967.

THE SIX-DAY WAR

In the summer of 1967, the Six-Day War in the Mideast diverted our attention from Vietnam and brought me a new and sensitive assignment. I sympathized with the reasons that led Israel to attack Egypt at a moment when they had every reason to believe that Nasser's Egypt was about to attack them. I was pleased the war was a complete success for Israel—especially after the Jordanians made the strange decision to enter the war, thus allowing Israel to take over East Jerusalem and unite the Holy City under their control.

But Israel's triumph was marred by a horrible and unnecessary tragedy, which put a dark cloud over American-Israeli relations—the attack, by Israeli aircraft and motor torpedo boats, on the USS *Liberty,* a state-of-the-art electronic intelligence ship. Thirty-four Americans died and 171 were wounded in the attack.

Through a serious failure in the Pentagon, one of many during this incident, President Johnson was not informed of the attack until two hours after it had taken place. He immediately called for an emergency meeting in the Situation Room; the White House called me at home around 6 A.M. and asked me, without further explanation, to come to the White House immediately.

We convened at 6:40 A.M. At first the President suspected the attack had been made by the Russians, and as we sat around the large wooden table in the Situation Room studying maps of the area, he dictated a hot-line message to Soviet Premier Kosygin warning him that our aircraft were investigating a serious incident in the area. Suddenly we were interrupted by a "flash" from Tel Aviv that the Israelis had just informed an American naval attaché that "maybe" they had attacked an American ship in error. With that astonishing report, we knew we were not facing a confrontation with Moscow, but something entirely different.

We were baffled. From the beginning, there was skepticism and disbelief about the Israeli version of events. We had enormous respect for Israeli intelligence, and it was difficult to believe the *Liberty* had been attacked by mistake. Every conceivable theory was advanced that morning. It became clear that from the sketchy information available we could not figure out what had happened. President Johnson asked me, as Chairman of the PFIAB, to chair a special investigation.

Assisted by Pat Coyne, I spent the next month reviewing information that had been gathered for a naval board of inquiry that had been convened at U.S. Navy headquarters in Valetta, Malta. The President asked me not to make an independent inquiry; because of this limitation, I was never fully satisfied with the results of my report, but these were some of the highlights of my still-classified report to the President:

- The *Liberty* was unquestionably in international waters when it was attacked, despite Israeli efforts to suggest otherwise.

- The *Liberty* was, at all times prior to the attack, flying a five-by-eight-foot American flag at the masthead, her distinguishing letters and number printed clearly on her bow and her name painted clearly on its stern. It was impossible that the *Liberty* could have been mistaken for the Egyptian ship *El Queir,* as the Israelis had suggested publicly and privately in their effort to excuse the attack. The physical differences between the two ships were simply too great for such a mistake to be made—especially by airmen and sailors as skilled as those in the Israeli Defense Force.

- There was no evidence that the highest levels of the Israeli government, headed by Levi Eshkol, were aware of the *Liberty*'s true identity or the fact that an attack was taking place. At the same time, however, no one could prove that they did not know.

- The best interpretation from the facts available to me was that there were inexcusable failures on the part of the Israeli Defense Forces. There was no justification for the attack, which constituted an act of gross negligence, and I recommended that the Israeli government should be held completely responsible, and Israeli military personnel involved should be punished.

When I submitted this report to the President, I considered my role in this terrible affair substantially completed. I do not know to this day at what level the attack on the *Liberty* was authorized, and I think it is unlikely the full truth will ever come out. Having been for so long a staunch supporter of Israel, I was particularly troubled by this incident: I could not bring myself to believe that such an action could have been authorized by Levi Eshkol. Yet somewhere inside the Israeli government, somewhere along the chain of command, something had gone terribly wrong—and then had been covered up. I never felt the Israelis made adequate restitution or explanation for their action. At the same time, though, I did not believe this tragic incident justified a break between the U.S. and Israel.

SUMMER, 1967

Vietnam did not allow us much time for other issues. Even before I had completed my study of the attack on the *Liberty,* the President had again redirected my attention to the war.

The officials in charge of the war thought it was going better than ever: a steady stream of optimistic reports came from the new American Ambassador in Saigon, Ellsworth Bunker. Most dramatically, General Westmoreland told a cheering joint session of Congress on April 28, 1967, that the allies would prevail. McNamara continued to advocate our policies with a personal dynamism and apparent conviction that disguised or minimized any underlying doubts he might have felt. At a meeting in July 1967,[4] after returning from another trip to Vietnam, he attacked a widely quoted and influential article by the Saigon bureau chief of *The New York Times,* R. W. Apple, which suggested the war was a stalemate; he asserted with great vigor that "there is no military stalemate in Vietnam." McNamara said the reporting from Vietnam was "cynical and skeptical" and should be heavily discounted: progress in the pacification program, he said, "has exceeded my expectations."

I asked McNamara if he agreed with what I felt was a growing public sentiment in this country that the war in Vietnam "can't be won."

"There is a limit to what the enemy can send into the South," McNamara replied. "We are destroying a significant number of the large units. For the first time, I feel that if we follow the same program we will win the war and end the fighting."

The President was so encouraged by McNamara's expressions of optimism that he wrote down, and saved, his response to my question.[5] But McNamara was not so positive when it came to the bombing of the

North: he no longer believed in its value, and said he opposed military requests to expand it. General Wheeler disagreed openly. It was the first time I had seen the normally amiable and mild-mannered Chairman of the Joint Chiefs take on his superior in the chain of command.

VISITING THE DOMINOES: THE CLIFFORD-TAYLOR MISSION

President Johnson said he agreed that more troops were needed, but he wanted McNamara and Wheeler to "shave the number." The best way to get the American public to accept another troop increase, he said, was to get more troops from the troop-contributing nations that had met with him at Manila. "I am going to ask Clark and Max Taylor to go out on a Presidential mission to see our allies, especially Prime Minister Holt in Australia. I want to get more support from our allies."

He had two clear goals in mind. First, he wanted another summit meeting, in 1967 or early 1968, preferably in Bangkok; second, having decided to increase American troop levels to 525,000 men, he desperately wanted new commitments from the nations of the region to show the American people we were not carrying the weight of an Asian war entirely on our shoulders. Before I set out, these seemed to me to be eminently reasonable, and achievable, objectives.*

As soon as the trip was announced, however, a serious problem arose. The first newspaper stories on our trip described all too accurately our primary purpose, and forced us to revise, at least for public consumption, our goals. The *New York Times* headline was typical: JOHNSON SENDING 2 AIDES TO PRESS ALLIES FOR TROOPS. Articles like this made us look, in Taylor's phrase, like "an arm-twisting delegation to squeeze more troops from laggard allies reluctant to do their fair share."[6] Every government we planned to visit except South Korea faced significant antiwar opposition of its own. As a result, most of the American Embassies on our route sent Washington urgent telegrams urging us not to portray the trip as a search for additional troops. Marcos went one step further: saying he "saw no need" for us to visit him so shortly after the Manila summit, he canceled our visit to the Philippines after it had been announced.

To minimize the damage, Taylor and I beat a quick retreat with the press, saying, somewhat disingenuously, that the purpose of the trip was simply to reassure our Asian allies, get a firsthand assessment of the situation, and discuss another summit.

*At the time of our trip, South Korea, in return for massive American military aid, had sent over 45,000 men to Vietnam; Australia had sent 5,465; Thailand had committed itself to send 2,500; the Philippines just over 2,000 in noncombat, civic action units; and New Zealand an artillery unit of 381 men.

The day after our trip was made public, I received a short note from Vice President Humphrey offering some suggestions, and wishing us well on our mission. What was most memorable about his note was its poignant opening sentence, which spoke volumes about the obscure role to which Lyndon Johnson had relegated his Vice President: "I read in the press this morning of the assignment given you by the President. I am so pleased. . . ."

Taylor and I left Andrews Air Force Base in an Air Force jet on the morning of July 22, 1967, accompanied by staff officers from State and the Defense Department, including Richard Steadman, an impressive young Deputy Assistant Secretary of Defense who was later to work closely with me in the Pentagon, and Freeman Matthews, a Foreign Service Officer representing the State Department.

We began in Saigon with the usual round of briefings. A national election was scheduled for September 3, and President Johnson had asked us to convey a strong personal message to Chief of State Thieu and Premier Ky as to the importance the U.S. attached to a fair and free election. This message we dutifully delivered over a lunch at the Presidential Palace, which included clear soup with birds' heads in it—a rare delicacy, our hosts told us. I gently sipped the broth and sought to avoid the delicacy itself, which stared up at me accusingly from the bottom of the bowl.

General Westmoreland and Ambassador Bunker gave us the most optimistic progress report I would receive in the course of the war. Both men told us that the tide had turned definitively in favor of Saigon. They believed that the level of communist activity was gradually but steadily decreasing, and—notwithstanding the tension evident between Thieu and Ky, they foresaw growing political stability in Saigon.

This was almost the last good news that Taylor and I received on our trip. To put it simply, the troop-contributing nations did not want to contribute any more troops. In fact, with the exception of Korea, they made it clear that they resented having had to send any soldiers to Vietnam in the first place. As we reported to President Johnson upon our return: "Our hosts liked to talk more about what they had done in the past rather than what they would be willing to do in the future."

Each country had a perfectly logical explanation for this—local conditions, either economic, political, or both. But the bottom line was always about the same:

- Thailand reacted negatively to our suggestion that they send 10,000 more troops—a figure chosen personally by President Johnson. Bangkok was busy with its own security problems, caused by communist guerrillas in their own northeast. The Thais also pointed out that they were already allowing us virtually unrestricted use of the bases in Thailand to stage raids over Laos and North Vietnam. A private meeting I had in Bangkok with Pote Sarasin, the Minister of National Development, whom I had known when he had served as the Thai Ambassador in Washington, was particularly troubling. We met alone in his house, elevated above the ground by pillars in the graceful Thai style, surrounded by plants and ancient Thai ceramics and statues. Sarasin gently blasted American ethnocentrism: "Your Secretary Rusk keeps talking about the 'yellow peril' from China, but we Thais simply do not see it that way here. You are afraid of Chinese soldiers entering the war as they did in Korea, but I don't think this will happen. Don't you Americans know that the Chinese and Vietnamese have hated each other for centuries?"

• In Australia, the President's good friend, Prime Minister Harold Holt, became extremely evasive when we told him that Johnson considered Australian participation in the war effort to be particularly critical, and that Australia's actions would strongly affect ours. He responded to my description of the American political landscape with a comparable portrait of Australian politics, designed to show that he, too, faced a difficult situation at home. In our report upon our return we noted, "Either the Australians do not believe that their vital interests are at stake to a point requiring immediate sacrifice, or they believe that we are so deeply involved that we must carry through to a conclusion satisfactory to them as well as to us."

• In New Zealand, the situation was much the same as in Australia. While this remote country of less than four million people had sent 120,000 men to fight in World War II, it felt that sending even 300 more men to Vietnam would be difficult. Wellington, the capital, was also the site of the only demonstrations against us during our trip. They were small in number and, as protesters go, well behaved—but I jokingly noted to Taylor that more people turned out in New Zealand to demonstrate against our trip than the country had sent to Vietnam.

• Even South Korea had its doubts. No Asian nation had contributed more to the war effort, and Washington had made it worthwhile by, in effect, paying Seoul twice for each soldier that went to Vietnam—once to cover his costs in Vietnam, a second time to cover the costs of his replacement in South Korea. But even President Park—a General who had seized power through a coup—made us sit through a dissertation on *his* political difficulties.

It was symbolic of our mission that, in the end, we did "visit" the Philippines, forced by engine trouble to land there while flying from Bangkok to Canberra. We made a safe landing north of Manila at the giant American air base at Clark Field, but Marcos pretended we were not in his country. After a nine-hour stop, we took off again into the night, past runways filled with American jets fueled, armed, and ready for more combat in Vietnam.

Taylor and I came home on August 5. As always, we had gotten on together very well, but we had interpreted our trip in significantly different ways. Taylor had more or less accepted the explanation that each nation had produced to avoid an additional commitment; I returned both puzzled and troubled, dismayed by our failure to get more support from our allies.

I could only hint at the level of my concern in our joint report to the President, since Taylor did not share it. Privately, though, I told President Johnson I was shocked at the failure of the countries whose security we believed we were defending to do more for themselves. Australia, which had given so much during World War II, dismayed us the most. Johnson, who remembered the country with special affection—from his brief service there in World War II—had counted on more from Down Under and his good friend Harold Holt.

A few weeks after my return to the U.S., I had another disturbing conversation, this one with the Asian leader most respected in Washington, Prime Minister Lee Kuan Yew of Singapore. Lee had literally carved his independent city-state out of the Malayan Federation, and turned it into one of the most successful states in the world—the Switzerland of Asia, as the press liked to call it. Lee regularly urged the U.S. to resist the spread of communism in Southeast Asia. When President Johnson asked me to join him for a meeting with Lee prior to a State Dinner, I asked the Singaporean if he would send a small contingent of soldiers to Vietnam. Without the slightest embarrassment or apology, Lee replied that his economy and his political situation could not stand the strain. After my trip to Southeast Asia, I was not entirely surprised: it seemed, as someone joked at the time, as if the Asians were ready to fight in Vietnam to the last American.

On the morning we returned to Washington, Robert Pierpoint of CBS News described our trip in a succinct and accurate commentary, which raised Lyndon Johnson's ire and led to a few hours of Presidential fury:

> It is not that President Johnson's two travelling emissaries are not highly competent men—they are. But all the evidence indicates their assignment was impossible. While it was never quite officially admit-

> ted, they went out to Asia to persuade the other Allied nations fighting in Vietnam to send more troops and to agree to the time and place for another Summit meeting. . . . As for the idea of an Asian Allies Summit Meeting this fall, the White House has already downgraded it from probable to possible, and after today's Taylor-Clifford report to the President, it could sink clear out of sight.[7]

As Pierpoint had suggested, there would be no more Asian summits, and few additional troops, during the Johnson Administration. The Asian and Pacific nations were beginning to distance themselves—some slightly, some openly—from America's efforts in Vietnam, although they would not say so publicly. Any effort to bring the leaders together again would only highlight the problem.

Taylor and I reported to President Johnson and his associates on August 5. Tom Johnson, a bright and engaging Presidential assistant who had begun his career as a White House Fellow and was to have a spectacular rise, took notes.*

I had returned from my trip to Asia with two points of view that were seemingly contradictory. On one hand, the trip had buried for me, once and for all, Washington's treasured domino theory; on the other hand, I continued to support the policy because it seemed to provide the best way out of the war. I had not yet reached the point where I could see that at the end of this particular tunnel there simply was no light—but serious doubts had been sown.

"If we continue the war at the same level of ground and air effort," I said, "I am unable to see that it will bring us any nearer to our goal. A year from now we will once again be taking stock, and we may well be no nearer our objectives than we are today." No one needed to be reminded that a year hence we would also be in a Presidential campaign.

"I found no concern anywhere in Asia," I continued, "that the Chinese might enter the war, and there was the same reaction to the possibility of the Soviets entering. There seems to be no diminution of Hanoi's will to continue the war. If we are to have a chance to get this war over with, we must hit them harder."

FALL, 1967: DEBATE OVER THE KISSINGER CHANNEL

The fall of 1967 was the last time that the Johnson Administration would be unified on Vietnam. Within weeks, McNamara would leave office, the

*Johnson later went into journalism, rising to become publisher of the *Los Angeles Times,* and later President of CNN.

communists would stun the world with a nationwide military offensive, the political landscape at home would change dramatically, and I would find myself back in the government—as Secretary of Defense.

None of this was stirring in the wind in October. Rostow, Bunker, Westmoreland, and the head of the pacification effort in Vietnam, Bob Komer, were all continuing to report significant gains in the war. The White House launched a multimedia public-relations campaign, climaxed by another trip to Washington by General Westmoreland and Ambassador Bunker, to persuade the American public that the war was being won. Westmoreland told the National Press Club that "the end begins to come into view," and it might be possible to phase down American troop levels in 1969. These statements and the trip by Westmoreland and Bunker proved, in light of subsequent events, to be a grievous error in both tactics and judgment. However, at the time, Westmoreland's briefings and predictions impressed almost everyone, including me.

Efforts to communicate with Hanoi were also intensified. During the late summer, the President made an effort to open secret communications directly with Ho Chi Minh through two left-wing European academics who had known the North Vietnamese leader for over twenty years. Their American contact was Henry Kissinger, who had survived the problems created in 1965 by the Foisie article. Kissinger's two friends saw Ho and Prime Minister Pham Van Dong in Hanoi during the summer; using Kissinger as the messenger, Johnson offered to stop the bombing of North Vietnam if Hanoi "would enter promptly into productive discussions with the United States." To give extra credibility to this secret message, Johnson publicly repeated his offer on September 27 in a major speech which contained what came to be known as the "San Antonio formula," after the city in which he had announced it. (The exact meaning of the San Antonio formula was to become an issue during my confirmation hearings a few months later.)

On the day before Kissinger was to return to Paris to see his two friends, October 18, I attended a meeting at the White House to discuss his instructions. Kissinger had sought a face-to-face meeting with the North Vietnamese in Paris, but they had refused to see him, replying to all his messages with strongly worded rejections. The President said he suspected the whole channel might be a trick to get us to reduce the bombing. Rusk wanted to keep the channel open, but opposed any halt in the bombing without a commitment from Hanoi in advance that they would take some de-escalatory action.

With the exception of Kissinger and me, almost everyone in the room was exhausted after close to seven years of government service, and I thought it showed in the confused discussion, and in the excessive attention being paid to a minor and ineffectual channel of communications to Hanoi. If one stripped away the drama of sending a message to Ho Chi Minh through a secret intermediary, I noted, Hanoi's position had not changed. I recommended terminating the Kissinger channel on the grounds that it would prolong the war by misleading and encouraging Hanoi. If Hanoi—or for that matter, Moscow—wanted to talk to us or change their position, it was easy for them to contact us more directly.

The President ended the discussion by turning to the academic from Harvard. "Professor Kissinger," he said, "I want to thank you for your efforts. Go back to Paris to meet with your friends as scheduled. In my own mind, I feel they have failed to indicate any desire to talk, but I see no necessity to break off the channel. Let's see what happens before deciding on another bombing pause."

The Kissinger channel never came to anything, but the San Antonio formula became the government's formal position. I remained convinced that if and when Hanoi was ready to change its position, we would not need any intermediaries.

THE WISE MEN: THE FIRST MEETING

In the first two days of November, two significant events took place that were to set the stage for the great drama of 1968. The first was the convening of a group of elder statesmen—the Wise Men—to advise the President on the war. The second was a dramatic change in Robert McNamara's position on the war.

The idea of convening a group of Wise Men originated during a discussion Walt Rostow and I had with President Johnson. Recalling the great comfort he had derived from earlier meetings with several elder statesmen, including Dean Acheson and John McCloy, the President said he wanted to hear from some of the senior statesmen again. He asked me to act as organizer and chairman of the effort. After much discussion, the final group was chosen by President Johnson from a list Rostow and I had assembled. Bob Lovett and John McCloy were unable to attend on the day chosen, but the rest of the group met for drinks and dinner with Rusk and McNamara at the State Department on the evening of November 1, 1967, and then met for four hours with President Johnson the next day. It was an impressive gathering: Acheson, General of the Army Omar Bradley, George Ball, McGeorge Bundy, Arthur Dean, former Treasury Secretary Douglas Dillon, Justice Fortas, and former Undersecretary of State Robert Murphy. They were joined by other elder statesmen still in the government: Averell Harriman, Henry Cabot Lodge, and Maxwell Taylor. Jim Jones, a White House assistant, kept notes of the meeting.*

(I learned later that, behind our backs, junior State Department officers called us the "WOMs," or Wise *Old* Men, but the mocking tone of the middle word was dropped from most subsequent reports of this group.)

The briefings that first evening, by General Wheeler and George Carver of the CIA, set an upbeat and optimistic tone. When the group convened with the President the next morning, each of the participants, led by Acheson, told the President he should stand firm. Asked by the President if we should get out, the group's response was, in the words of McGeorge Bundy's written summation, "a strong and unanimous negative." Even George Ball made only tactical suggestions for changing our policy, such as restricting the bombing of the North to the area around the Demilitarized Zone (DMZ). "No one in this group thinks we should get out of the war," Ball said, to the President's obvious pleasure.

Averell Harriman, I noticed, remained silent during this display of unanimity, looking straight ahead. At seventy-six, Harriman was the oldest man in the room. He wore a hearing aid, and on occasion liked to let people think he was too deaf to follow the conversation. But this was a sly trick. As soon as the discussion turned to the possibility of negotiations, Harriman suddenly seemed to wake up. Hoping to cap his long and distinguished career by heading the negotiating team, he had no intention of losing his access to the President by prematurely revealing the depths of his opposition to the war itself. A negotiation was "inevitable and necessary," he said.

When everyone else had finished, the President asked me to speak. "No matter what we do," I said, "this will never be a popular war. No wars have been popular, with the possible exception of World War II. But we must go on because what we are doing is right. Secretary McNamara said last night that perhaps his and Rusk's efforts since 1961 have been a failure. This is not true. . . . But any cessation of our efforts will be interpreted as a sign of weakness." As I finished my comments, Luci Baines Nugent brought the President's grandson, Patrick Lyndon Nugent, into the room and handed him to the President. For the rest of the meeting, as we continued to discuss such matters as the bombing of North Vietnam, the five-month-old child napped quietly in his grandfather's arms.

This first meeting of the Wise Men strengthened President Johnson's resolve at a critical moment. Unknown to anyone else in the room except Rusk and Rostow, Lyndon Johnson had received a severe shock the previous day: McNamara had virtually abandoned the policy he had played such a central role in creating.

*Subsequently a Congressman from Oklahoma (1973–1987), and chairman of the American Stock Exchange.

THE AGONY OF ROBERT S. McNAMARA

It was clear that, after almost seven years in the job, Bob McNamara was being pulled simultaneously in opposite directions by his deepening despair about the war and his loyalty to the President. During those long and grueling work days he would continue to oversee the war effort, selecting bombing targets, arguing with the Joint Chiefs, dealing with an increasingly distrustful Congress. In the evening he would share the growing doubts he had about the war with close friends—including, to Lyndon Johnson's special concern, Robert F. Kennedy.

Even though we worked together closely and remained friends, I find it hard to explain how McNamara's views on the war actually evolved. He never discussed the matter with me, but it obviously caused him great and continuing pain. Finally, after sixteen years of public silence and private anguish on the subject, he offered a limited insight into his own thinking when he testified in the libel trial brought by General Westmoreland against CBS in 1984. Asked under oath what he believed and when he believed it, McNamara said, "My view was that it was unlikely that the war could be won by military means. . . . I certainly held that view at times in 1966, if not earlier."[8] Yet, notwithstanding his ambiguous remarks about the difficulty of a military victory, McNamara did not share his underlying pessimism with the President until near the end of 1967. If he had spoken earlier, it would have had an enormous effect on the policy which he had done so much to create.

By the time he sent the President his memorandum on November 1, 1967, McNamara had been the focal point of the policy for so long, had made so many recommendations that had failed to produce the anticipated result, and had made so many projections that had turned out to be overly optimistic, that his credibility had begun to erode. In August, under intense grilling before the Senate Armed Services Committee, he had been unable to make a strong case for the continued bombing of the North; and for the first time the disagreements he was having in private with the Joint Chiefs became a matter of public record. Senator Stennis publicly charged McNamara with having "shackled" our air campaign against North Vietnam, and thereby caused higher American casualties.

Johnson publicly defended McNamara against Stennis, and said there was no "deep division" in the Administration over the air war against the North. In private, though, the President was deeply troubled, especially since McNamara's testimony had not been cleared by the White House. The President still liked and respected McNamara enormously, but he was losing confidence in the judgment of his tormented aide, and was increasingly suspicious of his relationship with Bobby Kennedy. Rather than examining the reasons for McNamara's growing doubts about the war, he began to express doubts, to Fortas and me, about his loyalty and stability. Johnson also worried about the strain the job had placed on McNamara and his family. Bob's gracious and intense wife, Margaret, had developed an ailment that was often described by friends as "Bob's ulcer." One of their children, Craig, had broken with his father over the war. (This was also true of Dean Rusk, whose younger son Richard also split with his father over the war. But unlike McNamara, Rusk, "the Iron Man," did not allow his family circumstances to affect his work.[9])

This situation might have festered for a long time before any action was taken. McNamara was still widely respected, and he continued to run the Pentagon with enormous skill. From a political point of view, there was value in keeping him in office through the 1968 election—but this option was foreclosed by McNamara himself, who precipitated the last act of the drama by airing the full dimensions of his doubts, for the first time, in the Tuesday Lunch on October 31, and following up the next day with his memorandum.

The Tuesday Lunch, President Johnson's most important regularly scheduled weekly meeting, had become a legend and a bit of a nightmare in Washington by the latter part of 1967. Because Johnson restricted it to "principals only," after every lunch the senior staff officers of the participants—Rusk, McNamara, Rostow, Helms, Wheeler, and later me—tried to reconstruct exactly what had been decided. Although a White House notetaker was usually present, disagreements and misunderstandings over what had been decided were still frequent.

On October 31, though, there could be no misunderstanding McNamara's position. He had come to the private conclusion that "continuation of our present course of action in Southeast Asia would be dangerous, costly in lives, and unsatisfactory to the American people." The next day, November 1, he sent the President a blockbuster memorandum, nine pages, single-spaced, and obviously prepared well in advance of the Tuesday Lunch. It argued for a radical change in policy. Because, he said dryly, the views in the memorandum "may be incompatible with your own," McNamara hand-delivered it to the President, bypassing Rusk and Rostow. Johnson was stunned. He knew he could no longer contain or control the "McNamara problem"; either his Defense Secretary or his Vietnam policy would have to be changed. Ironically, he ended up changing both—but that was not his intention.

McNamara's memorandum began by stating that while we would see "continued but slow progress" in Vietnam in the next eighteen months, "continuing our present course will not bring us by the end of 1968 enough closer to success, in the eyes of the American public, to prevent the continued erosion of popular support for our involvement in Vietnam." The memorandum recommended "stabilizing" the war at its present level, sending Westmoreland no new troops, refusing permission to expand the war into Laos or Cambodia, accepting "slow but steady progress for whatever period is required to move the North Vietnamese to abandon their attempt to gain political control in South Vietnam by military means," halting the bombing of North Vietnam before the end of 1967, and making an all-out effort to negotiate with Hanoi.

On November 2, the same day as the meeting of the Wise Men, the President asked for my reaction to this memorandum. In order to obtain the most objective response and to minimize the risks of a leak, he removed all identification from the memorandum, hoping to obscure its source.

My reply was heavily influenced by the meeting of the Wise Men. I stated that the memorandum's suggestions would probably retard "the possibility of concluding the conflict." I opposed, with "a loud and resounding 'no' " the suggestion that we suspend the bombing "without any effort to extract a quid pro quo." I objected to the suggestion that we "stabilize" our forces in the South on the grounds that it would be interpreted as "a resigned and discouraged effort to find a way out of a conflict for which we had lost both our will and dedication."

It is ironic that while my rebuttal of McNamara probably contributed to President Johnson's decision to ask me to become Secretary of Defense, I ended up eventually advocating positions similar in many respects to those in the memorandum I attacked in November 1967.

Some days after I sent my reply to the President, I learned that he had separately asked Rusk, Bunker, Rostow, Westmoreland, and Fortas for their views on the McNamara memorandum—and all had disagreed with its recommendations. The only document reaching the President that argued for a change in policy came from Nick Katzenbach, who sent him a long and thoughtful memorandum in mid-November, arguing for a bombing halt and a "shift of more of the weight of the war" to the South Vietnamese government in order to reduce American casualties. Katzenbach made an analogy that I was to remember later as both striking and prophetic:

> Hanoi uses time the way the Russians used terrain before Napoleon's advance on Moscow, always retreating, losing every battle, but eventually creating conditions in which the enemy can no longer function. For Napoleon it was his long supply lines and the cold Russian winter; Hanoi hopes that for us it will be the mounting dissension, impatience, and frustration caused by a protracted war without fronts or other visible signs of success. . . . Time is the crucial element at this

> stage of our involvement in Vietnam. Can the tortoise of progress in Vietnam stay ahead of the hare of dissent at home?

McNamara's memorandum removed all doubt that he had to leave the Pentagon. It was to Lyndon Johnson's great credit that he did this in a skillful and compassionate manner. Knowing McNamara was in a fragile emotional state, fearing even for his survival, the President found a perfect solution: he offered McNamara the job he knew most interested him, the presidency of the World Bank. The outgoing president, George Woods, had asked McNamara informally in the spring of 1967 if he would be interested in the position. McNamara was noncommittal at the time, but he mentioned the matter to President Johnson because, as he wrote him later, he felt it "might come to your attention and I did not want you to think I was planning to leave your Administration before you wanted me to do so."[10] During the summer, Woods asked the President if McNamara was available; failing to get any reply, Woods reluctantly agreed to stay on for at least another year. Perhaps at a subconscious level, McNamara's November 1 memorandum was a way of relieving the almost unbearable pressure building up within him. In any case, within days after the memorandum reached the President's desk, the U.S. had asked the World Bank's 107 member nations to approve McNamara's nomination as president.

Remarkably, the President never informed McNamara of his intention to nominate him—he simply did it. Perhaps he was concerned at the effect the news would have on Bob; perhaps he did not want to leave the decision in McNamara's hands at a time when he was almost paralyzed with indecision. McNamara found out that he had been nominated only when Woods called to tell him that, while the nomination was creating some controversy, he expected it to be approved. The news leaked shortly thereafter in the London *Financial Times,* to be confirmed after two hectic and confused days by the White House. At the time, Robert S. McNamara was only fifty-one years old.

ROBERT S. McNAMARA: AN APPRAISAL

In my years in Washington, only a handful of people below the Presidential level have dominated the scene: George Marshall, Dean Acheson, and Henry Kissinger all come to mind. But no one ever held the capital in greater sway than Robert S. McNamara did from 1961 until the end of 1967. Even at the end, beleaguered and exhausted, he remained, after the President, the dominant figure in Washington. The veteran journalist

Hugh Sidey, writing in *Life* magazine, captured the reaction to his departure with only slight exaggeration: "For Washington last week, waking up to the fact that Robert McNamara was leaving the Cabinet was like finding the Washington Monument missing one morning." *Newsweek* called him "a multifaceted genius," and described the news of his departure as striking Washington "with the force of a string of Claymore mines exploding along Pennsylvania Avenue."

Bob McNamara had transformed the Defense Department during his tenure. More than any of the men who had preceded him, he moved the military establishment toward what we had intended it to be during the battle for military reform in the late forties. It is no exaggeration to say that the history of the Department of Defense will always be divided into the pre-McNamara and post-McNamara eras. Bringing modern management techniques to the Pentagon's sacred fiefdoms was revolutionary, and like all revolutionaries, Bob McNamara made many enemies—especially among the uniformed services, who saw their private domains threatened by his drive toward increased efficiency and centralized management. Almost to a man, they were delighted to see him go.

In reforming the Pentagon, his talents had served him well, but in the prosecution of the war, they had sometimes failed him. Vietnam was not a management problem, it was a war, and war is about life and death, filled with intangibles that defy analysis. He had never been in a war, and perhaps he did not fully appreciate at first its stupid waste and its irrational emotions, and the elusiveness of facts and truth when men are dying. Nor did he did truly understand the political roots of the conflict until it was too late. He had tried to master the war as he had everything else in his remarkable career, using pure intellect and his towering analytical skills—but Vietnam defied such analysis. In the end, this man, who was probably our greatest minister of defense, was not as well suited to manage a war—yet this is precisely what was required by the circumstances.

Under his controlled exterior, Bob McNamara suffered as much as any man I ever knew. I cannot think of what he went through without an intense sense of sadness—for his pain, for his sincerity and commitment, for the dreadful cost in lives and national treasure of the policies that he and his colleagues followed for too long. From late 1965 until the end of 1967, after opposing them at the outset, I had supported those policies as a private citizen and personal adviser to the President. I was about to discover how wrong I had been.

27

"One Client from Now On"

Nineteen sixty-eight was the pivotal year of the sixties: the moment when all of a nation's impulses toward violence, idealism, diversity, and disorder peaked to produce the greatest possible hope—and the worst imaginable despair.

—CHARLES KAISER, *1968 in America*

JANUARY 19, 1968

It was one of those rare years that shape our lives, a year historians will reexamine and reinterpret for generations to come. It was the most difficult year of my life, a year of partial success and ultimate frustration. My secretary for so many years, Mary Weiler, later said to me, "That was a year that lasted five years. I thought it was going to kill you." But of course she did not tell me that at the time.

Less than three weeks into the new year, President Johnson nominated me to be Secretary of Defense. Four days later, the North Koreans seized an American intelligence ship, the USS *Pueblo,* in international waters. One week after that, on the day I was confirmed by the Senate, the communists fought their way into the American Embassy compound in Saigon, the spectacular opening of the Tet Offensive. The rest of the year kept pace with that dizzying start.

In late November, my name was listed in *Newsweek* and a number of newspapers as one of several possible successors to McNamara. When the President needled me about the publicity, I assured him I was not a candidate for the position. He laughed, giving no indication that I was under serious consideration.

But Abe Fortas told me I was on Johnson's short list. "Lyndon has got me serving my country, and now it's your turn," he said to me, only half-joking. Ironically, by the end of 1968, I would be fighting hard to save his doomed nomination as Chief Justice of the United States.

While I remained ambivalent about serving under Lyndon Johnson, the position of Secretary of Defense had an undeniable attraction to me: national security and foreign policy had always interested me more than domestic issues, and Vietnam was unquestionably the most difficult and important issue that had confronted the nation since the Korean War. I liked the idea of the challenge, and there was a certain personal logic in heading the Defense Department, in whose creation I had participated.

Shortly before Christmas, the President asked me to undertake an unusual and sensitive assignment. In October, several newspapers and magazines published charges that Walt Rostow had been denied a security clearance during the Eisenhower Administration because of family associations with the Socialist party. After Senator Thurmond repeated these charges in several speeches, demanding a Congressional investigation, the President asked me to make a private investigation.

After studying Rostow's security files, I concluded that these accusations were ridiculous, and stemmed from the mood of the McCarthy era in which they had first been made. The charges came from four CIA and FBI officers who charged that Rostow and his brother Eugene had "definitely pro-Russian" views. None of the four were willing to sign a formal accusation or appear before a loyalty board. After looking at every charge ever made against Rostow—and there were many others, equally absurd—I found them all to be irrelevant or without merit. "Walt W. Rostow," I wrote the President, "is now, and always has been, a loyal, dedicated citizen of this country."

With that assignment completed, I worked with the President and his staff on the drafting of the 1968 State of the Union Message. On January 18, the day after the speech, he asked to see me. It was almost two months since McNamara's departure had been announced, and there had been no movement toward naming a successor.

We met shortly after 7 P.M. "In the past," he said, "you've said your interest was foreign policy and national security. Now I've got exactly the right place for you—Secretary of Defense. It will suit you and you cannot possibly have any objection to it."

I knew that this time I could not refuse his request, nor did I wish to do so. I thanked him, and we shook hands. He told me not to tell anyone except Marny until he had a chance to discuss it with Rusk, McNamara, and Congressional leaders over the next few days.

The next morning, the President called shortly before eleven o'clock to say that McNamara, who was at that moment in the Oval Office, was "onboard and delighted." He intended to make the announcement that very day, before there were any leaks. Could I come over immediately to prepare for it?

My return to the government after eighteen years should have been preceded by a moment of reflection on what lay ahead; but in the real world, there is rarely time for such introspection. Practical questions imposed themselves, demanding immediate attention. When and how should the public announcement be made? What about detaching myself from the law firm? Were there any conflicts of interest? Which Congressional leaders should be notified in advance? Friends? Future associates? How does one prepare for the confirmation hearings? Security checks?

Such questions of detail drove larger considerations from my mind. In fact, my first thought, as I again walked across Lafayette Square to the White House, was about my appearance: I kicked myself for having worn an old suit to work that day. I had known LBJ all these years—*how* could I have failed to realize that, once started down a path, he liked to move fast?

Such sartorial considerations disappeared when I greeted McNamara, who was waiting for me in the Cabinet Room with warm and generous congratulations. He urged me to ask Paul Nitze to stay on as Deputy Secretary in order to assure an easy transition. He cautioned me, however, that Nitze had hoped for the top job himself, and believed he had been passed over for top positions by several Presidents, including both Kennedy and Johnson.

I had known Paul Nitze since the Truman Administration, and respected his abilities in the defense field. If he was willing to swallow his disappointment, I saw no reason to reject McNamara's recommendation. From that moment on McNamara and I worked as a team until, having completed the 1969 defense budget, he left the Pentagon at the end of February.

President Johnson made the announcement at 3:30 that afternoon. Then he departed, leaving me to face the White House press corps. Asked if I was a hawk or a dove, I replied: "I am not conscious of falling under any of those ornithological divisions. I think you will have plenty of opportunity to reach some conclusions if the Senate confirms me and I am in office for a while."

Another question concerned my law practice: how would I handle my law clients and "any private interests"? Anticipating this, I deliberately went further than the question required: "One, I will sever all connections with my law firm so that there will be no remaining association of any kind. Two, I will dispose of any asset, any stock or any security that would in any way interfere with my complete objective judgment in the conduct of the new post.* *I will have one client from now on—if confirmed—and that client will be the United States.*"

This last comment I meant literally. All three Democratic Presidents since the end of World War II had asked me for advice from time to time, and I had given it as best as I could. I was viewed, correctly, as a personal adviser to Presidents: the "client" had been the President. But now that I was subject to confirmation by the Senate and about to assume formal responsibility for the largest department in the government, I felt a responsibility to a larger constituency—the nation.

I closed the press conference by denying any desire to seek elective office: "I am sixty-one years old, and I'm sure this will finish me off." Then I settled back to await the reaction to my appointment.

REACTIONS

While I had tried to resist categorization, almost every article at the time described me as a hawk. *The New York Times* struck a particularly sour note, editorializing that "President Johnson has replaced a brilliant doubter with a confident confidante. The choice of Mr. Clifford seems particularly uninspiring in the shadow of his predecessor."

The most perceptive comment probably came from *The Boston Globe*, which wrote:

> Speculation as to the Secretary-Designate's hawkishness or doveishness is as pointless as it is confused. His friends have known him as a behind-the-scenes hawk and bombing advocate up to now. His peace friends are familiar also with his skilled lawyer's way of saying nothing intelligible when there is nothing to be gained. Mr. Clifford's counsel to his close friend of two decades will be persuasive. What it will be will depend entirely on what he senses as he takes the nation's pulse.

Moscow took a more predictable tack: "Clifford," wrote *Izvestia*, "is an out-and-out warmonger, a trusted man of Wall Street, and a stubborn opponent of stopping the air raids on the Democratic Republic of Vietnam."

Given all this speculation, what did Lyndon Johnson think was my position on Vietnam when he selected me as his new Secretary of Defense?

*After conferring at length with the general counsel of the Defense Department, I sent a letter to the Senate Armed Services Committee on January 24, 1968, outlining my intention to withdraw from all business and legal relationships, sell all securities in companies doing business with the Defense Department, and resign from all boards on which I then served. I accepted a lump sum payment from my law firm, and severed all relationships with it. This satisfied the committee.

And, for that matter, what *was* my position on Vietnam on the day I was named?

The answers are actually quite simple. The President wanted a Secretary of Defense who supported his policy, someone who could end the struggle between the Secretary of Defense and the Joint Chiefs, and who could improve relations with Congress. On January 19, 1968, I fit that job description. The President remembered, of course, my initial opposition to the buildup in 1965. But after that decision was made, I had consistently supported his policy in Vietnam. If, at the time of my appointment, I had held the views I was to develop only a few weeks later, I would have had an obligation to inform President Johnson, who might then have chosen someone else for the position.

THE *PUEBLO*

On January 23, four days after my nomination, the President invited me for the first time to the Tuesday Lunch, the weekly "principals only" meeting with his senior national security officials. It was a memorable harbinger of things to come, and began what was to be the most intense ten weeks of my life. On that day, the President and his advisers faced four major problems, ranging from very serious to crisis proportions. Normally, any one of these issues would have demanded full attention from the National Security Council, but these were not normal times. "Clark, this is a typical day around here," McNamara joked as we began to discuss the agenda for the day:

- Our troops had made a serious, inadvertent intrusion into Cambodia during a fierce firefight along the Vietnamese-Cambodian border. This violation of Cambodian neutrality, at a time when it was still important to us, would require both a public apology to Prince Sihanouk from Secretary Rusk, and tense internal discussions with General Westmoreland in order to prevent a recurrence.

- A B-52 carrying nuclear weapons had crashed seven miles short of the runway at an American air base in Thule, Greenland. A special rescue group, including nuclear weapons experts, was rushing to the scene before the plane sank through the ice into the depths of the North Atlantic. The question of what to say publicly was especially delicate because of Denmark's sensitivity on anything related to nuclear weapons.

- The largest battle of the Vietnam War seemed about to begin at Khe Sanh, in the far northwestern corner of South Vietnam, where 6,000 U.S. Marines were surrounded and—for the first time in the war—

outnumbered by the enemy. By the time of my first Tuesday Lunch, President Johnson had become obsessed by Khe Sanh, even setting up a sand table map and photo murals of Khe Sanh in the basement of the White House so he could follow personally every detail of the siege.

• Finally, there had been a major disaster overnight in the North Pacific: a few hours earlier, an American intelligence ship, the USS *Pueblo,* had been boarded by North Koreans and forced to proceed to the port of Wonsan with its eighty-three man crew, one of whom had been killed in the attack. Through a failure in Pentagon planning, there were no American planes or other naval vessels near enough to the *Pueblo* on January 23 to rescue it before it reached port.

To President Johnson, the seizure of the *Pueblo* was almost too much to bear. At first he was convinced it was part of a worldwide challenge to him and to the nation, a coordinated communist plan to smash our will and stretch our resources to the breaking point. Wearily, he said he expected the next blow to fall in Berlin.

The fear that the *Pueblo* was part of a worldwide crisis proved to be unfounded; the *Pueblo* seizure was simply part of the continuing brutality of North Korea, one of the world's most isolated and dangerous regimes. The effort to get the crew back would continue almost to the last day of my tenure at the Defense Department. We rejected retaliation because it would not have advanced our overriding objective: freeing the officers and crew, without subjecting them to an even greater risk of being killed. Eventually negotiations with the North Koreans began at Panmunjom. These talks started in an atmosphere of bitter propaganda and harsh, coercive treatment of the crew of the *Pueblo,* some of whom signed letters of "confession" stating that their ship had violated North Korean waters on a spy mission. Aware that these confessions had been obtained under duress, I reacted with pride when a photograph of some of the crew that was sent around the world by the North Koreans showed half the men in the photograph with their middle fingers discreetly but unmistakably extended in a gesture whose meaning, familiar to all Americans, had escaped North Korean notice.

The *Pueblo* negotiations continued for the rest of the year, under the direction of Paul Nitze and Richard Steadman, the very able Deputy Assistant Secretary of Defense who had accompanied me on the Clifford-Taylor trip the previous year. Together with the State Department, we devised one of the strangest solutions a hostage crisis ever witnessed. North Korea had demanded an American admission of guilt; we finally told them that, in return for the release of the crew, the U.S. would sign a "confession" but would repudiate it as a complete fabrication the moment we signed it. The North Koreans accepted our offer, presumably because they could control their own media completely and wanted to be rid of the problem. Accordingly, in December 1968, our negotiators signed a document, simultaneously telling the North Koreans "there is not one word of truth in the above statement." The North Koreans released the entire crew of the *Pueblo* on December 23, 1968, eleven months after they had been taken. The ship was never returned.

KHE SANH—AND TET

Despite the seizing of the *Pueblo,* the President was focused on "his" Marines at Khe Sanh. Haunted by the memory of the French defeat at Dienbienphu in 1954, he wanted reassurance that they could hold Khe Sanh. Wheeler and McNamara told the President that the Marines were ready for anything the North Vietnamese could throw at them.

The President read aloud part of a telegram from General Westmoreland describing developments in other regions of Vietnam. Westmoreland said he expected some "terrorism" in the Saigon area soon: "The enemy," he said, "is presently developing a threatening posture in several areas in order to seek victories essential to achieving prestige and bargaining power. He may exercise initiatives prior to, during, or after Tet."[1]

This telegram was to become part of a dispute that has continued ever since as to whether or not the military in Vietnam were prepared for the nationwide communist offensive that would start within a few days, on Tet, the Vietnamese New Year. Later, Westmoreland would say that he had predicted the offensive, supporting his claim with several public and private warnings he had made, among them the telegram the President had read to us. President Johnson, in his own memoirs, says he saw the Tet Offensive coming as early as the previous fall, and warned many people about it, including the Australian government during a trip to Canberra on December 21.*

There is a kernel of truth in these statements, but they are quite misleading. At the very last minute, Westmoreland had begun to cancel leave plans for Tet and alerted his troops that something big might be underway—but by that time, the evidence was overwhelming. But even then he did not anticipate the size and scope of the offensive: when I examined this question after I became Secretary of Defense, I concluded that his earlier warnings of attacks "prior, during, or after" Tet were part of the normal flow of intelligence messages from Saigon. Both President Johnson and Westmoreland had seen reports warning of the possibility

*The trip was to attend the memorial services for Prime Minister Harold Holt, who had drowned while swimming.

of a large enemy offensive in early 1968, but neither man, nor anyone else in the American intelligence community, predicted or foresaw anything approaching the extraordinary size and scope, or having the impact, of the Tet Offensive. An increase in enemy activity around Tet, yes, but not a massive offensive that could change the face of the war. Claims that the Administration and General Westmoreland had predicted the offensive—and that the prediction was ignored by the press—are self-serving; it is self-evident that, had anything resembling what actually happened been anticipated, the behavior and statements of most senior officials in the American government in the months preceding January 30, 1968, would have been markedly different.

In fact, in the three months prior to the offensive, Bunker and Westmoreland loudly proclaimed that enemy strength was decreasing. In the fall of 1967, they sent Washington a series of lengthy and forceful telegrams designed to demonstrate "that we are making solid progress and are not in a stalemate." These telegrams contained not one word of warning about the possibility of large-scale attacks in the future; on the contrary, they made proud assertions that were among the most erroneous ever sent by field commanders:

> FRIENDLY FORCES HAVE SEIZED THE MILITARY INITIATIVE FROM THE ENEMY. . . . HE HAS BEEN PREVENTED FROM EMPLOYING HIS PRIMARY STRATEGY OF MOUNTING LARGE SCALE OFFENSIVES BECAUSE OF STEADILY IMPROVING FRIENDLY MILITARY STRENGTH.[2]

Almost twenty years later, the debate over the quality and accuracy of American intelligence in Vietnam resumed in a most unlikely place, a Manhattan courtroom, when General Westmoreland sued CBS News over a documentary television program charging that he had deliberately understated the size of the enemy force in Vietnam—and deceived President Johnson—in order to suggest progress in the war. Although I did not think the CBS program justified a charge of libel, and was gratified that Westmoreland dropped the case at the last moment, the CBS interpretation of events was at variance with my own impression as Chairman of the PFIAB. Contrary to one of the key assertions of the CBS program, the President and his top advisers were aware of the intelligence community dispute, and Westmoreland could not have concealed it from them even if he had wanted to. Rostow himself had alerted the President to the existence of a "considerable debate in the intelligence community" in a memorandum of November 1967, which was not mentioned on the CBS program. Westmoreland, Rostow, and the DCI, Richard Helms, sincerely believed that, in the words of one memorandum to the President, "there has been a very substantial decline in the past year in enemy main force battalions rated as 'combat effective.' "[3] Such was the mood dominating official Washington on the eve of the Tet Offensive; a sense that events were moving in the right direction, and that the communists were on the defensive.

By the beginning of 1968, Westmoreland and Wheeler had decided that the major battle of the war was indeed about to take place. But they were certain it would come at Khe Sanh. In late January we met for three consecutive days at the White House to review the battle. General Wheeler, drawing from Westmoreland's messages, told the President "the most vicious battle of the entire war is about to begin at Khe Sanh." On January 29, the President met with all five Joint Chiefs solely to ask if, in his own words, "everything has been done to assure that General Westmoreland can take care of the expected enemy offensive against Khe Sanh." The Chiefs said that the Marines would be able to handle any communist assault. Their prediction about Khe Sanh proved to be correct—but at no time in those four meetings did anyone suggest that the battle in the northwestern corner of Vietnam might be part of a master communist strategy designed to *divert* American attention and resources from an offensive elsewhere. Yet only one week later, the full fury of the Tet Offensive descended on most of South Vietnam; as it turned out, *Khe Sanh* was the diversion, drawing troops to the remote highlands before the communists attacked the cities and towns of South Vietnam.

I never doubted General Westmoreland's sincerity, but I could not agree with his conclusion, written after the war, that his only real failure at Tet was in not "preparing the American public for it," so that "the offensive seemed to many in direct contradiction to President Johnson's campaign to demonstrate progress in the war, [and] a refutation of my remarks at the Press Club two months earlier."[4] General Wheeler was more candid when he told a military historian two years later: "I would say that no one really expected the enemy to launch the attack during Tet. . . . While we knew something was going to happen, we didn't know exactly when, nor did we know how extensive the attack was going to be."[5]

After studying the offensive, the PFIAB told the President that it represented a serious failure of military intelligence. A textbook prepared and used at West Point in the study of Vietnam expressed my view succinctly: "The first thing to understand about Giap's Tet offensive is that it was an allied intelligence failure to rank with Pearl Harbor in 1941 or the Ardennes offensive in 1944."[6]

CONFIRMATION AND THE SAN ANTONIO FORMULA

As the world seemed to spiral out of control, I still had to deal with my confirmation hearing before the Senate Armed Services Committee. This was a routine affair but for one important exchange with Senator Thurmond, which led in turn to my first disagreement with my new colleagues in the State Department and the White House.

The trouble centered around our conditions for stopping the bombing of North Vietnam. The President's speech at San Antonio in September 1967 had originally been designed to reinforce the negotiating effort conducted through Kissinger, but even when that channel dried up after his unproductive October meetings in Paris, the American position remained as stated by President Johnson in San Antonio:

> The heart of the matter is this: The United States is willing to stop all aerial and naval bombardment of North Vietnam when this will lead promptly to productive discussions. We, of course, assume that while discussions proceed, North Vietnam would not take advantage of this bombing cessation or limitation.

By the time my nomination went up for confirmation, I thought these forty-six words had been as much discussed, analyzed, and interpreted as the works of Shakespeare or the Bible. Dean Rusk viewed the "San Antonio formula" as "deliberately vague."[7] But before my hearings, which began shortly after 10:30 A.M. on January 25, no formal discussions had been held within the executive branch on the precise meaning of the San Antonio formula.

Just before noon, Strom Thurmond, our old adversary from the 1948 campaign and now the second-ranking Republican on the committee, began his round of questioning. In public comments prior to the hearings, Thurmond had been the only member of the committee to voice open hostility toward me. The questioning included the following exchange:

> SENATOR THURMOND: When you spoke of negotiating, in which case you would be willing to have a cessation of bombing, I presume you would contemplate that they would stop their military activities, too, in return for a cessation of bombing.
>
> MR. CLIFFORD: No, that is not what I said. I do not expect them to stop their military activities. I would expect to follow the language of the President when he said that if they would agree to start negotiations promptly and not take advantage of the pause in the bombing.
>
> THURMOND: What do you mean by taking advantage if they continue their military activities?

> CLIFFORD: Their military activity will continue in South Vietnam, I assume, until there is a cease fire agreed upon. I assume that they will continue to transport the normal amount of goods, munitions, and men to South Vietnam. I assume that we will continue to maintain our forces and support our forces during that period. So what I am suggesting, in the language of the President, is that he would insist that they not take advantage of the suspension of the bombing.

Most of the reporters covering the hearings had simply assumed, from my reputation, that anything I said would be hawkish. The next day most newspapers singled out some rather routine comments I had made supporting our overall policy, and overlooked my explanation of the San Antonio formula. James Reston wrote that I "took the hard line on the bombing of North Vietnam." Similarly, A *New York Times* editorial called my testimony "bellicose," and predicted that "conformity now seems likely to prevail." Only a few newspapers saw the significance of my remarks. One was *The Washington Post,* which editorialized, "Not nearly enough attention was paid to what Defense Secretary–designate Clark Clifford had to say about the Administration's terms for the Vietnam pause, nor is it yet clear whether Mr. Clifford was speaking authoritatively or expressing a personal view."

The *Post* had hit paydirt, although fortunately they did not know it; inside the Administration my comments had set off alarm bells, and more perceptive press coverage would have only made the situation more difficult. The morning after my testimony, Rusk and Rostow told the President that my testimony had weakened our negotiating position before Hanoi had even agreed to talk with us. They recommended a White House clarification retreating from my testimony, but he rejected the suggestion, and instead instructed Press Secretary George Christian to tell the press that my testimony correctly stated Administration policy. A few days later, during a meeting with White House correspondents, Johnson closed the issue: "Clark Clifford said what I stated in San Antonio and said it better."

As a lawyer, I had simply offered what I considered the most reasonable interpretation of the San Antonio formula. The words "not take advantage of" could mean only what I had outlined. Yet this had led to an immediate conflict with both Rusk and Rostow. Many more would follow.

JANUARY 30, 1968: WASHINGTON

Even in an eventful year, some days stand out. January 30, 1968, began for me simply as the day on which I expected to be confirmed by the Senate, but it ended as something quite different.

At midday, as the Senate confirmed me as Secretary of Defense, by a unanimous vote, I was attending the Tuesday Lunch.[8] The first item on the agenda was the President's obsession—Khe Sanh. General Wheeler reported that the area was quiet and the weather good. Wheeler had just talked to Westmoreland, who was still braced for an all-out attack there, although Wheeler noted that there had been a series of hit-and-run attacks by the communists in various other parts of Vietnam.

Wheeler surprised me by requesting authority for Westmoreland "to organize a feint of a full-scale landing north of the Demilitarized Zone." Westmoreland's plan was to move amphibious ships close to the North Vietnamese coast, then tell the South Vietnamese that we were planning to invade North Vietnam. Wheeler said he was confident that communist spies inside South Vietnam's high command would then "make sure the North Vietnamese learn of it." The objective, Wheeler explained, was to lessen the pressure on Khe Sanh by tricking Hanoi into moving troops away from Khe Sanh to defend their coastline against an invasion.

To my surprise, McNamara supported Wheeler's astonishing request. Responsibility for the Pentagon still rested entirely with McNamara, but I did not like getting caught off-guard on an issue that would soon fall within my purview. The idea made no sense to me—it could easily leak, backfire, or lead to actual ground combat in North Vietnam, and I said so.

The President, however, did not wish to reject a military request supported by McNamara, outright. "Go ahead and plan it," he said. "I want to give weight to the field commander's recommendation in this case."

As I was reflecting on how I might stop the planning for this strange idea, I noticed an aide enter and hand Walt Rostow a note. He slipped out of the room. A few minutes later Rostow returned and interrupted our discussion with a dramatic announcement: "We have just received a flash message from the National Military Command Center. We are being heavily mortared in Saigon. The Presidential Palace, our military installations, the American Embassy, and other parts of the city have been hit."

The brief silence was broken by the President: "This could be very bad."

"I hope," Rusk added, "that it is not Ambassador Bunker's residence."

No one in the room had any sense of the enormity of the event that was unfolding in the nighttime hours on the other side of the world. Wheeler thought it might be a series of small attacks. "This same type of thing has happened before," he said. "In a city like Saigon, people can infiltrate easily. They can fire and run. It is impossible to stop this in its entirety. This is about as tough to prevent as a mugging in Washington."

"This sounds like a public-relations problem, not a military one," McNamara said. "The answer to these mortar attacks is success at Khe Sanh. We are inflicting very heavy casualties on the enemy and we are not unprepared for the encounter. We must get our story across."

THE TET OFFENSIVE

By ordinary standards, the attempt to take over the Embassy was a complete failure: all nineteen of the communist sappers were killed after a dramatic all-night fight in which five Americans were also killed. But soon after we returned to our offices, we discovered that the dramatic assault on the Embassy compound was only a minor part of a nationwide offensive.

As a military campaign the outcome of the Tet Offensive may remain in dispute, but there can be no question that it was a turning point in the war. Its size and scope made mockery of what the American military had told the public about the war, and devastated Administration credibility. Five of South Vietnam's six major cities, 36 of its 44 provincial capitals, and 66 of the 242 district towns were attacked. American losses were heavier than ever before, 3,895 killed in eight weeks. South Vietnamese forces sustained 4,954 recorded deaths—proportionately the smallest loss of the major combatants. At least 14,000 noncombatant men, women, and children were also killed in the fighting. Almost one million new refugees, a third of them in and around Saigon, put the South Vietnamese government under a nearly intolerable strain.

The communists paid a fearful price for the offensive, losing an estimated 58,000 men, but their ruthlessness was evident in the type of losses they sustained: they kept most of their main force and regular units on the sidelines, sacrificing mostly local militia, irregular units, and hapless farmers forced into suicidal missions. Had they committed more of their regulars, they might well have achieved the one thing that eluded them at Tet—a clear-cut military victory in some area of the country. In fact, the communists failed to hold any of the major cities, except Hue, for more than a few days.

The American military and its defenders would later call the communist offensive a military defeat for the enemy that became, in General Wheeler's words, "a propaganda victory for the North Vietnamese here in the United States, [which] I attribute primarily to the press coverage at that time and to the dissident groups here in the United States."[9] Westmoreland would compare the Tet Offensive to Hitler's last-ditch gamble at the Battle of the Bulge in 1944.

In order to prove that Tet had been a communist setback it was also argued that the local Vietcong forces (that is, indigenous Southerners) had been so decimated that the enemy had been forced to send massive numbers of North Vietnamese regulars into the South to save the insurgency. I never understood why anyone should have regarded this as an indication of success. To me, it was bad news: it meant that from now on the U.S. and the South Vietnamese would be facing a better-trained, better-equipped enemy, and that casualties on both sides would increase.

In my view, the military reassessment of the Tet Offensive since it ended was incomplete and self-serving. At the time of the initial attacks, the reaction of our military leadership approached panic, and their intelligence failure was a critical factor in both the military setbacks suffered in the early phase of the offensive and the backlash in American public opinion. The military and its defenders later tried to ignore or minimize the heavy losses suffered by American troops, and the enormous damage the offensive had caused to the pacification campaign. Pacification—the program to create a strong government presence in the hamlets and villages of South Vietnam—was generally regarded as the most important long-term aspect of the war. Those in charge of the pacification program had predicted that 1968 would be a year of decisive success. Tet shattered more than this empty rhetoric; with the towns and cities of Vietnam under attack, most of the villages and hamlets were undefended, and the Vietcong forces were able to deal the pacification program a massive setback. When Westmoreland wrote his memoirs eight years after the offensive, he did not mention the damage to pacification, but in his official report on the war, written in June 1968 jointly with the Pacific commander, Admiral Ulysses S. Grant Sharp, he acknowledged "a substantial setback" to the pacification program.[10]

Supporters of the war would later single out inaccurate reporting by the press during the Tet Offensive as a major reason for the turnaround in American public opinion just when, they said, we were in a position to win in the field.[11] This view is misinformed: the press made errors in reporting, as it does in every war, but the bulk of the reporting from the war zone reflected the official position. Contrary to right-wing revisionism, reporters and the antiwar movement did not defeat America in Vietnam. Our policy failed because it was based on false premises and false promises. Had the results in Vietnam approached, even remotely, what Washington and Saigon had publicly predicted for many years, the American people would have continued to support their government.

Thus the most serious American casualty at Tet was the loss of the public's confidence in its leaders. Tet hurt the Administration where it needed support most, with Congress and the American public—not because of the reporting, but because of the event itself, and what it said about the credibility of America's leaders. Public confidence in General Westmoreland, high until Tet, was shattered, never to be rebuilt; for the rest of the American government, including President Johnson, it was severely damaged. In an unwise and costly initial comment, President Johnson heightened his own problem on February 2, when he pronounced the two-day old offensive "a complete failure." George Aiken of Vermont, the dean of the Senate Republicans, responded acidly: "If this is failure, I hope the Vietcong never have a major success."

Vietnam had always been a political war, and Hanoi had always fought with one eye fixed on domestic dissent, whether in France in 1954 or the U.S. in 1968. If, in a democracy, the public no longer has confidence in its leaders, they will be forced to change their policy or risk political defeat. Hanoi had planned the Tet Offensive to coincide with the beginning of the 1968 Presidential campaign, in order to affect the American electoral process.

Many of the Administration's severest critics wanted to see escalation, not de-escalation, of the war—but it mattered relatively little whether the Administration's opponents were hawks or doves; what was clear was that Americans had wearied of a war that seemed to have no end. The difference between hawks and doves mattered less politically than appeared on the surface; despite their mutual antipathy, both groups wanted to see an early end to the American involvement in the war—and both put pressure on the Administration for a dramatic change in the situation.

On my trip to the Pacific the previous summer, I had seen that Vietnam's neighbors were not anxious to contribute more forces to the war effort. Until the Tet Offensive, though, I still accepted the military's views that the war was being won in the field. I had never believed that our nation would be willing to fight a limited war for an unlimited time, in pursuit of uncertain and ill-defined objectives in a region of debatable national security importance. Now my faith in our ability to achieve our objectives within an acceptable period of time was shaken and began to erode.

FEBRUARY 1968

Even though I had been confirmed by the Senate on January 30, the President and I asked McNamara to stay at the Pentagon until March 1, when the budget process—which McNamara understood better than I ever could have—would be under control. In the month between confirmation and taking over the Pentagon, I was not burdened by any of the formal responsibilities of the Secretary of Defense, and thus, half–private citizen and half–Cabinet member, I was free to concentrate almost exclusively on Vietnam.

It is hard to imagine or re-create the atmosphere in Washington in the sixty days after Tet. The pressure grew so intense that at times I felt the government itself might come apart at its seams. Leadership was fraying at its very center—something very rare in a nation with so stable a governmental structure. In later years, almost every one of the men who lived through the crisis claimed that he had reacted calmly to events. In fact, everyone, both military and civilian, was profoundly affected by the Tet Offensive. This was true equally for those whose positions on Vietnam changed, and those who later viewed Tet as a great victory. There was, for a brief time, something approaching paralysis, and a sense of events spiraling out of the control of the nation's leaders.

My perceptions of the war were changing. Fundamental assumptions on which I had based my views crumbled—not with a single dramatic revelation, but slowly and unevenly. The policy implications of this change were complicated, and as my viewpoint evolved, I would sometimes support positions that seemed internally contradictory, in the intense and continuing discussions at the White House.

February 7. North Vietnamese forces overran the Lang Vei Special Forces Camp near Khe Sanh, using tanks for the first time in the war. Still convinced that the nationwide offensive was the diversion and Khe Sanh the main event, Westmoreland responded by holding a large number of his forces, including the 101st Airborne Division and the 1st Air Cavalry Division, in reserve in the northern part of the country to protect Khe Sanh.

February 8. For the first time since the offensive had begun, Wheeler told the President that Westmoreland would "welcome reinforcements at any time they can be made available."

I immediately expressed my concern: "There is a very strange contradiction in what we are saying and doing. We have told the American people that, first, the communist offensive was not a victory for Hanoi; second, there was no uprising of the Vietnamese people in support of the enemy; and third, it cost the enemy between 20,000 and 25,000 of their combat troops. But our reaction to all this is to say that the situation is more dangerous today than it was before all of this occurred. I think we should give some very serious thought to how we explain saying, on one hand, the enemy did not have a victory and, on the other, we are in need of many more troops, and possibly even an emergency call-up."

After the meeting, Wheeler sent Westmoreland a message, inviting him to ask for more troops: "My sensing is that the critical phase of the war is upon us, and I do not believe that you should refrain from asking for what you believe is required under the circumstances."[12] In order to prevent leaks, though, Wheeler told Westmoreland that any further messages concerning additional troops should be sent through the "back channel"—reserved for private communications between the Chairman of the Joint Chiefs and senior field commanders.

February 10. President Johnson removed some of the restrictions surrounding the bombing of the North, a move I favored, and American planes attacked targets in Haiphong for the first time since the offensive began. An additional 10,500 previously authorized airborne troops and marines were rushed to Vietnam. Meanwhile, American marines, in brutal house-to-house fighting in the central coastal city of Hue, began the effort to recapture the most historic site in Vietnam, the ancient imperial citadel.

Westmoreland still believed the Tet Offensive was probably an effort to take the pressure off Khe Sanh. "While it is always possible that the enemy buildup in the Khe Sanh–DMZ area is a diversion," he told Washington, "I consider this possibility remote."[13] This Khe Sanh obsession, which the President shared, had begun to trouble me: "All we have heard is about preparations for the North Vietnamese attack on Khe Sanh," I said. "I have a feeling that they are going to do something different. Our people were surprised by the twenty-four attacks on the cities last week. God knows the South Vietnamese were surprised. They had half their men on holiday. There may be a feint at Khe Sanh and a surprise coming up. . . . Giap may be trying to keep Westy's twenty thousand troops tied down up north."

McNamara told President Johnson that he was "trying to devise a plan that would get the men Westmoreland needs without the disastrous consequences of the action recommended by the JCS." I observed that this was a bad time to ask for any new program or buildup. The President made no comment.

February 11. The situation was so disturbing that President Johnson called an unusual Sunday meeting in the family quarters of the White House. Westmoreland had reported that the South Vietnamese Army (ARVN) was on the point of collapse. The President clearly did not wish to receive a formal request from the military for reinforcements, for fear that, if it leaked, he would be under great pressure to respond immediately. A delicate minuet took place to create the fiction that no request was being made. In response to a series of carefully phrased questions from the President, Wheeler and McNamara said neither Westmoreland nor the Joint Chiefs was, in fact, requesting more troops. Tiring of the charade, though, Maxwell Taylor interrupted the exchange: "I am quite out of tune with the tone of this meeting. I read Westy's message quite differently from you gentlemen." Taylor said it was clear to him that although Westmoreland had not yet asked for a specific number of troops, he was asking for reinforcements. Rusk observed dryly that if this was Westmoreland's way of requesting more troops, "he has an awfully poor colonel doing the drafting for him."

February 12. Alerted by Wheeler through the back channel that his earlier message had been unclear, Westmoreland removed any ambiguity in his position: "I am expressing a firm request for additional troops, not because I fear defeat if I am not reinforced, but because I do not feel that I can fully grasp the initiative from the recently reinforced enemy without them. On the other hand, a setback is fully possible if I am not reinforced." In a second private message to Wheeler, Westmoreland went further, saying that he "desperately needed" reinforcements "to contain [the enemy] and . . . seize the initiative." In the same message, however, he continued to focus on the besieged Marines: "I still see the enemy position in Khe Sanh," he said, "as the greatest threat."[14]

In a two-hour meeting over lunch, the President was frustrated and still fixed on Khe Sanh. Near the end of the meeting, he asked us if we all felt that Westmoreland should get more troops. McNamara, Rusk, Helms, Wheeler, Taylor, and Rostow each said yes. I remained silent. The President asked, "Is there any objection?" I continued to remain silent. McNamara still spoke for Defense, and I felt that my views should be given to the President in private until I was sworn in.

February 13. The Undersecretary of the Air Force, Townsend Hoopes, sent me—with, as he put it, "more candor than discretion"—a long personal letter, arguing that "the idea of a US military victory in Vietnam is a dangerous illusion," that de-escalation was a prerequisite for a settlement, and that cessation of the bombing was essential to start that process. Hoopes said Air Force reports showed that since the beginning of air strikes in 1965, the flow of men and matériel from the North to the South had "definitely increased." The bombing, he concluded, had caused "heavy damage" to North Vietnam's economy and society, but Hanoi's allies had more than made up for the damage with foreign aid. Hanoi's capacity to wage war at whatever level they wished had not been seriously impaired. Hoopes was critical of Westmoreland's attrition strategy, and argued he should be instructed to use American ground troops in a manner that would reduce American casualties. Why, he asked, did we choose to fight "in the worst possible terrain for American forces, at the time of the enemy's choosing"? It was a good question.

That same day, the President said he wanted some questions answered before making any decision on additional deployments. But he made clear he was inclined to send Westmoreland more troops and issue a limited call-up of the Reserves. Before he made any final decision, he asked Wheeler to go to Vietnam to confer with Westmoreland.

February 18. The Pentagon reported the highest one-week American casualty toll of the war, 543 killed, 2,547 wounded. We noted a new and disturbing trend: for the first time in the war, American casualties were significantly higher, proportionally, than those of the ARVN. The same day, as I feared, communist forces launched a new wave of attacks against forty-five cities and major installations across Vietnam, and attacked Saigon with 122-mm rockets.

February 21. American airplanes struck the main radio station near the center of Hanoi, another first.

February 23. The Selective Service announced it would draft an additional 48,000 men, the second-largest call-up of the Vietnam War, and Khe Sanh came under heavy artillery, rocket and mortar fire. The same day, Hanoi told its embattled troops in Hue to make a fighting withdrawal from the citadel.

February 25. Westmoreland told the Associated Press that additional troops would be needed in the war zone. That afternoon, a rare and welcome success: the Marines cleared the last enemy forces from the remnants of the citadel in Hue.

EARLE WHEELER AND THE REQUEST FOR 205,179 TROOPS

At the end of February General Wheeler returned from his three-day visit to Vietnam and submitted a report that was to frame the most dramatic policy debate of March. Wheeler's report contained an assessment of the situation so bleak, and a request for additional troops so large, that it had a profound effect on the course of the war and American politics.

Earle "Bus" Wheeler played a more important role in events and decisions than most outside observers and historians realized. Wheeler had a modest and low-key style: he lacked Westmoreland's theatrical appearance and carefully avoided the blustery personal style many military men adopt when dealing with civilians. He had spent most of his career in staff jobs and had held only one command in his career, a brief one as a battalion commander in World War II, but he was a talented administrator and skilled in Pentagon politics. Until the Tet Offensive, he had been an excellent intermediary between the field commander and the civilians in Washington, averting confrontations among the Chiefs or between the military and the President. For these abilities he was justly valued by most of the civilians with whom he worked. His personal standing with President Johnson and Bob McNamara was especially high, and at their request Congress had voted to extend his service as Chairman of the Joint Chiefs—although a heart attack in 1967, which was initially kept secret, had slowed him down somewhat. He would serve longer than any other Chairman in history, even staying for an additional year after the end of the Johnson Administration at the personal request of Richard Nixon.

Wheeler's trip report reached Washington by telegram the day before he returned. It had an enormous impact on the limited number of people who saw it. He presented an even grimmer assessment of the Tet Offensive than we had heard from Westmoreland and Bunker. It was clear that, although he avoided criticizing Westmoreland directly, he had lost some degree of confidence in his theater commander and no longer fully accepted Westmoreland's judgment of the war. Westmoreland was later to express dismay with Wheeler:

> Making no mention that I was considering more troops in hope of exploiting the enemy's defeat, nor making any allusion to the need to rebuild the strategic reserve, General Wheeler, probably as a tactic, emphasized uncertainty. Imbued with the aura of crisis in Washington, he at least partially discounted the sanguine briefings I and my staff had given him.[15]

Westmoreland's charge that Wheeler's assessment was based on such tactical or political considerations was unfair: he had given us his best judgment of the situation, and if it was grim, it was not defeatist. Wheeler still wanted to win, as the troop request in his report made clear, but his report damaged Westmoreland because in a disagreement between the two men, President Johnson and his advisers would unquestionably give far greater weight to the views of Wheeler.

Wheeler intentionally did not share his report with Westmoreland at the time. When Westmoreland saw it later, he acknowledged that many of the President's advisers were affected by "the incongruity between my public statements on the enemy's military defeat and General Wheeler's portrait of continuing crisis."[16] In somber language, Wheeler wrote:

> This offensive has by no means run its course. All commanders on the scene agree that [the enemy's] initial attack nearly succeeded in a dozen places and the margin of victory—in some places survival—was very small indeed. . . . There is some question as to whether the South Vietnamese Armed Forces have the stamina to withstand the pressure of a prolonged enemy offensive. . . . In many areas the pacification program has been brought to a halt. . . . The outcome is not at all clear. I visualize much heavy fighting ahead. Casualties will probably remain high. The government will have enormous problems with refugees, civilian casualties, morale, and recovery. . . . General Westmoreland's margin will be paper-thin. . . . For these reasons he is asking for additional forces as soon as possible during this calendar year.

Wheeler requested 205,179 additional troops in three phases. The size of his request astonished Washington, and triggered the first fundamental debate over the course of the war since the decisions of 1965—and a continuing dispute ever since about the origins and exact nature of the request.

Years later, Westmoreland was still deeply scarred by the assumption that the request came directly from him and reflected panic on his part. Looking back on these events, he blamed Wheeler for presenting his request for reinforcements in a tone so pessimistic as to

> exploit [Washington's] sense of crisis. [Wheeler] saw no possibility at the moment of selling reinforcements in terms of future operations. . . . Having read their newspapers, who among them would even believe there had been success? *Better to exploit their belief in crisis to get the troops, then argue new strategy later.*[17] (Emphasis added.)

Westmoreland's charge was a serious one: if true, the Chairman of the Joint Chiefs was guilty of deliberately misleading the President in order to get additional troops authorized for Vietnam. Wheeler, who died in 1975, apparently was never aware of Westmoreland's statement; he was an honorable man, though, and I do not believe the accusation.

General Westmoreland and others defended themselves by seeking to portray the request as a "contingency plan." Westmoreland put forward this surprising view in a paper he prepared in 1970, when he was Army Chief of Staff:

> I never considered the plan developed by General Wheeler and me to be a demand or a request for the deployment of additional troops. The plan submitted to Washington in the wake of the Tet offensive involving additional forces for the year 1968 was not, as had been

> alleged, an "emergency request for battlefield reinforcements." Instead, it was a prudent planning exercise designed to generate the military capability to support future tactical and strategic options.[18]

In his memoirs, written six years later, Westmoreland added that he had

> made no request for immediate deployment other than a Marine regiment and a brigade of the 82nd Airborne Division [because] I well knew that additional troops were unavailable without a call-up of Reserves. . . . [I] submitted no request per se for deploying 206,000 troops, [and was] not even aware that the total of the three increments General Wheeler and I had discussed came to 206,000.[19]

Wheeler's memory of the troop request was different. He agreed with Westmoreland that the first increment—totaling over 107,000 troops—constituted the only "firm request" in Wheeler's report. He claimed that half the additional forces requested were for the "strategic," not the "theater" reserve—an important distinction if true, since theater reserves were certain to end up in Vietnam, while strategic forces would be held for deployment anywhere in the world, with particular attention to Europe.[20]

In *his* version of the origins of the request, Maxwell Taylor said Westmoreland had asked for only 25,000 men: "Some of the individuals involved in the Clifford study group," which examined the troop request, "were not initiated in the jargon of military planners" and thus confused a "contingency plan" with a request.[21]

Taylor's statements were simply wrong. Almost every one of the officials who had access to Wheeler's report had worked with the military for years—they understood military language. Furthermore, the military, including Taylor, were present during the discussions and could have clarified, if necessary, any misunderstanding. The request was *never* presented as a "contingency," nor as troops for the "strategic reserve" (although a buildup of the strategic reserve was strongly desired by the Joint Chiefs).

Wheeler's memorandum was declassified in the mideighties, well after the memoirs of most of the participants in these events had appeared. It should have settled the dispute. Theories and interpretations are no longer needed: the memorandum speaks for itself, and can be read only as I understood it at the time: a joint request by Westmoreland and the Chiefs for 205,179 additional troops, to be deployed to Vietnam or held in a *theater reserve* earmarked for Vietnam by the end of 1968. This was what Wheeler wrote on troop requirements:

General Westmoreland wants, as a matter of urgency, a mechanized brigade consisting of one tank battalion and one mechanized battalion and one infantry battalion from the 5th Mechanized Division. He also wants an armored cavalry regiment and the remainder of the 5th Marine Division/Wing, and the acceleration of the deployment of certain supporting units now programmed for deployment under Program 5. These *immediately required* forces he hopes to receive before the first of May. . . .

As a matter of prudence, particularly in light of the protracted [North Vietnamese Army] buildup, *General Westmoreland states a requirement* during the calendar year for an additional infantry division to anticipate possible deterioration of some ARVN units, and to provide a reasonably available two-division theatre reserve at all times of the year.

It is my judgment that General Westmoreland *requires a theatre reserve of about two divisions. . . . If Hanoi deploys additional elements of the home army, this reserve might also be committed and additional force requirements would be generated.* The rough estimate of added strength required for the three force increments is:

	ARMY	NAVY	USMC	USAF	TOTAL
a. Immediate Increment, Priority One	54,000	8,060	37,132	8,791	107,983
b. Immediate Increment, Priority Two	31,600	4,446	—	5,750	41,796
c. Follow-on Increment	46,700	138	2,004	6,558	55,400
TOTAL	132,300	12,644	39,136	21,099	205,179

(Emphasis added.)

SPEECH-DRAFTING BECOMES POLICYMAKING

Sometimes the resolution of a controversial issue is deferred until a major speech is necessary, and the process of drafting the speech then becomes the process by which policy is decided. Such was the case with the Truman Doctrine speech in 1947; it would happen again now.

In early February, we began to discuss the idea of a major, nationally televised Presidential address on Vietnam. The original idea was to report to a nervous nation on the Tet Offensive and the *Pueblo* affair in order to put these events into perspective, defend the conduct of the war, and lay out a firm course for the rest of 1968. As the offensive grew in size, this speech proposal was set aside to await General Wheeler's return from Saigon.

On February 27, I joined McNamara, Katzenbach, Bill Bundy, Rostow, White House Special Counsel Harry McPherson, and the principal White House aide for domestic affairs, Joseph Califano* in Dean Rusk's dining room for our first discussion about a speech. This meeting began a process that led to one of the most dramatic speeches of our time, that of President Johnson on March 31, 1968, announcing that he would limit the bombing of North Vietnam and would not run again. But it did not start out as that kind of speech at all. It was intended originally as a tough speech supporting an aggressive response to the Tet Offensive.

The meeting in Rusk's office turned into a fierce discussion about what McNamara called "Westmoreland's request" for 205,000 troops. He said the troops would increase the budget by at least $10 billion in 1969, and more after that. These numbers, as part of a total federal budget then around $100 billion a year—roughly a tenth the size of more recent budgets—were staggering. They would lead to a big tax increase, more inflation, or both. "This is unbelievable and futile," Harry McPherson said. I noted with admiration McPherson's boldness in speaking in this manner in front of Rusk and Rostow.

As we talked, Nick Katzenbach left the room to take a telephone call over a secure line from Hawaii from Philip Habib, the Deputy Assistant Secretary of State for East Asian Affairs. A first-generation Lebanese Christian, Habib had made the enormous leap from the streets of Brooklyn to the very top of the American diplomatic service, and had served as the political counsellor in Saigon.** He was outspoken and unafraid to talk back to his superiors, and possessed a fine sense of timing and tactics. He was also a knowledgeable observer of the political scene in Saigon, and Rusk had sent him back to his old post for a firsthand assessment.

The secure telephone system was essential for sensitive conversations, but because it made voices sound vaguely like Donald Duck speaking under water, it was useful to take careful notes in order to focus on the substance of the conversation. Katzenbach returned to the meeting with his notes: Habib was "less optimistic" about the political situation in Saigon than before he had gone back. He was worried about the stability of the regime. Habib also told Katzenbach that there was "a serious disagreement among the Americans who know about the 205,000-troop request."

*Later Secretary of Health, Education, and Welfare in the Carter Administration.

**Habib was then in the middle of one of the most distinguished careers in the history of the Foreign Service. He served every President from Johnson to Reagan in posts that included Ambassador to Korea, Assistant Secretary of State for East Asian and Pacific Affairs, Undersecretary of State for Political Affairs, and Special Presidential Representative in the Mideast.

Rusk and Rostow argued that the enemy had taken a beating at Tet. I offered a different view: "Despite these optimistic reports, the American people and world opinion believe we have suffered a major setback. How do we gain support for major programs if we have told people that things are going well? How do we avoid creating the feeling that we are pounding troops down a rathole? What is our purpose? What is achievable?" I ended by asking for a review of "our entire posture" in Vietnam.[22]

As Rusk responded with a discussion of the need to intensify the bombing of North Vietnam, a remarkable event took place. Overcome with conflicting emotions, Bob McNamara's controlled exterior cracked. "The goddamned Air Force, they're dropping more on North Vietnam than we dropped on Germany in the last year of World War II, and it's not doing anything!" he said. His voice faltered, and for a moment he had difficulty speaking between suppressed sobs. He looked at me: "We simply have to end this thing. I just hope you can get hold of it. It is out of control." We were all stunned, but, out of a shared pain and sense of embarrassment, we went on with the discussion as though nothing out of the ordinary had occurred. Everyone in the room understood what had happened: this proud, intelligent, and dedicated man was reaching the end of his strength on his last full day in office. He was leaving the Pentagon just in time.

McPherson had advocated a major speech on Vietnam even before Tet, and he was assigned responsibility for drafting it. At the end of his notes of the February 27 meeting, he penned a personal comment to himself that accurately captured the mood at that time. "We are at a point of crisis," he wrote. "McNamara expressed grave doubts over military, economic, political, diplomatic and moral consequences of a larger force buildup in [South Vietnam]. Question is whether these profound doubts will be presented to President."

A native Texan who had worked for Johnson in the Senate and then served as an Assistant Secretary of State during the Kennedy Administration, Harry McPherson had been summoned to the White House in 1965, and by 1968 had become the President's chief speech writer. As the crisis deepened, I would increasingly come to regard this able, witty, and urbane man as my closest ally in the White House—"my silent partner," as I once put it.

February 28. President Johnson returned from the LBJ Ranch shortly after midnight. Four hours later, in a heavy rainstorm, General Wheeler slipped back into Washington from his trip to Vietnam, and went directly to the White House to join us for a gloomy early-morning breakfast. His weary tone and body language left the clear impression that the situation was worse than Bunker and Westmoreland had reported. While the Army of the Republic of Vietnam had survived better than some early reports had indicated, Wheeler said, the power and scope of the offensive had been greater than was realized in Washington. "Pacification is at a halt," he said. "The Vietcong can roam at will in the countryside. General Westmoreland has no theater reserve and needs one badly."

I had talked to the President privately before the meeting, urging him not to reach an immediate decision about additional troops under such pressure. I recommended a full-scale review of the policy before making any further decisions. Rostow separately made a similar suggestion, adding that the President might want to consider asking me to oversee such a review.

As the meeting came to an end, the President announced, as I had hoped, that he would not make any decision at this time. He said that he wanted "a new pair of eyes and a fresh outlook" to review the troop request, and asked me to chair an interagency review of the request for additional troops.[23] As we broke up he said to me: "Give me the lesser of evils. Give me your recommendations."

A MOVING FAREWELL TO McNAMARA

At the conclusion of the breakfast with Wheeler, we walked to the East Room of the White House for an immensely emotional and moving ceremony in which the President presented the nation's highest civilian award, the Medal of Freedom, to Robert McNamara. With the leaders of both parties, members of the Supreme Court, and friends, colleagues, and the press looking on, President Johnson praised McNamara as "the very best that we have."

McNamara took the podium to a sustained ovation. For seven years he had dominated Washington as few people ever do. To antiwar activists he had become a symbol of the war, to hard-liners, a symbol of ineffective half measures—but he had never regarded himself as a hawk, even when he advocated the troop buildup. In his own mind, he had simply addressed problems as they arose, applying his formidable intellect to the search for the best solution to each. His failure to achieve our objectives, either through military means or negotiations, had almost torn him apart.

The strain was evident as he accepted the medal from the President. He began to speak, but no words came out of his mouth. We stood silently watching his pain. Finally, in a choked voice similar to the one I had heard the previous day in Rusk's dining room, he said, "Mr. President, I cannot find words to express what lies in my heart today." He stopped completely, and struggled to gain control of himself. "I think that I had better respond on another occasion," he said. His mouth moved, but no further words came out of it. Gently, President Johnson came over to him, put his arm around him, and led him out of the room. For me, it was an eerie echo of what Jim Forrestal had gone through nineteen years earlier.

February 29. The last day of February was marked by Bob McNamara's formal departure ceremony, held at the River Entrance of the Pentagon in a driving wind and rainstorm. When the President and his entourage arrived at the Pentagon, they got stuck in an elevator for twelve minutes while McNamara and I waited for them. "At least this one didn't happen on your watch," someone quipped to me. After another ceremony, the President, McNamara, and I went to the State Department for a buffet luncheon with Rusk. Then I returned to the Pentagon to continue the meetings of the Vietnam Task Force (later to be known as the "Clifford Group"). I was not scheduled to be sworn in for two more days, but my work had begun.

28

The Most Difficult Month

We are conscious all the time that this is a moment in history. But it is very like falling down a mountain. One is aware of death and fate, but thinks mainly of catching hold of some jutting piece of rock.

—HAROLD NICOLSON

When does uncertainty undermine belief? With whom does one first share one's private doubts? When does inner skepticism surface, first tentatively, then as full-fledged apprehension?

In his memoirs, General Westmoreland reported that Lyndon Johnson said I had "disappointed" him.[1] I have no doubt there was a certain, but incomplete, truth to this statement: within weeks I had come to the conclusion that my overwhelming priority as Secretary of Defense was to extricate our nation from an endless war. I knew this would change my relationship with Lyndon Johnson, but I felt that my obligation to the nation—and to the President himself—required that I take the risk.

Our relationship did not change overnight. At first it remained close, but as time went on I found myself functioning on four different levels: deep in the privacy of my own mind, where disillusionment with the war was already well advanced by the time I took the oath of office on March 1; in private conversations with a tiny handful of close and trusted colleagues, especially Paul Warnke and Harry McPherson, with whom I could try to form a united front; in guarded dealings with those, such as Rostow and Rusk, who were still committed to the war; and finally, in my relations with the man who had appointed me. I constantly considered simply sitting down alone with him and trying to convince him that the entire policy had to be changed—and eventually I did just that. But in March, Lyndon Johnson would have rejected not only such flat statements but their messenger. I decided I could be most effective if I moved gradually; by summer, President Johnson understood that my opposition to his policy was no longer over tactics or strategy but over fundamental objectives. Our long friendship would never be the same again.

During the preparation of this book, Lady Bird Johnson was asked how she thought her husband felt about our relationship as the strain over Vietnam grew. "It made him sad, but not angry," she said, then paused—and added, speaking for herself, "It was a necessary and courageous thing to do, even if it hurt." I hope that the President felt the same way.

PAUL NITZE, PAUL WARNKE, AND THE TEAM AT DEFENSE

At noon on March 1, Chief Justice Earl Warren administered the oath of office to me from the same spot in the East Room where, two days earlier, Bob McNamara had received the Medal of Freedom. In his remarks before the swearing-in, President Johnson joked that it had taken a long time to prevail upon me "to move from the 'kitchen cabinet' to the East Room," and compared the appointment to a wedding: "After a very long and sometimes secret courtship, we are finally making an honest man out of him."

The ceremony was an anticlimax, coming, as it did, forty days after my nomination: I was psychologically already on the job—a job that after the Tet Offensive had an embattled quality. As soon as the ceremony was over, I rushed back to the Pentagon for a private luncheon with the Deputy Secretary of Defense.

Paul Nitze had come to Washington in 1940 with his partner and friend from Wall Street, James Forrestal, and would ultimately serve in a wide variety of positions over a fifty-year period under Presidents from Roosevelt to Reagan. He was genuinely knowledgeable in the field of arms control, and made important contributions to postwar American foreign and defense policy. Yet he was repeatedly frustrated in achieving his goal of becoming either Secretary of State or Secretary of Defense, and believed he had been denied these positions through the broken promises of Presidents and the maneuvering of his adversaries. His ambition and impatient intellect often manifested themselves in irritable peevishness and flashes of unveiled contempt for people whom he felt did not deserve the high government positions which they held. I knew he felt he should have had my job, but I was pleased when he agreed to stay on as my deputy. It was clear that it would take time to master the complexities of the huge job and deal with the crisis of Vietnam at the same time, so I delegated to Nitze responsibility for many important issues in order to concentrate on Vietnam.

Nitze served effectively and proved to be an excellent deputy. However, in the years after the end of the Johnson Administration, our paths diverged, as Nitze supported such bizarre ideas as a massive civil defense system, advocated huge defense budgets and adopted positions on some national security issues with which I wholly disagreed. Finally, in 1977, he made several statements concerning the patriotism of a former colleague; I found these inexcusable, and our relationship, once cordial, was permanently damaged (see Chapter 33).

For Nitze, the main arena—indeed, the only arena—that mattered was the confrontation with the Soviet Union, which had been his obsession since the midforties. In 1968, Rusk and Rostow still viewed Vietnam as a vital part of our worldwide struggle against Moscow, but Nitze had concluded that, in fact, the war was a diversion from that struggle. He was concerned that the Soviet Union might take advantage of Vietnam to challenge us in Europe, perhaps even try a surprise attack against us—an idea I thought farfetched.[2]

Nitze was only one member of the enormously impressive team McNamara had assembled at the Pentagon. Many of them had planned or expected to leave with McNamara, but I asked almost all to stay. My request was by no means automatically granted, however. Assistant Secretary of Defense for Public Affairs Phil G. Goulding, for example, a self-described "McNamara man," was typical in his attitude: he had assumed he would leave when I arrived because, as he wrote later, he regarded me as a "personal crony [of Johnson's] . . . who had never run anything except his law firm," and had "Neanderthal ideas on the war in Vietnam."[3] But after both McNamara and Vance talked to Goulding, he agreed to stay, performed splendidly, and became a lasting personal friend. I also kept McNamara's military assistant, Air Force Colonel Robert E. Pursley,* one of the most intelligent and broad-gauged military officers I have ever known, who proved to be an invaluable bridge to the military services and the rest of the Defense Department.

I brought only two people to the Pentagon from the outside world. My able, long-suffering, and loyal secretary, Mary Weiler, followed me across the Potomac. In addition, I asked my treasured colleague from the Truman White House, George Elsey, if he would take leave from Pullman, Inc., where he was working, to help me once more, this time as Special Assistant to the Secretary of Defense.

The most important member of the team I retained from McNamara turned out to be a forty-eight-year-old lawyer from Massachusetts named Paul Warnke, who was Assistant Secretary of Defense for International Security Affairs. I did not know him before I went to the Pentagon; he was to become my closest adviser and, after we both left the government, my partner in the law firm of Clifford and Warnke. His self-deprecating

*Pursley also served as military assistant to my successor as Secretary of Defense, Melvin Laird, and later, as a Lieutenant General, he became Commander of U.S. Forces, Japan.

manner and casual style made him easy to work with, but I learned quickly that behind that easygoing style lay an incisive mind that cut fearlessly through the circumlocutions and evasions of others in the government. For his courage in 1968, Warnke was to earn my deepest admiration—and the undying enmity of the American military services.

The positions of Warnke and Nitze on Vietnam—"the two Pauls"—were often parallel, but they approached the war from different starting points. Like Nitze, Warnke had concluded that the bombing of the North would neither force Hanoi to the negotiating table nor cut off the relatively small amount of supplies and forces the enemy needed in the South. Unlike Nitze, he did not relate our involvement in Vietnam to our Soviet policy; to Warnke, these were separate matters, connected only if Moscow could help in negotiating a way out of the war. He felt the U.S. had made a mistake in going into Vietnam in the first place, and he saw the war as unwinnable at any reasonable level of military commitment, to a large extent because of the ineffectiveness of the Saigon government.

Nitze, Warnke, Goulding, Elsey, and Pursley formed the inner team that I met with each day at 8:30 A.M.—the "8:30 Group," as they came to be called. Here I felt free to speak my mind, and to solicit the views of men I trusted and respected: they were my sounding board for ideas, and the meetings sometimes lasted for hours.

In his efforts to affect American policy, Warnke was assisted by an impressive group of younger civilians, among them Richard Steadman; a bright thirty-year-old Deputy Assistant Secretary, Morton Halperin; and an unusually gifted young academic, Leslie H. Gelb,* who had recently left the staff of Senator Jacob Javits. Warnke's staff also included some impressive midlevel military officers with experience in the field in Vietnam, who risked their careers by pointing out weaknesses in the official military reports from Saigon.

One other group in the Pentagon was especially important—the famous Systems Analysis division of the Pentagon, created by McNamara to bring to the Pentagon the modern analytical techniques he had learned at Harvard Business School and perfected at the Ford Motor Company. The Assistant Secretary of Defense for Systems Analysis, the original "McNamara whiz kid," was Alain Enthoven, an extraordinary thirty-seven-year-old economist trained at the Rand Corporation. He and his deputy for Vietnam, Phil Odeen, produced a weekly analysis of military activity which regularly cast doubt on, and frequently demolished, the military's own reporting. Needless to say, the military hated Enthoven and his fellow whiz kids, considering them smart alecks who had never seen

*Now a columnist for *The New York Times.*

"the real world,"—that is, the battlefield itself—but their analysis was important in pointing out the internal inconsistencies and weaknesses of the military's own assessments.

The "civilians in the Pentagon," especially Warnke and his staff, were attacked by many supporters of the war, including Westmoreland, Rostow, the columnist Joseph Alsop, and President Johnson himself, as having been responsible for spreading their biases against the war like an infectious virus, first to McNamara and then to me. "They excited [McNamara] with their brilliance," Johnson said bitterly after he had left the White House.[4]

Later, some of the right wing even charged that these men had welcomed America's defeat. These accusations often came from people who had been opponents of the war in the sixties (even, in several cases, evading the draft through academic or other deferments), who were trying to establish or reestablish their conservative credentials during the Reagan years.

Aside from the backhanded tribute to the influence of these men, these charges were ridiculous and patently false. For the most part, the young civilians in the Pentagon were imbued with the idealistic attitude toward public service that came from the Kennedy era. They had believed in our original objective in Vietnam, and they hated the idea of an American defeat in Vietnam just as much as their military colleagues did. Only with the greatest reluctance did they conclude that the war could not be won. They knew that the fight to change policy would be difficult and risky for their careers, but they undertook it out of a conviction and a patriotism every bit as profound as that of the military.

Warnke and his colleagues argued their case with logic, skill, and courage—but what changed my opinion on the war was, in the end, the failure of the war's supporters, especially the military, to make a convincing case that we could achieve our objectives at any acceptable cost to the nation. The simple truth was that the military failed to sustain a respectable argument for their position.

THE "CLIFFORD TASK FORCE"

My first few days as Secretary of Defense were devoted almost entirely to chairing the task force on Vietnam.[5] These meetings, which took place in my conference room, were attended by a large number of senior officials, including, at various times, Rusk, Katzenbach, Bill Bundy, Nitze, Warnke, Taylor, Helms, Wheeler, and Secretary of the Treasury Henry ("Joe") Fowler. Our primary assignment was to give the President a recommendation on the Wheeler-Westmoreland troop request. But the President's February 28 memorandum also asked that we produce, if possible, recommendations that "reconcile the military, diplomatic, economic, congressional, and public opinion problems involved."

I knew there would be no way to reach a consensus on such a range of issues in just five days. Furthermore, the main field of battle was not the Clifford Task Force, but the President's mind. In my first week in office, I had not yet reached a decision on how to handle several critical issues, including the bombing of the North and American ground strategy—but I was already unalterably opposed to the request for more troops.

I knew I had only a limited amount of time before my status as the "new boy in town" would end. For a few weeks, though, I could use relative ignorance as an excuse to ask questions that had not been raised in over three years in high-level meetings—questions so fundamental that, had they come from anyone else in the room, would have been dismissed instantly as being deliberately provocative. The others had worked together so long that perhaps only an outsider could break them out of their own stalemate—or so I hoped.

Task force meeting, March 2. The discussion was often confused and emotional. I questioned the military, politely but firmly asking them to justify the 205,000 troop request. Although there is no verbatim or precise record of our exchange, it went something like this:

- "Will 205,000 more men do the job?" *They could give no assurance that they would.*

- "If 205,000 might not be sufficient, how many more troops might be needed—and when?" *There was no way of knowing.*

- "Can the enemy respond with a buildup of his own?" *He could.*

- "Can bombing stop the war?" *No. Bombing was inflicting heavy personnel and matériel losses, but by itself it would not stop the war.*

- "Will stepping up the bombing decrease American casualties?" *Very little, if at all. Our casualties are a result of the intensity of the ground fighting in the South.*

- "How long must we keep on sending our men and carrying the main burden of combat?" *We do not know when, if ever, the South Vietnamese will be ready to carry the main burden of the war.*

This exchange, and many others like it, disturbed me greatly. The military was utterly unable to provide an acceptable rationale for the troop increase. Moreover, when I asked for a presentation of their plan for attaining victory, I was told that there was no plan for victory in the historic American sense. Although I kept my feelings private, I was appalled: nothing had prepared me for the weakness of the military's case.

Task force meeting, March 3. We met again, dressed in casual Sunday clothes rather than in our weekday business suits. Rusk wore a loud sport shirt he called his "Key West" shirt in honor of President Truman. Shortly before the meeting, Warnke and Gelb rushed to my office with the latest draft of the memorandum to the President—known in Pentagon jargon as a "DPM" (Draft Presidential Memorandum). It was the first time I had met Gelb, who was also the director of a top-secret group McNamara had established in 1967 to examine the origins and conduct of the war. Warnke later enjoyed teasing me that when he and Gelb tried to tell me about this project, I dismissed it as rather unimportant and a "dumb idea"; I did not understand why anyone in the office of the Secretary of Defense should be collecting historical material at this time. I should have paid the project more attention—when it was leaked to *The New York Times* in 1971, it was to become famous as the Pentagon Papers.

It was clear that the task force could not reach agreement on the question of additional troops. I was increasingly concerned that the President would agree to Westmoreland's request on the spot if it were debated in his presence. After the meeting broke up late in the afternoon, I asked Warnke to redraft the memorandum to the President, dropping the complete cessation of the bombing, and adding a recommendation for a limited call-up of Reserves and a small increase in Westmoreland's troop strength. When Warnke seemed disappointed, I told him the task force was not the right forum, nor was this the right time, to try to resolve the fundamental issues dividing the Administration; we needed to await a better time to present our case. After only four days at the Pentagon, I was not ready to take on the collective weight of Rusk, the Joint Chiefs, Westmoreland, and Rostow.

March 4. During a chaotic and frantic day, the final version of the DPM was cleared with Rusk and Wheeler. Some historians later interpreted it as a hard-line document; if read without knowledge of the context in which it was written, it could be interpreted as support for the Wheeler-Westmoreland request, because it recommended the deployment of 20,000 additional men to Vietnam before May 1, and a Reserve call-up "adequate to meet the balance of [Westmoreland's] request." But these were compromises with my colleagues; my real objective was contained—in a sense, concealed—in the third and last proposal, which I hoped would neutralize the first two by slowing down the military push for reinforcements, while granting them a relatively small number of additional troops and a limited Reserve call-up. I suggested that the final decision on the troop request be contingent upon three factors: a week-by-week reexamination of the situation, improved performance by the Saigon government and the South Vietnamese Army; and a complete review of our political and strategic options in Vietnam.

When the meeting with the President began in the Cabinet Room late Monday afternoon, it was the first time I presented my case as Secretary of Defense. What I said surprised some of those in the room who thought they knew my views. I was struck later by the fact that, without thinking about it, I had used some of the same phrases as I had at Camp David almost three years earlier in the debate with McNamara over the buildup. Tom Johnson recorded my words:

> This new request brings the President to a watershed: Do you continue down that same road of more troops, more guns, more planes, more ships? Do you go on killing more Viet Cong and more North Vietnamese? As we build up our forces, they build up theirs. The result is simply that we are fighting now at a higher level of intensity. . . . We recommend in this paper that you meet the requirements only for those forces that may be needed to deal with any exigencies in the next three or four months. . . . This is as far as we are willing to go. . . . We are not sure that a conventional military victory, as commonly defined, can be achieved. . . . If we continue with our present policy of adding more troops and increasing our commitment, it may lead us into Laos and Cambodia. . . . We seem to have gotten caught in a sinkhole. We put in more, they match it. . . . I see more and more fighting with more and more casualties on the U.S. side, and no end in sight. . . . Of course, if we in this room had to vote today on sending these 200,000 men or not sending them, we would come out all over the lot. We would be split. But all of us wonder if we are really making progress toward our goal.[6]

Treasury Secretary Joe Fowler followed me with a brutal description of the fiscal and economic implications of the buildup of the Reserves. I could see that it had a strong impact on the President, Rusk, and even Wheeler, who surprised me by backing away from the Wheeler-Westmoreland troop request in order to keep alive *his* primary objective, a call-up of the Reserves. Even though he still kept open the possibility of more troops at a later date, Wheeler disassociated himself from the request, referring to it throughout the meeting as "Westmoreland's request":

> If we could provide Westy with the troops he wants, I would recommend they be sent—but they clearly cannot be provided. Twenty-two

> thousand is the best that we can do by 15 June. I find nothing wrong with going along with this track. . . . With a call-up of the reserves, you can still meet Westmoreland's request by 1 September and 1 December, but not by 1 May.

The President asked about getting negotiations started. Rusk replied that the negotiating track was "quite bleak," a position he had taken often in the past. This time, though, Paul Nitze unexpectedly pressed Rusk on the need to consider a bombing halt: "We must . . . cease the bombing to see what happens," Nitze said. "We must choose the time ourselves."

Rusk was silent for a moment, then gave an unexpected reply. Nothing in our previous discussions had prepared me for it. "Well, we could try stopping the bombing during the rainy season in the north," he said. "It would not cost us much militarily, since our air sorties are way down at that time anyway."

President Johnson responded immediately, as if seeing a new life preserver in a stormy sea: "Dean, I want you to *really* get on your horse on that one—right away."

THE BOMBING-HALT DISCUSSION BEGINS

Countless articles, memoirs, and histories have already been written about March 1968, but because several proposals for a complete bombing halt had been circulating within the government for months, confusion has continued to surround the origins of President Johnson's March 31 decision to limit the bombing of North Vietnam. It is high time to clear up the confusion.

Both McNamara and Katzenbach had proposed a full bombing halt in November 1967, but their proposals had never received serious consideration. The first formal discussion of a bombing halt took place at the Tuesday Lunch on March 5, the day after the President had told Rusk to "get on your horse on that one."

When the President asked what he had done about a bombing halt, Rusk was prepared: "We have come up with an idea that would put additional responsibility on Hanoi for not seeking peace. We could do it during the period of bad weather coming up, when our bombing is limited in any case." Pulling a piece of paper out of his breast pocket, he read a draft Presidential statement he had prepared:

> After consultation with our allies, I have directed that U.S. bombing attacks on North Vietnam be limited to those areas which are integrally related to the battlefield. . . . Whether this step I have taken can be a step toward peace is for Hanoi to determine.

The President asked what Hanoi's reaction would be. Rusk said he did not expect a response to his proposal. "My guess is that a bombing pause would last about three days," he said. "It would not hold up if they attacked either Khe Sanh or the cities. If there is no response from Hanoi by the time the bad weather has ended, we could resume the bombing. We would not have lost much militarily, and we might regain the public initiative."

Rusk has often been portrayed by historians as oblivious to, or ignorant of, the domestic political aspects of foreign policy. In fact, though, in his career he had dealt repeatedly with those foreign policy issues that were the *most* political—including Israel, the Korean War, the fall of China, and relations with the Soviet Union. In suggesting that the bombing be restricted to "those areas which are integrally related to the battlefield," Rusk's primary motive was clearly to buy time at home for the war effort by showing the American people that we had "walked the last mile" for peace, while continuing the bombing in the area just north of the DMZ.

I listened in silent skepticism: for more than two years, I had opposed turning the bombing on and off as a way of influencing public opinion, on the grounds that it would only strengthen Hanoi and create pressure for heavier bombing from hard-liners at home. Rusk seemed to be making his proposal primarily as a public-relations move in order to justify an intensification of the war after its failure—the opposite of the direction I wanted to take. If, however, we could turn his proposal into part of a definitive change in America's direction in the war, *that* would be a different matter.

CONGRESS QUESTIONS THE RESERVE CALL-UP

Instead of responding directly to Rusk's proposal, the President returned to the issue of a Reserve call-up in a way that reflected his Congressional background: he said he would be guided by what key Senators had to say. "I want Bus [Wheeler] and Clark to go up and talk to Dick Russell and his colleagues. See if Russell can swallow a call-up of the Reserves, authority to call specialists, and an extension of enlistments. If he can, ask him if he can march it through the Senate and the House."

Thus the President put the size and nature of the Reserve call-up into the hands of the Senate leadership. These men were among Johnson's oldest professional colleagues and friends—he knew their strengths and weaknesses, and he could gauge changes in their positions down to the last centimeter. He paid especially close attention to the conservatives, and above all the man he respected most among his former Senate colleagues, Richard Russell of Georgia.

March 8. General Wheeler and I met with Russell and three of his most influential colleagues—John Stennis of Mississippi, Scoop Jackson of Washington, and Stuart Symington. Russell told me that getting into Vietnam was a mistake in the first place—and he did not wish to compound it by calling up the Reserves or extending tours of duty. None wished to support more reinforcements for Westmoreland or a large call-up. Jackson told us we could not proceed without Congressional support, and "we won't support you." When I met separately with Mike Mansfield, who had succeeded Lyndon Johnson as Senate Majority Leader and had opposed the war longer than most of his colleagues, he also warned, in his gentle manner, that we had reached the end of the line on increases in American troop levels.

Between meetings on Capitol Hill, I told Wheeler that I was disturbed by an article that had appeared in *The New York Times* the previous day, attributing a series of highly optimistic views, including the statement that the enemy did not have "any great capability to assume any general offensive in the near future" to "a senior military spokesman" in Saigon. I asked Wheeler to tell Westmoreland to put a stop to such ill-advised comments.

Wheeler carried out my request through a back-channel message to Westmoreland, which I did not see until some time later. It not only conveyed my instruction accurately but also offered Westmoreland some personal impressions, and hinted at the subtle tensions that had developed between Wheeler and Westmoreland:

> I HAD A MOST INTERESTING AND INFORMATIVE CONVERSATION TODAY WITH OUR NEW SECRETARY OF DEFENSE, MR. CLIFFORD. . . . IN MY JUDGMENT, APART FROM HIS IMPORTANT OFFICIAL POSITION, HE IS A MAN OF STATURE AND ACHIEVEMENT, ONE WHOSE VIEWS MUST BE ACCORDED WEIGHT. THE MAIN POINTS HE MADE WITH ME THIS MORNING WERE THE FOLLOWING:
>
> THE TET OFFENSIVE CAME AS A GREAT SHOCK TO THE AMERICAN PUBLIC. HE BELIEVES THAT SHOCK WAS THE GREATER BECAUSE OF THE EUPHORIA ENGENDERED BY OPTIMISTIC STATEMENTS IN PAST DAYS. . . . I MUST ADMIT THAT SECRETARY CLIFFORD'S ASSESSMENT IS SHARED BY ME, ALTHOUGH, NOT HAVING THE CONTACTS HE ENJOYS, I CANNOT DOCUMENT THE FEELINGS IN THE BUSINESS COMMUNITY AND AMONG THE NEWS MEDIA AS CAN HE. . . . [HE] BELIEVES OUR BEST COURSE OF ACTION IS TO BE CONSERVATIVE IN ASSESSMENTS OF THE SITUATION AND ENEMY CAPABILITIES. . . . I BELIEVE THIS GUIDANCE FROM THE SECRETARY OF DEFENSE IS SO CRITICAL TO OUR MILITARY EFFORT THAT YOU SHOULD DEVISE SOME WAY OF PASSING IT ON WITHOUT ATTRIBU-

TION AS COMMAND GUIDANCE TO YOUR COMMANDERS AND PUBLIC INFORMATION STAFFS.*

Late that day, we met at the White House to review the negative Congressional reaction to the Wheeler-Westmoreland requests. Without strong support from the Hill, a large call-up of the Reserves was impossible, and without this, a large troop increase would be virtually impossible—with our other worldwide commitments, the U.S. had reached the upper limit of what could be sent to Vietnam within the existing force structure. President Johnson realized the implications of the Congressional consultations immediately, and, for the first time, showed serious doubt about sending more troops to Vietnam. To his later regret, though, he did not make a final decision on how many troops he would send Westmoreland.

Prior to this meeting, Wheeler had cabled Westmoreland that there was still "substantial agreement" on an immediate deployment of at least 30,000 troops. But within hours, Wheeler sent Westmoreland a new reading of the darkening mood in Washington:

> I MUST TELL YOU FRANKLY THAT THERE IS STRONG RESISTANCE FROM ALL QUARTERS TO PUTTING MORE GROUND FORCE UNITS IN SOUTH VIETNAM. THE CALL-UP OF RESERVES AND THE CONCOMITANT ACTIONS THAT MUST BE TAKEN WILL RAISE UNSHIRTED HELL IN MANY INFLUENTIAL QUARTERS, AND I FIND THAT THERE IS SUBSTANTIAL SENTIMENT THAT THE 30,000 INCREMENT SHOULD NOT BE DEPLOYED. . . . I TELL YOU THIS BECAUSE I FEEL . . . YOU SHOULD NOT COUNT ON AN AFFIRMATIVE DECISION FOR SUCH ADDITIONAL FORCES.[8]

"THE FATAL LEAK"

Except for those people directly affected, most newspaper articles fade quickly from memory: only a few stories have any impact on events, and only a minuscule number of newspaper stories become a part of history itself. On Sunday, March 10, 1968, *The New York Times* printed such an article; it was later to be described, with reason, as "the fatal leak."[9]

My first warning of what was to come was contained in an urgent note from Phil Goulding on the afternoon of March 8:

*Westmoreland replied that *he* had been the source of *The New York Times* article, adding he would "do my best to conform" to the new guidance from Washington, "consistent with intellectual honesty as to my appraisal of the situation and in consideration of an essential attitude of command requiring a reflection of confidence." Wheeler understandably did not share this acerbic answer with me.[7]

> Nick Katzenbach called me this afternoon to say that Neil Sheehan has been calling various State people with the 206,000 figure, but without the detail that [Hedrick] Smith apparently has. . . . Paul, Nick and I are all surprised that it has taken this long for something to surface.

Goulding's note referred to two of the best—and therefore, most dangerous—reporters in Washington, Neil Sheehan and Hedrick Smith of *The New York Times,* who were at that moment contacting their sources at the State and Defense Departments to check out the details of an astonishing story they had been working on for several days. I talked to Goulding about the situation, and we agreed that there was nothing we could do.

March 9. It was Saturday, and much of official Washington had gathered to enjoy the annual Gridiron Dinner. I was the guest of the great *Washington Post* political cartoonist Herblock. President Johnson, who hated the barbs of the dinner, did not attend, but Vice President Humphrey did, along with most of the Cabinet.

As usual, the evening was long. I was trying to enjoy the jokes aimed at the Administration—including one that said "Clark Clifford is so used to dealing with General Electric that he demanded a retainer from General Wheeler." Sometime around 10 P.M., I was approached by Benjamin Bradlee, the executive editor of *The Washington Post,* who told me that *The New York Times* was leading its Sunday-morning edition with a story that a huge debate was under way within the Administration over a request from Westmoreland for 206,000 additional troops. (The *Times* headline, across three columns of its front page, read: WESTMORELAND REQUESTS 206,000 MORE MEN, STIRRING DEBATE IN ADMINISTRATION.)

After pressing me for confirmation of the story, Bradlee raced off in search of other Administration officials. I could see Chalmers Roberts, one of his best reporters, buttonholing other officials. George Christian, the President's press secretary, was surrounded by reporters. As other editors and publishers heard about the *Times* story, I watched them slipping out of the ballroom to call their newsrooms across the country. The normal atmosphere of the Gridiron Dinner—that of a relaxed off-the-record evening among journalists and government officials—was abandoned. As Smith proudly, and accurately, said later, the story "moved [across the room] like wind through a field of wheat"; it was the only time most of us ever "could physically see the impact of [a] story."[10]

Only two days remained before the New Hampshire primary, where Senator Eugene McCarthy of Minnesota, running against President Johnson on an antiwar platform, was trying to crystallize opposition to the war and the Administration. Because Johnson was not a declared candidate, he was not on the ballot in New Hampshire, but a vigorous write-in campaign was being waged on his behalf by most of the leading Democrats in the state, and polls had shown little support for McCarthy until the Tet Offensive.

I discussed the *Times* story with an angry President Johnson over the telephone the next morning. He viewed the story as a personal betrayal by someone in the Administration—he was sure it was a civilian in the Pentagon, and asked me to investigate.* He also tried to convince himself that he had rejected the Wheeler-Westmoreland troop request the previous week, although in fact he had not done so. In his heart, though, he knew that such details did not matter; the damage was done, and it would be virtually impossible to undo it. Finally, President Johnson instructed George Christian to state that "no specific request" from Westmoreland for additional troops had ever reached the President's desk. This might have been correct in the narrowest technical sense, but it fooled no one, and only added to the growing loss of confidence in the Administration.

NEW HAMPSHIRE—AND BOBBY KENNEDY

The next week was one of nonstop activity. On Monday, March 11, Dean Rusk began two days of previously scheduled, nationally televised testimony on Vietnam before the Senate Foreign Relations Committee. He performed superbly, showing cool courage in the face of a heavy barrage of criticism from Senators of both parties, and he won himself many new admirers. But admiration of Rusk's stoic calm was not convertible into support for the war.

March 12. As we gathered for the Tuesday Lunch, the citizens of New Hampshire were voting, and Rusk was still testifying before the committee. Low-key and subdued, Johnson spoke in an unusually reflective manner about the events of the previous week:

> I was ready a week ago to say that we should call up the reserves, to strengthen the strategic reserve, to ask Congress for authority to call up selected reservists, to use this as a basis for a new position on the tax bill, to ask for authority to extend enlistments. That session last Monday [March 4] did moderate my judgments some. I agree that we should reevaluate our strategy. I only hope we don't get overrun in the meantime.

*Oberdorfer's account of how *The New York Times* got the story suggests that it was not an intentional leak by a single "disgruntled Pentagon civilian," as President Johnson always believed, but was pieced together from a variety of sources. In another excellent reconstruction, Schandler decided that the key sources included Senators who had been briefed by President Johnson himself.[11]

come to reevaluate, in its entirety, our policy in Vietnam, this language would be sufficient for me, if coupled with the appointment of a board consisting of persons recommended by us."

"Who do you have in mind?" I asked. Kennedy and Sorensen had given some thought to this question, and offered a list that included Edwin Reischauer, the former Ambassador to Japan; Kingman Brewster, the President of Yale; Roswell Gilpatric, the former Deputy Secretary of Defense during the Kennedy Administration; Carl Kaysen, the former White House economic assistant; General Lauris Norstad, former NATO commander; General Matthew Ridgway, former U.N. commander in Korea; and four Senators—Republicans John Sherman Cooper and George Aiken, and Democrats Mike Mansfield and Kennedy himself. Bobby interjected to say that his own participation was not essential if the President objected.

I said I would have to talk to the President before making a formal reply, but I wanted to make three personal comments:

> First, it is my opinion that the possibility of your being able to defeat President Johnson for the nomination is zero. I went through a similar situation in 1948 with President Truman when the liberals had deserted him, his domestic and foreign policies were under attack, Henry Wallace was in the race, and leading Democrats were trying to persuade General Eisenhower to run.
>
> Second, I urge you to consider that the situation could change between now and the time of the convention in August. There are a number of factors under the President's direct control—such as the decision as to when to stop the bombing or get negotiations started.
>
> Finally, if by chance you are able to gain the nomination, it will be valueless because your efforts in displacing President Johnson would so split the party that the Republican nominee would win the election easily. I hope you consider with the greatest care whether it is worth going through what you will have to endure to gain a nomination which, in my view, would be worthless if you were to win it.

With absolute calm, Kennedy replied that he had considered all these points, but he still felt he would have to run unless President Johnson would agree to his proposal. With that, the meeting ended. In an atmosphere that remained polite but was now shadowed with a feeling that a confrontation could no longer be prevented, we parted.

At 3:30 P.M., I met with President Johnson, Vice President Humphrey, and Abe Fortas in the small lounge just off the Oval Office—the room the President used for his most private conversations. His reaction to my report was instantaneous and unequivocal: he could never accept the Kennedy-Sorensen proposal, for several reasons. First, no matter how it was handled, in the eyes of the world it would appear to have been a political deal; second, it would give comfort to Hanoi; third, he considered it an attempt to usurp Presidential authority: fourth, the proposed membership of the commission was composed entirely of men whose opposition to the war was already known: the deck, he said, was stacked against the policy.

Humphrey, Fortas, and I agreed with him. At his instruction, I placed a call to Sorensen, who was waiting in Kennedy's Senate office. Sorensen asked me to wait while he put Bobby on the line. President Johnson listened silently on a line in his office. I told them both that while the President believed in consulting outside advisers, this particular proposal was unacceptable. Bobby asked what the President's reaction would be if he were not on the commission, and I said that it would make no difference: from the President's point of view, it would still look like a political deal.

Kennedy said later that this was the precise moment he made the final decision to run. Other observers and friends of the Senator were not so sure: Arthur Schlesinger, Kenneth O'Donnell, Fred Dutton, and Jack Newfield all believed that Bobby never thought the commission idea would work, and simply went through the motions to satisfy both himself and Sorensen that he had made every effort to put the issue of Vietnam ahead of his own personal agenda. I was not privy to any of the discussions inside the Kennedy camp, but my impression was that Kennedy knew from the outset that the commission idea—especially in the form he had presented it—amounted to an ultimatum and was certain to be rejected.[14]

Two days later, on March 16, 1968, Kennedy announced his candidacy for the Democratic nomination for President. Lyndon Johnson's worst nightmare had come true: he was, he told me, trapped forever between the two Kennedys.

THE DECISION TO CALL THE WISE MEN—AGAIN

Within a day of Kennedy's announcement, bitter recriminations broke out between the Johnson and Kennedy camps over the events of the previous week. Much newspaper space was devoted to this, and, despite more pressing matters, it briefly obsessed the President; I too was drawn into a short public dispute with Sorensen and Kennedy over the events of the previous week. The squabble, however, was of importance neither to the political campaign nor to the crisis that had now almost completely enveloped Washington: a crisis in confidence in the government which—in those pre-Watergate days—was the most serious, in my opinion, since the Civil War.

I was particularly disturbed by the latest version of the draft for the President's Vietnam speech, now scheduled for March 31. Drafted by Harry McPherson under direct instructions from the President, it was even tougher than the first draft, and contained such phrases as "the American people . . . do not engage in craven retreats from responsibility, whatever the year." I told McPherson that it would further tear the nation apart. Meanwhile, Rusk cabled Ambassador Bunker in Saigon, asking for his and President Thieu's reaction to a full and unilateral bombing halt. Rusk had no hesitation in sharing his own view with Bunker that it "would be our best judgment that they [Hanoi] would not take any real step toward peace," he said.

As I continued my round of Congressional consultations, Senator Fulbright sent me a written request to testify before the Foreign Relations Committee. This presented me with a dilemma: I could not mislead the committee, but the differences between Rusk and me, if revealed publicly, would not only create an additional problem for the Administration, they would also make any effort to change the policy even more difficult.

The circumstances required that I be frank with Fulbright. This was made easier by the fact that we had become, over the years, golfing partners and friends. Determined to avoid testifying, I went to his office for a private talk. "Bill, I must talk to you in absolute confidence," I began. "I cannot testify before your committee because I can no longer support, in good conscience, the President's policy. I hope you will let me off the hook, because I can do more good if you leave me alone for a while." Fulbright understood completely. Expressing delight that I had "come around," he added, "Well, if you can't come up, please send your deputy."

But Nitze had no more desire to go before the committee than I did, and declined to appear. The President accepted my decision not to testify on the grounds that I was still new to the job, but he was unhappy that Nitze was unwilling to support a policy he had helped shape and implement for seven years. When I told Nitze that the President insisted he testify, Nitze drafted an angry letter to Johnson, stating he would resign if ordered to testify. I asked him to delete his threat to resign, and after a heated discussion, he agreed. On March 16 I forwarded to the President a revised letter from Nitze stating that, because he was not privy to every discussion being held in the White House, "I do not feel myself to be in a position properly to defend the Executive Branch in a debate before the Foreign Relations Committee." Fulbright dropped his request for a Pentagon witness, but Nitze had incurred the undying enmity of Senator

Fulbright, with long-term consequences on Nitze's career (see Chapter 33).

March 17. The President delivered one of the toughest speeches of his Administration, an extemporaneous address before a convention of the National Farmers Union in Minneapolis. With high emotion, he appealed to the nation:

> Your President has come to ask you people, and all the other people of this nation, to join us in a *total national effort* to win the war. . . . We will—make no mistake about it—win. . . . We are not doing enough to win it the way we are doing it now.

The speech created an uproar and reminded me that we were engaged in a tense struggle for the soul and mind of Lyndon Johnson. As I reflected on it, my initial shock turned to dismay: if he meant these words literally, he and I were much further apart than I had realized. *My God,* I thought, *after only eighteen days in office, am I in such fundamental disagreement with the man who appointed me?* I believed I had to try harder to persuade him; if I failed, then I would either carry out his policies without public complaint, or resign.

I looked for allies to help convince him to turn toward de-escalation or disengagement. When I realized the degree to which Dean Acheson had become disillusioned with the war, it occurred to me that, if presented in the right manner, a shift in the views of some of the other Wise Men, who had given the President such strong support in November 1967, might make an impression on President Johnson. I called a few of them and found they were no longer as confident of their position as they had been in the past. Of course, I could not be sure what positions the elder statesmen would take after briefings from government officials, but at the Tuesday Lunch on March 19, I suggested that the President reconvene his senior advisory group.

I hoped that another meeting would reflect a shift in the views of the Wise Men, but I did not tell this to the President, Rusk, or Rostow. The President was, of course, already aware of Acheson's change as expressed at their lunch a few days earlier, but he did not know the views of other influential members of the group, especially McGeorge Bundy and Vance.

At first, the President reacted negatively to my suggestion: "People would think we were complying with Kennedy's proposal," he said. Unexpectedly, my idea was rescued by Rusk and also by Fortas, who had been invited to the Tuesday Lunch for the first time. Rusk, who respected these men greatly—many were close former colleagues—said, "Since you have met with this same group before, it would not appear to be a cave-in to Kennedy." Fortas called it a good "public-relations move." After some further discussion, the President agreed, and we decided to convene the group on March 25, six days before his speech to the nation on Vietnam.

At this point, he still thought of the March 31 speech primarily as a justification for the decision to send Westmoreland more troops and call up the Reserves. There was no mention of a bombing halt in any of the drafts circulating from McPherson's office. Hanging over our heads as the drafting proceeded was the Wisconsin primary, which would take place only two days after the speech.

I knew that Dean Rusk would support a limited bombing halt, but nothing more, and that he was now deeply upset at the idea of sending more troops to Westmoreland. Thus, Rusk and I could be temporary and partial allies on two issues, even though a wide gulf continued to separate our motives and objectives.

March 20. At 11 A.M. I met with Bui Diem, the South Vietnamese Ambassador to the U.S., who was returning to Saigon for consultations. Fluent in English and knowledgeable regarding American ways, he represented his country in Washington with skill, and was adept at playing different Americans against one another. He was small and wiry, with bright eyes and an ever-present pipe, which gave him an air of great Oriental wisdom. Believing that an honest warning, even if blunt in tone, was probably the best way to make an impact in Saigon, I said to him:

> Tell your government we have run out of time for diplomatic niceties. We are sick to death of Thieu and Ky endlessly feuding while Americans die. Our people are sick and tired of this war, and our support is limited. Your government is facing a clear decision either to broaden the government, clean up the corruption, and take measures to gain wide support among the people, or face the loss of American support. We do not want to send additional forces to Vietnam. If this must be done, it can only be done if our public believes that your forces are doing the best job possible. This is not now the case. Tell your leadership that Saigon's best friends in Washington are deeply worried as to whether or not the American public will continue its support of our efforts in Vietnam. It is not clear to me that your leaders now understand this. We are losing supporters every day.

I ended by telling the Ambassador that I regretted that I did not have one optimistic comment to make to him. He was visibly stunned. He shared entirely my view of the public situation in the U.S., he said, but he was not sure it was similarly understood in embattled Saigon.

Because both the President and Dean Rusk also spoke to him in stern terms before he left for Saigon, Bui Diem received "the distinct impression that the three of them—Johnson, Rusk, and Clifford—had coordinated their messages."[15] But he was quite wrong. In fact, I had not discussed my presentation with the others beforehand.[16] It was so blunt that I withdrew from general circulation all copies of the record of the meeting made by the notetaker, Dick Steadman, who told me later it was the first time he realized how fully committed I was to trying to extricate us from the war.

THE FIGHT OVER THE SPEECH BEGINS IN EARNEST

Late in the afternoon of the same day, the President called a meeting to discuss the speech. Although it was only eleven days away, he had not yet decided how many reinforcements to send to Vietnam, how many Reserves to call up, whether to stop all or part of the bombing of the North, or whether to change our negotiating position. With so many overlapping issues to resolve, it was a chaotic meeting—but, for the first time, we focused on the bombing. Broadly speaking, three choices were presented to the President:

- A "hard" approach, opposing any reduction or cessation of the bombing of the North—backed by Fortas, Bunker, Rostow, Westmoreland, and the JCS.
- A "soft" approach, a complete and unilateral cessation of the bombing, and a reinterpretation of the San Antonio formula—supported by Arthur Goldberg and, in the course of the meeting, McGeorge Bundy.
- Several versions of a middle position, which involved cessation of the bombing of North Vietnam except for the area near the DMZ. With some variations, Rusk and I supported this position.

In my heart, I preferred a full bombing halt, but it was clear the President was not ready to approve a position that was opposed by Rusk, Bunker, Rostow, and the entire military leadership. Instead of pushing for a full halt, I decided to "lock" Dean Rusk into support for a limited bombing halt for the time being, and push for a "soft-line" speech—we could try for a full bombing halt later. Meanwhile, I would also encourage those in the second circle of access to the President, such as Goldberg and Bundy, to advocate a full bombing halt. This would serve as a counterbalance to Bunker and the military, who opposed *any* reductions in the bombing. As I explained to Paul Warnke, "We have to crawl before we can walk."

The strongest voice for increased military pressure was Abe Fortas, and he was backed by two absent but important parties, Ambassador Bunker and the Joint Chiefs of Staff. The President had Bunker's telegrams assembled in front of him, and quoted often from them. They contained strong language: the proposal for a full bombing halt would, Bunker said, "create the greatest difficulties for us here"; a limited bombing halt would create all the same negative effects but "would be easier to obtain [government] approval." The President quoted this and added, "I think that bombing keeps the lead out of our men's bodies."

"I don't think it's clear that the bombing results in lower American casualties, Mr. President," I replied. "Air power is not proving to be as effective in this war as I once thought."

Fortas objected, his voice rising in intensity: "This is not the time for a major negotiating offer. It will be seen as a sign of weakness. . . . I consider it most unfortunate to make any offers now."

I had to disagree with my old friend, but I tried to do it in an oblique and impersonal manner: "In World War II, 'prevail we will' worked because conditions were right for it. Now those conditions do not exist. In Vietnam continued application of strength and firepower does not show us the road to ultimate success. I don't know if any approach to Hanoi at this time will be accepted, but I am nonetheless for gradual de-escalation. Let's try stopping the bombing in the Northern part of North Vietnam and see what happens."

The President seemed unmoved by my comments and closed the meeting with an instruction addressed to Harry McPherson: "Let's get 'peace' out of the speech except [to say] that we're ready to talk. We are mixing up two different things when we include peace initiatives in this speech. Let's just make it troops and war. . . . Later on we can revive and extend our peace initiative." McPherson, who was convinced that the war was ruining his President, buried his head in his notepad, furiously taking notes, saying nothing.[17]

March 22. McPherson had sent out a new draft of the speech: still very tough in tone, it warned of a "grave challenge to our country," which we must "see through." It called for a surtax and reduced domestic spending to achieve our goal: "We have set our face against the enemy, and he will fail." We reconvened in the family quarters of the White House for a long luncheon to discuss this draft.

I suggested we reopen discussion on the idea of a bombing halt north of the 20th parallel. Someone had to break the logjam, and we should consider taking the first de-escalatory step. Rusk agreed with me, but added that he still believed Hanoi would not respond, and we would then be able to resume the bombing. Bill Bundy, citing Ambassador Bunker, said that my suggestion would cause major problems in Saigon, and Fortas flatly opposed my view. McGeorge Bundy closed the discussion by predicting that my proposal "would have a short life, but I am not against it."

Immediately after the meeting, the President announced that General Westmoreland would be reassigned to the Pentagon as Army Chief of Staff, effective July 2, replacing General Harold K. Johnson. McNamara had recommended the reassignment of Westmoreland prior to the Tet Offensive, but the delay in the announcement left the inevitable impression that Westmoreland had been relieved because of Tet. Concerned that Westmoreland needed to be talked to privately about both his reassignment and the question of reinforcements, I suggested we send General Wheeler to the Pacific for a quick meeting with him. Wheeler left the next day, met with Westmoreland for a few hours at Clark Air Force Base in the Philippines, and returned home immediately for the final week of discussions on the March 31 speech. With him came Westmoreland's deputy, General Creighton Abrams—the leading candidate to assume the command in Vietnam—and a request from Westmoreland for 13,500 additional men for Vietnam. As soon as Wheeler told me that Westmoreland would be satisfied with this relatively small increase, I decided I would support it, but try to ensure that it would be the last increase ever.

"THE MOST DISTINGUISHED DINNER PARTY . . ."

Historians and journalists have made much of the gathering of the Senior Advisory Group—the Wise Men—on March 25 and 26, 1968: in the words of various writers, "the high water mark of U.S. hegemony [at] one of history's turning points," "perhaps unique in American history," "possibly the most distinguished dinner party of the American Establishment ever held." The scene has become a dramatic part of the history of our times; the elder statesmen of the "Cold War Knighthood," proudly carrying their years and experience into one last meeting with a President in crisis.[18]

It was, in fact, an unhappy occasion; there could be no pleasure in participating in an event that required its participants to admit that their previous advice had been wrong, and that the President must change course, no matter what the consequences.

They began arriving in the State Department in the late afternoon of Monday, March 25. Some read background papers prepared by State and Defense; others talked privately to Katzenbach, Harriman, Bill Bundy, or Habib. George Ball spent part of the afternoon with Katzenbach, while

Cy Vance talked to some of his old colleagues in the Pentagon. Acheson dropped into Katzenbach's office late in the afternoon for a last chat. At 6 P.M., we gathered in the Secretary's Dining Room on the eighth floor of the State Department, a fairly small room a few yards from the large State Dining Room. President Johnson, who happened to be in the State Department that evening addressing a Conference on Farm Policy and Rural Life, almost gave away the secret session with a comment that the press missed entirely: "Secretary Rusk is having a meeting with some wise men in the next room," he said in his opening remarks, but no one picked up on his teasing hint. After his speech, Johnson dropped by Rusk's dining room to shake hands with the group, but he did not stay, saying that he would see us the next day.

As we sat around Rusk's dining-room table, the outside advisers questioned Rusk, Helms, Katzenbach, Bill Bundy, and me extensively. I told the group there were three choices open to the U.S.: first, granting Westmoreland a major troop increase, increasing the bombing of the North, and extending the ground war into Laos, Cambodia, and perhaps the lower part of North Vietnam; second, "muddling along" with roughly our present strategy, perhaps giving Westmoreland a few thousand more troops; or third, a "reduced strategy" of a bombing halt or a reduction in bombing of the North, abandonment of isolated military positions, and a new ground troop strategy which used American forces as a shield around populated areas in order to give the South Vietnamese time to assume the burden of the war. I said that, although I was willing to send Westmoreland a small number of additional troops, I strongly preferred the third course.

After dinner we took the Secretary's private elevator down one floor and walked a few steps to the State Department's nerve center, the Operations Center. These rooms, set up during the Kennedy Administration, provided the State Department with a capability it had never had before: a room manned twenty-four hours a day to deal with crises. Maps were set up for the Wise Men to examine, and then we settled down to hear briefings from Habib, Major General William E. DePuy, and the CIA's chief analyst for Vietnam, George Carver.

Like almost everything that happened in the month of March, there would be a heated debate later about these three briefings. President Johnson, Rostow, Taylor, and the military all felt that they had been betrayed by the briefings, if not by the briefers. Rusk would say the briefings were unbalanced and overly pessimistic. Maxwell Taylor would tell the President they were significantly different from the situation as he understood it. Wheeler, who did not attend the dinner because he was exhausted from his trip to the Philippines, would say that the briefers did not understand the true situation. Rostow would tell people later, "I smelled a rat." His military assistant, Major General Robert N. Ginsburgh, would say, "there is no question that if Wheeler and Rostow had briefed rather than DePuy and Carver, there would have been a different flavor to the briefings."[19]

These criticisms are unfair. The briefings came from three career government officials—chosen personally by Rusk, Wheeler, and Helms—who had substantial firsthand experience in Vietnam. Habib, DePuy, and Carver all presented their honest views. To the Wise Men, however, who had not been following events in Vietnam except through the media in the five months since their last meeting, the impact of the briefings was undoubtedly much greater than it was to those inside the government, who could see that the mood was somewhat less grim than it had been at the height of Tet.

General DePuy, who had commanded troops in Vietnam and was special assistant to the Joint Chiefs for counterinsurgency and special activities, portrayed the Tet Offensive as an allied victory—but his presentation was diminished in a telling exchange with Arthur Goldberg after the General had said that the communists had lost 80,000 men killed in action. What, Goldberg asked, was the normal ratio of wounded to killed? *A three-to-one ratio among the Vietnamese would be a conservative estimate,* DePuy answered. How many "effectives"—regular soldiers—do you think they now have, Goldberg asked. *Perhaps 230,000, maybe 240,000,* said DePuy. Well, said Goldberg, with 80,000 killed and a wounded ratio of three to one, that makes about 320,000 men killed or wounded. "Who the hell is there left for us to be fighting?" he asked.

The CIA briefer, George Carver, a frequent briefer of the PFIAB and a supporter of the war, presented a candid view of the difficulties involved, particularly in the pacification campaign, and said that it would take much longer than he had previously estimated to achieve our objectives—hardly a controversial conclusion by late March.

The most important briefing came from Phil Habib, who had already met secretly with Acheson several times to prepare him for the meetings. He presented a bleak but balanced picture of a South Vietnamese government unlikely to pull itself together within any reasonable amount of time, and guessed it might take five to seven years to achieve any lasting progress. His blunt and at times earthy Brooklyn style gave his words great credibility: with Habib, the elders felt that they were getting hard facts and honest opinions.

When Habib had finished, I asked, "Phil, do you think a military victory can be won?" Habib knew that to answer such a basic question in front of his three immediate superiors—Rusk, Katzenbach, and Bill

Bundy—put him in an exceedingly difficult position. But he was, above all, honest: pausing for just a moment, he replied, "Not under present circumstances."

I asked him one more question. He told me later that it was the toughest moment of his career. "What would you do if the decision was yours to make?" Another pause, then Habib's reply: "Stop the bombing and negotiate."

It was after 11 P.M. when the meeting broke up. The advisers retired to their own homes or hotel rooms to contemplate what they would tell the President the next day. I went back to my office at the Pentagon, where, after working for a while longer, I spent the night. From their comments, it was clear that the majority of the Wise Men had shifted position since November, but I was not yet certain whether or how they would convey this to the President, or what impact it would have on him.

I was especially gratified at the apparent shift of Cy Vance. President Johnson had great affection and respect for the former Deputy Secretary of Defense, and would listen to him carefully. Discreet and utterly loyal to the President, whom he had known since the fifties, he had listened intently during the evening session, taken careful notes, and asked only a few questions. But his comments, though guarded, convinced me he would be part of the consensus against escalation. Since he had left the Administration in 1966 because of a serious back problem, Johnson had asked Vance to undertake several difficult troubleshooting missions in Cyprus, Korea, and—in conditions of personal risk—Detroit during the racial disturbances in the summer of 1967. In each of these crises he had performed with distinction, precision, and rare courage—and this despite such back pain that he could not even bend down to tie his shoelaces without help. Yet he had accepted such difficult assignments without complaint, asking only that his wife Gay be allowed to travel with him to help him with his back.*

In the morning, I shuttled between another meeting of the Wise Men at the State Department and a briefing of the President and Rusk by Generals Wheeler and Abrams. I was particularly interested in getting a sense of Abrams, who was the leading candidate to replace Westmoreland.

I found an entirely different sort of man from either Westmoreland or Wheeler. Shorter, heavier, and less telegenic than Westmoreland, Creighton Abrams conveyed the strength of the World War II tank commander he had been—Patton's favorite tank commander, according to legend. There was nothing fancy about Abe—he was blunt and reassur-

*An operation and intensive physical therapy in the seventies enabled Vance to make a full recovery, and serve later as Secretary of State under President Carter.

ing where Westmoreland was dramatic and Wheeler cautious. He did not give off the scent of political ambition, like Westmoreland, who was even talked about as a possible Presidential candidate and later ran, without success, for Governor of South Carolina.

Wheeler and Abrams gave the President a far more optimistic picture of the situation than the Wise Men had heard at dinner the previous night. Perhaps encouraged by a reduced level of fighting in Vietnam and Abrams's positive personality, Wheeler had regained much of his confidence. He said Westmoreland still feared a "tactical defeat" if he did not receive adequate Reserves, but he and Westmoreland no longer worried about a broad defeat.

Abrams put heavy emphasis on intelligence reports that showed massive infiltration from the North, partly to replace the losses of Tet. To Wheeler and Abrams, there was only one answer to the increase in enemy strength: more American troops, an increase in the bombing, and an expansion of the ground war into Laos, Cambodia, and North Vietnam. Coming from a military tradition, they did not realize that, in the eyes of most members of Congress and civilians in the executive branch, the reports of massive North Vietnamese infiltration only strengthened the argument for seeking an alternative to what appeared to be endless escalation.

Impressed with Abrams, the President asked him and Wheeler to stay on to meet the Wise Men. He told Abrams to offer them "the whole picture, pros and cons" so as to counter what he said he had heard had been a "depressing" briefing by the CIA representative the night before on the low morale of the South Vietnamese Army.

"The civilians are cutting our guts out—" he began.

Rusk broke in. "The nation can't support a bottomless pit."

In response, President Johnson launched into a remarkable and painfully sad speech about his own difficulties. It almost seemed at times as if he were pleading for understanding, even forgiveness, from these two military officers, to whom he could no longer send reinforcements:

> What will happen if we cut housing, education, poverty programs? I don't give a damn about the election. I will be happy just to keep doing what is right and lose the election. There has been a panic in the last three weeks. . . . Warnke writes a paper for Clifford's group, and it's all over Georgetown. . . . I will have overwhelming disapproval in the polls. I will go down the drain. Goldberg wants us not to bomb North Vietnam for three weeks. Secretary Clifford had a plan to stop above the 20th parallel. We must have something. . . . Senators McCarthy and Kennedy and the left wing have informants in the State and Defense Departments.

> How can we get this job done? We need more money—in an election year. We need more taxes—in an election year. We need more troops—in an election year. And we need cuts in the domestic budget—in an election year. And yet I cannot tell the people what they will get in Vietnam in return for these cuts. We have no support for the war. This was caused by the 206,000-man request and the leaks, by Teddy Kennedy and Bobby Kennedy. I would have given Westy the 206,000 men if he said he needed them, and if we could get them.

There was nothing to say after this outburst. I felt immensely sorry for the President. None of the choices he faced was attractive. But his comments suggested to me that he understood the need for a dramatic change in policy.

Shortly after 1 P.M., the Wise Men arrived from the State Department. During luncheon, Wheeler and Abrams emphasized the substantial improvement in the situation since February, but the group of elders did not bother to question the two Generals closely. To a considerable degree, they had lost confidence in official assessments from the military—and, in any case, few of the Wise Men were thinking solely of Vietnam anymore: their eyes were fixed on disengagement now, not victory. After the plates had been cleared, the President asked McGeorge Bundy to summarize the group's views. Bundy began with a blunt statement that seemed to shock the President:

> Mr. President, there has been a very significant shift in most of our positions since we last met. The picture in November was one of hope for reasonably steady, slow but sustained, progress, especially in the countryside, which was then emphasized to us as an area of particular importance. The picture that emerged from the discussions last night was not so hopeful, particularly in the countryside. Dean Acheson summed up the majority feeling when he said that we can no longer do the job we set out to do in the time we have left, and we must begin to take steps to disengage. That view was shared by George Ball, Arthur Dean, Cy Vance, Douglas Dillon, and myself. . . . Four of us took a different position: General Bradley, General Taylor, Bob Murphy, and Justice Fortas. They all feel we should not act to weaken our position, and should do what our military commanders suggest. . . . On the question of troop reinforcements the dominant sentiment was that the burden of proof rests with those who are urging the increase. Most of us think that there should not be a substantial escalation, nor an extension of the conflict. This would be against our national interest.[20]

Almost wearily, the President asked for other comments. Acheson said he agreed with Bundy's summation, adding, "We should do something different no later than the summer." As Acheson spoke of the impossibility of achieving a military victory, Wheeler tried to correct him; we were not seeking a military victory in Vietnam, only helping the Vietnamese avoid a communist victory. This infuriated Acheson, and he answered with a flash of his old style: "Then what in the name of God are five hundred thousand men out there doing—chasing girls? This is not a semantic game, General; if the deployment of all those men is not an effort to gain a military solution, then words have lost all meaning."

One by one, the others spoke their piece. Henry Cabot Lodge advocated a new strategy that would lower American casualties as quickly as possible. Douglas Dillon supported both Lodge and Acheson, while Ball urged a complete bombing halt quickly. Cy Vance said he agreed with Ball.

General Omar Bradley, crusty and blunt as ever, supported the military, but with a significant qualification that was not lost on any of us: he would send *only* support troops to Vietnam at this time, and for the first time he expressed willingness to see the bombing stopped, if only as a "temporary" action that might shore up domestic support for the war.

Deeply alarmed, General Taylor tried to stop the trend of the discussion. "I am dismayed by what I have heard," he said. "The picture some of these gentlemen have in their minds is not the one that I have developed over a long period of time. Let's not concede the home front; let's do something about it." Robert Murphy, who had almost resigned in protest in 1948 when President Truman had refused to send an armored column through the Berlin Blockade, agreed, saying that while he was "shaken by the positions of my associates," he still supported the military. Fortas agreed with Murphy and Taylor, opposing, as he always had, any reduction in the bombing of the North: "I do not believe in drama for drama's sake."

Douglas Dillon and Arthur Dean both noted the difference between Wheeler and Abrams, on one hand, and General DePuy, on the other. Dean said, "Mr. President, all of us got the impression last night listening to General DePuy, Mr. Carver, and Mr. Habib that there is no military conclusion in this war—or any military end in the near future. I think all of us here very reluctantly came to the judgment that we've got to get out, and we only came to it after we listened to the briefing last night." There were general murmurs of assent from around the table.

Dean's comment greatly disturbed the President. He tried to make a joke—"The first thing I am going to do when you all leave is to find those people who briefed you last night"—but a moment later he passed a note to me on which he had scrawled, "Clark, could you and Dean come in a moment?" Then he rose, told the Wise Men that he would be back shortly, and left the room, trailed by Rusk and me.

As soon as we were outside the Cabinet Room he turned to us angrily: "Who poisoned the well with these guys? I want to hear those briefings myself." Then, telling us he wanted to continue the meeting with no government officials present, he sent us back to our offices.

I returned to the Pentagon tired but relieved. The impact of the Wise Men on him had been visible; I felt that Vance's change of views had particularly surprised him. (I learned later from Cy that, in fact, he had harbored serious doubts about the war for almost two years but had shared them only with McNamara.) Contrary to the conclusion most historians reached later, the President had known for almost two weeks that Acheson had started to change his views, and was thus less surprised by his shift than has generally been assumed. But speaking almost *ex officio* as the leader of the foreign policy establishment, and with his customary authority, Acheson had an unquestionable impact on the President. Still, nearly half the participants in the meeting had given the military full or partial support; it was hardly the nearly unanimous turnaround that later became part of the mythology of the Vietnam War.

The next day the President heard from two of the briefers, DePuy and Carver. Habib deliberately went ahead with a previously scheduled speech in Dayton, Ohio, thus avoiding the meeting with the President. I did not sit in on the repeat performances of DePuy and Carver, but the President pronounced himself satisfied that the well-poisoning had not come from them.* The debate over the briefings was, in any case, academic: even if they had been briefed by Westmoreland, Wheeler, and Bunker themselves, I believe that they would have reached the same conclusions, for one fundamental reason: even the strongest supporters of the war could no longer offer any credible plan or timetable for American withdrawal or a successful outcome. The men who had helped lay down the basic line of resistance to the expansion of communism in the world, the statesmen of Berlin and Korea, had decided they had had enough in Vietnam. The price was not commensurate with the goal.

It was not true, as later charged by critics on the Right, including Rostow, that this was the evening that the American Establishment came to an end.[22] In fact, the men in the room were still strong supporters of

*General Westmoreland's intelligence chief, Major General Phil Davidson, offered his own answer to President Johnson's memorable question in his memoirs: "The man who had 'poisoned the well' was, of course, Clark Clifford. . . . Clifford's use of the Wise Men to serve his dovish ends was a consummate stroke by a master of intrigue and it—more than anything else—convinced the President that he had to revise his policies on Vietnam. In a slightly blasphemous vein, what happened was that Johnson had fired a doubting Thomas (McNamara) only to replace him with a Judas."[21]

policies to contain the Soviet Union and China, and almost half of them still supported the war; opposition to the war was based solely on the belief that Vietnam was weakening us at home and in the rest of the world. And they were right.

THE FINAL DRAFTS

In just a few weeks, Harry McPherson had become one of my most trusted associates—on the White House staff, virtually the only man there with whom I could talk freely. Urging him to look for opportunities to reshape the speech from its dreadful early drafts, I suggested we work together closely in the coming days.[23]

We needed to turn the March 31 speech around. The latest draft was still a hard-line defense of the war ("Our will is being challenged. . . . We shall not quit. . . . I ask you now to support the new efforts I have described this evening . . . with determination to see this conflict through . . ."). It did not mention a bombing halt, partial or otherwise, and had a tone of belligerence that, I was certain, would cause nothing but difficulties for the President and the nation. On Wednesday, March 27, I sent McPherson a detailed set of suggested changes, and added a general comment:

> From a de-escalation standpoint, it still offers nothing. From a negotiating standpoint, it still offers nothing. The speech still locks us into a war that is pictured as being essential to our security but is not proven as being essential to our security. It offers nothing—neither hope nor plan for either victory or negotiated settlement.

Harry agreed with my reaction, but he said he was following guidance from the President and Rostow.

Thursday, March 28. Only three days remained until the speech. We met in Rusk's office at 11 A.M. for what I knew in advance would be the most critical speech-drafting session. I was beginning to despair; even the growing support for a limited bombing halt did not cheer me up, since I felt that such a step, if part of a hard-line speech, would look like another public-relations gimmick. The President had been shaken by the Wise Men, but he had not indicated any change in position. McPherson and I agreed to make an all-out effort to soften the speech and turn it around. I prepared for what I expected would be a contentious showdown with Rusk and Rostow—but it never came.

I began the meeting by stating my strong belief that the draft we were discussing was "warlike" and would, if delivered, be a disaster of the first magnitude for the President and the nation. Speaking directly to Rusk, I continued,

> I have a fundamental problem with this speech. It is still about war. What the President needs is a speech about peace. We must change it. We must take the first step toward winding down the war and reducing the level of violence. . . . I believe the first step should be an announcement that we have unilaterally restricted our bombing of the North to the area north of the DMZ. Not that we have paused, but that we have *stopped* bombing north of the 20th parallel. If there is a favorable response from the other side, we should be prepared to take other steps.

To my amazement, neither Rusk nor Rostow fought back, as they had in so many previous meetings; at the same time, though, neither said he agreed with the fundamental changes I had proposed. Instead, we began a calm and methodical exchange of what the President should accomplish with the speech. The hard-line draft lay ignored on the table. Rusk suggested we continue the discussion over luncheon in his dining room. As we ate, I looked for a way to move forward without forcing Rusk to take a clear-cut position. Finally, I had an idea: let McPherson draft a substitute, a softer speech, and let the President choose between the two. Rusk agreed; Rostow said nothing. Rusk suggested language for the new version of the speech on a partial bombing halt, to which I agreed immediately. Rusk asked Bill Bundy to prepare a message to Ellsworth Bunker informing him that we were considering a partial bombing halt, and instructing him to obtain President Thieu's agreement if necessary. It seemed clear that Rusk preferred the softer draft—although, characteristically, he refrained from saying so.

The alternative draft McPherson prepared had an entirely different tone from previous ones. This change was clear from the very first sentence, which, at my suggestion, was changed from

> I speak to you tonight in a time of grave challenge to our country

to

> Tonight I want to speak to you of the prospects for peace in Vietnam and Southeast Asia.

Rusk met alone for a few minutes with the President at eight, and told him we had decided to offer him an alternate draft which we both preferred. McPherson worked late into the evening on the new draft, sending it to the President around ten o'clock. We waited to see which version of the speech he would choose.

The next morning, shortly after ten o'clock, President Johnson called McPherson to discuss changes in the draft. As Harry began looking through the old draft for the places where the President wanted to make changes, he suddenly realized that the President was working on the alternate draft! Suppressing his excitement, he took the President's changes down one by one, but as soon as their conversation was over, Harry called me. *"We've won,"* he shouted. *"The President is working from our draft!"*

I was truly moved. The "turn toward peace" for which we had fought had been accepted. To be sure, there was still work to be done—I saw this as soon as I read Bill Bundy's telegram to Ambassador Bunker, instructing him to inform President Thieu of the new policy in the most negative way possible:

> [M]AKE CLEAR THAT HANOI IS MOST LIKELY TO DENOUNCE THE PROJECT AND THUS FREE OUR HAND AFTER A SHORT PERIOD. . . . IN VIEW OF WEATHER LIMITATIONS, BOMBING NORTH OF THE 20TH PARALLEL WILL IN ANY EVENT BE LIMITED AT LEAST FOR THE NEXT FOUR WEEKS OR SO—WHICH WE TENTATIVELY ENVISAGE AS A MAXIMUM TESTING PERIOD IN ANY EVENT. HENCE, WE ARE NOT GIVING UP ANYTHING SERIOUS IN THIS TIME FRAME. . . . INSOFAR AS OUR ANNOUNCEMENT FORESHADOWS ANY POSSIBILITY OF A COMPLETE BOMBING STOPPAGE IN THE EVENT HANOI REALLY EXERCISES RECIPROCAL RESTRAINTS, WE REGARD THIS AS UNLIKELY. . . .[24]

I was not happy with this language. It showed clearly that between State and me a large disagreement, only temporarily suppressed, still existed. But this was obviously not the moment nor the issue on which to start another argument.

Saturday March 30. "Victory" in these circumstances is a relative term and a temporary event. Several contentious issues arose during a lengthy speech review with the President, which lasted all afternoon and into the evening. Looking tired, he sat in shirtsleeves at the Cabinet table, hunched over his copy of the draft, reviewing every word. Around him were all his senior advisers, except for Rusk, who had left for New Zealand to attend the annual meeting of the foreign ministers of Australia, New Zealand, and the United States (ANZUS). Acting Secretary of State Katzenbach urged that the specific reference to the 20th parallel be replaced by language stating that the bombing would end in North Vietnam "except in the area north of the Demilitarized Zone, where the continuing enemy buildup directly threatens allied forward positions." Katzenbach's proposal, which we all accepted, was to cause a problem for us within twenty-four hours of the speech.

As the meeting was breaking up, the President asked McPherson why there was no ending to the speech. "It was too long, and it doesn't fit the speech any more," Harry replied. "I'll write a new ending that won't be so long."

"Go ahead, but don't worry about the length of it," he replied, with a knowing smile, as he headed out the door. "I may have a little ending of my own."

Harry turned to me with an astonished look. "Jesus, is he going to say sayonara?" For a moment, I did not understand what McPherson meant.

"Is he going to say good-bye tomorrow night?" Harry asked again. I looked back at him, McPherson recalled later, "with pity, as if I were too tired to be rational."

Shortly before 10 P.M., McPherson handed the President a new draft of a closing statement. He attached to it a note conveying my views, complete with a teasing attempt to capture in print my methodical speech pattern:

> Here is a closing peroration. It does not light up the sky with rockets. Clark Clifford feels strongly—I–would–say–vi–o–lent–ly—that it should *not* light up the sky. He argues that if you come on with a strong "we must resist aggression" line at the end of a peaceful initiative speech, people will say, "ah—now here comes the *real* Johnson, Old Blood and Thunder"; and that the purpose of the speech will be lost. I agree with him.

MARCH 31, 1968

Sunday, March 31. It began as the first relaxed day I had enjoyed since taking office a month earlier: the contentious preparation for the speech was finally over, the weather was mild and the sky overcast—but since it did not rain, I played golf for the first time in weeks, thinking as I played about the next steps in moving the President toward de-escalation.

Shortly before 5 P.M., the President called and asked if Marny and I would come to the White House before the speech and stay for dinner afterward. We arrived shortly after eight o'clock, and waited for a few minutes in the upstairs sitting room with the Rostows. We made the very smallest of small talk; after the previous month, Walt and I were guarded in our conversation with each other. President Johnson did not come out to greet us, however; instead, he asked his Army Sergeant to bring me into the bedroom alone.

The President was putting on a tie. He looked up, handed me a sheet of paper, and said, "I'd like you to read this—it is the ending to my speech, you have not seen it before." Nothing in my career ever surprised me so much as what I read:

> I have concluded that I should not permit the Presidency to become involved in the partisan divisions that are developing in this political year. . . . Accordingly, I shall not seek, and I will not accept, the nomination of my Party for another term as your President.

After a moment, I looked at him. "You've made up your mind?"

"Yes," he said, "I've made up my mind. Totally."

"I understand your decision, Mr. President," I said, "but that does not keep me from deeply regretting it. If this is your decision, then it becomes my decision. God bless you. I am very sorry." I shook his hand solemnly. As I left, Walt Rostow came in for a private moment with the President. I rejoined the wives, and told them the news. Tears came to Marny's eyes.

At about a quarter to nine, we gathered, burdened and subdued by the knowledge of a great secret about to become public, and made our way, almost like a funeral procession, toward the Oval Office, from which the President would speak. The President and his daughters led, followed by three aides, Jim Jones, Marvin Watson, and Walt Rostow. I walked slightly behind them with Lady Bird and Marny. When I reached the office of one of President Johnson's secretaries, Marie Fehmer, I stopped to watch the speech on her small television set. I was still having trouble believing what I was about to hear—but then, so would the rest of the nation.

When he had finished his speech, he wandered around the White House talking to people and viewing, with evident pleasure, the bewildered analysis of the commentators on television. After he took a few telephone calls from friends, he and I walked back to the family quarters together. "I never felt so right about any decision in my life," he said. A certain energy I had not seen in the past month had returned—he had, at least for a moment, regained the initiative and surprised the world.

As we talked, the President changed into a blue turtleneck shirt. Then we returned to the West Hall, where he joined the Rostows, Arthur and Mathilde Krim, and a few other friends. At 11 P.M. he held a brief press conference, stressing the finality of his decision. Then he rejoined us, making more calls and talking animatedly to everyone in sight. In one corner of the room Lady Bird sat quietly, eating dinner. Walt Rostow knelt at her side, talking softly with her. Lynda Robb came up to me to tell me how pleased she and her husband, Chuck, a Marine officer,* were that five hundred dollars of his pay was tax free because he was serving in Vietnam.

"I was never surer of any decision I ever made in my life," the President said again, "and I never made any more unselfish one. I have 525,000 men whose very lives depend on what I do, and I can't afford to worry about the primaries. Now I will be working full-time for those men out there. The only guys that won't be back here by the time my term ends are the guys that are left in the last day or two of my term."

It was after midnight. Marny and I said our good-byes and slipped out into the night. I had spent the evening in a crowd, but since the moment Lyndon Johnson had shown me his withdrawal statement almost four hours earlier, I had been alone with my thoughts.

The President had talked to me on one or two occasions about not running again in 1968. I knew he had had similar discussions with many other people, including one with Harry McPherson and Joseph Califano only a few weeks earlier. But even those who had helped him prepare the text of the withdrawal announcement—George Christian and Horace Busby—were not certain he would use it until he actually read it on television. Little wonder, then, that men like McPherson, Califano, and me had not believed President Johnson when he talked about giving up the job he had sought almost his entire life. We thought that his talk simply reflected his agony over the pressures and stress he was under.

I doubt that his intention to withdraw was firm as early as the late fall of 1967, when he discussed the issue with Westmoreland, or in January 1968, when he almost announced it during the State of the Union Address. Undoubtedly, he was considering it seriously then, even moving toward it—but he was still torn. Even as he was talking to some close advisers about withdrawing, he was involved with others in actively planning the 1968 campaign. He spent time with key advisers and fund-raisers such as Arthur Krim to discuss the details of the race. He had persuaded Charles Murphy, who had succeeded me in the Truman White House, to resign as Chairman of the Civil Aeronautics Board in order to become a special assistant at the White House working entirely on the 1968 campaign. And on the afternoon of the speech, I learned later, some of his family tried to talk him out of it at the last moment.[25]

Once I recovered from my shock, I remembered a Presidential request in the fall of 1967 to which I should have paid more attention. During a private talk one evening, President Johnson had asked me to write a memorandum concerning President Truman's decision not to run for

*Chuck Robb later became Governor and then a Senator from Virginia.

reelection in 1952. "I may do the same thing as Truman," he said, rather casually. I had prepared the memorandum for President Johnson, but I did not take seriously the possibility that he might not run in 1968. President Truman, a genuinely modest man, had renounced power with hardly a second thought. I could not then imagine Lyndon Johnson doing the same thing—but that was before Tet.

Now, reflecting on the stunning event I had just witnessed, I felt the President had made the right decision. If he had run, he would have been fully occupied in the fight for the nomination; if he had won the nomination, reelection after such a bitter internal fight would have been tough. In these unusual circumstances, it would have been difficult to campaign effectively and carry out his duties as President. His withdrawal broke the Gordian knot into which American politics in 1968 had been twisted; his sacrifice was a service to the nation. But when I had time later to reflect on the sequence of events, I had two deep regrets:

First, if he had really always intended to withdraw, as he told everyone, I wished he had done so earlier. By pulling out before his support in the polls had collapsed, he would have avoided a general impression he was driven from office by the Tet Offensive and Bobby Kennedy's entry into the race. Furthermore, by combining his withdrawal and the partial bombing halt in the same speech, President Johnson made inevitable the conclusion that both actions were caused by the same event—the Tet Offensive. Had he made the two announcements in different speeches, it would have reduced the impression that his political career had been ended by Hanoi, and perhaps strengthened him for the remainder of his term.

Second, and even more fundamentally, I felt that he had made a grievous error, and hurt himself greatly, by his decision to withhold from his closest policy advisers the fact that he was not going to run. We thought we were drafting a speech for an embattled candidate, not a man ready to sacrifice his career, in his own eyes, in pursuit of peace. We were at all times mindful of the fact that the critical primary in Wisconsin would take place two days after the speech. Had I known that the President would be a lame duck with ten months left in office, I would have argued for a full bombing cessation despite the difficulty of gaining his approval. The limited bombing halt I had supported was designed for another political scenario, and might not result in serious negotiations with Hanoi; a full bombing halt might have. With only ten months now left in his term, the President would need every day he had left in office to try to settle the war. As time passed, his political power would inevitably diminish. It is even possible that Rusk, who learned of his decision just prior to his departure for New Zealand—too late to take it into account in our deliberations—might have joined me in an effort to halt the bombing completely, if only on a trial basis. And, had Rusk and I joined forces, the President might have agreed.

Why did he not tell Rusk and me earlier? Perhaps he believed he had dropped enough hints so that we had been forewarned. Perhaps he did not tell us because he was uncertain himself until the last minute, or because he feared a leak, or because he enjoyed surprising everyone. But whatever the reason, we worked on the most important speech of the Johnson Presidency ignorant of information that would have changed at least some of our positions, and perhaps affected his own decision on the bombing.

29

The Long, Sad Summer

When the disinterested histories of the Johnson Administration come to be written 50 years from now, some of the most fascinating passages will have to do with the drama of the last few months, the civilized collision of Defense Secretary Clifford and Secretary of State Rusk.
—*The Washington Post,* JANUARY 3, 1969

WHAT HAD WE DONE? WHAT DID HANOI DO?

I left the White House on the evening of March 31 saddened for Lyndon Johnson personally, but deeply gratified that we had started on the road toward the end of the war. We had won a major victory—the end of escalation in Vietnam after a decade of a steadily increased commitment. I could not have imagined that from then on I would wage a constant struggle with some of my colleagues over Vietnam policy until the very last day of the Administration.

Despite his overwhelming personality and unique understanding of political power, Lyndon Johnson during this period often acted more like a legislative leader, seeking a consensus among people who were often irreconcilably opposed to each other, rather than a decisive Commander in Chief giving his subordinates orders. Faced with serious disagreement among his principal advisers, he approached the difficult decisions of 1968 cautiously, even hesitantly. Thus he had been much relieved when, near the end of March, Rusk, Bunker, the military, and I all agreed on a partial bombing halt.

This unity, however, masked a continuing and profound disagreement over what the President's March 31 speech meant and what our goal in Vietnam should be for the ten months remaining in Lyndon Johnson's Presidency. I believed that the stakes were transcendentally important.

During the late spring, the Administration split into two factions. In one camp were Dean Rusk, Walt Rostow, Ellsworth Bunker, Maxwell Taylor, Abe Fortas, and the entire American military command; in the other, Averell Harriman, Cyrus Vance, Nicholas Katzenbach, Arthur Goldberg, Paul Nitze, Paul Warnke, and me. Vice President Humphrey supported our group when he was consulted—which was not very often. Lyndon Johnson found himself at the center of this tug-of-war, and uncertain of what legacy he wanted to leave behind in Vietnam.

The roots of the dispute were inherent in his March 31 speech. What had Lyndon Johnson intended? Had he deliberately sacrificed his political career in order to seek an end to the war; or had he put forward a series of half measures designed to shore up domestic support, at a lower cost, without changing our objective in Vietnam? Did he know himself what his objective was?

There will always be disagreement on this complex and elusive question. I suspect that, in the inner recesses of his own mind, Lyndon Johnson was torn between a search for an honorable exit and his desire not to be the first President to lose a foreign war. Thus, during the remainder of his Presidency, he sent conflicting signals and possibly lost the opportunity to end the war during his term in office.

His speech was ambiguous. On one hand, none of its policy announcements were entirely new—limited bombing halts had been tried before, and there was nothing promising about a call-up of some Reserves. On the other, the tone and rhetoric of the speech, especially coupled with his withdrawal, was significantly more moderate than any other recent Presidential statement or speech. Rusk, Bunker, Rostow, and the military felt we had gone as far as we needed to in order to shore up domestic support for the war, and did not wish to show any additional enthusiasm for negotiations, for fear that we would weaken the Saigon government. I, however, wanted the speech to mark the beginning of an intensive search for a settlement of the war.

The day after the speech, American planes bombed Thanh Hoa, an important transfer point just south of the 20th parallel. This bombing fell within the unpublicized guidelines established by the President, but just barely—Thanh Hoa lay 205 miles north of the DMZ separating the two Vietnams. It produced an immediate uproar from people who felt the President had misled them into thinking the bombing would be restricted to a relatively small area just north of the DMZ. Senator Fulbright led the attack, even though I had told him the day before the speech that we would continue bombing up to the 20th parallel. He angrily charged on April 1 that, in light of Thanh Hoa, the speech constituted at best a "very limited change in existing policy." Other members of Congress and commentators joined in the attack.

We met April 2 to discuss the problem. The President lashed out furiously at Fulbright and other members of Congress "who start attacking us even before the communists do." Trapped by the uproar caused by the ambiguous wording of his speech, however, he decided to restrict the bombing still further, to the area north of the 19th parallel instead of the 20th, in order to bring policy back into line with rhetoric.

On the morning of April 3, 1968, the debate over the speech was swept aside by a stunning event that almost no one in Washington had expected: a message from North Vietnam, broadcast over Radio Hanoi. It began with a lengthy denunciation of the U.S. but contained the following sentence:

> However, on its part, the [Democratic Republic of Vietnam] government declares its readiness to send its representatives to make contact with U.S. representatives to decide with the U.S. side the unconditional cessation of bombing and all other war acts against the DRV so that talks could begin.

Hanoi's statement did not mention the President's March 31 speech, and, furthermore, it explicitly restricted any discussions with the U.S. to the subject of our "unconditional" cessation of the bombing of the rest of North Vietnam. It did not constitute an agreement to talk about ending the war. Nonetheless, it was the first time Hanoi had offered to meet with us on any basis at all, and for that reason alone, the statement created enormous worldwide excitement.

An argument, unfortunately foreshadowing many more along similar lines, immediately broke out among the President's senior advisers over how to respond to Hanoi. Harriman wanted to respond immediately so as to avoid "the public appearance of hesitancy." Rostow suggested we "improve the pace of the negotiations by military means"—that is, increase the level of American military activity—but the President rejected this. "It's easier to satisfy Ho Chi Minh than Bill Fulbright," he noted bitterly.[1] Ambivalent and wary, he warned against letting the public get its hopes up too high; but he wanted to respond during the same news cycle, so that the evening television news programs would carry not only Hanoi's offer but Washington's response. He asked Katzenbach and me to draft a statement that could be issued immediately.

Shortly after 5 P.M., the President walked into the West Lobby and read a short statement we had drafted reiterating the Administration's readiness "to send its representatives to any forum, at any time" to discuss ending the war. Less than seventy-two hours had elapsed since he had made his speech from the Oval Office.

At first, I assumed Hanoi's message was a direct response to the President's speech, but later I realized that this was probably not the case. Students of Hanoi's negotiating style pointed out that it would have been unusual for the North Vietnamese, with their methodical and collegial decision-making structure, to have responded so quickly. It is more likely that they had already decided to make a move of their own—and there is some evidence that this was in fact the case. Prior to the speech, the North Vietnamese had summoned to Hanoi several journalists, including Charles Collingwood of CBS, to hear an announcement of "international importance" on April 2. That statement was never issued. It seems probable that Hanoi's April 3 announcement was similar to the statement they had previously promised Collingwood.

If Hanoi had in fact intended to make an announcement, some may argue that the President's March 31 decisions were unnecessary. I do not agree. The importance of the March 31 speech was not its effect on Hanoi but its effect on the U.S.: it marked the end of the era of escalation, and the first step, however ambiguous, toward de-escalation and disengagement.

TRAGEDY IN MEMPHIS; ARGUMENTS OVER WHERE TO MEET

In his speech, the President had announced that if North Vietnam began talks with us, our negotiators would be Averell Harriman and the American Ambassador to the Soviet Union, Llewellyn Thompson, a Soviet expert who was very close to Rusk. After Harriman argued on April 3 for further de-escalatory steps in Vietnam, the President became concerned that he might be excessively conciliatory. (Taylor, who shared this view, even sent the President a memorandum after the meeting suggesting I replace Harriman as chief negotiator while remaining Secretary of Defense—an unworkable idea, but indicative of the distrust that Harriman had engendered among some of his hard-line colleagues.) When Rusk said that, in light of our efforts to get arms control discussions with the Soviets started (see Chapter 30), Thompson could not be spared from his Moscow post, the President decided to send Cyrus Vance to Paris as Harriman's conegotiator. So great were Vance's personal skills that he was able to maintain the trust of both Harriman and Johnson during the remainder of the year, even though the two men disagreed on almost every aspect of the negotiations.

On April 4, the day we began preparations for the talks, a great national tragedy occurred—the assassination of Martin Luther King, Jr. I had never met Dr. King, but I respected enormously what he had accomplished and stood for—both in the civil rights movement and in his early and strong opposition to the war. His death was an indescribable loss to the nation, and it set off, within hours, riots, followed by arson and looting, in Washington and 110 other cities across the nation. Before the riots ended, at least 39 people, mostly black, had been killed, and over 2,500 injured. For a moment, even Vietnam seemed to fade into the background. The riots required a federal response. Before they had died down, more than 75,000 National Guardsmen and regular military units had been sent into the streets of American cities. The Pentagon was heavily involved in every aspect of these events, and I found myself shuttling between meetings on Vietnam and emergency sessions on the riots in urban America.

Only two months after Tet, it seemed as if we were experiencing our own national uprising. As I drove from my house to the Pentagon the morning after Dr. King's death, I could see the smoke rising from the inner city, only ten blocks from the White House. Later that morning, only seventeen hours after Dr. King's death, I joined the President in a somber but emotional meeting with some of the nation's black leaders, including Roy Wilkins, Whitney Young, Jr., and Washington Mayor Walter Washington. During the meeting, President Johnson told them he would press for immediate passage of the long-stalled open housing bill as a tribute to Dr. King. The bill would pass both houses of Congress within a week, but it would be overshadowed by the fires burning across the land.

The following day, I sat with President Johnson at a moving memorial service at Washington National Cathedral, where Dr. King had preached the last Sunday sermon of his life only days earlier. On April 7, I joined the President in a helicopter survey of the riot damage in Washington, flying over streets that had been aflame only a day earlier. Federal troops were patrolling below us, and smoke still curled upward from the streets.

President Johnson had planned to fly to Honolulu during the first week of April to consult with General Westmoreland, who was still in command in Vietnam. Canceling this plan as soon as Dr. King was killed, he asked Westmoreland to fly to Washington instead. When the General arrived in Washington on April 6, he presented a glowing picture of confidence: "In the negotiations," Westmoreland said, stressing every word, "Governor Harriman will have a hand with four aces and the enemy will have two deuces."

"Under what conditions," I asked Westmoreland, "would a cease-fire be acceptable?" His reply alarmed me, showing how entrenched and unrealistic he was: "I do not see any acceptable cease-fire," he said. "We would just like the North Vietnamese to go home and turn in their weapons."

The day after Westmoreland left Washington the President commented almost sympathetically on Westmoreland's behavior during his visit. "Westy is bitter," Johnson observed. "He feels he has been made the goat of Tet and is being recalled because he got no support in Washington."[2]

The mood in Washington was ugly in the wake of the riots, and the pressure finally drove President Johnson to Camp David for a respite on the evening of Monday, April 8. The next day, Rusk, Wheeler, and I flew there with Ellsworth Bunker, who had just arrived from Saigon; at luncheon we were joined by Bill Bundy and Averell Harriman.

Ellsworth Bunker was a man with a style that bespoke the world of old New England. Tall, thin, and quiet-spoken, he was courteous and gentle at all times, no matter what the circumstances. A member of that group of Easterners who had dominated America's postwar foreign policy, Bunker had attended Yale at the same time as Harriman and Acheson, and, after a thirty-five year career in business, had been sent by Acheson to Argentina as Ambassador in 1951. He became a skilled professional diplomat, serving every President from Truman through Carter in senior posts.

He could not have been more different from Lyndon Johnson in style and background, but between the Texan and the New Englander there was a real affection—made the greater when, after the death of his first wife, Bunker married Carol Laise, an outstanding career Foreign Service Officer who was Ambassador to Nepal. This unique situation—two serving Ambassadors married to each other—pleased Johnson a great deal, and he took a special interest in seeing that they were able to spend time together. Bunker's age, combined with his firm but dignified demeanor, gave his presentations great force and credibility with President Johnson and Dean Rusk.

At seventy-four, Bunker was the oldest serving Ambassador in the world, older than anyone in the Cabinet, younger only than Averell Harriman (by two years). Yet he was holding down a job far more demanding than most Cabinet posts. He worked very hard, but at his age, working in the debilitating tropical climate of Southeast Asia, he had to choose his priorities carefully. In the absence of deep knowledge of either Vietnam or guerrilla warfare, he fell back on a simple position: if the flag is being shot at, we must rally behind our country. As the year wore on, Bunker was often to play the pivotal role in the three-ring circus between Washington, the Saigon government, and the negotiators in Paris—almost always, in my opinion, to the detriment of progress toward peace.

His style and Rusk's unswerving support made it extremely difficult to argue directly with him, especially in front of the President. In my limited previous contact with Bunker, I had always held him in high regard. Even when we disagreed, I still liked him and regarded him as a great patriot.

But during that April 9 meeting at Camp David, I realized that Bunker and I were never going to be on the same wavelength as far as Vietnam was concerned, and that his views would be a serious problem to those seeking to end the war.

Bunker told the President that the pacification program had been badly hurt by the Tet Offensive, although not so badly as stated in the press. Like Westmoreland, he felt that the press had badly misreported the outcome of the great battle. "In fact," he said, "we go into the negotiations from a position of strength." He stated that President Thieu was expecting another enemy offensive between May and October—an accurate prediction, as it turned out, of the offensive that took place in May. In a less accurate assessment, Bunker was also upbeat about Thieu, whom he said was now "acting like a leader." Finally, to my dismay, Bunker said we should move as slowly as possible in the negotiations. "Saigon is not at all ready," he said.

Supporting Bunker, Rusk said Hanoi's objective was to end all the bombing of the North. He predicted the first phase of the talks would be very tough: "We have to hang in there. Either get them to make concessions or get them to take the responsibility for breaking off the talks."

"Would they have made their feelers if we had not made our speech?" the President asked. "The quickness with which they responded, plus their invitations to Collingwood and the others, indicates they might have had in mind doing something, but probably not what has resulted. What happens if they are just fooling around with us?" I was ready for this question. "In that case," I replied, "Bus Wheeler and I will have some choice targets in the North ready for you." But I thought: *I will do everything possible to avoid having to make* that *recommendation.*

There was one problem: we had still not agreed on a negotiating site. On April 4, the President had proposed that talks begin in Geneva on April 8. At almost exactly the same time, Hanoi sent a message through Collingwood and two other Americans proposing that contacts begin at the Ambassadorial level in Phnom Penh, the capital of Cambodia. We had no embassy or representation in Cambodia, and this confronted us with the first dilemma of the new era of "dialogue" between Washington and Hanoi. Public pressure was beginning to build on the President to fulfill his pledge to go "anywhere, anytime" to meet with the representatives of Hanoi. This did not overly disturb me; I was confident we would reach an agreement with Hanoi on the site fairly soon.

THE FIRST PRESS CONFERENCE: SETTING LIMITS IN VIETNAM

I had avoided a formal press conference all during March, but my public affairs chief, Phil Goulding, felt it essential that I discuss the military aspects of the speech with the press. The President agreed, and Goulding scheduled a meeting with the press for April 11 at 10 A.M.

In considering ways to move our policy in Vietnam, I had already concluded that press conferences and Congressional testimony were generally more productive than formal speeches. This had been true during my confirmation hearings, when I had advanced our negotiating position during the discussion of the San Antonio formula. I hoped to repeat the same pattern occasionally in press conferences. Phil Goulding, who was responsible for preparing my press guidance, later wrote an accurate description of my method:

> Not once did [Clifford] oppose the President publicly. Not once did he suggest error in a past Presidential decision. Not once did he undercut a move the President was making or contemplating. And on every occasion possible he presented the President as the man in the world who had given more of himself to the quest for peace than any other. . . . Clark Clifford consistently . . . moved in public to occupy the ground the President had not yet reached.[3]

A Cabinet member must never contradict the President or undercut him in any way, but a President needs Cabinet members to clear a path ahead of him on delicate policy issues, testing public reaction. I was ready, at any time, to pull back or retract a statement if the President told me to—but he never did. While the previous warmth of our relationship took on a wary and guarded tone, he never criticized my positions directly.

The 8:30 Group—Nitze, Warnke, Goulding, Elsey, and Pursley—met for several hours before the press conference, reviewing press guidance. My press conference would allow me to focus on a critical issue: would we send any more troops to Vietnam after the small increment announced by the President on March 31?

In a background session on April 1 with a few Pentagon reporters I had mentioned a "limitation" on deployments to Vietnam. Although the President had not used similar language in public, I felt comfortable that my statement was consistent with his private views, as stated on the evening of March 31 and thereafter. There had been no reaction from the White House after my backgrounder, so I decided to repeat my point in public, using language that would not preclude the President's ability or right to send more troops at a later date, but suggesting strongly that we would send no more troops beyond the limited number already announced. In the same press conference, I decided to stress our intention to shift the burden of the war back to the South Vietnamese. My colleagues and I called this "de-Americanization." (A year later, my successor, Melvin Laird, would carry this theme further, and rename it "Vietnamization.")

I began the press conference by disclosing that the Reserve call-up previously announced would total 24,500 Reserves, 10,000 of whom would go directly to Vietnam. The first question concerned this deployment. In reply, I made two references to a troop ceiling, and linked it to an increased combat role for the South Vietnamese:

> I might add also in that regard that when these additional forces go, the total . . . in South Vietnam will be brought up to some 549,500, and it is the President's intention at this time not to increase those forces. . . . I would visualize that when the South Vietnamese troops were ready, they could be moved into areas where combat was taking place so that they could supplant some of the American troops . . . [who] might be drawn back in reserve. . . . This is part and parcel, I believe, of the President's decision to place a limitation at this time upon our troop level at a point not exceeding 550,000.

I had carefully qualified my statement with the words "at this time" twice. This phrase was ignored by the press, but *The New York Times*'s three-column headline captured my three objectives almost perfectly, announcing: U.S. CALLS 24,500 RESERVES; SETS G.I. CEILING AT 549,500, GIVING SAIGON MAJOR ROLE. *The Washington Post* called the announcement that we were shifting the burden back to the South Vietnamese a "monumental decision."

After my press conference, the overheated Washington grapevine was filled with rumors, some of which reached me, that the President had not been pleased by my statements, but I ignored the gossip. If he wished me to change my behavior, I knew he would inform me. I was to repeat my comments on a troop ceiling on April 22, June 20, and August 15, dropping the qualifying phrase "at this time" after the second press conference. He never objected.

The number of American soldiers in Vietnam was never to exceed the ceiling I had announced on April 11. Through repetition and lack of contradiction, my interpretation of the President's policy became the policy itself. Perhaps because he wished to maintain the support of the military, President Johnson had never made a similar statement, but it stood as policy, eventually confirmed by the White House.

My press conference surprised many people in Washington who had been unaware of my position during the battle over the President's March 31 speech. Under the headline CLIFFORD EMERGES AS THE PRESIDENT'S CHIEF SPOKESMAN ON VIETNAM; HIS MODERATE VIEWS COME AS SURPRISE TO CAPITAL, Neil Sheehan of *The New York Times* called me "the surprise of Washington." "Mr. Clifford," he wrote, "has spoken of Vietnam in terms of disengagement, accommodation, and a negotiated peace. . . . He has emerged as a new voice with a different approach."[4]

DEAN RUSK AND THE PARIS PEACE TALKS

As we prepared for the negotiations with North Vietnam, we could not ignore the upheaval taking place outside and the growing sense of social and political crisis. On April 23, a student uprising at Columbia University began a new cycle of violence on the campuses of America, which would spread overseas, to France and other parts of Europe.

Meanwhile, for close to a month the dance went on over where the peace talks would take place. A grand total of fifteen cities—as well as an Indonesian ship, the most inventive and, from the point of view of comfort, least attractive proposal—were eventually thrown into the discussion. But we deliberately kept one obvious choice, Paris, a city with which the Vietnamese were very familiar from their days as a French colony, off the list, hoping that if we did not suggest it, Hanoi eventually would. Our plan worked: after a month of sterile exchanges, on May 3, they offered to meet us in Paris a week later. The next morning, after middle-of-the-night telephone discussions between the President, Rusk, Rostow, and me, President Johnson went before the television cameras to announce the agreement.

As soon as a date and site had been selected, I noticed an unmistakeable hardening of Rusk and Rostow's position on the negotiations themselves. On May 6, I remarked to my colleagues in the 8:30 Group that I feared those closest to the President were turning against any compromise with Hanoi.

Late that day, I attended a frustrating meeting at the White House with our chief negotiators. Neither the President nor Rusk seemed to want to address pressing issues. "Suppose Hanoi says they want an agreement on stopping the bombing, and will discuss nothing else until that is done," I asked. "This is a real issue. Let's face this very real possibility." Rusk, however, immediately shifted the discussion toward other matters—the mutual withdrawal of forces, amnesty, the history of our earlier negotiating positions. I felt that such issues as these while important, were not going to be discussed in Paris until the bombing question was settled.

The next day, May 7, we met again with Harriman and Vance. Rusk pressed for an uncompromising opening position, saying we should press for more than what he deliberately called the "Clifford formula" in an effort to distinguish it from the San Antonio formula. Rusk wanted to tell Hanoi that the bombing would stop if *and only if* we knew in advance that North Vietnamese infiltration into the South would cease. This would constitute a significant retreat from the San Antonio formula as I had presented it in January, and I objected strongly.

Rusk was not simply being stubborn. Behind this—and many other—disagreements lay a fundamental and still unresolved question: what was our objective in Vietnam? He believed strongly in taking a tough initial line in any negotiations with communists, and holding to it indefinitely. He had spent many hours over many years across the table from such tough adversaries as Soviet Foreign Minister Andrei Gromyko, holding to his position as the Soviets clung to theirs. He had many examples, drawn from his own experiences since the end of World War II, of the perfidy and dishonesty of communist negotiators from Korea to Berlin.

As a general principle, I agreed with Rusk's view of communist negotiating techniques and ethics; indeed, as I sometimes pointed out, I had produced one of the earliest American government documents describing these techniques—the Clifford-Elsey report of 1946. But Rusk and I differed profoundly over how Vietnam fit into this pattern, and what our goal should be in the limited time left to the Johnson Administration. I had concluded that our objective should be to extricate our country from Vietnam before the end of the year, but Rusk did not agree. To him, the talks in Paris were simply another chapter in the long twilight struggle with communism throughout the world. He was unwilling to consider even as a possibility what I viewed as a fact—that the war was not an integral part of that worldwide struggle, and that our obsession with Vietnam was weakening us elsewhere in the world.

In our disputes, which grew in frequency and intensity during the summer, Rusk and I never raised our voices, and never attacked each other personally. We maintained a proper, if cool, personal relationship. But our substantive and stylistic differences, were deep—they went back as far as the forties, when we diverged over the question of a Jewish state in Palestine. Dean thought politics played too large a role in the positions I took on issues; I felt that domestic politics was a legitimate and unavoidable part of a successful policy.

Rusk was so determined to prevent any premature movement in Paris that he instructed the negotiating team not to discuss, or even prepare, fallback positions, or to look for possible areas of compromise with Hanoi, even as contingencies. He told Harriman and Vance to stick to their opening positions until instructed differently. Harriman—who had negotiated with Trotsky and every other Soviet leader except Lenin—was outraged at what he regarded as the excessive specificity and rigidity of these instructions. "When I went to Moscow in 1942," he told me angrily, "Roosevelt simply instructed me to accompany Churchill and explain our position to Stalin. I had no further guidance, I didn't need any then—*and I don't need any now!*"

On May 8, the President met with Harriman one last time to go over his instructions. Whatever lay ahead, the bureaucratic battles of the previous weeks had, at least, produced a reasonable compromise on our opening position. Harriman and Vance were given four negotiating objectives: first, "prompt and serious substantive talks looking toward peace in Vietnam, in the course of which an understanding may be reached on a cessation of bombing in the North under circumstances which would not be militarily disadvantageous"; second, the creation of some control mechanism to oversee any peace or cease-fire; third, the reestablishment of the DMZ as a genuine boundary; and fourth, the full involvement of the government of the Republic of Vietnam in any talks on the future of South Vietnam.

At the May 8 meeting another battle broke out between Rusk and me over the bombing. Rusk wanted to resume air strikes between the 19th and 20th parallels. I opposed this on the grounds that it was wrong to escalate our military activity on the eve of the Paris talks. The President agreed with me, but the issue was hardly dead. A week later, Rostow and Wheeler joined Rusk in raising the issue at the Tuesday Lunch. I stood my ground, arguing again that it made no sense to increase the bombing just as the talks in Paris were beginning, and again the President rejected Rusk's proposal; but he was upset that such a strong argument had broken out between his two top Cabinet members so soon after his withdrawal from the 1968 election. Deeply disturbed, he made an astonishing remark: "Sometimes I wonder if I should have made my speech on March 31 at all."

During that same meeting White House note-taker Tom Johnson recorded an exchange that showed how tense relations between Rusk and me had become:

> CLIFFORD: I have to appear on Friday before the Senate Foreign Relations Committee. They will want to get into sensitive areas.
>
> RUSK: I would just memorize the March 31 speech and not go beyond it.
>
> CLIFFORD: [You mean] I can't go into the San Antonio formula?
>
> RUSK: I would say to them what I have said to newsmen: "I [see] no point in my negotiating with you. We are trying to negotiate with Hanoi in Paris."

The mood in this meeting depressed me profoundly. Three days later, on Saturday, May 18, I closeted myself for the morning with Warnke, Elsey, and Colonel Pursley. Cautioning them that not a word of what we were about to discuss could leave the room, I expressed my deepest feelings to them. George Elsey, who made a record of my comments, later called this "Clifford's soliloquy":

> One reason why we have got our way [so far] on not resuming the bombing between the 19th and the 20th parallels was that I was well-prepared. Bus Wheeler said to me after the meeting was over, "I should have gone to law school instead of West Point." The next issue will be more basic: what is the future of the war in Vietnam? Rusk and Rostow are taking a very hard position, saying we must stay until we succeed militarily. This appeals to the President's "coonskin on the wall" mentality. It bothers him to have to side with me when Rusk, Rostow, and Wheeler are all against me. We are approaching the time when we will have to talk these things out like they have never been discussed before. . . . I must be prepared for such a meeting with a logical, airtight presentation. . . .
>
> If the President thinks he must stick to the search for a military victory, then there is no end to this war. . . . We have made more headway toward peace in the last three months than in the entire previous year. I think we can say that we made it around second base on March 31. But at the last Tuesday Lunch, the President worried about whether or not he should have even made that speech! . . . I want to impress upon the President that our posture is basically so impossible that we have got to find some way out. . . . We should come up with a memo that makes the case for a disengagement on our part as a matter of transcendent importance for this country. I know that the President is not going to be willing to settle the war by taking a terrible licking.[5]

A few days later, Warnke and Pursley responded to my request with a long and tightly reasoned memorandum. They pointed out that the absence of the "general uprising" predicted by the communists marked a significant failure of Hanoi's plans. They also noted that the communists were paying a fearful price for their efforts. This view, though, was overshadowed by a CIA assessment that Hanoi would be willing to pay this price for far longer than the American public would be willing to exact it. Warnke and Pursley drew particular attention to the CIA's judgment that Hanoi could receive sufficient military and economic assistance even if we mined the major harbors of North Vietnam, including the main port of Haiphong.

There was also more bad news in the pacification program. Even the usually optimistic Ambassador Bunker had reported to the President in a personal message on May 23 that

> SOMETIMES WE TEND TO OVERLOOK HOW MUCH CONTROL THE ENEMY ALREADY HAS OVER THE COUNTRYSIDE, ESPECIALLY SINCE TET. REGRESSION IN THE HAMLETS HAS BEEN SERIOUS. . . . SATISFACTORY PROGRESS IS HARD TO COME BY. . . .

The Warnke-Pursley memorandum argued that we could achieve our objective without seeking a clear-cut military victory:

> We should be able to contract our activities and still make it clear to the enemy that he cannot win. This is the best posture from which to negotiate an acceptable settlement or, if this proves unattainable, to buy for South Vietnam the time necessary for its government and armed forces to take over their own defense.[6]

This valuable memorandum, which I kept on my desk for the rest of the summer, made great sense to me; but I knew that at such a late date, the Administration lacked both the internal unity and the political will to adopt such a strategy. When I turned the Pentagon over to my successor, Melvin Laird, in January 1969, Warnke and Pursley gave him an updated version of their memorandum, which he used to help develop the policy of Vietnamization. (Wisely, he also retained Pursley as his military assistant, and asked Warnke to stay on for a transitional period.)

The Tuesday Lunch on May 21 was grim. Rusk began by suggesting again that we resume bombing up to the 20th parallel, while I continued to argue strongly against the expansion of the bombing: "If we escalate again," I said, "it will diminish the chance of success in Paris, and it would be catastrophic if Paris broke up and we had to go back to a purely military policy."

"Why is that so bad?" the President asked.

"It's bad," I replied slowly, "because we will lose more boys than ever before, and because I don't think we can win the war by military means."

The President seemed annoyed: "What do you mean?"

This was neither the ideal time nor the place to open a discussion of such basic questions, but I no longer had any choice; the dispute with Rusk over the bombing had forced me into areas of discussion I had originally planned to discuss only in private. I had to reveal the depths of my doubts to the President in front of three powerful opponents—Rusk, Rostow, and Wheeler:

> With the limitations now placed on our military, which I do not oppose—no invasion of the North, no mining of the harbors, no invasion of the sanctuaries—we have no real plans or chance to win the war. Our hopes must go with Paris. . . . In the fall of 1967, the North Vietnamese decided that their earlier plans were no good. They put in their stack; that was Tet. They didn't win, but they can still control the situation in the South: they can hit and run, they can attack the cities, they can control the level of casualties. Now, they may have concluded it is a good time to have a political settlement. They can't win the war militarily. But we can't win the war militarily.

"I disagree," said President Johnson, turning to General Wheeler for a comment. Quietly, Wheeler said, "I disagree to some extent." Rusk, showing greater emotion than I had ever seen before, turned toward me: "We sought to keep North Vietnam from overtaking South Vietnam with force. We have succeeded. We win when they know they can't win."

Determined not to yield, I replied:

> Hanoi cannot win the war militarily—they know that, we know that. But that doesn't mean we can win it. If Paris does not come off, we will be back where we were before. The CIA says they are not running out of manpower. They can continue at their present rate indefinitely. The Soviets and the Chinese will continue to help them. . . . Can anybody here tell me what our plan is if the Paris talks fail? If Paris fails, we have no alternative but to turn back to the military—and they have no plan to bring it to an end.[7]

Listening wearily to the arguments between Rusk and me, the President finally said, "I will put it [the expansion of the bombing] off again against my better judgement." Looking directly at me, he added grimly, "You're just carrying me along week-to-week on this one."

A few hours later, Rusk called me and, for the first time since I had become Secretary of Defense, asked to meet with me privately when it was convenient. When we met in his office three days later, there was none of the emotion that both of us had shown two days earlier. Rusk talked only about the need to bomb as far north as the 20th parallel. I listened to his suggestion that we send a few unannounced sorties north of the 19th parallel, and told him I still opposed the idea. Whatever his intention when he had asked for the meeting, he had decided he did not want to discuss any of the fundamental issues separating us. I saw no reason to raise them; I knew I could not convince him to change either his views or his style. From my point of view, the struggle was for the President's mind and heart, and Dean was always going to oppose me.

Nothing was happening in Paris, while in Vietnam, the communists launched a second wave of attacks, quickly dubbed the "mini–Tet Offensive." American casualties rose to an all-time high during the second week in May—562 killed, over 2,000 wounded. The pressure to bomb north of the 19th parallel increased once again.

Some of my colleagues, including Rusk, felt that in these circumstances the Paris talks hurt us. I believed that the opposite was true: even if we made no progress, we still gained more than Hanoi from the talks, as long as we continued to take a more reasonable position than they. Hanoi's continued insistence, for example, that there were no North Vietnamese troops in the South only made them look ridiculous in the eyes of the world. Furthermore, I believed that the concentrated air campaign aimed at interdicting supplies from the North was more effective than our previous bombing program of scattered major targets in the North. "I believe something important will come out of Paris," I said, "if we keep the talks going until after the end of the Democratic Convention."

I suggested we call Vance back from Paris to get his views. He returned to Washington May 27, and for the next three days he stayed at the White House and sat in on every meeting. He was extremely negative about any expansion of the bombing. With his calm, methodical, unemotional style, he had an enormous effect on the discussions, visibly cooling down the hawks around the table. For the first time in almost two months I had an influential ally. After the first day of meetings, I half-jokingly told him he should come home much more often, as "it makes it so much less lonely for me here."

In private, I explained to Vance why I opposed the relatively small step of bombing between the 19th and 20th parallels with such vigor: those supporting it, I said, would push for continued re-escalation if they got this first step.

Vance, backed by a cable from Harriman, succeeded in persuading Johnson to postpone any decision to move the bombing north to the 20th parallel again. The issue, though, was far from resolved in the President's mind.

A PROBLEM WITH GENERAL ABRAMS

In June, just before General Abrams was scheduled to take over the command in Saigon, I had a wholly unexpected argument with him, which raised the question of whether to reconsider his new assignment.

The incident, which never became public, was rooted in a field report from a young civilian named Charles Sweet, who worked for a special section of the Embassy run by the near-legendary guerrilla warfare expert, Edward Lansdale. Sweet's report described the "bitterly resentful" attitude of the local population toward the Americans for some of the death and destruction that had occurred in the countryside since Tet. It was short and hardly exceptional; such reports had been filed regularly by Embassy officers who had made field trips to the provinces. But because it described a pattern of activity by some American troops that had also come under some public criticism, it resonated with both the President and me.

I sent Sweet's memorandum to General Wheeler, noting that we must find a way to reduce civilian deaths without increasing American casualties. Wheeler forwarded my request to Abrams, adding his own observation that the issue was causing "very real concern" at high levels—a vague reference to the President—and "bad play in the news media."

In a rambling, emotional, and angry reply, Abrams objected not only to the content of the message but, apparently, to the authority of the Embassy to forward reports to Washington without his approval:

> THE COMMON US EFFORT IN [SOUTH VIETNAM], AS WELL AS THE ROLE OF [THE MILITARY], IS SERVED RATHER BADLY BY RAW DATA SENT DIRECTLY BACK TO WASHINGTON BY OTHER AGENCIES, AND GIVEN THE AUTHENTICITY OF CAREFUL, PROFESSIONAL WORK. I PREFER THAT SUCH REPORTING BE CAREFULLY EVALUATED BEFORE IT IS FLOATED AS AN OFFICIAL PAPER. WE HAVE NOTHING TO HIDE BUT NEITHER SHOULD WE BE CONSTANTLY ON THE REBUTTAL. . . . WHILE I DO NOT HAVE THE BENEFITS OF TV AND NEWSPAPERS THAT ARE AVAILABLE IN WASHINGTON, I LIVE HERE. I RIDE OVER THE CITY IN A HELICOPTER AND SEE PARTS BURNING. I WALK IN THE STREETS AND SEE THE DESTRUCTION. I WALK AMONG REFUGEES OVERWHELMED WITH THE PERSONAL DISASTER THAT HAS BEEN THEIR LOT; I VISIT AMONG THE DOG-TIRED AND GRIMY SOLDIERS WHO HAVE SURVIVED THE FIGHT. . . . I HAVE HAD TWO SONS SERVING HERE, ONE OF WHOM IS HERE NOW AND EXTENDING. IF SOMEHOW A SENSING HAS DEVELOPED THAT I HAVE BEEN IN TOO MANY WARS TO BE CONCERNED AND SENSITIVE TO ITS PAIN . . . LET ME SET THE RECORD STRAIGHT. . . . I LIVE WITH IT TWENTY-FOUR HOURS A DAY.[8]

The tone of Abrams's reply disturbed me. Did it indicate that Abrams was emotionally overwrought or potentially insubordinate? In theory, it was not too late to choose someone else to replace Westmoreland, although such a move would cause a major public-relations problem. On June 7 and 8, the President and I discussed Abrams's message and agreed it was unacceptable and required a frank reply. On June 8, I sent General Wheeler a memorandum stating that "I would be less than candid if I did not inform you that General Abrams's message has caused me real uneasiness." I went on:

> The phrasing of his statement and the context in which he placed it could lead to the implication that the military commander believes he should be the one to evaluate reports being sent by the Embassy to the Department of State. I would hope that General Abrams intended no such implications. . . . Am I to interpret [his message] to mean that I am not to ask him to look into an appropriate matter, or to investigate a situation, or to consider other ways of accomplishing the national purpose?

Abrams replied to my memorandum the next day with a full apology:

> I RECOGNIZE AMBASSADOR BUNKER AND AMBASSADOR BERGER AS THE SENIOR U.S. GOVERNMENT REPRESENTATIVES HERE. I AM WRONG IN THE STATEMENT [THAT I CANNOT BE] "CONSTANTLY ON THE REBUTTAL." THE COMMAND HAS IN FACT BENEFITTED FROM THE INVESTIGATION GROWING OUT OF THE SWEET REPORT. . . . IT IS MY INTENTION TO CARRY OUT THIS ASSIGNMENT WITHIN THE PARAMETERS OF POLICY AND COMMAND LINES ALREADY ESTABLISHED. . . . MY INTENTION IS TO DO THIS WITHOUT CREATING INTERNAL STRAINS OR EXTERNAL FIREWORKS.[9]

With this the storm blew over—General Abrams and I never had another problem. Later, I realized that his undiplomatic language was in fact a result of the same blunt, aggressive style that made him such a fine military commander. It had been important, however, to make clear to him at the beginning of his command that he was a part of a combined civilian-military mission which was not under his control, and that he must be responsive both to the Ambassador and to Washington. It was a lesson that would be vitally important in the month of October, when we faced the final, and most critical, set of decisions of the Johnson Administration.

THE DEATH OF ROBERT F. KENNEDY

And then, in an era of tragedies, yet another one enveloped the nation. On June 4, Robert F. Kennedy was shot and killed just after he had won the California Presidential primary. Once again, we were plunged into a period of national shock and grief. In personal terms, his death ended one of the most complicated relationships of my life. How could fate and history have bound me so closely to one brother and left such a strain with the other, when the two men had been so close to each other? I thought back to our last meeting less than three months earlier, which had ended with his fateful decision to run. I remembered the many occasions when John F. Kennedy had deliberately called me to the White House to argue some legal issue with the Attorney General. I thought back to the unsuccessful effort I had made, at Jack Kennedy's direction, to persuade his father that Bobby should not become Attorney General. In retrospect, I could see that, while I still felt my grounds for opposing the appointment had been entirely correct, Bobby had done an outstanding job at the Justice Department, assembling the finest team of lawyers I ever saw there. Bobby's friends—many also close friends of mine—had told me of his extraordinary growth as a human being in the last few years of his life, but I had not had occasion to witness this personally. Now history had closed its books on this remarkable man.

I regretted that Bobby Kennedy did not live long enough for us to reconcile. Even when our relationship was shadowed by tension, I recognized his unique value to President Kennedy, and his utterly single-minded devotion to his brother's career. In several crises, including the civil rights showdowns in the South and the Cuban Missile Crisis, he performed superbly. Sadly, though, sometimes circumstances cast people into hostile relationships that seem incapable of being corrected. This was the case with Robert F. Kennedy and me.

Lyndon Johnson's feelings about Bobby's death were complex. More deeply than before, Lyndon Johnson feared that history would always trap him between the martyred Kennedys. He had truly felt grief for the family of Jack Kennedy in 1963, and treated Jackie Kennedy with great courtesy. This was not true with regard to Bobby Kennedy's family.

At President Johnson's request, I went to the White House at about 6:30 P.M. on June 5 and stayed with him for the rest of the evening. At first, he did not wish to go on television to discuss the shooting in Los Angeles; perhaps, he said, a statement issued in his name would be sufficient. Every adviser in the room urged him to speak for himself; we pointed out that he had spoken after the death of Martin Luther King, Jr., and that not to do so now would seem small-minded. He *had* to set aside his own feelings and speak against the forces of hatred and prejudice that had cost us another great national figure. Finally, we persuaded him and settled down to produce an appropriate statement, which he read to the nation at 10:07 P.M.

Early the next morning, I received a telephone call from the President that began one of the saddest experiences of my long friendship and association with him. He wanted to discuss whether or not Bobby Kennedy had the right to be buried in Arlington Cemetery. I was stunned—not only was I unaware of the exact regulations concerning who was permitted burial in the increasingly crowded space of our most important national burial ground, but I was dumbfounded that he was concerned with such an issue. The regulations were irrelevant, and in any case could be suspended by the Commander in Chief. It seemed obvious that

Bobby should be buried near his beloved brother on the gentle slope below the Custis-Lee Mansion—the politician in Lyndon Johnson understood this, but his personal bitterness continued even after Bobby's death.

Robert F. Kennedy was buried at Arlington on June 8. I attended the moving ceremony, and wondered again how our nation would survive what was clearly the most serious challenge it had faced since the Civil War. We were increasingly divided along a fault line defined partially, but not entirely, by Vietnam; those mourning Bobby Kennedy versus those supporting the right-wing, racist candidacy of Alabama Governor George Wallace; those demonstrating against the war versus those calling for more bombing of the North; those asking for funds for the poor and a legislated end to discrimination versus those who felt threatened by change. Perhaps Bobby Kennedy had been the last Democrat who could have united the factions of the party, which was beginning to unravel; but now we would never know.

The Kennedy family asked Robert McNamara to advise them on various matters that arose after Bobby's death. One of these, seemingly routine, was a small appropriation of federal funds—less than $500,000—for the creation of a permanent gravesite near his brother's. For months, though, President Johnson refused to discuss it. McNamara, Joe Califano, and I all talked to him at various times about it, but he refused to put the request in the 1968 supplemental budget, the 1969 and 1970 budgets, or the 1969 supplemental budget. Finally, on January 12, 1969, during his last weekend at Camp David as President, he instructed the Bureau of the Budget to request an additional $431,000 in the President's contingency fund for 1970. In effect, President Johnson had simply turned the decision over to Richard Nixon, who routinely approved the request.

A MESSAGE FROM MOSCOW, A SUMMER CHILL

On June 4, the same day that Kennedy was shot, the President received a private message from the Soviet Premier, Alekser Kosygin, urging the U.S. to stop the rest of the bombing of North Vietnam. There was nothing unusual in this sentiment, which the Soviets had expressed publicly many times: what drew our attention was the opening phrase of his message: "My colleagues and I believe, *and have grounds to believe*" that if the U.S. stopped the bombing it would lead to a breakthrough and produce "prospects" for peace (emphasis added).

Harriman and Vance were excited, certain that the Soviet Union, which was giving Hanoi vast amounts of aid, could help settle the war. I favored a positive gesture that would put Moscow on the spot to produce results. It was already two months since the President's speech; there had been no movement in Paris—and many more deaths on the battlefield. On June 9 and again on June 11, I proposed that we take an action in Vietnam—perhaps lowering the level of the bombing of the North—based *directly* on the Soviet message, making clear to both Moscow and Hanoi that if there was no corresponding action by the North Vietnamese our action would be terminated. Rusk and Rostow, on the other hand, viewed the message as virtually meaningless unless it was backed up by a specific explanation of what Hanoi would do to reciprocate, and they wanted an explicit understanding in advance—not only from Moscow, but from Hanoi—as to what would happen if we stopped the bombing.

The President, again caught between his top advisers, wavered. Exasperated at my persistence, he called my recommendation "fantastically unrealistic." Finally he sent a noncommittal message to Kosygin asking what would happen if we stopped the bombing. Instead of a low-cost test of the prospects for peace, we began a sterile exchange of telegrams with Moscow. Kosygin's Russian message, I told the 8:30 Group in dismay, had not received a true test, and we might never know if it meant something or not.

"IS HE ONE OF US?"

Although for the most part the dissension within the Administration was unknown to the public—and was heatedly denied whenever it became the subject of speculation in the press—it was now a well-established fact. The distrust reached such a high level that the message from Kosygin to Johnson was withheld from me for almost a full day. At the end of a meeting at the State Department on June 7, I mentioned this to Rusk. He apologized and promised it would not happen again.

At the meeting's conclusion, Harry McPherson asked me to join him for a discussion in the small, glass-enclosed office of the powerful Executive Secretary of the State Department, Benjamin H. Read, located exactly halfway between the offices of Rusk and Katzenbach. I was uncertain how frank I could be about my views in Read's presence, and just before we entered the office, I pulled McPherson aside. Gesturing in Read's direction, I asked, "Is he one of 'us'?" Harry assured me that Read was "on our side." My question—"Is he one of us?"—became a shorthand phrase Harry and I used for the rest of the year when discussing our colleagues.

In June, Rostow told Read, who controlled the distribution of many of the most sensitive telegrams within the government, not to distribute to the Pentagon any of the sensitive telegrams from the Paris negotiating team. Read was one of the most respected officials in the government and was close to Dean Rusk—but he was also deeply committed to the search for a way out of the war. Read told Rusk that the Secretary of Defense could not do his job properly if he did not receive the telegrams from the negotiating team. Rusk, who believed deeply that government should function according to certain rules of rational and civilized behavior, agreed; without telling Rostow, Read set up a private messenger service, through Colonel Pursley, to keep me fully informed of events in Paris.*

At about the same time, Read, McPherson and a few other officials began to hear Rostow use my name as a regular noun or a verb. From time to time, they told me later, Rostow referred to someone as being "Cliffordized," meaning, apparently, someone he regarded as defeatist. Comments he felt were unduly negative were termed "Cliffordisms." Of course, Rostow never spoke in this manner in my presence, but I was not unaware that our disagreement had taken on an intensely personal tone.

Having lost the fight over the reply to Kosygin, I was in a gloomy mood when I met with the 8:30 Group on June 11. "I am constantly isolated in these meetings at the White House," I observed.

"Your goal is to get out of Vietnam," Elsey replied, "but Rostow and company still seek our original objective of 'a free, independent, and viable South Vietnam.' "[10]

In the Tuesday Lunch that day, the President was very emotional. He had just returned from a visit to some wounded American soldiers at Walter Reed Hospital, and he told us he felt "hornswoggled on the bombing pause" and would like "to knock Hanoi and Haiphong off the map." He told Rusk and me "to get out there and make speeches everywhere. You've got a big selling job to do."[11]

As requested, I held a press conference on June 20, in which I defended the Administration's position on the war in Vietnam; but because Vance and the North Vietnamese had just agreed to hold their first secret meeting, I also said that I saw "some bits and straws [in Paris] that indicate that there is some movement now, no matter how slight." Rusk, who believed that such positive statements only increased the pressure on us, complained to me, saying that my comments were an error. I responded that as long as they were not misleading, positive statements about the negotiations helped us. Furthermore, I saw no harm in telling the American public the truth, or at least alluding to it within limits

*As a result of this and similar incidents, in which the White House was unable to control the distribution of sensitive messages, the Nixon Administration made important changes in communications, creating a virtually foolproof "back channel" for themselves through the CIA. CIA communication channels had been used by previous Administrations, but the messages could be read at the CIA before being forwarded to the White House. Nixon and Kissinger installed their own code machines in the basement of the White House. From that time on, their most private messages were encoded or decoded for a second time on machines that were controlled solely by the White House. This capability was used by subsequent Administrations on a wide variety of matters, including the opening to China, the secret bombing of Cambodia, and, in the Reagan Administration, the Iran-*contra* affair.

imposed by security considerations; after all, all the other parties concerned—the South Vietnamese, the North Vietnamese, the Soviets, even our French hosts—knew secret talks were about to start. Why should the American public be the only ones kept completely in the dark?

As June stretched on, I sensed a change in the President's mood: he was more irritable than he had been in months, and spoke in a low, depressed, and muffled voice. He seemed to disagree with everyone. When I noted his strange disposition to Leonard Marks, a close friend of the President and Director of the USIA, Marks offered a simple explanation: "He knows he is presiding over a disintegrating Administration."

I felt as if a clock were ticking ever more loudly, counting down the days remaining in which the Administration could try to end the war. I was dismayed that the President, having ended his political career, in his own words, in order to devote himself to the pursuit of peace, continued instead to pursue a military victory. With a sinking heart I realized that the military had half-persuaded him that the war was going so well that he should stiffen his terms for a settlement.

Early on the evening of June 26, Cy Vance slipped out of a side door of the American Embassy in Paris, eased himself carefully and painfully—so as not to re-injure his back—into an unmarked sedan, and traveled by a circuitous route to a CIA "safe house" in the suburbs of Paris for a secret meeting with the second-ranking North Vietnamese representative in Paris, Ha Van Lau. After an intense argument within the Administration, Vance had been instructed to tell the North Vietnamese that we would stop the bombing on three conditions: if it led to "prompt and productive" talks involving the Saigon government, if the sanctity of the DMZ were respected, and if the communists agreed to refrain from rocket attacks on the major South Vietnamese cities. The North Vietnamese rejected this proposal immediately, stating they would never accept any conditions regarding the cessation of bombing. Nonetheless, we had opened a serious secret channel of discussion with Hanoi. I felt that my press conference statement of the previous week had been vindicated.

On the evening of June 30, at my invitation, I had a long talk with Walt Rostow about our differences at dinner at my home in Bethesda. For three hours we discussed our differences in a cordial manner. I could not, however, persuade him to take a more forthcoming view of the negotiating process; needless to say, he was equally unsuccessful in moving me away from my views.

A TRIP TO SAIGON, THE HONOLULU CONFERENCE

I had not visited the war zone since becoming Secretary. The summer months had seen a significant drop in the level of fighting in South Vietnam as the communists regrouped after the heavy losses they had suffered in the two offensives earlier in the year. Most intelligence analysts concluded that the lull foreshadowed another offensive in September or October, designed to influence the American election campaign. In mid-June, the President asked me to go to Vietnam in order to make my own assessment of the situation, then fly to Honolulu to join him for a summit conference with President Thieu scheduled for late July.

On Sunday, July 14, 1968, I flew into Saigon, which, in anticipation of the predicted enemy offensive, had been turned into a gigantic armed camp surrounded by a ring of Allied troops on full alert. American B-52s were flying missions against communist strongholds north and west of Saigon as I arrived, and a brigade of the 9th Division was engaged in a fierce firefight with North Vietnamese troops in Phu Vinh province.

My visits to the field once again convinced me of the courage and dedication of the American troops—but even as I praised them in public, in my heart I thought of how wasteful it was that they were still at such risk, when, with a different policy, we could be looking toward their withdrawal. In a press conference in Da Nang, I predicted enemy attacks in the next few months designed "to make an impression on the conference in Paris." Mindful of the problems other Americans had gotten into by predicting American withdrawals, I refused to offer a date when our forces might start to withdraw. At every opportunity, I stressed, however, the growing ability of the South Vietnamese Army to assume more responsibility for the fighting, and I frequently quoted President Thieu, who had said that Americans could start to go home in 1969.

But the highlight, if that is the right word, of my trip to Vietnam was two meetings I held in Saigon, one with President Thieu and Premier Ky, the other with Ambassador Bunker. Both were blunt, no-holds-barred sessions. The first convinced me that the leadership in Saigon did not really want any settlement with Hanoi; the second confirmed my worst fears about the attitude and role of the American Embassy.

I met with Thieu and Ky at the Presidential Palace, which was ringed with South Vietnamese Rangers. After listening to a long presentation by the Vietnamese, I began a frank discussion of the American commitment to the war. Flanked by Bunker, Wheeler, Abrams, Bill Bundy, and Pursley, I told the Vietnamese leaders that in the absence of visible progress the American public would simply not support the war effort much longer.

If we could not achieve a settlement in Paris, we expected the South Vietnamese gradually to take over the war. Bunker was shocked at my bluntness, but I was convinced that our gentle and dignified Ambassador had not made Thieu and Ky sufficiently aware of the degree of impatience and frustration felt by both the President and the American public. As the outsider from Washington, I could speak more frankly than a resident Ambassador.

Saigon's weakness was the major cause of our dilemma, and I saw no reason to indulge it. Bunker may have perceived growing stability in the government and discovered "statesmanlike" qualities in Nguyen Van Thieu—clearly his favorite among the South Vietnamese leaders—but I saw a group of squabbling and corrupt Generals, selfishly maneuvering for their own advantage while Americans and Vietnamese continued to die in combat.

My meeting with Bunker was unexpectedly emotional. We were joined by Deputy Ambassador Samuel Berger and Bill Bundy. I told the two Ambassadors that we would be derelict in our duty if we failed to make use of the six months left in the Johnson Administration to seek an honorable end to the war. Bunker and Berger were startled by my vehemence and unalterably opposed to my suggestions. Bunker considered it heresy to suggest that Saigon should bend a little to help get negotiations started. I expressed concern that Saigon appeared to oppose *any* agreement with Hanoi.

When I left Saigon for Hawaii I was depressed. With the exception of Nick Katzenbach in Washington and Averell Harriman and Cy Vance in Paris, I was an isolated voice among senior people in the Administration. The trip to Saigon had convinced me, more than ever, that the war was drifting along, out of control. I sent the President a message asking for a private meeting with him, Rusk, and Rostow as soon as I arrived in Honolulu. When we arrived, Bunker went to Rusk immediately and alerted him to the tone I was going to take with the President.

I made three points to the President, Rusk, and Rostow. First, I was more certain than ever that we could not win the war.

My second point shocked the President and visibly disturbed and offended Rusk. I was now "absolutely certain" that the South Vietnamese government did not want the war to end—not while they were protected by over 500,000 American troops and a "golden flow of money." While I wanted to strengthen the South Vietnamese Army, I was startled by the "shocking and outrageous list" they had given us of equipment they wanted—including between 300 and 400 helicopters, T-39 trainer jets to be used as private aircraft for senior officials, and so on. Thieu and Ky clearly feared the loss of American support the moment the war ended.

The entire American-Vietnamese relationship was riddled with corruption. The senior civilian in the government, Prime Minister Tran Van Huong, had put it well: corruption was the "national cancer."

Finally, I urged the President to inform the Vietnamese that we were going to make an all-out effort to settle the war in the next six months. I suggested we explain to Thieu that the next President, whether Nixon or Humphrey, would have a strong national mandate to end the war, and Thieu would have less bargaining power and less influence in Washington. I pointed out that every candidate of both parties, with the exception of George Wallace, was making statements that suggested moving away from support of the war. (Richard Nixon, the most likely Republican nominee, had referred to "phasing out" the American troop presence in South Vietnam, and the Republican platform would use the very words I had used earlier—"de-Americanizing" the war.[12])

Rostow said nothing after I finished. Rusk said he disagreed with all three of my points, and repeated his familiar arguments. I could see the President was again uncomfortable with such a fundamental rift between his top two Cabinet officers—this time only a few hours before he was scheduled to meet with the President of South Vietnam.

The two Presidents began their summit with a forty-five minute private meeting. This was followed by a larger meeting consisting of nearly worthless briefings by officials from both nations. I listened with little interest, wondering what had gone on in the private meeting between Johnson and Thieu. After the meeting ended, as we were preparing for lunch, President Johnson pulled me aside and told me that, impressed with my three points, he had raised all of them with Thieu.

THE SEEDS OF A FUTURE PROBLEM

We had given Saigon our word that we would not participate in serious talks on the future of South Vietnam without Saigon's representatives sitting at our side as a full participant. I believed this was the correct position to take: the very survival of our Saigon ally was at stake. In Honolulu, though, Thieu sought a further commitment from the U.S.: that we would not stop the bombing until all North Vietnamese troops had been withdrawn from the South. This position would have constituted a major hardening of our position. Yet the Paris talks seemed far away from Honolulu, and no one wanted to have a confrontation with Thieu over what appeared to be a theoretical point. We chose to treat his efforts as a propaganda ploy rather than an indication of serious trouble to come. We should have taken Thieu's views more seriously, and recognized that he and Ky were opposed (as I had tried to tell the President and Rusk) to any settlement at this time; but given the President's refusal to resolve our internal conflict, it was impossible to formulate a coordinated position, even as a contingency, to deal with Saigon. In the delicate balance within the Administration over how to deal with Saigon, the decisive vote went to the man on the ground, Ellsworth Bunker.

All factors considered, the Honolulu summit was a misguided venture that set back our negotiating efforts in Paris without advancing our military objectives in Vietnam. The big winner was Nguyen Van Thieu. He had failed to obtain his primary objective, but his rigid positions, which were supported by Bunker, stiffened the American position. We had gained nothing in return, not even a vague acceptance of the need for greater flexibility in Paris. Bunker returned to Saigon satisfied. I returned to Washington determined to continue the fight for the President's heart and mind—where the final decisions would be made.

30

More Disappointment and Tragedy

Hang 'em! They say!
They'll sit by the fire and presume to know
What's done i' the Capital. . . .
Who thrives and who declines.

—CORIOLANUS

Nineteen sixty-eight continued to be "the year everything went wrong."[1] Our problems went far beyond Vietnam, although the war's widening poison seemed to lie always at the core of events. Fast-breaking developments around the world—Prague, Hanoi, Saigon, Paris, Chicago—lay beyond even Lyndon Johnson's reach. By the middle of the summer he had become moody and difficult. Often his anger was directed at almost everyone around him, but the man who suffered most, and paid the highest price, was Vice President Humphrey. When, to survive politically, he explored ways to distance himself from the Administration on the war, the President was uncooperative. At the same time, Lyndon Johnson's last great dream, a summit conference with the Soviet Union to begin arms control negotiations, fell victim to the brutal Soviet invasion of Czechoslovakia. Perhaps most painful, in personal terms, was the setback the President suffered when the nomination of his close friend, Abe Fortas, to be Chief Justice of the United States had to be withdrawn. Johnson well understood that this disaster reflected his declining political strength in what was once his backyard—the United States Senate.

THE FORTAS TRAGEDY[2]

Normally, the Secretary of Defense does not get involved in matters outside the purview of Defense. However, during my tenure at the Pentagon, I was occasionally called in by the President on other matters. None had a sadder outcome or more long-term consequences than the nomination of Abe Fortas as Chief Justice.

On June 22, the President asked Fortas and me to follow him to the family quarters of the White House after a Saturday-morning session on Vietnam. He confirmed what I had already heard as a rumor, that he intended to nominate Fortas to succeed Chief Justice Earl Warren, who was resigning at the age of seventy-seven. I turned to Abe and shook his hand in silent, solemn congratulations.

But President Johnson was not satisfied simply with elevating his old friend to the position of Chief Justice. He also wanted to name Homer Thornberry, a judge on the U.S. Fifth Circuit Court of Appeals, to the Supreme Court seat that would be vacated in the shuffle. Thornberry was an affable and well-liked politician, but no one had ever considered him Supreme Court material. The only reason for his nomination was a friendship, going back over forty years, between the two men, who had met as teenagers when Lyndon Johnson's father was a member of the Texas legislature. When Johnson became a Senator, Thornberry took over his seat in the House of Representatives, and later, as Vice President, Johnson obtained a federal judgeship for his old friend, even swearing him in on the front porch of the LBJ Ranch.

Changing into pajamas as we talked, the President got into bed for one of those oddly timed rests that always seemed to refresh him. The enthusiasm that had long since drained out of him when discussing Vietnam came back in his voice, and his eyes were shining with pleasure at the thought of the wonderful honor he was going to bestow on two of his closest friends, and what they in turn could do for the country. He asked for my reaction.

"Mr. President," I said, "it is a splendid idea, but I am concerned that it may not survive in this form. I regret to say this, but I do not think you can sell that package to the Congress."

He seemed genuinely surprised. "What do you mean?" he asked. "Abe is already on the Court, he is well respected. What's wrong with it?"

"Mr. President," I replied, "the Republicans are convinced they are going to elect the next President. They would probably accept Abe on his own. But if his nomination is tied up with Homer Thornberry's, I am afraid that they will find some way to sidetrack it."

He protested: "Homer is a fine man, he has a good record, he has written some good decisions down there in Texas. Dick Russell will support him. They are not going to find anything wrong with him."

"That is not the point," I replied. "The Republicans will not get into the merit of the matter. They will oppose Homer simply on the grounds that you are trying to pack the court with your friends at a very late date in the political calendar. They will try to stall both appointments until after November."

"What do you suggest?" he asked.

"Here is how I would try to guarantee Abe's confirmation," I said. "For the opening on the Court, select a nonpolitical, prominent Republican, someone who stands high at the bar, who has been a practicing lawyer for years, but has not been down in the political pit fighting the Democrats. There are plenty of men who fill that description. Find one, and send his name up with Abe's, and my guess is that the Senate will confirm them both."

Looking at me sharply, he said, "Well, I don't intend to put some damned Republican on the Court."

Fortas sat silently through this discussion. The President looked at him for some comment. Fortas was in a tough spot: he did not wish to appear ungrateful by showing lack of support for Thornberry. "Mr. President, I would go along with your judgment," he said. "With the right handling and preparation, I am sure you can put it across."

The President was ready for his nap, and we drifted out of the bedroom. As we walked out of the White House, Fortas said to me, "I understand exactly what you were trying to do. I don't know if the President can bring this off, but I couldn't very well sit there and disagree with him when he wants to make me Chief Justice." I wished him good luck and said that I would do whatever I could to help—but I thought to myself, if only I had known about Thornberry before the meeting, perhaps I could have talked to Abe privately and convinced him to join me in opposing it.[3]

Within two days, I called the President and suggested an alternative to Thornberry: Albert Jenner, a prominent Chicago lawyer who was chairman of the American Bar Association's Committee on the Federal Judiciary. But the President was committed to Thornberry, and the die was cast.

Over the next few months, the fight to nominate Fortas was a recurring subtheme in my life. No matter what our tensions over Vietnam, the President continued to discuss the matter with me, and ask me to help with key members of the Senate, which I did. The initial hearings before the Senate Judiciary Committee took place while I was in Vietnam and Honolulu, and I did not realize until I returned how damaging Fortas's testimony had been to his own cause. He was given a very rough time by Republicans Robert Griffin of Michigan and Strom Thurmond, and by Sam Ervin, the North Carolina Democrat who a few years later was to become a national hero for his role in the Watergate hearings.

One of the charges against Fortas indirectly involved me: Did his dual role as an Associate Justice and a Presidential adviser violate his oath of office? Late in the evening September 11, Senator George Smathers of Florida called me at home to explain that, during a long day of procedural arguments in the Judiciary Committee, my old adversary Strom Thurmond had demanded my appearance before the committee. Thurmond believed that Fortas had violated the separation of powers of the two branches of government. I disagreed: while it may not have been wise for Johnson and Fortas to maintain their old relationship once Fortas had joined the Court, no laws had been violated by their friendship, which had many well-known historical precedents. As an old friend, Smathers advised me not to appear because the issue on which Thurmond wished to grill me was not central to the storm building around Fortas. He suggested that I reply with a letter. This I did on September 13, after extensive consultations with Deputy Attorney General Warren Christopher,* a man of excellent judgment. In a letter to James O. Eastland, Chairman of the Senate Judiciary Committee, I stated:

> I have attended numerous meetings at the White House during the past five years. . . . From time to time, Justice Fortas was present at such meetings. . . . In general, these meetings had to do with basic issues arising from our involvement in Vietnam. . . . I am sure that on none of these occasions was there discussed with Justice Fortas, or in his presence, any matter pending before the Supreme Court, or, indeed, any other judicial matter.

My letter was successful in stopping this particular line of inquiry. An article by Richard Goodwin and Daniel Yergin in *New York* magazine describing our involvement in the President's 1966 State of the Union Message created another momentary flutter, but what it described was neither important nor central to the mounting problems facing Fortas, which stemmed from new revelations that he had been paid for conducting a seminar at the American University Law School in Washington. It was a poor idea for any Supreme Court Justice to receive money for teaching, but what made the arrangement particularly damaging was that Fortas had been paid out of a fund set up by his former partner, Paul Porter, solely for this purpose, and collected from prominent businessmen. I had been unaware of the fund's existence until the hearings, and was astonished Fortas had allowed it. This new information doomed Fortas's nomination.

On October 2, after the White House had failed to cut off a Republican filibuster on the nomination, the President called me, deeply saddened at the collapse of his dream for Fortas and Thornberry. Fortas was at that

*As Deputy Secretary of State during the Carter Administration he negotiated the release of the hostages in Iran.

moment sitting forlornly in his office at the Court, waiting to hear from the President. Neither man seemed able to take the first step, and I suggested that the President call his old friend and discuss the most graceful way to withdraw the nomination. Then I called Abe, and told him that I thought he should call the President. I never found out who placed the call, but later that day, after the two men had talked, Abe Fortas formally asked that his name be withdrawn from consideration as Chief Justice of the United States.

It was a tragedy not only for Abe Fortas, but for the nation. As it turned out, the nomination of Abe Fortas to be Chief Justice marked the high-water mark of American liberalism on the Supreme Court. It was now impossible for the President to send up another name during his remaining time in office. Accordingly, the selection of a new Chief Justice was held over to the following year and fell to Richard Nixon, whose choice of Warren Burger began a historic shift toward a more conservative Court.

Within a year, with Nixon as President, Fortas faced more charges of financial impropriety. In its issue of May 9, 1969, *Life* magazine ran a devastating article outlining the financial relationship between Fortas and a Florida financier named Louis Wolfson who had gone to jail for conspiracy to violate securities laws and later pleaded no contest to making a false and misleading statement. Years before Wolfson's indictment, Fortas had accepted an arrangement from the Wolfson Family Foundation that would have provided him $20,000 a year during his life and his wife, should she survive him, with the same amount for the remainder of her life. He had canceled the arrangement and returned the money by the time *Life*'s reporter began his investigation, but the damage was done.

Nixon's Attorney General, John Mitchell, pursued Fortas relentlessly. Mitchell went to Earl Warren to present the evidence against Fortas; although the information did not include anything legally incriminating, it turned Warren from a supporter of Fortas into a reluctant believer that Fortas had to resign from the Court. The following week, *Newsweek* ran an article revealing Mitchell's "backstairs call" on the Chief Justice, adding that Mitchell had told Warren "there was still more damaging material in the Fortas file—and it was sure to surface unless Fortas withdrew."[4]

The *Life* and *Newsweek* articles set the rest of the Washington press corps on a chase after Fortas, staking out his home and following him to every public appearance. He asked to see me and his closest friend on the Court, William O. Douglas. For two days we talked, with Douglas arguing vehemently against resignation. Abe talked with the same calm, quiet logic and detachment with which he analyzed legal matters—it was as if he were discussing someone else. Listening to Fortas describe his own feelings, I concluded he had made up his mind before he came to see us. I never found out if Mitchell really had additional material against Fortas, but I felt that Fortas was concerned that the Nixon Administration would never let up in its pursuit of him. He said he had received a message from Mitchell that if he did not resign, Mitchell would institute criminal proceedings against him. I told Fortas I hoped he would stand and fight, but I could see that he clearly had made up his mind to leave.

I was saddened at Fortas's downfall. As intellectually fit for the Supreme Court and the Chief Justiceship as any man in this century, he had been destroyed through a combination of President Johnson's overreaching, his own bad judgment, and the Nixon Administration's attacks.

What had driven a man of such exceptional intelligence to bring himself down through such dubious financial arrangements? I would ask myself this question many times in the years that followed. Born poor, he wanted both the glory of public service and the wealth of a successful private lawyer. Because he was unwilling to live within the combined income of an Associate Justice and of his wife, a highly regarded Washington tax lawyer, the conditions were created for his downfall.

TWO MEETINGS ON A HOT DAY IN AUGUST

As I look back on 1968, all that year's hopes and heartbreaks seemed encapsulated in two meetings that took place a mere eight hours apart, on August 20. For once, the issue was not Vietnam.

The first was our regular Tuesday Lunch. It was one of the hottest days of the year, and everyone in Washington felt drained. In the air-conditioned White House, though, the mood was better than it had been in weeks. The President began the lunch by serving us each a glass of sherry. "Gentlemen," he said, "let us drink to a summit conference in the Soviet Union in October. This could be the greatest accomplishment of my Administration." He was as excited as I had ever seen him, and I shared in his pleasure.

During the summer, the President had pursued a dream for a dramatic final act to his Presidency—a summit meeting with the Soviets that would start arms control negotiations. But even after his withdrawal, it was impossible to separate the President and the political calendar. In a telegram in late July, Premier Kosygin suggested a meeting in Moscow in about one month. Kosygin had proposed a date for the summit that fell during the Democratic Convention, a coincidence that President Johnson noticed immediately. On July 29, Rusk and I met alone with him. "I'll be in Moscow in exactly one month," he said, turning Kosygin's general time frame into a specific date. For a moment both Rusk and I were silent.

I realized that he was seriously considering a summit designed to upstage the Democratic Convention. Rusk looked at me, and said, "Perhaps Clark would like to comment. . . ."

I made the obvious arguments against going to the summit during the Democratic Convention. I said it would look petulant and undercut the Democratic party and its nominee (whom we all assumed would be Hubert Humphrey), and the President would be seriously criticized for his behavior. He listened glumly, but did not object. Finally, he accepted the idea that the summit had to follow the convention, but instructed Rusk to continue planning for it.

Now one of the President's highest goals was within sight. Rusk had completed his negotiations, and agreement was reached for a summit in the Soviet Union during the first week of October. It would be the first real summit (not counting a brief meeting between Johnson and Kosygin the previous year in Glassboro, New Jersey, while Kosygin was speaking at the U.N. in New York) in seven years. At that time, summits were high-wire, high-tension affairs which the world watched with a combination of hope, fear, and fascination that is gone forever in this age when summitry has fortunately become routine. Only four had been held, two of which, the 1960 four-power summit in Paris and the 1961 Kennedy-Khrushchev meeting in Vienna, had led to significantly increased Cold War tensions.

Johnson knew he probably did not have enough time left to complete the complex negotiations needed for an arms control agreement, but he would get the talks started, and, at a minimum, try to commit his successor to some agreements. (He was not alone in seeing these talks as a form of salvation from Vietnam: during the summer Bob McNamara sent me a private message that he would leave the World Bank presidency immediately, if the President would appoint him our chief arms control negotiator.)

For once our Administration, so bitterly divided on Vietnam, was united. As we raised our glasses, I could see that arms control held the same importance to Lyndon Johnson in international affairs as civil rights did in the domestic arena. A promising new dawn in the Cold War, and not that dreadful war in Southeast Asia, would be his foreign policy legacy. A joint press announcement was planned for the next morning, and Tom Johnson was told to alert the press that afternoon for a statement of unusual importance.

After the congratulations, we turned to the crisis in Czechoslovakia. We had been watching the situation since the "Prague Spring," when the Czech Communist party chose the reformer Alexander Dubček to lead the party, and public demonstrations spread to the point where the survival of communism in Czechoslovakia was threatened.

It was thrilling to watch Czechoslovakia loosening the iron grip in which the Soviet Union had held it since 1948, but, remembering the brutal Soviet crackdown in Hungary in 1956, we were worried that Moscow might intervene. Rusk believed that Moscow would not have agreed to a summit announcement if they were planning to do something in Czechoslovakia; surely they knew that would lead to a cancellation of the meeting. CIA Director Helms noted with some concern, however, that the Communist party of the Soviet Union had just convened an emergency meeting of the Central Committee.

Less than eight hours later, at 10 P.M., I was back in the Cabinet Room for a meeting with a very different tone. Two hours earlier, Soviet Ambassador Anatoly Dobrynin had delivered to the President an urgent message from Moscow informing us that the Czech government had approached the Warsaw Pact nations with a request for "assistance by military forces" to deal with "a conspiracy of the external and internal forces of aggression against the existing social order in Czechoslovakia." This was, of course, a complete lie; in fact, a massive Soviet invasion of Czechoslovakia was underway. The Soviet note concluded with an expression of hope that "current events should not harm Soviet-American relations," a lame reference to the summit.

It was a shattering moment, not only for Lyndon Johnson and his dreams, but for the nation and the world. History was taking a turn in the wrong direction that day, and there was nothing that anyone could do about it.

The President said he felt "double-crossed" by Kosygin. "Maybe I was sucked in by honeyed messages about the summit from Kosygin," he said; but the evidence suggested the opposite, that the decision to invade had been made at the last minute. I said perhaps Kosygin had not been the central figure in the decision, and might be losing power to someone else—a guess that proved correct when it became clear later that power was passing to Leonid Brezhnev.

Was there anything that the U.S. could do to help Dubček and the forces of reform? The answer, unfortunately, was negative, except for strong statements and protests. We did not wish to repeat the Eisenhower Administration's tragic mistake in 1956, when the CIA gave the Hungarian resistance rhetorical encouragement which we were neither able nor willing to back up with more tangible support.

The most immediate problem was the summit announcement, which was still scheduled for the following morning. The President hated to lose his last great goal, and looked for ways to avoid a cancellation. But in fact, there was no choice. Rusk left the room to tell Dobrynin we were canceling the joint announcement. As the two men talked, over 200,000 Warsaw Pact troops were rolling into Czechoslovakia.

The saddest person in a sad room was Vice President Humphrey. He was on the eve of a moment he had waited for all his life: nomination by his party for the Presidency, yet it seemed nearly worthless that night, with Vietnam stalled and the summit dead. During the meeting, he said nothing, but his depression was almost physical. I tried to cheer him up on the way out, but I could not get through his veil of despair. All he could say was that this would help Nixon, who was already twenty points ahead in the Gallup poll.

The invasion of Czechoslovakia would have repercussions for the next generation. Talks on limiting strategic arms were delayed a year, during which time the development of new technologies accelerated. Both sides embarked on an expensive new round of the arms race that did not end, even with the first Strategic Arms Limitation Treaty (SALT I), negotiated by the Nixon Administration in 1972. That agreement and its successor, SALT II, negotiated by the Carter Administration in 1979, were only small steps, considering the size of the problem. I wish that we could have agreed on a complete ban on deployment of MIRVs—multiple-warhead missiles—a major objective from the beginning, but when Pentagon planners first realized, in the mid sixties, that MIRV technology was possible, they saw it as providing us with greater security. Only later did we see the dangers, costs, and complexities, to say nothing of the endless arguments over what was fair and what was not, created by this new technology.

HUBERT HUMPHREY AND THE CONVENTION

The invasion of Czechoslovakia took place on the eve of the Democratic Convention in Chicago, but the Democrats barely paused to notice it in their fierce battle over the Vietnam section of the platform. It was now clear that the Democrats, having lost Bobby Kennedy and not wishing to embrace Eugene McCarthy, were going to nominate Hubert Humphrey. Since his dramatic entry on the national stage in 1948, Humphrey had been one of the leading spokesmen for liberalism, but as Vice President, he had loyally supported a policy he played no role in creating. Now he was trapped between his natural constituency and the man to whom he owed his job. That he came so close to victory in November, despite all the difficulties he faced, was a tribute to both his personal popularity and his fundamental decency.

Humphrey and I saw little of each other in this period. He told me later that this was out of respect for the difficult position in which I would have been placed if I spent much time advising him on Vietnam. During the summer I heard that he was considering a limited declaration of independence from the Administration on the war. It was inevitable that this information would also reach the President, and equally inevitable that he would react furiously. In some of our meetings he branded Humphrey weak and "disloyal"; more important, the news stiffened the President's position against concessions to Hanoi and made him determined to obtain the backing of the Democratic Convention for his policy.

On August 8 one of Humphrey's closest advisers told me that Humphrey had decided to try to bridge the split within the Democratic party—that is, offer the doves an olive branch with conciliatory language in the platform. There was historical irony in the fact that Hubert Humphrey, who had risen to prominence in 1948 on his refusal to agree to a platform compromise on civil rights, was to pay such a heavy price for his efforts at a platform compromise in 1968. But for Humphrey to succeed, the President would have to accept a platform that differed, at least slightly, from that of the Administration. I wanted the President to treat the platform as the ephemeral document it was, but this was asking too much of Lyndon Johnson. He felt beleaguered and betrayed, and was determined to fight back.

His anger at Humphrey led him toward his old adversary, Richard Nixon. "I want to sit down with Mr. Nixon to see what kind of world he really wants," he told Rusk, Rostow, and me on July 24. "When he gets the nomination he may prove to be more responsible than the Democrats. He says he is for our position in Vietnam. . . . The GOP may be of more help to us than the Democrats in the next few months."[5] On August 10, the two men met at the LBJ Ranch.

Thus began a relationship between Johnson and Nixon, in which Nixon skillfully promoted himself as more sympathetic to the President's position in Vietnam than Humphrey. After the August 10 meeting, the President told me that Nixon had said that as long as the Administration did not "soften" its position, he would not criticize us. I was as appalled as the President was pleased. "This is good news for Nixon," I told the 8:30 Group on August 12, adding:

> If I were Nixon, the development that would worry me the most would be an announcement that the bombing was being stopped in response to indications that progress was being made in Paris. Nixon's game plan is to offer us his support in return for inflexibility in our negotiating position, and thereby freeze poor Hubert out in the cold. Humphrey wants to change the policy, but the President won't let him say so. I think the President has been so anxious to take a hard and inflexible line that he thinks he actually achieved an advantage by getting Nixon to go along with him. In fact, Nixon has outmaneuvered the President again, digging him in more deeply. Nixon is trying to hang the war so tightly around the Democrats' neck that it can't be loosened.[6]

So damaging was the situation to Humphrey that I could not help thinking the unthinkable aloud to my colleagues: at some inner level of his psyche, Lyndon Johnson seemed ambivalent about whom he preferred as his successor. George Elsey told me about a conversation he had had with Charles Murphy that appeared to confirm our worst fears. Murphy, still acting as liaison to the Humphrey campaign, told Elsey of a recent conversation in which President Johnson had said in Murphy's presence that if Humphrey did not stand firm on Vietnam a Nixon victory "would be better for the country." As he wrote later in his memoirs, Johnson considered Nixon "a much-maligned and misunderstood man, . . . a tough, unyielding partisan and a shrewd politician, but always a man trying to do the best for his country as he saw it."[7]

The next two weeks were a nightmare for the Vice President, as he searched for a position that would satisfy both the liberals and the President. Humphrey and his advisers actually achieved this seemingly impossible feat with a carefully worded draft statement that was accepted by Dean Rusk and Walt Rostow, on one hand, and the moderate liberals, on the other. But on the eve of the convention, in a fateful telephone call, the President told Humphrey he could not accept the compromise plank. In a critical decision, Humphrey acceded to the demands of his President and supported a plank unacceptable to the liberals, thus ensuring that there would be an up-or-down vote on the platform.

In order to bolster the Administration position prior to the vote, the White House took an action on August 22 to which I objected strongly because it pulled the military into partisan politics. Under Presidential instructions, Rostow sent General Abrams a back-channel message asking a series of questions about the value of the bombing of the North. Abrams did not know that this was a request for material that might be used in the battle over the Vietnam plank of the Democratic platform. Rostow's message went only to Abrams; it was clearly intended to bypass General Wheeler and Admiral Sharp, Dean Rusk, Ellsworth Bunker, and me. But ever since our altercation in June, Abrams had operated strictly within the chain of command, and he sent his reply to his military colleagues, Ambassador Bunker, and me. Within minutes after Abrams's answer reached the White House, Rostow realized that the channel had been "blown," and, in order to cover his earlier action, he sent Rusk, Helms, Wheeler, and me the same list of questions.

Predictably, Abrams's message reaffirmed the value of the bombing of the North. The White House gave carefully chosen portions of it to Congressman Hale Boggs, Chairman of the Platform Committee, who used it with great effect to win over delegates for a hard-line policy on the bombing. I protested vigorously on two grounds: it was highly improper to use military commanders, knowingly or unknowingly, in a political campaign, and the field commander should not communicate directly with the White House without the knowledge of the Joint Chiefs of Staff and the Secretary of Defense.

President Johnson's victory in the platform committee was a disaster for Humphrey. At a moment when he should have been pulling the party back together to prepare for the battle against Nixon, Humphrey had been bludgeoned into a position that had further split the party and given more evidence of his own weakness. But worse was to come: one of the low points in the history of American politics was about to unfold, the battle of Chicago. The scenes of police teargassing and clubbing young demonstrators senseless as the convention got under way drove a dagger into the heart of the Democratic party and its candidate. I watched from Washington, feeling helpless. Even a generation later, the 1968 convention was still haunting the Democratic party, and providing the Republicans with a potent symbol.

In the weeks preceding the convention, we discussed at length the difficult question of what role, if any, the federal government should play if civil disturbances, which radical groups were threatening, broke out in Chicago. I favored prepositioning Army troops, on the grounds that if there was an emergency requiring federal intervention, every minute would be critical, and it would take hours longer to transport troops from military bases. My position led me into a prolonged argument with Attorney General Ramsey Clark, who objected strenuously to prepositioning. With the concurrence of Chicago Mayor Richard Daley, we decided to move six thousand Army troops from Texas and Colorado to federal land just outside Chicago in case they were needed. When the disturbances did break out, though, Daley refused to use federal troops and decided to handle the problem solely with his own police force. Thus the origins of the enduring memory of the police terrorizing demonstrators in Lincoln and Grant Parks, which I believe might have been avoided if the federal troops had been used.

On the eve of the convention, the President began to talk about going to Chicago to defend his record. Everyone knew this was a poor idea, fraught with danger to him and to the party, but he persisted in considering it, and even insisted that a speech be prepared to deliver in Chicago. On Sunday afternoon, August 25, I joined Joe Califano and Harry McPherson at the White House, where we worked until after midnight on a speech that none of us believed should be delivered. McPherson told me he had made a secret trip to California the previous week to help edit a film commemorating the achievements of the Administration for possible use at the convention. We agreed it was tragic that Lyndon Johnson's domestic legacy was being undermined by the wrenching war within the Democratic party. It seemed particularly ironic to me that the President's most vocal opponents in Chicago included so many of the primary beneficiaries of the Great Society programs. In their anger at Johnson, they behaved in a manner that could only help Richard Nixon. Watching the war in the Chicago streets and the scene inside the convention hall, I would have said that Hubert Humphrey's chances to win the election in November were slipping away rapidly. But then, there was always the memory of 1948.

As I was driven through the streets of Washington to my office, I would sometimes see antiwar demonstrators through the thick bulletproof windows of the automobile. Even though I opposed the war, I could not relate to these people. I had spent my life trying to use reason and the power of persuasion to deal with problems. While I understood their desire to end the war, I was appalled that many of the demonstrators, in their anger at the government, seemed to side actively with the communists. Such acts as flying the Vietcong flag or burning the American flag were deeply offensive to me. The war was a tragic mistake, but it was wrong to glorify the enemy, who were at that moment killing Americans the same age as many of those demonstrating in the streets. The fact that we would not be able to achieve our original objectives was cause not for celebrating but for mourning.

31

History in the Balance

Things fall apart; the centre cannot hold;
Mere anarchy is loosed upon the world. . . .
The best lack all conviction, while the worst
Are full of passionate intensity.

—WILLIAM BUTLER YEATS,
The Second Coming

VIETNAM: THE PRESIDENT STIFFENS

During the summer, stunned by the violence in Chicago and elsewhere, Washingtonians quoted William Butler Yeats's immortal poem. It appeared to describe their condition. Leaders throughout the world seemed overwhelmed by events they could not control, and ugly new voices from the Left and the Right presented themselves. The war had come home to America and the talks in Paris were stalled. My hopes of convincing the President to stop the bombing had been set back by the Honolulu summit. Unaware of the change in his mood, Harriman and Vance boldly proposed on July 29 that, after consultations with Saigon and our other allies, we announce our intention to stop the bombing on the assumption that North Vietnamese would not take advantage of the halt. "If [these] assumptions are invalidated," they cabled, "we would resume the bombing."

It was the right proposal at the wrong time. The President would have none of it. He called the telegram "mush," and said it was part of a conspiracy designed to force him to stop the bombing. "The enemy is using my own people as dupes," he said bitterly.

On July 30, the President instructed Rusk to hold a press conference knocking down any efforts to add flexibility to our position. Rusk faithfully carried out his assignment, but at the regular Tuesday Lunch the President upbraided Rusk—something I had never seen before—for not taking a tougher line in his press conference. "You missed a lot of opportunities," he told an astonished Rusk. Moments later, he criticized me for a press conference comment I had made that the concentrated bombing had "in some respects produced more dividends" than the wider bombing prior to the limitation. I was trying, of course, to defend the policy and reduce pressure to resume bombing north of the 19th parallel, but he was annoyed, especially by an approving editorial in *The New York Times.* "Lay off that line," he said. "It's a damned lie."

Rusk was shaken by the President's mood. After the luncheon, I offered him a lift back to his office. Sitting in the back seat of the automobile, he said he was worried about the hard line the President was taking. I was even more distressed. "We are in danger of losing all that we have gained since March," I told the 8:30 Group on August 1.

Perhaps the President sensed the need to restore warmer relations, or perhaps it was just a coincidence, but the same day Lady Bird called Marny and invited us to spend the weekend at the LBJ Ranch. Determined to try to move the President, I began to formulate a bombing-halt proposal different enough from the Harriman-Vance recommendation to gain his acceptance.

On Friday, August 2, along with the Califanos, we boarded *Air Force One* for the flight to Texas. The mood seemed to warm up in the forward cabin as we approached the President's beloved ranch, and as Lady Bird's sunny disposition relaxed everyone. On Saturday he gave us the standard tour of his ranch, driving at breakneck speed across the Texas hill country. Finally, on Sunday afternoon, we sat down alone for a private discussion on Vietnam, our first in several months. He had left his rage behind in Washington, and seemed prepared to listen.

I argued that we had fulfilled our obligations to the South Vietnamese many times over. We had prevented their subjugation, prevented the enemy from taking over the cities, strengthened the South Vietnamese armed forces, and provided the South Vietnamese, to the extent we could, with the tools for self-determination. But we could neither outlast the North Vietnamese, nor bomb them into submission. We could not hope for the creation of a viable, stable, effective, and honest South Vietnamese government in the time that the American people would allow. Now was the last, best time for the Administration to seek a settlement in Paris. I recommended a variation of the Harriman-Vance proposal for stopping the bombing, with ways to resume immediately if the North Vietnamese took advantage of us.

When I had finished, the President said, in a pleasant manner, "Clark, it's very interesting, but I don't agree with a word that you have said." Nonetheless, he asked me to discuss my ideas with Rusk and put them down on paper. To those who did not know Lyndon Johnson, it may have seemed odd, but I found our discussion mildly encouraging, especially in contrast to his angry Washington performance.

The following week, when Vance returned to Washington to argue his case, we dined at my house. Vance complained bitterly about the effect the Honolulu summit had had on the peace process. On August 7, he and I went to Rusk's office to ask him to join us in a unified recommendation to the President on how to stop the bombing—but Rusk had again withdrawn into a hard shell of opposition to any movement in Paris. Disappointed at what I felt was Rusk's retreat, I said, "All you are suggesting is that we keep on fighting and having our men killed indefinitely." Rusk answered with a calm blandness I found maddening, "You never can tell when Hanoi will break and give in."

A few days later, the *New York Times* editorial page again mentioned a public comment of mine in a favorable context, and its news columns contained a story about disagreements between Rusk and me. That morning, the President called: "Every day I read something in the papers about deep policy differences between you and Dean," he said angrily. "I am telling both of you that I want it stopped." I thought to myself: *How fortunate for the Administration that the press hasn't learned how deep our policy differences* really *are.*

COUNTDOWN TO THE ELECTION AND THE SALT LAKE CITY SPEECH

As September began and Election Day neared, I hoped the President might become more flexible. He was clearly relieved that both parties had adopted platforms supporting the Administration's position in Vietnam. And he was beginning to smart under Nixon's attack on his domestic programs; perhaps the fact that the election was proceeding without him was beginning to sink in on the old campaigner.

In early September, I was awakened one night at 2:30 A.M. by a telephone call from a worried Hubert Humphrey, who wanted advice. He had just said publicly he would start bringing American troops home in 1969, and, once again, had been reprimanded by Presidential aides for his statement. The next morning, I hazily remembered having told him that he was on safe ground with the President as long as he based his comments on those of President Thieu, who had said American withdrawals could begin within a year.

I reported the call to the President, who questioned me sharply about it during the September 12 Tuesday Lunch. I explained the circumstances of the call and sought to calm him down.

"Look, I *want* the Vice President to win," he said. "I want the Democratic party to win. They are better for the country. I have told the

Cabinet not to let the records of their departments be distorted by the Republicans. I want the Cabinet to do whatever is appropriate to help the Vice President. Where I help depends on where the Vice President wants me to help." He paused, then added: "Humphrey wants space. In his heart he is with us, but he thinks it is politically wise to keep space."

I was encouraged by this declaration of support for Humphrey, but I knew that, in fact, in his heart, Humphrey was against the war, but thought it was still *necessary* to stick with the President.

On the weekend of September 14–15, Marny and I were invited to Camp David, and I spent almost four hours talking to the President about Vietnam. On Saturday afternoon, I tried *again* to get him interested in the plan I had first suggested at the LBJ Ranch in early August.

"You just want to stop the bombing without any concessions in return," he said. I tried to assure him that I was proposing a plan to test Hanoi's seriousness, and that we could resume the bombing if Hanoi did not respond. I also predicted flatly that Hanoi would enter into negotiations that included Saigon if we stopped the bombing.

On Sunday morning, while I was having a late breakfast, a three-thousand-word telegram from Harriman and Vance arrived at Camp David. They had just finished the first significant private conversation with Le Duc Tho and Xuan Thuy, the North Vietnamese negotiators. For the first time, they said, they were ready to begin serious discussions immediately after the bombing stopped.[1] The telegram arrived at a fortuitous moment. Even the President seemed impressed with the news of the first break in Paris.

A few days later, I met with Averell Harriman, who had returned from Paris for the funeral of his mother-in-law. He intended to launch another assault on the President; as usual, he was optimistic and tenacious. He hated the war in Vietnam, he hated Richard Nixon, and he was determined to fight for his beliefs. This magnificent old warrior, who had already lived a life filled with service to the nation, was just two months shy of his seventy-seventh birthday. He knew that the two jobs he wanted most in his career, President and Secretary of State, would never be his, but he never looked back—only forward.

He wanted to tell the President that we had to stop the bombing to save the nation from Nixon. I tried to prepare Harriman for the President's mood and the response he was likely to get.

"I'd quit if I thought I was just being used in Paris to hold the line until Nixon takes over," Harriman replied vehemently.

Harriman called immediately after his meeting to tell me that he thought he had made an impact on the President. In fact, he had not. The President felt his recommendations were compromised by his early and open commitment to the cessation of the bombing. I recognized that, in the President's eyes, I suffered from the same defect.

The calendar kept moving, but the negotiations did not. On September 24, Marny and I dined with the Johnsons. Before dinner the President invited me for a swim, and we discussed the Soviet summit and the war for almost an hour as we paddled up and down the White House pool. After dinner, with some Johnson family friends, we resumed our conversation until after midnight, leaving our wives alone in the hall. Seeing how tired Lady Bird looked, Marny urged her to go to bed. Always the gracious hostess, Lady Bird declined to leave her guests alone. In turn, seeing how exhausted her husband looked, Lady Bird tried several times to interrupt us and get him to go to sleep. But each time she approached us, he ignored her completely.

As Lady Bird tried to get her husband to bed, I made my case again for stopping the bombing. If we stopped the bombing, we could fight on, if necessary, and lower the costs at home. "Why shouldn't we risk giving up five percent of our total effort in Vietnam—the bombing—to get movement in Paris?" I asked. "I urge you to proceed on the assumption that your conditions will be met. The risk is minimal."

"Abrams says it would endanger our men," the President replied.

"No, Mr. President, that is not what Abrams says," I replied. "Abrams says his men would be *additionally* endangered only if the North Vietnamese took advantage of the bombing halt. If they do that, we can start bombing again, and you will not be blamed." I concluded, somewhat emotionally, that he should have the "honor" of settling the war, and not leave it to Nixon.

I had not mentioned Humphrey, but the President brought him into the conversation. He doubted, he said, that "Humphrey had the ability to be President." He would have respected Humphrey more, he said, if he "showed he had some balls." Johnson would not recognize, of course, that the best way for Humphrey to show personal strength was to do exactly what the President least wanted him to do—break with the Administration over Vietnam.

The next day, Rusk and I disagreed again at a formal meeting of the National Security Council. Rusk said that if we stopped the bombing without getting something substantial in return, Saigon could unravel, and Hanoi might intensify their efforts. I disagreed, stressing once again that if Hanoi acted dishonestly, we could resume the bombing. "We have not only an opportunity, but a responsibility, to test what would happen if we stopped the bombing," I concluded.

Once again, I was joined on the barricades by my eloquent comrade in arms from the 1965 debate, George Ball, who was resigning as U.N.

Ambassador. It was the last day of his distinguished government career. "The President has not heard my heresies in a while," he said, "but I want to associate myself fully with Clark Clifford. We are needlessly continuing the bombing and the war, without testing the chances for a settlement. The risks are low, as Clark says."

Rusk offered what I thought was an odd political judgment: "If we stop the bombing with no conditions, many Democrats would vote for Nixon."

The President's response was sharp: "Mr. Nixon shouldn't enter into this in any way. The North Vietnamese feel the same way about all of us. They are not hell-bent on reaching agreement. Earlier pauses didn't work. They took advantage of us. . . . A burned child dreads a fire. I am like that child. I need a wink or a nod or something from them. . . . Is it not possible to get a firm understanding?"[2]

The next day, Ball joined the Humphrey campaign team. Before he flew west, he called me to promise that he would try to free Humphrey from the "psychological grip" of President Johnson and lay out a policy of his own on Vietnam. Ball proposed to Humphrey a version of the same proposal that he and I had advocated in the NSC meeting; after a final late-night drama, Humphrey decided to go ahead with it.

Humphrey spoke in Salt Lake City on September 30. Although his speech was later remembered as a decisive break with the President, it was, in fact, a cautious proposal almost identical to recommendations Ball, Harriman, Vance, and I had made unsuccessfully for weeks—and not very different from the Administration's negotiating position.* Its tone, though, was unmistakably different from Lyndon Johnson's, and it was enormously important for the political signal it sent—Humphrey was setting out on his own for the first time.

The next day, the President asked me what I thought of Humphrey's speech. We could live with it, I said, and urged him not to attack his own Vice President.

"But he says he would stop the bombing without conditions," the President complained. I pointed out that Humphrey had stressed linkage between the bombing halt and the events that would follow it, and had reserved the right to resume the bombing. Humphrey's own staff was emphasizing the differences between their candidate and the President; in hoping to reduce the President's anger, I stressed the similarities with the Administration's position—to no avail. In the days that followed I listened to much talk at the White House about how Humphrey was undermining the negotiations.

*The key passage: "As President, I would stop the bombing of North Vietnam as an acceptable risk for peace. . . . In weighing that risk, and before taking any action, I would place key importance on evidence of communist willingness to restore the [DMZ]. . . . Now if the government of North Vietnam were to show bad faith, I would reserve the right to resume the bombing. . . ."

The Salt Lake City speech marked the beginning of an impressive comeback by Humphrey. Battling a shortage of funds and overwhelming odds, he gradually closed the gap in the polls. In its final week, despite every problem Humphrey had faced, the race was almost a dead heat. Any event near the end could have swung the election either way.*

OCTOBER 1968

It is a truism that American Presidential elections affect people throughout the world, and that other governments have preferences among candidates. But no other election in American history had ever seen, or probably will ever see, as much overt involvement by foreign governments as that of 1968.[4]

Even more astonishing, one of these governments, the Republic of Vietnam, *succeeded* in affecting the outcome. As *The New York Times* columnist, Bill Safire, then a Nixon speech writer, wrote later, "Nixon probably would not be President if it were not for [President] Thieu."[5] I agree: given the narrow margin of Nixon's victory—499,704 votes, or seven-tenths of one percent—it seems clear that the outcome of the 1968 election, and with it, the shape of politics in America for the next generation, was decided by the events of October.

As that decisive month began, it was clear that it was too late for Johnson to negotiate an end to the long war in Vietnam—but it was not too late to get negotiations started, and it was clear that if such talks began before November 5, they would help Humphrey. The final four weeks of the campaign were played out against a backdrop of almost unbelievable pressure and drama in Paris, Washington, and Saigon—and, I assume, Moscow and Hanoi as well.

The crisis of October 1968 was complicated by the distance and time differences between Washington, Paris, and Saigon. While one capital slept, the other two were working. Because Saigon was twelve hours and Paris six hours ahead of Washington, an entire day could be lost if Washington's instructions were not sent before the end of the day. We held frequent late-evening meetings and drafting sessions in Washington so that our messages would reach Bunker and Harriman at the beginning of their respective working days. In Paris, meanwhile, Harriman and Vance worked long hours, often spending their evenings at the Embassy,

*President Johnson wrote in his memoirs that the Salt Lake City speech cost Humphrey the election because it made the Saigon government "extremely nervous and distrustful of the Johnson-Humphrey administration and of the entire Democratic party" and thus encouraged Saigon to thwart the negotiations in Paris in the decisive phase that was about to begin. "That, I am convinced, cost Hubert Humphrey the Presidency."[3] I do not agree with this interpretation of Salt Lake City, nor do most of the people who participated in, or observed, the campaign.

sending us the results of the latest secret meeting with the North Vietnamese before catching a few hours sleep and resuming the cycle again. (Vance, unable to sleep on a soft mattress because of his back, often made do with the carpeted floor of his office in the Embassy.) In Saigon, Ellsworth Bunker would find instructions waiting for him as he arrived at work in the morning, and, after meeting with Thieu, he would spend the latter part of the day sending messages to Washington and Paris. I often slept in my office after these sessions—but, unlike Vance, not on the floor.

The President talked to Rusk and me about his hopes of making a spectacular farewell trip to Southeast Asia and Moscow. Nitze and Warnke both opposed this idea, but I said I would support anything that contributed to the cessation of the bombing and the beginning of serious talks with Hanoi on the war. Fortunately, there was little enthusiasm for another summit among the troop-contributing nations, and that idea died; but the President continued to hope for a summit in Moscow.

October 11. While I was in Bonn attending a Nuclear Planning Group meeting, the secret talks in Paris suddenly accelerated. Meeting with Harriman and Vance in a CIA-supplied "safe house" in the Paris suburbs, the North Vietnamese envoys asked whether we would stop the bombing if they agreed to the participation of the Saigon government.

October 12. Vance's counterpart at the Soviet Embassy in Paris delivered an urgent message from Moscow. Using language deliberately identical to Kosygin's June 5 letter to the President, he told Vance that if the U.S. stopped the bombing of North Vietnam, Hanoi would agree to the participation of the Saigon government in the negotiations that would follow immediately.

Bunker and Abrams cabled that they would support an end to the bombing of the North if there were prior understandings on the sanctity of the DMZ, no shelling of the major cities, "serious talks," and, of course, full participation by Saigon. Bunker predicted that Thieu would "find these instructions acceptable," but that he "must be given time to inform" Vice President Ky, Prime Minister Huong, and others.[6]

On this same day, unbeknownst to anyone in the Johnson Administration, Henry Kissinger secretly informed Nixon's campaign manager, John Mitchell, that there was a strong probability the Johnson Administration would stop the bombing before the election. Kissinger had met privately in Paris with Harriman, Vance, and other members of the delegation in mid-September, just before the first Harriman-Vance secret meeting with the North Vietnamese, and they had shared with him their frustration and brought him up to date on the state of the negotiations.[7]

October 13. The President and Rusk were so suspicious of the Soviet message to Vance that Rusk met with Ambassador Dobrynin simply to ask if the Soviet statement to Vance really came from Moscow. While Harriman and Vance waited in Paris for instructions on how to answer Hanoi, Bunker obtained, *or thought he had obtained,* agreement from Thieu for the American negotiating position. "Thieu concurs in instructions to be given Harriman-Vance," he cabled Washington.[8] The next day, he sent a more detailed report that included this passage:

> Thieu then said so long as we are going to press the offensive in the South and in Laos, and so long as we are prepared to resume the bombing if they violate the DMZ or attack the main cities, he is ready to go along. "After all," he said, "the main problem is not to stop the bombing but to stop the war, and we must try this path to see if they are serious." I thought this a statesman's view.

At the time of this message, we in Washington thought that Thieu had committed himself or his government to our negotiating position flatly, as Bunker had reported. But in light of Thieu's subsequent repudiation of the Administration's position and the breakdown in communications between Thieu and Bunker, it is worthwhile to reexamine this meeting and Bunker's cable. Thieu had "agreed" under extraordinary pressure: a ninety-minute meeting in which Bunker, General Abrams, and Deputy Ambassador Berger had presented an oral briefing on a highly complex negotiation and requested an immediate response. The entire conversation had been in English, which, I knew from personal experience, Thieu spoke adequately, but hardly with complete mastery. Furthermore, Asian style and courtesy may have led Thieu into a polite response that Bunker interpreted as more positive than it really was. Bunker and I had differed before on Thieu's motivation and style. Bunker's personal comment at the end of his report revealed again his excessive regard for Thieu:

> I must confess I thought Thieu would want to think over-night about [our presentation of the negotiating position] before providing an answer, but he responded immediately and unequivocally. Most times he thinks clearly and logically. This meeting was the latest demonstration of this, and it is also the answer to those who think he is indecisive.[9]

October 14. Dobrynin returned to the State Department with a message from Moscow confirming that the message to Vance was authoritative. I remembered Harriman's prediction that Moscow would try to prevent a victory by Nixon, whom they still regarded as an unreconstructed Cold Warrior.*

The President needed to send Harriman and Vance their instructions, but, as in March, he wanted to meet with the Joint Chiefs of Staff before making any final decisions. He even asked Westmoreland, who was in the hospital undergoing tests, to attend; he wanted to ensure that the former Vietnam commander supported the policy. He also invited Senator Richard Russell to the meeting. One by one, the Chiefs, including a reluctant Westmoreland, said they agreed with the new instructions to Harriman and Vance. Senator Russell seemed confused, and at first refused to take a position: "I am here because you asked me to come. I am here only to listen. This is the most agonizing decision any President or any Secretary of State or Defense could face. Whatever you do, you will be charged with politics. But everyone wants an end to the war. It's been miserable—worse than Korea."

The President looked at Russell and said, "I know I will be charged with doing this to influence the election. Nixon will be disappointed. The doves will criticize us for not doing this earlier. The hawks will say I shouldn't have done it at all. I don't have much confidence in the Soviets or the North Vietnamese. I don't think they will accept this. And if they accept, I don't think they will honor it. But if this doesn't work, I don't think I will have another opportunity."

"I guess it's worth a try," said Russell.

We assembled again that evening—our third meeting of the day. This time, only the President, Rusk, Rostow, Wheeler, Tom Johnson, and I were present. The President pledged us to *total* secrecy, then asked each of us, rather formally, if we agreed with the instructions to move forward with the North Vietnamese. After everyone concurred, he told Rusk to send the message to Paris that would start us toward a full bombing halt and formal negotiations on ending the war. It seemed we were finally on the road to a bombing halt.

During the day, however, Rusk and Rostow obtained Presidential approval for a new condition. In order to show the world that we had "gotten something" in return for the bombing halt, Harriman and Vance were instructed to tell Hanoi that negotiations *must begin within twenty-four hours after the cessation of the bombing.* I was not consulted.

October 15. As we waited at the Tuesday Lunch for a report from Paris on the talks with Xuan Thuy, the President mentioned a call he had

*This was to change dramatically in 1972, by which time the Soviet Union had concluded that Nixon's reelection was far more desirable than a victory by George McGovern, and took several steps, including the summit in May and the beginning of the era of détente, which benefited Nixon.

received from Florida Senator George Smathers, who said Nixon had told him that the Administration was going to try "to throw the election to Humphrey by pulling something in Paris." Then we went over a sixteen-point checklist of things that had to be done, both publicly and privately, in conjunction with the announcement of a full bombing halt: telephone calls to the candidates, consultations with the troop-contributing nations, Congressional and press briefings, and so on.

Bunker reported from Saigon that Thieu now wanted to delay our response to Hanoi while he conferred with his own government. It seemed to be a deliberate stall, and I urged that we press Thieu to honor his commitment to Bunker. Within hours, the delay in Saigon was matched by one from Hanoi. Our "next-day requirement" amounted to a new condition, Thuy said. He told Vance that, while Hanoi would be ready to meet with us the day after the bombing stopped, they could not guarantee the presence of the National Liberation Front—the political front organization of the Vietcong—within such a short time.

By the time I returned to the White House at 7:30, the President had fallen back into a dark mood over the setbacks in Saigon and Paris. He felt that the North Vietnamese request for more time to get the NLF to Paris was deliberately evasive: whatever its composition or regional character, he and Rusk said, the NLF was ultimately controlled by Hanoi. Meanwhile, Harriman and Vance recommended strongly that we proceed with the bombing halt even if we did not know when the NLF representatives would show up. I disagreed, reluctantly, with my friends in Paris, taking the position that we could not stop the bombing until we knew when the four-party talks would begin. However, I saw no reason to insist on a meeting within twenty-four hours after the bombing stopped; I thought that any reasonable "date certain" for the first meeting should be sufficient, and said so. The President and Rusk agreed with this position, and it was relayed to Paris.

October 16. The President placed a conference call to all three Presidential candidates, including the independent, George Wallace, to bring them up to date on the situation. Nixon promised he would make no statement that undercut the negotiations. Amazingly, there was no private discussion between Johnson and Humphrey; still in the doghouse for his Salt Lake City speech, the Vice President got exactly the same treatment as Nixon and Wallace.

October 17. Rumors that something big was about to happen in Paris began to spread through the world press. The first leak came from Australian Prime Minister John Gorton, who had been briefed as part of our obligation to keep our allies fully informed. Artfully worded and technically accurate denials kept the story under control—just barely—but the rumors put everyone, especially the Republicans, on full alert.

Calling Bunker to his office, Thieu raised a series of specific objections to the agreement we had reached with Hanoi. He said he was concerned that the NLF would be treated as a "separate government" in the Paris talks, with its own flag and other attributes of sovereignty. It was clear that we sought different objectives from a bombing halt: we wanted to ensure that it did not lead to increased deaths of American and South Vietnamese soldiers, whereas Thieu sought to prevent the NLF from gaining political advantage through the negotiations by obtaining recognition as a separate delegation. But Bunker said these were minor problems that would be cleared up quickly, and we failed to pay them sufficient attention.

October 21. In an emotional session with Bunker, Thieu stiffened his position again, stating that the NLF should participate in the Paris talks only as part of the North Vietnamese delegation. Whatever the logic in this proposal from Saigon's point of view, Thieu had never previously suggested this in more than five months of detailed discussions. As Thieu knew, Hanoi would never accept this; to introduce it now would mean a protracted delay in the start of the negotiations.

October 22. When the Tuesday Lunch began, I expressed my outrage: "I cannot understand what has happened in the last week. I thought we had an agreement. There is a missing factor here. We are facing an utter debacle."

"That's why we have diplomats," Rusk said dryly. "We are the Department of Debacles." He told the President he was still confident Bunker would bring Thieu around quickly.

October 23. In the morning, Wheeler and I visited General Eisenhower, who was at Walter Reed Army Hospital, in order to bring him up to date on the negotiations. He was cordial and supportive, but he was weakening. As is so often the case with people nearing the end, he was losing interest in issues that had preoccupied him for much of his life. If the President decided to stop the bombing, he would support him; if the President did not stop the bombing, he would also support him. He was always available if needed, he said pleasantly. It was the last time that I would see Eisenhower before he died early in 1969.

October 24. Twelve days remained in the campaign, and the latest Gallup poll showed Nixon leading Humphrey 44 percent to 36 percent, with Wallace at 15 percent. From Saigon, Bunker reported he was "making good progress getting rid of the underbrush." But once again, Bunker was overly optimistic: in fact, the underbrush was turning out to be a jungle.

October 25. In the morning, President Johnson received a letter from Kosygin, urging an early resolution of these "third-rate details which in reality have no meaning at all." The President wanted to hold an immediate meeting to discuss Kosygin's letter and the next instruction to Bunker, but, concerned that the sight of limousines converging unexpectedly on the White House would stimulate press speculation, he instructed Wheeler, Rusk, and me to meet in the State Department basement and drive to the White House together in an ordinary sedan.

We should have anticipated that such a request would backfire, and it did. Just as we were leaving the State Department garage, CBS State Department correspondent Marvin Kalb drove his car down the ramp, and saw an unlikely sight: Rusk, Wheeler, and me squeezed uncomfortably into the back seat of an old State Department Chevrolet, with a security man in front. Kalb did what any good reporter would have done: he backed up, turned around, and followed us to the White House. He got a nice story out of it, and our unsuccessful attempt at secrecy seemed to validate the Republican charge that LBJ was planning some kind of last-minute surprise for political purposes.

October 26. Near the end of a five-hour marathon meeting in Paris, Xuan Thuy told Harriman and Vance that if we stopped the bombing the next day, the first meeting could occur on November 2—a six-day interval. On instructions from Washington, Harriman and Vance replied that a three-day gap was our outside limit.

October 27. It was the next-to-last Sunday before the election. Harriman and Vance met again with Xuan Thuy. After further arguing over the wording of a joint announcement—an inconsequential issue, I thought—Thuy proposed that we stop the bombing on October 30. He could not promise if the NLF representatives would be ready for the meeting that would take place on November 2, but they agreed to meet "as early as possible." Hanoi's latest concession *almost* met our position, and meant the bombing would stop on Tuesday, only two days hence, with the first plenary meeting in Paris on Saturday. Returning to the Embassy shortly before midnight (Paris time), Harriman and Vance called Ben Read to alert him that a telegram of great importance was about to be sent. When we convened at the White House at 7:30 P.M., the President began with a simple question: "What do you think we should do?"

"We should go ahead," Dean Rusk said. "I smell vodka and caviar in this proposal. The Soviets have moved into this negotiation." I felt encouraged that Rusk and I were on the same side.

"Why do we have to yield now?" the President asked.

"If ten steps once separated us, they have taken eight and we have taken two," I replied.

"I would say it is even nine to one in our favor," Rusk said.

"I still think this is a political move to affect this election," the President said, still conflicted.

Before I could reply, Rusk stepped in with unusual strength: "Even if this were so, Mr. President, it is in our interests to do so." Then, for the first time, Maxwell Taylor supported us: "I have been a hard-nosed man, Mr. President, but I am for this, even if there are ulterior motives." He said he thought that Hanoi was ready to respect the DMZ and the cities.

The President still seemed reluctant. I could not tell if he was serious or trying to push us to the wall in defense of our position. "I think we are being herded into this under pressure," he said. "I want Soviet assurances on the DMZ and the cities. November 2 is a bad date, a dangerous date. Nearly everyone will think it is connected to the campaign."

"You have a good story to tell." I said. "For five months we have told Hanoi we couldn't go ahead without Saigon present. Finally, they changed their position. *They* chose the time—not us. We wanted substantive discussions. They capitulated." I concluded my arguments in favor of a full bombing halt with one of President Truman's favorite Mark Twain sayings: "When in doubt, do right. This will gratify some people and astonish the rest."

"We may be motivated by evils we know not of," the President replied. "I would rather be viewed as stubborn and adamant than be seen as a tricky, slick politician. Everyone will think we're working toward electing Humphrey by doing this. But this is not what motivates us. I want to take it slow."

Even the military agreed we had achieved our negotiating objectives with Hanoi. General Wheeler started to explain why the Joint Chiefs supported the deal in Paris: "The Soviets understand—"

The President interrupted Wheeler. He was very agitated. "I *want* the Soviets to understand it! I *want* Harriman and Vance to understand it! "And Nixon! . . . All of you are playing with this like you have been living in another world, with a bunch of doves. All of you know how much I want peace, but we don't have anything to show for it." Finally, he said that before he would agree to anything, he needed another discussion with General Abrams. "Abrams has the color of the field commander," he said.

"Russell tells me Abrams would be the most effective in selling a bombing halt. Let's get him back."

Why did the President take such a negative position? I could only conclude that, with the election only nine days away, he was determined not to let anyone conclude he was acting to help Humphrey. I pointed out to him that at this stage of the campaign, either action *or inaction* would benefit one candidate and hurt the other. So what if a bombing halt helped Humphrey? Continued bombing would help Nixon. The President needed to search for peace without worrying about its effect on the election. Obviously, I was not unaware of the benefits to Humphrey of a bombing halt, and I wanted Humphrey to win, but I would have taken the same position regardless of the political situation. It would be irresponsible to miss an opportunity for negotiations that might be lost after the election. I could not help asking myself, again, *In his heart of hearts, does Lyndon Johnson really want Humphrey to win?*

BUI DIEM AND THE "LITTLE FLOWER"

At about this time, a new and potentially explosive factor entered the picture: our discovery, through intelligence channels, of a plot—there is no other word for it—to help Nixon win the election by a flagrant interference in the negotiations.

History is filled with characters who emerge for a moment, play a critical, sometimes even decisive, role in a historic event, and then recede again into their normal lives. Such was the function of two people who played key roles in electing Richard Nixon in 1968: Bui Diem, South Vietnam's Ambassador in Washington, and Anna Chennault, the Chinese-born widow of General Claire Chennault, the commander of the famed Flying Tigers in Burma and China during World War II.

Mrs. Chennault, a small, intense, and energetic woman who was often seen in the company of her close friend Tommy Corcoran,* was chairwoman of Republican Women for Nixon in 1968. Early in the year, she took Bui Diem to New York to meet Nixon. When Diem alerted his closest friend in the Administration, Bill Bundy, to the meeting, Bundy raised no objections; it was quite appropriate for an Ambassador to meet with a former Vice President. But Bui Diem neglected to mention to Bundy that, at Nixon's request, he had opened a secret personal channel to John Mitchell and other senior members of the Nixon team through Chennault and John Tower, the Republican Senator from Texas.[10]

There was almost no one in Washington as well informed as the popular and affable Bui Diem. The State Department kept him informed

*To whom she dedicated her book, *The Education of Anna* (New York: Times Books, 1980).

of the negotiations in Paris, his own government sent him reports on the Bunker-Thieu talks in Saigon, and he maintained close relations with many prominent Americans, especially Republican conservatives such as Senator Tower and Everett Dirksen, the Senate Minority Leader. It was not difficult for Ambassador Diem to pass information to Anna Chennault, who was in contact with John Mitchell, she said later, "at least once a day."[11] Even more important, Diem could convey advice from the Nixon camp to Thieu.

In his memoirs, Diem claims he sent only two "relevant messages" to Saigon during October. While "they constituted circumstantial evidence for anybody ready to assume the worst," he wrote, "they certainly did not mean that I had arranged a deal with the Republicans." Some of Diem's messages to Saigon later became public. On October 23, he cabled Thieu: "Many Republican friends have contacted me and encouraged us to stand firm. They were alarmed by press reports to the effect that you had already softened your position." October 27: "The longer the present situation continues, the more we are favored. . . . I am regularly in touch with the Nixon entourage."[12] Despite his disclaimers, I believe there were other messages, delivered through other channels; Diem correctly suspected he was under surveillance by American intelligence, and tried to fool his watchers by using more secure channels.

Diem was not Anna Chennault's only channel to Saigon. As he wrote in his own memoirs, "My impression was that she may have played her own game in encouraging both the South Vietnamese and the Republicans." She took seriously Nixon's request that she act as "the sole representative between the Vietnamese government and the Nixon campaign headquarters,"[13] and she certainly found other routes of communicating with President Thieu, including the South Vietnamese Ambassador to Taiwan, who happened to be Thieu's brother.

What was conveyed to Thieu through the Chennault channel may never be fully known, but there was no doubt that she conveyed a simple and authoritative message from the Nixon camp that was probably decisive in convincing President Thieu to defy President Johnson—thus delaying the negotiations and prolonging the war. Rather proudly, she recounted one specific message she received from John Mitchell in the last few days of the campaign: "Anna," she quotes him as saying, "I'm speaking on behalf of Mr. Nixon. It's very important that our Vietnamese friends understand our Republican position and I hope you have made that clear to them."[14]

The activities of the Nixon team went far beyond the bounds of justifiable political combat. It constituted direct interference in the activities of the executive branch and the responsibilities of the Chief Executive, the only people with authority to negotiate on behalf of the nation. The activities of the Nixon campaign constituted a gross, even potentially illegal, interference in the security affairs of the nation by private individuals.

We first became aware of these activities through the normal operations of the intelligence community in the weeks prior to the election. Gradually we realized that President Thieu's growing resistance to the agreement in Paris was being encouraged, indeed stimulated, by the Republicans, and especially by Anna Chennault, whom we referred to as the "Little Flower." In total privacy—and, at the President's direction, without consulting Humphrey—the President, Rusk, Rostow, and I discussed what to do about this attempt to thwart the negotiations.

It was an extraordinary dilemma. On one hand, we had positive evidence that the Little Flower and other people speaking for the Republican candidate were encouraging President Thieu to delay the negotiations for political reasons. On the other, the information had been derived from extremely sensitive intelligence-gathering operations of the FBI, the CIA, and the National Security Agency; these included surveillance of the Ambassador of our ally, and an American citizen with strong political ties to the Republicans.*

In a decision filled with consequences for the election and for history, President Johnson, although furious at Mrs. Chennault, decided not to use the information or make it public in any way. There were several contributing factors to his decision:

- *Underestimation of the damage.* Bunker continued to predict that Thieu would accept our position within a few days. As a result, the President and Rusk seriously underestimated the harm the Chennault channel caused to the negotiating efforts.

- *Weakening of support for Saigon.* Johnson and Rusk still worried about losing American support for Thieu if information about his behavior and motives became public. For those who liked irony, there was plenty in Thieu's defiance of Johnson while the Administration continued to shield him from the wrath of American public opinion. President Johnson had sacrificed his political career as a result of his efforts to save South Vietnam, but as far as Thieu was concerned, Johnson was just a lame duck—the choice was between Humphrey and Nixon.

- *Effect on the negotiations.* Rusk was concerned that revealing the Chennault channel would reveal to Hanoi the strains between Saigon and Washington, stiffen Hanoi's position, and disrupt the negotiations.

*It should be remembered that the public was considerably more innocent in such matters in the days before the Watergate hearings and the 1975 Senate investigation of the CIA.

· *Ambivalence about Hubert Humphrey.* Finally, and most important, there was the question of President Johnson's feelings about Hubert Humphrey. Throughout the campaign, the President treated his Vice President badly, excluding him from National Security Council meetings, and threatening to break with him over the platform plank on Vietnam.[15] What mattered to President Johnson at that moment was not who would succeed him, but what his place in history would be.

Characteristically, the generous Humphrey does not even mention the incident in his memoirs,[16] even though one of his staff told him about Bui Diem's efforts on Nixon's behalf, and he could reasonably have claimed that these events cost him the Presidency.

* * *

Perhaps in the wake of a decade of post-Watergate revelations about intelligence activities, the decision not to go public may seem fussy and old-fashioned; but whether the President was right or wrong, it was an exceedingly tough call. Had the decision been mine alone to make, I would either have had a private discussion with Nixon, making clear to him that if he did not send a countervailing signal to Thieu immediately he would face public criticism from the President for interference in the negotiations; or I would have allowed the incident to become public, so that the American public might take it into account in deciding how to vote. Had he been the candidate himself, this is what I believed Lyndon Johnson would have done.

All this raises a critical question: what did Richard Nixon know, and when did he know it? No proof—in the terminology of the Watergate era, no "smoking gun"—has ever turned up linking Nixon directly to the secret messages to Thieu. There are no self-incriminating tapes from the campaign, and the whole incident has been relegated to the status of an unsolved mystery. On the other hand, this chain of events undeniably began in Richard Nixon's apartment in New York, and his closest adviser, John Mitchell, ran the Chennault channel personally, with full understanding of its sensitivity. Given the importance of these events, I have always thought it was reasonable to assume that Mitchell told Nixon about them, and that Nixon knew, and approved, of what was going on in his name.

THE LAST DAYS: HISTORY IN THE BALANCE

October 28–29. The new week began with one of the longest days of my life. While we slept, General Abrams secretly boarded a C-141 in Saigon to return to Washington. Bunker met with Thieu to go over the agreement negotiated in Paris. He reported that Thieu said, "I don't see how we can ask for anything more."[17] Kosygin weighed in again with a strongly worded message, stating that "doubts with regard to the position of the [North] Vietnamese side are without foundation."

In the early evening we met in the Cabinet Room to discuss our next steps. The President continued to withhold his final decision pending a discussion with Abrams, who was due to land at Andrews Air Force Base at 2:30 that morning. I argued that Hanoi had met every one of our original conditions, and that we could not keep adding new ones. Rusk agreed. "The record is as hard as it can be short of a contract," he said. As the President adjourned the meeting, he asked us all to return to the White House later for a meeting with Abrams. I went back to the Pentagon, worked a while, and then took a nap. At 2:30 A.M. we reassembled at the White House. As far as I could recall, I had not been there that late since November 16, 1946, when John Steelman and I had argued all night over how to respond to the nationwide coal strike.

In a sense, the meeting and Abrams's trip were unnecessary melodrama. On the other hand, if it pulled the President across the line—which the rest of his Administration had already crossed—it was well worth one sleepless night and Abrams's trip home.

The President began the meeting with a long review of the negotiations since Kosygin's June 5 note. Everyone in the room except Abrams had witnessed these events—we all understood that this was for the field commander's benefit. It was, I thought, a sort of dress rehearsal for the public defense of our actions if we were accused of stopping the bombing for political purposes.

The President began interrogating Abrams. "I am going to put more weight on your judgment than that of anyone else," he said. Rusk and I listened in silence for nearly an hour. We all knew the General's answers could still derail a bombing cessation, and, although Wheeler had reassured us that Abrams understood the situation, I was not entirely sure how he would respond. I listened intently to the President's questions and Abrams's replies:

"General, do you think they will violate the DMZ and the cities?"

"I think they will abide by it on the DMZ, Mr. President. On the cities, I am not so sure. I am concerned about Saigon."

"If the enemy honors our agreement, will this be an advantage militarily for us?"

"Yes, Mr. President."

"Will it compensate for lack of bombing north of the 19th parallel?"

"Yes, sir, it will."

"Can we return to full-scale bombing easily if they attack?"

"Yes, sir, very easily."

"In August you said that stopping the bombing would increase enemy capability severalfold. Why can we stop the bombing now?"

"First, our interdiction in the panhandle [of North Vietnam] has been successful. Second, they haven't replaced their losses in the region. He cannot cause the mischief he could have caused in August." Abrams's answer gave me a private sense of vindication after my long dispute with Rostow and the President over the effectiveness of the restricted bombing.

The President continued: "Can we do this without additional casualties?"

"Yes, sir, we can."

"If you were President, would you do it?"

"I have no reservations about doing it, even though I know it is stepping into a cesspool of comment. It is the proper thing to do."

Abrams has carried the ball across the goal line, I thought to myself. I looked back on our squabble in June, amazed that such a misunderstanding could have occurred, and gratified it had been resolved.

The President solemnly polled his senior advisers one by one, although he already knew their positions. First Rusk, then me, followed by Wheeler, Helms, and Taylor. Everyone urged him to proceed. He asked Rusk, McPherson, and me to draft a speech immediately.

While we met with Abrams, Bunker had been meeting with Thieu to gain his final approval. "When do we hear from Bunker?" the President asked. Rusk replied that we were waiting for a telephone call and a "flash" message. As we waited, we received an intelligence report that an NLF delegation had left Hanoi for Paris. At exactly 5 A.M. the President asked, "How long has Bunker been in there?" Looking at his watch, Rostow replied, "About an hour and a half." Looking weary, the President got up and started for the family quarters of the White House with General Abrams, Harry McPherson, and Jim Jones. Wheeler and I returned to the Pentagon, where he began preparing the orders to halt the bombing. I lay down for a nap as we awaited the report from Bunker.

I had been napping for about half an hour when, just after 6 A.M., Rusk called with terrible news: Thieu had reneged on everything to which he had previously agreed. We immediately reconvened in the Cabinet Room, weary, angry, and depressed.

What had happened in Saigon? According to Bunker's cable, Thieu had decided that November 2 was "too soon" for the first meeting, ignoring the fact that it was Washington and Saigon who had insisted on the shortest possible gap between the cessation of bombing and the first meeting. Thieu said he needed to consult the South Vietnamese National Security Council again. Bunker told Thieu that there was no reason for any further delay, but he ended his cable with a comment that suggested to me that he was neither sufficiently forceful nor committed to bringing Thieu around:

> WE HAVE PUT THIEU UNDER SUCH CONSTRAINTS OF SECRECY, WHICH HE HAS OBSERVED, THAT HE FEELS HE NEEDS MORE TIME TO BRING [his National Security Council] AND OTHERS ALONG. I THINK THAT THEY CAN BE BROUGHT AROUND TO A JOINT ANNOUNCEMENT TOMORROW OR NEXT DAY IF WE COULD OFFER THEM A SHORT POSTPONEMENT OF THE MEETING DATE.[18]

It was a shattering message—after a sleepless night, this unexpected disaster. I was furious. "They can get a man to Paris in twenty-four hours. They could use their Ambassador in Paris. . . . Their objection does not have merit. It seems to me they are playing extraordinary games. . . . It seems reprehensible and utterly without merit. We must *force* them to Paris."

The President immediately connected Thieu's intransigence to the secret channels operating on Nixon's behalf. "It would rock the world," he said, "if it were said that Thieu was conniving with the Republicans. Can you imagine what people would say if it were to be known that Hanoi has met all these conditions and then Nixon's conniving with them kept us from getting it?"

Rusk wavered between wanting to confront Thieu and agreeing to Bunker's request for a "short" delay, but gradually moved toward Bunker's position. He did not want to have an open break with Saigon. "Let's not give the orders to stop the bombing until we get one more bounce-back with Thieu out there," he said.

I was fed up with Saigon, and ready for the break: "We have two courses. One, we can wait another day to see what Thieu says. Two, we can tell Thieu that this is the plan we agreed to, and it is too late to turn back, that it is the will of the President and the American people. I much prefer the second."

Helms, who rarely offered operational advice, came to my support: "I feel you should go ahead. . . . It is undesirable to allow these people to believe they have hijacked us out of this."

Rusk felt we should not make an ally act against his will. He tried to take the long view. "President Kennedy said we would do battle to save South Vietnam. That set us on our course. We have lost 29,000 men killed and invested $70 billion to keep South Vietnam from being overrun. We should not flush all this down the drain." As he spoke, I felt myself tuning out: this history lesson was irrelevant. If Thieu refused to honor agreements he had made with us, we had to go it alone. A twenty-four hour delay was tolerable, but there was no reason to share Bunker's belief that Thieu might come around if given another day.

We instructed Vance to tell the North Vietnamese that we had certain "complexities" with which to deal. What were these complexities, Ha Van Lau asked Vance. Was it timing? If it was, Hanoi would take our problems into consideration. Even while carrying out these instructions, though, Harriman and Vance were up in arms. Harriman was particularly bitter and angry with Bunker. Over the secure telephone with Ben Read, he blistered his old Yale schoolmate. Looking at what might be his last days of public service, Harriman wanted to force Thieu to bend to our will. I agreed Bunker had done a poor job. But how could we physically force Thieu to send a delegation to Paris? In truth, we had only two choices: either go it alone, or allow Thieu to sink the negotiations in Paris. With this grim choice before us, I returned to the Pentagon utterly exhausted.

There was no time for even a short nap. Within hours we met again for the regular Tuesday Lunch. I expressed my disgust with the government in Saigon. Rusk tried to calm me down. "I am annoyed to beat hell," he said evenly, "but it is not unusual for this sort of thing to develop." Abrams, on the other hand, shared my anger: "Thieu made a decision. It was unequivocal. I was there. He took it, understood it, marched right up to the plate and swung."

In Saigon, Bunker waited through the night to see Thieu again, who was still closeted with his National Security Council. I felt sure they were stalling: "I am troubled by the fact that nothing has gone regularly. It looks ominous, even sinister. Thieu's excuse is totally lame—that he didn't have the time to get someone to Paris."

"We had the same problem with Hanoi in Paris," Rusk said. "There is a problem of 'face.' We can't say that Hanoi has face and Saigon doesn't. I recommend that you wait until you hear from Bunker. We should not sacrifice everything by creating a confrontation with our Asian allies."

I responded immediately: "I thought South Vietnam wanted to be at these talks. We have now reached an agreement. . . . I believe that they are trying to decide what is best for them—dealing with the Johnson Administration or waiting for a Nixon Administration to go on with the war. I fear that Bunker may not be putting it to them stiffly enough."

"They are being whipsawed too," Rusk said. "They also have a problem. The GOP may be giving them advice. The Vice President has also scared them."

"If I were Thieu I wouldn't feel very kindly about Hubert," the President said. "But I think we must go through with it [the bombing halt], making every effort to take Saigon with us. . . . I was eighty percent ready to go before General Abrams came here. *Now I am ready to go.* If we can't take South Vietnam with us, we may have to reassess the situation."

The President was belatedly showing anger at the Chennault-Bui Diem channel: "Nixon will double-cross them after November 5. All this publicity—Gorton, Hubert, McGeorge Bundy*—all had an effect on Nixon. When the GOP could not do it with us, they went to work on the South Vietnamese Embassy. They made Bui Diem think he could get a better deal from Nixon than us."

The President thanked Abrams for the long and tiring flight, and suggested he return to Saigon immediately. As Abrams left, I congratulated him warmly—I thought he had performed magnificently.

During the afternoon more bad news arrived from Bunker. Thieu had refused to see him again, but Foreign Minister Thanh had said that a plenary session of Parliament would have to authorize the government to send a delegation to Paris. The South Vietnamese government, Thanh said, would need "materially more time" to prepare for talks in Paris.

Bunker's reply to this insulting message from the Foreign Minister was, to my mind, again weak and inadequate. His report concluded:

> I PRESSED THANH AGAIN TO SAY WHETHER I SHOULD REPORT TO WASHINGTON THAT THE GVN [South Vietnamese government] IS NOT GOING TO COOPERATE WITH PRES JOHNSON'S REQUEST, AND AGAIN HE SAID IT WAS ONLY A MATTER OF TIME AND CLARIFICATION. . . . I THEN SAID I REGRETTED VERY MUCH TO CONCLUDE FROM OUR CONVERSATION THAT I HAD TO REPORT THAT THE GVN IS NOT PREPARED TO COOPERATE WITH US IN ENDING BOMBING AND SCHEDULING NEGOTIATIONS ON THE BASIS THAT WE HAD PROPOSED.

To my amazement, Bunker then suggested we give Thieu *another* twenty-four hour delay so that his government could "pull themselves together." I was appalled at the tone of Bunker's message. Where was the anger that should be shown when an Ambassador receives a message so insulting to the President and the nation?

*This was a reference to a widely publicized speech by McGeorge Bundy on October 12, 1968, at DePauw University, in which he broke with the Administration on Vietnam. Bundy's speech enraged some of his former colleagues, and was frequently mentioned by the President in scathing terms during October.

We met at the White House for the third time that day at 6:30 P.M. to consider Bunker's request. We had had almost no sleep for two days. Rusk and I had agreed before the meeting on a course of action we would both recommend. We both said it seemed self-evident that Saigon's delays were caused by their preference for Nixon over Humphrey and not by genuine substantive concerns. I stated my recommendation: "Bunker should tell Thieu that either he comes with us or we go it alone. Although sometimes doing nothing is the best course, this is not such a time. I feel it is inappropriate for us, after bearing these burdens for so many years, to turn this war over to Thieu and a new Administration in this manner."

President Johnson was once again uncertain as to how to proceed, as he said to his advisers:

> We don't want to tear ourselves to pieces over this. Doing it before the election would be interpreted as political. The Nixon forces have been working on South Vietnam. We must reassess this. We can't walk out, quit, split—we have to hold together. Sure, we must tell Saigon we won't stand for their vetoing this deal—but look at the Bundy speech, the Vice President's Salt Lake City speech, and you see the reasons for Saigon's concern. It may be better to wait until after the election. . . . I don't feel good about a quickie before the election. . . .
>
> Let's not go it alone. I know what forces are at work. I would be willing to agree to a postponement for a day or two before I broke up the alliance with South Vietnam. It is almost impossible with the people in our camp, Hubert, Bundy, making these speeches. Thieu and the others are voting for a man they see as the one who will stick with it—Nixon. . . . I think we have to give Thieu some more time.

He wanted to postpone the starting date of the Paris talks until November 4, as Bunker and Rusk had suggested. He asked that a strong message be sent to Bunker to deliver to Thieu, warning him that we might go it alone if he did not join us in those talks.

The long day, which had started with Abrams's enthusiastic support for the bombing halt, had ended dismally. I felt as if the President were snake-bitten by bad luck. As I lay down in my own bed for the first time in two days, I could hardly reconstruct the blur of events of the previous twenty-four hours.

October 30. Bunker's latest report was waiting when I arrived in the office. He had delivered a strong message to Thieu, who had replied "emotionally and disjointedly." However, when one stripped away the rhetoric, Thieu's answer amounted to a refusal to participate in any talks with Hanoi prior to Election Day. He said he needed a week between cessation and the first talk. He would give us a formal answer later that evening, but it seemed clear what that answer would be. Hoping for a Nixon victory, Thieu would stall.

Nonetheless, to my astonishment, Bunker still held out hope. If Thieu did not agree to our position in Paris, Bunker recommended we go ahead with the cessation of the bombing on October 31, but agree to a one-week delay for the first meeting in Paris.[19] It was the first time Bunker had recommended a break, even a small one, with Saigon.

I was reviewing this telegram and the discouraging developments of the previous twenty-four hours with the 8:30 Group when the telephone rang—it was the President. By custom, my staff left the room while the President and I talked.

The President, bone-tired the previous evening, had awakened refreshed. I had no idea what had moved him, but he seemed to have had a significant change of heart about the negotiations. He asked me to return at once to the White House. "We have to act, with or without Saigon," he said. "Let's start all over again, and see if a different approach will give us some sort of result." I thought—or did I hope?—that there was a new determination in his voice.

The meeting started with more desultory talk about Saigon's problems. Rusk criticized Harriman's brusque manner in a recent meeting with Saigon's representative in Paris. I began to wonder what had made the President sound so decisive only an hour earlier. Finally, I burst out, in language that I had not used before in the Cabinet Room: "Saigon's whole approach is delay. This latest message is thoroughly insulting. In fact, it is horseshit!"

After my outburst, the President took over: "Tell Bunker we are ready to go tonight," he said to Rusk. We would stop the bombing on the following day, October 31, and schedule the first plenary meeting for Wednesday, November 6, the day after the election. This would leave us, as he put it, "a hundred and sixty-eight hours until next Wednesday" to persuade Saigon to send someone to Paris, as Bunker had suggested.

We met again in the Cabinet Room at 4 P.M. With the decision to stop the bombing finally made, we focused, at long last, on such important details as logistics, notifying Congress and our allies, and the handling of the press. The President said he wanted to announce the complete cessation of the bombing to the nation the following day, October 31.

Near the end of the meeting, the President said something that I found utterly remarkable after the incredibly difficult year we had gone through:

> There are two things that caused me to make my decision. One was the constant harassing, and persuasive and eloquent argument of a fellow named Clifford. . . . The second thing is General [Abrams]

> saying here in this room what the other generals said to me—that this bombing halt does not hurt our men and really helps them.

Because he was coming down with a cold and was concerned that his voice was going to get hoarse, he wanted to tape his speech announcing a complete bombing halt a full day in advance. At the time of the taping, the speech could not answer two big questions: Would the Saigon government come to the peace talks in Paris? And when would those talks start? The President said he would tape an ending the following day, and set the broadcast for 8 P.M., October 31.

October 31. Would this finally be the day we stopped the bombing? I awoke believing it would, hoping it would be—but I could not forget that we had walked up this mountain several times in the last two weeks, only to be disappointed each time. Feeling as if I were on a roller coaster that was out of control, I predicted to the 8:30 Group that before the day was over Bunker would ask for another delay in the bombing halt.

While we talked, Ben Read called from the State Department. "Thieu is acting very badly," he said, sounding worried. While we slept, he said, Bunker had held three separate meetings with Thieu, Ky, and Thanh to make sure they understood that we were going to proceed with or without them. The South Vietnamese National Security Council was still in session and still objecting to our actions. Despite his own reports, Bunker, to my amazement, *still* thought Thieu was "coming around," and said there was a better than fifty-fifty chance the South Vietnamese government would go along with us.[20] I was furious, but not surprised.

My next call was from the President. He had just received, in response to his request, a written statement from the Joint Chiefs of Staff that stopping the bombing "constitutes a perfectly acceptable military risk." President Johnson wanted a stronger statement of support from the Chiefs. "They are weaseling out," he said. I almost begged him to forget about the Chiefs; this letter was sufficient, I said—and in any case, it was the most that I could get in writing from them.

At midday I went to the White House to help draft the final portion of the President's speech. As we reviewed the draft he was still worried that he might be making a mistake and asked me whether Hanoi's concessions might not be an indication that they were "washed up militarily." I said that, in my opinion, the enemy had been hurt, but they retained the capability to fight on indefinitely.

In Saigon, Bunker had completed a painful, seven-hour marathon session with Thieu that had been punctuated by outbursts of anger by the South Vietnamese. The two men failed to agree on a position that would satisfy both the U.S. and South Vietnam. The die was finally and irrevocably cast. We instructed Bunker to inform Thieu that the U.S. felt it had no choice but to proceed with a unilateral announcement.

I walked to the White House theater with the President to watch the first portion of the speech on tape. His voice had become noticeably huskier. He recorded three additional sentences, which were inserted into the speech tape:

> A regular session of the Paris talks is going to take place next Wednesday, November 6th, at which the representatives of the government of South Vietnam are free to participate. We are informed by the representatives of the Hanoi government that the representatives of the National Liberation Front will also be present. I emphasize that their attendance in no way involves recognition of the National Liberation Front in any form.

At 6 P.M., the President, his voice getting increasingly hoarse, placed a conference call to the three candidates to inform them of his speech. He made one particularly interesting comment: "Some old China hands are going around and implying to some of the Embassies and some others that they might get a better deal out of somebody that was not involved in this. Now that's made it difficult and it's held up things a bit, and *I know that none of you candidates are aware of it or responsible for it. . . .*"

Nixon wrote in his memoirs that he was not surprised at the news of the bombing halt because he had been kept informed through "a highly unusual channel," Henry Kissinger, who "continued to have entree into the Administration's foreign policy inner circles." He also said that his real reaction to Johnson's decision to stop the bombing was "anger and frustration."[21] But, ignoring the veiled allusion to the Chennault channel, Nixon told Johnson he would support the decision completely.

The decision to stop the bombing was long overdue, but at least it had been made. The next Administration would start business with the negotiations underway in Paris. I was sure Saigon would join those talks after the election. I took Warnke, Goulding, and two public affairs officers to dinner at Paul Young's restaurant in Washington, and we raised our glasses to hopes that all our efforts had helped bring the war closer to an end.*

*Unfortunately, the Nixon Administration did not learn from experience. Exactly four years later, just before the 1972 election, Thieu defied the Nixon Administration (and Ellsworth Bunker, who was still Ambassador) in a similar manner, refusing to sign the cease-fire agreement Kissinger had negotiated, even though they had previously agreed to each stage of the talks. This situation led directly to the Christmas bombing of 1972 and a revision of the cease-fire terms, after which Saigon accepted the agreement.

TO THE ELECTION

November 1. I told the 8:30 Group I could never have made it through the fall without their support and advice. Our meeting was interrupted by a continual series of telephones calls: the President wanted to read me the public reaction to the speech, which was more or less evenly split. He returned to a new-old subject: a summit with Kosygin. He still dreamed of visiting the Soviet Union after the election, and, at his request, I asked Warnke to draft a memorandum on why we should start nuclear arms control talks before he left office.

Unfortunately, though, another ominous note from Saigon intruded on our hopes and dreams. Thieu had announced a major speech to parliament, and he had flatly refused to see Bunker before he delivered it.

Saturday, November 2. On the last weekend before the election, Humphrey had closed the gap with Nixon; most polls showed the race as a dead heat, and Louis Harris showed Humphrey with a small lead. But in Saigon, Thieu played the single best card he had left to help Nixon: he announced flatly that he would not send anyone to the November 6 talks in Paris. It was a devastating blow to the Administration and to the Humphrey candidacy. Bunker, who had misread Thieu at every step, was powerless to stop him. So was the entire Johnson Administration.

Sunday, November 3. In growing fury, Johnson told Senator Dirksen that he knew all about Anna Chennault's activities. Dirksen, the man who probably came closest to being a true friend of both Johnson and Nixon (and who also knew Chennault well), immediately alerted Nixon to Johnson's fury, warning that Johnson might make it public. Nixon called the President, who was at the LBJ Ranch awaiting the arrival of the Humphreys. (Ironically, hours later, the Johnsons and the Humphreys would make their only joint appearance of the campaign, in the Houston Astrodome.) Sensitive to Johnson's mood, Nixon realized the danger to his floundering campaign if he could not placate Johnson, and the secret channel to Saigon became public. Anna Chennault and Bui Diem, at John Mitchell's suggestion, had convinced Thieu to boycott the November 6 meeting in Paris; Nixon now persuaded Johnson that he had had nothing to do with these activities. President Johnson again decided not to go public.

Monday, November 4. Gallup's final poll showed Nixon with a narrow lead. Harris showed Humphrey ahead by three points. In both polls the candidates were separated by less than the margin of error. Both men had scheduled telethons that evening. Thieu continued to hold Bunker off. I waited.

The President made a conference call to Rusk, Rostow, and me from the LBJ Ranch. His mail was running against the bombing halt, and he blamed it on Thieu's behavior. He wanted me to ask the American military commanders in Vietnam to defend him publicly. I told him this was not possible on the day before the election.

Tuesday, November 5. Election Day at last—I spent the day in the Pentagon, lunching with Nitze and Westmoreland, meeting with Air Force Secretary Harold Brown, and carrying out routine business. I was disgusted with the campaign—with Thieu's treachery, with Humphrey's vacillation, with Johnson's failure to give Humphrey enough support, with Nixon's clever deviousness, with Chennault's interference. I assumed Nixon would win, but still hoped for a miracle.

The day dragged on without shape or focus. We went about our work almost numb from fatigue and suspense. In the evening I went home to await the results with a few friends, thinking back to narrow victories in 1948 and 1960. But this time, the victory would go to Richard Nixon. With it came the beginning of a generation of Republican domination of the executive branch and the end of the great Democratic tradition that had begun with FDR in 1932 and run for thirty-six years.

AFTERMATH

We could have won. That was my initial reaction to the narrow victory by Nixon, and more than twenty years later, it remains my strongest impression of the 1968 campaign. Nixon's victory was not the result of a massive swing in American political sentiment, or the unleashing of great trends in voter sentiment. As in 1948 and 1960, it was a squeaker that could have gone either way had any one of a dozen events turned out differently. Yet the election did mark an undeniable watershed in American history: including 1968, five of the next six Presidential elections would be won by Republicans. I have never accepted the wisdom, so conventional in the Reagan years, that the Republicans achieved an "electoral lock" on the Presidency after 1968. It was clear, though, that the events of that year had created an opportunity on which the Republicans had skillfully capitalized.

Humphrey had lost to a man of shrewd cunning and inherent dishonesty, who had outmaneuvered him in the insider game of dealing with Lyndon Johnson. But Nixon did not ignite any great feeling of support, affection, or empathy among the voters. He came to office knowing he had barely won an election that, by all rights, should have been a Republican landslide. The Chennault–Bui Diem channel had been critical to his success, and it revealed a general behavioral and moral pattern that, once given the power of the Presidency, would lead to actions, some illegal, that were far more blatant than the secret messages to Thieu.

I felt sorry for Hubert Humphrey. He had made mistakes during the campaign, but they had been the result of his basic decency and his feeling of obligation to the man who had chosen him as his running mate four years earlier. Years later I was deeply touched to read in Humphrey's memoirs that, had he won, he would have appointed me his Secretary of State. Of this I knew nothing until his book appeared. I had always assumed George Ball would have received this honor, while I would have been asked to remain at the Pentagon. Humphrey wrote in 1976 that when he awoke on Election Day he lay in bed and "began to think more about what I might do as President."

> Clark Clifford would make a fine Secretary of State. He has surprised people with his views on the war. He's really good at the White House. I have a feeling he hasn't liked me, but he's so able—so sound. I'd appoint him right off the bat. He's first-rate.[22]

I was touched when I read this, but Hubert was wrong in one regard: I liked him very much, but my responsibilities, and his campaign, gave us very little time to be together in 1968.

This was as close, I suppose, as I ever came to the position in the executive branch that would have interested me most, but it was just as well that I was unaware in November 1968 of Humphrey's putative Cabinet (which also included Cy Vance at Defense). There were still over ten weeks left in the Johnson Administration, and the agenda was filled with unfinished business—most notably the continuing problems with Saigon.

Part VIII

THE REPUBLICAN ERA

32

Nixon and the End of the War

SAIGON KEEPS STALLING

With the election over, President Johnson revived his dream of a summit meeting with Kosygin. At first, I argued that the discussion on arms control should start at a lower level, with any summit awaiting the new Administration. But when the President refused to agree to any talks unless they began with a summit, I supported a last effort to arrange one, although both Rusk and I assumed that the Soviet Union would not be interested in such a meeting. Near the end of December, President Johnson learned, rather bitterly, that Nixon had secretly told the Russians he was opposed to a Johnson-Kosygin meeting. Thus the start of arms control talks was delayed for a year, while the new Administration organized itself and sorted out its policies and priorities.

President Johnson's power was waning as fast in Saigon as in Moscow. Almost contemptuously, Ky told Bunker on the day after the election that it might take two months—just about the time left to the Johnson Administration—to resolve his government's problems with the negotiating format. On November 7, I told the President that the only way to move the negotiations would be if Nixon sent word to Thieu that he wanted progress prior to January 20, 1969. I urged him to meet with his successor immediately and make clear that it was in everyone's interest to get the talks started.

President Johnson put the case for cooperation to the President-elect in a meeting November 11 in the Cabinet Room. Rusk, Wheeler, Helms, and I joined the discussion. Nixon came alone, pointedly leaving behind the man who had been his foreign policy adviser during the campaign, Richard Allen.* I was impressed with the controlled manner in which Nixon conducted himself: always polite and deferential to President Johnson, careful not to reveal his private thoughts on any issue that still lay within the responsibility of the President. Where Johnson liked to obscure his strategy with a stream of Texas stories and rhetoric, Nixon was self-controlled, and conveyed the impression of a man weighing every word. But one could easily overlook Nixon's skill with words, because he left such a strong impression of physical awkwardness.

Rather opaquely, Nixon said he found no significant differences between his own views on Vietnam and those of the Johnson Administration: "I will do nothing until the Inauguration unless it is seen to be helpful by you. We must present a united front"—this from the man whose agents had sung the song of dissension to Saigon only a few days earlier.

"You can be very helpful in the next sixty-five days, especially with Saigon," I said to Nixon. "I know you want to wind this up as much as we do."

"The quicker the better," the President-elect replied.

THE PRESS CONFERENCE—AND SOME RUMORS

The President's mood rose and fell. As his days in office waned, he alternated between a feeling that Saigon had prevented him from negotiating an end to the war and a feeling that he should never have made either of the March 31 or October 31 speeches.** Each meeting at the White House became a guessing game: which Lyndon Johnson would show up? At times, his rage, like mine, was directed at Thieu; at other times, he lashed out at those, including Harriman, Vance, and me, whom he feared might have pushed him in the wrong direction. Gradually, though, as he began to perceive Saigon's intransigence and Nixon's treachery more clearly, his impatience with Rusk and Rostow became manifest. I continued to push as hard as I could for instructions to Bunker to exert more pressure on Thieu and Ky. At the same time I felt immensely sorry as I watched Lyndon Johnson's thirty-two-year public career coming to an end in such disarray.

*Henry Kissinger had not yet been appointed Nixon's National Security Assistant. Allen later became the first of President Reagan's six National Security Assistants.

**He made the latter point, for example, in the Tuesday Lunch on December 3, 1968.

A week after the election, on November 12, the South Vietnamese Information Minister, Ton That Thien, stated publicly that the Johnson Administration had both halted the bombing of North Vietnam and agreed to the Paris talks without Saigon's approval. An enraged President Johnson called me early that morning to ask me to rebut this charge in a press conference.

No press conference I ever gave was more deliberately angry. Speaking calmly but using strong language to make sure Saigon's constant attempts to thwart the negotiations were understood, I said that we had had a "full and complete" understanding with Saigon until "the very last instant, [when] suddenly . . . Saigon change[d] its mind and decide[d] not to go ahead." Whether or not Saigon joined us at the Paris meetings, I said the President "owed it to the American people to proceed with the talks."

My remarks stunned Saigon and shocked many Americans, including some in the Administration. Until then we had carefully minimized in public our differences with Saigon; now they were out in the open. Thieu told his closest advisers that he feared I would attempt to overthrow or assassinate him "like Ngo Dinh Diem" before the Johnson Administration left office—a fanciful concern that Kissinger also mentioned in comments he made to William F. Buckley before he was appointed Nixon's National Security Assistant.*

Rostow was furious, but there was no criticism from either the President or his press spokesman, George Christian. On November 18, during a private lunch, I urged the President to send Thieu a letter—I had no confidence Bunker would deliver a firm message unless it was in writing—saying that we would begin talks with the communist representatives within a week, with or without Saigon. When consulted, Rusk opposed my suggestion, feeling that Bunker should continue to have the final word on how to present our position.

In the middle of my dispute with Saigon, I appeared on the CBS television program *Face the Nation,* and repeated some of my charges against the South Vietnamese government. Bunker sent a personal message to Rusk complaining that my statements had angered the South Vietnamese government. About ten days later, I received an amusing letter from Prentiss Childs, the producer of *Face the Nation,* describing the fuss Nguyen Cao Ky had put up when he appeared on the same program one week later. When asked to sign the program's guest book—immediately below my name, as it happened—Ky at first refused. Some-

*According to Buckley, Kissinger said, "Nixon should be told that it is probably an objective of Clifford to depose Thieu before Nixon is inaugurated. Word should be gotten to Nixon that if Thieu meets the same fate as Diem, the word will go out to the nations of the world that it may be dangerous to be America's enemy, but to be America's friend is fatal."[1]

one suggested that he draw a line between our names. *"No!"* Ky replied. He carefully drew two thick black lines on the page, wrote "DMZ!!!!" between the two lines and then signed his name.

On November 9, George Elsey reported in the 8:30 meeting that there were rumors "all over the Pentagon" that I would be asked to stay on in the Nixon Administration. Unlikely as the thought of my serving under Nixon may have appeared in retrospect, the rumor stayed alive for several weeks and was even reported in the press. Abe Fortas sent me a handwritten note that began, "I hope it's true that the President-elect is asking you to stay on." I told Goulding and his deputy, Dan Henkin, to deny all rumors that I might stay, yet the stories persisted until early December.

The only person who actually raised with me the possibility of staying on was the President-elect's transition chief, Franklin Lincoln. I had known Lincoln, both as a friend and a fine lawyer, since 1935, when he hired me to represent one of his clients in a St. Louis legal proceeding. He had served as an Assistant Secretary of Defense in the last year of the Eisenhower Administration, after which he joined the same New York law firm as Nixon and Mitchell. When he was asked to oversee the transition he asked to see me; we talked at length about how to make the changeover as smooth as possible, and I turned over to him my transition files from 1960.

In our first or second meeting, Lincoln asked if I would be willing to stay on for an unspecified period of time. I gave him several reasons why this was a bad idea. I would have liked to continue to work for the end of the war from within the government, but it was inconceivable, given our respective histories, that Richard Nixon and I could have worked together closely. I told Lincoln that I would ask only for the opportunity to present my views on Vietnam to the President-elect.

On the evening of December 2, Lincoln called me at home. He told me that while Nixon had been advised by several influential people in both parties to keep me on as Secretary of Defense—and had actually considered it—he had concluded that he could not select someone who represented an Administration whose policies he had been criticizing. I was neither surprised nor disappointed.

Later, the man who succeeded me, Melvin Laird, told me the background of the rumors. During discussions with Laird at transition headquarters at the Hotel Pierre in New York in November, Nixon had indicated that, given the narrowness of his victory, he wanted to consider a bipartisan Cabinet. Laird and another adviser, Bryce Harlow, told Nixon that I should be considered. At the same time, Franklin Lincoln independently put forward the same suggestion. But the idea was dead long before the rumor subsided. After desultory discussions, Nixon rejected it.* Still looking for a Democrat in his Cabinet, he turned to Senator Scoop Jackson of Washington for the job.

A SUCCESSOR IS NAMED

The day after Lincoln's call, Senator Jackson telephoned me from Hawaii and told me he had "stayed aloof" while I was under consideration, but he had just been offered the Pentagon job and had tentatively decided to accept. Nixon had gone to extraordinary lengths to get Jackson, even persuading Republican Governor Dan Evans of Washington to appoint a Democrat to Jackson's Senate seat. But Teddy Kennedy and other Democrats had warned Jackson that if he served in Nixon's Cabinet he could no longer pursue his goal: the Presidency. I agreed with this assessment, and said that while he would make a fine Secretary of Defense, he had to decide which career path to follow. Scoop finally decided not to go ahead, and Nixon, now far behind schedule in selecting his Cabinet, turned immediately to Melvin Laird, the powerful Republican Congressman from Wisconsin.

On December 12, I had luncheon alone with President Johnson. He spent much of the time analyzing Nixon's new Cabinet. He was disappointed by the choice of Laird, he told me, whom he considered "one of the ablest" but also one of the "meanest and most partisan" Republicans in the House. Giving vent to his extraordinary ability to tell a story, he launched into a half-humorous, half-serious monologue on how he hoped, for Nixon's sake, that William P. Rogers, the incoming Secretary of State, and Laird did not disagree as much as Rusk and I had. He added that he thought Rogers would be "tough" and effective. Later, it would be interesting to recall how the outgoing team underestimated Henry Kissinger—perhaps because we had seen him only as an academic intermediary during his Vietnam negotiations—and seriously overestimated the role Rogers would play as Secretary of State.

I met for the first time alone with Laird that same afternoon. After an initial wariness, we established an easy rapport, and in the last weeks of the Administration we met frequently in my office and my home, where Marny and I gave a large reception and a small dinner in his honor. I did not find him "mean," but rather an intelligent, likable, bluff, and astute politician. I was convinced from our first meeting that Laird would be far

*On December 9, 1968, Nixon dictated a personal note for his files on how he had chosen his Cabinet, part of which Bill Safire published in 1975. Referring to himself in the third person as "RN," Nixon dictated: "There was considerable pressure to keep Clark Clifford, but RN thought it would be a mistake to go forward with one who helped shape the policies which RN had been criticizing."[2]

tougher than Rogers, and I was particularly pleased to discover that he saw as his major task finding a way out of the Vietnam morass. He asked Paul Warnke to stay on for a few months to prepare him for trips to Vietnam and NATO and the opening of arms control talks with Moscow. In our talks with Laird, Warnke and I vigorously advanced our view that, whether or not the negotiations made progress, we should start withdrawing American forces from Vietnam so as to reduce our casualties and encourage some degree of South Vietnamese self-reliance. Laird, who needed little persuading on this point, became the leading advocate within the Nixon Administration for reducing the American role in Vietnam.

TABLE SHAPES

President Johnson still acted as if every one of his decisions mattered, but with each day that passed, our actions became less important. If Saigon could stall into mid-January, then the Johnson Administration would become irrelevant.

This was the real cause of the famously stupid argument over the shape of the table in Paris—a dispute that, understandably, subjected all parties to the negotiations to ridicule. How could diplomats argue over the shape of a table in Paris while young men were dying in Southeast Asia?

The whole matter, which ultimately lasted more than sixty days, would have been absurd had it not been so tragic. The South Vietnamese wanted Hanoi and the NLF to sit as a single delegation in Paris, and demanded a seating arrangement, table shape, flags, and nameplates that reflected their point of view. Hanoi insisted that the NLF and the North Vietnamese be seated as two separate delegations, at a square table, with two different nameplates and two different flags. Our position was simple: four delegations, a round table, no flags, no nameplates. In one meeting at the White House we looked at nine different table arrangements. I thought it was one of the silliest discussions in which I had ever participated.

On December 24, the day before my birthday, I received an unexpected letter from President Johnson. "I am convinced," he began, "that it was no coincidence that you were born on Christmas Day. For somewhere in your stars, it must have been written that your full and fruitful lifetime would be spent in selfless pursuit of peace and goodwill among all men." He was in a strange, bittersweet mood as he approached his last holiday season in public life. I interpreted the letter as indirectly expressing appreciation for my attempts to move the policy.

As 1969 began, we were acutely aware of the countdown to the end of the Administration. Farewells and letters were exchanged among old friends, as they always are at such a time. Of the many I received, one moved me most deeply. It came from McGeorge Bundy, whom I had always respected, although we had never been close. He wrote me, he said, as he sat at home in the last few hours of the last day of that difficult year:

> As I sit here thinking about 1968—not our best year on the whole—it becomes clear to me that there is one man with an outstanding claim to have done well for his country in this hard year—one real Man of the Year—and that's you. With just a little help from others in the case at critical moments, you would have done even more—but, as it is, you more than any other man have been brave and right at the right time and in the right place. You have been the President's brave and most tenaciously honest counselor, and you have got the damned thing turned around. . . . It's been a year worth five for you—and you once told me five is enough.* . . . Honest men who care and don't need anything are the most precious stones of the Republic—and forgive my high-flown language—it's how I feel.

In the same mood, I thanked Bundy profusely for his letter, and I tried to convey the pain the year had caused:

> It has been an incredible period. The road has been tortuous and painful and, at times, unbelievably lonely. The account that I had in the LBJ Bank stood me in good stead for awhile but it became dangerously low these last few months, and recently I have been tiptoeing on the brink of bankruptcy. It is better now, and it is even possible that there is the beginning of some recognition (on the part of the Bank) of where we would be today if the turn on Vietnam had not been made. I am worn out with it now, but I am convinced that we have gone so far down the road that those who follow cannot turn back.

The small note of encouragement—the "beginning of some recognition"—to which I referred had been based in part on a revealing remark the President had made to Rusk during the Tuesday Lunch of January 7: "I'm fed up with the South Vietnamese. I want these talks to start before January 20 even if we have to admit that Clark has been right all along."

The President instructed Rusk to send a stern letter to Thieu, warning that we would proceed without them if they continued to block agreement. When I read Rusk's telegram, however, I noticed that he had given Bunker discretionary authority to deliver the message *either* by letter or

*This was a reference to a discussion we had in 1965, when he was trying to decide whether or not to leave the Johnson White House, after almost five years as National Security Assistant.

orally. Fearing that Bunker would soften the message again, I protested to the President, who told Rusk he wanted the message delivered as a letter. The letter finally put an end to the last ridiculous details of the argument over the table shape—January 16, four days before the end of the President's term. Saigon, however, deliberately delayed the start of the talks until January 25, 1969, when Nixon was President and could receive the public acclaim for them.*

JANUARY 20, 1969

I had always remembered how President Truman had left Washington by train on January 20, 1953, ignored and almost forgotten in the excitement over Eisenhower's Inauguration. I did not wish Lyndon Johnson to suffer the same fate. Accordingly, in July I had asked President and Mrs. Johnson if they would let Marny and me give a luncheon in their honor on January 20, 1969. Despite the chill that Vietnam had caused between us, the Johnsons accepted and made up the guest list themselves, including their family, most of the Cabinet, some members of the White House staff, and a few friends. All told, we invited about fifty people; everyone accepted.

President Johnson, of course, had to attend the Inauguration of his successor, as did Hubert Humphrey. I stayed home and watched on television, as we prepared for the luncheon. When I looked out the window shortly after Nixon had finished his Inaugural Address, I saw, to my astonishment, that hundreds of people, who had read of the event in the press, had assembled on our front lawn. For a moment, I feared Lyndon Johnson was going to be subjected to one last, unnecessary antiwar demonstration, but then I saw signs in the crowd, saying, WELL DONE, LYNDON, and WE STILL LOVE YOU, LYNDON.

The Johnsons and the Humphreys came directly to our house from the Capitol. It was a raw, cold day, and a fine mist of rain was falling as they arrived. As the man who had been President only a few minutes earlier got out of his limousine the crowd surged across our soaked and frozen lawn and surrounded his car. He kissed a few babies, shook a few hands, and walked into the house, immensely pleased. "They didn't come to see the *President,*" he said to me, "they came to see Lyndon Johnson." He took his grandson out on the front porch and held him up to show the crowd, which cheered wildly.

Inside our house the party went on for several hours, a sort of last roundup before we all went back to our separate lives. "This was an

*The parallel to the release of the American hostages in Iran in 1981, which was delayed until just after Reagan had been sworn in as President, is striking.

assembly of old friends," Johnson wrote in his own memoirs, "who had . . . been with us in sunshine and in sorrow."[3] After luncheon, President Johnson asked me to join him and Lady Bird upstairs in one of the bedrooms, and told Marny to summon Dean Rusk, Averell Harriman, Walt Rostow, and William S. White, his oldest and closest journalist friend. Then, in classic LBJ fashion, he unveiled a final surprise—awarding the Medal of Freedom, the nation's highest civilian award, to each of us.

Most of the crowd had waited through the rain to say farewell. As we emerged, they surged forward again and gave Johnson one last cheer. We looked at the remains of our lawn, destroyed by the crowds that had camped on it for several hours. "Tell the press," Harriman said to George Christian, "that Marny Clifford regrets that she has but one lawn to give to her country."[4] We accompanied the President to the nearby Bethesda Naval Hospital and boarded a helicopter for Andrews Air Force Base, where an Army band awaited him. As the wind whipped across the chilly tarmac, close to a thousand people, including one lone Republican Congressman named George Bush, cheered the former President, who plunged into the crowd, hugging friends, reporters, and staff members. He said farewell to Dean Rusk and me, gave Humphrey one last hug, and boarded his plane—no longer *Air Force One,* a designation reserved for the President—to return to Texas. The plane circled Washington for one last look, then headed west—and home—to Texas.

THE NIXON ADMINISTRATION AND THE *FOREIGN AFFAIRS* ARTICLE

I had assumed that the next President, whether Nixon or Humphrey, would take rapid action to end the war, as President Eisenhower had done with Korea in 1953. It seemed irrational for a new President, unconstrained by his own past decisions, to continue the war. *Surely,* I thought, *we will be out within a year.*

In the first few months of 1969, I stayed in contact with several members of the new Administration, including Kissinger, Rogers, and especially Laird, who invited me regularly to luncheons and private meetings at the Pentagon. My conversations with them left me with the impression they were looking for ways to get out of Vietnam, either through negotiations or a gradual withdrawal of American forces while building up the South Vietnamese. This encouraged me, and without criticizing the Nixon Administration, I began speaking out frankly about the war—unconstrained, finally, by the limitations of public service.

My brief honeymoon with the Administration came to an abrupt and unexpected end in June, after I published the most important article of my career, "A Viet Nam Reappraisal: The Personal History of One Man's View and How It Evolved," in the Summer 1969 issue of *Foreign Affairs.* The U.S., I proposed, should withdraw 100,000 American troops by the end of 1969, and all ground combat forces by the end of 1970. Saigon would get serious about the negotiations in Paris only when they realized that our commitment was limited and some political compromise with Hanoi was unavoidable. Furthermore, the Saigon government could never create a strong political structure "while our presence hangs over them so massively." Wanting Saigon to use the time we gave them during a phased withdrawal to strengthen themselves and negotiate with Hanoi and the NLF, I proposed we leave behind air and logistical forces for an unspecified period of time. I refrained from advocating a complete pullout by a "date certain" because I felt such a suggestion would reduce the impact of the article among the moderate members of Congress and the public to whom it was primarily addressed.

All this created quite a sensation, and the article was widely reprinted. For the first time, a major participant in shaping the policy had admitted that we had been mistaken, and had outlined a strategy for American disengagement. Response to the article was mostly favorable. From General Ridgway to soldiers in Vietnam, I received letters that gave me hope the article might contribute to bipartisan support for a policy of gradual disengagement.

But two prominent men did not appreciate the article. From his ranch in Texas, former President Johnson acknowledged an advance copy of the article with a brief and cold note signed by his assistant Tom Johnson, who said LBJ "thought his opinion could not have weight of consideration and, therefore, he did not respond." From mutual friends, I heard that Lyndon Johnson was annoyed at what he considered a self-serving article. In this view he was, however, mistaken. There was nothing to be gained by further involvement in the bitter public debate over Vietnam, but I felt an obligation to the American public, and especially to the half-million Americans still in the war zone, to help solve the most important policy issue of our time.

The other person who did not like the article was President Nixon. Ironically, it was published only ten days after Nixon, during a summit meeting with Thieu at Midway Island in the Pacific, announced the first reduction in troop levels in Vietnam, pulling out 25,000 troops—over General Abrams's objections. I had welcomed the step publicly because I would have recommended similar actions had I still been at the Pentagon. So close, in fact, was Nixon's action to steps I had been advocating that General Pursley, who now worked for Mel Laird, had called me from Midway as soon as President Nixon had made the announcement, simply to share the moment.

But although the article contained not a word of criticism of the new Administration, President Nixon did not view the article as supportive. The day after it was published, he denounced both me and my proposal in a press conference comment later described by a writer in *The New York Times* as a "classic Nixonism—the pious disclaimer followed by the distortion and innuendo"[5]:

> I noted Mr. Clifford's comments in the magazine *Foreign Affairs*, and naturally, I respect his judgment as a former Secretary of Defense. I would point out, however, that for five years in the Administration in which he was Secretary of Defense in the last part, we had a continued escalation of the war. . . . In addition to that we found that in the year—the full year in which he was Secretary of Defense, our casualties were the highest of the whole five-year period. And as far as negotiations were concerned, all that had been accomplished—as I indicated earlier—was that we had agreed on the shape of the table. Now this is not to say that Mr. Clifford's present judgment is not to be considered because of the past record. It does indicate, however, that he did have a chance in this particular respect and did not move on it then.

Nixon finished with a sentence that made headlines and led later to charges that he had misled the public as to the pace of his withdrawals: "*I would hope that we could beat Mr. Clifford's timetable,* just as I think we've done a little better than he did when he was in charge of our national defense."

From then on, my relations with the Nixon Administration were virtually nonexistent; and, except for my continued friendship with Mel Laird, they collapsed completely when Nixon invaded Cambodia in May 1970.

LIFE MAGAZINE, AND MORE DISPUTES ON VIETNAM

On April 20, 1970, Nixon announced a reduction in troop ceilings of 115,000, and a further reduction of 150,000 by the spring of 1971, which would leave 284,000 Americans in Vietnam by mid-1971. I felt these withdrawals were too little and too late, and considerably slower than he had suggested a year earlier. Three days later, and only one week before the invasion of Cambodia, Secretary of State Rogers—presumably out of touch with his own President's thinking—told Congress that the Administration fully recognized "that if we escalate and get involved in Cambodia with our ground troops, our whole program is defeated."

Then came the stunning Presidential speech of May 1, 1970. After all these years, the military, supported by Ambassador Bunker, finally received permission to fight inside Cambodia—but they failed to destroy the military headquarters of the communists in the South (COSVN), which the President had said was the purpose of the action. By driving the communists further toward the populated center of Cambodia, the invasion brought the war to the heart of that previously peaceful nation, with tragic consequences that lasted into the nineties. Within days, campuses in the U.S. were aflame with demonstrations, student strikes, and a new wave of protests that culminated in the tragic deaths at Kent State and Jackson State. Outraged at the incomprehensible decision that had triggered these events, I wrote an article for *Life* magazine.

This time I was not bipartisan. I had been frank in accepting responsibility for errors I had made or been associated with, but I felt justified in publicly attacking the Nixon Administration for the Cambodian invasion. This was an action I had opposed throughout the Johnson years, including the final debate on the military's request to go into Cambodia in mid-December 1968. Calling President Nixon's action "reckless" and "foolhardy," I suggested that the Administration was "leading us more deeply into Vietnam rather than taking us out." The Cambodian incursion was "an infinitely greater mistake" than the Bay of Pigs. I was particularly concerned that the invasion had "greatly expanded the danger of the conflict spreading throughout Cambodia"—an all too accurate prediction, as it turned out.

I wrote that the Nixon Administration was now following "a formula for perpetual war," and I saw only one way to stop their pursuit of a "military victory that cannot be won": a public announcement that

> all U.S. forces are to be removed from any combat role anywhere in Southeast Asia no later than Dec. 31, 1970, and that all U.S. military personnel will be out of Indochina by the end of 1971, at the latest, provided only that arrangements have been made for the release of all U.S. prisoners of war.

The reaction to the *Life* article was even greater than to the *Foreign Affairs* article. It was reprinted around the world, and I was deluged with requests to speak. The White House, upset at the amount of coverage I received from the television networks, protested that they deserved equal time to defend their policies—as if the Administration did not have almost unlimited access to television. Administration spokesmen used the usual method to try to discredit my proposals—ignore the message and attack the messenger. In one fairly typical incident that came to my attention from a friendly British diplomat, the Nixon White House sent the British Ambassador a "compendium" of statements I had made in the sixties on Vietnam, in order to suggest what I had never tried to hide—that I had changed my position on the war.

In a speech in Cleveland, Vice President Spiro Agnew fired a venomous shot at Averell Harriman, Cyrus Vance, and me, calling us "men whom history has branded as failures. . . . Mr. Clifford's current writings seem to emanate from a deep desire to convince his friends that he was an early convert and not a late-blooming opportunist who clambered aboard the rolling bandwagon of the doves when the flak really started to fly." Agnew saw Harriman's "unmistakable footprints . . . in every great [international] conference that turned out to be a loss for the West and freedom." Finally, there was this: "It is Harriman, Vance, Clifford, the men who were bluffed, raised, called, whipped and cleaned out at the tables in Paris, who are the ones who are now standing behind President Nixon yelling, in effect, 'Fold, fold.' Well, the President isn't going to fold."[6]

THE PENTAGON PAPERS

On Sunday morning, June 13, 1971, I read *The New York Times* with more than usual interest. On the front page was a three-column headline—VIETNAM ARCHIVE: PENTAGON STUDY TRACES 3 DECADES OF GROWING U.S. INVOLVEMENT—and inside the paper, six pages of excerpts from the top-secret Vietnam Task Force study that Bob McNamara had commissioned.

The *Times* gave no indication of its source, but there was no questioning the authenticity of what they printed: excerpts from some of the most highly classified memoranda and documents of the Vietnam War. Other than authorizing the study to be completed, and having once told Paul Warnke I thought the project was a "dumb idea," I had never paid the study much attention, even though the Task Force had operated out of offices right behind mine in the Pentagon. In June 1969, the head of the project, Leslie Gelb, had sent me all forty-seven volumes of the Task Force Report, which I kept at my law office in a closet that Pentagon security officers had converted into a "security storage area," a common courtesy extended to former Secretaries of State and Defense after they leave the government in case they need to store classified material.

When the *Times* ran its articles, I had never looked at the massive collection of papers stored in my security area. The next morning, for the first time, I took a look at several of the volumes. Although I would never have initiated such a project, I was impressed with what I found. Gelb and his team* had assembled a remarkable collection of documents and produced some important analytical work. When it was finally made

*Including my associate in this work, Richard Holbrooke.

public in its entirety, the Pentagon Papers, as they came to be known, showed clearly the rationale by which every President, starting with Eisenhower, had increased America's role in the war in order to avoid defeat, but without any assurance of victory. The Pentagon Papers also showed that the American government had repeatedly overestimated the impact of its actions, both militarily and politically, on the communists. The report was later criticized by some people as biased. I saw no evidence to support such an accusation. In transmitting the study to me, Gelb had dealt forthrightly with this issue. "We had a sense of doing something important and of the need to do it right," he wrote. "Of course, we all had our prejudices and axes to grind and these shine through clearly at times, but we tried, we think, to suppress or compensate for them." I felt that he and his team had been successful.

VIETNAM: AN ASSESSMENT

At the end of the Vietnam War, there was much talk of the "lessons learned" in Vietnam. The implication was that, having suffered an undeniable defeat, we could agree on why it happened—and prevent it from ever happening again.

Unfortunately, history is not so simple. Almost two decades after the last American troops left Vietnam, the debate continues over *why* we lost. As President Bush rightly said in his Inaugural Address on January 20, 1989, Vietnam "cleaves us still." I am sure that on April 30, 2000, the twenty-fifth anniversary of the fall of Saigon, Americans will turn on the morning television programs and see aging veterans of the war once more arguing over what the lessons of Vietnam really were.

The unrepentant hawks and those who do not remember or never knew what the battlefield situation actually was offer an easy answer to explain the disaster: failure to use enough military force to achieve our objectives, and betrayal on the home front. For the first point, I have some sympathy, but only a limited amount. For the second, I have none.

As I have said, I do not believe we should send American military forces overseas to fight unless our national security is threatened. I believed that our national security *was* involved in Korea in 1950, but it was never at stake in Vietnam. I did not object to the advisory effort begun under Eisenhower and expanded greatly under Kennedy; I was prepared to risk the lives of a limited number of professional soldiers in pursuit of what I regarded as a legitimate foreign policy objective—to help the South Vietnamese defend themselves against communist aggression.

My objections to the decision to escalate in 1965 have been well documented elsewhere in this volume. Once that decision was made, though, I believed that the proper policy would have been to use greater military force immediately. The theories of "flexible response" and "graduated response" championed by Maxwell Taylor and Robert McNamara, and much in vogue in the midsixties, were based on the idea that, as Dean Rusk once put it to me, "if we gradually increase our military pressure, Hanoi will eventually have to cry 'uncle,' because they know they are facing the most powerful nation on earth." This theory worked splendidly in a nonshooting confrontation between the two nuclear superpowers in Cuba in 1962, but it was inappropriate to the circumstances of a shooting war on the other side of the globe against guerrillas. It made no sense to apply the theory of gradual escalation to the circumstances of Vietnam. If we could not convince the communists to negotiate or quit, we would have difficulty staying the course.

Yet our political and military leaders in several administrations and both parties insisted on a policy in which the light at the end of the tunnel kept receding. When the American public finally demanded the end of a war that seemed endless, the supporters and creators of the policy—the hawks in both parties—caved in, reached an agreement at the beginning of 1973 that doomed Saigon's chances of surviving—and blamed the outcome on the antiwar movement, Congress, and the American press, whom they accused of biased reporting.

This "betrayal theory" is perhaps the most dangerous of the new myths that the right wing has tried to perpetrate on the American public in regard to Vietnam. In fact, it was the hawks, not the doves, who weakened America by pursuing the war for so long. The hawks argued that America's worldwide strength and credibility were on the line in Vietnam, which was not true. They argued that Vietnam was another Munich, which was not true. By putting our national prestige on the line at the point where our ability to control events was at its weakest, the hawks undermined the very national strength and prestige they claimed to be protecting. Then, after the failure of their policies, they sought to blame America's defeat on those who had opposed the war, instead of accepting responsibility for the poor strategy and poor leadership they themselves had offered in Vietnam.

In this effort they were greatly aided by the nature of the antiwar movement in the U.S., much of which took on an ugly, unpatriotic and anti-American tone. But the facts of the war in Indochina remained: the war was unwinnable at any reasonable level of American participation, it was a tragic mistake, and it weakened us while it was going on, but not after it ended. The dominoes of Southeast Asia did not topple, as predicted, after Saigon and Phnom Penh fell in 1975; on the contrary, the noncommunist nations of the region began an era of cooperation and economic growth which had been held back by the war. Southeast Asia became the premier growth region of the world in the fifteen years following the end of the war, and our relations with almost every nation of the region, including Japan and China, improved.

Did this constitute the abandonment of a friend and ally, as so often charged by the hawks? Hardly. On the contrary, the length of time that the nation committed itself to Vietnam, and the price we were willing to pay in pursuit of our objectives, was impressive by any standard. We sent troops and military advisers to Vietnam from the late fifties until 1973, making Vietnam the longest war in American history. Even after our last combat troops were withdrawn in 1973, we continued to send massive aid and civilian advisers to South Vietnam for over two more years. All told, the U.S. sent over two and a half million Americans to Southeast Asia—over 55,000 of whom died. We spent well over $150 billion in pursuit of our objective. Over this long period of time, the U.S. gave the South Vietnamese an extraordinary amount of assistance—more than we ever gave any other nation. It was our South Vietnamese allies—fractious, corrupt, and poorly led—who failed, not the U.S. They were given every chance to survive and succeed. We should not draw the wrong lessons from Vietnam. It was a defeat, but not because we failed to stay the course. Rather than lacerate ourselves for our failure, I believe we can look back today and say that we demonstrated our willingness to make an enormous commitment to a friendly nation. We did everything we could reasonably do to help the South Vietnamese—more, for that matter.

The war was not lost at home, as is so often stated. It was lost where it was fought, in the jungles and rice paddies of Southeast Asia, and in the offices of a corrupt and incompetent ally. If the enemy had been reduced in strength or driven back into North Vietnam within a reasonable period of time, if there had been steady and sustained progress, the American public would have continued to support the policy and its Presidents. They did not wish to see America suffer its first defeat in a foreign war.

No event of my lifetime was as misguided or as tragic in its consequences as the war in Vietnam. Everyone who participated in the decisions between the late 1950s and 1975 must accept some responsibility for the errors in judgment, strategy, and tactics, and for the unnecessary casualties, both Vietnamese and American, resulting from those policies. Almost none of those involved have accepted any responsibility for what happened, preferring instead to look elsewhere for the reasons for the tragedy. But the facts are simple: we overestimated our allies, underestimated our adversary, and thought that the American presence on the battlefield would be sufficient to change the situation in our favor. We were wrong.

WATERGATE

By the spring of 1973, the break-in that had taken place at the Watergate in the summer of 1972 had replaced Vietnam as Washington's top subject of conversation. I watched with the same astonishment as the rest of the nation as revelations poured forth showing a pattern of conspiracy and illegality at the highest levels of the government.

In the summer of 1973, I discovered that I had not been quite as much of a passive observer as I had previously thought. The White House had kept something called an "enemies list"—people particularly despised by the President and his inner team. I suppose that by 1973 I would have been disappointed had I *not* made such a list; it was, in a sense, a badge of honor. *The New Yorker* drew wry attention to the list's "evident sloppiness;" noting that my name had appeared on the list misspelled as "Gifford," they observed, "The nation may have been heading in the direction of a police state, but at least it would have been an inefficient police state."[7]

A more sinister activity of the Nixon White House came to light a year later in 1974, as Nixon struggled through the last few months of his Presidency, when it was revealed that the White House had ordered seventeen illegal wiretaps of government officials and reporters for political purposes. I was apparently not under direct surveillance, but two of those who were, General Pursley and former Deputy Assistant Secretary of Defense Morton Halperin, had been in close contact with me and had helped draft my article for *Life* magazine. A Republican, Halperin had moved from the Pentagon to Kissinger's National Security Council staff in 1969, but, distrusted by the White House because of his close association with the Democrats, he was soon cut off from access to most sensitive matters; he left the White House in September 1969. Once he left the White House, Halperin became part of a small group of people that included Gelb and Warnke, on whom I relied for advice on Vietnam. They were joined later by Tony Lake, an outstanding young Foreign Service Officer who had resigned as Henry Kissinger's aide in protest against the invasion of Cambodia.

Curiously, Halperin's tap, which had been placed only on his home telephone, never produced any direct conversations between Halperin and me. Our conversations had taken place only over his office telephone. The FBI had, however, listened to conversations between Halperin and Gelb concerning the *Life* article. The transcripts of these conversations were read with great interest by senior members of the White House staff, whose resulting memoranda on the subject, later declassified during legal proceedings, revealed much about the mentality of the Nixon White

House. On January 15, 1970, White House Assistant Jeb Magruder wrote Nixon's top two aides, Bob Haldeman and John D. Ehrlichman:

> J. Edgar Hoover's memorandum to the President regarding the potential problem that is developing with Clark Clifford has been checked out thoroughly. He is going to write an article for *Life*. . . . We are in a position to counteract this article in any number of ways.

Ehrlichman was impressed with the value of the wiretap on Halperin. "This is the kind of early warning we need more of," he wrote Haldeman. "Your game planners are now in an excellent position to map anticipatory action [against Clifford]."[8] In a handwritten reply to Magruder, Haldeman instructed him to assemble "from [Department of Defense] all the facts of the Clifford secretaryship and leak what is bad about this re Vietnam to Joe Alsop et al. . . ."[9]

When I learned of these illegal wiretaps in the late seventies, I reacted with a combination of outrage and amusement; outrage at the gross violation of the rights of Halperin and Lake and anyone who happened to call them, and amusement at the heavy-handed counterattack Haldeman, Ehrlichman, and Magruder deemed necessary. In personal terms, I was not worried about the contents of the wiretaps. My opposition to the war was no secret, and my discussions with Halperin on the telephone were usually confined to Vietnam and politics. For Halperin and Lake, though, the surveillance was a gross violation of their Constitutional rights. Both men sued Nixon, Mitchell, Haldeman, Kissinger, and others over the wiretaps; Lake settled for an apology from Kissinger in 1989, but Halperin's suit against Kissinger and Haldeman continued into the nineties.

The illegal wiretaps were part of one of the general counts in the impeachment resolution approved by the Senate Judiciary Committee and pending before the full House when Richard Nixon resigned the Presidency in August 1974. I was much relieved that we would not have to go through the entire judicial process before reaching what was, by then, a foreordained conclusion—Nixon's departure from office.

Richard Nixon's defenders have credited him with an outstanding foreign policy record, but with the exception of China, the Soviet Union, and the Sinai agreements negotiated by Kissinger after the 1973 war, Nixon's record in that area is hardly as distinguished as myth would have it. The roll call of the Nixon-Ford years in foreign policy is not a good one, and includes several major disasters: disdain for human rights, the panic over the now-forgotten threat of Eurocommunism, the mishandling of the situation in Cyprus and the eastern Mediterranean, the blank check issued to the Shah of Iran even while he supported OPEC's inflationary oil policies, African policy (especially in Angola), and the encouragement and support of repressive regimes in Chile, South Korea, the Philippines, Romania, Greece, Brazil, and elsewhere. The disastrous legacy of strengthening these oppressive governments was bequeathed to the Administrations of Jimmy Carter and, ironically, Ronald Reagan, both of whom compiled better records in this area. At home, Nixon had demeaned and weakened our greatest institution, the Presidency, more than any other man who had ever held the office. This in turn weakened our nation, not only at home, but abroad. I did not share in the sense, a decade and more later, that Nixon's foreign policy achievements deserved acclaim and somehow offset Watergate on the ledger sheet of history.

33

President Carter: Promise and Disappointment

There is no question in my mind that history will acknowledge Jimmy Carter's accomplishments as President and deal more kindly with him than the American people and most of the press did at the end of his term. He left behind a substantial body of achievements that history will recognize and praise, but because of a spectacularly unfortunate series of events that, with a surprising lack of political acumen, he emphasized rather than minimized, he left the Presidency with his reputation and image much diminished. A Presidency that began with remarkable promise ended in disappointment.

The attainment of true greatness slipped through Carter's hands, due to a combination of errors, inexperience, poor staff, and bad luck. No one ever came to the White House with a greater opportunity to lead the nation, and it was heartbreaking to watch when his Administration failed to live up to that promise. He reminded me of Churchill's description of Russia: "a riddle wrapped in a mystery inside an enigma."

Four years earlier, in 1972, impressed with Edmund Muskie's performance as a Senator, I had been deeply involved in his campaign for the Democratic nomination. After Senator George McGovern won the nomination by running against Washington, though, I realized that the very reason Muskie had attracted me and other former government officials—that he was a seasoned Washington professional—had damaged him in the primaries, where people were looking for a way to vote *against* Washington. Muskie's public statements, prepared in campaign strategy sessions run like Cabinet meetings, looked like official government documents, while his chief opponent, George McGovern, campaigned as an outsider, even though he had almost as much Washington experience as Muskie. But McGovern had taken positions during the primaries far too radical for the general electorate, and his defeat in the general election by Nixon was inevitable. Nonetheless, there were important lessons in both McGovern's successful primary campaign and his general election disaster—lessons that Jimmy Carter absorbed and applied superbly four years later.

Carter's astonishing emergence from obscurity resulted from his vision, drive, and brilliant exploitation of the forces that were reshaping American politics in 1976, after Vietnam and Watergate. I hardly knew Carter before his nomination, and played little role in his campaign. We first met at a dinner in March 1976 given by close friends of mine, the columnist Clayton Fritchey and his wife Polly. Despite victories in the Iowa caucus and the New Hampshire primary, Carter was still almost unknown in Washington, and he accepted an invitation from the Fritcheys to meet some of the capital's leading citizens. About twenty people, including a half-dozen former Cabinet members, were invited. There, in a lovely candlelight setting in one of Georgetown's most gracious homes, the candidate dined with men and women who had seen the capital survive three wars and the Great Depression—but had never met anyone quite like this former Governor of Georgia, then in the process of shattering almost every assumption Washington believed about Presidential politics.

Carter, after all, was the ultimate outsider. If he succeeded in winning the Presidency, he would be the first Southerner to reach the White House on his own since Zachary Taylor in 1848, and the first man to sit in the Oval Office without any prior Washington experience since Woodrow Wilson. At the same time, he was immensely attractive, a fresh and intelligent personality, with the will and strength to reach his goal. With the nation fed up with Washington insiders and searching for change after thirteen years of disasters and tragedies, Carter seemed to offer something new, different, and promising.

I left the Fritcheys' house that evening convinced I had met the next President of the United States. He conveyed the single-minded drive and focus I have always believed was the most important ingredient—besides luck—required to be a successful Presidential candidate. I was particularly impressed with his strategy, which was based on a bold and brilliant analysis of the Democratic party's new rules of delegate selection. Carter and I sat next to each other for part of the dinner, and as we spoke I found him well prepared on every question and adept at conveying a general impression without being excessively precise.

During the campaign, Carter asked for my views on the defense budget, the restructuring of the intelligence community, and the television debates with President Ford. After each memorandum I sent him or his staff, I received a polite handwritten note from Carter, thanking me for my efforts, written in his curiously impersonal style. His notes always began "To Clark Clifford," never "Dear Clark," and I later learned that he used this peculiar salutation—presumably a way of seeming neither excessively formal nor familiar—in notes and letters to almost everyone.

Just after Carter achieved front-runner status, *Newsweek* ran an article listing me, among others, as a member of Carter's advisory team. His reaction was revealing: Carter, *The Washington Star* reported a few days later, had been

> particularly miffed because *Newsweek* had carried pictures of former Johnson advisor Joseph Califano and of old Washington hand Clark Clifford and described them as having a major role in the planning of his administration. Califano and Clifford, the candidate noted, hardly squared with the image he is trying to project as a different kind of candidate who would bring a fresh breeze into the White House.[1]

This was more than imagery and politics. It was an early sign of Carter's extreme sensitivity to any implication that he needed advice from people identified as part of the Washington power structure.

During the summer, the chief of his transition task force, Jack Watson, came to see me several times. Watson, a bright and energetic Georgian, did not accept my view that if he headed the transition team he should neither seek nor accept a position in the government. Unwisely, he proposed for the Carter White House a structure that included a major role for himself, setting off an immediate power struggle with Hamilton Jordan, the new President's closest aide. Not surprisingly, Watson lost, although he did stay on in the White House.

A month after his election, on December 9, 1976, Carter invited me to the Blair House to discuss the Presidency and some of his senior appointments. He told me he identified most closely with President Truman—"one of my heroes," he said. I was, of course, glad to hear this, but thought it interesting that, after revealing this admiration, he asked not a single question about him or his Administration.

Carter appointed to the key position of White House liaison with Congress one of his closest aides, a genial Georgian with no prior Hill experience and limited political skills. This was obviously a mistake, but what troubled me more than the appointment itself was what it seemed to reveal about the new President's attitude toward Congress and Washington. He entered office without obligations to anyone. This was a source of tremendous strength for him; but he misunderstood his own achievement and seemed to think that if he could win without Washington, he could govern without Washington. In this he was wrong: alienating the powers of the capital city served no purpose and could only cause unnecessary difficulties.

This problem was evident even in that first meeting in December. I suggested that he include in his circle of advisers some experienced Washington hands. Concerned he might think I wanted a job myself, I stressed that I was too old for a position in the government, but that I deeply wished to see him succeed. Carter nodded and took notes, but he did not ask me for any names. I felt he neither liked nor fully understood my suggestion, and may have viewed it as an attempt to penetrate and weaken his loyal inner team.

In the national security area, he was more open, perhaps because there were no serious candidates from Georgia for the top posts. It was vitally important to assemble a group of people for the top positions who could work together closely as a team, and avoid the feuds that had broken out among Kissinger, Rogers, and Laird. The President-elect planned to nominate Cyrus Vance as Secretary of State, Harold Brown as Secretary of Defense, and Ted Sorensen as Director of Central Intelligence. I applauded all three appointments, but I objected strongly to another key appointment in the national security field—Zbigniew Brzezinski as Assistant for National Security Affairs. Brzezinski, an articulate and combative academic from Columbia University, seemed to me too much of an advocate and not enough of an honest broker to fill this post in the way I believed appropriate. Also, I was certain he would clash with the gentle and collegial Vance. This I stated frankly to the President-elect, who was not pleased; Brzezinski had been one of the earliest and closest members of his team. Even after Carter told me Vance had said he could work with Brzezinski, I persisted in my objections. Finally, he said, "Well, if we don't put Zbig there, what should I do with him?" With deliberately exaggerated seriousness, I replied, "Make him the first American Ambassador to the Bermuda Triangle." The President-elect laughed, and our discussion was over.

SORENSEN AND THE CIA

More than any other single factor, senior personnel determine the character and course of an Administration, yet often selections are made without sufficient thought as to what kind of a team is being assembled or how people will get along with each other. Sometimes the right person is offered the wrong job. Such, I regret to say, was the case when Carter chose Theodore Sorensen, the most impressive of President Kennedy's aides, to succeed George Bush as Director of Central Intelligence. The nomination ran into immediate difficulty.

As we were all soon to learn, no one on the Carter transition team had gone through the tedious but necessary process of checking the candidate's background—another price of the inexperience of Carter's team. Senators who disliked Sorensen seized on several aspects of his background of which the Carter team was unaware. When he had registered for the draft in 1946, he had asked, on moral and ethical grounds, for noncombatant status as a conscientious objector. Sorensen's stance had been highly moral and completely proper, but some Senators who had fought in World War II did not like the idea of an intelligence chief who, they inferred, might oppose the use of force in defense of our national security. (Sorensen rightly objected to this characterization of his views.) In addition, he was unfairly accused of having taken with him, when he left the Kennedy White House in 1964, certain classified material to help in writing his book on the Kennedy Administration. Thus, a newly elected President faced the rejection of a senior appointee even before his Inauguration, a highly unusual event.

Instead of rallying immediately to Sorensen's support, the Carter team began to back away from their nominee, telling Sorensen, in effect, that the fight for confirmation was his to wage. Sorensen wanted to fight, for his reputation and for the job. Once I knew what the problems were, I concluded, rather sadly, that while Sorensen was extremely well qualified to serve again in high office, perhaps in the State Department, he probably should have been offered some position other than the CIA post. Despite these misgivings, though, I wanted to assist him, as a friend and because the charges against him were political and misguided. I agreed to testify on his behalf in the hearings, scheduled to begin on Monday, January 17.

Sorensen spent the weekend before the hearings in Washington trying to rally Senatorial support. On Saturday, I received a telephone call from Hamilton Jordan, followed by one from the President-elect himself, who was spending the weekend at his home in Plains, Georgia. Based on the information they had received from their operatives on Capitol Hill, including Senator Walter F. Mondale, the new Vice President, they concluded that the fight for confirmation would be long, drawn-out, costly—and probably unsuccessful. Carter asked if I would be willing to tell Sorensen how bleak his situation was and urge him to withdraw.

Later that evening, Sorensen called, at the suggestion, he said, of the President-elect. It was a painful conversation. Carter had told him that the decision as to whether or not to proceed was entirely up to him, and he was thinking about withdrawing. Did I have any suggestions?

I stressed that I was still ready to testify on his behalf. While I could not tell him what to do, I had to tell him, in all candor, that the new President did not appear to have the stomach for a fight over the nomination. If Sorensen wished to see it through, he might still be confirmed, I said—but without the personal involvement and commitment of Jimmy Carter, it would be tough going. Whatever he decided, I urged him to go before the committee and rebut the charges against him.

Without the slightest sign of emotion, Sorensen thanked me for my time and ended the call. On Monday, after a day of rumors that Sorensen was going to withdraw, he appeared before the Senate Select Committee on Intelligence. Averell Harriman and I sat directly behind him as he defended himself with deftness and precision, and then withdrew from the field of battle with dignity.

Twelve years later, I was reminded of this sad, short chapter in the history of the Carter Administration when Senator John Tower faced far more serious difficulties as President Bush's nominee for Secretary of Defense. Even when it was clear Tower was going to be defeated, the Bush Administration stuck with their man, forcing a vote in the Senate. It was a bitter defeat, but by refusing to withdraw, Bush showed he was willing to fight with the Congress. By pulling away from its very first confrontation with Congress, the Carter Administration had offered an early sign it could be intimidated. Later, President Carter would win some big fights with Congress—notably over the Panama Canal Treaties—but the failure to support Sorensen, win or lose, was a mistake.

THE TWO PAULS

I had hoped Paul Warnke would be offered one of the top two spots in the State Department. He was eminently qualified for either. Instead, he was offered a dual appointment as Director of the Arms Control and Disarmament Agency (ACDA) and chief negotiator for the Strategic Arms Limitation Talks (SALT) with the Soviet Union. I urged him to decline, feeling that this particular offer did not justify his return to government; as time went on, I was sure, other positions would open up. I was also worried he would find himself in the position of carrying out instructions which he had played only a minor role in formulating. But he had thoroughly enjoyed his service in the Pentagon, and after initially declining the offer, he finally accepted it under heavy pressure from Carter and Vance.

Everyone expected a routine confirmation hearing—but no one had counted on Paul Nitze. As soon as our former colleague heard about Warnke's nomination, he set out to stop it in the most personal and nasty fashion. Nitze later explained his venomous behavior by saying that while he "had considerable respect for [Warnke's] intelligence," the more he studied Warnke's positions on arms control issues, the more "I became convinced that he was not the right man for either role or both."[2]

This was nonsense. Nitze's differences with Warnke on arms control were real enough, but they did not remotely excuse the personal nature of the attack against his former colleague. Some people believed that at the root of Nitze's behavior lay his deep disappointment that Carter had not offered him a position in the new Administration. His thwarted ambition had turned into rage, exploded, and focused itself on his former associate.

What made this all the more puzzling was that Warnke and I had supported Nitze eight years earlier, in 1969, in roughly similar circumstances: President Nixon had asked him to serve as Ambassador to West Germany, and Senator Fulbright objected because he was still angry at Nitze's refusal to testify on Vietnam in 1968. At Nitze's request, both Warnke and I had urged Fulbright to drop his objection to Nitze's nomination—unsuccessfully.*

On February 28, 1977, Nitze's attacks on Warnke reached their low point. Warnke's views, he testified before the Senate Foreign Relations Committee, were "asinine," "screwball," and "demonstrably unsound." Astonished at Nitze's venom, Senator Thomas McIntyre, a New Hampshire Democrat who supported Warnke, asked, "Are you saying that you impugn [Warnke's] character as an American citizen?"

Nitze replied, "If you force me to, I do."

"That is very interesting. Do you think you are a better American than he is?" McIntyre asked.

"I really do."

It was one of the most outrageous and inexcusable statements I ever encountered in Washington; this was not, after all, an attack by a Joe McCarthy on a political opponent, it was an assault upon a close former colleague. Warnke and I both hoped Nitze had weakened his own credibility by the extreme and personal nature of his attack. I concluded, after telephone calls and private visits with members of the Senate, that Warnke would be confirmed, but it was clear that Nitze's attacks had damaged Warnke with some Senators.

Unlike the Sorensen nomination, President Carter fought hard for Warnke, and he was confirmed as Director of ACDA by a vote of 70 to 29. For chief SALT negotiator, however, he was approved by a vote of 58 to 40. Since, in the latter vote, Warnke had received less than the two-thirds Senate majority that an arms control treaty would require for

*Nitze then accepted a lesser position which did not require Senate confirmation, that of Defense Department representative on the SALT delegation headed by Warnke's predecessor, Gerard Smith. He later quit in a dispute with Henry Kissinger.

ratification, Warnke's opponents considered this vote a symbolic victory and a warning to the Administration that any treaty negotiated by Warnke would probably face additional difficulty.

Nitze's attack may have weakened Warnke politically, but it never touched his integrity or the deep respect in which he was held by his many friends and associates. He performed splendidly and with distinction, negotiating most of the SALT II Treaty before resigning in 1979. Nitze later tried to reinterpret the record so as to deny having attacked Warnke's patriotism, but the despicable words were there.

MISSION TO THE EASTERN MEDITERRANEAN

My first assignment from President Carter came less than a month after his Inauguration, when he asked me to act as his special envoy to the eastern Mediterranean. Every Administration since Kennedy's had tried to deal with the problems of this region, where the ancient enmity between Greece and Turkey had exploded with Turkey's invasion of Cyprus in 1974. President Carter hoped I could ascertain what contribution, if any, the U.S. could make toward solving the bitter dispute.

Cyprus was a small island republic divided into two distinct and hostile communities, a Greek majority and a Turkish minority. Because there was a real danger of a war between Greece and Turkey over Cyprus, the situation threatened the entire eastern flank of NATO. The Greek government had already withdrawn from the NATO command structure and refused to participate in any NATO military exercises. They had even refused to meet with Secretary of State Kissinger only a few months earlier. Jimmy Carter's election, though, had excited them. He had successfully courted the Greek-American vote, and they expected a policy change in Washington.

The Turks, on the other hand, were angry at the U.S. Overcoming strenuous Ford Administration opposition, Congress had imposed an arms embargo on Turkey for using American weapons in the invasion of Cyprus. In retaliation the Turks had closed or severely restricted important American intelligence listening posts.

My only previous involvement with the region had been during the drafting of the Truman Doctrine thirty years earlier. Nevertheless, I welcomed the opportunity. Vance assigned a first-rate team to work with me: Matthew Nimetz, a lawyer from New York who had just been appointed Counselor of the State Department, and Nelson Ledsky, a career diplomat with substantial experience in the area. Nimetz and Ledsky spent long hours in my office educating me on the complexities of Greek-Turkish relations and Cyprus. It was clear that, left to themselves, the two

Cypriot communities would never make progress. It was by no means clear that our efforts could solve the problem—but it was worth a try.

I called on a dozen members of Congress who had special interest in the region. This group, all strongly pro-Greek, had assembled the majority that had surprised Kissinger in 1974–1975 by imposing the Turkish arms embargo. After meeting with the President to get my final instructions, I left Washington on February 16, 1977, and flew to Athens, Ankara, Nicosia, and London.

I concentrated first on repairing American relations with Greece and Turkey, and sought to defuse heightened tension between the two nations over Cyprus and several other issues, including drilling rights to oil and mineral deposits in the Aegean Sea and sovereignty over the Dodecanese Islands.

In Athens, Prime Minister Constantine Karamanlis treated me to a complete history of Greek-American relations, with emphasis on the alleged misdeeds of the Johnson Administration and the Nixon-Kissinger team. Two or three times, he alluded to the possibility of war with Turkey. In Ankara, Turkish Prime Minister Suleiman Demiral appeared willing to try to help the new Administration. His position was simple: Turkey had been humiliated by the United States Congress, Cyprus had nothing to do with the basic problems in Turkish-American or NATO relations, and the Greek lobby in Washington was "impossible." They attached great importance to my visit, and promised to put pressure on the head of the Turkish community in Cyprus, Rauf Denktash, to be flexible on intercommunal issues—provided I could produce some flexibility from the most important figure in the region, Archbishop Makarios, the President of Cyprus. It was clear that both Athens and Ankara were awaiting the results of my meetings with this legendary man, who had virtually created the modern nation of Cyprus and had dominated it since 1960. I, too, looked forward to meeting him, but I had no idea what to expect.

What I found when I got to Nicosia was a crafty but likable politician, tough and single-minded in his objectives, flexible in tactics. He and I began the meeting sizing each other up warily. After about thirty minutes, the Archbishop suggested we leave the rest of the group for a private talk. It was a very hot day, and he led me to an outside terrace of the Presidential Palace, which was still covered with the scaffolding from repair work after the fighting in 1974. We began by reviewing each other's careers and talking about President Kennedy—whom Makarios admired greatly—only later coming to the Cyprus question. As we talked, Makarios gradually stripped down, taking off first his religious robes, then his impressive religious hat, finally even his white shirt. The result was a dramatic downscaling of the Archbishop. Minus the full religious garb which made him recognizable throughout the world, he became a fairly short, balding man in an undershirt; but the partial disrobing also had the effect of humanizing him and gave our talks a more informal air.

The more I talked to Makarios, the more I felt he was ready to bargain. After I said we would support a federal division of Cyprus in order to reduce tensions, Makarios said he would support such a "bizonal" solution. This was unexpected. He cooled considerably, though, when I warned that delay in seeking a solution would work against him in the U.S.

I drove across the heavily fortified Green Line dividing the two communities, to meet in Kyrenia with Rauf Denktash, the leader of the so-called Turkish Republic of Northern Cyprus. He treated us to a magnificent lunch, and as his grandchildren scampered beneath the table I received another lecture, this one on the grievances of the Turkish community on Cyprus. I shuttled back to see Makarios again, and again, he unexpectedly offered to make some concessions in order to get talks restarted.

I returned to Washington with a slightly optimistic report. I recommended that we defer lifting the arms embargo on Turkey, but, to improve U.S.-Turkish relations immediately, release for delivery some fighter jets that Turkey had paid for but never received. The President approved this recommendation and asked me to carry the case in testimony before Congress. This led to several difficult sessions with some old Congressional friends like Congressman John Brademas, but I tried to assure them that their interests were not going to be jeopardized.

Congress eventually agreed to the lifting of the arms embargo. As Makarios had promised, the intercommunal talks started in Vienna in April. I joined President Carter at the U.N. and later in London for meetings with the Greek and Turkish leaders. Sadly, though, in August 1977, the man whom I believed held the greatest promise for solving the problem, Archbishop Makarios, died at the age of sixty-three. I had developed a sincere affection for him. He had fought for his beliefs all his life, and he had vision. Had he lived longer, I believe that we might have seen progress on the all-important intercommunal issue.

I went to Makarios's funeral in Nicosia as part of a large American delegation that included Chief Justice Warren Burger, several members of Congress, and Ruth Stapleton, the President's sister. On one of those hot August days that sears one's insides, we walked through the streets of Nicosia for almost two miles through enormous crowds of grief-stricken mourners. One by one, the members of the American delegation approached the open coffin to pay final respects. Some impulse within me caused me to lay my hands upon those of the Archbishop for a brief moment, causing the crowd around the coffin suddenly to hush. Congressman Paul Simon, a member of the delegation, told me later that he felt the crowd was waiting for their leader to rise from his coffin.

Makarios's death dealt a severe setback to the intercommunal talks, and the hatreds in the region defied a negotiated solution. Nevertheless, the strain in our relations with both Greece and Turkey had been significantly reduced, and the threat of war gradually abated. I continued my involvement in the Cyprus issue for the next two years, but the progress for which I had hoped never fully materialized. More than fifteen years later, Denktash was still arguing with Makarios's successors over the same issues.

THE BERT LANCE AFFAIR

Jimmy Carter had presented himself as a completely different sort of political leader. In two of the most effective campaign pledges I ever heard, he had promised "never to lie" to the American people, and said that they "deserve a government that reflects their own decency and generosity and common sense and honesty." This was not the sort of rhetoric people expected from politicians, but coming after the worst political scandal in the nation's history, it constituted one of Carter's greatest strengths. Thus the Bert Lance affair, while not in substance as serious as problems many other Administrations have encountered, was a major blow to the new President.

Like everyone else in Washington, I had followed the difficulties of the Director of the Office of Management and Budget during the hot summer of 1977. But I did not know Lance well, and was unprepared for his telephone call on Labor Day weekend.

By the time Lance called, his situation had deteriorated badly. He had promised during his confirmation hearings to divest himself of all stock he owned in two Georgia banks before the end of 1977. Rather unwisely, he had asked the Senate six months later for permission to delay the sale because of a downturn in the value of his stock. His request triggered demands that the Senate Governmental Affairs Committee, which had voted for his confirmation unanimously only nine months earlier, reexamine his banking activities. At the same time, the Comptroller of the Currency made an independent investigation of Lance which did not find him guilty of anything illegal, but did list a series of "unresolved questions" about his banking activities. Although these problems had nothing to do with Lance's activities as Director of the OMB, they included charges that he had abused his authority and violated banking regulations as President of the National Bank of Georgia and the Calhoun First National Bank. The President—badly misled by his White House counsel (another inexperienced Georgian), who told him that the report was a full exoneration of Lance—held a joint press conference with Lance on August 18, and made a soon-to-be-famous remark. "Bert," he said, "I'm proud of you."

I was impressed with Lance when we met at the Old Executive Office

Building on Labor Day morning. He struck me as the smartest and the most politically astute of the Georgians who had accompanied Jimmy Carter to Washington. A large and jovial man with a keen sense of political power, he had been a close friend and ally of Jimmy Carter since they had first met in Georgia years earlier.

I could see that he was almost at the end of his rope. Although in public, Carter was still supporting him, Lance understood that the President, Hamilton Jordan, and Charles Kirbo, a close and influential Presidential adviser from Atlanta, all wanted him to resign—probably that day. Somewhat startled by this news, which contradicted public statements by the White House, I stressed that, if I became Lance's lawyer, I would be thinking of his interests, which might no longer be identical to those of the President. For starters, I said I would recommend against his resignation at this time: "If you resign, no one will ever pay any attention to your defense. If I am to represent you, I want to fight for your chance to defend yourself against each and every charge that has been made against you. If you defend yourself while Director of OMB, you will have national attention, and we may be able to force your attackers to retreat publicly on many of these false charges."

Lance was gratified to find someone who thought he should stand and fight. He said that he and his wife had been asked to meet with the President later that afternoon, and he expected at that time to be asked to resign. Because I was his new lawyer, he asked if I would meet immediately with Hamilton Jordan to try to head this request off.

We walked across the street to the White House, where I explained to Jordan why asking Lance to resign without the benefit of hearings would be viewed as an admission of guilt and could injure Lance for the rest of his life. Jordan asked me to return later to the White House to repeat my argument to the President.

I met with President Carter on Labor Day in his small private office just off the Oval Office shortly after 3 P.M. As I presented my position, he showed no emotion. After I had finished, he asked a few questions, then said in a flat, tired tone of voice aimed in Jordan's general direction, "This is the right course of action." Barely saying good-bye to me as he rose, he asked Jordan to bring in Bert and his wife, LaBelle.

I waited to see the Lances after their meeting with the President. They were both relieved that Bert had been given an opportunity to defend himself, although he realized his survival was still in doubt. As we conferred, the President met with the two ranking Senators on the committee that was investigating Lance's financial situation, Abraham Ribicoff, Democrat of Connecticut, and Charles Percy, Republican of Illinois. Ribicoff and Percy were usually fair-minded men, but in the heat of the moment, they made an error. After the meeting with the President,

Ribicoff and Percy went out on the lawn of the White House and repeated to the press some ludicrous charges a convicted Georgia felon had made to Congressional investigators about Lance being involved in a criminal bank embezzlement. Citing "alleged illegalities," the two Senators said they had asked the President to fire Lance. The next day, the Ribicoff-Percy press comments dominated the nation's newspapers. In the eyes of the public, Lance was already convicted, but I felt that the action of the two Senators threatened to deprive him of his right of due process. That Labor Day evening, I brought the most promising young lawyer in my firm, Robert Altman, into the case. From then on, Altman worked closely with me and Lance.

Lance was scheduled to appear on Thursday, September 8, 1977. On September 6, I called on Ribicoff and Percy in Ribicoff's office to discuss the hearings, and obtained a one-week delay in the hearings so we could prepare Lance's defense.

The President, much relieved that he could turn the Lance affair over to outside counsel, was able to focus on an event of far greater long-term importance, the battle to ratify the Panama Canal Treaties, on which he also asked for my support. In the middle of the Lance deliberations, I went to the White House for a breakfast in which the two American negotiators, Ellsworth Bunker and Sol Linowitz, defended the treaties. It was a significant foreign policy achievement for the Administration, but the fight for ratification would be long and costly. I also spent several hours preparing for the meetings scheduled for later that month at the U.N. with the leaders of Greece, Turkey, and Cyprus. Always, though, I came back to the Lance case, working every evening until past midnight preparing his statement. The combination of events made me feel as if I were temporarily back in full-time government service.

At first, Lance wanted to spend his time on the witness stand discussing his close relationship with President Carter, but I believed Lance had to address each allegation. I pointed out that it was not the President, but Bert Lance, who was under examination. The best overall approach was to object strongly to the treatment he had received from the press and the Senate, and to counterattack vigorously in those areas where he had been unfairly accused. The White House also wished to participate in the preparation of the statement, but, telling Jordan that my obligations were to my client, I declined to show the statement to anyone in the White House until it had been completed. A week later, the evening before it was to be delivered, I finally invited Jordan to my office to read it. When he had finished it, he turned to Lance: "This is the toughest statement I have ever seen. You are attacking both the chairman and the ranking minority member. I think it goes much too far. I hope you know what you are doing." Bert just smiled and said he was comfortable with the statement and the advice of his counsel.

The statement Lance presented to the Senate Governmental Affairs Committee and a national television audience on September 15, 1977, was very strong indeed. We heightened its impact by not releasing it to the Senate and the press in advance, thus forcing everyone to listen to Lance deliver it. For the next three days, Lance rebutted each charge. I sat next to him, occasionally interrupting the questioning to make a technical or legal point.

Lance succeeded in putting the Senate committee on the defensive. Members of the Committee—especially Senators Sam Nunn and Tom Eagleton—supported Lance. Across the nation, particularly from his native South, people rallied to his defense, viewing him as a victim of unfair press coverage. Mail, which had been running over two to one against him at the White House, now ran heavily in his favor. *The Washington Star* columnist Mary McGrory described the hearings as a "stunning reversal." James Reston wrote, "Mr. Lance turned the whole controversy around. He was not the accused, but the accuser." But Reston added, "Nobody knows better than Mr. Lance's lawyer, Clark Clifford, the survivor of many tragic struggles in Washington, that you can defy the Senate or live with the Senate, but you can't do both for long."

Lance's triumph was, as we had expected, short-lived. On Sunday, September 18, the Senate Majority Leader, Robert Byrd of West Virginia, told President Carter that despite Lance's testimony, he felt Lance had to resign in order to avoid a protracted struggle that would end with his departure. That same day, Charles Kirbo flew to Washington from Atlanta to consult with me.

I conferred with Lance repeatedly during the weekend and on Monday. It was clear that with the hearings over, his attackers would resume their investigations: other charges against him were surfacing or about to surface, and the press was still relentlessly pursuing the story. I went over the situation in detail with him, pointing out several areas in which he faced further difficulties. On Tuesday, September 20, after what he later described as an almost sleepless night,[3] President Carter met privately with Lance and hinted strongly that the time had come to step down. Lance called me afterward: he was ready to go, but his wife, LaBelle, was furious at the President for not sticking up for him—she wanted Bert to stay and fight. I gently tried to help LaBelle through the difficult realization that the game was over, that Bert had done as much as he could to defend his reputation. Gradually, Altman and I began to focus Bert on his letter of resignation, which we completed late that afternoon. On September 21, 1977, the sad story ended, as so many Washington dramas do, with a

President sorrowfully "accepting" the resignation of a trusted and valued aide. That day, as the press trumpeted the news that the "deputy President" had resigned, both Bert and LaBelle Lance wrote me touching personal letters of appreciation for my advice and support.

Lance returned to Georgia, where he faced legal investigations into his banking affairs. He asked me to represent him before the courts in Georgia, but I felt he needed a local lawyer. Altman and I gave him advice on a regular basis and assisted him on matters relating to federal regulatory agency proceedings. For a time, Altman flew to Atlanta once a week to counsel Lance. After several years of legal proceedings, all criminal charges against Lance were dismissed or rejected by the jury.

The cost of the Lance affair was immense to Carter. The press—especially *The Washington Post*—may have vastly overcovered the story, but Carter had stimulated the problem by inviting the world to judge him by higher standards than it did normal politicians. After its role in Watergate, the press was bound to scrutinize the first such problem in the next Democratic Administration.

There was another cost to Carter: he lost his most savvy political adviser and never found anyone again whom he trusted as much, and whose political judgment was as good, as that of Bert Lance.

"MALAISE" AT CAMP DAVID

Three weeks after Lance resigned, on an evening when Marny was out of town visiting one of our daughters, I was at home alone on a Saturday evening, reading, when I felt an extremely sharp pain in my chest. Calling my doctor, I said I thought I was having a serious problem with my heart, perhaps even a heart attack. He asked if I could drive myself to the hospital. When I said I thought I could, he told me to go immediately to the Georgetown Coronary Care Unit. The diagnosis was, indeed, a heart attack, and the prescription was rest and a reduced work schedule for the rest of the year, and beyond. For several months, I worked only part-time.

As a result, my involvement with the Carter Administration declined greatly for a while. I kept myself informed on the Greek-Turkish situation through Nimetz and Ledsky, but canceled another trip to the region. My contact with the White House—including involvement in the ratification of the Panama Canal Treaties—dropped off while I regained full strength.

So, partially sidelined, I watched the second year of the Carter Presidency with admiration. It was a year of spectacular, even historic, accomplishments. Although the political costs were high, the Panama Canal Treaties passed the Senate by the narrowest of margins, after an all-out effort led by the President himself. Progress was made toward a second

SALT treaty with Moscow. Six months of secret negotiations led to the establishment of full diplomatic relations with the People's Republic of China, after twenty-nine years of nonrecognition. The Administration's commitment to human rights, while criticized by conservatives, stirred people living under repression from South Africa to Czechoslovakia. But the greatest achievement of this productive year was, without question, the agreements between Israel and Egypt made possible by the remarkable negotiations at Camp David in September 1978.

The peace treaty was signed at the White House on March 25, 1979, in one of the most moving ceremonies I ever attended. Everyone present knew that this impossible event owed a enormous amount to the persistence, courage, and faith of Jimmy Carter. It was ironic that Israel's Menachem Begin and Egypt's Anwar Sadat would receive the Nobel Peace Prize, while President Carter, without whom it would never have been possible, was passed over. Marny and I returned to the White House that evening for a glittering and unforgettable State dinner for over 1,300 guests—the largest State dinner ever held there. I was seated with Israeli Foreign Minister Moshe Dayan and Cyrus Vance. In his toast, as Begin paid an eloquent tribute to Vance, who had played a crucial role at Camp David, I glanced at Cy. That normally controlled man, exhausted and moved, was weeping silently.

At that moment, the future of the Carter Administration seemed bright. After a decline in his approval ratings, which had started with the Lance affair, he had regained considerable support. Yet that beautiful dinner turned out to be the high-water mark. Never again did the Administration look so good.

* * *

It has often been said that politicians are better off lucky than smart, and this is certainly borne out by the last twenty-two months of the Carter Presidency. Everything seemed to go wrong for the Administration: double-digit inflation, rising interest rates, skyrocketing oil prices, the taking of the hostages in Iran, the Soviet invasion of Afghanistan. But several embarrassing events—including the messy departure of Andrew Young from the post of Ambassador to the U.N., the even messier mishandling of an American vote condemning Israel in the U.N. Security Council, and the botched attempt to rescue the hostages—were self-inflicted, the results of poor political judgment or poor planning.

At the beginning of this decline, in July of 1979, President Carter retreated to Camp David for ten days and summoned a wide variety of national leaders and opinion-makers to offer him advice. The nation watched the daily trek to Camp David with growing astonishment. More in wonderment than criticism, *Time* magazine observed that "In the whole history of American politics, there had never been anything quite like it."

I participated in what turned out to be the longest and probably the most painful of these meetings, a two-day session on July 7–8, 1979, which ended at 1 A.M. on Saturday night—only to resume seven hours later over breakfast. My group, only one of many summoned to Camp David during those ten days, was described by *The Washington Post* as the " 'A' list." It included AFL-CIO chief Lane Kirkland, Panama Canal negotiator Sol Linowitz, the Reverend Jesse Jackson, and Wellesley College President Barbara Newell. We arrived late Saturday afternoon, just as a group of Governors were leaving.*

Former Secretary of Health, Education, and Welfare John Gardner, with whom I was sharing a cabin, noticed two bicycles sitting on our porch. Rather rashly, I allowed him to talk me into joining him for a bike ride. As we toured Camp David, we came to a hill, where I began accelerating rapidly. I could not get the brakes to work, and, noticing I was rapidly approaching some trees, I slid off the back of the bike and landed unceremoniously on my backside. Gardner asked me why I had not put on the brakes. "Well, I reversed the pedals, just as I always do when I ride a bike," I answered. Gardner, vastly amused, pointed out that the brakes on bikes were on the handlebars. "Clark," he asked, "when was the last time you rode a bike?" I thought for a moment. "About sixty years ago," I replied.

I was still sore when we gathered in the late afternoon at Laurel Lodge, and Gardner recounted the story for the amusement of the group before we got down to the serious purpose of our session. The President of the United States, in blue jeans and a polo shirt, sat on the floor, a yellow legal pad perched on his knees.

He began with an admission that I thought both revealing and unnecessary: "I feel I have lost control of the government and the leadership of the people"—and this from the man who only a few months earlier had orchestrated one of the greatest diplomatic achievements of the postwar era. He invited comments on almost any subject. As he filled page after page with his own careful notes, I became increasingly disturbed at the formlessness of the exercise. Hugh Sidey captured my concerns in a thoughtful column in *Time:* "From such a mishmash of people, prejudice, and points of view," Sidey asked, "could an executive distill any rational policy in so short a time?"[4]

Many of our comments were highly critical, but the man on the floor with the yellow pad never flinched, methodically taking notes as, one by

*Some of President Carter's closest advisers and aides, including Charles Kirbo, Hamilton Jordan, Press Secretary Jody Powell, Communications Assistant Gerald Rafshoon, and the President's chief pollster, Patrick Caddell, also attended parts of the meetings.

one, most of his guests told him that the nation was drifting and disappointed in his leadership. Sitting above President Carter's head on a straight-backed chair, I thought back to my meetings on Vietnam with Lyndon Johnson at Camp David fourteen years earlier, and tried, for a moment, to imagine Lyndon Johnson sitting on the floor and saying, "Tell me what I am doing wrong."

After a steak dinner, the President asked his staff to leave so that he could discuss the operations of the White House. The conversation became even more frank. I made the point that President Carter seemed to want to do everything himself; while this might work in situations like the Camp David negotiations on the Mideast, one could not lead the nation singlehandedly. I told him that he had a deep reservoir of goodwill among the American people, but that basic doubts existed as to his effectiveness and competence. I observed that the Administration suffered from a lack of discipline, and I wondered if anyone would ever be dismissed for incompetence or insubordination. Once again, I urged him to open up his White House to a few experienced outsiders—not to replace the Georgians, but to assist them. Finally, I suggested that, in order to bring more order to the sloppy operation of the White House, someone needed to be given the authority, if not the title, of Chief of Staff. I recognized that this last recommendation was at variance with the advice I had given both Presidents Kennedy and Johnson, but I felt that two factors—the growth in the size of the Office of the President, and the different style of Jimmy Carter—argued for a Chief of Staff.

It was impossible to tell what effect the Camp David sessions had on the President, although Jordan was soon appointed Chief of Staff. They were part political theater, part an earnest attempt to learn what he should do to revamp his Administration and regain public confidence. But even if the President did learn something during these meetings, they were a political mistake. The entire exercise had begun to work against itself as soon as the White House staff decided to turn it into a public event. While President Carter was admirable in listening to so much criticism, I felt that such frank criticism—which every President needs to hear—should come only in total privacy. Advertised to the world, it worsened the very problem it was designed to solve, conveying the sense that the President was confused and had lost confidence in both himself and the American people.

The day after the Camp David meeting, I described the session to Martin Schram of *The Washington Post,* using a word that would become shorthand for the entire episode. "President Carter," I told Schram, "had the feeling that the country was in a mood of widespread national malaise." When the President spoke to the nation after his ten days at Camp David, he never uttered these two words. He had used them in his private comments to us, though, and thanks to the headline writers at the *Post*, who put the word "malaise" in the headline to Schram's article, it stuck and became an unfortunate part of the language of politics during the Carter years.

Despite my bewilderment at the Camp David exercise, I felt sorry for the President. He aspired deeply to national and world leadership, and had run a remarkable campaign to reach the White House. He was always best in pursuit of a single objective—whether it was the Democratic nomination, the election, or the historic agreements between Israel and Egypt. When confronted with the subtler tasks of sorting out the nation's priorities from a myriad of competing claims and leading the nation, he had more difficulty. To the end, his good intentions and genuine achievements were undermined by the inexperience of the people around him, and by his reluctance to widen his circle of advisers. Of course, as I have said before, in the end every President gets the advice—and the advisers—that, in his heart, he really wants.

THE LOST BRIGADE

No incident in which I was involved during the Carter Administration was handled more ineptly than the case of the Soviet brigade in Cuba. The fault for this fiasco could be apportioned between the American intelligence community, several senior members of the Administration, and Senator Frank Church. Had it not been for this dreadful episode, I believe the SALT treaty—which had been signed by President Carter and Soviet leader Leonid Brezhnev in Vienna in June 1979—probably would have been ratified by the Senate before the Soviet invasion of Afghanistan in December killed its chances entirely.

It began on August 14, 1979, during a routine briefing of the President by Brzezinski, in his own words, on "intelligence reports [that] there is now an actual Soviet brigade in Cuba." Instead of double-checking or asking for additional information, Brzezinski reacted instantly, telling the President "that this is an extremely serious development which could most adversely affect SALT."[5]

The intelligence report leaked, and events quickly slipped out of the Administration's control. Several Senators of both parties charged that by introducing new troops into Cuba, Moscow had violated the agreement between the Soviet Union and the United States that followed the 1962 Missile Crisis. Fighting for his political life against a conservative challenger in Idaho who eventually would unseat him, Democratic Senator Frank Church, the Chairman of the Senate Foreign Relations Committee, held a press conference in Boise to demand that the Soviet Union remove the brigade from Cuba. A few days later, he added that SALT could not be ratified unless the brigade was withdrawn. Even though senior State Department officials had known that Church was about to make his statement, they made no serious effort to dissuade him.

Church's statement attracted wide attention. Overwrought comparisons were made by conservative columnists and Congressmen to the Cuban Missile Crisis. Pressed by reporters, the normally precise Cy Vance made an unusual verbal slip, saying, "I will not be satisfied with maintenance of the status quo." This compounded the damage done by Church's statement and seemed to mean that the Administration would insist on the withdrawal of the Soviet brigade. Vance later regretted "not having used words less open to misinterpretation."[6]

Washington swung into full speed after Labor Day, and the issue of Soviet troops in Cuba began to obstruct the SALT treaty. The President unwisely raised the ante: "There are two ways to change the status quo. One is by the action of the Soviet Union. . . . The other way is by action on the part of the United States, and I want to report to the nation probably within the next week [on] what action I will take." Reacting to this ominous rhetoric, "Crisis time in Washington" had arrived, *Time* commented, in the "most baffling, potentially the most explosive" issue that Jimmy Carter had faced as President.

The President asked me to convene and chair a board of senior advisers to review the issue. The Citizens Advisory Committee on Cuba, as it was officially called, was intended to be a 1979 version of the now-famous Wise Men of 1968. For the core group, I selected two former national security advisers, McGeorge Bundy and Brent Scowcroft;* former CIA Director John McCone; Ambassador Sol Linowitz; John J. McCloy, still active at the age of eighty-four; and a former Republican Deputy Secretary of Defense, David Packard.

During the last week of September, Vance met several times at the U.N. with Soviet Foreign Minister Andrei Gromyko. In both public and private, Gromyko urged us to drop the entire issue; it was, he said, "artificial," "propaganda without foundation." The troops in question, Gromyko said, had been in Cuba continuously since 1962.

Meanwhile, our advisory group spent a full day at CIA headquarters, grilling the experts on the nature of the Soviet brigade in Cuba. I was appalled as the truth emerged during an extensive examination of long-ignored CIA records: Gromyko *was* correct. The Soviet brigade had indeed been sent to Cuba in 1962 and had never left after the Missile Crisis—with the full knowledge of the American government at the time. It had become an issue in 1979 only because the intelligence community had lost track of the brigade sometime during the previous sixteen years.

*Scowcroft, of course, returned to the NSC position under President Bush in 1989.

The full dimensions of the intelligence failure was captured in an angry and eloquent memorandum McGeorge Bundy prepared for me on September 26:

> The present crisis over a Soviet infantry brigade in Cuba is the product of internal accident and error in the United States. It should be ended mainly by American good sense. . . . Soviet ground troops have been continuously present at Santiago since 1962. . . . I find it unbelievable that this would have happened. . . . We would not have made the brigade a *cause célèbre* if we had known its full history; we should not make it so because we did not.

The 1979 version of the Wise Men met with President Carter on Saturday, September 29. We added to our ranks all three living former Secretaries of State, Dean Rusk, William Rogers, and Henry Kissinger, as well as George Ball, Averell Harriman, Nicholas Katzenbach, and former Secretary of Defense James R. Schlesinger. I asked Bundy to summarize the errors that the intelligence community had made, and then offered my own conclusions:

> This entire business about the Soviet brigade in Cuba is a false issue. We have no right to object to the brigade. Odd as it sounds, I cannot disagree with Gromyko in this instance. Statements that the status quo is 'unacceptable' or that we face 'a very serious matter' are incorrect. We must disengage from this issue.

Not everyone in the Advisory Group agreed. McCone thought we should "take steps to rectify the situation"; Kissinger said he felt Gromyko's statements were "disdainful" of the U.S. and required a response. But neither man specified what response he would favor.

The President listened carefully, asked a few questions, and left for Camp David to work on his speech, which was scheduled for Monday, October 1. A serious argument broke out between Vance and Brzezinski over the best way to handle the issue publicly. I recommended that the President simply tell the nation the truth, but instead, he presented a convoluted and almost unintelligible explanation of events:

> Recently, American intelligence obtained persuasive evidence that some . . . Soviet forces had been organized into a combat unit. When attention was focused on a careful review of past intelligence data, it was possible for our experts to conclude that this unit had existed for several years, probably since the midseventies and possibly even longer. . . . Nonetheless, this Soviet brigade in Cuba is a serious

> matter. It contributes to tension in the Caribbean and Central American region. . . .

I regretted deeply that President Carter had not simply told the American people that the experts had blundered, but it was too late now: politicized with implications far beyond its origins, the issue had become a useful tool with which conservatives of both parties could attack the Administration's alleged "weakness" toward the Soviet Union. The damage could not be undone.

The hearings on ratification of the SALT treaty were delayed until after the Christmas recess. Then, before they could be resumed, the Soviet Union took a genuinely dangerous and destabilizing step: it invaded Afghanistan. With that, the Administration had no choice but to withdraw the treaty from active consideration by the Senate. Although it was still substantially honored by both nations without ratification, it never entered into legal force.

MISSION TO INDIA

The Soviet invasion of Afghanistan led to my final mission for the Carter Administration. Concerned that our strong opposition to the Soviet action would stimulate an anti-American backlash in India, the President asked me to go to New Delhi as his personal emissary and seek to establish a closer relationship with Indira Gandhi. This tenacious daughter of India's first Prime Minister, Jawaharlal Nehru, had ruled first as a democratic Prime Minister from 1966 to 1975, then governed India under a "state of emergency" for twenty months. When she lost power in 1977, she was expelled from Parliament and was imprisoned twice for misuse of power. Just as her state of emergency had been a major blow to freedom and democracy, her return to power in a restored democratic process in 1979 was a major event, not only for India but for the cause of democracy everywhere.

Mrs. Gandhi, in her youth a recluse who felt humiliated and culturally inferior to the sophisticated women on her father's side of the family, was an only child, much closer to her mother than her father. The intelligence briefers told me that, as a child, she had identified with Joan of Arc. In a personal message to me, the American Ambassador to India, Robert Goheen, described her as "lonely and insecure, distrustful of all but a handful of intimates." In her first term as Prime Minister, she had been particularly hostile toward the U.S.

My mission was to convince Mrs. Gandhi that we genuinely wished to improve relations with India, and that our relationship with Pakistan should not be seen as anti-Indian in any way. It was particularly difficult to present this position convincingly because, at about the same time of my visit, a high-level mission, headed by Deputy Secretary of State Warren Christopher and National Security Assistant Brzezinski, was in Pakistan, urging a common front against the Soviets in Afghanistan. Moreover, Harold Brown had just completed the first trip by an American Secretary of Defense to India's other much-despised and feared neighbor, China.

During our lengthy meeting on January 31, 1980, Mrs. Gandhi was surprisingly charming and friendly. She listened carefully to my presentation, and spoke warmly of President Carter and his mother, "Miss" Lillian, who had been a Peace Corps volunteer in India. I told her that, in light of the Soviet action in Afghanistan, we were sending Pakistan some arms to strengthen them, but that we were also prepared to sell arms to India. She replied at length, in a manner that the India experts in our government considered positive. "I am neither pro-Soviet, nor pro-American," she said with great force. "I am pro-Indian."

I was struck by her strength and the sense she conveyed that she *and she alone* knew what was best for India. She had reached the top, of course, because of her famous father, but there was no doubt in my mind after meeting her that her return to power was based on her own strength, determination, and skill.

After the meeting, I held a press conference in New Delhi that was to lead to the only public disagreement I ever had with Cyrus Vance. Eight days earlier, the President had enunciated what became known immediately as the Carter Doctrine:

> An attempt by any outside force to gain control of the Persian Gulf region will be regarded as an assault on the vital interest of the United States, and *such an assault will be repelled by any means necessary, including military force.*

In answer to a question about how the U.S. viewed Soviet actions in the region, I said that our first objective was to get them out of Afghanistan, and added:

> The Soviets must know that if part of their plan is to move toward the Persian Gulf, that means war.

My comment made headlines around the world. Vance took exception to them. "I cannot speak for what Mr. Clifford had in mind," he said to reporters while I was en route back to Washington. "I would have used different language. I believe that Mr. Clifford was being more dramatic than necessary. . . . I think it draws lines that tend to confuse people on the other side."

When I spoke to Vance after my return, I realized he thought I had sided against him in his bitter struggle with Brzezinski, which had reached a crescendo after the Soviet invasion of Afghanistan. This was, of course, not my intention, as I explained, but Vance still disagreed with my use of words; he understood my statement was rooted in the President's own statements, but he was concerned that it went beyond the President's. I felt that it was necessary to emphasize to Moscow and to the world that we would view any further Soviet action as far more serious than their move into Afghanistan. Ambiguity might encourage further Soviet adventurism, with disastrous results.

On February 6, I met for almost an hour with President Carter. Well aware of the difference between Vance's remarks and my own, he called the press in at the end of our meeting to thank me for "a very successful and fruitful mission." When asked about the minicontroversy between Vance and me, the President supported me, saying, "The clarity of the American position is crucial, not only for our friends and allies, but for those who might be tempted to use military force or aggression in the future." That same week, several public opinion polls showed that the American public, by a large majority, was ready to send American troops to the Persian Gulf to protect our interests in the region and "to face up to the Russians, even if that could lead to war."[7]

On March 18, 1980, I was invited to testify on my trip before the Senate Foreign Relations Committee, and I used the occasion to restate my views, adding, "Perhaps more diplomatic language could have been used. But in this area, I felt diplomacy is not so much what is needed as specificity." I likened the situation in Southwest Asia to Europe in the thirties: failure to stand up to the Soviets in an area of such vital importance could have disastrous consequences for world peace. I was critical of our European allies, whose dependence on Mideast oil was greater than ours, for treating the situation as "business as usual. . . . I would have hoped they would have recognized that the Soviet invasion of Afghanistan is naked aggression." Given my views, it was not surprising that I later backed President Carter's policy in support of the Afghan resistance—a policy that continued in the Reagan and Bush Administrations and succeeded in forcing a withdrawal of Soviet troops from Afghanistan in the late eighties.

Afghanistan was one of a number of issues on which Carter followed the right policy, but got almost no credit from the American people. The same was true for the deployment of the Pershing II missiles in Europe, a courageous and much-disputed decision central to the achievement of the Intermediate Range Nuclear Forces Treaty with the Soviet Union that was signed in December 1987. In both cases the public identified the policy with Reagan and overlooked its origins under Jimmy Carter.

Jimmy Carter had entered office with great dreams, for himself and for his country, but in 1980 events overwhelmed his Administration. The last of the Kennedy brothers unwisely challenged him for the nomination, doing the President, the party, and himself great damage. The Republicans nominated a man the Carter White House thought would be easy to defeat, but Ronald Reagan surprised them with his political skill, and changed the face of American politics. The Carter era, begun only four years earlier with such promise, ended in sadness and confusion.

34

Reagan—and Beyond

Had anyone predicted when Richard Nixon barely defeated Hubert Humphrey in 1968 that in the next twenty-four years the Democrats would control the White House for only four years, I would have thought that he was crazy. I assumed that the American public had settled into a pattern of changing the party in power every four to eight years, and assumed, as did most political observers, that Jimmy Carter's election in 1976 was part of that process, and not a single Democratic term amid five Republican victories.

One of the few Democrats who rose to the challenge after Carter's defeat in 1980 was the party's senior statesman, Averell Harriman. In his late eighties and early nineties, the old warrior continued to fight indefatigably for everything in which he had always believed, and two issues were preeminent for him: American-Soviet relations, and the Democratic party. To deal with the former, he continued to speak out, and made several trips to the Soviet Union, accompanied by his wife Pamela, to meet Brezhnev and his successor, Yuri Andropov. Helping the Democratic party revitalize itself was a task that Pamela Harriman, the British-born former daughter-in-law of Winston Churchill, increasingly assumed. Shortly after the first Reagan victory in 1980, she and Averell formed a political action committee named "Democrats for the '80s," which raised money for Congressional campaigns. Many seasoned Washington political hands scoffed at first at the small organization operating under her direction out of offices adjacent to the elegant Harriman home in Georgetown, but it soon developed into one of the Democratic party's most successful efforts. After Averell died in 1986, Pamela continued their work on her own, and made a signal contribution to the party.

The Harrimans also started a series of "Issues Dinners" at their home, which brought together prominent Democrats from all over the country. The dinners were always off the record, but on September 15, 1981, unknown to me, the discussion was taped so that Mrs. Harriman, who was unable to attend because she was in the hospital as a result of a riding accident, could listen to the discussion later. At that dinner I made a chance remark about Ronald Reagan that endured.

Felix Rohatyn, the noted and articulate New York investment banker, delivered a scathing critique of the Reagan Administration's economic policies. As moderator, I commented that President Reagan's economic policies were internally contradictory. It was impossible to cut taxes, increase the defense budget, and balance the federal budget by 1984—as he had promised to do. I predicted that we were going to face budget deficits far larger than any in our history. In concluding my comments, I said that, unless these policies succeeded, which I thought unlikely, the feeling would grow over time that President Reagan was "an amiable dunce." Everyone laughed at the phrase, and the evening went on.

Somehow the transcript of the tape reached a reporter at *The Wall Street Journal,* who found my description of President Reagan interesting. It appeared, slightly out of context, in an October 8, 1981, front-page story otherwise concerned with the Harrimans' political activities. Republicans were offended; Democrats amused. I was not pleased. I had been quoted out of context, and the privacy of an off-the-record dinner had been violated. But the remark lived on, and was much quoted.

* * *

Six years later, in 1987, President Reagan had what several of my friends decided was his revenge during White House ceremonies celebrating the fortieth anniversary of the Marshall Plan. Before a gathering of people connected in some way with the European Recovery Program, he read prepared remarks in which he was supposed to acknowledge me for having worked with President Truman and General Marshall in formulating the original speech. When Reagan came to my name, he announced that among the distinguished guests at the White House this very day was one of President Truman's closest aides, "Clark M. Gifford." The press enjoyed the thrust and considered the duel a draw.

MONDALE, JACKSON, DUKAKIS, AND BUSH

Reagan's performance as President was effective, but I viewed it as just that—a performance. He was more skillful in *acting* like a President than anyone since Franklin Roosevelt; but, after all, he was an actor. At the same time, he showed less interest in the art of governance than any President since Calvin Coolidge, who happened to be one of his personal heroes. He enjoyed and had a talent for articulating and reaffirming grand conservative themes—even if his Administration sometimes veered off in the opposite direction, as in the case of the budget deficit.

In 1984 Carter's Vice President, Walter F. Mondale, won the Democratic nomination. He had been the most influential and effective Vice President in my experience, the first to have an office inside the White House,* and perhaps the first to be consulted on almost every major issue. He was well qualified to be President, and waged a determined and respectable campaign—but against Ronald Reagan, who was at the height of his popularity and adept at avoiding identification with problems, he never had a chance.

The same could not be said about the Democratic candidate four years later, Governor Michael Dukakis of Massachusetts, who had a good chance to win and conducted one of the most inept campaigns American politics has ever seen. Like many observers, I had thought 1988 would be a Democratic year: structurally, it bore a resemblance to 1960, when an old and popular Republican President retired, and his less popular Vice President sought to succeed him, running against a younger man from Massachusetts. Dukakis even accentuated the similarity by choosing a running mate from Texas, Senator Lloyd Bentsen, and trying to revive talk of another "Boston-Austin axis." But he then went on to run an absolutely themeless campaign filled with easily avoidable errors.

During the primaries, I had no contact with Dukakis, although several other candidates, including Senator Albert Gore, Jr., the son of my old associate from the Kennedy campaign, kept in touch with me. The most unusual meetings I had during the campaign were with the Reverend Jesse Jackson, whom I had known since President Carter's 1979 domestic summit. I saw him from time to time at Democratic party functions, introduced him at one of Pamela Harriman's "Issues Dinners," and was generally impressed by his brilliant speaking style. In late 1987, he approached me during a large political dinner and asked if he could get advice about the campaign. Encouraged especially by his friend, Bert Lance, who hoped I might be helpful in encouraging Jackson to be more

*The office assigned to him was, by coincidence, the same one I had occupied as Special Counsel to President Truman.

of a party supporter and less of a one-man band once we got to the general election, I agreed to see him on December 9.

Jackson was widely, and not inaccurately, viewed by the party as a two-edged sword: a galvanizing and charismatic leader of many black and other disenfranchised Americans, but also someone who scared many moderates away from the party with overheated and melodramatic positions. This presented the Democrats with a dilemma since they needed both the moderates and the black vote to win the Presidency.

Jackson arrived in my office accompanied by one of his sons and an associate. He was close to an hour late, which I was told was typical of his style. From the moment he arrived I could see that he was overscheduled and distracted. Although the force of his personality was evident, he struck me as quite volatile and undisciplined. I encouraged him to pursue the nomination but *within* the framework of the party, which would need unity after the convention.

Three months later, a few days after Jackson had won the Michigan caucus and emerged as one of the three surviving contenders for the nomination, along with Dukakis and Gore, Lance asked me if I would introduce Jackson at a breakfast in Washington, and act as host. The purpose, as *The Washington Post* explained, was for the candidate to meet with "elder Democratic statesmen," in order to reduce Washington's "fear" of Jesse Jackson.

A couple of those invited refused to attend, but I went ahead with the breakfast. Restrained throughout, Jackson began with a clever and pointed observation about the number of losing campaigns with which the people in the room had been associated. The toughest questions concerned whether Jackson had been strong enough in repudiating Louis Farrakhan, the racist leader who had embarrassed him in the 1984 campaign. Jackson offered what I thought was a clever but evasive answer: that he believed in "redemption, not condemnation."

Because Jackson was at the very height of his success, the event received wide coverage. I was criticized by some old friends for participating in the breakfast, but I did not agree. From the outset of my contact with Jackson, I had made the decision that it was worth risking some criticism from friends in order to try to encourage him to operate in a manner that minimized the damage to the Democratic party. "I take the long view of the Jackson candidacy," I wrote in a letter to several friendly critics. "I feel strongly that Jackson should be given the same opportunities by our Party to run for President that we would give to any other person. We either have a democracy or we don't have one."

Dukakis was clearly headed for the nomination. Although I talked to him at a Harriman dinner in Washington, I watched his dreadful campaign mostly from the sidelines, hardly believing that so many mistakes could be made by one candidate. But Dukakis's advisers—especially after a shake-up in the middle of the campaign—were too insecure to use the expertise available within the Democratic party and the candidate, resisting even his own staff, seemed content to run a colorless and enervated campaign. At the Harriman dinner, Dukakis was polite and pleasant, but he made little impression on the guests. If Jesse Jackson could dominate a room merely by his presence, one had to search the room simply to find Dukakis.

In contrast to the stumbling Dukakis campaign, George Bush exhibited unexpected political skill in 1988. His father, Connecticut Senator Prescott Bush, had been one of my frequent golfing partners in the fifties, and I had both liked and respected him. Senator Bush had a splendid singing voice, and particularly loved quartet singing. In the fifties, he organized a quartet that included my daughter Joyce, who had a lovely singing voice. They would sing in Washington, and on occasion, he invited the group to Hobe Sound in Florida to perform. His son, though, had never struck me as a strong or forceful person. In 1988, he presented himself successfully to the voters as an outsider—no small trick for a man whose roots wound through Connecticut, Yale, Texas oil, the CIA, a patrician background, wealth, and the Vice Presidency. Bush managed to portray his opponent, who was a *true* outsider (son of Greek immigrants, never worked in Washington, serious student of government, married to a member of the Jewish faith, simple lifestyle), as a member of the "Harvard Yard elite." This successful role reversal was critical to Bush's victory over Michael Dukakis. I thought I recognized a few ploys, conscious or unconscious, from our campaign strategy of 1948, when a President ran as an outsider against a challenger from Albany. But I felt that Bush's campaign was directed to the public's fears and prejudices, rather than to their hopes and aspirations. Its misrepresentation of Dukakis's position on many issues, from the prison furlough program (especially the infamous "Willie Horton" advertisement) to the environmental issue, was disgraceful. It was, moreover, wholly at variance with President Truman's campaign in 1948, in which he almost never mentioned his opponent by name. Bush's famous pledge—"Read my lips: No more taxes"—was an irresponsible act taken for short-term gain without measuring how much it might diminish his ability to govern if he reached office. It was an action for which Bush, but more important, the nation, would pay later.

In 1976, 1980, and 1988, each challenger—Jimmy Carter, Ronald Reagan, and Michael Dukakis—had emphasized his record as a Governor. But while Ford in 1976, and Carter in 1980 ignored their opponents' records as Governor and emphasized instead their own experience as

President, George Bush had responded with a strong attack on his opponent's gubernatorial record. It is no accident, in my view, that only the last of these three elections resulted in a defeat for the challenger.

THE ORDEAL OF SPEAKER WRIGHT

Once again, in 1989, a friend in political trouble came to me for counsel and advice. This time it was the Speaker of the House of Representatives, the third man in the line of succession to the Presidency and the highest-ranking Democrat in the nation, Congressman Jim Wright of Texas. Once again, it was very late in the game.

By the time Wright called me, he had been under scrutiny for eleven months because of certain business transactions. The allegations principally concerned Wright's alleged receipt of gifts from persons with an interest in legislation, and a financial arrangement relating to a book he had published, as well as questions as to whether Wright had improperly intervened with bank regulators on behalf of Savings and Loan owners in Texas. Under pressure from House Republicans, the House Committee on Standards of Office and Conduct—known as the Ethics Committee—had voted unanimously to conduct an inquiry into these charges.

In February 1989, the outside counsel of the Ethics Committee, a Chicago lawyer named Richard J. Phelan, presented the committee with a 279-page report. Its wide-ranging charges put Wright on the defensive, and a few weeks later, hoping to turn his situation around, he went before television cameras with an emotional appeal for fairness and a point-by-point rebuttal of the charges. But on April 17, the Ethics Committee announced it had "reason to believe" Wright had repeatedly violated the rules of Congressional conduct. The continuing political damage to Wright was severe. He responded again before the Democratic Caucus on April 18, but the pressure continued to build relentlessly. Two days later, Jim Wright asked Robert Altman to see if I would be available to help him.

Wright had entered the House of Representatives in 1955, and quickly decided that this was to be his life. His mentor and role model was Sam Rayburn, and after many years, he had finally risen to the Speaker's chair that "Mr. Sam" had occupied with such power and distinction. Now, only one year into his Speakership, he was facing the possible end of his political career.

I thought Wright's situation contained elements of a Greek tragedy. Having just achieved his lifelong goal, he looked forward to taking a place alongside the Speakers he considered the greatest in history, Henry Clay and Sam Rayburn. He had begun by taking the most activist position of any senior legislator in opposition to the Reagan Administration's policies in Central America. All his hopes were jeopardized, though, by questionable financial decisions. In an earlier era, these charges would probably have been brushed aside or buried without serious consequences. But in 1989, President Bush had lost his nominee for Secretary of Defense, Senator John Tower of Texas, in a brutal confirmation battle that included discussion of Tower's drinking, his behavior with women, and his business interests. Revenge was in the air—a Texas Democrat for a Texas Republican. How much rougher and more personal the game had gotten since I arrived in Washington in 1945! Jim Wright knew the rules and how they had changed, and he knew how difficult his situation was.

When Altman and I initially met with Wright on April 19, with his staff present, I found a still-defiant man. Five days later, he asked to see us again, but this time kept his staff outside for most of the meeting. After I evaluated both his legal and political problems, Wright spoke with greater candor: "I realize that I must face up to the possibility that I might have to resign."

I responded, "Resigning means not only the Speakership but also resigning from the House, because you are being investigated as a member of the House, not as Speaker. Only your resignation from the House would stop the entire investigation." I did not, then, recommend resignation. I said that while Wright had credible legal arguments on the merits, his political position was indeed tenuous. Moreover, as I looked ahead, I was reluctant to subject him and his wife, Betty, to a searching cross-examination in a trial of the charges—with the predictable damage that might ensue.

Wright asked me to head up his legal team, but I declined. I told him he needed a full-time legal defense team to combat each of the charges, led by someone who would master every detail of the situation, and I was not the man for that job. Meanwhile, I told him, Altman and I would be available at all times as advisers. Within hours, his staff had announced publicly that we had joined his defense team.

From the outset, I thought Wright's situation would probably lead to his resignation, but, as with Bert Lance, I believed strongly that a public figure should not walk away under attack without presenting his side of the story. The same attitude that had led me to urge Lance to make a full statement of his position led me to offer Wright similar advice.

We met again on April 26. After a few minutes, Wright dismissed his staff and pulled a small chair up close to Altman and me. "I want to tell you something I have not yet told any other person," he said. "I am conscious of the fact that I may have been so badly damaged that I may have lost my ability to serve effectively as Speaker even if I am completely vindicated."

At that moment, I felt immensely sorry for him. As gently as I could,

I replied, "I am gratified, Jim, that you are able to face that reality, for as we proceed, if we were to conclude that even if you were vindicated you would feel you should resign because your leadership has been impaired, then we would wish to give consideration to the possibility of avoiding the trauma of a trial altogether."

On May 2, Wright summoned several members of the Democratic leadership of the House, without their staff, to a secret meeting in a private room tucked away in the Capitol to ask their advice and counsel on how to proceed. Altman and I attended, but we deliberately did not sit at the table with the Congressmen, choosing instead two chairs along the wall. All eight said the Wright matter did not yet appear to be a big political issue in their districts, and they did not feel under heavy pressure to seek his ouster. Only Congressman John Dingell of Michigan was openly pessimistic. The other Congressmen present, including House Majority Leader Tom Foley, all told Wright that he should present, in the words of Dante Fascell of Florida, Chairman of the Foreign Affairs Committee, a "spirited defense." I sympathized with Foley, who was likely to succeed Wright. He could do or say nothing that seemed to encourage the Speaker's departure. Wright said he was greatly comforted and moved by their support, and the meeting broke up, leaving Altman and me alone with Wright and his closest friend in the House, Jack Brooks of Texas. I felt that the meeting had backfired, and left Wright with a false sense of support from well-meaning colleagues who had not wished to tell him how precarious his situation really was.

Two days later, there was a blow from an unexpected direction. *The Washington Post* ran a long article recounting the horrifying details of the near-fatal assault, sixteen years earlier, of a woman in Washington. Her assailant had been John Mack, who had later become one of Jim Wright's closest aides. At the time of Mack's trial, Wright had written a letter asking the sentencing judge to consider a reduced sentence for Mack. The story was not new, but it was the first time that the woman had come forward, identified herself, and told her story in detail. Mack resigned almost immediately from Wright's staff, but the story received national attention, and its effect on the Speaker's situation was devastating. From that point on it spiraled steadily downhill. By this time, Wright's defense team had split roughly into three groups: his legal co-counsels, his supporters in the House (led by Congressman Robert Torricelli of New Jersey), and Altman and me.

In this situation, it was not surprising that Wright's defense strategy became confused. Some of his advisers wanted him to fight it out to the end. In one meeting, I actually heard a Texas colleague exhort him, "Remember the Alamo, Jim!" Other advisers, particularly Torricelli, wished to plea-bargain with the Ethics Committee counsel on Wright's behalf—a position which I opposed. On May 10, 1989, Wright filed a motion for dismissal to test his legal arguments without the trauma of an extended hearing. Eight days later, he informed me he was under great pressure from some of his advisers to file a motion that day asking for an expedited—and televised—trial. Concerned that Wright was damaging himself, I hurried to the Hill. When I arrived, the Speaker was in his office with his legal team and other advisers who were pressing Wright to ask for a trial. I disagreed and pointed out that requests for a hearing were inconsistent with the pending motion to dismiss. The stalemate continued.

Following arguments on the motion to dismiss—and while the matter was pending—the issue of a "deal" with the committee was again raised by some of Wright's lawyers. I again reiterated my total opposition to any negotiation with the committee's counsel, which would surely backfire. This was a matter of ethics for Wright and his fellow Representatives, and the lawyers had no business offering or considering deals. Despite my views, some of Wright's legal team approached the committee to discuss a settlement and the results were immediately public—and disastrous. All further consideration of Wright's position on the merits by the media quickly ceased.

The Speaker and his loyal wife, Betty, were clearly losing heart for the battle. He began looking for a graceful way to exit, while retaining his honor and the privileges of a former Speaker and member of the House. On May 31, he called me in the morning. "The pressures on the Hill have become intolerable," he said simply. "I'm going to resign, unless you disagree. I thank you for all your help and friendship." I replied that while I deeply regretted the circumstances, I could not disagree.

Wright chose the most appropriate forum for the announcement, a speech from the well of the House of Representatives. He defended himself, recounted his career, and announced he would resign before the end of June. "Let that be a total payment for the anger and hostility we feel toward each other," he said to the Republicans. "God bless this institution. God bless the United States."

35

Reflections

A LAWYER WHO LOVED WASHINGTON

World War II divided my life neatly in half. Before the war I lived in the center of our continent nation, not only physically but psychologically, assuming I would spend my entire life practicing law there. But the war did for me what it did, on a gigantic scale, for the country: it ended a period of relative insularity. It was an accident of friendship with an aide to the new President that brought me to Washington in 1945. Once there, I saw a new world opening up, filled with opportunity and challenge for both the nation and me. Although I still retained a love for the city of my youth, I knew that I wished nothing more than to spend the rest of my working days in the city that, by the end of World War II, had become the capital of the world as well as the center of our political life. It was good fortune that fate allowed me to live out so much of that dream.

By the sixties, I was sometimes described as a pillar of the Washington power structure, a quintessential member of the Washington establishment. I was not displeased with the compliment implicit in such a description, but at the same time it always amused me. After all, in those days Washington was still filled with alumni of the New Deal, and it was not hard to find men who even remembered the Presidency of Woodrow Wilson. I was a comparative newcomer to Washington, who, after five years of service to President Truman, resumed my profession, which I had practiced for sixteen years in St. Louis. I did not consider myself an old Washington hand. In my own mind, I was what I had always been, a lawyer. I loved the law, both for the discipline it taught me and the opportunities it had given me.

On June 1, 1990, I had been a lawyer for sixty-two years. My relationships with men in power had almost always begun with legal matters. Despite what was written about me, I always considered myself an amateur in politics, a professional in the law.

Yet I could not deny that I loved participating in Washington's great contest. Only six years of my life, not counting the Navy, were spent in full-time government service. But substantial portions of my time while a private citizen had involved working on a private basis with government officials or politicians, or participating in part-time governmental activity. I carefully organized and compartmentalized my life so as to devote as much time as necessary to public affairs while continuing to run a law firm, and keep the two activities separate. Extra discipline was, of course, needed in order to attend properly to each area of interest. I worked long hours, took very short vacations, and frequently worked on Saturdays. This was what I wanted to do, though, and I never lamented the leisure time I might have sacrificed, except insofar as it came out of time with my family.

To me, government represented both the best and the worst of our society. It could be boring, bureaucratic, and self-serving, in Emerson's phrase, a "riot of mediocrities and dishonesties and fudges."[1] It could produce inaction when action was required, and, no matter how justified, some of its procedures and regulations—the very part of government that our law firm spent much of its time dealing with on behalf of clients—were often deadening in their effect on individual initiative. Yet, when solving a great crisis or creating a far-reaching policy, government could be a noble endeavor, and the White House the most majestic and exhilarating place on earth.

WHAT WE GAINED, WHAT WE LOST: EQUALITY AND SOCIETY

The most important domestic achievement during my lifetime has been the systematic elimination of legal and institutional barriers based on race or sex, and the opening of opportunities to all Americans. In my youth we lived with prejudices and assumptions that were unexamined, but which prevented members of minority groups of every description, as well as women, from having an equal opportunity in the world. Today we are far more sensitive to these biases, and the law has been rewritten by the Congress, or reinterpreted by the Supreme Court, to eliminate almost every form of legalized or institutionalized discrimination. This magnificent achievement has strengthened America by giving it the benefit of the hitherto untapped energy and talents of millions of citizens who had previously been denied an opportunity to participate on an equal legal footing in society.

Yet these successes have not eliminated the underlying problems that exist. Equal opportunity in theory has not created equal opportunity in reality, nor has it eliminated poverty, ghettos, crime, or stopped the spread of drugs. Above all, it has not eliminated prejudice as a way of thinking. By this I mean prejudice of all sorts—not just antiblack feelings among many whites, but antiwhite feelings among many blacks. The white racists who have opposed the civil rights movement have their black counterparts: all are to be equally condemned.

I grew up in a different America, and I regret the decline of civility that was part of that world. But the kinder and gentler world of my youth was not open to everyone, and could not be sustained. It was based to an excessive degree on a passive acceptance of class and race distinctions that ran counter to our professions of full equality for all Americans. Our failure, in the last third of this century, is that we have not moved fast enough to eliminate the economic and social barriers that still exist after the initial wave of legal decisions and legislation raised hopes to such a high level. Vietnam, by diverting and dividing us, contributed greatly to the problem, but I believe it would have worsened in any case. The overriding task for the next generation is to deal with this problem. I recognize full well what a daunting assignment this is. In recent years the nation has moved toward a two-tier society, in which a relatively few members of each minority have moved upward into positions of leadership and influence, leaving behind an underclass of disadvantaged and increasingly alienated people. Drugs and their inevitable partner, organized crime, have created a situation both explosive and divisive to our society, seriously exacerbated by continued racism. Americans *can* live as two separate nations under one roof, divided by class and fearing each other, the richer portion of our society always erecting physical and psychological walls to insulate themselves from the rest of the population—but this is not the "city on a hill" to which Americans have so fervently aspired.

I have not been impressed by the quality of leadership on this issue in recent years. Most advances in civil rights in this century have been effected by the Democratic party, in response to the efforts led by black Americans themselves. The Democrats, however, paid a serious price at the polls by alienating many white voters. The nation would be better served if the race issue did not break down so clearly along party lines, as it has especially since 1948.

PRESIDENTS

Throughout my lifetime, it has been the Democrats who stood for innovative leadership. It is not axiomatic, however, that the Democrats will always be the party of innovation. Leaders can come from either party, from the halls of Congress or from the heartland. However, with the exception of the first Roosevelt, who was still in the White House when I was born, the Presidents I would categorize as progressive or innovative in this century have all been Democrats. (I do not include Ronald Reagan among the innovative Presidents, as some observers do, because I believe his Administration will be viewed as having left behind a disastrous legacy of fiscal and social irresponsibility, and because he made no effort to deal with the nation's real problems.)

Of the Presidents I have known, the two who were most willing to take on the big issues were Harry Truman and Lyndon Johnson. Both men were willing to take on the toughest questions, despite warnings from conservative advisers. In 1946–1947, President Truman's domestic advisers, led by an influential and conservative Secretary of the Treasury, sought to disassociate the Administration from Roosevelt's New Deal. But after a year of indecision, President Truman, liberated by the GOP sweep in the 1946 Congressional elections, decided to finish FDR's term as a New Dealer and run for election in his own right as a liberal activist at home, an internationalist abroad. In so doing, he established an enduring identity for himself and won the unforgettable victory of 1948.

Some will question my inclusion of Lyndon Johnson among courageous Presidents. After all, his Presidency was damaged almost irretrievably by the Vietnam War. But this should not obscure the fact that he had a clear vision of what he wanted to accomplish, and the drive and courage to seek it. His domestic achievements were among the most impressive in our history. Many of his advisers warned him in the midsixties that he could not undertake so many domestic reforms while he was escalating the war in Vietnam. But Johnson dreamed great and noble dreams for the nation, and he was not going to trim his sails because of Vietnam on issues he had cared about all his life: equal rights for all Americans, a better educational system, medical care for the elderly, fair housing, and the war on poverty. That he overextended himself, brought on an inflationary spiral, and demanded too much of a nation already in turmoil, is clear. But he still deserves commendation and admiration for his boldness, and his desire to identify and tackle the problems that faced the nation.

President Kennedy was more cautious than either President Truman or President Johnson, due in part to the narrowness of his victory. In his heart he was neither a New Dealer nor a liberal; pragmatism was his watchword. He did little for the civil rights movement before 1963, although I believe that he would have become a leader in this area had he lived. For him, the Presidency was above all about foreign policy, a field in which he felt comfortable. He understood the intangible aspects of Presidential leadership better than any other President except Franklin Roosevelt. He left behind a role model for the Presidency which everyone since has tried to emulate. Ironically, only Reagan, in every other way Kennedy's antithesis, equalled him in this respect. When people talk of the unfulfilled promise of John F. Kennedy, I do not consider this mere rhetoric: he had more capacity for growth than any other President I knew, and I believe that had he lived he would have been one of our most illustrious Presidents.

If President Johnson was the most complex President I knew, President Carter was the greatest mystery. Like Presidents Truman and Johnson, Carter was committed to equality for all Americans, and he ranks close to them as a great civil rights President. He wanted to solve every problem the nation faced, and at first set out a bold agenda to do so, but he squandered the power of the Presidency by failing to establish his own authority and power early in the unavoidable struggle with Congress, and by failing to establish clear priorities. For, the truth is, even a President cannot do everything at once.

Our Chief Executive must function as the leader of the nation, not the manager of the executive branch. At times, Jimmy Carter seemed to see himself as the CEO, the chief executive officer, of the federal government. His engineering and naval background, and his impressive single-mindedness in pursuit of specific objectives—the Camp David agreements, the SALT II treaty, normalization of relations with China—produced a collection of impressive achievements; but, as many people have pointed out, his Administration seemed to lack a theme. This was all the more unfortunate because during the 1976 campaign he had established a clear image in the minds of the voters as a man of honesty, determination, intelligence, and strength. His defenders may respond that it is not necessary to conduct the nation's affairs for four years within a single "theme," but at its core the Presidency is about politics, not programs, and Presidents must do more than propose solutions to problems. They must summon the nation to share their vision and their values, and, by their priorities, symbolize their definition of what they want the nation to be. At the dawn of the century, Theodore Roosevelt coined his famous phrase to describe the Presidency: "the bully pulpit." More than seventy years later, with the greatest good intentions and values in the world, Jimmy Carter failed to grasp this essential aspect of the Presidency.

Reagan and Carter were in most ways absolute opposites, but there are striking parallels in the manner in which they won the Presidency, and important lessons in the way one man succeeded politically while the other failed. Both were outsiders distrusted by the Washington establishment, both capitalized on public discontent with the established parties. But Reagan understood what Carter did not—that it was essential to keep faith with one's original electoral base. No matter what position Reagan took on issues, he found a way to appear to have stuck to his principles. Carter, on the other hand, seemed to forget how and why he had been elected; once in the White House, he took positions on the problems he faced with little attention to their cumulative impact on his image. The beginning of the end came for him, in my opinion, when he spoke to the nation from Camp David in the summer of 1979 and showed bitterness and anger in complete contrast to his campaign image. Carter had broken an unwritten compact with his supporters, in effect blaming them for his own difficulties while presenting the nation with a new and significantly different Jimmy Carter. Why he did this mystified me; it seemed to violate a basic rule of politics. Months before the hostages were seized in Iran, the Camp David speech conveyed the impression that the job was overwhelming him. At a subconscious level, he was setting into motion the seeds of his own downfall.

Not so with Ronald Reagan. During a Presidency filled with mistakes and corruption, ranging from the Iran-*contra* scandal (which I believe involved a cover-up fully as serious as that of Watergate) to the unnecessary deaths of over two hundred Marines in Beirut, Reagan understood exactly how to protect himself. His policies left innumerable problems behind for his successors, but he protected his own political standing. I do not praise him for this; the nation will suffer as a result. But the Democrats, indeed all politicians, can learn from Reagan's performance how important it is—to paraphrase Polonius's words in *Hamlet*—to be true to one's public self in public.

The other Republican Presidents I knew covered as wide a range as the Democrats. President Eisenhower was the right man for the nation at the time he was elected, but I was disappointed that he did not do more with his immense popularity. He had the opportunity, working with the most skilled Congressional leadership of my lifetime, Sam Rayburn as Speaker of the House and Lyndon Johnson as Senate Majority Leader, to start our nation toward a gradual solution of our racial dilemma. Instead, he did nothing that was not forced upon him, and later lamented his most inspired decision, the selection of Earl Warren as Chief Justice of the United States. Similarly, he was passive in the face of Senator Joe McCarthy's attacks not only on General Marshall, but on the most fundamental values of the Bill of Rights.

I do not agree with the "hidden hand" theory of the Eisenhower Presidency, now fashionable among some writers. Advocates of this theory offer the concept that throughout his Administration Eisenhower maneuvered almost invisibly with great skill to achieve his objectives. I find this concept mostly an academic invention designed to explain outcomes and events that in fact happened with little or no involvement by Eisenhower. The one exception is the skillful way he defused pressure to get more heavily involved in Indochina on the French side in 1954. In this case, Ike's passivity was probably intentional, and succeeded in distancing the nation from the disaster in Indochina—alas, not for long enough.

Of Eisenhower's Vice President, what more can be said? I never liked Richard Nixon, and he never liked me. Yet he put on the longest-running political show of my lifetime, from his first appearance as J. Edgar Hoover's ally in 1947 to his regular attempts, continuing into the nineties, to restore his reputation through books and carefully calibrated public appearances. I do not question Nixon's three major foreign policy achievements: the opening to China; his attempt to reduce the chances of nuclear tragedy by establishing a framework of relations with the Soviet Union; and the effort to bring peace to the Mideast. All three of these accomplishments received well-deserved bipartisan support, and set the stage for Carter's own foreign policy achievements—the completion of the normalization process with China; an effort, ultimately unsuccessful, to expand and extend American-Soviet détente; and the climax of his Presidency, the Camp David agreements. Still, these accomplishments were accompanied by significant failures and errors of policy in Chile, Cyprus, Iran, the Philippines, South Africa, and elsewhere.

* * *

It will not come as a surprise to the reader that I judge the Nixon Administration to be one of the low points in our nation's history. Watergate alone left a scar on our political system that can hardly be measured. To be sure, Nixon's removal from office for cause, through orderly and Constitutional processes, was a triumph for the genius of the original design of the Founding Fathers—but at what cost in the spread of cynicism, the legacy of recriminations and myths, and the loss of respect for the noblest institution in American life? By demeaning the Presidency, Richard Nixon disgraced himself and the nation.

Beyond that, I find fundamentally dishonest his efforts to portray himself as having brought "peace with honor" to Vietnam, only to have it snatched away by a defeatist Congress. The deal that the Nixon Administration offered North Vietnam in 1972 contained a concession so massive that it is not surprising President Thieu rejected it in October before having it crammed down his throat after the Christmas bombing. That concession—far greater than anything the Johnson Administration ever considered—was to permit the North Vietnamese to leave their regular troops in the South after the withdrawal of all American troops. At the time of this deal, there were over 135,000 North Vietnamese regulars in the South, and no method to verify either that number or its increase. (That number exceeded by 75,000 the estimated number of North Vietnamese regulars in the South in 1968–1969.*) Nixon had resisted such a deal for the first four years of his Presidency, withdrawing American troops unilaterally instead of negotiating with Hanoi to get something in return. These delays in negotiating for an American withdrawal—for that is all that Nixon actually negotiated, the rest of the 1973 cease-fire agreement being worthless from the outset—resulted in over 20,000 additional American deaths during the Nixon years, as well as an enormous number of Vietnamese casualties. Nothing was gained by this, and much was lost: the war spread into a country that the Johnson Administration had always kept off limits, Cambodia, with the most disastrous results.

Gerald Ford inherited this legacy in 1974, but about his brief Presidency there is little that can be said. In almost every way, it was a caretaker government trying to bind up the wounds of Watergate and get through the most traumatic act of the Indochina drama. Ford himself was a likable person who deserves credit for accomplishing the one goal that was most important, to reunite the nation after the trauma of Watergate and give us a breathing spell before we picked a new President. On his most controversial decision, the pardon of Richard Nixon, I believe that he made the correct decision. The nation would not have benefited from having a former Chief Executive in the dock for years after his departure from office. His disgrace was enough.

WHO WON THE COLD WAR?

"Ideology is the curse of public affairs because it converts politics into a branch of theology and sacrifices human beings on the altar of dogma."[3] In its name, tens of millions of people died during this bloodiest of all centuries, in the furnaces of the Third Reich and in the Gulag, in Cambodia and Mao's China. We are living at the end of a century which saw the rise and fall of two of the most pernicious ideologies in history, fascism and communism. They each portrayed themselves as the antithesis of the other, but in fact they had a great deal in common. I lived much of my life watching one, then the other, grow in power. From the twenties through the seventies—half a century, more than half a lifetime—one or both of these alien philosophies threatened not only our freedom, but the very concept of freedom. That the century ends with the apparent triumph of the idea of freedom is a tribute, above all, to the human spirit.

*In January 1969, the Military Assistance Command, Vietnam (MACV), estimated that there were 125,000 North Vietnamese regulars in the South. In the spring of 1972, MACV estimated that this number had risen to at least 200,000.

Today, in the wake of the collapse of communism in Eastern Europe, its near (and I hope imminent) collapse in the Soviet Union, and its return to a police state in China, we can begin to look back on the policies that were put into place by the U.S. after World War II as a completed period of world history. Now that it has come to an end in the region in which it began—Eastern Europe—it is timely to address the question of who won the Cold War.

The events with which the eighties ended and the nineties began were, above all, a result of the failure of communism as both an economic theory and a political system. Neither the theory nor the system worked, and all that was left was a collection of police states which had lost the ability to use limitless force and repression to retain control. Mikhail Gorbachev recognized this and let Eastern Europe go, although that could not have been his original intention. Thus, credit for the liberation of Eastern Europe—the second end to the Second World War, so to speak—should go first and foremost to their own skillful and courageous leaders, and to Mikhail Gorbachev's decision not to intervene.

American policy, though, made an important contribution to these events. Many will step forward to seek credit for the triumph of freedom in Eastern Europe. The Reagan conservatives will claim that the bloated defense budgets of the eighties and President Reagan's muscular rhetoric turned the tide in Eastern Europe. Others will credit President Carter's human rights policies or his support of the resistance in Afghanistan, and some may even search the debris of Vietnam for evidence that our stand there, however costly, bought time for freedom to take root in other corners of the world.

Perhaps, in some minor incremental manner, all these events contributed to the flow toward freedom. But the policy that truly succeeded was born during the great era of American foreign policy, when, in less than three years, President Truman unveiled the Truman Doctrine, the Marshall Plan, NATO, and Point Four. Over the next forty years, the essential core of President Truman's policies survived fierce domestic debate, domestic politics, even the four great challenges of the last forty years—the Korean War, McCarthyism, Vietnam, and Watergate—and was accepted as the framework of our foreign policy by every President from Eisenhower to Bush.

President Truman knew we were embarking on a long and difficult struggle with an uncertain outcome, but he and most of his advisers nevertheless believed that if we held the line against further Soviet expansion, eventually communism would start its own painful transformation into something less dangerous and more open. He could not imagine then that his policy would require a commitment of more than forty years, that it would at times threaten to tear our own nation apart, that we would veer from overinvolvement to neo-isolation, and that it would be misapplied and overextended in Vietnam. With characteristic directness, President Truman did not agonize over the details. He simply announced the policy because he felt it was right. In my years in Washington, this was the most enduring event with which I was associated. Its consequences and its legacy would keep the fires of freedom burning until communism reached the point of collapse from within.

As I watched the collapse of communism, I thought back to the report George Elsey and I had produced for President Truman in 1946, and to George Kennan's prophetic writings of the same era. We had both argued for resistance to Soviet expansion, and offered the hope that if we could "restrain," or "contain," the Soviets, the country would eventually be transformed by internal pressures. In America, both the Left, with its readiness to accept communism as inevitable, and the Right, which searched for the enemy within and advocated a swollen and wasteful American military establishment, had been wrong. In the forty-fifth year after our report, I believed that communism was not only morally and intellectually bankrupt and discredited—as it had been for a long time—but it was also dying as a framework for government. It will survive for a while longer in certain areas, perhaps including North Korea, Vietnam, Cuba, and China, neither as an economic system nor as a viable ideology, but only as a justification for a police state. Its death, however, seemed to me virtually certain. In the eloquent words of the Yugoslav dissident and former communist Milovan Djilas:

> Communism is contrary to human nature. . . . Human nature is pluralistic in its being. Human nature is sinful. If human nature were perfect, communism might be possible, but that would be a "dead" society. Human nature is evil and at the same time gentle and good. The constant struggle of different tendencies in us is essential for the existence of humanity. . . . Capitalism functions better than communism because it is closer to human nature. Communism has failed and will fail because human nature cannot live without freedom, without choices, without facing alternatives. . . . Man can be restricted for a while, but not for generations.[4]

Now that this period of American history has apparently come to an end, what should now be the basis of our foreign policy? Beyond the Cold War, we still have global interests, both economic and strategic, and a new set of major international issues that could affect our national security as much as the Cold War. With international borders no longer the barrier they once were, we face a host of problems that are both domestic and international at the same time. Such issues as drugs, hunger, international terrorism, and the protection of the environment all treat international frontiers with contempt; their solution can come only with a level of international cooperation not yet achieved.

And what of our role in political and strategic issues in the future? I favored the American role in protecting freedom in Europe, Japan, Korea, and elsewhere over the last forty-five years. I do not believe, though, that we should attempt to play this role indefinitely. If our real interests are threatened, by all means let us do whatever is necessary to defend them. In other areas of the world, let us take a stand in favor of our own principles, let us assert our own values, and let us act in accordance with them—for that can be our greatest source of strength. Let us strengthen international institutions and promote movement toward a world of law, but let us refrain from excessive unilateral involvement in events around the world.

I am not making a neo-isolationist argument. The world we live in is shrinking; problems that were once internal to a society today cross international boundaries as if they did not exist. International cooperation to solve those problems which know no frontiers is, without question, the greatest conceptual challenge for the next generation of statesmen in the U.S. and abroad. The world leaders of the nineties will be seen by historians, I believe, as a transitional generation between a seventy-five year era of World Wars and Cold War, and an era in which global problems will compel intergovernmental cooperation. The great nations, which have spent so much of their time and national treasure in this century fighting each other or preparing for war, will have to recognize that the era of armed *major* power confrontation has come to an end.

This requires Americans to move beyond their obsession with such questions as our decline in power. The national fixation with whether or not we are still Number One belongs more suitably on the sports page than the front page. It was relevant when our national security was potentially threatened by the existence of a hostile power, be it Nazi Germany, Japan, or the Soviet Union. We must retain enough military force to protect our interests in important places around the world.

This brave new era toward which we are stumbling is not without dangers, the greatest of which is that we may be unable to see where our true interests lie. Nations, like people, have a tendency to fight the last war long past its end and to fail to recognize where the new dangers are until they have exploded. I pray that this will not be the case for my beloved country.

I was brought up in a world where the idea of America was in itself special. Our nation had been created in a unique manner, wholly different from any other nation on earth, and I believed it had a unique destiny. That destiny was not as an international crusader, but as the creator of a different and unique society within our own borders. The great irony of the postwar period is that we have been increasingly successful in exporting some of our most basic values, while risking the loss of them at home. Around the world, in nations under both communist and right-wing rule, America's ideals and values, and the vitality and openness of our society, have inspired people. It is no accident that when they free themselves from repressive regimes, leaders like Corazon Aquino, Lech Walesa, and Vaclav Havel come to America to address our Congress and celebrate our values.

This is a tribute to our greatest basic strengths—our ideals, our values, and our character—not to our military might. Eastern Europe freed itself. Our role was to encourage them, to offer an inspiring example from afar, and to prevent any further Soviet expansion into Western Europe after 1948. We never used, or threatened to use, force; if we had, we could have started a war without helping the people of the region, as President Eisenhower belatedly recognized during the Hungarian uprising in 1956. Even in the Philippines, where our influence is as great as anywhere else on earth, our influence in the 1986 overthrow of the dictatorship of President Marcos was through skillful diplomatic and public activity; we did not use force, even though our two largest bases in the world were located near Manila.

Even as we deal with problems that none of our fathers or forefathers could have imagined, it would be well to be guided by the words of John Quincy Adams in his famous Fourth of July address in 1821. Adams was not averse to the use of American power to protect our own interests, and he would not have objected to the use of the tools of modern diplomacy, had they been available then. But he feared that if we took on the task of intervening in foreign lands in order to promote our views and values, we would get sucked into the internal affairs of nations to a degree that could distort our original ideals. "Wherever the standard of freedom and independence has been or shall be unfurled," he said, referring to our country,

> there will her heart, her benedictions and her prayers be. But she goes not abroad, in search of monsters to destroy. She is the well-wisher to the freedom and independence of all. She is the champion and vindicator only of her own. She will commend the general cause by the countenance of her voice, and the benignant sympathy of her example. She well knows that by once enlisting under other banners than her own, were they even the banners of foreign independence, she would involve herself beyond the power of extrication, in all the wars of interest and intrigue, of individual avarice, envy, and ambition, which assume the colors and usurp the standard of freedom.

> The fundamental maxims of her policy would insensibly change from *liberty* to *force*. . . . She might become the dictatress of the world. She would no longer be the ruler of her own spirit.

THE CYCLES OF AMERICAN HISTORY

I have always been a liberal activist in regard to the role of government. At an early age, I acquired from my crusading uncle and my parents a belief that the government had a responsibility to try to solve the intractable problems that lay beyond the reach of individuals. I regretted those periods in our history when the government was passive and conservative, although I recognized that there is a certain cyclical nature to our history, that a certain tension would always exist—in another lovely phrase of Emerson's, between "the party of Conservatism and that of Innovation." These two parties "divide the state," he wrote,

> and have disputed the possession of the world ever since it was made. . . . Innovation is the salient energy; Conservatism the pause of the last movement. . . . Its fingers clutch the fact, and it will not open its eyes to see a better fact.[5]

By the measurement that I prefer,[6] I have lived through three cycles of Innovation and Conservatism. The first President of whom I was conscious was Woodrow Wilson, one of the century's few innovative and visionary leaders. As I grew up in the twenties, the pendulum swung to a conservative era, marked by attention not to public affairs but to private interests. The second progressive cycle, which began in 1933 with the century's greatest and most successful innovators, Franklin Roosevelt and Harry Truman, encompassed twenty extraordinary years in the life of our nation. The New Deal, World War II, the Cold War and the Marshall Plan, the Korean War, and the Fair Deal were all events of historic dimensions. They shaped the world in which we live today. They left the nation exhausted, however, ready for the calming leadership of President Eisenhower.

Although the narrowness of John F. Kennedy's victory eight years later made it impossible to view the result as a clear mandate for innovation, the challenges of the time and the dynamic personality of the young President led the nation into another period of extraordinary change. But the events of that era—President Kennedy's assassination, the Vietnam War, domestic turmoil, racial crisis, and Watergate, to name just a few—reached such a disruptive level that the nation seemed to be coming apart at the seams. In the words of Arthur M. Schlesinger, Jr.,

> So much trauma and exhaustion compressed in so short a time produced national disillusion and exhaustion in less than the customary two decades. By the later 1970s Americans were once more, as they had been in the 1950s and 1920s, fed up with public action and disenchanted by its consequences. The compass needle now swung toward private interest and the fulfillment of self.[7]

And so we moved into the Reagan-Bush era.

I have no doubt that the pendulum will swing back again. With the reforms of the New Deal fully absorbed into the mainstream of our society, and the civil rights battles of the sixties largely won, new and, in many ways, more complex problems have arisen. During the eighties, Washington virtually ignored these problems, among which I would include the many aspects of the environmental crisis, the budgetary disaster, the decay of our nation's infrastructure, the drug problem, AIDS, the decline in our educational system, the deficiencies in health care, our lack of competitiveness overseas, and the most enduring and serious of all our social problems, the continuing racial crisis in America. The preceding is by no means a complete list. These are, in my view, the real national issues for the rest of this century and beyond; the future strength of our nation will depend absolutely on solving them. This will demand leadership of a level that has not been seen in Washington in many years. But I am convinced that at a certain point in the historical cycle the American people will demand it, and a new era of change and innovation will begin.

Acknowledgments

I would like to acknowledge the large number of people and institutions whose support, advice, encouragement, and assistance were indispensable over the last three years.

Above all, I wish to acknowledge the assistance of George M. Elsey, the president-emiritus of the American Red Cross, whose own archives, memories, and commitment to historical precision were vital throughout these efforts, as they were at many critical times during my career.

I was deeply touched by the number of people who agreed to search their own memories and answer my questions about events that are now receding into the past. The following contributed their time, some in extended or repeated interviews, others in response to questions on specific events: Robert A. Altman, Dr. William O. Baker, George W. Ball, Benjamin C. Bradlee, Charles Brannan, McGeorge Bundy, William P. Bundy, Joyce Clifford Burland, Jimmy Carter, George Christian, Richmond Coburn, Margaret Truman Daniel, C. Gerard Davidson, Frederick G. Dutton, Ahmet Ertegun, Jack Foisie, Yolande Fox, Clayton Fritchey, J. William Fulbright, Katharine Graham, Philip Geyelin, David Ginsburg, Carson Glass, Albert Gore, Sr., Mrs. Freeman Gosden, Phil G. Goulding, Philip C. Habib, Morton H. Halperin, Ken Hechler, Richard Helms, Lady Bird Johnson, W. Thomas Johnson, Hamilton Jordan, Jim Jones, Nicholas deB. Katzenbach, George F. Kennan, Henry A. Kissinger, Melvin Laird, Bert Lance, Nelson Ledsky, Franklin W. Lincoln, Martin Lipton, Samuel D. McIlwain, Robert S. McNamara, Harry C. McPherson, Jr., David A. Morse, Richard E. Neustadt, Matthew Nimetz, Jacqueline Kennedy Onassis, Dudley Orr, Robert E. Pursley, Elwood "Pete" Quesada, Kate Davis Quesada, Benjamin H. Read, Abraham A. Ribicoff, Mrs. James H. Rowe, Jr., Dean Rusk, Herbert Y. Schandler, Hugh Sidey, Senator Paul Simon, Theodore C. Sorensen, Richard C. Steadman, Arthur O. Sulzberger, Jr., James Symington, Stuart Symington, Stuart Symington, Jr., Jack Valenti, Cyrus R. Vance, William Walton, Paul C. Warnke, James E. Webb, Mary Weiler, Nancy Wexler, Fraser Wilkins, Edward Bennett Williams, Tim Wirth, and Barry Zorthian.

I am especially indebted to Arthur M. Schlesinger, Jr., who reviewed the entire manuscript with great care. His vast historical knowledge and encouragement were of constant value and comfort to me. Leslie H. Gelb, Brooke Shearer, and Peter Tarnoff also reviewed the entire manuscript and made many helpful suggestions. Morton Abramowitz, Daniel I. Davidson, Stephen R. Fenster, Frances FitzGerald, John Guare, James Hoge, Townsend Hoopes, Peter Grose, Pamela Harriman, Maxine Isaacs, James A. Johnson, Howard Kaminsky, Stanley Karnow, Anthony Lake, Sol Linowitz, Anne Mandelbaum, Kati Marton, Bob Mrazek, Maynard Parker, Norman Pearlstine, Naomi Rosenblatt, Jack Rosenthal, Strobe Talbott, and Frank G. Wisner also commented on portions of the work. Several of those who were interviewed also reviewed portions of the manuscript, including Messrs. Altman, Fritchey, Ginsburg, Glass, Halperin, Lance, Ledsky, McPherson, Neustadt, Nimetz, Orr, Pursley, Read, Sorensen, and Valenti. Not every suggestion they made was taken, but all were listened to and deeply appreciated. Any errors of fact are, of course, my responsibility.

Many people offered other forms of assistance or encouragement during our research. They included: James Albrecht, Robert L. Bernstein, Sidney Blumenthal, Joan Ganz Cooney, Fred R. Demich, Jr., Dick Ebersol and Susan Saint James, Harry Evans, Joni Evans, Abraham Feinberg, Alfred Friendly, Jr., Doris Kearns Goodwin, Bobby Ray Inman, Walter Isaacson, Linda Janklow, Henry Muller, S. I. Newhouse, Nathan W. Pearson, Peter G. Peterson, Evan Thomas, William vanden Heuvel, and Alberto Vitale. Professor Fritz Stern of Columbia University helped locate Brian VanDeMark at UCLA and urged us on at all times.

My collaborator, Richard Holbrooke, wishes to express gratitude for the forbearance and support he received from many of his present and former colleagues at Lehman Brothers and American Express, especially Vincent A. Mai, James D. Robinson III, Sherman Lewis, J. Tomilson Hill, Roman Martinez IV, and Peter Cohen. He also expresses special thanks to his sons, David Dan and Anthony Andrew Holbrooke, who showed marvelous understanding, enthusiasm, and support when it mattered most.

At every stage of our efforts, I relied on the good judgment and advice of my literary agent, Morton Janklow, whose enthusiasm for this project was instrumental in bringing it to fruition.

My sincere appreciation to our editor, Peter Osnos. He has been wise and supportive and deeply involved from the beginning, and brought to bear, in a most valuable way, his own extensive knowledge of Washington. To him and all his colleagues at Random House, especially Amy Edelman and Ken Gellman, my deepest appreciation. To William Novak, special thanks for his invaluable advice on how to make a collaboration work. I am also deeply indebted to three government officials who assisted in gaining access to material that was still either classified or restricted at the time: former Secretary of Defense Frank C. Carlucci, and General Colin L. Powell and Ambassador John D. Negroponte during their tours of duty at the National Security Council.

Among the most important resources for this work were three collections of papers that were previously restricted or unavailable: the official minutes of many important White House meetings in 1968, taken by White House Assistant Tom Johnson; and notes taken at the 8:30 Group staff meeting during my tenure as Secretary of Defense, by George Elsey and Colonel (later Lieutenant General) Robert Pursley. I am deeply grateful to all three men for allowing me complete access to these documents. To Eileen Carver, Beverly Snyder, and Toby Godfrey, special thanks for many administrative and secretarial tasks, large and small but always "urgent," which they performed with continual good cheer.

My own memory and files were augmented by over three thousand pages of material from one of the nation's greatest treasures, the Presidential Libraries and the National Archives of the United States. This material included most of my own papers, which I have deposited, as appropriate, at the libraries of the four Presidents with whom I worked. I wish to acknowledge the assistance from the following people and institutions: THE NATIONAL ARCHIVES AND RECORDS ADMINISTRATION OF THE UNITED STATES: Don Wilson, Archivist of the United States; John T. Fawcett, Judy Koucky, Nancy Kegan Smith, and David Van Tassel; FRANKLIN D. ROOSEVELT LIBRARY, Hyde Park, New York: John Ferris; HARRY S TRUMAN LIBRARY, Independence, Missouri: Benedict K. Zobrist, Dennis E. Bilger, George H. Curtis, Anita Heavener, Niel Johnson, Philip D. Lagerquist, Erwin J. Muller, Doris Pesek, Elizabeth Safly, and Pauline Testerman; DWIGHT D. EISENHOWER LIBRARY, Abilene, Kansas: Herbert Pankrapz and Martin M. Teasley; JOHN FITZGERALD KENNEDY LIBRARY, Boston Massachusetts: Michael Desmond, Megan Desnoyers, Allan Goodrich, Henry Gwiazda, William Johnson, and Ron Whealan; LYNDON BAINES JOHNSON LIBRARY, Austin, Texas: Harry J. Middleton, David C. Humphrey, Claudia W. Anderson, Charles W. Corkran, Katherine H.

Frankum, Theodore D. Gittinger, Regina Greenwell, Linda M. Hanson, Tina Houston, Irene Parra, E. Philip Scott, Bob Tissing, Steve Young, Jennifer Warner, and Shellynne Wucher; NIXON PRESIDENTIAL MATERIALS STAFF, National Archives, Alexandria, Virginia: Anita O. Happoldt and Joan L. Howard; JIMMY CARTER LIBRARY, Atlanta, Georgia: Martin Elzy, David Stanhope, and James Yancey, Jr.; ARMY CENTER OF MILITARY HISTORY, Washington, D.C.: Vincent Demma; MISSOURI HISTORICAL ASSOCIATION: Ken Wynn and Barbara Stole; RICHARD B. RUSSELL MEMORIAL LIBRARY, Athens, Georgia: Sheryl B. Vogt; ST. LOUIS LAW LIBRARY: Rosa Wright; ST. LOUIS MERCANTILE LIBRARY ASSOCIATION: David E. Cassens; ST. LOUIS MUNICIPAL COURTS RECORDS: William C. Friedrich; SEELEY G. MUDD MANUSCRIPT LIBRARY, Princeton University: Jean Holliday; WASHINGTON UNIVERSITY, St. Louis, Missouri: John Drobak, Beryl Manne, and Bernard Reams. Also, a special word of appreciation to Bruce Stark of ComputerTutor, in New York City, who helped set up the WordPerfect program, which enabled us to complete this manuscript within the alotted time, and who helped on several occasions to retrieve material we feared had been lost to computer gremlins.

Finally, I wish to thank my closest collaborator over the last sixty years, my wife, Marny, who saw most of the events described in this book. She read the manuscript with her usual precision, and added her memories to my own. To Marny, I owe the deepest debt of all, not only for this book, but for so much more.

Works Consulted

Acheson, Dean. *Present at the Creation: My Years in the State Department.* New York: W. W. Norton, 1969.

Allen, Robert S. and William V. Shannon. *The Truman Merry-Go-Round.* New York: Vanguard Press, 1950.

Ball, George W. *The Past Has Another Pattern: Memoirs.* New York: W. W. Norton, 1982.

Berman, Larry. *Lyndon Johnson's War: The Road to Stalemate in Vietnam.* New York: W. W. Norton, 1989.

Bernstein, Carl. *Loyalties.* New York: Simon and Schuster, 1989.

Bickerton, Ian J. "President Truman's Recognition of Israel," *American Jewish Historical Quarterly,* v. 58, n. 2, Dec. 1968, pp. 173–240.

Bingham, Jonathan B. *Shirt-Sleeve Diplomacy: Point 4 in Action.* New York: John Day, 1954.

Blum, John Morton, ed. *The Price of Vision: The Diary of Henry A. Wallace, 1942–1946.* Boston: Houghton Mifflin, 1973.

Bontecou, Eleanor. *The Federal Loyalty-Security Program.* Ithaca, N. Y.: Cornell University Press, 1953.

Bradlee, Benjamin C. *Conversations with Kennedy.* New York: W. W. Norton, 1975.

Braestrup, Peter. *Big Story: How the American Press and Television Reported and Interpreted the Crisis of Tet 1968 in Vietnam and Washington.* 2 vols. Boulder: Westview Press, 1977.

Branch, Taylor. *Parting the Waters: America in the King Years, 1954–63.* New York: Simon and Schuster, 1988.

Brauer, Carl M. *Presidential Transitions: Eisenhower through Reagan.* New York: Oxford University Press, 1986.

Brayman, Harold. *The President Speaks Off-the-Record: Historic Evenings with America's Leaders, the Press, and Other Men of Power, at Washington's Exclusive Gridiron Club.* Princeton: Dow Jones Books, 1976.

Brewin, Bob, and Sydney Shaw. *Vietnam on Trial: Westmoreland vs. CBS.* New York: Atheneum, 1987.

Brzezinski, Zbigniew. *Power and Principle: Memoirs of the National Security Adviser 1977–1981.* New York: Farrar Straus and Giroux, 1983.

Bundy, McGeorge. *Danger and Survival: Choices on the Bomb in the First Fifty Years.* New York: Random House, 1988.

Byrnes, James F. *Speaking Frankly.* New York: Harper and Brothers, 1947.

Caro, Robert A. *The Years of Lyndon Johnson: Means of Ascent.* New York: Alfred A. Knopf, 1990.

Carter, Jimmy. *Keeping Faith: Memoirs of a President.* New York: Bantam Books, 1982.

Caute, David. *The Great Fear: The Anti-Communist Purge under Truman and Eisenhower.* New York: Simon and Schuster, 1978.

Chennault, Anna. *The Education of Anna.* New York: Times Books, 1980.

Christian, George. *The President Steps Down: A Personal Memoir of the Transfer of Power.* New York: Macmillan, 1970.

Clifford, Clark M. "A Viet Nam Reappraisal: The Personal History of One Man's View and How It Evolved." *Foreign Affairs,* v. 47, n. 4, July 1969, pp. 601–622.

———. "Factors Influencing President Truman's Decision To Support Partition and Recognize the State of Israel," Speech to American Historical Association and American Jewish Historical Society, Washington, D.C., Dec. 28, 1976.

Clodfelter, Mark. *The Limits of Air Power: The American Bombing of North Vietnam.* New York: The Free Press, 1989.

Davidson, Philip B. *Vietnam at War: The History, 1946–1975.* Novato, Cal.: Presidio Press, 1988.

Destler, I. M., Leslie H. Gelb, and Anthony Lake. *Our Own Worst Enemy: The Unmaking of American Foreign Policy.* New York: Simon and Schuster, 1984.

Diem, Bui, with David Chanoff. *In the Jaws of History.* Boston: Houghton Mifflin Company, 1987.

Donovan, Robert J. *Conflict and Crisis: The Presidency of Harry S Truman, 1945–1948.* New York: W. W. Norton, 1977.

———. *Tumultuous Years: The Presidency of Harry S Truman, 1949–1953.* New York: W. W. Norton, 1982.

Eisenhower, Dwight D. *White House Years: Waging Peace, 1956–1961.* Garden City, N.Y.: Doubleday, 1948.

Elsey, George M. "Some White House Recollections, 1942–53," *Diplomatic History,* v. 12, n. 3, Summer 1988, pp. 357–364.

Ferrell, Robert H., ed. *Dear Bess: The Letters From Harry to Bess Truman, 1910–1959.* New York: W. W. Norton, 1983.

———, ed. *Off the Record: The Private Papers of Harry S Truman.* New York: Harper and Row, 1980.; repr., New York: Penguin, 1982.

Flapan, Simha. *The Birth of Israel.* New York: Pantheon, 1987.

Foreign Relations of the United States: 1948, v. 5, *The Near East, South Asia, and Africa, Part 2.* Washington: Government Printing Office, 1976.

Freeland, Richard M. *The Truman Doctrine and the Origins of McCarthyism.* New York: Alfred A. Knopf, 1972.

Gaddis, John Lewis. *The United States and the Origins of the Cold War, 1941–1947.* New York: Columbia University Press, 1972.

Gelb, Leslie H., with Richard K. Betts. *The Irony of Vietnam: The System Worked.* Washington, D.C.: The Brookings Institution, 1979.

Gilbert, Martin. *Winston S. Churchill* vol. 8, *Never Despair: 1945–65.* Boston: Houghton Mifflin, 1988.

Goulding, Phil G. *Confirm or Deny: Informing the People on National Security.* New York: Harper and Row, 1970.

Grose, Peter. *Israel in the Mind of America.* New York: Alfred A. Knopf, 1983.

Halberstam, David. *The Best and the Brightest.* New York: Random House, 1972.

Hamby, Alonzo L. *Beyond the New Deal: Harry S Truman and American Liberalism.* New York: Columbia University Press, 1973.

Hechler, Ken. *Working with Truman: A Personal Memoir of the White House Years.* New York: G. P. Putnam's Sons, 1982.

Hersh, Seymour. *The Price of Power: Kissinger in the Nixon White House.* New York: Summit Books, 1983.

Hoopes, Townsend. *The Limits of Intervention: An Inside Account of How the Johnson Policy of Escalation in Vietnam Was Reversed.* New York: David McKay, 1969.

Humphrey, Hubert H. *The Education of a Public Man: My Life and Politics.* Norman Sherman, ed. Garden City, N.Y.: Doubleday, 1976.

Hung, Nguyen Tien, and Jerrold L. Schecter. *The Palace File.* New York: Harper and Row, 1986.

Isaacson, Walter, and Evan Thomas. *The Wise Men: Six Men and the World They Made.* New York: Simon and Schuster, 1986.

Johnson, Lady Bird. *A White House Diary.* New York: Holt, Rinehart, and Winston, 1970.

Johnson, Lyndon Baines. *The Vantage Point: Perspectives of the Presidency, 1963–1969.* New York: Holt, Rinehart, and Winston, 1971.

Jones, Joseph M. *The Fifteen Weeks (February 21—June 5, 1947).* New York: Viking, 1955.

Kaiser, Charles. *1968 In America.* New York: Weidenfeld and Nicolson, 1988.

Kalman, Laura. *Abe Fortas.* New Haven: Yale University Press, 1990.

Karnow, Stanley. *Vietnam: A History.* New York: Viking, 1983.

Kearns, Doris. *Lyndon Johnson and the American Dream.* New York: Harper and Row, 1976.

Kernell, Samuel, and Samuel L. Popkin, eds., *Chief of Staff: Twenty-five Years of Managing the Presidency.* Berkeley, Cal.: University of California Press, 1986.

Kissinger, Henry A. *White House Years.* Boston: Little, Brown, 1979.

Kolsky, Thomas A. *Jews Against Zionism: The American Council for Judaism, 1942–1948.* Philadelphia: Temple University Press, 1990.

Krock, Arthur. *Memoirs: Sixty Years on the Firing Line.* New York: Funk and Wagnalls, 1968.

Lash, Joseph P. *Dealers and Dreamers: A New Look at the New Deal.* New York: Doubleday, 1988.

Lilienthal, David E. *Journals of David E. Lilienthal,* vol. 2, *Atomic Energy Years, 1945–1950.* New York: Harper and Row, 1964.

Lowenthal, Max. *The Federal Bureau of Investigation.* New York: William Sloane Associates, 1950.

McLellan, David S. and David C. Acheson, eds. *Among Friends: Personal Letters of Dean Acheson.* New York: Dodd, Mead, 1980.

McPherson, Harry. *A Political Education: A Washington Memoir.* Boston: Houghton Mifflin, 1988 (rev. ed.).

Manchester, William. *The Glory and the Dream: A Narrative History of America, 1932–1972* Boston: Little, Brown, 1974.

Millis, Walter, ed. *The Forrestal Diaries.* New York: Viking, 1951.

Murphy, Bruce Allen. *Fortas: The Rise and Ruin of a Supreme Court Justice.* New York: William Morrow, 1988.

Neustadt, Richard E. *Presidential Power and the Modern Presidents: The Politics of Leadership from Roosevelt to Reagan.* New York: Macmillan, The Free Press, 1990.

——— and Ernest R. May. *Thinking In Time: The Uses of History for Decision-makers.* New York: The Free Press, 1986.

Newfield, Jack. *Robert Kennedy: A Memoir.* New York: E. P. Dutton, 1969.

Nitze, Paul H., with Ann M. Smith and Steven L. Rearden. *From Hiroshima to Glasnost: At the Center of Decision. A Memoir.* New York: Grove Weidenfeld, 1989.

Nixon, Richard. *RN: The Memoirs of Richard Nixon.* New York: Grosset and Dunlap, 1978.

Oberdorfer, Don. *Tet!* New York: Doubleday, 1971. Repr. New York: Da Capo Press, 1984.

Oshinsky, David M. *A Conspiracy So Immense: The World of Joe McCarthy.* New York: The Free Press, 1983.

Palmer, General Bruce. *The 25-Year War: America's Military Role in Vietnam.* Lexington: University Press of Kentucky, 1984.

Parmet, Herbert S. *JFK: The Presidency of John F. Kennedy.* New York: Dial Press, 1983. Repr. New York: Penguin, 1984.

Patterson, Richard S., and Richardson Dougall. *The Eagle and The Shield: A*

History of the Great Seal of the United States. Washington, D.C.: Government Printing Office, 1976.

Perry, Mark. *Four Stars.* Boston: Houghton Mifflin, 1989.

Phillips, Cabell. *The Truman Presidency: The History of a Triumphant Succession.* New York: Macmillan, 1966.

Podhoretz, Norman. *Why We Were in Vietnam.* New York: Simon and Schuster, 1982.

Pogue, Forrest C. *George C. Marshall: Statesman 1945–1959.* New York: Viking, 1987.

Rearden, Steven L. *Formative Years, 1947–1950,* vol. 1 in Alfred Goldberg, ed., *History of the Office of Secretary of Defense.* Washington, D.C.: Government Printing Office, 1984.

Reedy, George E. *The Twilight of the Presidency from Johnson to Reagan.* New York: New American Library, 1987. Rev. ed.

Roberts, Chalmers. *First Rough Draft: A Journalist's Journal of Our Times.* New York: Praeger, 1973.

Ross, Irwin. *The Loneliest Campaign: The Truman Victory of 1948.* New York: New American Library, 1968.

Rusk, Dean, as told to Richard Rusk. *As I Saw It.* New York: W. W. Norton, 1990.

Safire, William. *Before the Fall: An Inside View of the Pre-Watergate White House.* Garden City, N.Y.: Doubleday, 1975.

Schandler, Herbert Y. *The Unmaking of a President: Lyndon Johnson and Vietnam.* Princeton: Princeton University Press, 1977.

Schlesinger, Arthur M., Jr. *A Thousand Days: John F. Kennedy in the White House.* Boston: Houghton Mifflin, 1965.

———. *Robert Kennedy and His Times.* Boston: Houghton Mifflin, 1978.

———. *The Cycles of American History.* Boston: Houghton Mifflin, 1986.

Sharp, Admiral U.S.G., and General W. C. Westmoreland. *Report on the War in Vietnam (As of 30 June 1968).* Washington, D.C.: U.S. Government Printing Office, 1969.

Sherwin, Martin J. *A World Destroyed.* Repr. New York: Random House, 1987.

Sidey, Hugh. *John F. Kennedy, President.* New York: Atheneum, 1963.

Smith, Gaddis. *Dean Acheson.* New York: Cooper Square, 1972.

Smith, Richard Norton. *Thomas E. Dewey and His Times.* New York: Simon and Schuster, 1982.

Smith, Timothy G., ed. *Merriman Smith's Book of Presidents: A White House Memoir.* New York: W. W. Norton, 1972.

Sorensen, Theodore C. *The Kennedy Legacy.* New York: Macmillan, 1969.

Talbott, Strobe. *The Master of the Game: Paul Nitze and the Nuclear Peace.* New York: Alfred A. Knopf, 1988.

Taylor, Maxwell. *Swords and Plowshares.* New York: W. W. Norton, 1972.

Thayer, Mary Van Rensselaer. *Jacqueline Kennedy: The White House Years.* Boston: Little, Brown, 1967.

Troy, Thomas F. *Donovan and the CIA: A History of the Establishment of the*

Central Intelligence Agency. Frederick, Md.: University Publications of America, 1981.

Truman, Harry S. *Memoirs,* vols. 1 and 2. Garden City, N.Y.: Doubleday, 1955 and 1956.

Truman, Margaret. *Harry S Truman.* New York: William Morrow, 1973.

Valenti, Jack. *A Very Human President.* New York: W. W. Norton, 1975.

Vance, Cyrus. *Hard Choices: Critical Years in America's Foreign Policy.* New York: Simon and Schuster, 1983.

VanDeMark, Brian. *Into the Quagmire: Lyndon Johnson and the Escalation of the Vietnam War.* New York: Oxford University Press, 1991.

Wallace, Mike, and Gary Paul Gates. *Close Encounters.* New York: William Morrow, 1984.

Westmoreland, General William C. *A Soldier Reports.* Garden City, N. Y.: Doubleday, 1976.

White, Theodore H. *The Making of the President—1960.* New York: Atheneum, 1961.

Witcover, Jules. *85 Days: The Last Campaign of Robert Kennedy.* Repr. New York: William Morrow, Quill Books, 1988.

Notes

AUTHOR'S NOTE

1. Brian VanDeMark, *Into the Quagmire: Lyndon Johnson and the Escalation of the Vietnam War* (New York: Oxford University Press, 1991).

1. SHOWDOWN IN THE OVAL OFFICE

1. See Walter Issacson and Evan Thomas, *The Wise Men: Six Men and the World They Made* (New York: Simon and Schuster, 1986).
2. Max Lowenthal, *The Federal Bureau of Investigation* (New York: Sloane Associates, 1950).
3. My account of the May 12, 1948, meeting is drawn from my memory and notes, as well as the official memorandum of conversation draft by Robert McClintock (and reviewed and signed by Secretary Marshall). I am grateful as well to the late Fraser Wilkins for adding his own recollections to mine regarding this meeting. See *Foreign Relations of the United States: 1948,* v. 5, *The Near East, South Asia, and Africa, Part 2* (Washington: Government Printing Office, 1976), pp. 972–978.
4. Forrest Pogue, *George C. Marshall: Statesman 1947–59* (New York: Viking, 1987), p. 377.
5. *FRUS,* 1948, vol. 5, pp. 972–78.
6. This movement, which is almost forgotten today, carried weight until the establishment of Israel. For a useful account, see Thomas A. Kolsky, *Jews Against Zionism: The American Council for Judaism, 1942–1948.* (Philadelphia: Temple University Press, 1990), pp. 4 and *passim.*

7. Iphigene Ochs Sulzberger had become ardently pro-Zionist after the war but her husband Arthur "held to his anti-Zionist position. He did not believe in the concept of a Jewish nation. . . . The wiser course, he thought, was to help the refugees find new homes in countries where they would be welcome. Arthur contributed to an organization dedicated to resettling Jews in northern Australia." *Iphigene: My Life and The New York Times,* as written by Susan W. Dryfoos (New York: Times Books, 1981), pp. 223–224.

8. Michael Bar-Zohar, *Ben-Gurion,* 3 vols. (Tel Aviv: Am Oved, 1977); manuscript, *Ben-Gurion Remembers,* Hebrew University, Jerusalem; and Dan Kurzman, *Ben-Gurion: Prophet of Fire* (New York: Simon and Schuster, 1983), p. 416.

2. ST. LOUIS

1. *St. Louis Post-Dispatch,* Nov. 7, 1916, p. 1.

3. TO THE WHITE HOUSE

1. Shevardnadze was speaking before the Foreign Policy Association: see *The Washington Post,* Oct. 3, 1989, p. A20.

2. Margaret Truman, *Harry S Truman* (New York: William Morrow, 1973), p. 290.

3. *Time,* April 22, 1946, p. 21.

4. A LITTLE GAMBLING AMONG FRIENDS

1. Dean Acheson, *Present at the Creation: My Years in the State Department* (New York: W. W. Norton, 1969), pp. 717–18.

2. Samuel Rosenman, Oral History Transcript, Harry S Truman Library, p. 40.

3. Interview with Richard E. Neustadt, Dec. 28, 1955. Richard E. Neustadt Papers, John Fitzgerald Kennedy Library.

5. THE LABOR WARS OF 1946

1. Cabell Phillips, *The Truman Presidency: The History of a Triumphant Succession* (New York: Macmillan, 1966), p. 119.

6. CHURCHILL AT FULTON

1. The statement, made on January 5, 1952, is quoted by William Leuchtenberg, "Give 'Em Harry," *The New Republic,* May 21, 1984, p. 22.

2. Martin Gilbert, *Winston S. Churchill,* vol. 8, *Never Despair, 1945–65* (Boston: Houghton Mifflin, 1988), pp. 204–206.

7. THE CLIFFORD-ELSEY REPORT AND THE FIRING OF HENRY WALLACE

1. Acheson, *Present at the Creation,* p. 213.

2. Letter dated Sept. 20, 1946, in Robert H. Ferrell, ed., *Off the Record: The Private Papers of Harry S Truman* (reprint ed., New York: Penguin, 1982).

3. Arthur Krock, *Memoirs: Sixty Years on the Firing Line* (New York: Funk and Wagnalls, 1968), pp. 419–482. Sixteen of the original twenty copies are at the Truman Library, and several have never been located.

8. THE TRUMAN DOCTRINE AND THE MARSHALL PLAN

1. See Harry S Truman, *Memoirs,* vol. 2 *Years of Trial and Hope* (Garden City, N.Y.: Doubleday, 1956), pp. 103–104; Dean Acheson, *Present at the Creation,* p. 219; Joseph M. Jones, *The Fifteen Weeks* (New York: Viking, 1955), pp. 138–144; Forrest Pogue, *George C. Marshall: Statesman, 1945–1959* (New York: Viking, 1987), pp. 164–165.

2. Many historians, not understanding the system of speech preparation in the Truman Administration, viewed the drafting of this speech as a unique event. This view was unintentionally encouraged by two important firsthand accounts, Joseph Jones's *The Fifteen Weeks,* and Dean Acheson's *Present at the Creation,* which drew heavily on Jones. Both works, while indispensable for understanding events at State, do not accurately describe the White House role in the evolution of the speech.

3. Thanks to George Elsey's fine sense of history, copies of every draft are preserved at the Truman Library. These include numerous handwritten changes and additions, including those of President Truman himself. They are essential material for anyone who wants to understand how this most important of Presidential speeches was produced.

4. Harry S Truman, *Memoirs,* vol. 1 *Year of Decisions* (Garden City, N.Y.: Doubleday, 1955), p. 105.

5. In *The Fifteen Weeks,* Jones writes that, "except for three additions, [Clifford] had made no material change in organization, content, or phraseology" (page 156). A similar misstatement appears in *Present at the Creation.* I suspect these errors of fact were a result of the fact that, given the pressure under which everyone was working, no one ever made a careful comparison between the State draft of March 9 and the heavily revised draft I sent back to State the next day.

6. Nixon's first comment was made on October 27, 1952 in Texarkana, the second in Los Angeles on October 30, 1952.

9. THE BIRTH OF THE NATIONAL SECURITY SYSTEM

1. Letter to Congressman Gordon L. McDonough, Aug. 29, 1950.

2. Letter to Robert Sherwood, Aug. 27, 1947, quoted in Steven L. Rearden, *History of the Office of Secretary of Defense,* v. 1, *Formative Years, 1947–1950* (Washington, D.C.: U.S. Government Printing Office, 1984).

3. Harry S Truman, *Memoirs,* vol. 2, *Years of Trial and Hope,* pp. 59–60.

4. These articles both appeared on Feb. 9, 1945.

5. Testimony before the Senate Select Committee on Intelligence, Dec. 16, 1987.

10. J. EDGAR HOOVER AND THE LOYALTY PROGRAM

1. Eleanor Bontecou, *The Federal Loyalty-Security Program* (Ithaca, New York: Cornell University Press, 1953), p. 28.

2. See *Journals of David E. Lilienthal, Atomic Energy Years, 1945–1950* (New York: Harper and Row, 1964), p. 163, for Lilienthal's account of our conversation.

3. Quoted in Richard Gid Powers, *Secrecy and Power: The Life of J. Edgar Hoover* (New York: Free Press, 1987), p. 275.

11. 1948: THE BEGINNING

1. Letter to Dr. W. R. Underhill (author of *The Truman Persuasions),* Jan. 31, 1981. See also Cabell Phillips, *The Truman Presidency,* pp. 197–99.

2. The phrase later became the title of a fine book on the 1948 campaign: Irwin Ross's *The Loneliest Campaign: The Truman Victory of 1948,* (New York: New American Library, 1968).

12. CIVIL RIGHTS AND THE DESEGREGATION OF THE ARMED FORCES

1. See Lee Nichols, *Breakthrough on the Color Front* (New York: Random House, 1954), p. 97.

2. Edwin Dorn, the Joint Center for Political Studies, "Truman and the De-Segregation of the Military," *Focus* (May 1988), p. 3.

13. UPSET

1. Letter to Clark Clifford, Oct. 15, 1948.

2. Truman, *Memoirs,* vol. 2, *Years of Trial and Hope,* p. 215.

3. *The New York Times,* Nov. 4, 1948.

14. LAST YEAR AT THE WHITE HOUSE

1. See M. Truman, *Harry S Truman,* pp. 400–401, for a similar comment.

2. Jonathan B. Bingham, *Shirt-Sleeve Diplomacy: Point 4 in Action* (New York: The John Day Company, 1954), pp. 11–12.

3. *Parade,* Jan. 26, 1958, p. 14.

4. David E. Lilienthal, *Journals of David E. Lilienthal,* vol. 2, *Atomic Energy Years, 1945–1950,* pp. 433–35.

15. A WASHINGTON LAWYER

1. *Phillips Chemical Company* v. *Dumas Independent School District,* Feb. 23, 1960.

16. THE YEARS BETWEEN: 1950–1960

1. A reference to Robert McNutt McElroy, *Grover Cleveland, the Man and the Statesman: An Authorized Biography* (New York: Harper and Brothers, 1923).

2. *Off the Record: The Private Papers of Harry S Truman,* Robert H. Ferrell, ed. (New York: Penguin, 1980), pp. 268–69.

3. *Ibid.,* pp. 263–64 (Aug. 16, 1952).

17. MCCARTHY AND HIS -ISM

1. Hearing before the Special Subcommittee on Investigations of the Committee on Government Operations. Special Senate investigation on charges and countercharges involving: Secretary of the Army Robert T. Stevens, John G. Adams, H. Struve Hensel and Senator Joe McCarthy, Roy M. Cohn, and Francis P. Carr, June 4, 1954, pp. 2226–7.

2. John Hersey, *Aspects of The Presidency* (New York: Ticknor and Fields, 1980), p. 138.

3. Hearings, p. 2903.

18. THE BEGINNING, 1957–1960

1. Letter from Sherman Adams, White House Chief of Staff, to Senator Kennedy, Jan. 11, 1956, on behalf of President Eisenhower, and letter from President Truman to Senator Kennedy, Jan. 5, 1956.

2. Hearings before the Subcommittee on Reorganization of the Committee on Government Operations, on the proposal to create position of Administrative Vice President, United States Senate, Eighty-fourth Congress, Second Session, Jan. 24, 1956, p. 60.

3. Mike Wallace and Gary Paul Gates, *Close Encounters* (New York: Berkley Books, 1985), p. 63.

4. Tyler Abell, ed., *Drew Pearson Diaries: 1949–1959* (New York: Holt, Rinehart, and Winston, 1974), p. 420.

5. See, for example, Bill Moyers's comments to me during "Bill Moyers' Journal: An Interview with Clark Clifford," first broadcast on PBS, January 6, 1981.

6. Theodore H. White, *The Making of the President—1960* (New York: Atheneum, 1961), pp. 45–51.

20. THE TRANSITION

1. Carl M. Brauer, *Presidential Transitions: Eisenhower through Reagan* (New York: Oxford University Press, 1986), p. 226.

2. Theodore C. Sorensen, *Kennedy,* (New York: Harper and Row, 1965), p. 284.

3. Arthur M. Schlesinger, Jr., *A Thousand Days: John F. Kennedy in the White House* (reprint ed., Greenwich: Fawcett, 1965), p. 308.

21. THE PRESIDENCY AND FOREIGN CRISES

1. See William Safire, "Preserve Your 'Piffiab,' " *The New York Times,* Feb. 16, 1989, p. A35.

2. Letter from President Kennedy to Clark Clifford, April 20, 1963.

3. *The New York Times,* April 29, 1963.

22. THE PRESIDENCY, CLOSER TO HOME

1. Arthur M. Schlesinger, Jr., *A Thousand Days,* pp. 406–407.

23. LYNDON JOHNSON TO 1965

1. *Newsweek,* January 15, 1969.

2. Letter from Dean Acheson to Clark Clifford, April 15, 1968.

3. Laura Kalman, *Abe Fortas* (New Haven: Yale University Press, 1990), p. 2.

4. Lyndon Baines Johnson, *The Vantage Point: Perspectives of the Presidency, 1963–1969* (New York: Holt, Rinehart and Winston, 1971), p. 100.

5. White, *The Making of the President—1964,* pp. 348–49.

24. VIETNAM: THE DRAMA BEGINS

1. Clark M. Clifford, "A Viet Nam Reappraisal: The Personal History of One Man's View and How It Evolved," *Foreign Affairs,* vol. 47, no. 4 (July 1969), p. 602.

2. Quoted in Arthur S. Link, *Wilson the Diplomatist: A Look at His Major Foreign Policies* (Baltimore: The Johns Hopkins Press, 1957), p. 5.

3. Memorandum of Telephone Conversation: 10:55 A.M., July 2, 1965, by Lillian H. Brown (Eisenhower's confidential secretary), Eisenhower Post-Presidential Papers: Augusta Series, Box 10, Dwight D. Eisenhower Library.

4. George Ball, *The Past Has Another Pattern: Memoirs* (New York: W. W. Norton, 1982), p. 402.

5. EMBTEL (Embassy Telegram) 2699, from Ambassador Taylor to Washington, Feb. 22, 1965.

6. In the detailed description of the meetings that follows, I have relied on three sources: first, the official White House memoranda of the meetings; second, my own notes and recollections; and third, the memories and writings of others who participated in the meetings. This is not, of course, the full record, which is available at the Lyndon Baines Johnson Library at the University of Texas in Austin.

25. ON THE TEAM

1. General William C. Westmoreland, *A Soldier Reports* (New York: Doubleday, 1976; reprint ed., New York: Dell, 1980,), p. 137.

26. THE YEARS OF THE HAWK

1. *The Washington Post,* Oct. 26, 1966.

2. Johnson, *The Vantage Point,* p. 363.

3. Chalmers Roberts, *First Rough Draft: A Journalist's Journal of Our Times,* (New York: Praeger, 1973), p. 265.

4. Report of the President's meeting in the Cabinet Room to hear Secretary McNamara's report on his mission to Vietnam, July 12, 1967. Based on notes by Tom Johnson (in the LBJ Library) and my own notes of the meeting.

5. See LBJ Handwriting File, LBJ Library.

6. General Maxwell Taylor, *Swords and Plowshares* (New York: W. W. Norton, 1972), p. 376.

7. CBS Morning News, Aug. 5, 1967, as transcribed in a memorandum to President Johnson from White House assistant Tom Johnson at the President's request.

8. Robert S. McNamara in a sworn deposition during the *Westmoreland v. CBS News* trial. See Bob Brewin and Sydney Shaw, *Vietnam on Trial: Westmoreland vs. CBS* (New York: Athenaeum, 1987), pp. 102–103.

9. Dean Rusk (as told to Richard Rusk), *As I Saw It,* (New York: W. W. Norton, 1990), contains a moving and valuable account of their relationship.

10. Memorandum from Robert S. McNamara to the President, Nov. 28, 1967, LBJ Library. Also, James Reston, in *The New York Times,* "Washington: Why McNamara? And Why Now?," Nov. 29, 1967.

27. "ONE CLIENT FROM NOW ON"

1. Quoted in Westmoreland, *A Soldier Reports,* p. 319. Westmoreland emphasizes (by italicizing) the word "during" in his own memoirs, but he did not do so in the cable at the time. Other references are documented in the minutes of the White House meetings, including the January 23 Tuesday Lunch (on file at the LBJ Library). The notetaker was Tom Johnson.

2. EMBTEL 7867 and 10573, from General Westmoreland to Washington, Nov. 7, 1967 (transmitted to the President by Walt Rostow November 10, 1967).

3. Memorandum to the President from Walt Rostow, Nov. 15, 1967, enclosing a Memorandum from the Director of Central Intelligence, November 14, 1967 (Top Secret).

4. Westmoreland, *A Soldier Reports,* p. 321.

5. Interview of General Earle G. Wheeler by Dorothy Pierce McSweeny, May 7, 1970, at the Pentagon, part 2, pp. 1–2 (LBJ Library).

6. Lieutenant Colonel Dave R. Palmer, *Readings in Current Military History,* p. 103. Palmer later became superintendent of the United States Military Academy.

7. Herbert Y. Schandler *The Unmaking of a President: Lyndon Johnson and Vietnam* (Princeton: Princeton University Press, 1977), p. 130.

8. The accounts of most of the White House meetings during 1968 are drawn from notes taken during these meetings by the White House staff (usually

by Tom Johnson), from notes taken at the 8:30 Group meetings (by Colonel Pursley and George Elsey), and from my own records.

9. Interview with General Wheeler part 2, p. 2.

10. *Report of the War in Vietnam (as of 30 June 1968),* (Washington: U.S. Government Printing Office, 1969), p. 170.

11. See, for example, Peter Braestrup, *Big Story: How the American Press and Television Reported and Interpreted the Crisis of Tet 1968 in Vietnam and Washington,* (Boulder, Col.: Westview Press, 1977), 2 vols.

12. Wheeler to Westmoreland, JCS 01589, and Westmoreland to Wheeler, MAC 01849 (both Feb. 9, 1968): "Eyes Only" Message File, Papers of General William C. Westmoreland, LBJ Library.

13. Westmoreland to: Sharp and Wheeler, MAC 1901, DTG 101114Z (Feb. 10, 1968), "Eyes Only" File, Westmoreland papers.

14. Westmoreland to Wheeler, MAC 02018 (Feb. 11, 1968), "Eyes Only" File, Westmoreland papers.

15. Westmoreland, *A Soldier Reports* pp. 356–57. General Palmer on the same subject: "Regrettably, General Wheeler, who engineered and in reality was responsible for Westmoreland's abortive request, did little to set the record straight," General Bruce Palmer, *The 25-Year War: America's Military Role in Vietnam* (reprint ed., New York: Touchstone Books, 1984), p. 80.

16. Westmoreland, *A Soldier Reports,* p. 357.

17. *Ibid.*

18. "The Origins of the Post-Tet 1968 Plans for Additional American Forces in RVN," a special paper prepared by General William C. Westmoreland, Nov. 9, 1970, and endorsed by General Earle G. Wheeler, Chairman, Joint Chiefs of Staff, Admiral U. S. G. Sharp, former Commander in Chief, Pacific, and Ambassador Ellsworth Bunker, pp. 25 and 28.

19. Westmoreland, *A Soldier Reports,* pp. 357–58.

20. General Earle Wheeler, oral history, May 7, 1970, LBJ Library, tape I, p. 18. See also John B. Henry II, "February 1968," in *Foreign Policy* (Fall 1971): "But Wheeler had a 'clear understanding' with Westmoreland that the first increment was the only increment earmarked for Vietnam, and that the other increments were to be kept in the strategic reserve" (pp. 16–17). Henry attributes this to an interview with Wheeler in February 1971, but, in light of his own memorandum, Wheeler may have confused "strategic" and "theater" reserve forces.

21. Taylor, *Swords and Plowshares,* p. 388.

22. Notes of Feb. 27, 1968, meeting, taken by Harry McPherson, LBJ Library.

23. Johnson, *The Vantage Point,* pp. 392–93.

28. THE MOST DIFFICULT MONTH

1. Westmoreland, *A Soldier Reports,* p. 233.

2. See Strobe Talbott, *The Master of the Game: Paul Nitze and the Nuclear Peace* (New York: Knopf, 1988), pp. 99–101.

3. Phil G. Goulding, *Confirm or Deny: Informing the People on National Security* (New York: Harper and Row, 1970), pp. 308–309.

4. See, for example, Johnson, *The Vantage Point,* p. 398; Westmoreland, *A Soldier Reports,* p. 358; Palmer, *The 25-Year War,* p. 74; and Doris Kearns, *Lyndon Johnson and the American Dream* (New York: Harper and Row, 1976), p. 320.

5. Herbert Y. Schandler, *The Unmaking of a President: Lyndon Johnson and Vietnam* (Princeton: Princeton University Press, 1977), contains the most detailed description of the Clifford Group.

6. Tom Johnson was the notetaker for this meeting; his notes are on file at the LBJ Library.

7. Wheeler to Westmoreland and Sharp, CJCS 02721, March 8, 1968, "Eyes Only"; Westmoreland to Wheeler, MAC 03280, DTG 0813572, "Eyes Only."

8. Wheeler to Westmoreland, JCS 2767, March 9, 1968, "Eyes Only."

9. Don Oberdorfer, *Tet!* (New York: Doubleday, 1971), pp. 266–70.

10. Schandler, *The Unmaking of a President,* p. 201.

11. *Ibid.*, pp. 202–205.

12. David S. McLellan and David C. Acheson, eds., *Among Friends: Personal Letters of Dean Acheson* (N.Y.: Dodd, Mead, 1980), p. 293.

13. Oral History interview with Theodore C. Sorensen, by Larry J. Hackman, July 23, 1970, for the Robert F. Kennedy Oral History Program of the Kennedy Library, p. 34.

14. Statement of Senator Robert F. Kennedy, March 17, 1968. See also Jules Witcover, *85 Days: The Last Campaign of Robert Kennedy* (N.Y.: Quill repr., 1988), p. 80; Theodore C. Sorensen, *The Kennedy Legacy* (N.Y.: Macmillan, 1969), p. 138; Jack Newfield, *Robert Kennedy: A Memoir* (N.Y.: E.P. Dutton, 1969), p. 217; Arthur M. Schlesinger, Jr., *Robert Kennedy and His Times,* (New York: Ballantine, 1978), p. 917.

15. Bui Diem with David Chanoff, *In the Jaws of History* (Boston: Houghton Mifflin, 1987), p. 225.

16. See notes taken by Richard Steadman, March 20, 1968, LBJ Library.

17. Notes taken by both McPherson and Tom Johnson, LBJ Library.

18. Walter Issacson and Evan Thomas, *The Wise Men: Six Men and the World They Made* (New York: Simon and Schuster, 1986), p. 699; Don Oberdorfer, *Tet!* p. 308.

19. See Townsend Hoopes, *The Limits of Intervention* (New York: David McKay, 1969), p. 216, for Wheeler; Isaacson and Thomas, *The Wise Men,* p. 700, for Rostow; Schandler, *The Unmaking of a President,* pp. 260–61, for Ginsburgh; notes of meetings with the President, LBJ Library, for Rusk and Taylor.

20. See handwritten notes by McGeorge Bundy, March 26, 1968, LBJ Library.

21. Isaacson and Thomas, *The Wise Men,* p. 700.

22. General Phil Davidson, *Vietnam at War: The History, 1946–1975* (Novato, Cal.: Presidio Press, 1988), p. 525.

23. See Harry McPherson, *A Political Education* (Boston: Atlantic–Little, Brown, 1972), p. 431.

24. DEPTEL (Department Telegram) 138438, March 29, 1968, drafted by William P. Bundy, March 28, 1968, "Top Secret, Literally Eyes Only for Ambassador from Secretary."

25. See George Christian, "The Night Lyndon Quit," *Texas Monthly,* April 1988, for details of this little-known aspect of the President's withdrawal.

29. THE LONG, SAD SUMMER

1. In *The Vantage Point* President Johnson credits this remark to one of his advisers (p. 497), but the original notes of this meeting, taken by Tom Johnson, show that this was said by the President. This is also my recollection.

2. George Christian took notes, now on file at the LBJ Library, of this meeting, April 8, 1968.

3. Phil G. Goulding, *Confirm or Deny,* p. 329.

4. *The New York Times,* April 28, 1968.

5. Throughout the summer and fall of 1968, both Pursley and Elsey took extensive notes at the 8:30 Group and other meetings. These notes have made it possible to assemble a far more complete record than would otherwise have been imaginable. I am indebted to both men for permitting me to use these notes, which are in their private papers.

6. Undated memorandum entitled "How Can We Best Achieve Our Objective in South Vietnam," at the LBJ Library. Both Pursley and Warnke helped me to identify this memorandum as the one that they wrote for me in mid-May 1968 in response to the May 18 meeting.

7. The record of this meeting comes from three sources, all previously unavailable: Tom Johnson notes, on file at the LBJ Library; and the notes of George Elsey and Bob Pursley at the 8:30 Group meeting May 22, 1968, based upon my description to them of the meeting.

8. General Abrams to General Wheeler, 7404, DTG 051132Z, "Secret Eyes Only."

9. Abrams to Wheeler, MACV 7600, DTG 090948Z, June 9, "Secret Eyes Only."

10. Notes of George Elsey, June 11, 1968, meeting of the 8:30 Group.

11. Notes of George Elsey and Robert Pursley, June 12, 1968.

12. Richard J. Whalen, *Catch the Falling Flag: A Republican's Challenge to his Party* (Boston: Houghton Mifflin, 1972), p. 194.

30. MORE DISAPPOINTMENT AND TRAGEDY

1. William Manchester, *The Glory and the Dream: A Narrative History of America, 1932–1972* (Boston: Little, Brown, 1974), p. 1122.

2. I have limited my account of the Fortas nomination only to matters that directly involved me. For a detailed examination of this complicated affair, see Bruce Allen Murphy, *Fortas: The Rise and Ruin of a Supreme Court Justice,* (New York: William Murrow, 1988).

3. Immediately after this meeting, I described it to George Elsey, who made notes of the conversation.

4. *Newsweek,* May 19, 1969, p. 29.

5. Notes of July 24, 1968, meeting at the White House, Tom Johnson notetaker, LBJ Library.

6. Notes of George Elsey and Robert Pursley, 8:30 Group, August 12, 1968.

7. Johnson, *The Vantage Point,* p. 548.

31. HISTORY IN THE BALANCE

1. Paris 20872 (Secret), NODIS/HARVAN/PLUS, September 15, 1968, "Flash."

2. Summary Notes of 591st NSC Meeting, Sept. 25, 1968: 12:05 to 1:40 P.M., taken by Bromley Smith, Secretary to the NSC. National Security Council File, Vol. 5, Tab 73, Box 2, LBJ Library.

3. Johnson, *The Vantage Point,* p. 548.

4. Less has been written about October than March 1968, partly because documentary material has been less available. I am especially indebted to Tom Johnson, Benjamin H. Read, Robert Pursley, and George Elsey for allowing me to examine previously unavailable material.

5. William Safire, *Before the Fall: An Inside View of the Pre-Watergate White House* (Garden City, N.Y.: Doubleday, 1975), p. 88.

6. Cited in Rostow to the President, CAP82546, Oct. 12, 1968, "Sensitive Literally Eyes Only," and Saigon 40117 (Secret), NODIS/HARVAN/DOUBLE PLUS, Oct. 12, 1968.

7. Unless noted, we were unaware of the activities of the Republican camp at the time. I have included in this narrative some of what is now known because it is impossible to understand the events of October without an understanding of these actions.

In their memoirs, Nixon and Kissinger disagreed over the origins, frequency, and nature of Kissinger's contribution to the Nixon campaign. According to Kissinger, "Only one question was ever put to me by the Nixon organization. Early in October 1968, Bill Buckley introduced me to John Mitchell, Nixon's campaign manager. Mitchell asked me if I thought the Johnson Administration would agree to a bombing halt in Vietnam in return for the opening of negotiations before the election. I replied that it seemed to me highly probable that the North Vietnamese wanted a bombing halt on these terms and . . . therefore I believed that Hanoi was likely to agree to it just before the election. . . . Mitchell checked that judgment with me once or twice more during the campaign."

Nixon's version of events is considerably longer: On September 12, 1968 (before Kissinger's trip to Paris), H. R. ("Bob") Haldeman "brought me a report that Rockefeller's foreign policy advisor, Henry Kissinger, was available to assist us with advice. . . . I told Haldeman that Mitchell should continue as liaison with Kissinger and that we should honor his desire to keep his role completely confidential . . . [On September 26] Kissinger called again. He said that he had just returned from Paris, where he had picked up word that something big was afoot regarding Vietnam." Henry Kissinger, *White House Years* (Boston: Little, Brown, 1979), p. 10; Richard Nixon, *RN: The Memoirs of Richard Nixon* (New York: Grosset and Dunlap, 1978), pp. 323–24.

8. Saigon 40178, Bunker to Rusk, NODIS/HARVAN/DOUBLE PLUS, Oct. 13, 1968.

9. Saigon 40220, Bunker to Rusk, NODIS/HARVAN/DOUBLE PLUS, Oct. 14, 1968.

10. Most of those involved in this extraordinary episode have told their version of it; none strike me as completely candid, but they are all useful. See Anna Chennault, *The Education of Anna* (New York: Times Books, 1980), p. 174; Diem and Chanoff, *In the Jaws of History*, pp. 235–46; Nguyen Tien Hung and Jerrold L. Schecter, *The Palace File* (New York: Harper and Row, 1986), pp. 23–30.

11. *The Education of Anna,* p. 174.

12. *In the Jaws of History,* pp. 244–45.

13. *The Education of Anna,* p. 176.

14. *Ibid* p. 190; and *The Palace File,* p. 29.

15. Carl Solberg, *Hubert Humphrey: A Biography* (New York: W. W. Norton, 1984), pp. 391 and 394.

16. Hubert H. Humphrey, *The Education of a Public Man: My Life and Politics* (Garden City, N.Y.: Doubleday, 1976).

17. Johnson, *The Vantage Point,* p. 517.

18. Saigon 41449, Bunker to Rusk, NODIS/HARVAN/DOUBLE PLUS, Oct. 29, 1968.

19. Saigon 412521, NODIS/HARVAN/DOUBLE PLUS, Oct. 30, 1968.

20. Saigon 41586, Saigon 41618, and Saigon 41589, all NODIS/HARVAN/DOUBLE PLUS, Oct. 31, 1968.

21. Nixon, *RN,* pp. 322–28.

22. Humphrey, *The Education of A Public Man* p. 7.

32. NIXON AND THE END OF THE WAR

1. William F. Buckley, Jr., *United Nations Journal: A Delegate's Odyssey* (New York: G. P. Putnam's Sons, 1974), pp. 56–57; see also Hung and Schecter, *The Palace File,* pp. 30 and 80.

2. Safire, *Before the Fall,* p. 108.

3. Johnson, *The Vantage Point,* p. 567.

4. George Christian, *The President Steps Down: A Personal Memoir of the Transfer of Power* (New York: Macmillan, 1970), p. 276.

5. Patrick Anderson, "Clark Clifford 'Sounds the Alarm,' " *The New York Times Magazine,* Aug. 8, 1971, p. 55.

6. *The New York Times,* June 21, 1970, p. 1.

7. "The Talk of the Town," *New Yorker,* July 16, 1973.

8. Undated handwritten memorandum (believed to have been written sometime in January 1970), from John Erlichman to H. R. Haldeman. I am indebted to Morton Halperin for bringing this material to my attention.

9. Papers of Morton Halperin.

33. PRESIDENT CARTER: PROMISE AND DISAPPOINTMENT

1. *The Washington Star,* June 20, 1976. Despite this attitude, Carter appointed Califano Secretary of Health, Education, and Welfare.

2. Paul H. Nitze with Ann M. Smith and Steven L. Rearden, *From Hiroshima to Glasnost: At the Center of Decision, A Memoir* (New York: Grove Weidenfeld, 1989), p. 354.

3. Jimmy Carter, *Keeping Faith: Memoirs of A President* (New York: Bantam Books, 1982), p. 134.

4. *Time,* July 23, 1979, pp. 20 and 22.

5. Zbigniew Brzezinski, *Power and Principle: Memoirs of the National Security Advisor, 1977–1981* (New York: Farrar, Straus and Giroux, 1983), pp. 346–49.

6. Cyrus R. Vance, *Hard Choices: Critical Years in America's Foreign Policy* (New York: Simon and Schuster, 1983), p. 362.

7. *The Washington Post,* Feb. 3, 1980; *Time,* Feb. 11, 1980; and the AP News Poll, released Feb. 3, 1980.

35. REFLECTIONS

1. Ralph Waldo Emerson, "The Fortune of the Republic," in *Miscellanies* (Boston: Houghton Mifflin, 1904), p. 537. I am indebted to Arthur M. Schlesinger, Jr., for reminding me of the remarkable, relevant insights of Emerson, whom I studied in my youth.

2. 1969 estimate: Jeffrey Clarke, *Advise and Support: The Final Years* (Washington, D.C.: U.S. Army Center of Military History, 1988), p. 345; 1972 estimate: Hung and Schecter, *The Palace File,* p. 499.

3. Authur M. Schlesinger, Jr. *The Cycles of American History* (Boston: Houghton Mifflin, 1986), p. 67.

4. Milovan Djilas, *Aspects of Communism,* May-June 1988.

5. Emerson, "The Conservative," lecture delivered in Boston, Dec. 9, 1841, in *Essays and Lectures* (New York: Library of America, 1983), pp. 173–74.

6. See Arthur M. Schlesinger, Jr., *The Cycles of American History* (Boston: Houghton Mifflin, 1986), for an analysis of these cycles which I find most closely approximates my own.

7. *Ibid.,* p. 32.

Index

About the Co-author

RICHARD HOLBROOKE was a Foreign Service Officer who served in Vietnam, the Johnson White House, and the State Department. He wrote one volume of the Pentagon Papers and was a member of the American delegation to the Paris Peace Talks on Vietnam in 1968. He was Assistant Secretary of State for East Asian and Pacific Affairs during the Carter Administration. He is currently a Managing Director at the investment bank of Lehman Brothers and lives in New York.